The Science of Compassionate Love

The Science of Compassionate Love

Theory, Research, and Applications

edited by
Beverley Fehr, Susan Sprecher,
and Lynn G. Underwood

A John Wiley & Sons, Ltd., Publication

This edition first published 2009
© 2009 Blackwell Publishing Ltd

Blackwell Publishing was acquired by John Wiley & Sons in February 2007. Blackwell's publishing program has been merged with Wiley's global Scientific, Technical, and Medical business to form Wiley-Blackwell.

Registered Office
John Wiley & Sons Ltd, The Atrium, Southern Gate, Chichester, West Sussex, PO19 8SQ, United Kingdom

Editorial Offices
350 Main Street, Malden, MA 02148-5020, USA
9600 Garsington Road, Oxford, OX4 2DQ, UK
The Atrium, Southern Gate, Chichester, West Sussex, PO19 8SQ, UK

For details of our global editorial offices, for customer services, and for information about how to apply for permission to reuse the copyright material in this book please see our website at www.wiley.com/wiley-blackwell.

The right of Beverley Fehr, Susan Sprecher and Lynn G. Underwood to be identified as the authors of the editorial material in this work has been asserted in accordance with the Copyright, Designs and Patents Act 1988.

Library of Congress Cataloging-in-Publication Data
The science of compassionate love : theory, research, and applications / edited by Beverley Fehr, Susan Sprecher, and Lynn G. Underwood.
  p. cm.
  Includes bibliographical references and index.
  ISBN 978-1-4051-5393-5 (hardcover : alk. paper) – ISBN 978-1-4051-5394-2 (pbk. : alk. paper) 1. Compassion. I. Fehr, Beverley Anne, 1958– II. Sprecher, Susan, 1955– III. Gordon, Lynn Underwood.

BJ1475.S39 2008
177′.7–dc22
                                                    2008003440

A catalogue record for this book is available from the British Library.

Set in 10.5/12pt Galliard by SPi Publisher Services, Pondicherry, India
Printed in Singapore by Fabulous Printers Pte Ltd

1 2009

Contents

Contributors

Arthur Aron, PhD, is Professor of Psychology and Director of the Interpersonal Relationships Laboratory at the State University of New York at Stony Brook.

Jorge A. Barraza, MA, is a doctoral student at the School of Behavioral and Organizational Sciences, Claremont Graduate University, Claremont, California.

Becka Bowden, MA, is presently working in industry.

Salena Brody is Professor of Psychology at Collin County Community College, Frisco, Texas.

Matthew C. Butler, MA, is currently working as an analyst in the State Budget Office for the State of Michigan.

Edward Downs, MA, PhD Candidate (Penn State University), is an Instructor and Coordinator for the Media Effects Research Lab in the College of Communications at Penn State University, University Park, Pennsylvania.

Lori L. DuBenske, PhD, is Investigator in the Center for Health Enhancement Systems Studies, College of Engineering, University of Wisconsin-Madison.

Nancy Eisenberg, PhD, is Regents Professor of Psychology in the Department of Psychology at Arizona State University, Tempe, Arizona.

Beverley Fehr, PhD, is Professor of Psychology at the University of Winnipeg, Winnipeg, Manitoba, Canada. She is currently Associate Editor of the *Journal of Personality and Social Psychology* and former president of the International Association for Relationship Research.

Amber Ferris, MA, is a doctoral candidate at Kent State University, School of Communication Studies, Kent, Ohio.

Doran C. French, PhD, is Chair and Professor of Psychology in the Department of Psychology at Illinois Wesleyan University, Bloomington, Illinois.

Norman D. Giesbrecht, PhD, RPsych, is Professor in the Graduate Division of Educational Research, University of Calgary, Alberta, Canada.

Omri Gillath, PhD, is Assistant Professor in the Department of Psychology at the University of Kansas, Lawrence, Kansas.

David R. Graber, PhD, MPH, is Associate Professor and Director of the Bachelor of Health Sciences Program in the Department of Health Administration and Policy at the Medical University of South Carolina, Charleston, South Carolina.

Benjamin R. Karney, PhD, is an Associate Professor in the Department of Psychology at the University of California, Los Angeles.

Denise E. Kennedy, PhD, is a Postdoctoral Research Fellow in the Department of Psychology at the University of Michigan, Ann Arbor, Michigan.

Amy M. Kolak, PhD, is Assistant Research Scientist in the Department of Psychology at the University of Michigan.

Anna M. Malsch, PhD, is a Research Associate at the Research and Training Center on Family Support and Children's Mental Health within the Regional Research Institute for Human Services at Portland State University, Portland, Oregon.

Nadine F. Marks, PhD, is Professor of Human Development and Family Studies at the University of Wisconsin-Madison.

Tracy McLaughlin-Volpe, PhD, is Assistant Professor of Psychology at Boston College.

Mario Mikulincer, PhD, is Professor and Dean of the New School of Psychology at the Interdisciplinary Center (IDC) Herzliya, Herzliya, Israel.

Maralynne D. Mitcham, PhD, OTR/L, FAOTA, is Professor and Director of the Occupational Therapy Educational Program in the Department of Rehabilitation Sciences at the College of Health Professions, Charleston, South Carolina.

Lisa A. Neff, PhD, is an Assistant Professor in the Department of Psychology at the University of Toledo, Toledo, Ohio.

Allen M. Omoto, PhD, is Professor of Psychology and Director of the Institute for Research on Social Issues in the School of Behavioral and Organizational Sciences at Claremont Graduate University, Claremont, CA.

Daniel Perlman, PhD, is a Professor and Chair of the Department of Human Development and Family Studies, School of Environmental Sciences at UNCG, the University of North Carolina at Greensboro.

Sri Pidada (deceased) was formerly a senior lecturer and researcher in the Department of Psychology at Universitas Padjadjaran, Bandung, Indonesia.

Katherine M. Pieper, MA, PhD candidate (the Annenberg School for Communication at the University of Southern California), is currently working with World Relief, and is based in Phnom Penh, Cambodia.

Urip Purwono, Drs MS, PhD, is the Head of the Laboratory of Psychometric and Information System in the Faculty of Psychology at the Universitas Padjadjaran, Bandung, Indonesia.

Linda J. Roberts, PhD, is Professor and Chair in the Department of Human Development and Family Studies and Investigator in the Center for Health Enhancement Systems Studies at the College of Engineering, University of Wisconsin-Madison.

Rozzana Sánchez Aragón, PhD, is a Professor in the Department of Social Psychology at the National Autonomous University of Mexico, Mexico City, Mexico.

Phillip R. Shaver, PhD, is Distinguished Professor of Psychology in the Department of Psychology at the University of California, Davis, and President of the International Association for Relationship Research.

Sandi W. Smith, PhD, is Professor in the Department of Communication and Director of the Health and Risk Communication Center at Michigan State University.

Stacy L. Smith, PhD, is an Associate Professor of Entertainment at the Annenberg School for Communication, University of Southern California.

Tom W. Smith, PhD, is Director of the General Social Survey and Director of the Center for the Study of Politics and Society at the National Opinion Research Center, University of Chicago.

Jieun Song, PhD, is a postdoctoral Research Associate with the Institute on Aging and Human Development and Family Studies at the University of Wisconsin-Madison.

Susan Sprecher, PhD, is Professor of Sociology and Anthropology (also holding a joint professorship appointment in psychology) at Illinois State University, Normal, Illinois.

Telie A. Suryanti, SPsi, a bachelor of psychology from Universitas Padjadjaran, Bandung, Indonesia, is an associate consultant for various psychological consulting agencies in Bandung.

Lynn G. Underwood, PhD, Fellow of the Academy of Behavioral Medicine (FABM), is Professor of Biomedical Humanities at Hiram College, Hiram, Ohio.

Julie Vaughan, MA, is a graduate research associate in the Department of Psychology at Arizona State University, Tempe, Arizona.

Brenda L. Volling, PhD, is Professor of Psychology and Research Professor at the Center for Human Growth and Development, University of Michigan, Ann Arbor.

Meg Wise, MLS, PhD, is an Assistant Scientist at the Center for Health Enhancement Systems Studies at the College of Engineering, University of Wisconsin-Madison.

Stephen C. Wright, PhD, is Professor of Psychology and Canada Research Chair in Social Psychology at Simon Fraser University, Burnaby, British Columbia, Canada.

Jina H. Yoo, PhD, is Assistant Professor in the Department of Communication at the University of Missouri, St. Louis.

Preface and Acknowledgments

The primary purpose of this edited volume is to present cutting-edge, outstanding scholarship on the topic of *compassionate* love. Compassionate love is the term we have chosen to refer to various forms of other-oriented cognitions, affect, and behavior. It is the kind of love that is a central feature in many religious traditions: a self-giving, caring love that values the other highly and has the intention of giving full life to the other. It is associated, but not synonymous with, concepts such as empathy, perspective-taking, altruism, social support, volunteerism, attachment, romantic love, and familial love. Although the central focus of the book is on compassionate love, many of the chapters also refer to one or more of these related other-oriented concepts.

Compassionate love can be experienced for close others such as family members, romantic partners, and friends; however, it can also be experienced for peripheral ties and unknown others, even all of humanity. In fact, it is distinguishable from other types of love, such as romantic love or maternal love, by the degree to which it is a universal type of love that can be experienced in all types of relationships and settings. A collected volume on compassionate love seems timely and important in the midst of a world filled with hate, violence, and devaluation of the person.

The goal of the present volume was to create a "state-of-the-art" compendium that would document what is presently known about compassionate love and provide a basis for future research. The book provides insight into the nature of compassionate love, how we might better understand it, and, importantly, how to encourage its appropriate expression in our intimate relationships and to strangers. The chapters were designed to create a varied, but cohesive, body of knowledge on the antecedents of compassionate love, its manifestations, and its consequences. This book takes a significant step toward covering previously uncharted territory and provides a relatively detailed analysis of the landscape. More specifically, this volume examines conceptual frameworks for studying compassionate love, the measurement of compassionate love, compassionate love as experienced in a variety of relationship contexts, compassionate love as manifested in a variety of situations (e.g., medical, care-giving, social support), directions for future research, and finally, suggestions for interventions aimed at promoting compassionate love in today's world.

Many disciplines, with unique foci and methods, contribute to our understanding of compassionate love: psychology, sociology, communication studies, family studies, epidemiology, and medicine. This volume uses the model of compassionate love articulated by Lynn Underwood (2002, 2005, see also Chapter 1, this volume) to enable these disciplines to communicate with each other. This model also provides cohesiveness for this volume, as each chapter links its work to the model. By including a diverse group of scholars and research traditions, incorporating a common model, and having editors representing psychology, sociology, and epidemiology, this book synthesizes knowledge in a way that will be informative for both teaching and research. It also lays out a variety of methods and measures that will help this field progress. It is intended to be a practical book, grounded in solid scientific findings and methods.

The volume is organized into six major sections and a final commentary. Each chapter includes reviews of the literature, original empirical work – often previously unpublished findings – and suggestions for future research.

Part I is focused on *Definition, Theory, and Measurement*. Chapter 1, by Underwood, sets the stage for the rest of the volume. In this chapter, she presents a working definition and model of compassionate love. The model begins with the individual – affected by the environment, the situation, relationships, and his or her own internal dispositions. Individual factors, in turn, contribute to motivation and discernment in a dynamic process that ultimately results in "compassionate love fully expressed." Underwood also presents findings using items from her Daily Spiritual Experiences scale that measure compassionate love for others. Beverley Fehr and Susan Sprecher, in Chapter 2, discuss a program of research on conceptual, measurement, and relational issues pertaining to compassionate love. This research includes an analysis of laypeople's conceptions of compassionate love, as well as a description of the development of the Compassionate Love Scale that measures, in different versions, compassionate love for a variety of targets (e.g., all of humanity, a specific partner). The chapter presents studies on correlates of compassionate love, gender differences, and relationship type differences in compassionate love. People's beliefs about the outcomes of compassionate love also are examined, including whether it is better for individual well-being to give versus receive this kind of love. The final chapter in Part I, written by Stacy Smith, Sandi Smith, and colleagues, focuses on the measurement of acts of compassionate love on American television. The authors extracted key features of altruism from extant literature to create a coding scheme for identifying compassionate love on television. They document the extent to which each of these aspects of altruism/compassionate love is displayed in entertainment programs, making the point that conclusions about the frequency of acts are highly dependent upon how the construct is measured.

Part II of the book, on the *Sociodemographics of Compassionate Love*, consists of two chapters. Tom Smith, in Chapter 4, examines trends and correlates of empathy, altruism, and related constructs with data collected in the General Social Survey. Variations in loving and caring in the United States based on sociodemographic variables such as age, gender, marital status, urban–rural residence, and so forth, are examined. In Chapter 5, Nadine Marks and Jieun Song review life-course and sociological perspectives on social support and care-giving and present data on compassionate attitudes and acts across the adult life course, based on two US national studies: the National Survey of Midlife in the United States and the National Survey of Families and Households. The authors demonstrate that compassionate attitudes and acts (toward primary kin, secondary kin, friends, and others) vary as a function of several sociodemographic variables, including gender and stage in the adult life course.

Part III addresses *Compassionate Love in Close Relationships*. In Chapter 6, Brenda Volling, Amy Kolak, and Denise Kennedy examine the development of empathy and compassionate love in early childhood, focusing on the influences of family members. They first review the extensive literature on the development of children's moral development, compassionate behavior, empathy, and prosocial behaviors. In the latter part of the chapter, they present findings from their own multi-method research on compassionate behavior, conducted with families. Lisa Neff and Benjamin Karney, in Chapter 7, focus on compassionate love in early marriage. They define compassionate love as accurate understanding of one's partner – positively evaluating one's partner at a global level while perceiving accurately the partner's positive and negative traits. They summarize their research conducted with newlywed couples over the first four years of marriage, including how compassionate love is associated with support-giving, marital efficacy, and the likelihood of divorce.

The theme of Part IV of the book is *Compassionate Love for Non-Close Others* and contains three chapters. Chapter 8, by Mario Mikulincer, Philip Shaver, and Omri Gillath, provides an attachment theory perspective on compassion and caregiving. After reviewing research on the link between secure attachment and caregiving, the authors highlight their research findings. Specifically, they show how dispositional attachment and experimentally-created security are associated with compassion and empathy for strangers, minority group members, and people with special needs. Allen Omoto, Anna Malsch, and Jorge Barraza, in Chapter 9, present their model of volunteerism and make the case that volunteer behavior can be construed as a behavioral manifestation of compassionate love. Correlates of, and motivations for, volunteerism were examined in several samples of older volunteers. In Chapter 10, Salena Brody, Stephen Wright, Arthur Aron, and Tracy McLaughlin-Volpe extend self-expansion theory (particularly the inclusion of other in self model) to cross-group friendships. The authors report several correlational and experimental studies in which they examine factors that increase positive intergroup attitudes (a proxy for compassionate love). They conclude that close cross-group friendships can foster compassionate love for members of other groups.

Part V of the book focuses on *Compassionate Love in Health Care and other Caregiving Contexts*. Linda Roberts, Meg Wise, and Lori DuBenske, in Chapter 11, examine compassionate caregiving in an end-of-life context. They report the results of three qualitative studies on compassionate love between family caregivers and terminally ill patients. Several themes, exemplifying compassionate love in this caregiving context, are extracted from these end-of-life accounts. Chapter 12, by David Graber and Maralynne Mitcham, is on exemplary care in hospital settings. These authors highlight findings from in-depth interviews conducted with clinicians in two US hospitals who had been nominated as particularly compassionate. The authors develop a model that elucidates characteristics of the care provider and the kinds of situational factors that promote exemplary care.

Chapter 13, by Norman Giesbrecht, examines the influence of the the sociocultural context on giving care to adults with disabilities. Two different types of health-care organizations are compared, one with an interdependent care ethic (*l'Arche* communities) and the other with an independent care ethic (the Community Living Organization). The author develops and tests a complex model of caregiving based on quantitative and qualitative data gathered from a large sample of caregivers in these two organizations. Constructs included in the model are: attachment, empathy, perspective-taking, to name a few.

In Part VI, *Compassionate Love in an Intercultural Context*, we highlight research on compassionate love in a collectivist culture. Julie Vaughan, Nancy Eisenberg, Doran French, Urip Purowano, Telie Suryanti, and Sri Pidada, in Chapter 14, examine the relations between empathy, sympathy, perspective-taking, and prosocial behavior in children and adolescents from two subcultures in Indonesia. Building on Underwood's model, they propose a model in which empathy-related responding leads to positive behavior and compassionate love.

The final section of the book is a *Commentary*, in Chapter 15, by Daniel Perlman and Rozzana Sánchez Aragón. We asked these distinguished scholars to read the chapters and reflect on them, once again using Underwood's model as a guiding framework. The authors highlight key findings in the volume, situate them in the larger context of social science research, and discuss the contrast between compassionate love and the dark side of relationships. They end their chapter by offering several directions for future compassionate love research.

We want to express our deep gratitude to the authors for their research, expertise, tenacity, and willingness to work together with us on this volume. Their research into previously uncharted territory and their extensive work in crafting the chapters have made this volume possible. We thank the funders of the research: the Fetzer Institute, in particular, as well as the Templeton Foundation, the National Institutes of Health, the National Science Foundation, and the Social Sciences and Humanities Research Council of Canada. We thank our colleges and universities for supporting us in our research endeavors: the University of Winnipeg, Illinois State University, and Hiram College. We thank Blackwell Publishing, and editor Christine Cardone, for their belief in this project and editorial advice. Finally, we want to thank our families, who have been understanding of our need to work on this project and are supportive in so many other ways: Marvin, Genevieve, Everett; Charles, Abigail, Katherine, and Samuel; Anna, Michelle, and Zoë, Marie, and Gerald.

References

Underwood, L. G. (2002). The human experience of compassionate love: Conceptual mapping and data from selected studies. In S. G. Post, L. G. Underwood, J. P. Schloss & W. B. Hurlbut (Eds.), *Altruism and altruistic love* (pp. 72–88). New York: Oxford University Press.

Underwood, L. G. (2005). Interviews with Trappist monks as a contribution to research methodology in the investigation of compassionate love. *Journal for the Theory of Social Behavior*, 35, 285–302.

Beverley Fehr
Susan Sprecher
Lynn G. Underwood

Part I

Definitions, Theory, and Measurement

I

Compassionate Love: A Framework for Research

Lynn G. Underwood

Introduction

Compassionate love is that particular kind of love that centers on the good of the other. It's that kind of love that feels so good to be on the receiving end of – good in a lasting way, one that sticks to the ribs and doesn't give indigestion. It is a caring love which has a weight, a nourishing quality. To be loved when it is the choice of the other, and at some emotional or physical cost, can make a special impact. In giving this kind of other-centered love one tries to truly understand and accept the conditions and state of the recipient in order to enable the recipient to become more fully alive. "Altruistic love," "unconditional love," and "agape" are other terms sometimes used to describe this kind of love (Post, Underwood, Schloss, & Hurlbut, 2002; Underwood, 2005). The working definition of compassionate love presented here describes the kind of love that ultimately centers on the good of the other.

This love is *not* identical with the often hormonally driven romantic drive, the natural bonding with offspring, the tit-for-tat of the business world, or financial and emotional support given out of obligation. Nor is it captured by the platitudes of love and forgiveness trotted out by the religious and nonreligious alike.

Both scientific and nonscientific resources can help us to identify this kind of love and to illuminate its trajectory. The scientific research included in this volume is designed to help us further our understanding about the conditions, behaviors, and attitudes associated with compassionate love and to investigate what might get in the way of forming those attitudes and behaviors and what might promote them. The ultimate end is to discover ways to appropriately encourage the expression of this other-centered love in the world. This research supplements what religious thinkers, ethicists, and philosophers contribute to the understanding of these issues (Vacek, 1994).

The main purpose of this chapter is to lay out a working definition of compassionate love and a model to reveal the mechanism of this other-centered love. These are designed to provide a common reference for the chapters included in this volume and a guide for the reader.

Working Definition and Key Features

The working definition of compassionate love includes both the attitudes and actions related to giving of self for the good of the other. The term as used here is meant to identify a self-giving, caring love that values the other highly and has the intention of giving full life to the other. Compassionate love can be seen in actions, expressions, and words, but at the core of the construct are motivation and discernment, facets of free choice to stretch and to give. The "why" of the action, the reason for the behavior, the motivation behind the action – all are important to categorizing something as compassionately loving in nature. The ultimate focus is the giving of self for the good of the other. Compassionate love can be expressed in the context of other kinds of love and altruistic behaviors, but somehow reaches beyond them. Compassionate love as used in this volume is not necessarily always in response to the suffering of another, but also includes attitudes and actions centered on the flourishing of another at a cost to self. This kind of love is a central feature in many religious traditions, but is not conceived of in this volume as essentially tied to any particular religion.

Compassionate love is not synonymous with empathy, attachment, or bonding, but can relate to these. The word "compassion" alone is not a synonym, as it might imply a focus limited to those who are suffering, and it can imply detachment, whereas compassionate love implies some degree of emotional engagement as appropriate, and also emphasizes the enhancement of human flourishing.

Research on "altruism" also has relevance to this work, but "altruism" is not identical to "compassionate love." Throughout this volume altruism is discussed in various chapters and definitions vary. For example, sociobiologists and many evolutionary biologists tend to see altruism as ultimately self-serving either for individual survival or for that of the ingroup, or genetically related group. In evolutionary theory, altruism means behavior that reduces the actor's fitness while enhancing the fitness of others. If the total contribution of the altruist to the fitness of others is greater than the fitness lost by the altruist, altruism will increase the prospects of the group's surviving in competition with other groups (Barkow, Cosmides, & Tooby, 1992). Economists, on the other hand, frequently write about bounded rationality and how altruism, or "choice to act for the good of the other rather than for one's own perceived benefit" operates in the context of limited knowledge (Simon, 1993). Some psychological definitions describe "empathic altruism" as something done for the other that is ultimately directed at benefiting the other rather than oneself (Batson and Oleson, 1991). In a recent volume on altruism in world religions, the conclusion was that although compassionate behavior was important in many religions, the concept of altruism was not a particularly relevant one in the religious context (Neusner & Chilton, 2005).

Rather than quibble over the distinct line between altruism and compassionate love, given the multiple understandings of altruism, it is of more use to describe how compassionate love as here defined stretches beyond altruism as we often think of it. Compassionate love is more rich conceptually than altruism. An altruistic act may be done merely from habit or natural inclination or a sense of duty or to engender obligation. As seen below (the section articulating the definitional features), a true act of compassionate love involves more cognition, more freedom, more explicit *choosing* than "mere" altruism would imply (see also Post et al., 2002).

Romantic love, too, is not synonymous with the construct of compassionate love, though research on romantic love can have relevance to the topic (see Chapters 2 and 10 in this volume). "Falling in love" with someone can reflect hormonal flux and physical attraction that can actually lead to giving of self for the good of the other. But on the other hand, fulfillment of one's own needs or desires through the relationship can dominate feelings of caring for the other. Recent brain-imaging studies have suggested that the circumstances of romance may be particular to that state rather than generalizable beyond it (Bartels & Zeki, 2000). Compassionate love can exist in romantic contexts, as it can in familial affection, and in the midst of basic altruistic action, but these contexts can also lack compassionate love.

Although I start here with a central working definition of compassionate love defined by the qualities outlined below, throughout this volume each group of researchers has operationalized this construct somewhat differently, or has addressed constructs that overlap, but are not identical with, compassionate love. The key unifying principle for this volume is to inform our understanding of this other-centered love, and produce work that can have practical application. If we visualize a series of concentric circles, with scientific research on compassionate love as the bull's-eye, basic research in the outer rings can provide supports for research closer to the bull's-eye even though distant from the exact construct of interest. For example, research on "fairness" using economic theory could be on the outer edges of the concentric circles. Some of the work using animal models to investigate empathy in apes or pair bonding in prairie voles can give us insight into basic mechanisms, even though the work does not directly address compassionate love (Insel, 1997; Preston & de Waal, 2002).

At the first scientific meeting on this topic, at the Massachusetts Institute of Technology (MIT) in 1999, I was responsible for delivering opening remarks to set the stage for presentations from philosophers, theologians, economists, psychologists, sociologists, and biologists. In remembering a talk by Ian Stewart, the mathematician, on patterns in mathematics and nature, such as animal stripes and gait, I recalled that he once brought a live tiger into the room for a talk. I wanted so much to bring the tiger into the room, and say, "Here it is. Here is compassionate love, that special kind of love we are trying to capture in this meeting." To try to do this I devised the following exercise that I shared then, and suggest that you, the reader, try to do this now before reading on.

> Reflect on a time in the past when you personally felt truly loved, loved for who you truly are, beyond the momentary circumstances, beyond what was expected of you. Pick a time that still holds particular importance for you. What was the relationship context and what were the circumstances? Close your eyes and try to relive it.

This is the construct that the researchers in this volume are informing us about. Although for each individual the specifics of the event remembered were different, the premise of this volume is that there is something in common at a fundamental level. After doing this exercise at the MIT meeting, Dame Cicely Saunders, the founder of the hospice movement, came up to me and thanked me for that moment of connection to being loved that brought the experience vividly back to her. Some of the scientists present did the same. I have been teaching undergraduates about this topic and we use poetry, film, and visual art to flesh out the construct, in addition to scientific research. However, at the end of the course, many students return to this initial exercise as a key to defining compassionate love.

It was necessary to develop a definition of compassionate love in the context of the original meeting on the topic, so the book, then, proceeded from that meeting, and from the requests for proposals for scientific research funded by various foundations and the National Institutes of Health. To address the depth and complexity of the topic, a number of qualities were articulated as necessary to varying degrees for compassionate love to be present (Underwood, 2002). These were: free choice for the other; some degree of cognitive understanding of the situation, the other, and oneself; valuing the other at a fundamental level; openness and receptivity; and response of the "heart." (For more on how these were developed, see Underwood, 2002.)

Free Choice for the Other

Free choice, although constrained by biological, social, environmental, and cultural factors, is a key element for compassionate love to be present. When one reflects on being loved in this way by another, the selfless motive of the other is important, but it is often the fact that he or she made the deliberate choice to "love" rather than to "be indifferent" that touches our heart. For example, much altruistic behavior in parenting results simply from instinctual or ingrained responses to the child's need. To cuddle a smiling baby may be instinctual; to stay up through the night with a baby with colic takes us beyond the instinctual response, to choose to give of oneself for the ultimate good of the other.

Some Degree of Accurate Cognitive Understanding of the Situation, the Other, and Oneself

This includes understanding one's self – one's natural inclinations and constraints. It also includes understanding something of the needs and feelings of the person to be loved, and what might be appropriate to truly enhance the other's well-being. Again, in a parenting situation, a parent will frequently impose his or her own notion of the child's good on the child. While this is obviously unavoidable when dealing with infants and small children, an important element of compassionate love in parenting involves allowing increasing space for the child or adolescent to choose his or her own notion of the good. And it is also important for the parent to have an accurate perception of the parent's understanding of the child, and the parent's own personality and tendencies.

Valuing the Other at a Fundamental Level

Some degree of respect for the other person is necessary to articulate love rather than pity in situations of suffering, and to enable one to visualize potential for enhancing human flourishing. People do not generally like to be pitied, although help in those circumstances is usually better than no help at all. To be pitied does not elevate us as human beings. But to be respected in the midst of the imperfections of being human, to be known for who we are and still valued, enables us to truly flourish (Vanier, 1998). This attitude also protects the giver from delusions of superiority, which may get in the way of love being ultimately centered on the good of the other.

Openness and Receptivity

Although specifically religious inspiration is not a necessary component of compassionate love as used in this volume, there is an "inspired" quality of this kind of love for many people. So the definition needs to leave room for this kind of divine input or open receptive quality that many feel is a central feature of this kind of love (Neusner & Chilton, 2005; Vacek, 1994). For instance, during interviews with Trappist monks that explored their experience and practice of compassionate love, "openness" was mentioned as a central feature of compassionate love (Underwood, 2005). In a religiously diverse group interviewed in the inner city of Chicago as part of a scale development study, for many it was only "grace" that enabled love to emerge in the midst of difficulties (Underwood, 2006).

Response of the "Heart"

Heart here is used as "coeur," or the core of one's being. Some kind of heartfelt, affective quality is usually part of this kind of attitude or action. Not that everyone will feel gushing emotion when giving compassionate love to another, but some sort of emotional engagement and understanding seem to be needed to love fully in an integrated way. The central features of motivation and decision-making rely on both cognitive and affective dimensions. Moral decision-making has been seen in empirical studies to involve affective as well as cognitive areas of the brain and body (Roskies, 2006).

Background for the Use of the Term "Compassionate Love"

As a body of scientific research was being developed we needed to find a word or phrase to provide a common language for communication. The term "compassionate love" first emerged in the context of scientific research at a meeting of the World Health Organization (WHO) when working groups were trying to develop an assessment tool for "quality of life" to be used in diverse cultures (WHOQOL SRPB Group, 2006). The goal of this particular series of meetings was to develop a module to measure spiritual, religious, and personal belief factors involved in "quality of life." The group was composed of people from all over the world, from multiple religious and nonreligious backgrounds, particularly social scientists and health professionals. One of the "facets" identified for the module was loving-kindness, or love for others (Saxena, O'Connell, & Underwood, 2002). There was considerable discussion of the appropriate wording for this aspect. The Buddhists were not happy with the word "love" but wanted "compassion" to be used, which for them fit the concept. The Muslims in the group (from Indonesia, India, and Turkey) were adamant that compassion was too "cold" and that "love" needed to be there as it brought in the *feeling* of love, the element of *affect*. As others weighed in from various cultural, religious, and atheist positions, "compassionate love" was the compromise phrase arrived at to portray this aspect of quality of life. "Altruistic love" was a close second. For the members of the WHO group and many others interviewed on this topic, "compassionate love" captures both aspects, addressing human suffering *and* encouraging human flourishing. "*Passio*" can mean suffering but can also express positive feelings, as in "I am passionate about my work," or "I am passionate about my spouse." So "*cum-passio*" means to "feel with" (Underwood, 2005). Compassionate love is not the perfect wording, but for most people it pointed in the right direction, and provided a common language with which to move forward.

Scientific research began to focus on this particular construct owing primarily to the intense interest of two philanthropists in this subject. Sir John Templeton believed that "unlimited love" is a central motivating force to be harnessed for the good of humankind, and John Fetzer felt that "unconditional love" is at the center of the universe. Both of these philanthropists were interested in pursuing scientific research as a way of exploring this powerful factor in order to better enable humans to enhance the well-being of humankind. They were willing to provide money through their respective foundations to key scientists to explore this topic with openness and rigor. The construct of "compassionate love" (also called "altruistic love") and the model described in this chapter fit the topic of interest for both of these philanthropists, and this definition and model have provided an anchor for specific research solicitation and the selection of projects for funding.

As research continues in this area, now supported both by private foundations and federal funding agencies, various new measures and operational definitions are being established and tested, some of which appear in various chapters in this volume. New words are being included and constructs fleshed out. This process will enrich and build on this working definition to enable the sciences to contribute to a greater understanding of compassionate love, and what it means for compassionate love to be fully expressed in various relationships, across situations, and among different individuals.

Research Model

To enable various researchers' work on this topic to fit together despite differences in focus and disciplinary starting points, I articulated a working model that appeared in *Altruism and Altruistic Love* (Underwood, 2002).

This model, as shown in Figure 1.1, has usefully provided a structural framework over the years for those from a variety of disciplines. Researchers in the present volume were encouraged to relate their work to this model, to provide a unifying framework for the work presented here. Many of them used the model initially to develop some of their research. Of course any model only provides a starting point for exploring the messiness of human interaction. The model is incomplete and there are interactions between various parts that are not drawn in. For example, feelings and emotional content cannot be entered into the model in a linear sequential manner, but exist throughout the model. The same is true of a possible interaction with the transcendent. But the model still can provide an effective tool to bring together disparate research and translate from one discipline to another, even communicating with humanities disciplines such as philosophy, theology, and the arts.

On the left-hand side of the figure is the individual person nested in the environment. The individual encounters specific situations and relationships. He or she engages in the situation or relationship with motivation and discernment, shown in the center of the diagram. And on the right-hand side is the resulting action, or attitude expressed in words.

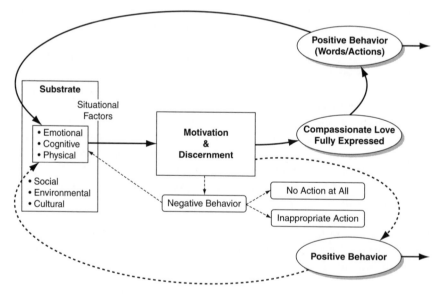

Figure 1.1   Working Model of Compassionate Love
Note. From *Altruism and altruistic love: Science, philosophy and religion in dialog*, ed. S. G. Post, G. Underwood, J. P. Schloss, and W. B. Hurlbut (New York: Oxford University Press, 2002). By permission of Oxford University Press, Inc.

The Substrate: Individual, Physical, Cultural, Environmental, Social, Emotional, and Cognitive

An individual expressing compassionate love begins with a base of individual variations in personality, biology, and developmental patterns. This is nested within and shaped by cultural, historical, family, and social environments. An example of this substrate might be whether the person as a child was provided with a secure and nurturing environment. Being loved well as children may affect our subsequent capacity to love others (see Mikulincer, Shaver, & Gillath, Chapter 8, this volume). The religious and cultural environment also shapes the starting point (see Smith, Chapter 4, and Vaughan et al., Chapter 14, this volume). Individual inherited dispositions may also play a role. For example, it has been shown that empathic concern, but not perspective-taking empathy, may be inherited to some extent (Davis, Luce, & Kraus, 1994). Another example of these dispositional individual differences is that extroverts may find it easier to reach out to a stranger than introverts (Kagan, 2002). Impairment of empathy secondary to neural damage or congenital situations can limit ability to express compassionate love appropriately (Damasio, 2002). Rushton (2004) has made the case, via twin studies, for the heritability of various altruistic tendencies. There are also obvious physical constraints. For example, if one is old or disabled, one is less likely to be able to offer physical assistance to a person in need, even if one desires to do so.

Cross-cultural studies of altruism can help to inform work on compassionate love (Johnson et al., 1989, Vaughan et al., Chapter 14, this volume). The WHO has produced data specifically on loving-kindness and giving love that could help inform the examination of the cultural substrate in which we operate (Saxena et al. 2002). Cross-cultural work on helping behaviors has used structured, social psychology experiments to test the likelihood of helping behaviors in real-life settings throughout the world and has developed theories for why people may be more likely to help strangers in various cultures (Levine, 2003). Certain cultures or religions value helping more than others (Batson & Gray, 1981), and other features, such as lower population density, can contribute to the increased likelihood of helping behaviors in daily life (Levine, 2003).

While none of these factors necessarily determine one way or the other whether a person will be compassionately loving, they can increase or decrease the possibility of such behavior. We do not all start with the same initial conditions. We start from different places. These substrate factors can be thought of as "limitations of freedom." These differences at the individual level lead to unique responses to individual situations or individual relationships in which love can be expressed. This is one reason why compassionate love cannot be measured purely by behavior.

The left-hand side of Figure 1.1, from a theological perspective, might also include the divine, God, or the transcendent as part of the greater environment and within the person and within relationships. The presence of the transcendent might also be present in each of the other parts of the model, depending on one's theological framework.

It is not obvious from Figure 1.1 itself that the substrate can change over time, but of course this can be the case. An example would be social support. The kind of nurturing a child has affects his or her ability to engage in compassionately loving actions as an adult. But also current support as an adult received from a spouse or a religious or other community can shape the substrate in the present moment of action. Other aspects of the substrate, such as the cognitive, emotional and cultural, can change over time as well, and this needs to be taken into account in research that uses this model as a base.

Specific Situation and Particular Relationship

The expression of compassionate love can also be affected by the specific situation and the relationship to the person being loved. For example, people typically express different attitudes and behaviors to "ingroup" members (e.g. family, friends, similar religious or racial groups) than to "outgroup" members. How each of us defines our "outgroup" varies, but most people do have a distinct sense of the "stranger" that affects how they relate to people (Pfeifer et al., 2007). Whether an action addresses an "ingroup" or "outgroup" member can play a role in the likelihood of helping others in specific circumstances (see Vaughan et al., Chapter 14, this volume). And the way that compassionate love is expressed in marriage is going to be different than in interactions with strangers (see in this volume Fehr & Sprecher, Chapter 2; Brody, Wright, Aron, & McLaughlin-Volpe, Chapter 10; and Neff & Karney, Chapter 7).

Both situational factors and specific relationships can affect how compassionate love is expressed. Nitschke et al. (2004) examined the neural correlates of mothers looking at photos of their newborns and photos of other babies. Functional magnetic resonance imaging of the brain shows responsiveness in the orbital-frontal cortex correlated with positive mood when mothers were viewing photos of their own babies, but not when viewing strange babies. The relationship and the situation affect the degree to which this area of the brain was engaged, and the level of positive affect generated. Nitschke went on to do additional research that showed that when a mother thinks about getting up in the night to attend to a crying child, the areas implicated in moral decision-making "light up" on the brain scans. Linking the affective and moral decision-making areas may point toward compassionate love being expressed by the mother, especially at times when the cost to the self is higher, for example when she is tired, and the baby is less immediately attractive.

When I was preparing for the 1999 MIT conference, I explained to my daughter Anna, who was 9 years old at the time, that I couldn't play with her right then, as I was preparing a talk on compassionate love, trying to explain to those at the meeting exactly what it was. She said to me, "Mummy, it's simple. You just take me up on the stage with you in front of everyone and give me a big hug." Yes, that would definitely be one way of demonstrating love. But as I further thought about why this wouldn't be an adequate explanation, I reflected on my teenage daughter, whom I loved just as much. A demonstration of that love as expressed in a particular situation might be a moment of confrontation, firm words, saying no, or a severe expression. This contrast is a good example of why just examining an action is not sufficient to fully describe whether and to what extent compassionate love is being expressed.

Another situational element was identified by Darley and Batson (1973). They found that urgency (i.e., time pressure) was the most predictive of helping behaviors in a structured experiment. The more hurried someone is, the less likely he or she is to help someone perceived to be in need.

How compassionate love might be expressed in a professional situation provides another example of situational and relational variables. In this volume, Graber and Mitcham discuss compassionate love as expressed by physicians. In the health-care systems of the United States and many other countries, a fee-for-service or fee-for-time arrangement results primarily in action from duty and obligation. However, there is flexibility even within this operating system that provides opportunity to "go the extra mile for the patient," or engage in compassionate caring for the sick person (Underwood, 2004).

Motivation and Discernment

Although both the substrate and final actions are important parts of the model, at the center of the model are motivation and discernment. Motivation and discernment are integral parts of the moment of choice. At some point a person internally reflects and makes a choice to move, to act, to express something, centered on the good of the other. In this moment the person balances the various aspects of the situation, for example their own needs, priorities of obligation, fairness assessments, and perceived urgency. They also discern the appropriateness of action, sometimes explicitly and analytically, and sometimes with more of a "gut" sense, a more implicit process. Thus both motives and discernment are key in this moment of choice. Behaviors flow from that choice. The model also shows the negative results possible for the other person when motives for self outweigh those for others (motive not centered on the good of the other), or there is an inappropriate action given the various factors to be considered (poor discernment). To some extent, motivation and discernment are mixed in decision-making but it is still worth considering them separately in this discussion.

Motivation. Motives are always mixed, so in compassionate love as expressed in daily life, there are frequently motives that obstruct orientation toward the good of the other. As revealed in interviews, so many self-centered motives can get in the way, such as the need for reciprocal love and affection, the need to be accepted, guilt, fear, seeing others as an extension of one's own ego, the control of others through indebtedness, a desire to avoid confrontation, a desire to look well in the eyes of others. When we reflect on our own motives in daily life, these kinds of motives frequently are a part of our actions for others (Underwood, 2002). Our motives are always mixed. This is why the phrase, "centered on the good of the other" is used. That the "ultimate aim" is the good of the other might be another way to phrase this. The central thrust, the dominating force, of motivation is one of the key definitional features of compassionate love.

Given the individual and environmental starting points, as one encounters a specific person in a specific situation, one must make a decision to act (shown centrally in Figure 1.1), and a motive drives that decision. No motive is totally free of self-interest, but in this definitional model the motive needs to be *centered* on the good of the other to count as compassionate love. Motive is particularly hard to research and many researchers have relied on observation of behaviors to indirectly tap into motive (Post et al., 2002). However, there are starting to be some innovative ways to investigate it, such as experimental models from economics, game theory, cognitive science, and social psychology (Batson & Shaw, 1991; Fehr & Gächter, 2002), measurement of implicit attitudes such as the Implicit Association Test (Fazio & Olson, 2003), and observational studies with multiple actions, insightful self-report, and neural imaging (Moll et al., 2006). Techniques to enhance abilities for self-reflection on "what is driving the bus" can help identify how motives can be colored more than one would like by self-serving interests, enabling one to clear out some excessively self-serving motives if so desired. Recent work suggests how these kinds of self-reports in the area of motivation can be refined and selected for (Underwood, 2005).

Discernment. Discernment, as well as motivation, is important, and these two features are not clearly differentiated in decision-making. The process of discernment is reflected in weighing things cognitively, implicitly or explicitly, to make the right decision for the other. Compassionate love fully expressed is not just good intentions, but doing what is really good for the other, or at least aiming to do so. One can mean well, be well-intentioned towards the other, but do something that will ultimately harm him in some way.

In the context of focus on this topic and in other health studies, intensive interviews were held over time with a wide variety of people: students, inner-city women of diverse ethnic and religious backgrounds, Trappist monks, and others (Underwood, 2005, 2006). The responses of the Trappist monks were particularly informative in identifying the cognitive processes and subtleties involved in choices. It was found that some people tended to be quite analytical about their choices to give of self for the good of the other, weighing various articulated factors. Others described themselves as "just acting," without giving much conscious thought to the action for the good of another, somehow having the motive wrapped up in their definition of self or worldview in such a way that action automatically flows – either in an other-centered way or in a self-centered way. Some combined the two approaches.

It is not easy to discern the appropriate behavior in given situations. From the interviews, some of the often competing factors that need to be balanced, that are involved in the more consciously analytic approach, included:

1. *Self interests vs. those of others.* Appropriate self-care in a long-term caring relationship, for example, requires us to balance our own needs with those of the other. Putting the oxygen mask on oneself and then assisting others in an aircraft emergency is important. Protecting oneself first, in this case, is the best choice to maximize the benefit to self and others.

2. *Short term vs. long term considerations.* In health-care settings, it is frequently obvious that short-term distress of the patient may be necessary in order to serve the longer-term interests of a sick person. "Tough love" may be another example of this as discipline in the short term is aimed to truly enhance the flourishing of the individual being cared for in the long run.

3. *Benefits to those we are close to vs. benefits to strangers or more distant others.* An example of this is that we frequently balance the needs of our family members with the never-ending needs of those in various parts of the world in dire circumstances. Often, as we try to act in self-giving

ways, we are faced with conflicting demands that are mutually exclusive, and we have to negotiate the way through them.

4.   *Giving vs. receiving.* Usually, in the context of compassionate love we focus on making sure we are giving enough. However, in helping those in need we often need to create space for them to give to us, and not be too comfortable with the power-balance that is often established if giving becomes a one-way street.

5.   *Justice vs. mercy.* An example of this is the altruistic punishment research of Fehr and Gächter (2002). One may judge that it is ultimately loving to establish a more just society which promotes more caring behavior overall even when it requires less than compassionate behavior toward an individual. One may even do this at cost to oneself. This is not a simple call, and emphasizes the challenges of discernment.

The less analytic approach is emphasized in the work of Kristen Monroe, a political scientist, studying rescuers in the Holocaust and Carnegie "heroes" (Monroe, 1996), where she found that many people carried out heroic acts just because "it was the only thing I could do." A similar approach was reported in the monastic interviews, where a few of the monks felt that caring actions flowed primarily from a basic "attitude of love" engendered by their faith and lifestyle, not primarily articulated as conscious decision-making processes (Underwood, 2005).

Most people, however, use a combination of these ways of going about decision-making in the area of compassionate love, which fits with explorations by others of selfless motivational cognitions (Lengbeyer, 2005). It may be that we all combine a mode of analytical choice with a more automatic decision-making process that reflects how we see or define ourselves and an underlying orientation. However discernment occurs, whether more or less intuitively or explicitly, it is a crucial component to ensure loving action.

Actions and Attitudes

The right-hand side of the model shows the resulting actions and attitudes. Positive behavior can result from compassionate love (upper loop) or from non-loving choice (lower-outer loop). Because of this, it is very difficult to judge the compassionately loving quality of an action. Observing altruistic actions such as organ donation, volunteering, helping behaviors, and supporting or caring for others in the social context are important ways to assess compassionate love. But any of these seemingly altruistic results can also be cases of non-loving choices.

An example of the complexity of judging compassionate love by actions is the case of someone who wants to donate money to a university, but will only do so if it goes toward a specific building, and that building must have the name of the donor on the front. One question is, what is the central motive of the giver – is it love, "centered on the good of the other," or is it "centered on the good of oneself"? This is not an easy call, but if the money will be given only if the name appears on the building, then that is a tip-off regarding motivation, but one that can not always be tested empirically.

Much has been written in the scientific literature on volunteering, prosocial behavior, and altruism (Post, Johnson, McCullough, & Schloss, 2003). Much of that work relies on external measures of actions and words to categorize the behavior to be studied. Compassionate love cannot always be so clearly seen. One of the outcome measures in Neff and Karney's Chapter 7 in this volume is whether the marriage lasts. The ups and downs of actions in the midst of daily situations might not be the best gauge of compassionate love, and a particular situation might not reflect the general drift. However, longevity and long-term satisfaction may be better outcomes to measure, and these are the ones they select. As research proceeds on this topic, outcomes can be selected that can more accurately assess the actions of compassionate love.

Attitudes expressed in subtle ways through facial expression, body language, or words can also be included among the "behavioral actions" indicating compassionate love. We can express a loving attitude to someone even without more concrete actions, and this can lead to a positive effect on the person. When we view someone with fundamental respect, it can produce in us words or expressions toward the person which in and of themselves can bring out the best in the person. A caring attitude can in and of itself soothe the suffering of another even before we take any action. The mere willingness to give of oneself for the good of another can produce a positive result in another person even when the actions and expressions are quite subtle, possibly not even consciously perceived by the recipient, and not always obvious to the observer.

Feedback Loops

The model also includes feedback loops in which expressing other-centered love can develop the capacity and desire to continue with such expressions. The expression of compassionate love is a dynamic process. It is a process of action, internal feedback, inner correction, and action. Feedback from compassionately loving others can expand the capacity to love, transforming a person's self-identity and developing a greater capacity to love others fully (De Wit, 1991). The feedback can be intrinsic (the effect of the choice and action on the agent him- or herself) or extrinsic (feedback from others regarding one's actions and apparent motivations). The feedback can be from others – other-centered actions can provide kudos from others. The feedback can also be internal – the good feeling on more than a superficial level, or sense of integrity, provided by other-centered actions can encourage one to engage in such actions in the future.

Good actions can also emerge from motives not full of compassionate love, such as the motive to look good in the eyes of others or to feel needed, but ultimately the intrinsic feedback of repeating these kinds of behaviors on the moral development of the agent can be detrimental (Vacek, 1994). The donor who primarily donates the money for the name on the building, the credit, and kudos, could find that kind of behavior reinforced, and continue to do it. On the other hand, honest feedback from self and others could help the donor see his or her motives and reevaluate them, leading to more other-centered behavior in the future. This is represented in the outer lower loop of Figure 1.1.

It is also possible that if the more self-centered, condescending, or less respectful motive is noticed by the person being loved and cared for, the care is not as effective. Work in the area of social support has shown that the perceived motive of the giver can affect the benefit of the action to the person on the receiving end (Ronel, 2006).

Selfless Caring and Accepting Others: Qualitative and Quantitative Research

Use of two self-report items on selfless caring and accepting others has provided some qualitative and quantitative empirical contributions to better understanding compassionate love. Throughout this volume a variety of measures are used to assess different aspects of the compassionate love model, compassionate love itself, and other variables that are more at the outer circles of the bull's-eye target. (Fehr and Sprecher discuss these at length in Chapter 2, this volume.) As part of this growing set of measures, a number of the chapters in this volume use two items from the Daily Spiritual Experience Scale (DSES) which focus on the motivation involved in expressing compassionate love and some of the attitudes and feelings involved (Underwood, 2006; Underwood & Teresi, 2002). These items were developed in 1996 as part of a 16-item scale of ordinary spiritual experiences. Compassionate love was seen as a vital part of spiritual experiences that might occur in daily life. These two items were designed to tap the experiences and feelings of extending compassionate love toward others (two other items on the scale address the receipt of compassionate love), and in that context it may be useful here to discuss some of the background to these items. They were not designed to fully address the construct of compassionate love, but do address some elements of its expression.

The two DSES items discussed here address the felt experience of desire to give of self for the good of the other and a valuing and accepting of the person at a fundamental level, not depending on their superficial actions or characteristics. The DSES items have been included in two waves of the General Social Survey and they have been used extensively in health research (e.g., Fowler & Hill, 2004; Holland & Neimeyer, 2005; Koenig, George, Titus, & Meador, 2004; Zemore & Kaskutus, 2004). In studies published here and in other, unpublished work the two love items have been used separately from the instrument as a whole to examine other-centered attitudes and motives.

The items in the DSES were developed using a number of techniques, one being in-depth interviews with a number of populations to ensure that the language was in fact getting at the desired constructs, using a "back translation" technique (Underwood, 2006). The interviews themselves also provided helpful qualitative research on the nature of compassionate love itself, as well as refining two appropriate items to tap the construct. Some of the most valuable results from these items came from the qualitative research used in their development.

The first "compassionate love" item in the DSES is: "I feel a selfless caring for others." (All items are scored on a six-point frequency scale from "many times a day" to " never or almost never.") One initial concern in the construction of the item was with the word "selfless," with the item not designed to measure total self-abnegation, and this word in the abstract might indicate this. However in the interviews it emerged that positive responses to the item did not portray self-abnegation, but rather attitudes centered on the good of the other. The goal of the item was to identify times in daily life when caring was centered on the other, rather than for primarily selfish reasons. The interviewees talked about times when they acted in a caring way to look good, or because they were paid for it, and those didn't really "count" in the tally of frequency. Examples the interviewees "counted" included doing something for a child when exhausted, or buying groceries for a sick neighbor, or helping someone when you did not initially want the person to succeed. When asking people whether they lost themselves in the act, whether self and other merged, they usually said no. Using the word "selfless" as an adjective for caring enabled the interviewees to describe the kind of caring that was centered on the other. I asked specifically if responding positively to the item meant that you could not think at all about your own welfare. No one stated that they had to be completely selfless to answer positively to the item.

Table 1.1 Distribution of Compassionate Love Items in the General Social Survey, 2005

	Many times a day 1	Every day 2	Most days 3	Some days 4	Once in a while 5	Never/ almost never 6	Total	Mean	s.d.
Selfless caring	50 (3.8)	100 (7.7)	229 (17.6)	338 (26.1)	398 (30.7)	183 (14.1)	1298	4.14	1.30
Accept others	20 (1.5)	123 (9.4)	214 (16.4)	452 (34.6)	360 (27.5)	140 (10.7)	1309	4.09	1.17

Note. Rounded percentages of the frequency count to the total respondents for each item are shown in parentheses. Means are weighted averages (sum of percentage multiplied by the score). From Davis, Smith, & Marsden, 2005.

One of the groups interviewed in the process of developing the DSES was a group of Christian monks. The selfless caring items did seem to sum up the concept well for them. If anything, the monks were perhaps more critical of their motives than some people in the general population sample. "There are times during the day that I don't express this kind of caring but I should," said one of the monks. "If I am not acting with the same amount of respect for each person, it signals to me that I am not being selflessly caring." One mentioned the situation of helping out another monk that he didn't particularly like.

The second item in the DSES directly relating to compassionate love states, "I accept others even when they do things I think are wrong," tapping into the concept of mercy. The underlying attitude addressed by this item is that of dealing with others' faults in the light of one's own: mercy and acceptance. This item addresses the felt sense of mercy, rather than the mere cognitive awareness that mercy may or may not be a good quality. Mercy, as presented in this item, is closely linked to forgiveness, yet is a deeper experience than isolated acts of forgiveness. In the monastic interviews one monk said, "People are foolish and stupid, and it is so important to accept them anyway." "My own awareness of my own failings really helps me have this experience," said another. And, "Self-knowledge helps me not to judge others" (Underwood, 2005). This element of mercy is connected to the insight brought out in Neff and Karney's Chapter 7 in this volume: that accepting another at a fundamental level – knowing the person's flaws but loving them anyway – predicts longevity of the healthy marriage.

Those who responded "never or almost never" to the mercy item felt that not accepting others when they did wrong was "right" and justified. "Of course I don't accept others when they do things I think are wrong – they don't deserve it." And on the other hand, those who reported being often merciful thought it was the "right" thing to do. This willingness to answer at both ends of the spectrum helped to demonstrate that the responses are not significantly affected by social desirability bias. In the interviews overall it seemed easy for most people to identify moments when people did things thought to be wrong.

The qualitative results give valuable information, and help to confirm the construct validity of the items; however, the use of the DSES in quantitative studies also has provided a rich body of data, much of which still awaits analysis. Table 1.1 shows the distribution of the two items on the 2005 General Social Survey, a random sample of the US population funded by the National Science Foundation and others (Davis, Smith, & Marsden, 2005; see also Smith, Chapter 4, this volume). The two compassionate love items have been administered in two waves of this data set.

These two items have also been translated into a variety of languages (Hebrew, Spanish, Lithuanian, French, Vietnamese, Korean, and Chinese) and incorporated into a variety of health studies, as they are a part of the 16-item DSES. For example, the Chinese version has been incorporated into a study of burnout in health professionals in Hong Kong, and the entire DSES is part of the Jackson Heart Study, a major longitudinal study of African American health (Loustalot, Wyatt, Boss, May, & McDyess, 2006). Higher levels of these experiences have also shown correlation with better adjustment to distressing circumstances in Muslim Afghan refugees in the United States (Dean, 2006). Because of the wide use of this scale in such a variety of studies, the items have substantial population distribution and correlational data. The two DSES items do not fully operationalize compassionate love, but they do begin to get at the assessment of the internal elements involved in the model. Together with measures of behaviors, other attitudes, substrate, and conditions, they can help us to operationalize compassionate love. More measures over time will add to our capacity to assess this construct fully.

Conclusion

The solid science presented in this volume represents the results of cutting-edge work exploring the nature of giving of self for the good of the other, other-centered love. The chapters also review the progress of relevant research from the past, and other work currently being undertaken in some related fields. There is much to be learned here about the nature of compassionate love, what hinders it, and what facilitates its expression. As you read through this volume as a researcher, student, or interested professional, I would encourage you to also reflect on the "tiger" itself, the construct of compassionate love, in your own life. Giving love to others and receiving it ourselves can be such a vital part of a full life. This rich, full kind of love is the love that the editors and authors are exploring scientifically in this volume. Given the potential of work in this field to make a difference, exploring this topic scientifically is difficult, but worth it.

References

Barkow, J., Cosmides, L., & Tooby, J. (Eds.) (1992). *The adapted mind: Evolutionary psychology and the generation of culture.* New York: Oxford University Press.
Bartels, A., & Zeki, S. (2000). The neural basis of romantic love. *NeuroReport, 11,* 3829–3834.

Batson, C. D., & Gray, R. A. (1981). Religious orientation and helping behavior: Responding to one's own or to the victim's needs? *Journal of Personality and Social Psychology, 40*(3), 511–520.

Batson, C. D., & Shaw, L. L. (1991). Evidence for altruism: Towards a pluralism of prosocial motives. *Psychological Inquiry, 2*(2), 107–122.

Damasio, H. (2002). Impairment of interpersonal social behavior caused by acquired brain damage. In S. G. Post, L. G. Underwood, J. P. Schloss, & W. B. Hurlbut (Eds.), *Altruism and altruistic love* (pp. 272–284). New York: Oxford University Press.

Darley, J. M., & Batson, C. D. (1973). From Jerusalem to Jericho: A study of situational and dispositional variables in helping behavior. *Journal of Personality and Social Psychology, 27*(1), 100–108.

Davis, J., Smith, T., & Marsden, P. (2005). General Social Surveys, 1972–2004 ICPSR04295-v2. Chicago, IL: National Opinion Research Center [producer]. Storrs, CT: Roper Center for Public Opinion Research, University of Connecticut/Ann Arbor, MI: Inter-university Consortium for Political and Social Research.

Davis, M. H., Luce, C., & Kraus, S. J. (1994). The heritability of characteristics associated with dispositional empathy. *Journal of Personality, 62*, 369–391.

Dean, M. (2006). *Islam and psychosocial wellness in an American Afghan community*. Unpublished master's thesis in International Health, Curtin University of Technology, Perth, Australia.

De Wit, H. F. (1991). *Contemplative psychology*. Pittsburgh, PA: Duquesne University Press.

Fazio, R. H., & Olson, M. A. (2003). Implicit measures in social cognition research: Their meaning and use. *Annual Review of Psychology, 54*, 297–327.

Fehr, E., & Gächter, S. (2002). Altruistic punishment in humans. *Nature, 415*, 137–140.

Fowler, D. N., & Hill, H. M. (2004). Social support and spirituality as culturally relevant factors in coping among African American women survivors of partner abuse. *Violence against Women, 10*, 1267–1282.

Holland, J. M., & Neimeyer, R. A. (2005). Reducing the risk of burnout in end-of-life care settings: The role of daily spiritual experiences and training. *Palliative & Supportive Care, 3*, 173–181.

Insel, T. R. (1997). A neurobiological basis of social attachment. *American Journal of Psychiatry, 154*, 726–735.

Johnson, R. C., Danko, G. P., Davill, T. J., Bochner, S., Bowers, J. K., Huang, Y-H., et al. (1989). Cross-cultural assessment of altruism and its correlates. *Personality and Individual Differences, 10*, 855–868.

Kagan, J. (2002). Morality, altruism and love. In S. G. Post, L. G. Underwood, J. P. Schloss, & W. B. Hurlbut (Eds.), *Altruism and altruistic love* (pp. 40–50). New York: Oxford University Press.

Koenig, H. G., George, L. K., Titus, P., & Meador, K. G. (2004). Religion, spirituality, and acute care hospitalization and long-term care use by older patients. *Archives of Internal Medicine, 164*, 1579–1585.

Lengbeyer, L. A. (2005). Selflessness and cognition. *Ethical Theory and Moral Practice, 8*, 411–435.

Levine, R. (2003). The kindness of strangers, *American Scientist, 91*, 226–233.

Loustalot, F. V., Wyatt, S. B., Boss, B., May, W., & McDyess, T. (2006). Psychometric examination of the Daily Spiritual Experiences Scale. *Journal of Cultural Diversity, 13*(3), 162–167.

Moll, J., Krueger, F., Zahn, R., Pardini, M., de Oliverira-Souza, R., & Grafman, J. (2006). Human fronto-mesolimbic networks guide decisions about charitable donation. *PNAS, 103*, 15623–15628.

Monroe, K. R. (1996). *The heart of altruism: Perceptions of a common humanity.* Princeton, NJ: Princeton University Press.

Neusner, J., & Chilton, B. (Eds.). (2005). *Altruism in world religions.* Washington, DC: Georgetown University Press.

Nitschke, J. B., Nelson, E. E., Rusch, B. D., Fox, A. S., Oakes, T. R., & Davidson, R. J. (2004). Orbitofrontal cortex tracks positive mood in mothers viewing pictures of their newborn infants. *NeuroImage, 21*, 583–592.

Pfeifer, J. H., Ruble, D. N., Bachman, M. A., Alvarez, J. M., Cameron, J. A., & Fuligni, A. J. (2007). Social identities and intergroup bias in immigrant and nonimmigrant children. *Developmental Psychology, 43*(2), 496–507.

Post, S., Johnson, B., McCullough, M., & Schloss, J. (Eds.). (2003). *Research on altruism and love: An annotated bibliography of major studies in psychology, sociology, evolutionary biology, and theology.* Radnor, PA: Templeton Foundation Press.

Post, S. G., Underwood, L. G., Schloss, J. P., & Hurlbut, W. B. (Eds.). (2002) *Altruism and altruistic love: Science, philosophy and religion in dialogue.* New York: Oxford University Press.

Preston, S. D., & de Waal, F. B. M (2002). Empathy: Its ultimate and proximate bases. *Behavioral and Brain Sciences, 25*(1), 1–20.

Ronel, N. (2006). When good overcomes bad: The impact of volunteers on those they help. *Human Relations, 59*(8), 1133–1153.

Roskies, A. (2006). A case study in neuroethics: The nature of moral judgment. In J. Illes (Ed.), *Neuroethics* (pp. 17–32). Oxford: Oxford University Press.

Rushton, J. P. (2004). Genetic and environmental contributions to pro-social attitudes: A twin study of social responsibility. *Proceedings of the Royal Society, 271*(1557), 2583–2585.

Saxena, S., O'Connell, K., & Underwood, L. (2002). Cross-cultural quality of life assessment at the end of life: A commentary. *The Gerontologist, 42* (Special Issue III), 81–85.

Simon, H. A. (1993). Altruism and economics. *American Economic Review, 83*(2), 156–161.

Underwood, L. (2004). Compassionate love. In S. G. Post (Ed.), *Encyclopedia of Bioethics* (3rd ed.) (pp. 483–488). New York: Macmillan Reference USA.

Underwood, L. G. (2002). The human experience of compassionate love: Conceptual mapping and data from selected studies. In S. G. Post, L. G. Underwood, J. P. Schloss, & W. B. Hurlbut (Eds.), *Altruism and altruistic love* (pp. 72–88). New York: Oxford University Press.

Underwood, L. G. (2005). Interviews with Trappist monks as a contribution to research methodology in the investigation of compassionate love. *Journal for the Theory of Social Behavior, 35*, 285–302.

Underwood, L. G. (2006). Ordinary spiritual experience: Qualitative research, interpretive guidelines, and population distribution for the Daily Spiritual Experience Scale. *Archive for the Psychology of Religion/Archiv für Religionspsychologie, 28*, 181–218.

Underwood, L. G., & Teresi, J. (2002). The Daily Spiritual Experience Scale: Development, theoretical description, reliability, exploratory factor analysis, and preliminary construct validity using health-related data. *Annals of Behavioral Medicine, 24*, 22–33.

Vacek, E. (1994). *Love, human and divine: The heart of Christian ethics.* Washington, DC: Georgetown University Press.

Vanier, J. (1998). *Becoming human.* Mahwah, NJ: Paulist Press.

WHOQOL SRPB Group (2006). A cross-cultural study of spirituality, religion, and personal beliefs as components of quality of life. *Social Science and Medicine, 62*, 1486–1497.

Zemore, S. E., & Kaskutus, L. A. (2004). Helping, spirituality and Alcoholics Anonymous in recovery. *Journal of Studies on Alcohol, 65*(3), 383–391.

2

Compassionate Love: Conceptual, Measurement, and Relational Issues

Beverley Fehr and Susan Sprecher

When asked to think about a person who exemplifies compassionate love, we suspect that for many, Mother Teresa would come to mind. Her life was dedicated to helping the "poorest of the poor" – those who were neglected, shunned, and cast aside by their society. Mother Teresa won a litany of humanitarian awards for her selfless dedication to, and love and care for those who were homeless, sick, and dying. She articulated her view of love in many of her public speeches and lectures. One prominent theme in her lectures and writing was the necessity of sacrifice. In her words, "It is very important for us to realize that love, to be true, has to hurt. I must be willing to give whatever it takes" (address to the US Senate and House of Representatives, February 3, 1994). Although Mother Teresa dedicated her life to the service of strangers (e.g., homeless people found on the streets of Calcutta), she maintained that love must originate in the family. "We must remember that love begins at home and we must also remember that 'the future of humanity passes through the family'." She exhorted people to find the poor in their homes and in their neighborhoods.

Theologians and others interested in the study of religion have called for scientific research on altruistic or compassionate love – love that is centered on the good of the other (e.g., Post, Underwood, Schloss, & Hurlbut, 2002; Underwood, 2002). This kind of love, exemplified by Mother Teresa, has been overlooked by social scientists – a surprising omission, given the voluminous literature on other kinds of love, particularly romantic love (see, for example, reviews by Aron, Fisher, & Strong, 2006; Felmlee & Sprecher, 2006; Hendrick & Hendrick, 2000; Noller, 1996). However, recently, social scientists have begun to apply methodological tools and theories originally developed in the close relationships field to the study of compassionate love. As the present volume attests, this is proving to be a valuable and worthwhile endeavor.

We are among the social scientists who have turned our attention to this kind of love. We began our research on compassionate love with several guiding questions, including: How do people conceptualize compassionate love? Can compassionate love be measured? What are the distinctions, if any, between compassionate love as experienced for close others versus compassionate love as experienced for strangers and humanity? Are there individual differences in the experience of compassionate love? And, finally, does the experience of compassionate love differ, depending on whether one is the giver or the recipient of this kind of love? In this chapter, we present findings from our program of research on compassionate love that speak to each of these issues. We set the stage by presenting conceptualizations of compassionate love – both experts' definitions and lay conceptions. We then turn to measurement issues and describe the development of a self-report instrument to assess compassionate love, namely the Compassionate Love Scale (Sprecher & Fehr, 2005). In the remaining sections, we focus on the experience of compassionate love. Topics we cover include whether compassionate love differs depending on the target (e.g., close others versus strangers or all of humanity) and individual differences in the experience of compassionate love. In our final section, we explore how the experience of compassionate love differs, depending on whether one is the giver or the recipient. We close the chapter with a discussion of future research directions.

Conceptualization of Compassionate Love

Compassionate love remains largely uncharted territory in the social sciences. Scholars in this fledgling area seem to agree that an important first step is to address the basic question: What is compassionate love? Indeed, it is commonly assumed that in any scientific investigation, the first and most fundamental step is to provide a definition of the target concept. As we discuss next, social scientists have taken on this challenge.

Experts' Definitions

The term *compassionate love* was selected by Underwood and others (see Underwood, 2002, 2005; Chapter 1, this volume) to capture a kind of love that involves a giving of the self for the good of the other. Underwood articulated five basic elements of this kind of love: free choice for the other; valuing the other at a fundamental level; openness and receptivity; an accurate cognitive understanding of the other, oneself, and the situation; and, finally, a "response of the heart" – an accurate emotional understanding of the situation. This conceptualization of compassionate love, along with the formulation of a broader model that includes antecedents, consequences, and so on (see Underwood, 2002, 2005; Chapter 1, this volume), led to a targeted research initiative, funded by the Fetzer Institute, focused specifically on compassionate love. (Many of the contributions to this volume were part of this initiative.) This funding program and a subsequent conference on compassionate love (2003, co-sponsored by the International Association for Relationship Research) led to the formulation of a number of definitions and conceptualizations of compassionate love. These were compiled by Shacham-Dupont (2003), who also examined the extent of commonality across definitions. Compassionate love was variously defined as: an attitude, specific behaviors, cognitive predispositions, an expression of the neural-based bonding system, a dyadic phenomenon, and as a "complex functional whole including appraisals, appreciations, patterned physiological responses, action tendencies, and instrumental behaviors" (p. 14).[1] Features or elements of compassionate love included: altruism (e.g., "Compassionate love is a type of sharing that is selfless"), helpfulness ("Helping, or willingness to help, someone in distress"), care and concern ("observable, meaningful behaviors that demonstrate concern and care for the welfare of the others"), empathy, sympathy, tenderness, and so on. In addition, the theme of selflessness and sacrifice was prominent ("put the needs of others over individual needs"). Although there were some similarities in these definitions, equally striking was the diversity – both in terms of what compassionate love is (e.g., an attitude, behavior, cognition) and in terms of its elements or features.

Laypeople's Conceptions of Compassionate Love

The failure of experts to agree on a definition suggests that compassionate love, like other kinds of love, may not be amenable to a classical definition, whereby concepts are defined in terms of a set of individually necessary and jointly sufficient criterial attributes. Instead, compassionate love may be better understood as a prototype concept. The founder of prototype theory, Eleanor Rosch (1973), argued that many natural language concepts lack classical definitions, but rather, are organized around their clearest cases or best examples. Members of a category can be ordered in terms of their degree of resemblance to these prototypical

---

[1] Lazarus (1991) defined *compassion* as emotion that involves "being moved by another's suffering and wanting to help" (p. 289), which is highly similar to some of the definitions of compassionate love in Shacham-Dupont's (2003) compendium. Underwood (2002) preferred the term compassionate love because "*compassion* alone left out some of the emotional and transcendent components which the word *love* brings in" (p. 78).

cases. Boundaries between categories therefore are blurry, with members of one category shading into members of neighboring categories. For example, Rosch (for a review, see Mervis & Rosch, 1981) found that although the concept of fruit cannot be precisely defined, people agree that apples and oranges are better examples than are mangoes and apricots. Instances such as olives and avocados lie at the fuzzy boundary between fruit and the neighboring category of "vegetable." Although Rosch's work focused primarily on natural-object categories, her theory inspired prototype analyses of a variety of concepts, including emotion, as well as specific types of emotion such as anger and love (e.g., Aron & Westbay, 1996; Fitness & Fletcher, 1993; Shaver, Schwartz, Kirson, & O' Connor, 1987; for a review, see Fehr, 2005). In fact, love is the concept that has been most extensively analyzed from a prototype perspective. An example is Fehr and Russell's (1991) prototype analysis of types of love. In their first study, participants were asked to list the varieties of love. (Compassionate love was listed as a kind of love, albeit with relatively low frequency.) Consistent with a prototype perspective, some of the types (e.g., maternal love, friendship) were considered highly representative of the concept, whereas others were considered less so (e.g., patriotic love, infatuation). Moreover, this prototype structure affected information processing in predictable ways. For example, in a reaction-time study, participants were quick to verify that prototypical instances were types of love, but required more deliberation to confirm the category membership of nonprototypical instances.

In other research, Fehr (1988) hypothesized that the *features* of love might show a similar prototype organization such that some features would be considered more representative of the concept than others. In her first study, participants were asked to list the attributes or features of the concept of love. Consistent with a prototype conceptualization, features such as trust, caring, friendship, respect, and compassion were regarded as central to the concept; features such as excitement, uncertainty, and gazing at the other were regarded as peripheral. This prototype structure was found to influence the cognitive processing of category-relevant information. For example, prototypical features were more salient in memory than were nonprototypical features. Interestingly, the prototype structure of love also affected people's judgments about the dynamics of close relationships (e.g., violations of prototypical features were regarded as more damaging to a relationship than violations of nonprototypical features). The prototype of love identified in this research proved replicable by other researchers, using diverse samples (for reviews, see Fehr, 1993, 2006).

Subsequently, researchers conducted prototype analyses of the features of specific kinds of love, including romantic love (e.g., Button & Collier,

1991; Regan, Kocan, & Whitlock, 1998) and the concept of "being in love" (Lamm & Wiesmann, 1997; Luby & Aron, 1990). Once again, there was evidence that these kinds of love were organized as prototype concepts. Some features were regarded as more central to the concept than others. Moreover, this internal structure was reflected in various kinds of information-processing tasks.

Thus, there is substantial evidence that the concept of love is organized as a prototype concept. There is also evidence that a few specific types of love are organized as prototype concepts. However, the question of whether compassionate love is structured as a prototype concept remains an empirical one. We therefore set out to test the hypothesis that the concept of compassionate love would be more amenable to a prototype than a classical conceptualization.

Six studies were conducted (Fehr & Sprecher, under revision). In our first study, participants were asked to generate characteristics or features of compassionate love. The responses were subjected to a coding procedure in which identical and highly synonymous responses were combined. This procedure resulted in a final set of 59 features. The prototype of compassionate love, derived in this way, included cognitions (e.g., worrying, think about the other all the time), feelings and emotions (e.g., feel happiest when with the person, feel sad when apart), behaviors (e.g., do anything for the other, hugging), and motivations (e.g., want to make the other happy, want to spend time with other). The feature "caring" was listed most frequently, followed by trust, helping, understanding, and wanting to spend time with other.

In Study 2, we gathered prototypicality ratings to test whether compassionate love is structured as a prototype concept, such that some features are considered more central to the concept than others. The features that received the highest prototypicality ratings were: trust, honesty, caring, understanding, and support. Thus, in the minds of ordinary people, it is these characteristics that capture the meaning of compassionate love. Interestingly, these features also are seen as central to the concept of love itself (Fehr, 1988). The features that received the lowest prototypicality ratings were: doing anything for the other, putting other ahead of self, and making sacrifices for the other. In other words, these characteristics were regarded as part of the concept, but on the periphery. This stands in contrast to experts' definitions, many of which focus on sacrifice and selflessness. Our findings suggest that in the minds of laypeople, compassionate love is, at its core, a kind of love.

In Study 3, we again gathered prototypicality ratings, but this time we manipulated the target of compassionate love (close other versus stranger). The features of compassionate love received higher prototypicality ratings when rated in the context of a close other compared to a stranger. Thus, the prototype of compassionate love seems most applicable to close relationships – more so than strangers. Put another way, ordinary people seem to agree with Mother Teresa's declaration that love begins at home.

In the remaining studies, we sought to verify the prototype structure of compassionate love, using a variety of methodologies. In Study 4, we used reaction-time methodology to test the hypothesis that participants would be quick to confirm that prototypical features are part of the concept, but would require more deliberation when deciding whether nonprototypical features belonged. The results supported this hypothesis. In our next study (Study 5), we focused on memory for prototypical versus nonprototypical features of compassionate love. As predicted, participants were more likely to "recall" prototypical features, even when they had not been presented. False memory effects were less likely to occur for nonprototypical features.

In our final study, we hypothesized that when the concept of compassionate love is activated in cognitive representation, people would be more likely to infer that prototypical, than nonprototypical features, were applicable. Results supported predictions. For example, when told that "Pat experiences compassionate love for Chris" participants inferred that Pat was likely to trust Chris, care about Chris, be concerned about Chris's well-being, and so on. They were less likely to assume that prototypical features, such as Pat would make sacrifices for Chris or put Chris first, would apply.

In conclusion, these studies suggest that laypeople have a rich and complex knowledge of the concept of compassionate love. The findings are consistent with the view that compassionate love is organized as a prototype concept, such that some features are seen as more representative of compassionate love than others.

Development and Validation of the Compassionate Love Scale

Although the identification of the features that laypeople regard as central or peripheral to compassionate love is an important step for understanding the concept, the advancement of research in any new area is facilitated by the availability of measurement instruments. Thus, in another line of work, we undertook the development of a scale to assess the degree to which people experience compassionate love for a variety of targets (Sprecher & Fehr, 2005). In constructing our scale, labeled the Compassionate Love Scale (CLS), we drew on social science research on love and related concepts (see the earlier section on conceptualizations of compassionate love), items from existing scales that appeared to portray compassionate love, as well as our ongoing research on lay conceptions of compassionate love. Our goal was to develop a scale that assesses the many facets of compassionate love for others, where "others" can refer to people in general, strangers/humanity, close others (friends, family), or a specific close other. One benefit of such a scale is that mean levels of compassionate love can be compared across targets. Another advantage is that the predictors, correlates, and consequences can be compared across relational contexts. For example, the factors that may contribute to compassionate love for all of humanity may differ from those that contribute to compassionate love for a specific close other such as a romantic partner. The Compassionate Love Scale can be tailored to address such issues.

We began by examining existing love scales. Most of the well-known, multifaceted love scales include at least one or two items that pertain to some aspect of compassionate or altruistic love (although the focus generally has been on intimacy, passion, and commitment). For example, the following items from standard love scales portray at least some aspect of compassionate love:

1. "I would do almost anything for my partner."
This is a caring item from Rubin's (1970, 1973) Love Scale, which measures three components of love: caring, intimacy, and need/attachment.

2. "I feel happy when I am doing something to make ___ happy."
"If ___ were going through a difficult time, I would put away my own concerns to help him/her out."
These are items from the long version of the Passionate Love Scale (Hatfield & Sprecher, 1986).

3. "I give considerable emotional support to ___."
This is an intimacy item from Sternberg's (1986, 1997) Triangular Love Scale, which assesses three components of love: intimacy, passion, and commitment.

4. "I try to always help my lover through difficult times."
"I would rather suffer myself than let my lover suffer."
"I cannot be happy unless I place my lover's happiness before my own."
"I am usually willing to sacrifice my own wishes to let my lover achieve his/hers."
"Whatever I own is my lover's to use as he/she chooses."
"When my lover gets angry with me, I still love him/her fully and unconditionally."
"I would endure all things for the sake of my lover."
These items comprise the agape love-style scale. Agape is defined as a selfless, caring kind of love, characterized by high levels of self-sacrifice (Hendrick & Hendrick, 1986). An instrument to measure this love style,

along with five others, was originally developed by Lasswell and Lasswell (1976), but later modified and refined by Hendrick and Hendrick (1986; Hendrick, Hendrick, Foote, & Slapion-Foote, 1984).[2]

We also combed the literature for scales that measure love for non-intimate others. Love experienced for strangers, peripheral ties, or all of humanity has generally been overlooked by researchers, although there are a few recent exceptions, as discussed below:

5.   "I feel a selfless caring for others."

"I accept others even when they do things I think are wrong."

These are items from the Daily Spiritual Experience Scale (Underwood & Teresi, 2002; see Underwood, Chapter 1, this volume). The first item is intended to assess compassionate love. The second item is intended to measure the closely related construct of mercy (defined as an acceptance and understanding of others' faults).

6.   "To what extent are you able to feel love and compassion for others?"

"How much are you able to accept others?"

"To what extent are you able to help others without being interested in anything in return?"

These items, worded as questions, are part of the Given Love Scale, a scale that is being developed by the World Health Organization (see Underwood, Chapter 1, this volume). The purpose of this measure is to examine associations between giving love and spirituality/religiosity (WHOQOL SRPB Group, 2006).

7.   Finally, we note that Campos, Logli, and Keltner (2006) have recently developed a Feelings toward Others Scale that includes a Love for Humanity subscale. This subscale is intended to measure a kind of love centered on the inherent good of all people and the desire to engage in benevolent action toward others, particularly unknown others. For example, the scale includes items such as "I believe that people are inherently good" and "Doing kind things for others is a reward in itself." Although several items on this scale appear to portray compassionate or altruistic love, this measure was not available when we constructed the Compassionate Love Scale.

In sum, standard love scales tend to include items that refer to altruistic or compassionate love. In addition, there are a few scales that directly attempt

---

[2]   The purpose of the agape love-style scale is to measure an altruistic type of love, which we do not regard as synonymous with compassionate love. Moreover, the two scales have different purposes. The agape love-style scale is intended for use in a romantic context, whereas the CLS is intended to assess compassionate love for a variety of targets. Thus, we do not see our scale as redundant with the agape love-style scale.

to measure other-oriented kinds of love. However, in our view, there was still a need for a multifaceted scale to assess compassionate love, per se.

The Compassionate Love Scale: Item Generation

To begin our scale development, we adapted the compassionate and mercy items from Underwood (2002, Underwood & Teresi, 2002) and an item from the Hendrick and Hendrick (1986) Agape scale ("I would rather suffer myself than let my lover suffer."). In addition, we wrote several items, drawing on findings from our prototype studies, other love scales (see above) and the literature on love and altruism. The first few items that we generated referred directly to compassion or compassionate love (e.g., "I feel considerable compassionate love for people from everywhere"). Next, we crafted items to assess the cognitive elements of compassionate love (e.g., "I spend a lot of time concerned about the well-being of humankind," emotional aspects (e.g., "It is easy for me to feel the pain (and joy) experienced by my loved ones"), and behavioral predispositions (e.g., "If a person close to me needs help, I would do almost anything I could to help him or her"; see Sprecher & Fehr, 2005). Based on a psychometric analysis of our initial item pool (e.g., item-to-total correlations, inter-item correlations) we eliminated a few of our original 19 items and added several others (see Sprecher & Fehr, 2005, for details). Table 2.1 presents the final 21-item Compassionate Love Scale in three different versions (family and friends, strangers/humanity, a specific close other), along with means and standard deviations for each. The Compassionate Love Scale has demonstrated high levels of internal consistency. For example, across three studies and across different versions of the scale, Cronbach's alpha has exceeded .90 (Sprecher & Fehr, 2005; Studies 1–3). In general, the scale is uncontaminated by social desirability biases, although in one study, the strangers/humanity version of the scale was positively correlated ($r = .28$) with the Impression Management subscale of the Balanced Inventory of Desirable Responding (Paulhus, 1991; see Sprecher & Fehr, 2005; Study 2). However, the association between compassionate love for strangers/humanity and other variables (e.g., spirituality) remained significant when controlling for impression management.

Convergent Validity

We sought to demonstrate the validity of the Compassionate Love Scale (CLS) by correlating scores on this scale with established scales that measure constructs that theoretically should be related to compassionate love. We focused on the following variables: empathy, social support, helpfulness, including volunteerism, and altruistic love/agape.

Table 2.1 Mean Ratings for Different Versions of the Compassionate Love Scale

	Close others version	Stranger/humanity version	Intimate partner version
1. When I see family members or friends feeling sad, I feel a need to reach out to them	6.1 (1.20)	4.18 (1.64)	6.36 (1.18)
2. I spend a lot of time concerned about the well-being of those people close to me	5.89 (1.07)	3.93 (1.52)	5.75 (1.30)
3. When I hear about a friend or family member going through a difficult time, I feel a great deal or compassion for him or her	6.16 (99)	4.61 (1.49)	6.36 (.86)
4. It is easy for me to feel the pain (and joy) experienced by my loved ones	5.89 (1.47)	4.33 (1.56)	5.99 (1.18)
5. If a person close to me needs help, I would do almost anything to help him or her	6.41 (.81)	4.51 (1.42)	6.61 (.78)
6. I feel considerable compassionate love for those people important in my life	6.48 (.73)	4.04 (1.52)	6.15 (1.28)
7. I would rather suffer myself than see someone close to me suffer	5.80 (1.23)	3.70 (1.61)	5.61 (1.28)

Item			
8. If given the opportunity, I am willing to sacrifice in order to let the people important to me achieve their goals in life	5.39 (1.29)	3.92 (1.52)	5.10 (1.52)
9. I tend to feel compassion for people who are close to me	6.28 (.85)	4.53 (1.53)	6.20 (1.12)
10. One of the activities that provides me with the most meaning to my life is helping others with whom I have a close relationship	5.82 (1.26)	4.19 (1.59)	5.25 (1.44)
11. I would rather engage in actions that help my intimate others than engage in actions that would help me	5.28 (1.26)	3.78 (1.54)	4.84 (1.54)
12. I often have tender feelings toward friends and family members when they seem to be in need	5.92 (1.06)	4.41 (1.45)	6.02 (1.17)
13. I feel selfless caring for my friends and family	5.59 (1.21)	3.91 (1.45)	5.47 (1.58)
14. I accept friends and family members even when they do things I think are wrong	5.68 (1.08)	3.58 (1.52)	5.34 (1.48)
15. If a family member or close friend is troubled, I usually feel extreme tenderness and caring	5.84 (1.05)	4.01 (1.47)	5.96 (1.23)
16. I try to understand rather than judge people who are close to me	5.91 (1.03)	4.80 (1.47)	5.97 (1.14)

(*Continued*)

Table 2.1 (*Continued*)

	Close others version	Stranger/humanity version	Intimate partner version
17. I try to put myself in my friend's shoes when he or she is in trouble	5.77 (1.12)	4.57 (1.50)	5.69 (1.08)
18. I feel happy when I see that loved ones are happy	6.38 (.85)	5.01 (1.40)	6.47 (.85)
19. Those whom I love can trust that I will be there for them if they need me	6.54 (.74)	5.43 (1.32)	6.60 (.80)
20. I want to spend time with close others so that I can find ways to help enrich their lives	5.57 (1.19)	3.82 (1.55)	5.88 (1.25)
21. I very much wish to be kind and good to my friends and family members	6.42 (.82)	5.54 (1.36)	6.49 (.83)

1. The items for the Close Others version of the Compassionate Love Scale are listed in column 1. The wording for the strangers/humanity and the intimate partner versions is available upon request from the authors.
2. The means in columns 1 and 2 are taken from Sprecher & Fehr (2005). The means in column 3 are taken from Fehr & Sprecher (2006).

Empathy. Empathy has been defined as the perception of another's emotional state and a response on the part of self that is highly similar to that experienced by the other (e.g., Batson & Oleson, 1991). Empathy is especially likely to be experienced in response to another's suffering. We believe that compassionate love includes tenderness, caring, and other aspects of empathy, but is a broader construct that also entails behavioral predispositions such as self-sacrifice (Sprecher & Fehr, 2005). Thus, empathy may be a component of compassionate love, or perhaps a precursor to compassionate love. Underwood (2005) has argued that although empathy facilitates the expression of compassionate love, it is possible to express compassionate love without necessarily experiencing empathy. The point is that empathy should be related to, but not synonymous with, compassionate love.

Consistent with this expectation, we found that scores on the CLS were positively associated with empathy, assessed by scales such as the Other-oriented Empathy scale (e.g., "When I see someone being taking advantage of, I feel kind of protective towards them"; Penner, Fritzsche, Craiger, & Freifeld, 1995) and a version of the Davis (1996) empathy scale (e.g., "I am usually aware of the feelings of other people") used by Schieman and Van Gundy (2000). The correlations were in the moderate range for both the close others and the strangers/humanity versions of the CLS (rs = .45 to .68; Sprecher & Fehr, 2005; Studies 1–2), suggesting that compassionate love and empathy are related, but distinguishable, concepts.

Social support. We also examined the relation between compassionate love and the provision of social support for others. Because social support is generally enacted in a relational context, we expected that scores on the close others version of CLS would be more highly correlated with the provision of social support than scores on the strangers/humanity version. To test this hypothesis, participants were asked to report the degree to which they had offered others various kinds of social support (e.g., emotional, instrumental). These were combined to form a total social support score. Scores on the close others version of the CLS were positively correlated with provision of social support assessed in this way ($r = .51$; Sprecher & Fehr, 2005; Study 2). Similarly, in a study of compassionate love directed toward a specific close other (generally a romantic partner), CLS scores were moderately correlated with the level of social support provided to that individual ($r = .56$; Sprecher & Fehr, 2005; Study 3). Scores on the strangers/humanity version of the CLS also were positively correlated with social support, but, as expected, this relation was weaker than that found for the close others versions ($r = .27$; Sprecher & Fehr, 2005; Study 2).

Helpfulness. As the life of Mother Teresa attests, helpfulness is often regarded as a manifestation of compassionate love. Thus, we anticipated that scores on the CLS would be positively correlated with self-reports of helpfulness. However, again, we did not expect these relations to be substantial. As Underwood (2002, this volume) has argued, even though an individual may be experiencing compassionate love, there are numerous factors that may inhibit him or her from acting on those feelings. Furthermore, helpfulness is only one of many possible outcomes of experiencing compassionate love. We found that scores on the CLS were, indeed, positively correlated with scores on Penner et al.'s (1995) Helpfulness factor (rs = 23 to .25 for close others; rs = 30 to .32 for strangers/humanity; Sprecher & Fehr, 2005; Studies 1–2). Given that the helpfulness scale items generally refer to strangers (e.g., "I have offered to help a handicapped or elderly stranger across a street"), it is not surprising that the correlations were somewhat higher for the strangers/humanity version of the CLS than for the close others version.

We also examined another form of helping, namely reports of volunteerism. Volunteerism was assessed across several domains (assisting the homeless, charitable giving, supporting social causes, community service), as well as with a global assessment of volunteering compared to peers, based on a measure developed by Gillath et al. (2005; see also Mikulincer, Shaver, & Gillath, Chapter 8, this volume). Compassionate love scores were positively correlated with these measures (rs = .19 to .35; Sprecher & Fehr, 2005; Study 2), and, again, the correlations tended to be higher for the strangers/humanity version of the CLS. The one null finding was that compassionate love was unrelated to reports of the number of hours volunteered in the past three months. Thus, it appears that compassionate love can predict whether or not one engages in helpful behaviors, but not necessarily the frequency with which one does so.

Altruistic love/agape. These terms altruism and compassionate love are often used interchangeably. However, Underwood (2005) has argued that the two concepts can and should be distinguished. In her words, "The word 'altruism' ... does not capture the fullness of the construct. It is nested within the wider concept, but compassionate love captures an investment of self deeper than 'altruism' suggests, a dimension that cannot be fully assessed through external evaluations of actions" (p. 292). The Greek word *agape* is also used to describe altruistic love. According to Hendrick and Hendrick (1992), agape can be defined as "selfless and giving, concerned with the partner's welfare and untroubled for the self" (p. 66). Some have questioned whether this kind of love is actually experienced in human relationships (e.g., Noller, 1996). For example, the Trappist monks interviewed by Underwood (2005) reserved the term "agape" for the kind of love that God extends to humankind. We expected that scores on the CLS would be related to altruistic love/agape, but only moderately so. We examined these relations in a sample of dating relationships, using a relationship-specific measure of the CLS (Sprecher & Fehr, unpublished raw data). Altruistic love was assessed with the agape love-style scale (Hendrick & Hendrick, 1989) as well as a measure of self-sacrifice adapted from Randall, Fedor, and Longenecker (1990). As predicted, compassionate love as experienced for one's romantic partner was moderately correlated with the agape love style ($rs = .49$ to .61) and with self-sacrifice ($rs = .54$ to .66).

Discriminant Validity

We have focused our psychometric efforts on convergent validity because it seemed most important to demonstrate that our compassionate love scale was not simply another measure of empathy, social support, helpfulness, or altruism. However, it must also be shown that CLS scores are not correlated with measures of constructs that should not be associated with compassionate love (or inversely correlated with measures of constructs that should be negatively associated with compassionate love). We have examined discriminant validity in a preliminary way in a sample of dating partners (Sprecher & Fehr, unpublished raw data). Specifically, we hypothesized that scores on the CLS (as experienced for a romantic partner) would be negatively correlated with a manipulative, game-playing approach to love (ludus love style). The results supported this prediction: $rs = -.26$ to $-.27$. We also expected that compassionate love would be unrelated to obsessive-dependent love (mania love style). These relations were nonsignificant: $rs = .09$ to .13. Similarly, compassionate love was not associated with a practical, "shopping-list" approach to love (pragma love style), in which relationships are formed only with those who possess the proper credentials (e.g., earning potential, $rs = -.02$ to $-.21$). Thus, although further demonstrations of discriminant validity are required, these initial findings are promising.

Behavioral Validation

The gold standard for scale validation is whether scale scores can predict behavior. In other words, it is important to demonstrate that people who score high on the CLS actually behave more compassionately than those who score low. We addressed this issue by conducting a laboratory study in which participants first completed the CLS (close others and the strangers/humanity versions; Fehr & Sprecher, unpublished raw data). Then, several days later, they were invited to participate in a supposedly unrelated study on the effects of rewards on performance. A ring-toss game was set up in the laboratory and participants were told that they would receive one Canadian dollar for every successful toss, ostensibly to see whether rewards increase accuracy. The experimenter discontinued the ring-toss trials when a participant had earned $10. Upon leaving the laboratory, participants were given the opportunity to engage in a compassionate act. A confederate was stationed at a table that was set up with a large display, obtained from the Red Cross, to solicit donations for tsunami relief. After the participant passed by the table, the confederate recorded whether or not a donation was made, and if so, the amount. (All of the money collected was, in fact, donated to the Red Cross.) Consistent with predictions, participants who scored high on the CLS, especially the strangers/humanity version, contributed more to tsunami relief than those who scored low (Fehr & Sprecher, unpublished raw data).

In sum, the evidence so far suggests that the CLS is a reliable, valid measurement instrument for assessing compassionate love as experienced for multiple targets. The convergent validity findings reinforce that those who experience high levels of compassionate love are more likely to report experiencing empathy and altruistic love (agape) and to report the provision of social support and help. However, in all cases, the correlations were not so high as to suggest that these were redundant constructs. We also obtained preliminary evidence of discriminant validity. Compassionate love as experienced for a romantic partner was negatively correlated with a game-playing love style and uncorrelated with obsessive-manic and pragmatic love styles. Perhaps most important, compassionate love, particularly as experienced for strangers/humanity, was associated with prosocial behavior, specifically the act of making a charitable donation.

Interestingly, the strength of the association between compassionate love and these other constructs was dependent on the relational context. Compassionate love as experienced for close others was more strongly linked with empathy and the provision of social support than was compassionate love for strangers/humanity. Compassionate love for strangers/humanity was more strongly related to helpfulness (toward strangers) and volunteerism than was compassionate love toward close others. Although the correlational nature of these findings prevents causal conclusions, the findings suggest that the outcomes or consequences of compassionate love may well vary, depending on the context in which compassionate love is experienced.

Compassionate Love as Experienced for Different Targets

According to Underwood's (2002, Chapter 1) model, situational factors, such as the social, environmental, or cultural context, influence the degree to which compassionate love is expressed. In our research, we have focused on the social or relational context in which compassionate love is experienced. As reported above, compassionate love scores show a differential pattern of correlations, depending on whether the target is close others, a specific close other (romantic partner), or strangers/humanity. However, these findings do not speak to the question of whether people experience different levels of compassionate love, depending on the target. In studies designed to address this issue, we have found consistently that people report significantly higher levels of compassionate love for close others than for strangers/humanity (Sprecher & Fehr, 2005). For example, in one study, the mean score on the close others version of the CLS was 5.96 (on a seven-point scale) versus 4.32 on the strangers/humanity version (Sprecher & Fehr, 2005; Study 1). In another study, we administered a relationship-specific version of the scale in which respondents were asked to focus on "a special person to whom you are currently close" (Sprecher & Fehr; 2005; Study 3). The mean score on this version was 5.92 – similar to the mean score for close others obtained in our earlier studies (Sprecher & Fehr, 2005; Studies 1–2). When we partitioned the data, based on whether participants reported on a romantic relationship or a close friendship, we found that compassionate love scores were significantly higher for those who had completed the scale with reference to a marital or dating partner than for those who had focused on a close friend ($M = 6.11$ vs. 5.45).

The finding that people report more compassionate love for close others than for strangers/humanity is consistent with theorizing and research in the close relationships literature. For example, research on lay conceptions of love has found that people tend to associate the concept of love with close others – more so than with humanity and strangers (e.g., Fehr & Russell, 1991). Several major theories in psychology point to the same conclusion. According to evolutionary theory, much of human behavior is motivated by the goal of survival and the successful transmission of one's genes (e.g., Burnstein, Crandall, & Kitayama, 1994; Crawford & Krebs, 1998). From this perspective, people should feel higher levels of compassionate love for family members and close friends than for strangers/humanity because close others play a more direct role in ensuring their survival. Attachment theory posits that the caregiving system, which includes compassionate love, is activated when loved ones demonstrate attachment-seeking behaviors (e.g., Mikulincer, Shaver, Gillath, & Nitzberg, 2005; Chapter 8, this volume; Shaver, Hazan, & Bradshaw, 1988). Those who are not close are less likely to activate the attachment system. In short, the findings from diverse literatures converge on the conclusion that close others are the most likely recipients of compassionate love.

Individual Differences in Compassionate Love

According to Underwood (2002; Chapter 1, this volume), there are individual characteristics that encourage the expression of compassionate love in people. We have conducted several studies to examine individual differences in the propensity to experience compassionate love, focusing on variables such as gender, religiosity/spirituality, and attachment. Regarding gender, we have consistently found that women score higher on the CLS than do men (Sprecher & Fehr, 2005; Sprecher, Fehr, & Zimmerman, 2007). This gender difference holds across targets (family and friends, strangers/humanity).[3] Other research has shown that women express more empathy and emotional support for others (e.g., Eagly & Crowley, 1986; Penner et al., 1995; Taylor, 2002). Our findings suggest that compassionate love should be added to this list.

Given that compassionate love is encouraged and promoted by many religions, we expected that compassionate love would be correlated with religiosity and spirituality. This hypothesis has been confirmed using multiple measures, including frequency of church attendance, self-ratings of religiosity and spirituality, and Underwood and Teresi's (2002) multi-item Daily Spiritual Experience Scale (Sprecher & Fehr, 2005; Study 2). The correlations tend to be small to moderate ($rs = .22$ to $.47$) and are generally higher for the strangers/humanity version of the CLS than for the close others version. In fact, measures of religiosity and spirituality are uncorrelated with compassionate love for a specific close other (generally a romantic partner; Sprecher & Fehr, 2005; Study 3). Typically, in religious teachings, when people are exhorted to show kindness and compassion to others, the "others" are portrayed as strangers or the downtrodden (e.g., the parable of the Good Samaritan). This may account for why the strongest link between spirituality and compassionate love is found when the target is strangers or all of humanity.

We have also examined whether variability in compassionate love is linked to individual differences in attachment style. According to attachment theory (see e.g., Hazan & Shaver, 1987; Mikulincer et al., 2005; Chapter 8, this volume), secure attachment is associated with the ability

---

[3]   We note that although women report experiencing higher levels of compassionate love than do men, we did not obtain gender differences in prototypicality ratings of the features of compassionate love. This finding is consistent with other research on love in which it has been shown that women and men agree on the *conceptualization* of love (and therefore do not differ significantly when providing prototypicality ratings), but do differ in their *experience* of love (see e.g., Fehr & Broughton, 2001; Fehr, 2005).

to extend love, including compassionate love, to others. So far, empirical examinations have focused on compassionate acts toward strangers (e.g., Mikulincer et al., 2005; Chapter 8, this volume) and on compassionate love between caregivers and their clients (e.g., Giesbrecht, Chapter 13, this volume). We extended this work by examining the relation between attachment and compassionate love toward close others. Consistent with predictions based on attachment theory, we found that secure attachment was positively correlated with compassionate love toward close others ($r = .32$; Sprecher & Fehr, 2007). Conversely, insecure attachment was negatively correlated with compassionate love ($rs = -.17$ to $-.20$). We also derived positive model of self and positive model of other scores from people's self-reported attachment style ratings (see Bartholomew & Horowitz, 1991), and found that both were positively associated with compassionate love ($rs = .23$ and $.25$, respectively). Thus, attachment security is associated with the capacity for compassionate love.

Effects of Giving and Receiving Compassionate Love

In our final section, we focus on the consequences of giving and receiving compassionate love. Mental health officials and clinicians have long claimed that giving to others has positive effects on the self (e.g., Caprara & Steca, 2005; Simmons, 1991). Similarly, theories in social psychology, such as the negative-state relief hypothesis (e.g., Cialdini, Darby, & Vincent, 1973), suggest that doing good to others can lift one's negative mood. In Underwood's (2002; Chapter 1, this volume) model, compassionate love, fully expressed, leads to positive outcomes for the self, including moral and spiritual growth, wisdom, and a realistic perspective on the self (see also Dovidio & Penner, 2001). Thus, the experience of giving compassionate love to others should lead to positive outcomes for the self.

It is less clear whether being a recipient of compassionate love is a uniformly positive experience. On one hand, there is evidence in the psychology literature that being on the receiving end of others' benevolent actions can have negative effects on the self, particularly if it is difficult to reciprocate (Hatfield & Sprecher, 1986) or if the need for help implies a lack competence on the part of self (e.g., Nadler & Fisher, 1986). On the other hand, Underwood (2002; Chapter 1, this volume) has argued that compassionate love, when offered with wisdom and for the right motives, need not create feelings of powerlessness and indebtedness in the recipient. Indeed, there is evidence that being loved by others can be a highly rewarding experience (Sedikides, Oliver, & Campbell, 1994).

We explored the effects of giving and receiving compassionate love in a series of studies (Sprecher & Fehr, 2006). Specifically, we asked participants to describe an experience in which they either extended compassionate love to another person (giving condition) or were the recipient of compassionate love (receiving condition). They then answered a number of questions about the effect that this experience had on them.[4] The results indicated that there were a number of positive consequences associated with giving compassionate love. Participants reported that the experience resulted in increased self-esteem, positive mood, self-awareness and, to some extent, heightened spirituality. They also believed that giving compassionate love increased their feelings of closeness to the recipient. We found no evidence of a "dark side" to compassionate love – participants reported only a moderate level of self-sacrifice and gave low ratings to the item "made me feel bad."

Interestingly, the same pattern of findings was obtained in the receiving compassionate love condition. These participants also reported positive outcomes as a result of receiving compassionate love. In fact, the items "increased my self-esteem" and "made me feel good" received significantly higher ratings in this condition than in the giving compassionate love condition.[5]

Finally, in follow-up research, we focused on the outcomes that people anticipate as a result of giving and receiving specific compassionate acts. We found that women were more likely than men to expect enhanced positive emotion when engaging in, and receiving, compassionate acts (Sprecher et al., 2007). Similarly, those who scored high on the Compassionate Love Scale anticipated more positive emotion in response to giving and receiving compassionate acts than those who scored low.

In sum, our research indicates that the experience of passionate love is associated with a number of positive benefits to the self, including increased self-esteem, self-awareness, spirituality, and positive affect. Interestingly, we find no evidence that being the recipient of compassionate love is perceived as humiliating or demeaning. If anything, participants report more positive outcomes when on the receiving end. Thus, when it comes to compassionate love, it may actually be better to receive than to give!

---

[4]   In these studies, we assessed participants' perceptions of how the experience of compassionate love affected them. We cannot tell from these studies whether people do, in fact, gain self-esteem, self-awareness, and so on as a result of giving or receiving compassionate love. However, we believe it is important to examine such perceptions because they may well influence whether or not people seek out opportunities to give or receive compassionate love.

[5]   Participants in the receiving compassionate love condition also reported higher levels of self-sacrifice than those in the giving condition, although it is not clear whether they interpreted this item as sacrifice on the part of self or the other.

Future Research

There are a number of avenues for future research in this fertile area. With regard to conceptualization, we encourage further research on the model of compassionate love articulated by Underwood (2002; Chapter 1, this volume). The present volume represents an important step in this direction. As research on the individual components of this model continues to progress, it will become possible to conduct large-scale, extensive studies to test the model in its entirety.

With regard to measurement, we plan to continue to refine and validate the CLS. Some specific areas for future attention include examination of other kinds of reliability (e.g., stability of CLS scores over time), as well as more extensive demonstrations of discriminant validity. We also plan to conduct further research to clarify what, exactly, the different versions of the scale are measuring. The close others and strangers/humanity versions of the CLS, in which the participants focus on more than one person, may be measuring a general disposition (i.e., an individual's stable predisposition to love others in a compassionate way). In contrast, the relationship-specific version of the scale may be assessing a state-like experience of compassionate love, which could change if the individual entered a different type of relationship or if conditions changed in the present relationship (e.g., the partner becomes ill). An analogy can be drawn with the attachment literature in which it has been shown that people hold both general attachment representations (e.g., their general proclivity to be secure, anxious, or avoidant) as well as relationship-specific attachment styles (e.g., Baldwin, Keelan, Fehr, Enns, & Koh-Rangarajoo, 1996; Ross & Spinner, 2001). Moreover, there is evidence that, over time, relationship-specific attachment tends to change in the direction of global attachment, rather than vice versa (Pierce & Lydon, 2001). It would be fascinating to explore whether a similar dynamic occurs for compassionate love.

We would also like to expand the base of individual difference variables explored in compassionate love research. In particular, it will be important to examine the relation between compassionate love and standard personality variables, such as the Big Five (extroversion, agreeableness, openness to experience, conscientiousness, and neuroticism; McCrae & Costa, 1997). One might expect, for example, that those who experience compassionate love for others would be high in agreeableness, open to experience, and low in neuroticism.

Finally, we plan to conduct further research on how compassionate love varies, depending on the target, and whether this variability is linked to individual difference variables. In our studies, greater compassionate love was reported for close others than for strangers/humanity, overall. However, we also observed considerable variability at the individual level. For some participants, compassionate love was experienced primarily for close others and only moderately for strangers and humanity. Others reported high levels of compassionate love across targets. Some questions to explore in future research include: Do people who experience high levels of compassionate love for close others and all of humanity exhibit extraordinarily high levels of prosocial behavior? Are they more likely to experience "compassion burnout"? Is the propensity to experience compassionate love "across the board" the product of particular socialization practices, or is it an inherited trait?

In conclusion, compassionate love may be the most universal type of love, experienced for multiple others in a variety of relational and non-relational contexts. Important conceptual and methodological contributions have already been made in this flourishing area of research and will continue to be made. As we begin to understand this kind of love, and who is most likely to show it, we move increasingly close to the goal of understanding how to promote it.

Acknowledgment

The authors would like to thank the Fetzer Institute for supporting the research described in this chapter. The assistance and encouragement from Wayne Ramsey and Heidi Ihrig throughout this project are greatly appreciated.

References

Aron, A., Fisher, H. E., & Strong, G. (2006). Romantic love. In A. Vangelisti & D. Perlman (Eds.), *The Cambridge handbook of personal relationships* (pp. 595–614). New York: Cambridge University Press.

Aron, A., & Westbay, L. (1996). Dimensions of the prototype of love. *Journal of Personality and Social Psychology, 70,* 535–551.

Baldwin, M. W., Keelan, J. P. R., Fehr, B., Enns, V., & Koh-Rangarajoo, E. (1996). Social-cognitive conceptualization of attachment working models: Availability and accessibility effects. *Journal of Personality and Social Psychology, 19,* 746–754.

Bartholomew, K., & Horowitz, L. M. (1991). Attachment styles among young adults: A test of a four-category model. *Journal of Personality and Social Psychology, 61,* 226–244.

Batson, C. D., & Oleson, K. C. (1991). Current status of the empathy-altruism hypothesis. In M. S. Clark (Ed.), *Review of personality and social psychology (Vol. 12): Prosocial behavior* (pp. 62–85). Newbury Park, CA: Sage.

Burnstein, E., Crandall, C. S., & Kitayama, S. (1994). Some neo-Darwinian decision rules for altruism: Weighing cues for inclusive fitness as a function of the biological importance of the decision. *Journal of Personality and Social Psychology, 67,* 733–789.

Button, C. M., & Collier, D. R. (1991, June). *A comparison of people's concepts of love and romantic love.* Paper presented at the Canadian Psychological Conference, Calgary, Alberta.

Campos, B., Logli, M., & Keltner, D. (2006). *The love of humanity: Emotional underpinnings and social consequences of the disposition to affiliate toward the human collective.* Unpublished manuscript, University of California, Los Angeles.

Caprara, G. V., & Steca, P. (2005). Self-efficacy beliefs as determinants of prosocial behavior conducive to life satisfaction across ages. *Journal of Social and Clinical Psychology, 24,* 191–217.

Cialdini, R. B., Darby, B. L., & Vincent, J. E. (1973). Transgression and altruism: A case for hedonism. *Journal of Experimental Social Psychology, 9,* 502–516.

Crawford, C., & Krebs, D. L. (1998). *Handbook of evolutionary psychology.* Mahwah, NJ: Lawrence Erlbaum.

Davis, M. H. (1996). *Empathy: A social psychological approach.* Boulder, CO: Westview.

Dovidio, J. F., & Penner, L. A. (2001). Helping and altruism. In G. J. O. Fletcher & M. S. Clark (Eds.), *Blackwell handbook of social psychology: Interpersonal processes* (pp. 331–356). Oxford: Blackwell.

Eagly, A. H., & Crowley, M. (1986). Gender and helping behavior: A meta-analytic review of the social psychological literature. *Psychological Bulletin, 100,* 283–308.

Fehr, B. (1988). Prototype analysis of the concepts of love and commitment. *Journal of Personality and Social Psychology, 55,* 557–579.

Fehr, B. (1993). How do I love thee...? Let me consult my prototype. In S. Duck (Ed.), *Understanding personal relationships (Vol. 1): Individuals in relationships* (pp. 87–120). Newbury Park, CA: Sage.

Fehr, B. (2005). The role of prototypes in interpersonal cognition. In M. W. Baldwin (Ed.), *Interpersonal cognition* (pp. 180–206). New York: Guilford Press.

Fehr, B., (2006). A prototype approach to studying love. In R. J. Sternberg & K. Weis (Eds.), *The new psychology of love* (pp. 225–246). New Haven, CT: Yale University Press.

Fehr, B., & Broughton, R. (2001). Gender and personality differences in conceptions of love: An interpersonal theory analysis. *Personal Relationships, 8,* 115–136.

Fehr, B., & Russell, J. A. (1991). The concept of love viewed from a prototype perspective. *Journal of Personality and Social Psychology, 60,* 425–438.

Fehr, B., & Sprecher, S. (under revision). *Prototype analysis of the concept of compassionate love.* Personal Relationships.

Fehr, B., & Sprecher, S. Unpublished raw data, University of Winnipeg.

Felmlee, D., & Sprecher, S. (2006). Love: Psychological and sociological perspectives. In J. E. Stets & J. H. Turner (Eds.), *Handbook of sociology of emotions* (pp. 389–409). New York: Springer.

Fitness, J., & Fletcher, G. J. O. (1993). Love, hate, anger, and jealousy in close relationships: A prototype and cognitive appraisal analysis. *Journal of Personality and Social Psychology, 65*, 942–958.

Gillath, O., Shaver, P. R., Mikulincer, M., Nitzberg, R. E., Erez, A., & Van IJzendoorn, M. H. (2005). Attachment, caregiving, and volunteering: Placing volunteerism in an attachment-theoretical framework. *Personal Relationships, 12*, 425–446.

Hatfield, E., & Sprecher, S. (1986). Measuring passionate love in intimate relations. *Journal of Adolescence, 9*, 383–410.

Hazan, C., & Shaver, P. (1987). Romantic love conceptualized as an attachment process. *Journal of Personality and Social Psychology, 52*, 511–524.

Hendrick, C., & Hendrick, S. (1986). A theory and method of love. *Journal of Personality and Social Psychology, 50*, 392–402.

Hendrick, C., & Hendrick, S. S. (1989). Research on love: Does it measure up? *Journal of Personality and Social Psychology, 56*, 784–794.

Hendrick, C., Hendrick, S. S., Foote, F. F., & Slapion-Foote, M. J. (1984). Do men and women love differently? *Journal of Social and Personal Relationships, 1*, 177–195.

Hendrick, S. S., & Hendrick, C. (1992). *Romantic love.* Newbury Park, CA: Sage.

Hendrick, S. S., & Hendrick, C. (2000). Romantic love. In S. Hendrick & C. Hendrick (Eds.), *Close relationships: A sourcebook* (pp. 203–215). Thousand Oaks, CA: Sage.

Lamm, H., & Wiesmann, U. (1997). Subjective attributes of attraction: How people characterize their liking, their love, and their being in love. *Personal Relationships, 4*, 271–284.

Lasswell, T. E., & Lasswell, M. E. (1976). I love you but I'm not in love with you. *Journal of Marriage and Family Counseling, 38*, 211–224.

Lazarus, R. S. (1991). *Emotion and adaptation.* New York: Oxford University Press.

Luby, V., & Aron, A. (1990, July). *A prototype structuring of love, like, and being-in-love.* Paper presented at the Fifth International Conference on Personal Relationships, Oxford, UK.

McCrae, R. R., & Costa, P. T., Jr. (1997). Personality trait structure as a human universal. *American Psychologist, 52*, 509–516.

Mervis, C. B., & Rosch, E. (1981). Categorization of natural objects. *Annual Review of Psychology, 32*, 89–115.

Mikulincer, M., Shaver, P. R., Gillath, O., & Nitzberg, R. A. (2005). Attachment, caregiving, and altruism: Boosting attachment security increases compassion and helping. *Journal of Personality and Social Psychology, 89*, 817–839.

Nadler, A., & Fisher, J. D. (1986). The role of threat to self-esteem and perceived control in recipient reactions to help: Theory development and empirical validation. In L. Berkowitz (Ed.), *Advances in experimental social psychology* (Vol. 19, pp. 81–122). New York: Academic Press.

Noller, P. (1996). What is this thing called love? Defining the love that supports marriage and family. *Personal Relationships, 3*, 97–115.

Paulhus, D. L. (1991). Balanced inventory of desirable responding (BIDR). In J. P. Robinson, P. R. Shaver, & L. S. Wrightsman (Eds.), *Measures of social psychological attitudes (Vol. 1): Measures of personality and social psychological attitudes* (pp. 37–41). San Diego, CA: Academic Press.

Penner, L. A., Fritzsche, B. A., Craiger, J. P., & Freifeld, T. S. (1995). Measuring the prosocial personality. In J. N. Butcher, & C. D. Spielberger (Eds.), *Advances in personality assessment* (Vol. 12; pp. 147–163). Hillsdale, NJ: Lawrence Erlbaum.

Pierce, T., & Lydon, J. E. (2001). Global and specific relational models in the experience of social interactions. *Journal of Personality and Social Psychology, 80,* 613–631.

Post, S. G., Underwood, L. G., Schloss, J. P., & Hurlbut, W. B. (Eds.). (2002). *Altruism and altruistic love.* New York: Oxford University Press.

Randall, D. M., Fedor, D. B., & Longenecker, C. O. (1990). The behavioral expression of organizational commitment. *Journal of Vocational Behavior, 36,* 210–224.

Regan, P. C., Kocan, E. R., & Whitlock, T. (1998). Ain't love grand! A prototype analysis of the concept of romantic love. *Journal of Social and Personal Relationships, 15,* 411–420.

Rosch, E. (1973). On the internal structure of perceptual and semantic categories. In T. E. Moore (Ed.), *Cognitive development and the acquisition of language* (pp. 111–144). New York: Academic Press.

Ross, L. R., & Spinner, B. (2001). General and specific attachment representations in adulthood: Is there a relationship? *Journal of Social and Personal Relationships, 18,* 747–766.

Rubin, Z. (1970). Measurement of romantic love. *Journal of Personality and Social Psychology, 16,* 265–273.

Rubin, Z. (1973). *Liking and loving.* New York: Holt, Rinehart & Winston.

Schieman, S., & Van Gundy, K. (2000). The personal and social links between age and self-reported empathy. *Social Psychology Quarterly, 63,* 152–174.

Sedikides, C., Oliver, M. B., & Campbell, W. K. (1994). Perceived benefits and costs of romantic relationships for women and men: Implications for exchange theory. *Personal Relationships, 1,* 5–21.

Shacham-Dupont, S. (2003). Compassion and love in relationships – can they coexist? *Relationship Research News, 2,* 13–15.

Shaver, P. R., Hazan, C., & Bradshaw, D. (1988). Love as attachment: The integration of three behavioral systems. In R. J. Sternberg & M Barnes (Eds.), *The psychology of love* (pp. 68–99). New Haven, CT: Yale University Press.

Shaver, P., Schwartz, J., Kirson, D., & O'Connor, C. (1987). Emotion knowledge: Further explorations of a prototype approach. *Journal of Personality and Social Psychology, 52,* 1061–1086.

Simmons, R. G. (1991). Altruism and sociology. *Sociology Quarterly, 32,* 1–22.

Sprecher, S., & Fehr, B. (2005). Compassionate love for close others and humanity. *Journal of Social and Personal Relationships, 22,* 629–652.

Sprecher, S., & Fehr, B. (2006). Enhancement of mood and self-esteem as a result of giving and receiving compassionate love. *Current Research in Social Psychology, 11,* 227–242. http://www.uiowa.edu/~grpproc/crisp/crisp.html

Sprecher, S., & Fehr, B. (2007). *General and relationship-specific attachment as predictors of compassionate love for a romantic partner.* Unpublished manuscript, Illinois State University.

Sprecher, S., & Fehr, B. Unpublished raw data, Illinois State University.

Sprecher, S., Fehr, B., & Zimmerman, C. (2007). Expectation for mood enhancement as a result of helping: The effects of gender and compassionate love. *Sex Roles, 56,* 543–549.

Sternberg, R. J. (1986). A triangular theory of love. *Psychological Review, 93,* 119–135.

Sternberg, R. J. (1997). Construct validation of a triangular love scale. *European Journal of Social Psychology, 27,* 313–335.

Taylor, S. E. (2002). *The tending instinct: Women, men and the biology of our relationships.* New York: Henry Holt.

Underwood, L. G. (2002). The human experience of compassionate love: Conceptual mapping and data from selected studies. In S. G. Post, L. G. Underwood, J. P. Schloss, & W. B. Hurlbut (Eds.), *Altruism and altruistic love* (pp. 72–88). New York: Oxford University Press.

Underwood, L. G. (2005). Interviews with Trappist monks as a contribution to research methodology in the investigation of compassionate love. *Journal for the Theory of Social Behavior, 35,* 285–302.

Underwood, L. G., & Teresi, J. (2002). The Daily Spiritual Experience Scale: Development, theoretical description, reliability, exploratory factor analysis, and preliminary construct validity using health-related data. *Annals of Behavioral Medicine, 24,* 22–33.

WHOQOL SRPB Group (2006). A cross-cultural study of spirituality, religion, and personal beliefs as components of quality of life. *Social Science and Medicine, 62,* 1486–1497.

3

Measuring Prosocial Behavior, Altruism, and Compassionate Love on US Television

Stacy L. Smith, Sandi W. Smith, Katherine M. Pieper,
Edward Downs, Jina H. Yoo, Becka Bowden,
Amber Ferris, and Matthew C. Butler

Because positive role models on television can foster the learning and imitation of their actions (Hearold, 1986; Mares & Woodard, 2001; Rushton, 1979), quantifying the presence of characters who are truly concerned with the good of the other is an important first step in understanding the prosocial impact that these portrayals may have on individuals at any age in the life span. Given this, we sought to measure acts of compassionate love on US television. However, very little was known about compassionate love at the time this research was being conducted. As a result, we had to rely heavily on media-based research and on theorizing on two concepts that are closely aligned with loving acts of compassion: prosocial acts and altruistic behavior. In this chapter, we detail the thinking behind our novel approach to conceptualizing altruism and compassionate love and highlight a few of our key research findings.

To this end, the chapter is divided into six sections. In an effort to provide a backdrop to our work, previous television content analyses on prosocial acts in general and altruistic behaviors in specific will be reviewed first. Summarizing past research will illuminate some of the choices we had to make when developing our coding scheme. Our approach to tapping prosocial and altruistic acts on television will be explicated in the second section of the chapter. We will highlight stipulations surrounding our definition and illustrate the impact these limiting conditions may have on our results. The third section will focus on the operationalization of a series of variables which allow us to quantify multiple definitions of altruism. Because altruism is a multidimensional construct that is hotly debated in the literature (see Post, Underwood, Schloss, & Hurlbut, 2002), we have created a series of variables which allow us to capture different conceptualizations of this phenomenon. The fourth section is devoted to explaining how we constructed different definitions of altruism using these variables. It could be argued that the most stringent definition may reflect compassionately loving behavior. In addition to assessing the prevalence of altruistically loving acts on television, we created a series of contextual variables designed to examine the nature or meaning surrounding these incidents. These will be highlighted in the fifth section. The sixth section is a brief overview of a few of the findings of our content study, given that the focus of this chapter is on the conceptualization and measurement of prosocial behavior and altruistic acts on television. Readers interested in the details surrounding our findings should see Smith et al. (2006).

Previous Content-Analytic Research

Many of the previous content analyses of television have focused on potentially negative content features such as aggression (for reviews, see Smith et al., 1998; Wilson et al., 1997, 1998) or risky sexual behaviors (for reviews, see Kunkel et al., 1999, 2001, 2003). Only a handful of studies have examined positive social behaviors on entertainment television (Greenberg, Edison, Korzenny, Fernandez-Collado, & Atkin, 1980; Lee, 1988; Potter & Ware, 1989; Poulos, Harvey, & Liebert, 1976).

One of the earliest studies was conducted by Poulos et al. (1976). These researchers assessed positive social behaviors on Saturday-morning programs ($n = 50$) across four broadcast networks and two independent stations. The results revealed that altruism occurred most frequently at a rate of roughly six acts per half-hour, followed by sympathy/explaining feelings at two and a quarter incidents per hour. As stated by the authors, "the remainder of the positive social behaviors (*reparation of bad behavior, resistance to temptation*) seldom appeared, with control of aggressive impulses being the least frequent of all" (1976, p. 1053; emphasis added).

Greenberg et al. (1980) also were interested in the presence of prosocial behavior on television. Prosocial acts were defined as "affiliative interpersonal acts ... those deemed appropriate, redeeming, and legal by society" (p. 109). The sample spanned three years (1975/6, 1976/7, 1977/8), and included one episode each from chosen primetime and Saturday-morning series ($n = 248$). The results revealed that prosocial behaviors were very common on television, with 42.7 acts occurring per hour. Altruistic acts (i.e., sharing, helping, cooperating) occurred at a rate of 14.3 per hour, followed by explaining feelings of self and other (e.g., 11.5 and 8.7, respectively). Time of day and genre also contributed to variance in the findings. Prime time featured more prosocial acts than did

Saturday-morning television programming. Situation comedies presented a higher hourly rate of prosocial acts than did family drama or action/crime series.

Roughly a decade later, Lee (1988) assessed prosocial acts or "models of positive social relations" (p. 239) across four weeks of primetime programs (n = 235) during the 1985/6 viewing seasons. A full 97% of the programs featured at least one prosocial behavior. Over a thousand (n = 1,035) prosocial acts were coded, with affection (i.e., feelings of sympathy/empathy) being the predominant act type (57%), followed by actions controlling negative predispositions (22%) and altruism (21%).

Finally, Potter and Ware (1989) examined prosocial acts and their surrounding contexts on two weeks of primetime television shows (n = 88 hours). Prosocial behavior was defined as "any attempt by one character to help another character" (p. 363). Acts could be classified as physical (e.g., tangible aid) or symbolic (e.g., verbal support, providing information, enhancing esteem). A few contextual variables associated with the prosocial act also were assessed, such as the presence of rewards and initiator motivation (i.e., internal, external). The results revealed that 20.2 prosocial acts occurred per primetime hour, with symbolic acts (83.5%) being significantly more common than physical acts (16.5%). A majority of the prosocial acts were rewarded (93.5%) and internally motivated (58.5%). Episodic series featured the most acts per hour, followed by situation comedies. Of all genres, continuing series had the fewest incidents of prosocial actions per hour.

Looking across these studies, prosocial behavior seems to be conceptualized as a superordinate type of behavior that may or may not be categorized as altruistic in nature. Very simply, altruistic acts seem to be a smaller subset of broader, positive social behavior. In terms of results, prosocial and altruistic acts occurred quite frequently on television programming. Genre and time of day also exerted an influence on the number of acts depicted. At least one study (Greenberg et al., 1980) showed that prime time featured more prosocial content than did Saturday morning. Situation comedies and episodic series were the most likely genres to feature prosocial behavior.

The previous work also has a few limitations. First, the definitions of prosocial behavior, in general, and altruism, in specific, vary from investigation to investigation. Such variability in conceptualization undoubtedly contributed to the vast differences in rate per hour found across studies. In a similar vein, the definitions of altruism fail to take into account the complexity of altruistic behavior. Some scholars have argued that such acts must be devoid of external benefits (Oliner & Oliner, 1988), whereas others have stated that they must involve a cost to the initiator (Oliner, 2002; Sober, 2002), and/or be motivated by empathy (Batson, 2002). Unfortunately, none of the previous content studies captured any of the complexities of the different conceptualizations of altruism offered currently in the psychological or sociological literature.

Second, the studies minimally captured the context or meaning surrounding prosocial acts and altruistic incidents. Yet a large and growing body of empirical research reveals that the nature or way in which acts are presented on television influences viewers' interpretation of and responses to such content (see Gunter, 1994; Smith et al., 1998; Wilson et al., 1997). For example, an altruistic act occurring in the situation comedy *Will & Grace* may be interpreted very differently from one occurring in the dramatic movie *Philadelphia*. Thus, simply counting the number of "prosocial" or "altruistic" acts on television does little to enhance our understanding of how viewers might make sense of and thus react to such portrayals.

Third, the sampling frames included only a limited number of channels. Most of the previous studies sampled only programming content on the broadcast networks. Roughly 70% of US households subscribe to at least basic cable packages (Nielsen Media Research, 2000). As such, we know virtually nothing about the frequency and context surrounding prosocial behaviors and altruistic acts on popular cable outlets. The previous research also relied primarily on sampling shows from prime time and Saturday morning, undoubtedly because these are the most popular viewing times. We still know virtually nothing about the rate or nature of altruistic acts during other times of day (i.e., early morning, afternoon, late night) when we know countless numbers of individuals are in the viewing audience. Examining this content is also important with the advent of easy-to-use time-shifting devices such as digital video recorders (DVRs) to capture television programming that airs when viewers may be at work or school. Clearly, a complete picture of altruism on television is still missing from the social science literature.

In response to these issues, we developed a content-analytic framework uniquely sensitive to capturing the frequency and context surrounding both prosocial and altruistic behaviors on television. Rather than looking at the presence of such acts on prime time or Saturday morning, we coded program content across 18 popular broadcast and cable outlets from early in the morning (6:00 a.m.) until late at night (11:00 p.m.). The main contributions from this investigation are outlined below, starting with our general definition of what constitutes prosocial behavior.

Defining Prosocial Behavior

Although research has been conducted on the impact of seeing televised portrayals of altruistic behavior on prosocial outcomes (for reviews, see Hearold, 1986; Mares & Woodard, 2001), few scholars have conceptually defined these phenomena. Many of the definitions of prosocial behavior in previous research are by categorical examples such as, but not limited to, sharing, explaining feelings, friendly interaction, and resistance to temptation. Because our ultimate interest was to examine a subset of prosocial behaviors (e.g., altruism) on television, we crafted a definition that is narrower than the ones employed in previous research. This definition was the first threshold which informed coders to "stop the tape" and begin evaluating the prosocial event.

Our definition of prosocial behavior is "a voluntary action, independent of motive, that is intended to benefit others beyond simple sociability or duties associated with role (i.e., family or work). All prosocial behaviors, by definition, must be legal." We follow Greenberg et al. (1980) in focusing on behaviors that are appropriate and legal in a particular social context. Although one could conceivably engage in an illegal behavior that is prosocial, the behaviors chosen from media portrayals that reach a large audience and have a positive impact on them should be those that are sanctioned by that society. Two aspects of our definition, we believe, set it apart from the conceptualizations used in previous content studies. The first aspect addresses a character's role in a program. Many characters perform positive actions that are associated with their occupations in a show. For example, doctors on *ER* operate on the sick and police officers on *NYPD Blue* apprehend suspected criminals. Because such prosocial occupations are depicted routinely on television, the behaviors associated with these jobs might artificially inflate the number of positive acts on television. Thus, all prosocial actions associated with an occupation (i.e., paycheck) are not coded in our study.

However, there are times when characters within a particular occupation go above and beyond the call of duty. To illustrate, a fireman may run into an inferno to save a pregnant mother despite the fact that all of his training would suggest he should not. A doctor may be shown reading to an unconscious child in intensive care hours after performing surgery for a congenital heart defect. Such acts, provided that they rise above expected duties associated with an occupation or role, would be coded as prosocial, because they not only are attempts at benefiting another character but also defy/exceed norms associated with a particular vocation.

The second aspect addresses a character's sociability in a program. Some of the previous content studies have coded verbal and physical acts of affection as examples of prosocial behavior (see Greenberg et al., 1980; Lee, 1988). Many affectionate acts are simply scripted rituals of politeness for interpersonal, family, and/or professional contexts. For example, family members and friends often display affection when greeting or leaving one other with hugs and/or kisses. Some scholars may consider such polite interaction as prosocial or even altruistic in nature (Drabman & Thomas,

1977; Fryrear & Thelen, 1969), especially in relation to children's imitation and social learning. Others, however, may not (Eisenberg & Miller, 1987), arguing that sociable behavior may not intentionally benefit the other (p. 92) or that such acts are just norm-based rules of greeting (Burgoon, Buller, & Woodall, 1996). Such behaviors are *not* captured in our definition.

There are instances, however, when characters show purposeful affection outside norms or rituals that would be coded as prosocial. To illustrate, an affectionless father may break down and communicate love for his daughter by hugging her as she departs for college. A child may befriend a new student at school by putting her arm around the stranger and welcoming her to the new environment. Such behavior that exceeds role expectations, provided that it is intended to benefit another character, would constitute instances of prosocial action.

These stipulations render our conceptualization of prosocial behavior more conservative in nature than definitions used in previous content-analytic work. As a consequence, the total number of prosocial acts (i.e., rate per hour, proportion of shows with such actions) we find should be substantially *lower* than the number found in other content studies. In terms of type, we categorized prosocial behaviors as instances of helping and/or sharing.

Our definition of prosocial behavior was simply a starting point. Our interest was to examine a smaller subset of altruistic and compassionate acts on television. Because general instances of helping and/or sharing may or may not be altruistic in nature, we had to turn to other researchers' conceptualizations of this construct to inform our work. It became clear that a series of variables have guided how scholars define and think about what constitutes altruistic behavior. In the next section, we review those variables and illustrate how they influenced our own content-analytic study.

Others' Conceptualizations of Altruism

In 1851, Auguste Comte penned the term "altruism," derived from the Latin word "alter" (i.e., meaning other) and the Italian adjective *altrui*. Comte (1875) believed that altruism signified benevolence or living for others. Decades have passed and debates ensued since Comte originally defined the term and its selfish counterpart, egoism. Now, there is much disagreement on the limiting conditions surrounding altruistic acts (see Post et al., 2002). We believe that the variability in definitions is something to embrace rather than eschew. Instead of wrestling over what constitutes an "altruistic act," we decided to operationalize aspects of different definitions offered in the literature. Our final estimates of altruistic acts on television were not dependent on *our* conceptualization of this construct, but rather on different *researchers'* conceptualizations. Therefore, our answer to the central question, "How many altruistic acts appear across the landscape of television programming?" is, "it depends." As shall be seen, it depends on what definition of altruism one embraces, and different conceptualizations can be assessed with our coding scheme.

After reviewing the literature, five key aspects came to the fore of altruism that some scholars include and some exclude in their conceptual definitions.[1] It is important to note that much of this literature is grounded in theorizing that is yet to be empirically tested. The five key aspects of altruism include: direction of concern (self versus other), initiator cost, recipient benefit, empathy on the part of the initiator for the recipient, and ease of escape from self and/or social censure.

Concern. One of the common definitional elements of altruism involves individuals' intentions in performing altruistic acts. Some theorists have argued that the primary concern of the altruist is for the other (Batson, 2002; Eisenberg & Miller, 1987; Kagan, 2002; Latane & Darley, 1970; Oliner, 2002; Rushton, 1976) and not the self (see Monroe, 2002, p. 107). For example, Post (2002) argues that: "By the strictest definition, the altruist is someone who does something for the other and for the other's sake, rather than as a means to self-promotion or internal well-being" (p. 53). Whether we label the motivational state a "goal" or "concern," theorists are arguing that the primary intent behind helping behavior is to facilitate an "other" – over self – in some way.

Theorists also have been quite clear that there may be secondary concerns (i.e., motivational pluralism) associated with altruistic acts (Post, 2002, p. 53; Sober, 2002, p. 19). For example, a young boy may rescue a scared and injured dog that had accidentally fallen into a storm drain. After rescuing the animal and trying to find its owner, the boy may wonder whether a reward will be given for the dog's return. Such a self-motivated concern, provided that it is not the primary reason for performing such an act, does not disqualify a behavior as being altruistic in nature for some empathy theorists. Other self-concerns may include, but are not limited to, self-promotion, internal well-being, alleviation of a negative state, and avoidance of punishment (see Batson, 2002; Post, 2002).

---

[1]   Two additional attributes – voluntary and intentional – are generally agreed upon in the literature and were captured in our basic definition of altruistic behavior (see Monroe, 2002; Oliner, 2002).

To capture these issues, our coding scheme included a variable which assesses whether benefit to the self or other is the primary force behind a character's decision to act altruistically. Therefore, coders were trained to decipher concern based not only on verbal utterances made by the initiator of the act, but also their nonverbal responses and the context of the unfolding plot. Each helping and/or sharing action was coded as either primary concern for self or primary concern for the other.

Cost. The word altruism often conjures up extreme images of individuals risking life and limb for the sake of saving another from death. Central to this idea is the belief that altruistic acts involve a sacrifice or cost on the part of the initiator. Several theorists hold this view (Monroe, 2002; Sober, 2002; Wyschogrod, 2002). Oliner (2002), one of the most notable sociologists in this area, arranges costly altruism on a continuum from heroic acts to more conventional daily experiences.

Many of Oliner's ideas about altruism are derived from hundreds of interviews with rescuers of Jews during the time of the Holocaust (see Oliner & Oliner, 1988). The researchers found that many individuals risked not only their own lives but also the lives of family and friends in an effort to save those destined for death. Some of the instances involved single, extraordinary acts of heroism that saved lives, whereas other efforts involved extended acts of generosity and hospitality (i.e., hiding Jews in their home) in the continued face of fear. Similar results were found in Monroe's (1996) study, which involved a substantially smaller sample of interviews with rescuers of Jews from World War II.

In an effort to measure this aspect of altruism, we created a variable designed to tap whether the initiator experienced a "cost" for helping and/or sharing with another character. Costs were defined broadly and could be physical (e.g., injury/death), emotional (e.g., embarrassment, grief), and/or material (e.g., loss of home, car) in nature. Altruism encompasses all types of "costs" ranging from the tragic to the trivial. However, we captured only the presence or absence of a cost rather than asking coders to determine the degree or intensity of the potential loss on some sort of scale.

Benefit to the recipient. A logical extension to an act that is motivated by concern for the other and that is costly to the actor is the fact that the recipient should actually benefit from the act. Some scholars argue that altruism cannot occur without actual benefit accruing to the recipient as a result of the act.

Recipient benefit refers to something that actually promotes or enhances the life of the recipient. Benefits may be emotional (e.g., confidence, self-esteem), physical (e.g., the ability to walk), material (e.g., car, house), or spiritual (e.g., faith). Each act of helping and/or sharing was coded as recipient benefit present or absent.

Empathy. It has been argued that one of the reasons individuals help distressed others is because of empathy (Batson, 2002). In fact, several studies have found that empathy evoked by witnessing others in distress facilitates helping behavior (Batson, Duncan, Ackerman, Buckley, & Birch, 1981; Coke, Batson, & McDavis, 1978; Fultz, Batson, Fortenbach, McCarthy, & Varney, 1986). Yet meta-analyses of multiple studies reveal that the strength of the relationship between empathy and prosocial and cooperative socially competent behavior may vary depending on the operationalization of altruistic action. In explanation, altruistic action is often measured as (1) prosocial behavior that is voluntary and intentional which benefits others but with no motive for the action specified; or (2) altruistic behavior which is performed without expecting benefits or avoiding punishment. In addition, the strength of the relationship can be altered depending on the method of measuring (e.g., self-report, picture indices, physiological markers) empathy, and age of the participant in the study (Eisenberg & Miller, 1987).

However, just what constitutes empathy? This is a controversial construct in the social science literature that is defined in multiple ways (Eisenberg & Miller, 1987; Feshbach & Feshbach, 1997; Hurlbut, 2002; Zillmann, 1991). Some researchers define empathy in terms of affect matching (e.g., facial mimicry), emotional responding (e.g., sharing the same or similar emotional state), cognitive reactions (e.g., ability to take the perspective of the other, concern for other's plight), and/or some combination of these categories. Most scholars agree that cognitive and affective factors are both at work in empathic reactivity (see Eisenberg & Strayer, 1987; Feshbach & Feshbach, 1997). The most extreme reaction to another's need is emotional contagion, whereby the individual not only perceives the need in the other but is so overwhelmed by the emotion that it becomes self-focused, not other-focused (Preston & de Waal, 2002).

Given this literature, a series of measures arise which assess different approaches to empathy. The coding scheme used dichotomous variables to examine whether the initiator of a helping and/or sharing act (1) had the capacity to take the perspective of the character in need; (2) showed empathic concern for the other; and (3) became self-focused in his/her emotional responsiveness (i.e., contagion effect). These measures were combined so that empathy occurred when "1" and "2" are present but "3" is absent.

It is important to note, however, that it is possible that measuring internal cognitive states such as perspective-taking may be impossible to ascertain with television characters. Just because a character has the "capacity" or shows signs of perspective-taking, it may be impossible to know if this is in fact what s/he is doing.

Ease of escape. Central to much of the empathy-altruism hypothesis is the notion of ease of escape (see Batson, 2002). Batson (1991, 2002) has argued and experimentally tested other motives that might drive helping behaviors such as aversive arousal, reward seeking, or punishment avoidance. All are considered egoistic in nature; the basic premise is that when empathy is low or nonexistent, any one of these other self-focused motives may drive positive social action. He has tested these egoistic alternatives with the variable "ease of escape" or the relative effort it takes one to withdraw from potential helping situations.

Ease of escape was operationally defined in two ways. The first was self-blame or internal, negatively valenced emotions such as guilt or shame. These were punishment-based feelings that emerged in the face of helping. Ease of escape was high if one can remove the self from the potential helping situation without feeling bad, guilty, or remorseful in some way. The inability to escape in the absence of empathy might suggest that one is helping to reduce aversive arousal or internal punishment.

The second was social censure or external factors that may evoke condemnation from others. Ease of external escape occurred if one can remove the self from the potential helping situation without enduring the condemnation of others for failing to help. Consequently, the inability to externally escape the helping scene – in the absence of empathy – might suggest that one was helping to avoid punishment or receive rewards from bystanders.

Studies have typically found that egoistic motivations for helping operate in the absence of empathy (for a review, see Batson, 2002). The two measures in the present research that capture ease of escape are the presence or absence of internal (i.e., self-censure) and external blame (i.e., other censure) for each helping incident. Taken in combination with the empathy measure outlined above, the ease of escape variables enabled us to ascertain egotistic reasons for helping when empathic reactivity is not present.

In sum, five variables capture differences in scholars' definitions of altruistic behavior. By combining these variables, the prevalence of diverse definitions of altruism on television can be estimated. We looked at the prevalence of four different possible conceptualizations of altruism using the five variables outlined above. These variables were assessed for each prosocial act or instance of helping and/or sharing on television. In the next section, our four conceptualizations or "composites" of altruism are detailed.

Composites of Altruism

Owing to the aforementioned ambiguity surrounding the conceptual definition of altruism, four specific composites were created. (See Table 3.1 for an overview of the variables and composites that result from grouping

Table 3.1   Variables Used to Create Altruism Composites

	Composite 1: Liberal altruism	Composite 2: Initiator focus	Composite 3: Recipient focus	Composite 4: Loving acts of compassion
Helping/sharing	Yes	Yes	Yes	Yes
Other concern		Yes		Yes
Cost		Yes		Yes
Other benefit			Yes	Yes
Empathy			Yes	Yes
Ease of escape				Yes

Note. Helping/sharing are simply prosocial acts. The remaining five dimensions (other concern, cost, other benefit, empathy, and ease of escape) are elements of altruism.

them as described below.) The first composite simply involved instances of helping and/or sharing. No additional stipulations were added to these types of acts. Put differently, none of the five variables outlined above were added to helping and/or sharing acts. Thus, this composite really reflects prosocial behavior or the most *liberal* approach to defining altruism.

The second and third composites were informed by the work of Krebs. Arguing for a framework of altruism, Krebs (1970) asserts:

> To begin with, the prototypical altruistic situation involves someone who gives (a benefactor), and someone who receives (the recipient). In some cases, characteristics of the benefactor affect altruism, and in other cases it is characteristics of the recipient ... The first dimension of classification, then, separates variables which relate to the characteristics of benefactors that cause or correlate with altruism from the altruism-eliciting characteristics of recipients. (p. 262)

Using Krebs's logic, the second composite tapped key variables related to the *initiator* of altruistic acts such as the locus of concern and cost. Instances of helping and/or sharing that were motivated out of a primary concern for the other over self and involved personal cost to the initiator were included in the second composite. Conceptually, we labeled this composite "initiator-focused" altruism. The third composite tapped key variables related to the *recipient*. Acts of helping/sharing that benefited the recipient and were the byproduct of empathy were featured in this composite. These acts were motivated by initiator projection into the emotional state and need of the recipient so that they could act in such a way that actually benefited him/her. Thus, the third composite was called "recipient-focused" altruism.

The fourth composite is the most conservative, and is where we believe that the "Compassionate Love Fully Expressed" shown in Underwood's model (see Chapter 1, Figure 1.1) is evidenced. Only acts of helping/ sharing that feature all five dimensions were included; those instances in which the initiator is primarily concerned with the other, there is a cost to the actor, the recipient actually benefits, the act is the byproduct of empathy, and ease of escape from self-censure or social censure is available. It is our belief that this stringent composite captures the most conservative other-oriented instances of altruistic behavior or the "Positive Behavior (Words/Actions)" that emanate from "Motivation & Discernment" in Underwood's model. Such acts have been described in the literature to be on par with the actions of receivers of the Carnegie Hero Commission Award, hospice volunteers, and rescuers of Jews in Nazi Europe during World War II (Monroe, 2002, p. 108; Oliner, 2002, pp. 123–133).

In sum, we defined prosocial acts as instances of helping and sharing. Five variables that theorists identify as critical components of altruism also were presented. Using the five variables, different definitions of altruism on television can be examined. The most "liberal" form may involve any instance of helping and/or sharing. As a result, *liberal altruism* may actually resemble "prosocial action." The "purest" or most "stringent" form of altruism may involve those acts of helping and/or sharing that stem from a primary concern for the other, actually benefit the recipient, involve empathy, incur a cost to the initiator, and from which the actor could escape self-censure or social censure relatively easily. These acts might be termed *compassionately loving behavior.* Put another way, only acts that include helping and/or sharing as well as the five dimensions of altruism were considered to be compassionate love. We anticipated that these acts would be the most infrequent on television, given the high threshold that had to be crossed.

Context of Prosocial and Altruistic Behavior

Over the last two decades, researchers have begun assessing the context or way in which portrayals are presented on television (for reviews, see Potter & Ware, 1987; Wilson et al., 1997). The context or nature of the depiction influences the meaning viewers construct while watching, as mentioned above. Although most of the previous work on context has examined the nature of violent (Potter & Ware, 1987; Smith et al., 1998; Wilson et al., 1997, 1998) or sexual portrayals on television (Kunkel et al.,

1999, 2001, 2003), we believe that many of the same contextual variables should influence viewers' interpretations of prosocial behavior and/or altruistic acts.

Six major contextual variables were included in the present research. The first was *type of character*. Characters on television come in all shapes, forms, and colors. For example, *SpongeBob SquarePants* is a young, anthropomorphized, yellow sponge whereas *Sabrina* is a white, teenaged witch. Research reveals that attributes of the characters, in particular, demographic markers, can have a pronounced impact on individuals' parasocial interaction and identification (Bandura, 2002; Hoffner, 1996; Hoffner & Cantor, 1991). Studies show that identification can foster imitation and modeling of behavior with both children and adults (Leyens & Picus, 1973; Paik & Comstock, 1994; Perry & Perry, 1976). Because of this research, we included variables which assessed not only the type of character (e.g., human, anthropomorphized animal, supernatural creature) involved with altruistic incidents but also typical demographic (e.g., gender, ethnicity) features.

The second variable is the *relationship* between the initiator of the altruistic act and the target. Altruism, in a biological sense, refers to actions which decrease the reproductive fitness of the initiator but increase the robustness of fitness for the target (Post, 2002). Such acts are supposed to be especially strong for genetically linked individuals such as mother and child. Other theorists have examined altruism and "inclusive fitness," or kind acts that extend to siblings, and other relatives outside the parent–child bond. Altruistic acts also have been found to be particularly likely toward specific ingroups, which were labeled by Sorokin (1950) as "tragedy of tribal altruism" or outgroup egoism (c.f. Post, 2002, p. 7). Given the theoretical interest in the genetic and/or ingroup bond between altruist and recipient, it seemed prudent to code the nature of their relationship. Our measure captures complete strangers on one hand, similar to many of the rescuers of Jews during the Holocaust (Monroe, 1996; Oliner & Oliner, 1988) and acquaintances, friends, family members, and co-workers on the other.

The third measure was *reinforcements*. Initiators of altruistic acts may be rewarded for their actions with money, praise, and/or affection. For example, a character may rescue a woman trapped in a car fire. Because of his heroism, the rescuer might be given a key to the city by the mayor. Characters may also experience feelings of self-adulation and pride because of their helping behaviors. Studies show that rewards are important incentives in the acquisition of information and fostering imitation among both children and adults (Bandura, 1986; Bandura, Ross, & Ross, 1961; Lando & Donnerstein, 1978). For example, children exposed to aggressive models that were rewarded behaved significantly more violently after viewing than did those exposed to aggressive models that were punished (see Bandura, 1965; Bandura et al., 1961).

Clearly, the presence of rewards and punishments are important vicarious cues that influence social learning. This is impressive given that at least one study (Bandura, 1965) used simple *mediated* rewards such as verbal praise and treats (e.g., candy, soda pop) and punishments such as adult verbal disapproval and spanking. Consistent with this line of research, we assessed the reinforcements for altruistic actions at the end of each scene. This examination includes the presence of different types of verbal, nonverbal, and material rewards and punishments.

The fourth measure assesses the presence of *bystanders*. Research reveals that in ambiguous situations, the presence of bystanders seems to *decrease* the likelihood of helping (Latane & Darley, 1970). These findings have been explained (Krebs & Miller, 1985) by the fact that inactive onlookers may communicate that (1) the situation is not serious enough to warrant helping; (2) it is inappropriate to help; or (3) responsibility surrounding who should assist is not clear. To date, we know virtually nothing about how bystanders are portrayed in helping situations on television. Given this, we simply measure the presence or absence of bystanders in altruistic scenes.

The fifth measure is *humor*. Altruistic acts may occur in the context of a humorous plotline or in the midst of a joking comment. Much of children's educational programming (e.g., *Sesame Street*) uses humor as a stylistic device to capture and regain attention to important pedagogical components and promote interest in learning (Zillmann, Williams, Bryant, Boynton, & Wolf, 1980). To date, we know very little about the impact of including humor in an altruistic scene. The presence of humor may facilitate enjoyment of viewing altruistic acts, thereby functioning as a reward. As noted above, positive reinforcements heighten the likelihood of learning (Bandura, 2002). Cracking a joke or firing off a sarcastic quip may also trivialize the seriousness of helping behavior. Such trivialization may decrease the likelihood of imitation or learning, presumably because the viewer disregards the helping or encodes it as unimportant. Or the use of humor in a helping scene may short-circuit empathic reactivity, a motivator of altruistic actions. Because our knowledge in this area is still in its infancy, we simply code each altruistic scene for the presence or absence of humor.

The last measure is *realism*. Characters, settings, and events may take place in realistic, fictional, and/or fantastic worlds. Studies have shown repeatedly that the level of perceived realism affects both children's and adults' reactions to programming content (Atkin, 1983; Geen, 1975; Thomas & Tell, 1974). Generally, these studies reveal that realistic violent portrayals have a greater impact than do fictional violent portrayals on aggressive behavior immediately after viewing. Similar findings have been documented with longitudinal research as well (Huesmann, Moise, Podolski, & Eron, 1998). Other studies have documented that perceived realism influences youngsters' perceptions of and reactions to sexual content (Baran, 1976).

The realism of the portrayal may also influence individuals' responses to altruistic content. Viewers may perceive altruistic acts as directly relevant to their lives or informative when such behaviors occur in more realistic formats and settings. As a result, we measured not only the level of realism associated with the portrayal (i.e., real, re-created reality, fictional, fantasy) but also the method of presentation (i.e., live action, animation, or both) and program genre (i.e., reality show, movie, children's show, music video, drama, comedy).

Overall, then, we assessed six different contextual features associated with prosocial behavior and altruistic actions on television. The presence or absence of these features may exert an influence on the probability of imitation effects for viewers. In the next section, we overview the sample of television content used in our investigation, as well as a few of the major findings.

Content-Analytic Results

The goal of our study was to examine prosocial behavior and altruistic acts on US television. To this end, we assessed the prevalence of and context surrounding each of the composites outlined above. In terms of television content, we randomly sampled programs from April 7 to June 30, 2003 from 6:00 a.m. to 11:00 p.m. across 18 broadcast (ABC, CBS, NBC, Fox), independent (WB, UPN), public broadcasting (PBS), and basic/premium cable (A&E, Cartoon Network, CNN, Disney, HBO, Lifetime, MTV, Nickelodeon, TBS, TNT, USA) outlets. Only entertainment programs were coded for altruism, thereby excluding news, sports, informational content, and religious programming. In total, 2,227 programs (1,763 hours) were sampled and coded to build a constructed week of television content (for complete study details see Smith et al., 2006).

To capture the prevalence and context of prosocial acts and altruistic behavior on television, we used two units of analysis: the incident and the program. As Smith et al. (2006, p. 711) indicated, an incident involved an actor (initiator) engaging in a specific type of helping action (e.g., sharing, giving, donating) directed toward a specific recipient. Whenever the initiator, type of act, or recipient changed, a new altruistic line of data or unit was created. Multiple measures were captured at the incident level, such as character demographics (e.g., type, age, sex, ethnicity), composite variables (e.g., empathy, ease of escape, cost, concern), and the adjacent context to each act (e.g., rewards, punishments, secondary benefit, humor). The second unit of analysis was the program, which referred to a time block featuring one or more unfolding storylines (see Smith et al., 2006). Contextual variables also were measured at the program level, such as realism (i.e., actual reality, re-created reality, fictional, fantastic) and style of presentation (i.e., live action, animated action, both).

What did we find? Our results are in Tables 3.2–3.4. Rather than reviewing the findings for each composite, we would like to highlight four major trends across all of the data (for detailed findings see Smith et al., 2006). The first trend is that *liberal altruism* (e.g., composite 1) is pervasive on US television (see Table 3.2). To reiterate, liberal altruism involves *all* instances of helping and/or sharing. Almost three-quarters (73%) of all shows in the sample feature one or more instances of helping and/or sharing. Overall, there were 5,152 acts of liberal altruism across the composite week, which translates into 2.92 behaviors per hour (see Smith et al., 2006).

These findings suggest that viewers are likely to encounter a good deal of positive social behavior on television. If the average child viewer is exposed to two to three hours of television content per day, then s/he will see roughly 6 instances of liberal altruism each day, 30 per week, 120 per month, or 1,440 per year. Such depictions may be powerful exemplars of positive social modeling. It must be noted that our results are more conservative than those found in other studies examining the number of shows featuring prosocial and/or altruistic actions (Lee, 1988), or the rate of such acts per hour (Greenberg et al., 1980; Potter & Ware, 1989; Poulos et al., 1976). Presumably, our lower estimates are

Table 3.2 Industry Averages by Composite Type

	Composite 1: Liberal altruism	Composite 2: Initiator focus	Composite 3: Recipient focus	Composite 4: Loving acts of compassion
Prevalence variables				
Programs	73% (1,621)	49% (1,082)	26.4% (588)	5% (107)
No. of incidents	5,152	2,508	1,059	162
Rate per hour	2.92	1.42	0.6	0.09

Note. The numbers in parentheses refer to the total number of shows in the sample featuring one or more instances of the composite.

due to the fact that we chose to exclude acts of sociability and normative behaviors involving helping and/or sharing in occupational contexts.

The second major trend is that altruism varies on television greatly depending on how it is conceptualized. As shown in Table 3.2, the prevalence of altruism decreases on television as the definitional stringency increases. For instance, almost three-quarters of all shows on television feature one or more instances of liberal altruism, whereas fewer than half feature initiator-focused behavior (e.g., composite 2) and less than one-third feature recipient-focused acts (e.g., composite 3). Interestingly, the prevalence of compassionate love (composite 4) occurs quite infrequently on television. These types of behaviors only appear in 5% ($n = 107$) of all shows across 18 different broadcast, independent, and cable channels. This trend is consistent with not only some scholars' narrow definition of compassionate love, but also media-based content studies which show that prosocial messages of social responsibility (i.e., antiviolence themes, risk and responsibility messages surrounding sexual behavior) are very infrequent in television programming (Kunkel et al., 1999; Smith et al., 1998; Wilson et al., 1997).

The third major trend is that the context surrounding altruistic acts varies – to some degree – by composite type (see Table 3.3). While most altruistic acts involve white adult males, some notable deviations occur across the composites. For instance, initiator-focused altruism (e.g., composite 2) is more likely than the other composites to feature children as initiators and recipients of altruistic acts. Recipient-focused altruism (e.g., composite 3), on the other hand, is the most likely to present a balanced view of gender, with 58.5% of the initiators coded "male" and 41.5% coded "female." These differences are important given that viewers are more likely to attend to and identify with characters who demographically look and act like themselves (Hoffner, 1996; Jose & Brewer, 1984). Moving beyond demographics, we also see that the composites depict different types of relationships between initiator and recipient (see Table 3.4). To illustrate, liberal altruism (e.g., composite 1) is most commonly directed at strangers, whereas recipient altruism is most likely targeted toward friends and family members.

Examining loving acts of compassion (composite 4) reveals that these acts seem to take place in a unique context, which is the fourth major trend. As shown in Table 3.3, compassionate acts of love are the most likely of all the composites to feature adult initiators and targets. Further, these acts are very likely to be presented in live action contexts (see Table 3.4). This stringent form of altruism is the least likely of all the composites to feature a bystander and most likely to depict rewards and secondary benefits to the initiator of the selfless act (see Table 3.4). Together, the portrayal of compassionately loving acts on television

Table 3.3   Character Demographics by Composite Type (%)

	Composite 1: Liberal altruism	Composite 2: Initiator focus	Composite 3: Recipient focus	Composite 4: Loving acts of compassion
Initiator variables				
Type				
Human	80.4	81.2	85.8	90.1
Anthro	12.8	13.0	9.1	6.8
Age				
Child	30.6	30.8	25.3	24.2
Adult	69.4	69.2	74.8	75.8
Gender				
Male	66.1	67.0	58.5	63.4
Female	33.9	33.0	41.5	36.6
Ethnicity				
White	79.5	80.4	76.5	75.2
Black	14.3	12.2	16.0	13.8
Recipient variables				
Type				
Human	80.1	80.7	83.8	89.5
Anthro	12.4	12.9	9.5	8.0
Age				
Child	38.8	39.3	33.6	30.2
Adult	61.2	60.7	66.4	69.8
Gender				
Male	58.4	59.1%	52.1%	51.0%
Female	41.6	40.9%	47.9%	49.0%
Ethnicity				
White	79.3	80.7%	77.0%	77.1%
Black	14.5	12.8%	15.7%	13.6%

involves two contextual elements that have been found in previous research to increase the likelihood of imitation: realistic characters and settings and positive reinforcements.

A few other general patterns are worth noting. As illustrated in Table 3.4, acts are shown in a humorous setting from one-quarter (24.7%, compassionate love or composite 4) to over one-third (36.2%, initiator-focused altruism or composite 2) of the time. If humor functions as a positive reinforcement, then its presence in an altruistic context could facilitate learning. When mirthful moments make light of instances of helping and/or sharing,

Table 3.4   Context by Composite Type (%)

	Composite 1: Liberal altruism	Composite 2: Initiator focus	Composite 3: Recipient focus	Composite 4: Loving acts of compassion
Relationship				
Stranger	19.7	19.6	15.5	15.6
Friend	31.7	32.6	34.6	33.1
Family	13.8	13.7	16.2	14.3
Bystander	60.1	61.8	55.0	51.2
Secondary benefit	28.1	29.1	34.7	58.6
Rewards	31.3	33.6	25.9	37.7
Punishments	13.9	14.0	14.5	17.9
Humor	35.6	36.2	29.4	24.7
Realistic settings	72.0	71.6	76.8	76.6
Live action format	64.7	64.4	72.9	74.8

however, the impact on learning may be hindered. That is, the humor may function as a cue to inform the audience that the action is to be taken lightly or less seriously. Anywhere from 25.9% (recipient altruism, composite 3) to 37.7% (compassionate love: composite 4) of altruistic actions on television are rewarded and roughly three-quarters (71.6% to 76.8%) are shown in realistic contexts (see Table 3.4). As noted above, these variables have been found to heighten the probability of learning effects. Therefore, many of the altruistic acts shown on television may be contributing to the acquisition and learning of prosocial social action.

Conclusion

We believe that our research contributes to the literature in significant ways. First, our results provide a current assessment of altruistic acts on both broadcast *and* cable television across multiple time slots. As noted earlier, not one study has examined positive social influences on popular cable outlets. Second, the findings reveal which types of altruistic behaviors are most prevalent on television and the types of contexts that surround those actions. Although much of the violence literature has focused on the nature of mediated aggression (Potter & Ware, 1987; Wilson et al., 1997), mediated altruistic behavior remains unexamined. Third, the results reveal how different definitions affect the prevalence and rate of altruistic actions per hour. Fourth, this scheme can be easily adapted to code actual behavior in a variety of contexts.

We believe that this research should spawn future empirical investigations. In terms of content studies, future scholars may want to examine more closely character attributes (i.e., attractiveness, strength, funniness) associated with altruists. We did not include any of these variables in the present study. Yet research suggests that character variables influence identification and modeling effects (Bandura, 2002; Hoffner, 1996).

Scholars also may want to examine how viewers interpret different aspects of altruistic scenes. It was mentioned above that the presence of humor in an altruistic scene may facilitate or inhibit helping responses. Examining the role of humor as well as different types of mirth used in altruistic contexts would contribute substantively to our understanding of individuals' interpretations of and reactions to positive television content.

Our novel approach to conceptualizing altruism should also be tested in the laboratory. Though we defined altruism in different ways by creating four separate composites, lay observers may have very different ideas about what constitutes an altruistic act. As such, testing how individuals perceive and make sense of altruistic acts is an important next step. Further, scholars could use our coding scheme to categorize different types of altruistic behaviors that may be evoked in self-reports or in more naturalistic, observational settings.

The conceptualizations and findings from this study can be overlaid on Underwood's (2002) model of compassionate love. A content analysis, such as ours, by definition begins with behavior. Here, we begin with a focus on positive behavior and move back toward the Substrate where our contextual variables fall. Direction of concern (self versus other), initiator cost, recipient benefit, empathy on the part of the initiator for the recipient, and ease of escape from self and/or social censure fall within Motivation & Discernment, or the internal processes involved with making decisions regarding action, and when all five are present Compassionate Love Fully Expressed is present.

Our approach is not without its limitations, however. We did not assess altruistic actions on actual news programming. This may be a tragic oversight, given some of the amazing acts of heroism and altruism of volunteers since September 11, 2001. Additionally, we sampled programs during the onset of the War on Iraq. Because our sample dovetailed with the beginning of this international conflict, some of our programming may have been preempted. Finally, we embraced a rather conservative definition of prosocial behavior owing to our interest in altruistic actions that occur above and beyond role-related behaviors. The consequence is that many actions that are perceived as altruistic (e.g., acts of affection, acts of public servants) to both viewers as well as other researchers may not be coded by our scheme.

Overall, we have developed an original content-coding scheme of altruistic behavior on television. As such, our findings should contribute substantively to the extant literature on altruistic behavior and its impact on individuals, society, and culture.

Acknowledgment

This project was supported by funding from the Fetzer Institute awarded to the first two authors of the manuscript. We would like to thank the Institute for its support.

References

Atkin, C. (1983). Effects of realistic TV violence vs. fictional violence on aggression. *Journalism Quarterly, 60*, 615–621.

Bandura, A. (1965). Influence of models' reinforcement contingencies on the acquisition of imitative responses. *Journal of Personality and Social Psychology, 1*(6), 589–95.

Bandura, A. (1986). *Social foundations of thought and action: A social cognitive theory*. Englewood Cliffs, NJ: Prentice-Hall.

Bandura, A. (2002). Social cognitive theory of mass communication. In J. Bryant & D. Zillmann (Eds.), *Media effects* (pp. 121–154). Hillsdale, NJ: Lawrence Erlbaum.

Bandura, A., Ross, D., & Ross, S. A. (1961). Transmission of aggression through imitation of aggressive models. *Journal of Abnormal and Social Psychology, 63*, 575–582.

Baran, S. J. (1976). Sex on TV and adolescent sexuality. *Journal of Broadcasting, 20*, 61–68.

Batson, C. D. (1991). *The altruism question: Towards a social psychological answer.* Hillsdale, NJ: Lawrence Erlbaum.

Batson, C. D. (2002). Addressing the altruism question experimentally. In S. G. Post, L. G. Underwood, J. P. Schloss, & W. B. Hurlbut (Eds.), *Altruism and altruistic love: Science, philosophy, and religion in dialogue* (pp. 89–105). New York: Oxford University Press.

Batson, C. D., Duncan, B. D., Ackerman, P., Buckley, T., & Birch, K. (1981). Is empathic emotion a source of altruistic motivation. *Journal of Personality and Social Psychology, 40*, 291–302.

Burgoon, J. K., Buller, B., & Woodall, W. G. (1996). *Nonverbal communication: The unspoken dialog.* New York: McGraw Hill.

Coke, J. S., Batson, C. D., & McDavis, K. (1978). Empathic mediation of helping: A two-stage model. *Journal of Personality and Social Psychology, 36*, 752–766.

Comte, A. (1875). *System of positive polity (Vol. 1).* London: Longmans, Green, & Co.

Drabman, R. S., & Thomas, M. H. (1977). Children's imitation of aggressive and prosocial behavior when viewing alone and in pairs. *Journal of Communication, 27*(3), 199–205.

Eisenberg, N., & Miller, P. A. (1987). The relation of empathy to prosocial and related behaviors. *Psychological Bulletin, 101*(1), 91–119.

Eisenberg, N., & Strayer, J. (1987). Critical issues in the study of empathy. In N. Eisenberg & J. Strayer (Eds.), *Empathy and its development* (pp. 3–16). New York: Cambridge University Press.

Feshbach, N. D., & Feshbach, S. (1997). Children's empathy and the media: Realizing the potential of television. In S. Kirschner & D. A. Kirschner (Eds.), *Perspectives on psychology and the media* (pp. 3–28). Washington, DC: American Psychological Association.

Fryrear, J. L., & Thelen, M. H. (1969). Effect of sex of model and sex of observer on the imitation of affectionate behavior. *Developmental Psychology, 1,* 298.

Fultz, J., Batson, C. D., Fortenbach, V. A., McCarthy, P. M., & Varney, L. L. (1986). Social evaluation and the empathy-altruism hypothesis. *Journal of Personality and Social Psychology, 50*(4), 761–769.

Geen, R. (1975). The meaning of observed violence: Real vs. fictional violence and consequent effects on aggression and emotional arousal. *Journal of Research in Personality, 9,* 270–281.

Greenberg, B. S., Edison, N., Korzenny, F., Fernandez-Collado, & Atkin, C. K. (1980). Antisocial and prosocial behaviors on television. In B. S. Greenberg (Ed.), *Life on television: Content analyses of U.S. TV drama* (pp. 99–128). Norwood, NJ: Ablex.

Gunter, B. (1994). The question of media violence. In J. Bryant & D. Zillmann (Eds.), *Responding to the screen: Reception and reaction processes* (pp. 163–211). Hillsdale, NJ: Lawrence Erlbaum.

Hearold, S. (1986). A synthesis of 1043 effects of television on social behavior. In G. Comstock (Ed.), *Public communication and behavior* (Vol. 1, pp. 65–133). New York: Academic Press.

Hoffner, C. (1996). Children's wishful identification and parasocial interaction with favorite television characters. *Journal of Broadcasting and Electronic Media, 40,* 389–402.

Hoffner, C., & Cantor, J. (1991). Perceiving and responding to mass media characters. In J. Bryant & D. Zillmann (Eds.), *Responding to the screen: Reception and reaction processes* (pp. 63–101). Hillsdale, NJ: Lawrence Erlbaum.

Huesmann, L. R., Moise, J., Podolski, C. L., & Eron, L. (1998). *Longitudinal relations between children's exposure to television violence and their later aggressive and violent behavior into adulthood 1977–1992.* Paper presented at the annual conference of the International Society for Research on Aggression, Mahwah, NJ.

Hurlbut, W. B. (2002). Empathy, evolution, and altruism. In S. G. Post, L. G. Underwood, J. P. Schloss, & W. B. Hurlbut (Eds.), *Altruism and altruistic love: Science, philosophy, and religion in dialogue* (pp. 309–327). New York: Oxford University Press.

Jose, P. E., & Brewer, W. F. (1984). Development of story liking: Character identification, suspense, and outcome resolution. *Developmental Psychology, 20*(5), 911–924.

Kagan, J. (2002). Morality, altruism, and love. In S. G. Post, L. G. Underwood, J. P. Schloss, & W. B. Hurlbut (Eds.), *Altruism and altruistic love: Science, philosophy, and religion in dialogue* (pp. 40–50). New York: Oxford.

Krebs, D. L. (1970). Altruism – an examination of the concept and a review of the literature. *Psychological Bulletin, 73*(4), 258–302.

Krebs, D. L., & Miller, D. T. (1985). Altruism and aggression. In G. Lindzey & E. Aronson (Eds.), *Handbook of social psychology* (Vol. 3, pp. 1–73). New York: Random House.

Kunkel, D., Biely, E., Eyal, K., Cope-Farrar, K., Donnerstein, E., & Fandrich, R. (2003). *Sex on TV 3.* Menlo Park, CA: Kaiser Family Foundation.

Kunkel, D., Cope, K., Farinola, W., Biely, E., Rollin, E., & Donnerstein, E. (1999). *Sex on TV: Content and context.* Menlo Park, CA: Kaiser Family Foundation.

Kunkel, D., Cope-Farrar, K., Biely, E., Farinola, W. J. M., & Donnerstein, E. (2001). *Sex on TV 2.* Menlo Park, CA: Kaiser Family Foundation.

Lando, H. A., & Donnerstein, E. I. (1978). The effects of a model's success or failure on subsequent aggressive behavior. *Journal of Research in Personality, 12,* 225–234.

Latane, B., & Darley, J. M. (1970). *The unresponsive bystander: Why doesn't he help?* New York: Appleton-Croft.

Lee, B. (1988). Prosocial content on prime-time television. *Applied Social Psychology, 8,* 238–246.

Leyens, J. P., & Picus, S. (1973). Identification with the winner of a fight and name mediation: Their differential effects upon subsequent aggressive behavior. *British Journal of Social and Clinical Psychology, 12,* 374–377.

Mares, M. L., & Woodard, E. (2001). Prosocial effects on children's social interaction. In D. G. Singer & J. L. Singer (Eds.), *Handbook of children and the media* (pp. 183–205). Thousand Oaks, CA: Sage.

Monroe, K. R. (1996). *The heart of altruism: Perceptions of a common humanity.* Princeton, NJ: Princeton University Press.

Monroe, K. R. (2002). Explicating altruism. In S. G. Post, L. G. Underwood, J. P. Schloss, & W. B. Hurlbut (Eds.), *Altruism and altruistic love: Science, philosophy, and religion in dialogue* (pp. 106–122). New York: Oxford University Press.

Nielsen Media Research (2000). Nielsen Media Research: 2000 Report on Television: The First 50 Years. New York: Author.

Oliner, S. P. (2002). Extraordinary acts of ordinary people: Faces of heroism and altruism. In S. G. Post, L. G. Underwood, J. P. Schloss, & W. B. Hurlbut (Eds.), *Altruism and altruistic love: Science, philosophy, and religion in dialogue* (pp. 123–139). New York: Oxford University Press.

Oliner, S. P., & Oliner, P. M. (1988). *The altruistic personality: Rescuers of Jews in Nazi Europe.* New York: Free Press.

Paik, H., & Comstock, G. (1994). The effects of television violence on anti-social behavior. *Communication Research, 21,* 516–546.

Perry, D. G., & Perry, L. C. (1976). Identification with film characters, covert aggressive verbalization, and reactions to film violence. *Journal of Research in Personality, 10,* 399–409.

Post, S. G. (2002). The tradition of agape. In S. G. Post, L. G. Underwood, J. P. Schloss, & W. B. Hurlbut (Eds.), *Altruism and altruistic love: Science, philosophy, and religion in dialogue* (pp. 51–64). New York: Oxford University Press.

Post, S. G., Underwood, L. G., Schloss, J. P., & Hurlbut, W. B. (Eds.). (2002). *Altruism and altruistic love: Science, philosophy, and religion in dialogue.* New York: Oxford University Press.

Potter, W. J., & Ware, W. (1987). An analysis of the context of antisocial acts on prime time television. *Communication Research, 14,* 664–686.

Potter, W. J., & Ware, W. (1989). The frequency and context of prosocial acts on primetime TV. *Journalism and Mass Communication Quarterly, 66*(2), 359–366, 529.

Poulos, R. W., Harvey, S. E., & Liebert, R. M. (1976). Saturday morning television: A profile of the 1974–75 children's season. *Psychological Reports, 39,* 1047–1057.

Preston, S. D., & de Waal, F. B. (2002). The communication of emotions and the possibility of empathy in animals. In S. G. Post, L. G. Underwood, J. P. Schloss, & W. B. Hurlbut (Eds.), *Altruism and altruistic love: Science, philosophy, and religion in dialogue* (pp. 284–308). New York: Oxford University Press.

Rushton, J. P. (1976). Socialization and the altruistic behavior of children. *Psychological Bulletin, 83*(5), 898–913.

Rushton, J. P. (1979). Effects of prosocial television and film material on the behavior of viewers. *Advances in Experimental Social Psychology, 12,* 321–351.

Smith, S. L., Wilson, B. J., Kunkel, D., Linz, D., Potter, W. J., Colvin, C., & Donnerstein, E. (1998). Violence in television programming overall: University of California, Santa Barbara Study. *National television violence study* (Vol. 3, pp. 5–220). Newbury Park, CA: Sage.

Smith, S. W., Smith S. L., Pieper, K., Downs, E., Yoo, H. J., Bowden, B., Ferris, A., & Butler, M. C. (2006). Altruism on American television: Examining the amount of, and context surrounding, acts of helping and sharing. *Journal of Communication, 56,* 707–727.

Sober, E. (2002). The ABCs of altruism. In S. G. Post, L. G. Underwood, J. P. Schloss, & W. B. Hurlbut (Eds.), *Altruism and altruistic love: Science, philosophy, and religion in dialogue* (pp. 17–29). New York: Oxford University Press.

Sorokin, P. A. (1950). *Altruistic love: A study of American 'good neighbors' and Christian saints.* Boston: Beacon Press.

Thomas, M. H., & Tell, P. M. (1974). Effects of viewing real versus fantasy violence upon interpersonal aggression. *Journal of Research in Personality, 8,* 153–160.

Underwood, L. G. (2002). The human experience of compassionate love: Conceptual mapping and data from selected studies. In S. G. Post, L. G. Underwood, J. P. Schloss, & W. B. Hurlbut (Eds.), *Altruism and altruistic love science, philosophy, and religion in dialogue* (pp. 72–88). New York: Oxford University Press.

Wilson, B. J., Kunkel, D., Linz, D., Potter, W. J., Donnerstein, E., Smith, S. L., Blumenthal, E., & Berry, M. (1998). Violence in television programming overall: University of California, Santa Barbara Study. *National television violence study* (Vol. 2, pp. 3–204). Newbury Park, CA: Sage

Wilson, B. J., Kunkel, D., Linz, D., Potter, W. J., Donnerstein, E., Smith, S. L., Blumenthal, E. Y., & Gray, T. E. (1997). Violence in television programming overall: University of California, Santa Barbara Study. *National television violence study* (Vol. 1, pp. 1–268). Newbury Park, CA: Sage Publications.

Wyschogrod, E. (2002). Pythagorean bodies and the body of altruism. In S. G. Post, L. G. Underwood, J. P. Schloss, & W. B. Hurlbut (Eds.), *Altruism and altruistic love: Science, philosophy, and religion in dialogue* (pp. 29–39). New York: Oxford.

Zillmann, D. (1991). Empathy: Affect from bearing witness to the emotions of others. In J. Bryant & D. Zillmann (Eds.), *Responding to the screen: Reception and reaction processes* (pp. 135–168). Hillsdale, NJ: Lawrence Erlbaum.

Zillmann, D., Williams, B. R., Bryant, J., Boynton, K. R., & Wolf, M. A. (1980). Acquisition and information from educational television programs as a function of differently paced humorous inserts. *Journal of Educational Psychology, 72,* 170–180.

Part II

The Sociodemographics of Compassionate Love

4

Loving and Caring in the United States: Trends and Correlates of Empathy, Altruism, and Related Constructs

Tom W. Smith

Introduction

Throughout the arts and sciences, from philosophy to neuroscience, constructs dealing with empathy, altruism, compassion, love, and related caring concepts have been widely studied. Just within the social sciences there have been very diverse research traditions within economics, psychology, political science, sociology, and related disciplines (Batson, 1991, 1998; Eisenberg, 1986; Kangas, 1997; Penner, 1995; Piliavin & Charng, 1990; Sawyer, 1966; Staub, Bar-Tal, Karylowski, & Reykowski, 1984; Underwood, 2002; Wispe, 1978; Wrightsman, 1974). One of the main limitations of social science research on altruism and other caring concepts is that most research has been based on very restricted, small, nonrepresentative samples, mostly of undergraduate students.[1] Although convenience samples can be useful when working with students, especially when experimental designs are used, they suffer from serious problems of external validity and do not accurately reveal the extent of behaviors and values in society at large.

A host of related terms have been employed to describe the constellation of interrelated concepts dealing with helping and caring (Post, Underwood, Schloss, & Hurlbut, 2002; Underwood, 2002, 2005). Some center around the concept of "love" and include agape, altruistic love, compassionate

---

[1] Some prosocial behaviors, such as giving and volunteering to organized groups, have been examined in large-scale, national studies such as the Giving and Volunteering Surveys by Independent Sector and on the 1996 General Social Survey. However, most research on empathy and altruism has been restricted to small samples of students. For example, in the bibliography by Post and others (2002), 43 studies were exclusively based on students, 3 on students plus some others, 8 on people in various types of voluntary associations, 3 on twins, 3 on other convenience samples, and 2 on state-wide probability samples. Their sample sizes were less than 100 (21), 100–199 (19), 200–499 (13), and 500+ (9).

love, self-giving love, unconditional love, and unlimited love. Others concentrate on the idea of "altruism" and involve terms such as selflessness, self-sacrifice, and charitableness. Still others focus on the feelings that the caregiver has for others and include such concepts as empathy and compassion. While they cannot cover all of the rich and important elements encompassed by these concepts, four central aspects were examined in this research: altruistic love, altruistic values, altruistic behaviors, and empathy. Altruism is thought of as dealing with both values/preferences and behaviors "motivated mainly out of a consideration for another's needs rather than one's own" (Piliavin & Charng, 1990, p. 30), and altruism "provides benefits to its recipients but also provides no benefits to the actors and even incurs some costs" (Howard & Piliavin, 2000, p. 114). Empathy was examined in addition to the direct altruism measures because, as Batson (1998, p. 300) has noted, "the most frequently proposed source of altruistic motivation has been an other-oriented emotional response congruent with the perceived welfare of another person – today usually called empathy."

To expand knowledge about the level, nature, and associates of empathy, altruism, and related concepts in American society, measures of these constructs were included on national full-probability samples of adult Americans. Based on those data, this chapter first discusses the measures of empathy, altruistic love, altruistic values, and altruistic behaviors. Second, it describes the five scales constructed from the items. Third, it tracks trends in empathy and altruism. Fourth, it analyzes the bivariate associations between these scales and other measures. Specifically, it examines (a) validating measures; (b) variation across sociodemographic groups; and (c) various hypotheses about how empathy and altruism are related to other measures. Many of these indirectly touch on what Underwood (2002) refers to as "motivation and discernment." The principal hypotheses examined are drawn from the extant literature and hold that empathy and altruism will be greater among:

(1) those who are socially and civically engaged.
(2) those who see interpersonal, social obligations between people.
(3) the religious rather than the nonreligious, and that among the religious empathy and altruism will rise with level of involvement.
(4) those with higher psychological and physical well-being.
(5) those who are not misanthropic.
(6) those less fearful of crime and victimization and with a less punitive attitude toward crime and criminals.
(7) those supporting more spending for social welfare programs and the expansion of government policies to assist disadvantaged groups.

Finally, a series of multivariate models are developed to test the contributions of the sociodemographics and other variables controlling for the others. In particular, these models allow the partial testing of Underwood's compassionate-love model that the contexts of people's lives (physical, social, emotional, and cognitive) influence their ability to express compassionate love fully. The multivariate models also can partially test the part of Underwood's model of motivations and discernment which may lead to "compassionate love fully expressed" and then to positive actions, or on the other hand, certain motivations and discernment which may instead lead to either negative actions (inappropriate action) or positive action done "for the wrong reasons" (Underwood, 2002, p. 76).

Data

The empathy and altruism items were administered on random subsamples of the 2002 and 2004 General Social Surveys (GSSs). The GSSs are in-person, full-probability samples of adults living in households in the United States. Each GSS is a new cross-sectional sample. The 2002 GSS had a response rate of 70.1% and 1,366 completed cases and the 2004 GSS had a response rate of 70.4% and 1,329 completed cases. For a full description and methodology of the 2002 and 2004 GSSs see Davis, Smith, and Marsden (2005).

Levels of Empathy and Altruism

Empathy

Empathy is measured by the seven-item Davis Empathy Scale (Davis, 1994). As the combined 2002–4 figures in Table 4.1A show, a solid majority of Americans indicate that the empathic response to each item describes themselves: 81% say they feel protective of someone being taken advantage of, 76% describe themselves as "a pretty soft-hearted person," 74% are often touched by things that happen, and 74% often have tender, concerned feelings for the less fortunate. In addition, 75% say not feeling pity for the unfairly treated does not describe them, 62% that not being disturbed by the misfortunes of others is not typical, and 58% indicate that not feeling sorry for people having problems does not describe them.

The seven-item Davis Empathy Scale has values running from 7 (for someone giving the least empathic response to all items) to 35 (for the most empathic). The mean for the total sample is 28 and the sample size

Table 4.1 Empathy and Altruism

	Doesn't describe well				Describes well	
	1	2	3	4	5	Prob.
A. *Davis Empathy Scale*						
a. I often have tender, concerned feelings for people less fortunate than me.	4.1	4.5	17.6	28.4	45.4	
2002	4.8	4.7	19.3	25.9	45.3	
2004	3.4	4.3	15.9	30.9	45.5	.010
b. Sometimes I don't feel very sorry for other people when they are having problems.	34.1	23.4	24.5	11.5	6.4	
2002	36.7	22.0	23.8	11.1	6.4	
2004	31.4	24.9	25.3	12.0	6.4	.057
c. When I see someone being taken advantage of, I feel kind of protective toward them.	3.3	3.9	11.4	34.2	47.1	
2002	4.1	4.1	12.0	33.0	46.8	
2004	2.5	3.7	10.8	35.6	47.4	.110
d. Other people's misfortunes do not usually disturb me a great deal.	35.3	26.3	22.2	10.0	6.2	
2002	35.7	25.6	22.7	10.3	5.8	
2004	35.0	27.1	21.7	9.6	6.6	.749
e. When I see someone treated unfairly, I sometimes don't feel very much pity for them.	46.6	28.1	13.4	6.5	5.4	
2002	45.7	27.6	14.6	6.7	5.4	
2004	47.5	28.6	12.3	6.3	5.4	.485
f. I am often quite touched by things that I see happen.	3.0	4.6	18.0	28.5	45.8	
2002	3.6	3.6	17.8	26.7	48.3	
2004	2.3	5.7	18.3	30.4	43.3	.002

Table 4.1 (*Continued*)

	Doesn't describe well 1	2	3	4	Describes well 5	Prob.
g. I would describe myself as a pretty soft-hearted person.	2.9	5.2	16.6	27.8	47.5	
2002	3.7	5.0	18.0	24.8	48.5	
2004	2.1	5.4	15.2	30.9	46.4	.001

Note. 2002/2004 GSSs; N = 2,654–2,669.

	Strongly agree	Agree	Neither agree nor disagree	Disagree	Strongly disagree	Prob.
B. *Altruistic values*						
a. People should be willing to help others who are less fortunate.	43.4	46.3	8.7	0.9	0.8	
2002	42.8	46.3	9.2	1.1	0.7	
2004	44.0	46.3	8.1	0.7	0.9	.567
b. Those in need have to learn to take care of themselves and not depend on others.	10.5	40.3	26.0	19.4	3.9	
2002	12.0	41.4	23.5	19.2	3.9	
2004	8.9	39.2	28.5	19.6	3.9	.009
c. Personally assisting people in trouble is very important to me.	25.0	51.5	18.7	4.1	0.7	
2002	25.1	49.5	19.9	4.8	0.7	
2004	24.9	53.5	17.5	3.4	0.7	.108
d. These days people need to look after themselves and not overly worry about others.	5.6	23.1	22.8	39.9	8.6	
2002	6.6	25.6	21.8	37.2	8.8	
2004	4.7	20.5	23.9	42.7	8.4	.001

(*Continued*)

Table 4.1 (*Continued*)

	Strongly agree	Agree	Neither agree nor disagree	Disagree	Strongly disagree	Prob.
C. Altruistic love						
a. I would rather suffer myself than let the one I love suffer.	63.4%	26.4	6.9	2.6	0.7	
b. I cannot be happy unless I place the one I love's happiness before my own.	34.8%	37.4	14.9	9.2	3.7	
c. I am usually willing to sacrifice my own wishes to let the one I love achieve his/hers.	37.8%	43.5	11.7	5.5	1.6	
d. I would endure all things for the sake of the one I love.	42.7%	36.5	10.0	7.6	3.1	

Behaviors	Mean number of times[a]	% doing 1+ times
D. Altruistic behaviors per annum		
Talked to depressed person	24.0	93.6
Helped others with housework	16.1	79.0
Allowed someone to cut ahead	12.3	88.2
Gave directions	10.8	88.8
Gave money to charity	10.0	79.0
Volunteered for charity	6.9	46.9
Give to homeless	6.5	64.5
Helped someone find job	4.9	61.0
Helped someone who was away	4.2	58.9
Gave up seat	4.0	47.2
Carried belongings	3.8	46.5
Loaned item	3.5	41.7
Lent money	3.2	51.8
Returned extra change	2.2	50.7
Gave blood	0.6	17.3

Table 4.1   (Continued)

Behaviors	Mean number of times[a]		
	2002	2004	Prob.
Talked to depressed person	23.9	24.1	.824
Helped others with housework	16.6	15.7	.358
Allowed someone to cut ahead	10.9	13.7	.000
Gave directions	10.6	11.0	.541
Gave Money to charity	9.5	10.5	.117
Volunteered for charity	6.4	7.5	.111
Give to homeless	6.1	6.9	.162
Helped someone find job	4.6	5.2	.233
Helped someone who was away	4.2	4.3	.782
Gave up seat	3.5	4.5	.052
Lent money	3.2	3.8	.197
Carried belongings	3.1	4.4	.003
Loaned item	2.6	3.8	.197
Returned extra change	1.7	2.6	.004
Gave blood	0.6	0.6	.730

N = 1329–1357 for 11-item battery and 1138–1140 for 4 items.
[a] Original categories converted to get estimated mean number of times per year as follows: not at all = 0; once = 1; at least 2 or 3 times = 3; once a month = 12; once a week = 52; more than once a week = 75.

is 2,635. The inter-item correlations (Pearson's r's) average .296 and Cronbach's reliability coefficient is .75. Items a, c, f, and g were reverse-coded to give the empathic responses the high scores.

Altruistic Values

Four items measure altruistic values (Nickell, 1998; Webb, Green, & Brashear, 2000). As Table 4.1B shows, 90% agreed that people should be willing to help the less fortunate, with 2% disagreeing; 77% agreed that assisting those in trouble is personally important and only 5% disagreed; 49% disagreed that people "need to look after themselves and not overly worry about others," with 29% agreeing; and 23% disagreed that the needy should help themselves rather than depend on others, with 51% agreeing with this sentiment.

The four-item altruistic values scale runs from 4 (for someone giving the least altruistic response to all items) to 20 (for the most altruistic). The mean for the total sample is 14.2 and the sample size is 2,660. The inter-item correlations average .24 and Cronbach's reliability coefficient is .55. Items a and c were reverse-coded to give the altruistic responses high values.

Altruistic Love

Four items measure interpersonal, altruistic love or agape. Agape is one of six types of love measured by the Love Attitudes Scale (Butler, Walker, Skowronski, & Shannon, 1995; Davies, 2001; Hendrick & Hendrick, 1986, 1987, 1991; Montgomery & Sorell, 1997; Murthy, Rotzien, & Vacha-Haase, 1996; Sorokin, 1950; Taraban & Hendrick, 1995; Yancey & Eastman, 1995). Based on analysis of past studies (Butler et al., 1995; Hendrick & Hendrick, 1986; Montgomery & Sorell, 1997; Yancey & Eastman, 1995) and a GSS pretest, four of seven original items were selected. As Table 4.1C shows, altruistic love is widely endorsed. Ninety percent agree that they would suffer themselves rather than let their loved one suffer, 81% agree that they usually put their loved one's wishes above their own, 79% agree that they would "endure all things for the sake of the one I love," and 72% agree they cannot be happy unless they place their loved one's happiness first. The agape scale runs from 4 for someone who strongly disagreed with each statement (the lowest on altruistic love) to 20 for someone who strongly agreed with each (the highest on altruistic love). The mean for the total population is 16.6 and the sample size is 1,316 (having been asked only in 2004). The inter-item correlations average .52 and Cronbach's reliability coefficient is .81.

Altruistic Behaviors

There are two altruistic behavior batteries. The first has 11 items asked as part of the GSS empathy and altruism study. These items were based on various baseline studies (Amato, 1990; Johnson et al., 1989; Khanna, Singh, & Rushton, 1993; Rushton, Chrisjohn, & Fekken, 1981; Rushton & Sorrentino, 1981). The second has four similar items asked as part of the International Social Survey Program (ISSP) module on social networks. These 15 items are presented in Table 4.1D. A majority of Americans performed 10 of the 15 altruistic acts during the previous year. Four actions were carried out by 42–47% and only one activity was relatively infrequent, with only 17% giving blood. In terms of estimated number of times an activity was done in the previous year, talking to a depressed person was the most common of these altruistic behaviors (24 times per annum). This was followed by helping others with housework (16 times), allowing someone to cut ahead in line (12 times), giving directions (11 times), giving money to charity (10 times), volunteering (7 times), helping the homeless (6.5 times), assisting someone to find a job (5 times), taking care of things for someone who is away (4 times), giving up a seat (4 times), lending money (3 times), carrying belongings (4 times), loaning items (3.5 times), returning extra change (2 times), and giving blood (less than once).

Two scales were made from these behavioral items. The first scale uses the 11 items that were part of the empathy and altruism study. Values range from 0 (for someone who did none of the altruistic acts during the previous 12 months) to 825 (for someone who did all acts more than once a week during the previous year). The mean for the total population is 64.1 and the sample size is 2,623. The inter-item correlations on the original response scale average .126 and Cronbach's reliability coefficient is .61. The second scale consists of the 11 items plus 4 similar items from the ISSP module. These 4 items differ from the other 11 items because (a) they refer to things done "for people you know personally, such as relatives, friends, neighbors, or other acquaintances" which the former does not; and (b) in 2002 they were asked only of people doing the ISSP supplement, which reduced the sample size as indicated below. Values range from 0 (for someone who did none of the altruistic acts during the previous 12 months) to 1,125 (for someone who did all acts more than once a week during the previous year). The mean for the total population is 114.3 and the sample size is 2,418. The inter-item correlations average .127 and Cronbach's reliability coefficient is .68.

Trends in Empathy and Altruism

Several changes occurred on empathy and altruism between 2002 and 2004 (Table 4.1). Using chi-square tests, three of the seven empathy items show statistically significant change. People were more likely to describe themselves as having tender, concerned feelings toward the less fortunate in 2004 than in 2002 (+ 5.2 percentage points at 4 or 5 on the scale) and as more soft-hearted (+ 4.0 points), but as less "touched by things that I see" (– 0.9 points). Next, the empathy scale showed no significant change (27.9 in 2002 and 28 in 2004). Two of the four altruistic value measures showed increases. Agreement that people have to take care of themselves and not depend on others dropped by 5.3 points and those saying that "people need to look after themselves and not overly worry about others" fell by 7 points. Overall, altruistic values rose from 14 to 14.3 (prob. = .002). Likewise, 9 of the 15 altruistic behaviors were higher in 2004 (returning change, allowing cutting in, giving up a seat, helping someone who is away, carrying something, loaning an item, helping with housework, lending money, and talking to someone). However, using t-tests, there were significant increases in the means for only three actions (allowing cutting in, carrying something, and returning change). Overall, the 11-item scale showed an increase in the mean number of altruistic behaviors from 58.8 to 69.4 (prob. = .000) and the 15-item scale rose from 109.3 to 118.6 (prob. = .029). Altruistic love was measured only in 2004, so no trend is available.

While several statistically reliable shifts in the pro-altruistic occurred with only two time points just two years apart, it is not possible to know if this is a long-term societal shift or merely some short-term fluctuation.

Intercorrelations of Empathy, Altruistic Values, and Altruistic Behaviors

As anticipated, the empathy and altruistic scales are significantly associated to each other (Batson, 1998; Eisenberg et al., 1989; Morgan, Goddard, & Givens, 1997; Piliavin & Charng, 1990; Post et al., 2002; Romer, Gruder, & Lizzadro, 1986; Sprecher & Fehr, 2005). Empathy is strongly related to altruistic values (r = .46, prob. = .000). It is more moderately associated with altruistic behaviors (.13/prob. = .000 with the 11-item scale and .15/.000 and with the 15-item scale). Altruistic values are also moderately related to altruistic behaviors: by .14/.000 for the 11-item scale and .17/.000 for 15-item scale. Agape has the lowest associations, but is positively related to empathy (.14/.000), altruistic values (.18/.000), and altruistic behaviors (11-items = .08/.003; 15-items = .07/.008).

The somewhat higher inter-scale correlations for the 15-item scale compared with the 11-item scale suggests that on average the longer version has somewhat less measurement error and more reliability.

The comparatively modest associations of both empathy and altruistic values and altruistic behaviors reflect both the imperfect connection between values/attitudes and behaviors that prevails in general and the particular difficulties in reliably measuring altruistic behaviors. First, doing many of the behaviors depends on the specific opportunity of the act occurring (e.g., being asked for directions, getting extra change, being asked to help when someone is away) or knowing someone needing help (e.g., who is depressed, or needs a job or loan). One has to have an opportunity for doing these good deeds before one can act altruistically and it is likely that exposure to such opportunities is largely unrelated to a person's likelihood to assist, so this is essentially a random factor that attenuates associations with other empathy and altruistic values. Second, many of the incidents asked about are relatively minor and difficult to recall and report accurately. Both forgetting and misestimating the occurrence of good deeds also tends to reduce correlations. Third, altruistic acts are dependent to a notable degree on situational and contextual factors (Piliavin & Charng, 1990; Romer et al., 1986). For example, the presence or absence of others, time pressures, and framing (e.g., the nature of the need or its reason) will all influence whether a particular individual will act altruistically.

The even more modest associations of agape with both the attitudinal and behavioral measures probably indicates that one's altruistic attachment toward a loved one has only limited association to more generalized empathy and altruism which either involve people in general or often strangers. The low association of agape with behaviors reflects the factors delineated in the previous paragraph.

Correlates of Empathy and Altruism

Overall the five empathy and altruism scales were associated with 54 other variables. Of a total of 259 comparisons 154 or 59.5% were statistically significant (Table 4.2). The number of statistically significant associations were similar for the empathy (related to 35 variables), altruistic values (40), and the 15-item altruistic behaviors scale (36), but the altruistic love and 11-item behavioral scales were related to fewer variables (21 and 22, respectively).

First, two validation variables that measure cooperation and helpfulness independent of self-reports were considered (Table 4.2A). The first is the interviewer's ratings of how helpful and cooperative respondents were. One would expect that the more empathic and altruistic would be more cooperative with the interviewer. The analysis shows that for four variables empathy and altruism rose with rated level of cooperation and that in each case the association was largely linear.[2] Altruistic love was not significantly associated with cooperation, but showed a similar, monotonic relationship. The second validation variable is whether respondents reported their household income to interviewers. Altruistic behavior was associated with

---

[2]   The statistical analysis first tested whether there is statistically significant variation in empathy and altruism across the categories of the other variables. If not, no model is listed. If significant and the other variable is nominal, then the model is not constant (NC). If significant and the other variable is ordinal or interval, then the possible models are: linear (L) – no significant variation from the best linear fit; significant linear component (SLC) – linear fit is significant, but also significant variation from the best linear fit; and not constant, not linear (NCNL) – linear fit is not significant and deviation from best linear fit is significant.

Table 4.2 Altruism and Empathy Scales by other Variables

Variables[a]	Davis empathy	Altruistic love	Altruistic values	Altruistic behaviors 11-items	15-items
A. *Validation*					
Interviewer-rated cooperation (COOP)					
Friendly and eager	28.3	16.7	14.3	67.7	119.0
Cooperative, not eager	26.6	16.4	13.7	47.5	89.7
Indifferent/hostile	25.7	15.6	12.7	46.7	99.9
Prob.	.000	.068	.000	.000	.000
Model[b]	L	—	L	L	SLC
	(2630)	(1314)	(2655)	(2618)	(2414)
Reported income (INCOME98)					
Gave	27.9	16.6	14.1	65.3	116.0
Refused	28.6	17.0	13.9	55.9	96.6
Prob.	.107	.165	.126	.101	.032
Model	—	—	—	—	L
	(2499)	(1247)	(2522)	(2490)	(2300)
B. *Demographics*					
Gender (SEX)					
Men	26.6	17.0	13.6	65.8	109.4
Women	29.2	16.2	14.6	62.4	119.2
Prob.	.000	.000	.000	.223	.021
Model	L	L	L	—	L
	(2635)	(1316)	(2660)	(2623)	(2418)
Age (AGE)					
18–29	26.9	16.2	13.6	71.0	134.5
30–39	27.8	16.8	14.0	60.4	110.7
40–49	28.3	16.4	14.3	65.1	111.9
50–59	28.6	16.6	14.7	66.0	116.1
60–69	28.8	16.9	14.4	61.1	103.1
70+	28.0	17.4	14.2	52.9	88.3
Prob.	.000	.005	.000	.019	.000
Model	NCNL	L	SLC	L	SLC
	(2623)	(1311)	(2648)	(2610)	(2406)
Degree (DEGREE)					
LT high school	27.7	17.3	13.9	60.6	119.6
High school	27.9	16.6	14.1	63.8	114.8
Jr. college	27.8	16.6	14.2	64.1	112.2
4-yr. college	28.0	16.3	14.3	62.2	105.8
Grad. school	28.2	16.0	14.7	74.8	119.8
Prob.	.769	.006	.001	.166	.407
Model	—	L	L	—	—
	(2634)	(1315)	(2659)	(2622)	(2417)

Table 4.2 (*Continued*)

Variables[a]	Davis empathy	Altruistic love	Altruistic values	Altruistic behaviors 11-items	Altruistic behaviors 15-items
Income (INCOME98)					
LT 20 K	27.7	16.4	14.1	66.9	128.4
20–40 K	27.8	16.4	14.1	60.7	115.7
40–75 K	28.0	16.9	14.2	66.4	111.5
75 K+	28.2	16.4	14.4	67.3	112.4
Refused	28.6	17.0	13.9	55.9	96.6
Prob.	.216	.131	.039	.200	.016
Model	—	—	NCNL	—	L
	(2499)	(1247)	(2522)	(2490)	(2300)
Marital Status (MARITAL)					
Married	28.2	17.2	14.3	63.9	108.0
Widowed	28.9	16.8	14.6	50.8	92.9
Divorced	28.3	15.8	14.4	64.8	118.8
Separated	27.6	15.6	14.1	63.2	118.4
Never married	27.0	15.5	13.6	67.6	131.3
Prob.	.000	.000	.000	.123	.000
Model	NC	NC	NC	—	NC
	(2635)	(1316)	(2660)	(2623)	(2418)
Residence (SRCBELT)					
Big cities	27.4	15.1	13.8	78.1	141.5
Med. cities	27.4	16.3	13.7	60.2	111.8
Subs. big	27.6	16.3	14.1	63.6	114.1
Subs. medium	28.2	16.6	14.3	64.9	111.6
Other urban	28.1	16.9	14.3	65.2	114.8
Other rural	28.4	17.3	14.3	56.3	103.1
Prob.	.026	.000	.001	.029	.001
Model	L	L	L	NCNL	SLC
	(2635)	(1316)	(2660)	(2623)	(2418)
Region (REGION)					
New England	28.3	16.4	14.6	66.6	108.0
Mid-Atlantic	27.6	15.9	14.0	65.3	116.4
E. No. Cen.	28.3	16.9	14.3	56.5	107.7
W. No. Cen.	27.5	16.9	13.7	58.0	99.5
So. Atlantic	28.4	17.0	14.4	70.6	125.5
E. So. Cen.	28.5	16.4	14.4	52.1	102.9
W. So. Cen.	28.1	16.6	14.2	67.7	125.7
Mountain	27.8	16.4	14.2	62.7	108.3
Pacific	27.1	16.5	13.8	67.9	115.1
Prob.	.001	.024	.000	.028	.035
Model	NC	NC	NC	NC	NC
	(2635)	(1316)	(2660)	(2623)	(2418)

(*Continued*)

Table 4.2 (*Continued*)

Variables[a]	Davis empathy	Altruistic love	Altruistic values	Altruistic behaviors 11-items	15-items
Race (RACECEN1)					
White	28.1	16.8	14.2	62.3	109.9
Black	27.7	15.0	14.0	76.5	146.1
Prob.	.131	.000	.238	.001	.000
Model	—	L	—	L	L
	(2412)	(1184)	(2432)	(2396)	(2202)
Hispanic (HISPANIC)					
Is Not	28.0	16.6	14.2	64.1	113.2
Is Hisp.	27.7	16.5	13.8	64.4	126.5
Prob.	.365	.714	.007	.947	.072
Model	—	—	L	—	—
	(2634)	(1315)	(2659)	(2622)	(2417)
Labor-force status (WRKSTAT)					
Full time	27.8	16.7	14.1	66.1	116.8
Part time	28.1	15.9	14.2	68.0	121.9
Temp. off	29.0	16.7	14.3	46.6	100.2
Unemployed	26.9	15.3	13.9	62.7	121.5
Retired	28.1	17.2	14.3	54.7	90.4
Student	26.2	15.6	13.6	71.4	122.9
Homemaker	29.3	17.0	14.6	64.8	117.9
Other	28.5	17.6	14.8	54.6	114.3
Prob.	.000	.000	.001	.051	.006
Model	NC	NC	NC	—	NC
	(2635)	(1316)	(2660)	(2623)	(2418)
C. *Social/civic engagement*					
Socializing with friends (SOCFREND)					
Daily	27.4	16.0	14.1	106.2	181.8
Weekly	28.1	16.3	14.2	69.9	133.5
Monthly+	28.2	16.5	14.2	69.1	124.0
Monthly	28.1	16.5	14.2	64.2	112.3
Several times	27.8	16.8	14.2	60.0	106.2
Yearly	28.0	17.1	14.0	50.9	81.0
Never	28.4	17.2	14.0	47.3	92.9
Prob.	.723	.207	.916	.000	.000
Model	—	—	—	SLC	SLC
	(1767)	(891)	(1778)	(1749)	(1611)
Socializing with neighbors (SOCOMMUN)					
Daily	27.0	16.5	13.7	74.7	154.2
Weekly	28.1	16.2	14.3	79.7	143.2
Monthly+	28.6	16.7	14.3	71.5	123.4

Table 4.2 (*Continued*)

Variables[a]	Davis empathy	Altruistic love	Altruistic values	Altruistic behaviors 11-items	Altruistic behaviors 15-items
Monthly	28.1	16.8	14.4	69.3	117.1
Several times	28.7	16.8	14.4	67.9	109.1
Yearly	27.2	16.4	14.2	54.9	102.6
Never	28.2	16.6	14.0	54.8	104.3
Prob.	.004	.598	.057	.000	.000
Model	NCNL	—	—	L	L
	(1766)	(891)	(1776)	(1747)	(1609)
Socializing with relatives (SOCREL)					
Daily	28.6	16.4	14.3	79.4	157.3
Weekly	28.2	16.9	14.2	72.3	133.4
Monthly+	28.2	16.4	14.2	58.4	103.4
Monthly	28.1	16.8	14.3	63.1	107.6
Several times	27.8	16.2	14.2	59.9	101.9
Yearly	27.1	17.0	13.6	57.4	91.6
Never	27.6	15.9	13.9	55.9	107.2
Prob.	.133	.203	.345	.003	.000
Model	—	—	—	L	SLC
	(1768)	(893)	(1779)	(1750)	(1612)
Socializing at bar (SOCBAR)					
Daily	27.7	16.7	14.1	118.4	170.0
Weekly	27.5	16.5	14.1	63.6	120.8
Monthly+	27.2	16.1	13.7	62.8	114.9
Monthly	27.4	16.1	13.6	64.9	120.0
Several times	28.0	16.4	14.2	68.6	118.8
Yearly	27.7	16.1	14.4	62.2	110.1
Never	28.6	17.0	14.3	66.2	119.2
Prob.	.001	.027	.000	.175	.535
Model	L	L	SLC	—	—
	(1768)	(893)	(1779)	(1750)	(1612)
Friends (COWRKFRD, NEIFRD, OTHFRD)					
None	25.9	—	12.9	56.1	86.5
1	26.5	—	13.3	48.4	99.3
2	27.5	—	13.6	54.6	97.2
5–9	28.2	—	14.2	55.6	99.1
10–19	27.7	—	14.3	63.7	115.0
20–34	29.1	—	14.5	65.4	124.0
35+	28.5	—	14.6	83.5	144.9
Prob.	.001	C	.000	.015	.000
Model	SLC	—	SLC	L	L
	(1118)	C	(1121)	(1105)	(1102)

(*Continued*)

Table 4.2 (*Continued*)

Variables[a]	Davis empathy	Altruistic love	Altruistic values	Altruistic behaviors 11-items	15-items
Vote in 2000 (VOTE00)					
Did	28.2	16.6	14.3	65.8	113.4
Didn't	27.9	16.7	13.9	59.3	112.5
Not eligible	26.2	16.0	13.6	71.6	131.6
Refused	24.8	19.0	13.7	32.3	50.6
Prob.	.000	.129	.000	.063	.121
Model	NC	—	NC	—	—
	(2621)	(1305)	(1335)	(2608)	(2402)
Group activity (GRPPOL to GRPOTH)					
Low (7–9)	26.7	—	13.4	43.1	86.6
Medium (10–13)	28.4	—	14.0	55.4	100.7
High (14+)	28.4	—	14.7	81.9	137.5
Prob.	.000	—	.000	.000	.000
Model	SLC	—	L	L	L
	(1127)	C	(1131)	(1114)	(1110)
D. Obligations					
Adult children's duty to care for parents (KIDPARS)					
Agree str.	28.4	—	14.3	59.5	117.4
Agree	27.6	—	14.0	60.8	102.5
Neither	27.0	—	13.7	59.3	100.5
Disagree	27.8	—	14.3	71.2	119.3
Dis. str.	30.2	—	13.9	73.8	122.2
Prob.	.003	—	.022	.572	.117
Model	NCNL	—	L	—	—
	(1108)	C	(1112)	(1097)	(1094)
Parents live with children (AGED)					
Good idea	27.8	16.6	14.3	64.9	116.8
Depends	27.9	16.7	14.0	53.6	98.6
Bad idea	28.0	16.8	14.0	60.1	106.7
Prob.	.649	.641	.055	.036	.018
Model	—	—	—	NCNL	SLC
	(1729)	(868)	(1747)	(1719)	(1592)
Help self, family first (FIRSTYOU)					
Agree str.	27.6	—	13.8	59.5	111.0
Agree	28.1	—	14.0	58.4	100.9
Neither	28.2	—	15.0	71.8	124.8
Disagree	28.8	—	14.9	70.7	129.9
Dis. str.	29.5	—	18.3	101.2	171.0
Prob.	.352	—	.000	.210	.053
Model	—	—	L	—	—
	(1124)	C	(1128)	(1112)	(1110)

Table 4.2 (*Continued*)

Variables[a]	Davis empathy	Altruistic love	Altruistic values	Altruistic behaviors 11-items	15-items
Family, friends make demands (DEMANDS)					
No	27.7	—	14.0	58.1	101.2
Yes, seldom	27.4	—	13.9	62.2	106.6
Yes, sometimes	28.4	—	14.1	64.9	117.5
Yes, often	28.5	—	14.2	58.6	129.2
Yes, v. often	30.3	—	15.3	64.9	157.5
Prob.	.006	—	.059	.729	.006
Model	L	—	—	—	L
	(1125)	C	(1127)	(1112)	(1111)
Better should help friends (HELPFRDS)					
Agree str.	29.7	—	15.1	70.9	147.9
Agree	27.7	—	14.2	58.0	104.0
Neither	27.3	—	13.5	59.9	99.0
Disagree	27.0	—	13.3	63.9	107.6
Dis. str.	23.9	—	12.3	40.3	54.6
Prob.	.000	—	.000	.191	.000
Model	SLC	—	L	—	SLC
	(1104)	C	(1105)	(1092)	(1089)
E. Religion					
Religion (RELIG)					
Protestant	28.4	16.9	14.4	62.6	113.1
Catholic	27.8	16.8	14.0	64.7	115.9
Jewish	27.0	14.3	14.3	67.7	119.7
None	26.6	15.5	13.6	63.8	109.6
Other	27.7	16.6	13.9	74.3	126.5
Prob.	.000	.000	.000	.339	.489
Model	NC	NC	NC	—	—
	(2628)	(1313)	(2652)	(2615)	(2411)
Religion raised in (RELIG16)					
Protestant	28.3	16.8	14.3	63.7	113.7
Catholic	27.7	16.7	13.0	67.2	118.1
Jewish	26.9	14.5	14.2	60.1	107.9
None	27.3	15.8	13.5	56.5	100.4
Other	26.8	15.8	13.9	65.3	122.5
Prob.	.001	.000	.000	.405	.292
Model	NC	NC	NC	—	—
	(2628)	(1312)	(2650)	(2614)	(2410)

(*Continued*)

Table 4.2 (*Continued*)

Variables[a]	Davis empathy	Altruistic love	Altruistic values	Altruistic behaviors 11-items	15-items
Theology (FUND)					
Fund.	28.6	17.1	14.4	67.0	120.2
Moderate	28.0	16.8	14.1	64.7	116.1
Liberal	27.2	15.9	14.0	60.1	104.8
Prob.	.000	.000	.012	.170	.019
Model	L	SLC	L	—	NCNL
	(2518)	(1272)	(2538)	(2500)	(2310)
Religion (RELIG)					
Has	28.2	16.8	14.2	64.2	115.2
None	26.6	15.5	13.6	63.8	109.6
Prob.	.000	.000	.000	.913	.364
Model	L	L	L	—	—
	(2628)	(1313)	(2652)	(2615)	(2411)
Religion raised in (RELIG16)					
Had	28.0	16.7	14.2	64.9	115.5
None	27.3	15.8	13.5	56.5	100.4
Prob.	.064	.008	.000	.115	.063
Model	—	L	L	—	—
	(2627)	(1312)	(2650)	(2614)	(2410)
Religiousness (RELITEN)					
Strong	28.9	17.0	14.6	74.6	129.9
Somewhat	28.1	16.6	14.2	63.0	111.3
Not strong	27.6	16.6	13.9	54.9	102.6
No religion	26.6	15.5	13.6	63.8	109.6
Prob.	.000	.000	.000	.000	.000
Model	L	SLC	L	SLC	SLC
	(2611)	(1298)	(2634)	(2596)	(2394)
Attend church (ATTEND)					
Never	27.1	15.7	13.6	54.2	102.1
LT yearly	27.0	16.6	13.7	54.6	104.8
Once year	27.2	16.7	13.8	54.9	96.8
Sev. times	28.4	16.6	14.3	62.5	116.7
Monthly	27.4	14.4	14.1	58.7	112.0
2–3 month	27.5	16.8	14.4	66.0	118.4
Al. weekly	28.3	16.7	14.1	68.0	116.4
Weekly	29.0	16.9	14.4	77.2	128.4
Weekly+	30.0	17.5	15.4	85.1	144.0
Prob.	.000	.001	.000	.000	.000
Model	SLC	L	SLC	L	L
	(2629)	(1314)	(2652)	(2616)	(2412)

Table 4.2 (*Continued*)

Variables[a]	Davis empathy	Altruistic love	Altruistic values	Altruistic behaviors 11-items	15-items
Praying (PRAY)					
Daily+	29.3	17.0	14.8	76.7	138.0
Daily	28.5	16.7	14.4	67.2	118.4
Weekly+	27.7	16.9	14.0	60.4	104.7
Weekly	27.0	16.1	13.6	49.6	82.9
LT weekly	26.1	16.0	13.5	47.0	90.2
Never	25.5	15.6	13.2	60.2	101.6
Prob.	.000	.000	.000	.000	.000
Model	L	L	L	SLC	SLC
	(2617)	(1311)	(2641)	(2606)	(2403)
F. Psychological well-being					
Marital happiness (HAPMAR)					
Very happy	28.4	17.4	14.4	68.0	112.6
Pretty happy	27.9	16.9	14.2	58.2	101.0
Not too hap.	27.7	15.4	14.3	52.5	102.3
Prob.	.088	.000	.516	.020	.121
Model	—	L	—	L	—
	(1461)	(774)	(1477)	(1453)	(1340)
Life is (LIFE)					
Exciting	28.3	16.5	14.4	74.8	128.8
Routine	27.5	16.5	14.0	57.1	101.3
Dull	28.2	17.1	13.7	51.0	104.5
Prob.	.008	.572	.001	.000	.000
Model	L	—	L	L	L
	(1746)	(863)	(1763)	(1746)	(1609)
Health (HEALTH)					
Excellent	28.1	16.4	14.4	70.3	120.6
Good	27.8	14.4	14.9	63.4	110.8
Fair	27.7	16.7	14.2	62.8	113.4
Poor	28.8	17.6	14.5	61.9	122.5
Prob.	.260	.222	.070	.314	.393
Model	—	—	—	—	—
	(1770)	(869)	(1789)	(1771)	(1629)
Happiness (HAPPY)					
Very happy	28.2	17.0	14.3	72.5	125.2
Pretty happy	27.8	16.4	14.1	58.5	105.9
Not too happy	28.0	16.5	14.1	65.7	122.6
Prob.	.103	.002	.031	.000	.000
Model	—	SLC	L	SLC	SLC
	(2634)	(1315)	(2659)	(2621)	(2417)

(*Continued*)

Table 4.2 (*Continued*)

Variables[a]	Davis empathy	Altruistic love	Altruistic values	Altruistic behaviors 11-items	15-items
Financial satisfaction (SATFIN)					
Pretty well empathy	27.8	16.6	14.2	65.9	113.5
More or less	27.9	16.5	14.1	62.8	112.2
Not at all	28.1	16.7	14.2	64.3	119.2
Prob.	.606	.604	.271	.635	.403
Model	—	—	—	—	—
	(2629)	(1312)	(2653)	(2616)	(2413)
Job satisfaction (SATJOB)					
Very sat.	28.2	16.6	14.3	65.9	119.6
Mod. sat.	27.6	16.5	14.0	61.4	107.5
Little dis.	28.1	16.2	13.9	73.3	131.1
Very dis.	29.0	16.8	14.2	69.6	131.1
Prob.	.013	.586	.083	.196	.015
Model	NCNL	—	—	—	NCNL
	(2045)	(1023)	(2066)	(2043)	(1899)
G. Misanthropy					
Rosenberg Scale (TRUST, FAIR, HELPFUL)					
3 (Low)	28.5	16.6	14.7	60.9	105.3
4	27.8	15.7	14.3	60.8	97.5
5	27.9	16.4	14.1	51.2	91.8
6	27.8	17.1	13.9	70.8	120.0
7	27.7	16.8	14.1	63.3	114.9
8	27.6	16.8	14.0	57.9	105.6
9 (High)	27.5	16.9	13.8	67.6	128.6
Prob.	.155	.313	.000	.044	.000
Model	—	—	L	NCNL	SLC
	(1724)	(867)	(1744)	(1718)	(1589)
Trust few (TRUSTED)					
Agree str.	27.9	—	14.0	64.6	116.3
Agree	27.7	—	14.0	55.3	100.1
Neither	27.7	—	13.9	62.1	111.8
Disagree	28.6	—	15.1	70.8	117.5
Dis. str.	29.3	—	14.2	67.0	117.8
Prob.	.378	—	.000	.152	.136
Model	—	—	SLC	—	—
	(1118)	—	(1122)	(1105)	(1104)
People take advantage (ADVANTAGE)					
Agree str.	27.9	—	14.0	62.8	128.1
Agree	27.9	—	13.8	58.3	101.6
Neither	27.3	—	13.9	62.1	100.6

Table 4.2 (*Continued*)

Variables[a]	Davis empathy	Altruistic love	Altruistic values	Altruistic behaviors 11-items	15-items
Disagree	28.5	—	15.1	64.0	107.6
Dis. str.	27.9	—	15.4	101.2	161.2
Prob.	.336	—	.000	.229	.001
Model	—	—	SLC	—	NCNL
Want best (WANTBEST)					
Agree str.	28.6	—	15.0	65.0	132.4
Agree	28.0	—	14.0	60.6	105.9
Neither	27.3	—	13.9	61.6	105.1
Disagree	27.6	—	13.7	62.1	107.9
Dis. str.	29.2	—	14.7	46.8	102.7
Prob.	.050	—	.000	.811	.046
Model	NCNL	—	SLC	—	NCNL
	(1113)	—	(1116)	(1100)	(1099)
H. Crime					
Courts are: (COURTS)					
too harsh	27.1	15.6	14.4	77.8	138.9
about right	27.3	16.4	14.2	61.9	107.2
too easy	28.2	16.8	14.1	62.7	113.0
Prob.	.000	.000	.291	.007	.001
Model	L	L	—	SLC	SLC
	(2481)	(1234)	(2498)	(2468)	(2284)
Fear walking at night (FEAR)					
Yes	28.4	16.2	14.4	64.1	117.5
No	27.7	16.7	14.1	65.3	112.7
Prob.	.005	.036	.003	.742	.399
Model	L	L	L	—	—
	(1764)	(866)	(1785)	(1765)	(1624)
Death penalty (CAPPUN)					
Yes	27.7	16.7	13.9	62.2	109.4
Don't know	28.2	16.5	13.9	53.8	99.0
No	28.6	16.3	14.7	70.5	128.4
Prob.	.000	.118	.000	.008	.000
Model	L	—	L	L	—
	(2616)	(1303)	(2639)	(2602)	(2403)
Police hit (POLHITOK)					
Approve	27.8	16.7	14.2	62.9	108.6
Disapprove	28.1	16.4	14.2	60.9	117.5
Prob.	.334	.235	.758	.593	.129
Model	—	—	—	—	—
	(1639)	(820)	(1649)	(1629)	(1511)

(*Continued*)

Table 4.2 (*Continued*)

Variables[a]	Davis empathy	Altruistic love	Altruistic values	Altruistic behaviors 11-items	Altruistic behaviors 15-items
I. *Social welfare*					
Govt social spending[c]					
Low	27.2	16.6	13.5	66.0	113.6
Middle	28.1	16.7	14.2	61.5	111.4
High	28.6	16.3	14.6	70.1	129.0
Prob.	.000	.223	.000	.062	.007
Model	L	—	L	—	SLC
	(2211)	(1282)	(2230)	(2212)	(2041)
Govt aid to old (AIDOLD)					
Def. should	28.8	—	14.4	62.7	117.6
Prob. should	27.3	—	13.8	57.7	105.9
Prob. not	26.8	—	13.9	68.2	105.1
Def. not	27.7	—	13.7	55.5	80.7
Prob.	.000	—	.001	.386	.056
Model	SLC	—	L	—	—
	(1081)	—	(1084)	(1069)	(1066)
Govt aid to children (AIDKIDS)					
Def. should	28.3	—	14.3	66.5	133.1
Prob. should	28.0	—	14.1	57.5	107.7
Prob. not	27.7	—	14.1	61.3	105.0
Def. not	28.0	—	14.0	61.0	100.7
Prob.	.686	—	.678	.647	.007
Model	—	—	—	—	L
	(1032)	—	(1033)	(1021)	(1019)
Equalize wealth (EQWLTH)					
Govt should	28.8	16.5	14.5	71.9	127.4
2	28.4	16.8	14.6	55.6	105.2
3	27.6	16.8	14.3	55.5	98.7
4	27.6	16.8	13.9	57.0	108.7
5	27.7	16.9	14.1	59.7	107.4
6	27.6	16.7	13.8	61.0	103.3
Govt shldn't	27.2	16.1	13.5	66.1	115.0
Prob.	.001	.506	.000	.035	.026
Model	L	—	L	NCNL	NCNL
	(1718)	(862)	(1735)	(1709)	(1581)
Govt help poor (HELPPOOR)					
Govt help	28.6	16.9	14.9	68.1	128.4
2	28.3	16.9	14.6	59.7	103.3
3	27.9	16.6	14.1	58.4	106.1
4	27.1	16.2	13.6	61.7	103.4

Table 4.2 (*Continued*)

Variables[a]	Davis empathy	Altruistic love	Altruistic values	Altruistic behaviors	
				11-items	15-items
Help self	27.3	17.1	13.2	66.0	115.3
Prob.	.001	.229	.000	.268	.017
Model	L	—	L	—	NCNL
	(1699)	(857)	(1715)	(1692)	(1567)
Govt do more (HELPNOT)					
Govt do more	28.7	16.5	14.6	69.7	133.0
2	27.4	16.6	14.6	56.3	96.7
3	27.8	16.7	14.0	56.2	102.9
4	27.6	16.9	14.1	65.0	112.1
Govt do less	27.7	16.6	13.7	70.6	120.7
Prob.	.041	.891	.000	.007	.000
Model	NCNL	—	L	NCNL	NCNL
	(1694)	(852)	(1709)	(1688)	(1560)
Govt help sick (HELPSICK)					
Help sick	28.7	16.9	14.6	62.1	115.7
2	27.6	16.4	14.3	60.7	102.6
3	27.6	16.8	13.9	60.6	111.1
4	27.5	16.2	13.9	62.9	109.3
Not help	26.6	16.8	13.2	63.0	108.9
Prob.	.000	.364	.000	.991	.486
Model	L	—	L	—	—
Govt help blacks (HELPBLK)					
Help blacks	29.1	15.8	14.4	70.5	134.2
2	28.2	16.6	14.9	59.5	108.3
3	28.0	16.6	14.2	64.3	113.3
4	27.8	16.8	14.3	55.7	98.7
Not help	27.5	17.0	13.7	61.4	110.7
Prob.	.018	.063	.000	.228	.023
Model	L	—	SLC	—	NCNL
	(1703)	(855)	(1722)	(1697)	(1570)

[a] The GSS variables names are in parentheses and their wordings can be found in Davis, Smith, & Marsden, 2005.

[b] This ANOVA approach compares means across groups and places the results in one of 5 outcomes: (1) C = no statistically significant variation at the .05 level; (2) NC = not constant; (3) L = linear; (4) SLC = significant linear component; and (5) NCNL = not constant, not linear.

[c] This is a 5-item scale based on support for government spending for health (NATHEAL, NATHEALY), blacks (NATRACE, NATRACEY), children (NATCHLD), social security (NATSOC), and welfare/the poor (NATFARE, NATFAREY). Scores range from 5 for someone who thought the government was spending too much on all areas to 15 for someone who thought the government was spending too little in each case. Low is 5 to 10, middle is 11 to 13, and high is 14 to 15.

reporting income (but significant only for the 15-item scale), but the attitudinal measures showed no association.

Second, the demographic profile of empathy and altruism or what Underwood (2002) refers to as one's "social and physical environment" was looked at (Table 4.2B).

The literature is inconsistent on gender's relationship to empathy (Chou, 1998; Davis, 1994; Giesbrecht, 1998; Gilligan & Attanucci, 1988; Piliavin & Charng, 1990; Post et al., 2002) and altruism (Amato, 1990; Batson, 1998; Howard & Piliavin, 2000; Johnson et al., 1989; Khanna et al., 1993; Penner, Dovidio, Piliavin, & Schroeder, 2005). Batson (1998, p. 289) summarized research as "sometimes men help more than women, sometimes women help more than men, and sometimes the sex of the helper makes no difference." Similarly, Howard and Piliavin (2000, p. 117) observe that, with regard to gender differences, "who helps depends heavily on the nature of the help required." In this study gender is strongly associated with empathy and altruistic values, with women leading men on both. Likewise, the 15-item altruistic behaviors scale showed more helping by women, but there was no difference on the 11-item scale. Altruistic love showed the counter-results of men outscoring women.

Few studies on altruism have examined age since most research involves students with little variation in age. Some research suggests that altruism may be greater among the middle-aged and less for the young and old (Penner et al., 2005; Rushton et al., 1989). There are some signs of such a relationship here. Empathy rises with age, but perhaps falls among those over 65. A similar pattern exists for altruistic values. Altruistic love, however, shows no drop-off among the elderly and basically increases across age groups. Both altruistic behavior scales show that helping declines with age. The decline among the elderly probably reflects less exposure to requests for assistance because of both less social interaction and because more are physically less able to render the needed help (e.g. giving blood, carrying articles, offering a seat). Thus, the age patterns for altruistic love and values tend to be the opposite of that for altruistic behaviors.

Stratification variables in general and education in particular have not been extensively examined in the main empathy and altruism literature, but other research indicates that the better educated are more supportive of social welfare policies and more likely to be volunteers (Berkowitz & Lutterman, 1968; Penner et al., 2005; Webb et al., 2000). Here the associations are mixed and generally weak. Empathy is unrelated to the stratification variables. Altruistic values increase with education and income, but the income relationship is statistically significant only because of the lower altruism of those refusing to give their income. Altruistic love does not vary by income, but is higher among the less educated (the reverse pattern to altruistic values). The 11-item behavioral measure is unrelated to education or income and the 15-item scale is not associated with education, but helping is higher among those with lower incomes.

Marital status has rarely been considered as a predictor variable. Here empathy, altruistic values, and altruistic love are greater among the married and widowed (in the later case because there are more widows than widowers) and lowest among the separated and never married. It may be that people with these tendencies are more likely to opt into marriage and/or their marriages are more likely to last. Altruistic behaviors are not consistently related, but the scores on the 15-item scale are highest among the never married and lowest among the married and widowed.

Research on helping, neighborliness, and interpersonal relations finds these to be stronger in less densely populated areas (Howard & Piliavin, 2000). Here empathy, altruistic love, and altruistic values are greater in the more rural areas, but altruistic behavior tends to be greater in the largest central cities and least in the most rural areas, counter to both the prior research and the empathy and attitudinal measures. The higher level of assistance in large cities may largely reflect greater opportunities to render assistance as one is likely to come into contact with more people, and certain situations may be more common in urban areas (e.g., being approached by a homeless person, encountering strangers with various needs).

Regional differences appear, but they are somewhat scattered and mostly modest in size. The South Atlantic tends to lead overall, being first on altruistic love and the 11-item altruistic behavior scale, second on empathy and the 15-item altruistic behavior scale, and tied for second on altruistic values. No region consistently anchors the opposite end.

Ethnicity and race have been little examined in the empathy and altruism literature, although some cross-cultural differences have been found (Johnson et al., 1989).[3] Here Hispanic ethnicity is unrelated to empathy or altruism except for non-Hispanics having marginally higher altruistic values, and race is only related to altruistic love being higher for whites and altruistic behaviors being higher for blacks on both scales.

Labor-force status has not been examined by most empathy and altruism research. In this study empathy is highest among homemakers (because they are overwhelmingly female) and lowest among students, followed by the unemployed. The lower empathy among the unemployed may reflect the negative impact of hardships on people's worldviews, but there are too few unemployed respondents to examine this hypothesis. Similarly, altruistic values are highest among those whose labor-force

---

[3] Race of helper and helped interactions have been examined (Batson, 1998).

status is "other" (mostly disabled people) and homemakers and lowest among students and the unemployed. Altruistic love was highest for the others (disabled) and retired (both older groups) and then among home-makers. The higher level among homemakers was surprising, given that almost all homemakers are women and women have lower scores than men do. Looking at labor-force differences by gender showed that among men altruistic love did not vary by labor-force status, but among women those in the labor force had lower scores than homemakers or the retired (full time = 15.8; part time = 15.5; homemaker = 17.0; retired = 17.2). This suggests that women in traditional roles have higher expressions of altruistic love than women in more modern roles. Altruistic behaviors on the 11-item scale do not vary, but are highest among students, part-time workers, and the unemployed and lowest among the retired (owing to their greater age) on the 15-item scale.

The structure of the family of origin may relate to empathy (Piliavin & Charng, 1990). As Table 4.3 shows, empathy is highest for those raised in two-parent families, almost as high for those raised by females only, and lowest for those raised by males. This pattern holds overall and for being raised by one's own parents, parents and stepparents, and other relatives.

Table 4.3 Empathy Scale by Family of Origin

	Parent(s)/caregiver(s)		
	Both genders	Female	Male
A. Respondents by gender			
Parents	28.0	27.6	26.1
Parent/stepparent		28.4	26.5
Relatives	29.3	28.8	24.1
All	28.0	27.9	26.0

Parents = raised by both parents or one parent alone.
Parent/stepparent = raised by parent of specific gender plus stepparent.
Relatives = raised by one or more relatives of both or one gender.
All = raised by parents, parent + stepparent, or relatives of both or one gender.

	Parent(s)		
Child	Both genders	Female	Male
B. Respondents by gender			
Male	26.6	26.6	25.1
Female	29.4	28.6	26.6

Consistent with the large gender differences discussed above, these results suggest that mothers and other female guardians are more likely to engender empathy in their offspring and charges than father/male caregivers are. Moreover, if one looks at the child's gender (i.e., the gender of respondents in the GSS), it appears that empathy is lowered more for females than for males when a mother/mother substitute is missing (Table 4.3B). This suggests that the development of empathy is reduced more for females than for males when a maternal model is absent. However, even when raised by fathers/father substitutes, females still have more empathy than males.

Third, the hypothesis that social and civic engagement is associated with empathy and altruism is considered (Bolle, 1991) (Table 4.2C). Regarding social engagement, empathy, altruistic love, and altruistic values have little relationship. For altruistic behaviors, helping generally increases as socializing rises. Going to bars, on the other hand, is unrelated to altruistic behaviors while empathy, altruistic love, and altruistic values tend to be highest among those rarely going to bars. Having more friends is associated with more empathy, altruistic values, and altruistic behaviors. Altruistic love could not be compared to number of friends because friendship was not measured in 2004. On civic engagement, empathy and altruistic values are greater among voters, but altruistic love and altruistic behaviors are unrelated to voting. Empathy and altruism are higher among those active in voluntary groups on all four relevant scales (altruistic love could not be compared).

Fourth, the idea that empathy and altruism would be higher when obligations are seen as existing between various socially related groups is examined (Table 4.2D). Empathy proved to have a complex relationship. The two items on the duty of children to their parents showed inconsistent patterns, no association for one and a curvilinear association for the other. Empathy was unrelated to a general measure about putting self and family first. It was higher among those reporting that friends and family often made demands on them and those feeling that the better-off should help their friends. Altruistic values were somewhat stronger among those believing children have a duty to elderly parents, but the association was not strong. It was also higher among those who disagree that one should help their family and selves first. Altruistic values were also greater among those believing that the better-off should help their friends. Altruistic behaviors were somewhat more frequent among those saying elderly parents should live with their children, but were unrelated to the other variable about parental obligations. They were also unrelated to the self/family first variable. The 11-item measure was unrelated to demands on people from family and friends and on friends helping friends, but the 15-item measure, which includes items referring to family and friends, was higher among those receiving demands

_..._ others and among those favoring friends helping friends. Altruistic love could not be meaningfully related to this dimension.

Fifth, the hypothesis that empathy and altruism would be greater among the religious is tested (Amato, 1990; Dillon, 2002; Post et al., 2002; Smith, Fabricatore & Peyrot, 1999; Sprecher & Fehr, 2005; Underwood, 2005) (Table 4.2E). First, whether these constructs vary by the religious tradition in which one was raised or which one currently practices was looked at. Most of the variation across religious groups was due to the lower empathy and altruistic values of those with no religion. Protestants tend to outscore Catholics and other religious adherents. Altruistic behaviors, however, do not meaningfully vary by major religious groups. On empathy, altruistic love, altruistic values, and the 15-item altruistic behavior scale, fundamentalists scored higher than moderates and liberals did, both with the nonreligious included and excluded from the analysis. Secondly, religiosity was looked at. In terms of all three indicators (self-rated strength of religious attachment, attending church, frequency of praying), more religious involvement was associated with greater empathy and more altruism on all five scales. The relationships were strong and linear or nearly linear.

The strong, consistent, and positive relationship of praying with empathy and altruism compared to the much more modest associations with religious adherence or religious attendance suggests that one's personal spiritual engagement rather than participation in organized religion may be of greater importance. On the 2004 GSS the Daily Spiritual Experience (DSE) scale was asked (Underwood, 1999; Underwood & Teresi, 2002). The 15 items ask about how often one has these spiritual experiences.[4] The 15-item scale correlates significantly with all of the empathy and altruism measures (empathy = .24/.000; altruistic love = .17/.000; altruistic

---

[4] Wording: The list that follows includes items you may or may not experience. Please consider if and how often you have these experiences and try to disregard whether you feel you should or should not have them. A number of items use the word "God." If this word is not a comfortable one, please substitute another idea to mean the divine or holy for you.

Many times a day/Every day/Most days/Some days/Once in a while/Never or almost never

a. I feel God's presence. b. I experience a connection to all of life. c. During worship or at other times when connected to God I feel joy which lifts me out of my daily concerns. d. I find strength in by religion or spirituality. e. I find comfort in my religion or spirituality. f. I feel inner peace or harmony. g. I ask God's help in the midst of daily activities. h. I feel guided by God in the midst of daily activities. i. I feel God's love for me, directly. j. I feel God's love for me, through others. k. I am spiritually touched by the beauty of creation. l. I feel thankful for my blessings. m. I feel a selfless caring for others. n. I accept others even when they do things I think are wrong. o. I desire to be closer to God or in union with Him.

Table 4.4 Daily Spiritual Experience (DSE) and Empathy and Altruism

DSE	empathy	Altruistic love	Altruistic values	Altruistic behavior 11-items	15-items
Low	26.8	16.0	13.7	57.5	98.2
Medium	28.2	16.7	14.2	60.1	103.6
High	29.0	17.0	15.0	90.5	154.3
Prob.	.000	.000	.000	.000	.000
Model	L	L	L	SLC	SLC
	(1220)	(1227)	(1230)	(1221)	(1218)

values = .25/.000; 11 behaviors = .18/.000; 15 behaviors = .22/.000). If the DSE scale is divided into thirds to show the details of the relationship and each empathy and altruism scale is broken down by DSE, strong and mostly linear associations are revealed (Table 4.4).

Moreover, when one looks at only the ten items that are explicitly religious (with seven mentioning God and three mentioning spirituality or spirituality and religion) vs. the five items less explicitly religious (items b, f, l, m, and n – see footnote 4), the religion DSE sub-scale correlates as high as or higher than the whole scale does (e.g. .24/.000 with altruistic love and .24/.000 with empathy). The not explicitly religious items have notably lower associations (e.g., .11/.000 with altruistic love and .08/.000 with empathy). This occurs despite the fact that they still have a strong implicit spiritual component (e.g. references to "inner peace or harmony" and being "thankful for my blessings") and two items have strong empathic/altruistic elements ("accept others even when they do things I think are wrong" and "selfless caring for others"). Thus, it especially seems to be the explicitly religious and/or God-centric elements that establish the connection to empathy and altruism. Coupled with the association of praying with empathy and altruism, this indicates that one's personal religious feelings and daily practice play important roles in promoting empathy and altruism.

Sixth, whether better health and psychological-well being were associated with more empathy and altruism was examined (Table 4.2F). The relationship of these measures to empathy and altruism was mixed. Empathy was only irregularly related to job satisfaction. Altruistic love was associated with greater happiness in general and especially with more marital happiness. Altruistic values are modestly associated with more excitement and more overall happiness. More altruistic behaviors were done by those who are happier and living more exciting lives.

Seventh, the hypothesis that the misanthropic would be less empathic and altruistic was tested (Table 4.2G). The misanthropy measures showed rather weak and scattered relationships, but where statistically significant associations emerged, they were in the hypothesized direction. Empathy and altruistic love are not meaningfully related to misanthropy, but altruistic values are higher among those with low misanthropy. The measures of altruistic behaviors are not consistently related to the misanthropy items.

Eighth, whether concern about crime or punitive attitudes toward criminals would be related to lower empathy and altruism was considered (Table 4.2H). Counter to expectations, empathy was higher among those fearful of crime. The two measures of punitive attitudes showed opposite results, with empathy higher for those wanting tougher courts, but also among those opposed to capital punishment. This may be partly related to the fact that women are both more fearful and less punitive than men are and more empathic than men are. Altruistic love was also higher among those thinking courts are too lenient, but was greater among the fearless than the fearful. Altruistic values were higher among those fearful of crime (counter to expectations), unrelated to whether courts should be tougher or the police should hit people, and higher among those opposed to the death penalty (as expected). Altruistic behaviors were unrelated to fear of crime or capital punishment, but more frequent among those who found courts too harsh.

Finally, the hypothesis that those who were empathic and altruistic would also be liberal on social welfare policies was examined (Table 4.2I). In general these expectations were supported. Empathy was higher among those backing more government spending for health care, blacks, children, social security, and welfare/the poor. It was also higher among those in favor of more government efforts to help the elderly, the poor, the sick, and blacks, for reducing inequality in wealth, and for more government action in general. It was unrelated to expanding government aid to children. Altruistic values were higher among those for more social welfare spending, more government assistance to the old, the poor, the sick, and blacks, equalizing wealth, and more government action in general. It was not related to more assistance for children. Altruistic love was not related to any of these social welfare measures. The 11-item scale was unrelated to support for most of these social welfare programs and the two relationships that did appear were irregular. The 15-item scores were higher among those favoring more social welfare spending, wanting the government to assist children, blacks, and the poor more, backing more government action in general, and supporting the equalization of wealth, but most of these associations were not linear.

Looking at the results that are statistically significant, consistent across the empathy and altruistic scales, and that apply to all measures within each of the domains, reveals the following main patterns. Empathy is greater among women than men and for the widowed and homemakers because of the gender of these groups. It is higher among the connected – those with more friends and those belonging to more voluntary associations, those who see more obligations between groups of people, and those getting more demands from others. It is greater among the religious than the nonreligious and those actively engaged in their religion (by self-assessment, frequency of praying, and church attendance). Counter to expectations, empathy is higher among those who think courts are too easy and who are afraid of crime, but as expected, it is greater among opponents of the death penalty. Empathy is higher among those for more social welfare spending and for expanded governmental programs for the disadvantaged.

Altruistic love is greater among groups that tend to be mainstream and traditional (the married vs. the never married, older adults, whites, residents of the South Atlantic states). The traditionalist connection is also evident by the higher scores that women who are homemakers have vs. women working outside the home. It is also higher for men than women. This may be because there is an element of heroic stoicism and being a protector rather than passive self-sacrifice in this construct. This element may also explain why measures of "compassionate love," which lack this aspect, show women scoring higher than men (Sprecher & Fehr, 2005). Altruistic love also is higher among the religious than the nonreligious, among evangelical Protestants rather than other adherents, and among those actively engaged in religion as measured by self-evaluation, attending church, praying, and DSE. It is greater among those who are happy and especially among the happily married. In differences that may reflect the gender difference and traditionalist tendencies noted above, agape is greater among those thinking courts are too easy and who are not fearful of crime.

Altruistic values are related to many of the same factors as empathy is. Values are higher among women, the widowed, the better educated, and those living outside central cities. The more connected (those with friends and members of groups) have more altruistic values, as do those seeing obligations across social groups (but more weakly than for empathy). The religious and the religiously involved have more altruistic values. Those scoring low on misanthropy also are more altruistic. As with empathy, altruistic values are higher among those fearful of crime (counter to expectations) and among those against the death penalty (as expected). Those with a liberal position on social welfare spending and programs also have more altruistic values.

Altruistic behaviors show relatively few notable relationships. Altruistic acts occur more frequently among the never married than among the l or widowed (counter to the pattern on empathy and altruistic values) iong blacks (race is unrelated on empathy and altruistic values). As with the other constructs, altruistic behaviors are related to having more friends and belonging to more groups (and also with socializing more often). Helping is also more frequent among the religious and the religiously involved.

Multivariate Models of Empathy and Altruism

Various multivariate models using OLS regression were run corresponding to the variables in Table 4.2. The basic demographics model included gender, age, education, income, marital status, residence, race, and labor-force status. The other model included these background variables, plus variables from each of the topics outlined in Table 4.2. Details are presented in Smith (2005) and summarized below.

For the empathy scale only one demographic variable consistently mattered; women are more empathic than men. Gender is also by far the strongest demographic predictor. In the demographics-only model and two other models, empathy moderately increases with age. Likewise, in three models empathy moderately rises with income. The only other demographic variable to show up in at least two models is size-of-place, with empathy being somewhat higher in more rural areas. In the various other models, empathy was also greater among those rated as more cooperative by interviewers, those belonging to voluntary associations, those thinking that one should help friends, those praying more frequently, the less misanthropic, those opposed to the death penalty, but those for tougher courts, and those for more social welfare spending. With the exception of the positive association between supporting tougher courts and being more empathic, these all follow expected directions.

Expressions of altruistic love are greater among men, the less educated, those who are not divorced/separated or never married, rural residents, and non-blacks. The absence of a difference between the currently married and the widowed indicates that it is not the mere lack of a spouse that depresses altruistic love sentiments among the divorced/separated and never married. Being a homemaker is related to more altruistic love in two models. In other models greater altruistic love is expressed by those rated as cooperative, those who pray more and are more religious, the more misanthropic, those for tougher courts, and those for more social spending. The misanthropy and courts results were counter to expectations.

Given the strong association with marital status and the bivariate association with marital happiness discussed above, a model was tested with agape as a predictor variable and marital happiness as the dependent variable. It showed that with controls for the same demographics utilized in general that altruistic love was related with more marital happiness (beta = .16, prob. = .000).

For the values scale, altruism is greater among women for all models. The basic demographic model and most other models also show more altruism among older adults and the college educated. The basic demographic model and some of the other models also show more altruism among the never married and rural residents. Almost all of the non-demographic correlates of empathy are also related to altruistic values: being rated as cooperative by interviewers, belonging to groups, agreeing that one should help friends, praying, attending church, being less misanthropic, opposing the death penalty, and favoring social welfare spending.[5]

Models differ for the two behavior scales. For the shorter scale nothing was a consistently statistically significant predictor across all models. Being black was associated with more helping in four models, more education in two models, men were more helpful than women in the religion model involving the religious variables, and rural residents were less helpful in the engagement model involving the social and personal contact variables. Helping was also greater among the cooperative, those belonging to groups, those opposed to the death penalty, more frequent church attenders, more frequent prayers, and those disagreeing that one has a duty to assist one's parents. The last is counter to expectations.

The 15-item scale is also not consistently related to any demographics. In four models helping is greater among younger adults, the never married, and being black. In two models help is greater in larger cities. In the engagement model alone more helping is associated with less education. Among non-demographics helping is also more frequent among the cooperative, those with more friends, those belonging to more groups, those who believe one should help friends, those who receive heavy demands from others, the more misanthropic (counter to expectations), opponents of capital punishment, and those praying more.

Looking across the empathy, altruistic love, altruistic values, and altruistic behaviors shows the following patterns:

(1) Women are more empathic than men are and have higher altruistic values, but men are more likely to express sentiments of altruistic love. Gender is not notably related to altruistic behaviors. (2) Age is

---

[5] All of these are treated as independent predictors of empathy and altruism, but in some cases the causal order is unclear. For example, it probably makes more sense to say that empathy predicts social spending than the other way around. However, to facilitate comparisons across models empathy and altruism have been consistently made the dependent variables in the models.

largely unrelated to empathy, but older adults tend to have more altruistic love and altruistic values. On the longer altruistic-behavior scale the young show more acts of helping, at least in some models, but age is unrelated to the shorter scale. (3) Income is unrelated to empathy and altruism. (4) Marital status has little relationship to empathy, but altruistic love is higher among the married than among the divorced/separated or never married and altruistic values greater among the married than the never married. The never married are more likely to engage in altruistic acts on the longer scale, but marital status does not differentiate on the shorter scale. (5) Living in more rural areas is weakly related with more empathy, modestly associated with more altruistic values, and most consistently related to more sentiments of altruistic love. But altruistic behavior on a few models is associated with living in more urban areas. (6) Race is largely unrelated to empathy or altruistic values, but blacks are less likely to endorse altruistic love. On both the short and long altruistic-behavior scales blacks report more helping in several models. (7) Labor-force status is essentially unrelated to empathy or altruism. (8) Empathy and altruism are generally greater among people rated as cooperative respondents, among those belonging to groups, those agreeing that one should help friends, those actively involved in religion (especially frequent prayers), and those opposed to the death penalty.

Other non-demographic variables are related to some, but not all or almost all, scales. Empathy, altruistic love, and altruistic values are higher among those favoring more governmental social spending, but altruistic behavior is unrelated to attitudes on governmental social spending. Attitudes about obligations toward parents are related to the shorter behavior scale in one model only. The more misanthropic have lower empathy and altruistic values, but greater altruistic love, and on the 15-item scale, more altruistic behaviors.

Conclusion

The 2002 and 2004 GSSs provide basic data on the prevalence and structure of empathy and altruism in contemporary American society. They indicate that empathic feelings, sentiments of altruistic love, altruistic values, and helping behaviors are all common. Moreover, over this two-year span there was an increase in altruistic values and behaviors.

Empathy is closely related to altruistic values, but both empathy and altruistic values are only moderately positively associated with altruistic behaviors. Moreover, they are better predictors of helping behaviors involving those close to the helper rather than more "random acts of assistance" directed mostly toward those without ties to the helper. Altruistic love is less related to the other constructs primarily because of its personal rather than general reference (for a similar result on compassionate love, see Sprecher & Fehr, 2005).

Among demographics, gender has the main impact on empathy. Moreover, gender plays an important role in socializing empathy in children with those raised without a mother or female caregiver tending to be less empathic as adults. Empathy also tends to be greater among older adults, the well-to-do, and, to a lesser extent among rural residents. Among non-demographics empathy was also greater among those rated as more cooperative by interviewers, those belonging to voluntary associations, those thinking that one should help friends, those praying more frequently, those with more frequent daily spiritual experiences, the less misanthropic, those opposed to the death penalty, but those for tougher courts (counter to expectations), and those for more social welfare spending.

Expressions of altruistic love are greater among men, the less educated, those who are not divorced/separated or never married, rural residents, and non-blacks. Many of these groups are more traditionalist and the association with homemakers also supports such a characterization, but the lack of any relationship to age questions this interpretation. The gender difference may reflect an element of protective stoicism that is more prevalent among men, and this construct should be examined more closely. The fact that the divorced/separated score lower while the widowed do not indicates that it is not only the absence of a spouse that is associated with fewer expressions of altruistic love. The connection between sentiments of altruistic love and greater marital happiness also establishes another important linkage between marriage and sentiments of altruistic love. Among non-demographics, greater altruistic love is expressed by those rated as cooperative, those who pray more and are more religious, those with very happy marriages, the more misanthropic, those for tougher courts, and those for more social spending. The associations with misanthropy and courts were counter to expectations.

Altruistic values are greater among women, older adults, and the college-educated. To a lesser extent altruistic values are higher among the never married and rural residents. Almost all of the non-demographic correlates of empathy are also related to altruistic values: rated cooperative by interviewers, group memberships, agreeing that one should help friends, praying, attending church, less misanthropy, opposing the death penalty, and for social welfare spending.

The correlates of altruistic behavior depend in good measure on which scale is being used. In general, the 11-item scale shows fewer associations compared with the 15-item scale. For the shorter scale nothing was a consistently statistically significant predictor across models. Both showed that blacks tended to help more and the 15-item scale showed more helping among the young. Other demographic associations were scattered. Among non-demographics, helping was also greater among the cooperative, those belonging to groups and/or having friends, more frequent church attenders and/or more frequent prayers, those with greater misanthropy (counter to expectations), and those opposed to the death penalty.

Overall, empathy and altruism are common values and behaviors in contemporary society. Among their most important and consistent predictors are gender, religious engagement (especially praying and daily spiritual experiences), contact with other people and groups, and interpersonal and social obligations. Likewise, they are tied to and probably causes of such other important facets of society as marital happiness and support for social welfare policies.

Finally, future research should first of all continue the time series started in 2002 to determine whether a notable pro-altruistic societal trend is underway. Second, while the basic hypotheses in the literature on altruism have been tested, a particular strength of the GSS is its wide-ranging content, and more connections to altruism can and should be explored. Third, altruistic behaviors have proven to be challenging to measure even with 11–15 indicators, with many results being inconsistent across measures. This indicates that more development of an even better behavioral scale would be useful. Likewise, the altruistic-love scale has been administered only once and its replication is needed to more fully examine its role. In brief, both more extensive analysis of the existing data and the collection of additional data are indicated by this research.

References

Amato, P. R. (1990). Personality and social network involvement as predictors of helping behavior in everyday life. *Social Psychology Quarterly, 53(1)*, 31–43.

Batson, C. D. (1991). *The altruism question: Toward a social-psychological answer.* Hillsdale, NJ: Lawrence Erlbaum.

Batson, C. D. (1998). Altruism and prosocial behavior. In S. T. Fiske, D. T. Gilbert, and G. Lindzey (Eds.), *Handbook of social psychology* (pp. 282–316). Boston: McGraw-Hill.

Berkowitz, L., & Lutterman, K. G. (1968). The traditional socially responsible personality. *Public Opinion Quarterly, 32*, 169–185.

Bolle, F. (1991). On love and altruism. *Rationality and Society, 3*, 197–214.

Butler, R., Walker, W. R., Skowronski, J. J., & Shannon, L. (1995). Age and responses to the love attitudes scale: Consistency in structure, differences in scores. *International Journal of Aging and Human Development, 40*, 281–296.

Chou, K.-L. (1998). Effects of age, gender, and participation in volunteer activities on the altruistic behavior of Chinese adolescents. *Journal of Genetic Psychology, 159*, 195–201.

Davies, M. F. (2001). Socially desirable responding and impression management in the endorsement of love styles. *Journal of Psychology, 135*, 562–570.

Davis, J. A., Smith, T. W., & Marsden, P. V. (2005). *General Social Survey, 1972–2004: Cumulative codebook.* Chicago: NORC.

Davis, M. H. (1994). *Empathy: A social psychological approach.* Madison, WI: WCB Brown & Benchmark.

Dillon, M. (2002, August). *Religion, cultural change, and altruism in American society.* Paper presented at the meeting of the American Sociological Association, Chicago.

Eisenberg, N. (1986). *Altruistic emotion, cognition, and behavior.* Hillsdale, NJ: Lawrence Erlbaum.

Eisenberg, N., Miller, P. A., Schaller, M., Fabes, R. A., Fultz, J., Shell, R., et al. (1989). The role of sympathy and altruistic personality traits in helping: A reexamination. *Journal of Personality, 57*, 41–67.

Giesbrecht, N. (1998). Gender patterns of psychosocial development. *Sex Roles, 39*, 463–478.

Gilligan, C., & Attanucci, J. (1988). Two moral orientations: Gender differences and similarities. *Merrill-Palmer Quarterly, 34*, 223–237.

Hendrick, C., & Hendrick, S. S. (1986). A theory and method of love. *Journal of Personality and Social Psychology, 50*, 392–402.

Hendrick, C., & Hendrick, S. S. (1991). Dimensions of love: A sociobiological interpretation. *Journal of Social and Clinical Psychology, 10*, 206–230.

Hendrick, S. S., & Hendrick, C. (1987). Love and sex attitudes and religious beliefs. *Journal of Social and Clinical Psychology, 5*, 391–398.

Howard, J. A., & Piliavin, J. A. (2000). Altruism. In E. F. Borgatta (Ed.), *Encyclopedia of sociology.* New York: Macmillan.

Johnson, R. C., Danko, G. P., Darvill, T. J., Bochner, S., Bower, J. K., Huang, Y.-H., et al. (1989). Cross-cultural assessment of altruism and its correlates. *Personality and Individual Differences, 10*, 855–868.

Kangas, O. E. (1997). Self-interest and the common good: The impact of norms, selfishness and context in social policy opinions. *Journal of Socio-Economics, 26*, 475–494.

Khanna, R., Singh, P., & Rushton, J. P. (1993). Development of the Hindi version of a self-report altruism scale. *Personality and Individual Differences, 14*, 267–270.

Montgomery, M. J., & Sorell, G. T. (1997). Differences in love attitudes across family life stages. *Family Relations, 46*, 55–61.

Morgan, M. M., Goddard, H. W., & Givens, S. N. (1997). Factors that influence willingness to help the homeless. *Journal of Social Distress and the Homeless, 6*, 45–56.

Murthy, K., Rotzien, A., & Vacha-Haase, T. (1996). Second-order structure underlying the Hendrick–Hendrick Love Attitudes Scale. *Educational and Psychological Measurement, 56*, 108–121.

Nickell, G. S. (1998). *The Helping Attitude Scale.* Paper presented at the meeting of the American Psychological Association, San Francisco.

Penner, L. A., Dovidio, J. F., Piliavin, J. A., & Schroeder, D. A. (2005). Prosocial behavior: Multivariate perspectives. *Annual Review of Psychology, 56,* 365–392.

Penner, P. S. (1995). *Altruistic behavior: An inquiry into motivation.* Amsterdam: Rodopi.

Piliavin, J. A., & Charng, H.-W. (1990). Altruism: A review of recent theory and research. *Annual Review of Sociology, 16,* 27–65.

Post, S. G., Underwood, L. G., Schloss, J. P., and Hurlbut, W. B. (Eds.). (2002). *Altruism and altruistic love: Science, philosophy, and religion in dialogue.* New York: Oxford University Press.

Romer, D., Gruder, C. L., & Lizzadro, T. (1986). A person–situation approach to altruistic behavior. *Journal of Personality and Social Psychology, 51,* 1001–1012.

Rushton, J. P., Chrisjohn, R. D., & Fekken, G. C. (1981). The altruistic personality and the Self-Report Altruism Scale. *Personality and Individual Differences, 2,* 293–302.

Rushton, J. P., Fulker, D. W., Neale, M. C., Nias, D. K. B., & Eysenck, H. J. (1989). Ageing and the relation of aggression, altruism and assertiveness scales to the Eysenck Personality Questionnaire. *Personality and Individual Differences, 10,* 261–263.

Rushton, J. P., & Sorrentino, R. M. (Eds.). (1981). *Altruism and helping behavior: Social, personality, and developmental perspectives.* Hillsdale, NJ: Lawrence Erlbaum.

Sawyer, J. (1966). The Altruism Scale: A measure of co-operative, individualistic, and competitive interpersonal orientations. *American Journal of Sociology, 71,* 407–416.

Smith, L. H., Fabricatore, A., & Peyrot, M. (1999). Religiosity and altruism among African American males: The Catholic experience. *Journal of Black Studies, 29,* 579–597.

Smith, T. W. (2005). *Altruism and empathy in America: Trends and correlates* (GSS Report No. 38). Chicago: NORC.

Sorokin, P. A. (1950). *Altruistic love: A study of American "good neighbors" and Christian saints.* Boston: Beacon Press.

Sprecher, S., & Fehr, B. (2005). Compassionate love for close others and humanity. *Journal of Social and Personal Relationships, 22,* 629–651.

Staub, E., Bar-Tal, D., Karylowski, J., & Reykowski, J. (Eds.). (1984). *Development and maintenance of prosocial behavior.* New York: Plenum.

Taraban, C. B., & Hendrick, C. (1995). Personality perceptions associated with six styles of love. *Journal of Social and Personal Relationships, 12,* 453–461.

Underwood, L. G. (1999). Daily spiritual experiences. In R. Ables, C. Ellison, L. George, E. Idler, N. Krause, J. Levin, M. Ory, K. Pargament, L. Powell, L. Underwood, & D. Williams (Eds.), *Multidimensional measurement of religiousness/spirituality for use in health research: A report of the Fetzer Insitute/ National Insitute on Aging Working Group.* Kalamazoo, MI: John E. Fetzer Institute.

Underwood, L. G. (2002). The human experience of compassionate love: Conceptual mapping and data from selected studies. In S. G. Post, L. G. Underwood, J. P. Schloss, & W. B. Hurlbut (Eds.), *Altruism and altruistic love: Science, philosophy, and religion in dialogue.* London, England: Oxford University Press.

Underwood, L. G. (2005). Interviews with Trappist monks as a contribution to research methodology in the investigation of compassionate love. *Journal for the Theory of Social Behaviour, 35,* 285–302.

Underwood, L. G., & Teresi, J. (2002). The Daily Spiritual Experience Scale: Development, theoretical description, reliability, exploratory factor analysis, and preliminary construct validity using health related data. *Annals of Behavioral Medicine, 24,* 22–33.

Webb, D. J., Green, C. L., & Brashear, T. G. (2000). Development and validation of scales to measure attitudes influencing monetary donations to charitable organizations. *Journal of the Academy of Marketing Science, 28,* 299–309.

Wispe, L. (Ed.). (1978). *Altruism, sympathy, and helping: Psychological and sociological principles.* New York: Academic Press.

Wrightsman, L. S. (1974). *Assumptions about human nature: A social-psychological analysis.* Monterey, CA: Brooks, Cole.

Yancey, G. B., & Eastman, R. L. (1995). Comparison of undergraduates with older adults on love styles and life satisfaction. *Psychological Reports, 76,* 1211–1218.

5

Compassionate Motivation and Compassionate Acts across the Adult Life Course: Evidence from US National Studies

Nadine F. Marks and Jieun Song

... The human being is so constructed that he presses toward fuller and fuller being and this means pressing toward what most people would call good values, toward serenity, kindness, courage, honesty, love, unselfishness, and goodness. (—Abraham Maslow (1968, p. 155))

Introduction

"Compassionate love" is not yet a phrase typically in wide use in the fields of adult development and life-course sociology, yet related theoretical work in these areas of scholarship has led to population assessment of constructs related to the model of compassionate love guiding this volume (see Underwood, Chapter 1). For example, inclusion of measures for some types of compassionate norms that may be viewed as motivating factors for compassionate love, as well as measures for some types of compassionate acts (i.e., positive behaviors directed toward others) have become increasingly included in contemporary social science surveys (see also Tom Smith, Chapter 4, this volume).

The first aim of this chapter is to discuss links between the scientific study of compassionate love and other theoretical and empirical work related to adult development and life-course studies that has included attention to issues of generativity, social responsibility, and giving to others (both social support and caregiving). Specifically, we suggest that the biopsychosocial model of compassionate love is compatible with contemporary overarching biopsychosocial theories of human development, and we describe core ideas from Maslovian theory, Eriksonian theory, and social exchange theories that have led to measurement of constructs relevant to the science of compassionate love in US population surveys. Next, with the aim of contributing to an adult life-course population perspective on compassionate love, we provide exemplary descriptive analyses of how selected compassion-related norms (i.e., motivational factors: altruistic normative obligation, normative obligation to family and friends) and compassionate acts of love (i.e., positive behaviors: overall assessment of one's contribution to the well-being of others; volunteer work; giving emotional, instrumental, and caregiving support to kin and nonkin) vary by sociocultural location as indexed by age, gender, race/ethnic, educational, and income-group status among US adults participating in the National Survey of Midlife in the United States 1995 and the National Survey of Families and Households 1987–1993. We conclude with a discussion of directions for future complementary research.

Links between Constructs in the Compassionate Love Model and Constructs in Other Adult Developmental and Life-Course Research

The most prevalent contemporary overarching theoretical orientations to life-course development are biopsychosocial systems frameworks that emphasize biological, psychological, and social factors in reciprocal interaction over time to shape human development and action. Two major examples of such frameworks are Bronfenbrenner's bioecological systems theory (Bronfenbrenner, 1989; Bronfenbrenner & Morris, 1998) and the life-course perspective (Elder, Johnson, & Crosnoe, 2003; Featherman, 1983; Settersten, 2003).

The model of compassionate love guiding this volume is also very much a biopsychosocial model, and therefore is very compatible with these overarching models of human development and behavior. The biological element in the compassionate love model involves a consideration of the biological substrate that provides the basis for a socioemotional capacity for compassionate love, possibly through an evolutionarily adaptive capacity for empathy (e.g., Preston & de Waal, 2002) and/or attachment (Mikulincer & Shaver, 2005; Mikulincer, Shaver, & Gillath, Chapter 8, this volume).

The psychological domain in the compassionate love model emphasizes cognitive, motivational, and emotional factors whereby individuals consciously choose to be sensitive and responsive to the needs of others, value others, and sometimes respond to others at cost to self (see, Underwood, 2002; Underwood, Chapter 1, this volume). At least two theoreticians of life-span development have contributed ideas that lead to an expectation that compassionate love would be psychologically expectable among healthy adults – Abraham Maslow and Erik Erikson.

Maslovian Theory and Compassionate Love

Maslow was a germinal figure in helping to provide a foundation for what is today called "positive psychology" – that is, the study of positive subjective experience, positive individual traits, and positive institutions (Aspinwall & Staudinger, 2003; Keyes & Haidt, 2003; Peterson & Seligman, 2004; Seligman & Csikszentmihalyi, 2000; Seligman, Steen, Park, & Peterson, 2005; Snyder & Lopez, 2002). Maslow is most famous for his theory of human motivation, which posited a "hierarchy of needs." Specifically, Maslow suggested that individuals will be first motivated to satisfy basic physiological needs (e.g., for food and drink). Given satisfaction of physiological needs, motivation to satisfy safety needs comes into play; subsequently, belongingness and love needs, followed by esteem needs, predominate as motivating factors. When all of these basic needs are reasonably satisfied, Maslow suggested that the individual is motivated to further move toward "self-actualization" – i.e., the unique expression of a person's innate potentials (Maslow, 1954).

What is less understood about Maslow's work and theorizing is that when he empirically studied self-actualizers, he found that they almost invariably reported that they became intrinsically motivated by what he called the "Being-needs" – the needs for beauty, truth, justice, love, and care for others (Maslow, 1968). When self-actualizers described how they thought about what they felt most deeply "called" to do in their lives, there was almost always a theme of "service to others" in whatever the activity might be – whether it was homemaking, statemaking, art, or prayerful contemplation. Maslow became intrigued with the fact that among self-actualizers there was a synergetic process whereby doing what was most expressive of the highest potential of the individual self was also serving the greatest good of others and the community (Maslow, 1968).

Maslow's last book, *The Farther Reaches of Human Nature* (published posthumously after his sudden death in 1970) outlined even more of his ideas about how society might be structured to provide for basic needs and thereby contribute toward the evolution of more self-actualizers who, in turn, would also be expected to act synergetically to promote the greatest good of others (Maslow, 1971). Maslow's theoretical orientation and empirical work is therefore compatible with the view that human nature is intrinsically designed to facilitate greater motivation toward compassionate acts if basic survival, safety, psychological, and social needs are satisfied.

Eriksonian Theory and Compassionate Love

In a somewhat kindred vein, Erik Erikson (1950) developed a very influential developmental theory in the early 1950s that emphasized stages of development with potential relevance for conceptualizing the evolution of compassionate love in adulthood. For Erikson, the first developmental stages of childhood included resolving challenges of security (vs. insecurity), autonomy (vs. shame and doubt), initiative (vs. guilt), and industry (vs. inferiority). In adolescence and young adulthood the challenges shifted to establishing a coherent identity (vs. role confusion), and then moving on to intimacy (vs. isolation). The next developmental challenge, expected to occur after identity and intimacy were achieved in adulthood, was generativity (vs. stagnation). (The final posited developmental challenge was ego integrity vs. despair, expectable in late adulthood.) Generativity was defined by Erikson as a stage characterized by "care for the next generation."

It is important to remember that when Erikson was first formulating this theory, it was one of the first developmental theories to attempt to map out developmental expectations across the entire life span. Historically, as Erikson developed his theory in the late 1940s and early 1950s, he was doing so during a period when the vast majority of US adults were getting married in their early 20s and beginning to have children quite quickly thereafter. The typical challenge of life after getting married (i.e., resolving the challenge of intimacy) that he observed for adults around him was concern for taking care of children – i.e., taking care of the next generation. Erikson noted that in taking on the social role of parent, most adults made what he postulated to be a healthy adult developmental shift to a focus beyond the self, to self-sacrifice, and to the expression of compassionate love toward children. Parenting was then and is still now a significant role experience for the vast majority of adults (about 90% of current middle-aged US adults are biological, adoptive, and/or step-parents; Marks, Bumpass, & Jun, 2004).

However, Erikson (1950) also expanded his concept of generativity beyond parenting – suggesting that work in the world on behalf of future generations and other contributions to society were also evidence of the generativity that is developmentally appropriate during middle adulthood. For example, he wrote a psychobiography of Gandhi (Erikson, 1969) to illustrate generativity that was instantiated in other work in the world in service and care for others that might well also be considered self-transcending compassionate love for others.

Dan McAdams and his colleagues have led the way in bringing renewed conceptual and empirical attention to generativity (de St. Aubin, McAdams, & Kim, 2004; McAdams 2001, 2006; McAdams & de St. Aubin,

1992; McAdams, Hart, & Maruna, 1998). McAdams and de St. Aubin's (1992) theoretical formulation conceptualizes generativity as a "configuration of seven psychosocial features constellated around the personal (individual) and cultural (societal) goal of providing for the next generation" (p. 1004). *Cultural demand* and *inner desire* are posited as motivational sources for generativity. These two factors then combine to promote a conscious *concern* for the next generation. If grounded in a supportive *belief* in the goodness of the human species, concern may stimulate generative *commitment*. Generative *action* may be motivated directly by cultural demand or inner desire, but also can be derived from the adult's commitments to generative activities and goals. Generative action – which includes the behaviors of creating, maintaining, and offering to others – may reciprocally influence later generative commitments. Finally, the model suggests that a person's *narration* (i.e., subjective verbal account) of their life story related to generativity is important to consider, because it holistically synthesizes the meaning of the complex relations among the other six features of the generativity model for a given individual.

Generativity, with its focus on providing for the next generation as outlined by the McAdams and de St. Aubin model, is not synonymous with the concept of compassionate love guiding this volume. Yet the two concepts do share some overlap in their emphasis on care for others and action that moves beyond a focus only on care for self.

Anthropological and Sociological Theory and Research on Giving to Others

The social components of the compassionate love model enter most prominently as part of the situational factor substrate, where social, environmental, and cultural factors (including norms) are posited to influence compassionate motivation and discernment, which, in turn, influence positive behaviors (compassionate acts, e.g., giving to others). Sociologists and anthropologists have specialized in considering such factors and have had a longstanding interest in studying giving to others – yet this interest has been guided by diverse additional theoretical models.

Sociologists and anthropologists have long recognized the ubiquity of social exchange – both giving and receiving – in all human societies (Sabatelli & Shehan, 1993). Various motives and functions for social exchange have been posited. Often, guided by utilitarian social exchange theory with links to classical economic theory, social exchange theory has emphasized the importance of giving so that you also receive (e.g., Homans, 1961; Thibaut & Kelley, 1959). Guided by a more functionalist approach to social exchange, sociologists and anthropologists have also posited that giving and receiving have a structural benefit for society by linking people together and promoting social solidarity (Lévi-Strauss, 1969; Mauss, 1954). The benefit of giving in this view is more global and societal – and is not so isolated to an individual benefit. In contrast to a biological basis for motivation, sociologists and anthropologists emphasize the importance of socially generated socialization processes that lead to the internalization of cultural norms that motivate behavior. Most sociologists conceptualize norms as consisting of widely acknowledged rules that specify what a society or social group considers appropriate or inappropriate behavior in particular circumstances (Blake & Davis, 1964). Further, norms are considered to be statements of obligatory actions or evaluative rules (Rossi & Rossi, 1990). The actual measurement of social norms can be challenging, but one approach is to infer norms from strength of perceived obligation to action in specific situations (Rossi & Rossi, 1990).

In life-course studies, interest in social exchanges has led to a considerable literature studying what is often labeled "social support." The main interest here typically has been to see how receipt of social support can be of benefit to individuals – both in routine daily life as well as a protective factor under risk. Life-course sociologists, influenced by both utilitarian and structural-theoretical social exchange models, have therefore often included measures of giving and receiving social support in studies of adults (e.g., Eggebeen & Hogan, 1990; Rossi & Rossi, 1990; Spitze & Logan, 1992). Psychologists interested in adult resilience have also often included measures of receiving support in their studies (although less often measures of giving support; for a review see Cohen & Wills, 1985).

Interestingly, in work on aging, where social support has been expected to be a critical factor in maintaining well-being for the elderly, empirical work has begun to suggest that even among elders, it is usually more valuable for well-being to be on the giving end of social support than on the receiving end. For example, at least for US midlife and older adults, overall, being able to give to adult children, whether reciprocated or not, is associated with better psychological well-being than being overbenefited in exchanges with adult children (Davey & Eggebeen, 1998; Marks, 1995; Mutran & Reitzes, 1984; Stoller, 1985). This finding does not fit with what utilitarian social exchange theory might predict.

Evidence that "it is better to give than to receive" for adult well-being has also led to additional interest in the role that volunteering and other productive activities may provide for well-being (e.g., Keyes & Ryff, 1997; Krause, Herzog, & Baker, 1992; Musick, Herzog, & House, 1999). Research is increasingly documenting that volunteering for others is an important way in which adults may continue to age well and successfully – mentally and physically (Greenfield & Marks, 2004; Moen, Dempster-McClain, & Williams, 1992; Morrow-Howell, Hinterlong,

Rozario, & Tang, 2003; Musick et al., 1999; Oman, Thoresen, & McMahon, 1999; Omato, Malsch, & Barraza, Chapter 9, this volume). Individuals report various motives for volunteering (Allison, Okun, & Dutridge, 2002) – but the finding that volunteering leads to better mental and physical well-being is congruent with an Eriksonian developmental perspective that might view volunteering as an instantiation of generativity (broadly construed, as providing care to others), and perhaps even a Maslovian perspective that might guide us to consider volunteering as activity chosen, in some cases, to instantiate elements of self-actualization.

In addition to growth in interest in social support and volunteering, life-course scholars have begun giving more attention to caregiving for persons of all ages who are not able to take complete care of themselves owing to a mental or physical illness or disability. Demographic trends toward greater longevity, more years spent with potentially chronic diseases (in contrast to quick deaths due to acute illnesses), smaller families, and higher rates of marital dissolution (leading to a larger number of single adults, especially women, at midlife and older ages) have all contributed to a relatively high prevalence of caregiving by adults in contemporary societies (Biegel, Sales, & Schulz, 1991; Caregiving in the US, 2004; Marks, 1996). Health-care institutional changes emphasizing earlier hospital discharge and greater reliance on informal health care also have contributed to a greater need for family and friend caregivers (Biegel et al., 1991). Caregiving research has mushroomed since the early 1980s, and there is now more inclusion of measures of caregiver status in social science surveys (Hirst, 2005; Marks, 1996; Turner, Killian, & Cain, 2004; Wolff & Kasper, 2006).

In sum, although population studies of human development and human behavior have not typically assessed "compassionate love" per se, guided by contemporary psychological and sociological theoretical and empirical interest in adult development and aging, constructs related to caring about others and giving to others (both kin and nonkin) *have* been included in some larger population studies. Analyses of data from extant studies that include such related measures can contribute to the current scientific understanding of compassionate love and may also help inform the future scientific study of compassionate love. Likewise, continued explicit research on compassionate love stands to make a major contribution to future work on life-course development and aging.

Constructs from Contemporary Social Science Surveys Considered in this Chapter

The social elements of the compassionate love model emphasize the fact that compassionate love is expressed *in relation to others* and that motivation, discernment, and actions are shaped, in part, through *interaction with others in specific cultural settings and milieux* (social, environmental, cultural factors of the situational factor substrate; see Underwood, Chapter 1, this volume). This chapter aims to contribute to understanding how both *motivation* and *positive behaviors* may be contingent on *physical, social, and cultural factors* (also denoted in Underwood's Compassionate Love model) as indexed by *age, gender, race/ethnic status, educational status,* and *income status* across the US adult population.

In the next section, we describe analyses of US national data focusing on three constructs related to *motivation* for compassionate love. Specifically, we examine similarities and differences across age, gender, race/ethnic, educational, and income groups in *altruistic normative obligation* (sense of obligation to contribute to the "common good"), *normative obligation to family,* and *normative obligation to friends,* using data from the National Survey of Midlife in the United States (MIDUS) 1995.

We then focus on similarities and differences across age, gender, race/ ethnic, educational, and income groups in one global perceptual construct and seven behavioral constructs assessing *positive behaviors* (compassionate acts). These include *overall self-assessment of one's contribution to the welfare and well-being of other people; formal volunteer work; giving emotional support to primary kin; giving emotional support to secondary kin and friends; giving instrumental support to primary kin;* and *giving instrumental support to secondary kin and friends* (using data from the MIDUS); as well as *providing unpaid caregiving to family;* and *providing unpaid caregiving to friends and other nonkin* (using data from the National Survey of Families and Households [NSFH] 1987–93).

Biopsychosocial overarching theoretical frameworks guided the development of both these national population studies. The Eriksonian and Maslovian concepts of adult generativity and self-actualization, as well as sociological social exchange perspectives emphasizing social solidarity expressed through the giving and receiving of social support, led scholars developing the MIDUS and NSFH to include these measures of compassionate norms and compassionate acts in these surveys.

Compassionate Norms and Compassionate Acts in the US Adult Population

Compassionate Norms across the Adult Life Course

MIDUS data and sample. MIDUS 1995 was undertaken by the John D. and Catherine T. MacArthur Foundation Network on Successful Midlife Development (MIDMAC). This interdisciplinary research network was a research initiative of the MacArthur Foundation beginning in the late

1980s and continuing for more than a decade. Its goal was to foster greater understanding of optimal and successful functioning during the relatively understudied midlife decades – roughly ages 40–60 (Brim, Ryff, & Kessler, 2004).

MIDUS 1995 respondents are a nationally representative US population sample of noninstitutionalized persons ages 25 to 74 who have telephones. The sample was obtained through random digit dialing, with an oversampling of older men to guarantee a good distribution on the cross-classification of age and gender. We used a sample weighting variable for our population estimates, which allows the MIDUS sample to match the proportionate composition of the US population on age, sex, race, and education in 1995, and thus helps to correct for differential sample selection probabilities and nonrandom nonresponse to the survey.

MIDUS respondents first participated in a telephone interview that lasted approximately 40 minutes; response rate for the telephone questionnaire was 70%. Respondents to the telephone survey were then asked to complete two self-administered, mail-back questionnaires. The response rate for the mail-back questionnaire was 86.8% of those answering the telephone questionnaire. This yielded an overall response rate of 60.8% for the analytic sample used here, which includes respondents who responded to both parts of the survey (N = 3,032; 1,318 men, 1,714 women). (See http://midmac.med.harvard.edu/research.html for more details on survey design and weighting.)

MIDUS measures of compassionate norms. In the development of MIDUS, MIDMAC member Alice Rossi took leadership in formulating several new measurement items and indices related to social responsibility. (See also Rossi, 2001 for an overview of all the domains and dimensions of social responsibility included in MIDUS, as well as complementary descriptive analyses of some measures included here.) Using the measurement precedent of inferring social norms from the assessment of levels of obligation endorsed across specific situations (Rossi & Rossi, 1990), the new MIDUS measures included some new measures of normative obligation to others.

There is no one consistently agreed-upon definition of altruism (see Post, Underwood, Schloss, & Hurlbut, 2002), but most definitions include some compatibility with Comte's early formulation of altruism as a type of motivational state with the ultimate goal of increasing another's welfare (Batson, 2002). The newly developed MIDUS assessment of *altruistic normative obligation* analyzed for this chapter consisted of a four-item scale. Respondents were asked, "Here is a list of hypothetical situations. Please rate how much obligation you would feel if they happened to you using a 0 to 10 scale where 0 means 'no obligation at all' and 10 means 'a very great obligation.' If the situation does not apply to you, please think about how much obligation you would feel if you *were* in this situation." "How much obligation would you feel (a) to pay *more* for your health care so that *everyone* had access to health care? (b) to vote *for* a law that would help others worse off than you but would increase your taxes? (c) to volunteer time or money to social causes you support? (d) to collect contributions for heart or cancer research if asked to do so?" (Cronbach's alpha = .80).

Normative obligation to primary kin was assessed with a five-item index also new to MIDUS. Respondents were asked (using the same instruction as for altruism items), "How much obligation would you feel (a) to drop your plans when your children seem very troubled? (b) to call, write, or visit your adult children on a regular basis? (c) to drop your plans when your spouse seems very troubled? (d) to take your divorced or unemployed adult child back into your home? (e) to call your parents on a regular basis?" (Cronbach's alpha = .76).

Normative obligation to friends was assessed with three items (developed for MIDUS). Respondents were asked (using the same instruction as for altruism items), "How much obligation would you feel (a) to raise the child of a close friend if the friend died? (b) to take a friend into your home who could not afford to live alone? (c) to give money to a friend in need, even if this made it hard to meet your own needs?" (Cronbach's alpha = .79).

The correlations among the three measures of compassionate norms ranged from .36 (altruistic normative obligation with normative obligation to primary kin) to .57 (normative obligation to kin with normative obligation to friends). These moderate levels of association indicate that these indices are related, yet relatively distinct measures of compassionate norms.

A description of results from analyses of altruistic normative obligation, normative obligation to family, and normative obligation to friends across US adults aged 25–74 in 1995 is provided in Table 5.1. This table provides crosstabulations of weighted means for each of these indices by gender, age, race/ethnic, educational attainment, and household income groups. *T*-tests (across gender groups) and analyses of variance (ANOVA) across other sociodemographic groups were evaluated for each crosstabulation (column of subcategories of a demographic status); where significant overall differences were noted for groups with more than two categories (i.e., all sociodemographic statuses other than gender), post hoc Scheffe tests were conducted to identify significant group differences.

Altruistic normative obligation. The second column of Table 5.1 provides results related to the four-item index of altruistic normative obligation. The overall mean score on the altruistic normative obligation scale was 5.86 (*SD* = 2.23), indicating a relatively normal distribution for this scale. Women reported a significantly higher level of altruistic obligation than men (M = 6.10 vs. 5.56). This gender difference finding is congruent with some related previous work that has indicated women rate higher on compassionate love for strangers as well as close others (Sprecher & Fehr, 2005).

An evaluation of differences across age groups also revealed significant effects. Young and early midlife adults (ages 25–44) reported significantly less altruistic obligation than later midlife and young-old adults (ages 45–74). This result may reflect the fact that, on average, later midlife and older adults have greater resources than younger adults, and that this more secure resource base is conducive to developing more sense of altruistic obligation; this interpretation would be consistent with Maslovian theory. It may also be that younger adults are still focusing mainly on their own identity and intimacy issues, whereas later midlife and older adults have moved on developmentally to become more concerned with caring for others, as Eriksonian theory would predict. We must be cautious, though, about making developmental inferences here and in other cases of age differences; we cannot rule out cohort differences as an alternative explanation of any age differences found with these cross-sectional data.

Considering levels of altruistic normative obligation across different race/ethnic groups, results revealed that African Americans reported higher endorsement of altruistic normative obligation than both non-Hispanic whites (i.e., all Caucasians other than Latinos) and Latinos. There were no significant differences, however, in altruistic obligation across educational or income status groups.

The fact that African Americans, a historically very disadvantaged group in the United States, report higher altruistic obligation than either non-Hispanic whites or Latinos is noteworthy. (Supplementary analyses also confirmed that African Americans had the highest means on all four items comprising the scale.) Faced with greater structural constraints, Maslovian theory might have predicted that altruistic obligation ratings would be lower among African Americans. The fact that, instead, ratings are higher suggests there may be a particularly high cultural valuing of communitarianism and altruism in the African American community that is being reflected in this result (Baldwin & Hopkins, 1990). Such a normative explanation would be consistent with a structural social exchange perspective.

Normative obligation to primary kin. The third column of Table 5.1 provides results related to the normative obligation to primary kin index. The overall rating of normative obligation to primary kin for this sample was 8.18 (SD = 1.67). This relatively high rating on a scale of 0 to 10 is consistent with previous research that has demonstrated that the highest normative obligation ratings reported are for primary kin (Rossi & Rossi, 1990).

Table 5.1 Weighted Means for Altruistic Normative Obligation, Normative Obligation to Primary Kin, Normative Obligation to Friends, and Overall Self-Assessment of Personal Contribution to the Well-Being of Others by Gender, Age, Race/Ethnicity, Education, and Household Income

	Unweighted N	Altruistic normative obligation (weighted mean (SD))	Normative obligation to primary kin (weighted mean (SD))	Normative obligation to friends (weighted mean (SD))	Overall personal contribution to the well-being of others (weighted mean (SD))
Gender					
Women	1561	6.10 (2.18)[a]	8.45 (1.55)[a]	6.81 (2.18)[a]	6.85 (2.26)[a]
Men	1471	5.56 (2.26)	7.85 (1.75)	6.21 (2.30)	6.32 (2.19)
Age					
25–34	627	5.61 (2.08)A	8.33 (1.52)B	6.98 (1.89)C	6.40 (2.26)A
35–44	727	5.62 (2.16)A	8.09 (1.50)AB	6.57 (2.11)BC	6.68 (2.09)AB
45–54	720	6.11 (2.28)B	8.10 (1.79)AB	6.46 (2.30)B	6.75 (2.17)AB
55–64	596	6.21 (2.25)B	8.37 (1.73)B	6.41 (2.45)B	6.91 (2.35)B
65–74	335	6.13 (2.46)B	7.98 (2.01)A	5.80 (2.79)A	6.37 (2.48)A
Race/ethnicity					
Non-Hispanic white	2513	5.72 (2.19)A	8.22 (1.61)[b]	6.50 (2.24)[b]	6.56 (2.19)[b]
African American	201	6.89 (2.27)B	7.95 (1.96)	6.84 (2.34)	7.06 (2.52)
Latino	139	5.72 (2.19)A	8.31 (1.60)	6.78 (2.11)	6.82 (2.34)
Other race/ethnicity	91	6.24 (2.17)AB	7.95 (1.92)	6.56 (2.39)	6.57 (2.30)

Education					
Less than 12 years	300	5.83 (2.43)n.s.	7.77 (2.00)A	6.55 (2.61)[b]	6.41 (2.54)A
12 years	888	5.83 (2.26)	8.29 (1.66)B	6.67 (2.30)	6.69 (2.26)AB
13–15 years	945	5.79 (2.24)	8.17 (1.66)B	6.54 (2.12)	6.45 (2.26)A
16 years and more	897	6.02 (2.06)	8.25 (1.44)B	6.36 (2.09)	6.81 (2.01)B
Household income					
Lowest quarter	720	6.02 (2.39)n.s.	7.96 (1.91)A	6.76 (2.27)B	6.50 (2.53)n.s.
2nd quarter	737	5.86 (2.18)	8.31 (1.59)B	6.63 (2.27)AB	6.63 (2.25)
3rd quarter	777	5.74 (2.18)	8.17 (1.61)AB	6.36 (2.29)A	6.65 (2.11)
Highest quarter	798	5.83 (2.16)	8.30 (1.50)B	6.45 (2.17)AB	6.71 (2.06)
Total sample	3032				
Mean		5.86	8.18	6.55	6.62
SD		2.23	1.67	2.25	2.25
Range		0–10	0–10	0–10	0–10

Note: From the National Survey of Midlife in the US (MIDUS), 1995.

[a] T-test revealed a significant gender difference.

[b] One-way ANOVA revealed a significant overall difference in mean scores among group (column) categories; no specific significant group differences revealed by post-hoc Sheffe test.

A, B, C: Overall ANOVA was significant and post-hoc Scheffe test revealed groups with the same letter to be a homogeneous subset (i.e., no different in means); groups with distinct letters have significantly different means.

n.s.: One-way ANOVA revealed no difference in mean scores among group (column) categories.

Similar to the results for altruistic normative obligation, an evaluation across gender groups demonstrates that women report significantly higher normative obligation to primary kin than men ($M = 8.45$ vs. 7.85). This is consistent with previously reported gender differences in normative attitudes toward "kinkeeping" (Rossi & Rossi, 1990).

In terms of age differences, the youngest age group (ages 25–34) and the later midlife group (ages 55–64) report the highest normative obligation to primary kin, and their levels of reported obligation are significantly higher than that of the young-old group (ages 65–74). It may be that upon reaching young-old age adults are beginning to feel they have "paid their dues" already at younger ages, and may feel that some other younger members of the family may now be able to carry more of the burden of family obligations, especially if health and other resources of the older adult are not optimal. Overall, however, the mean of 7.98 of 10 for young-old adults is evidence that normative obligation to primary kin is quite high for all young, midlife, and young-old adults.

ANOVA revealed overall significant race/ethnic group differences in mean scores of normative obligation to primary kin; in post hoc Sheffe analyses, however, significant specific between-group differences did not emerge. Latinos reported the highest mean score among race/ethnic groups ($M = 8.31$), consistent with a cultural emphasis on familism in Latino families (Vega, 1990).

Among educational groups, the lowest education group (less than 12 years) reported significantly less obligation to primary kin than the other three groups with higher education. A somewhat similar pattern emerged with income, where persons with household incomes in the lowest quarter of the population distribution reported lower normative obligation to primary kin than persons in the second quarter or the highest quarter of the distribution (persons in the third quarter were not significantly different from any of the other groups). These results suggest that having limited educational or income resources may reduce feelings of basic security that might be necessary to generate enhanced feelings of obligations to primary kin; this interpretation would be consistent with a Maslovian theoretical perspective.

Normative obligation to friends. For normative obligation to friends the overall mean is slightly lower than for the other measures of normative obligation – 6.55 ($SD = 2.25$). This finding is congruent with research indicating that normative obligation to nonkin tends to be lower than normative obligation to primary kin (Rossi & Rossi, 1990), as well as from other research on altruism and compassionate love that emphasizes the greater ease with which individuals tend to report compassionate love for family and "ingroup" members in contrast to nonkin and "outgroup" members (Sprecher & Fehr, 2005). Another possible methodological reason for the lower rating is the potentially greater commitment suggested by the items tapping nonkin obligation in contrast to kin obligation – e.g., raising the child of a friend who has died vs. dropping your plans when your child is in trouble. Nonetheless, the mean rating for nonkin obligation is still well above the half-way point of the scale – indicating a considerable sense of obligation to support persons not closely linked by genes or marriage.

Consistent with the pattern observed across the other norm measures, women reported significantly higher normative obligation to friends than men (M = 6.81 vs. 6.21). Additionally, the highest normative obligation to friends occurred for the youngest age group (ages 25–34, M = 6.98); the lowest levels of normative obligation to friends was reported by the oldest age group (ages 65–74, M = 5.80). Young adults are more likely to be unmarried and without children, and therefore more involved in activities with nonkin (Gerstel & Sarkisian, 2006); this structural situation may lend itself to more salience of normative obligation to friends. Additionally, an item that asks, for example, about willingness to raise the child of a friend who died may also be more hypothetical and easier to idealistically affirm for younger adults than for older adults who know from more life experience the heavy burden such an actual commitment would entail. The lower ratings among older adults also might be due to their greater likelihood of health and/or structural constraints (e.g., low income, lack of transportation) that could interfere with their ability to generate an extremely high sense of obligation to persons outside the family. This latter interpretation would be consistent with Maslovian theory.

ANOVA results suggested there were overall race/ethnic group and educational attainment group differences in normative obligation to friends; however, post hoc analyses did not yield evidence of specific intergroup differences. Among race/ethnic groups, African Americans had the highest mean score on normative obligation to friends – 6.84. Among educational groups, high-school graduates reported the greatest normative obligation to friends (M = 6.67).

Examining household income group differences, there was evidence that persons in the lowest quarter of the population income distribution reported higher levels of obligation to friends than those in the third quarter of the income distribution (and the highest mean score overall). The second and top income quarter groups were not significantly different from other groups. Similar to the result for African Americans and altruistic obligation, the finding that lower-income persons report the highest obligation to friends is contrary to what a structural constraint or Maslovian perspective might suggest. However, structural need owing to lower income might also provoke more sense of interdependence with friends, and thereby lead to more sense of obligation to friends to promote joint well-being.

Compassionate Acts across the Adult Life Course

MIDUS measures of compassionate acts. One global perceptual item assessing *overall personal contribution to the well-being of others* was also included in MIDUS. Respondents were asked, "Using a scale from 0 to 10 where 0 means 'worst possible contribution to the welfare and well-being of other people' and 10 means 'the best possible contribution to the welfare and well-being of other people,' how would you rate your contribution to the welfare and well-being of other people these days? Take into account all that you do, in terms of time, money, or concern, on your job, and for your family, friends, and the community."

Table 5.1 reports results for this global assessment. The overall rating for this item across the entire sample was relatively high ($M = 6.62$, $SD = 2.25$), with women scoring higher than men ($M = 6.85$ vs. 6.32). Across age, the highest rating of contribution was from persons aged 55–64 who rated this significantly higher than either the youngest adults (aged 25–34) or the young-old adults (aged 65–74). This may reflect, in part, the structural role expectations – and opportunities – that go along with the considerable range of family, work, and community roles that adults are typically enacting during the midlife years (Brim et al., 2004). For example, within families, midlife adults often occupy "sandwich-generation" family roles that involve giving support to both children and adults. (See also Fleeson, 2001, for expanded age-related analyses related to the MIDUS measure of overall contribution to the welfare of others.)

ANOVA analyses suggested overall significant differences by race/ethnicity, although post hoc analyses did not yield evidence of specific between-group differences. The mean rating of African Americans was the highest among race/ethnic groups – 7.06.

Among educational status groups, there was clear evidence that persons with the highest education (16 or more years) rated their contribution to others significantly higher than persons with the lowest level of education (under 12 years) or third highest level of education (13–15 years). This finding may be a result of the greater leadership opportunities in work and community roles that are afforded to persons with higher education. Interestingly, however, there were no significant differences in ratings of personal contribution to others across household income groups.

Additional analyses of behavioral measures of compassionate acts across the adult life course were conducted using data from the MIDUS. *Volunteering* was assessed with four items. Respondents in MIDUS were asked, "On average, how many hours per month do you spend doing formal volunteer work of any of the following types: (a) hospital, nursing home, or other health-care-oriented volunteer work, (b) school or other youth-related volunteer work, (c) volunteer work for political organizations or causes, (d) volunteer work for any other organization, cause or charity?" A dichotomous measure of "any volunteering" was created where respondents were coded 1 if they reported one or more hours of volunteering in any of these contexts. Additionally, a continuous measure of volunteering was created across all respondents (volunteers and non-volunteers) where hours were summed across the four items. In many cases respondents to the MIDUS self-administered questionnaire only answered questions where they had something other than zero hours to report. Therefore, for this variable and all other variables that included multiple items assessing hours for different types of related activities, if respondents provided a valid answer (i.e., 0 to any number of hours) to *any* of the questions, a zero was imputed for any questions left without an answer, and they were assigned a valid score for the respective index. If respondents did not provide an answer for *any* of the questions for a respective index, they were considered missing on the index and were excluded from analyses.

Emotional support to primary kin was assessed with four items, and two measures (dichotomous and continuous) were created in a manner similar to the volunteering measures. Respondents were asked, "On average, about how many hours per month do you spend giving informal emotional support (such as comforting, listening to problems, or giving advice) to each of the following people? (If none, or if the question does not apply because, for example, you have no spouse or partner, enter "0"): (a) to your spouse or partner, (b) to your parents or the people who raised you, (c) to your in-laws, (d) to your children or grandchildren?"

Emotional support to secondary kin and friends was assessed with two items that were used to create both a dichotomous and a continuous measure. Respondents were provided the same prompt as for emotional support to primary kin, but were additionally queried about providing emotional support (a) to any other family members or close friends and (b) to anyone else (such as neighbors or people at church).

Dichotomous and continuous measures of *instrumental support to primary kin* were created using data from three items. Respondents were asked, "On average, about how many hours per month do you spend providing unpaid assistance (such as help around the house, transportation, or childcare) to each of the following people? (If none, enter "0"): (a) to your parents or the people who raised you, (b) to your in-laws, (c) to your grandchildren or grown children?"

Two similar measures of *instrumental support to secondary kin and friends* were created using data from two items. Respondents were queried similarly as for primary kin about instrumental support, but were additionally asked about giving instrumental support (a) to any other family members or close friends, and (b) to anyone else (such as neighbors or people at church).

Correlations among the dichotomous MIDUS measures of compassionate acts ranged from .04 (volunteering with instrumental support to kin) to .42 (emotional support to kin with emotional support to nonkin). Correlations between compassionate norm measures and dichotomous measures of compassionate acts ranged from .02 (altruistic normative obligation with emotional support to primary kin) to .30 (altruistic normative obligation with overall contribution to the well-being of others).

The weighted percentage of respondents reporting any volunteering or giving support, as well as means for hours of volunteering and provision of support, are provided in Table 5.2. In addition to t-test and ANOVA analyses of group differences with follow-up post hoc Sheffe tests for continuous measures, chi-square tests of group differences were conducted for categorical (proportion) estimates.

Volunteering. The first column of Table 5.2 provides information about the weighted percentage of persons indicating they provided any amount of formal volunteering during the last month; the second column provides information about the mean number of hours of volunteering reported per month. Across the entire sample, 40.8% of adults ages 25–74 reported some level of volunteering. This overall proportion is somewhat less than the 56% reported in a 1998 Gallup Poll for the Independent Sector (Wilson, 2000), but relatively comparable to prevalence rates in the 1989 Americans' Changing Lives Study, which used somewhat similar items to measure the construct (Wilson & Musick, 1997). The mean number of hours of volunteering during the last month reported across the entire sample (volunteers and nonvolunteers) was 5.8 ($SD = 16.4$).

A significantly higher proportion of women than men reported volunteering (40.1% vs. 36.0%), although mean hours spent volunteering per month did not differ by gender. There were significant differences across age groups in proportion volunteering, with midlife adults (ages 35–54) evidencing the highest rates. However, mean hours of reported volunteering did not differ across age groups.

There were race/ethnicity differences in proportion of respondents who volunteer, suggesting that non-Hispanic whites and persons of other race/ethnicity had the highest rates, and Latinos the lowest rates. Among race/ethnic groups, Latinos reported the fewest hours of volunteering, and this was significantly less than persons of "other" race/ethnicity.

Among education groups, there was a positive linear relationship between education and proportion of respondents reporting volunteering. In terms of mean hours spent volunteering during the last month, persons

Table 5.2 Weighted Percentage Any and Mean Hours of Volunteering, Providing Emotional Support to Primary Kin, Providing Emotional Support to Secondary Kin or Friends, Providing Instrumental Support to Primary Kin, Providing Instrumental Support to Secondary Kin or Friends During the Last Month by Gender, Age, Race/Ethnicity, Education, and Household Income

	Volunteering (hrs/month)		Emotional support to primary kin (hrs/month)		Emotional support to secondary kin/friends (hrs/month)		Instrumental support to primary kin (hrs/month)		Instrumental support to secondary kin/friends (hrs/mo)	
	% any	mean (SD)	% any	mean (SD)	% any	mean (SD)	% any	mean (SD)	% any	mean (SD)
Gender										
Women	40.1[c]	6.2 (16.6)[n.s.]	93.6[n.s.]	95.7 (242.5)[a]	88.6[c]	28.7 (91.3)[a]	59.6[n.s.]	23.6 (79.1)[a]	56.3[c]	15.0 (51.6)[a]
Men	36.0	5.2 (16.1)	91.8	54.2 (115.7)	78.6	11.4 (27.8)	59.1	15.4 (56.4)	61.6	9.7 (31.1)
Age										
25–34	33.8[c]	6.4 (21.9)[n.s.]	95.1[c]	105.1 (234.4)C	92.2[c]	28.7 (70.3)B	56.6[c]	19.9 (67.9)[n.s.]	66.7[c]	17.7 (59.9)C
35–44	44.8	5.7 (15.0)	94.4	86.6 (202.0)BC	85.2	21.1 (76.3)AB	57.1	22.6 (82.0)	62.4	15.5 (46.3)BC
45–54	40.7	6.1 (15.1)	95.9	63.6 (204.6)AB	84.4	18.9 (84.6)AB	65.5	19.9 (75.5)	55.7	8.2 (30.0)AB
55–64	32.7	4.1 (10.0)	89.4	63.1 (169.3)AB	78.3	18.5 (71.1)AB	64.7	22.0 (67.5)	50.0	8.8 (34.2)AB
65–74	37.3	6.2 (13.5)	83.5	34.2 (68.6)A	71.0	11.8 (24.8)A	53.1	10.3 (24.5)	47.5	6.4 (16.5)A

(*Continued*)

Table 5.2 (Continued)

	Volunteering (hrs/month)		Emotional support to primary kin (hrs/month)		Emotional support to secondary kin/friends (hrs/month)		Instrumental support to primary kin (hrs/month)		Instrumental support to secondary kin/friends (hrs/mo)	
	% any	mean (SD)	% any	mean (SD)	% any	mean (SD)	% any	mean (SD)	% any	Mean (SD)
Race/ethnicity										
Non-Hispanic white	39.3c	5.5 (15.1)AB	94.1c	73.3 (180.8)n.s.	84.7n.s.	19.4 (64.0)b	59.9n.s.	16.9 (53.1)b	58.5n.s.	11.5 (37.1)b
African American	35.3	8.4 (26.2)AB	86.4	97.1 (293.1)	81.8	35.9 (123.4)	58.6	33.3 (122.0)	57.1	21.6 (80.1)
Latino	25.6	3.5 (9.1)A	90.2	93.6 (196.5)	84.9	16.7 (33.2)	59.2	34.6 (88.9)	58.3	9.3 (20.5)
Other race/ethnicity	46.8	8.5 (15.6)B	91.7	68.5 (171.5)	85.5	20.5 (54.4)	54.1	27.2 (113.0)	73.1	14.7 (50.8)
Education										
Less than 12 years	18.1c	3.5 (24.0)A	85.2c	93.9 (270.4)B	70.3c	33.1 (116.8)C	58.2c	30.6 (104.9)B	51.2c	15.3 (42.9)AB
12 years	32.8	4.9 (12.3)AB	92.5	81.3 (194.6)B	82.5	19.8 (58.5)AB	62.3	19.8 (56.9)AB	55.7	10.9 (29.5)AB
13–15 years	40.9	6.4 (18.1)BC	94.6	92.6 (229.0)B	89.4	25.1 (81.2)BC	61.3	24.7 (87.3)B	62.4	17.6 (67.7)B
16 years and more	55.8	7.8 (14.9)C	95.5	44.7 (80.9)A	88.7	12.7 (40.3)A	53.3	9.5 (37.1)A	63.0	8.8 (28.5)A

Household income

Lowest quarter	30.2[c]	5.6 (22.5)*n.s.*	84.3[c]	70.5 (204.4)*n.s.*	79.4[c]	23.9 (62.8)*n.s.*	55.7*n.s.*	20.8 (80.3)*n.s.*	54.3[c]	13.6 (39.9)*n.s.*
2nd quarter	36.9	5.4 (11.8)	93.5	88.0 (206.1)	86.5	21.0 (58.3)	62.0	23.3 (72.3)	61.7	12.7 (36.1)
3rd quarter	41.3	6.2 (17.0)	95.8	76.7 (211.6)	83.5	21.1 (93.7)	60.4	16.7 (56.6)	57.3	13.3 (61.4)
Highest quarter	45.0	5.9 (11.7)	97.6	73.5 (162.8)	87.4	18.6 (65.1)	59.3	19.1 (69.5)	61.3	11.1 (32.0)
Total sample Percent	40.8	5.8 (16.4)	92.3	77.3 (197.5)	84.2	21.2 (71.5)	59.0	20.0 (70.2)	59.0	12.7 (44.0)
Range	0–416		0–2880		0–1440		0–1440		0–800	

Note. From the National Survey of Midlife in the US (MIDUS), 1995.

[a] T-test revealed a significant difference between gender groups (column) at p < .05 level.

[b] One-way ANOVA revealed an overall significant difference in mean scores of continuous variables among group categories (column) at p < .05 level; no post hoc Sheffe test evidence of specific group differences.

[c] Chi-square test revealed significant differences in proportions among group categories (column) at p < .05 level.

A, B, C: Overall ANOVA significant across groups (column) and post-hoc Scheffe test revealed groups with the same letter to be a homogeneous subset (i.e., no different in means); groups with distinct letters have significantly different means.

n.s.: One-way ANOVA (means) or Chi-Square test (proportions) revealed no significant differences among group categories (column).

with some college or more reported more volunteering than persons without schooling beyond high school (12 years). These results are consistent with other research indicating that more highly educated groups do more formal volunteering (Wilson, 2000; Wilson & Musick, 1997).

There was evidence of proportion differences across income groups – with a linear pattern where higher-income groups were more likely to report formal volunteering. However, the actual mean hours of formal volunteering did not significantly vary across income groups. Finding higher proportions of higher-educated, higher-income, middle-aged, and non-Hispanic white persons volunteering is consistent with what we might expect from a Maslovian perspective, which emphasizes the importance of having basic needs met before being able to give additionally to others.

Emotional support to primary kin. Within the overall sample the prevalence of reporting at least some emotional support to primary kin during the last month was extremely high; 92.3 % of sample respondents reported providing some such support; the average number of hours of support provided in the last month across the entire sample was also quite sizeable: 77.3 hours.

There was a significant gender difference in number of hours provided (although not in the proportion providing *any* support). Women averaged about 95.7 hours of emotional support to primary kin in the last month; men reported an average of 54.2 hours of emotional support during the same period of time. These results are consistent with other work that provides evidence that women provide higher levels of emotional support than men (e.g., Almeida & McDonald, 2005; Rossi & Rossi, 1990; see also Taylor et al., 2000).

Proportions of persons providing emotional support to kin varied by age – with younger adults reporting higher rates. Additionally, younger adults aged 25–34 reported the highest levels of mean hours of providing emotional support to primary kin ($M = 105.1$), significantly more than the young-old adults (ages 65–74) in this sample who reported the lowest mean hours of support ($M = 34.2$). It may be that younger adults (in contrast to young-old adults) have more living and/or coresident primary kin members – spouses, parents, parents-in-law, and children – to whom they may provide considerable support. Older adults may also be less healthy and less able to focus on providing support to others owing to their own needs.

A significant difference across race/ethnic groups in proportions of persons giving emotional support to primary kin was noted; the rate for African Americans was the lowest. Yet there were no significant race/ethnic differences in mean hours of providing emotional support to primary kin (mean hours of African Americans were actually highest

(97.1 hours) but with an extremely large standard deviation (293.1 hours), suggesting some exceptionally intense cases of support provision within this group).

There was evidence that proportions of persons providing emotional support to primary kin also differed across education – with the higher rates in evidence at each step up the educational ladder. Yet persons with the highest level of education reported the lowest mean number of hours of emotional support to primary kin ($M = 44.7$), which was significantly different from the level of providing support reported by any other educational group. This latter result is puzzling, given the fact that more highly educated people tend to report having more kin as well as nonkin persons with whom they discuss important matters (McPherson, Smith-Lovin, & Brashears, 2006). Persons with higher income were found to provide emotional support to primary kin at higher proportional levels than persons with lower income. There were no differences across income groups, however, in terms of mean number of hours of providing such support.

Emotional support to secondary kin and friends. Overall, 84.2% of the sample reported providing some degree of emotional support to secondary kin or friends during the last month. Mean hours of such support provided was 21.2 – a much lower number of hours than the mean for primary kin (77.3). Women were more likely to report providing emotional support to secondary kin or friends in the last month than men (88.6% vs. 78.6%). Women also reported more than twice the number of hours reported by men ($M = 28.7$ vs. 11.4). This is convergent with other evidence that women are more engaged in emotional support exchange with friends, neighbors, and co-workers (Liebler & Sandefur, 2002).

There was a clear linear trend by age in proportions of adults reporting providing emotional support to secondary kin or friends – with younger adults reporting the highest levels. An evaluation of age differences across mean hours of support also suggested that congruent with their higher level of reported obligation to friends noted previously, younger adults (ages 25–34) reported providing significantly more hours of emotional support to secondary kin and friends than did young-old adults (ages 65–74; $M = 28.7$ vs. 11.8).

While no proportion differences were in evidence across race/ethnicity, there were significant differences across race/ethnic groups in mean hours reported of providing support to secondary kin and friends. Post hoc Sheffe tests did not reveal significant differences in two-group comparisons, but African Americans, on average, reported the highest mean number of hours of emotional support to secondary kin and friends – 35.9 (although the standard deviation was also extremely high, at 123.4, suggesting great variation in reports).

Although higher proportions of persons with more than a high-school education reported providing "any" emotional support to secondary kin and nonkin, there was evidence that the highest educational group reported significantly fewer hours of emotional support than the lowest educational group or the group with some college education. This suggests that the time-intensity of providing emotional support to secondary kin and nonkin may be greater when it occurs for persons with lower education. There were no significant differences across household income groups.

Instrumental support to primary kin. Overall, about three out of five adults (59%) in our sample reported providing some degree of instrumental support to primary kin, with an average of about 20 hours provided per month. There was no gender difference in the proportion of persons reporting provision of instrumental support to primary kin, but women did report significantly more hours per month than men (23.6 hours vs. 15.4 hours). A methodological issue may be contributing to this result; the instructions for considering types of instrumental support (e.g., childcare, help around the house, transportation) may have cued the types of activities that women are more likely to undertake. Other research has also suggested that women tend to report giving more instrumental support overall than men, but not necessarily more across every type of support; for example, sons in Rossi and Rossi's (1990) study reported "fixing things" for mothers and fathers more often than daughters did.

Proportions providing instrumental support to primary kin differed by age – with the highest proportions in evidence during the midlife decades (ages 45–64). Again, this may reflect the greater likelihood of midlife adults being in family roles of partner, parent, and adult child, which call upon them to respond in significant ways to needs for instrumental support to primary kin. There were no age differences, however, in reports of mean hours of support provided.

No difference in proportions across race/ethnic groups was found. ANOVA provided evidence of a global difference in mean hours across race/ethnicity, but post hoc tests did not reveal specific group differences. Latinos reported the highest level of hours of providing instrumental support to primary kin – 34.6; non-Hispanic whites were lowest, reporting a mean of 16.9 hours.

Persons with 16 or more years of education evidenced the lowest rate of providing instrumental support to primary kin. Similar to the pattern observed for emotional support, the highest educational group reported a lower level of provision of instrumental support to primary kin (9.5 hours) compared to the lowest educational group (30.6 hours) or the some college education group (24.7 hours). Persons with higher education tend to live further away from kin in adulthood than persons with lower education (Fischer, 1982); this structural factor may contribute to less instrumental support exchange with kin (Rossi & Rossi, 1990). Neither proportions nor means differed across income groups.

Instrumental support to secondary kin and friends. Interestingly, the overall rate of report of instrumental support to secondary kin and friends in the last month was similar for secondary kin and friends to that found for primary kin – 59%. Yet the mean number of hours reported was less – 12.7 hours for secondary kin and friends vs. 20 hours for primary kin – as might be expected, owing to differences in normative obligation typically reported for secondary kin and friends in contrast to primary kin (Rossi & Rossi, 1990).

Although a higher proportion of men than women reported providing any instrumental support to secondary kin and friends during the last month (61.6% vs. 56.3%), women were found to provide more hours of instrumental support to secondary kin and friends than men ($M = 15.0$ to 9.7). The youngest age groups provided instrumental support to secondary kin and friends at higher rates than the oldest age groups. The oldest age group (65–74) also reported providing fewer hours of instrumental support to secondary kin and friends per month (6.4 hours) than the youngest age groups (17.7 for ages 25–34 and 15.5 for ages 35–44).

There were no proportion differences by race/ethnic group status. ANOVA suggested overall mean hour differences by race/ethnicity, but post hoc tests did not reveal a specific group difference. African Americans reported the highest mean hours of instrumental support to secondary kin and friends (21.6); Latinos reported the lowest mean hours (9.3).

At each progressively higher level of education, a higher proportion of persons reported the provision of instrumental support to secondary kin and friends during the last month. Yet in terms of mean number of hours provided, persons with the highest education (16 or more years) provided fewer hours of instrumental support to secondary kin and friends than persons with some college. It may be that the higher prevalence of providing support is because persons with higher education have larger numbers of nonkin (as well as kin) in their social networks (McPherson et al., 2006; Moore, 1990), and a higher proportion of nonkin to kin (Moore, 1990). Yet owing to homophily in social networks (McPherson, Smith-Lovin, & Cook, 2001), it may be that the secondary kin and friends in the networks of persons with higher education also have more resources and do not require and therefore elicit the same intensity of instrumental support.

There were overall differences across household income status in proportions providing instrumental support to secondary kin and nonkin. The lowest rate (54.3%) was found for the lowest income group. There were no significant differences across income groups in mean hours of support provided.

NSFH data and analytic sample. We turn next to population analyses of informal caregiving to kin and nonkin owing to a mental or physical illness, disability, or condition. Data for analyses of caregiving came from the National Survey of Families and Households (NSFH), which includes information from personal interviews conducted in 1987–88 (NSFH1, T1) and 1992–93 (NSFH2, T2; five years later) with a nationally representative primary respondent sample of 13,007 noninstitutionalized US adults, 19 years old and older. The response rate at NSFH1 was 74%, and at NSFH2, 82% of first-wave respondents, yielding national population coverage at a rate of about 60% for data from both waves. Again, we used a sample weight variable available in these data that allowed us to generate estimates that correct for selection probabilities and nonresponse, thereby allowing the NSFH2 sample used here to match the composition of the US population on age, sex, and race in 1992 (for more design details see Sweet & Bumpass, 1996; Sweet, Bumpass, & Call, 1988). The analytic sample for this study consisted of NSFH primary respondents who reported caregiving information at both NSFH1 and NSFH2 (N = 9,620; 5,893 women and 3,727 men).

NSFH measures of caregiving. In-household caregiving at NSFH1 was assessed by asking the question: "Does anyone living here require care or assistance because of a disability or chronic illness?" If respondents answered "yes," they were asked for the age and relationship to them of up to four disabled or chronically ill persons in their households. Because of the way this question was asked at NSFH1, it should be noted that some inference of caregiving must be made with these data; persons who live with a disabled person are inferred to provide at least some degree of help with care for that coresident person.

Out-of-household caregiving at NSFH1 was evaluated by a more direct question: "Sometimes people help take care of relatives who are seriously ill or disabled, and who do not live with them. Have you provided such care at any time during the last 12 months?" For those who answered "yes," the age and relationship of up to four persons was reported by respondents.

To assess in-household caregiving at NSFH2, respondents were asked, "During the last 12 months have you, yourself given anyone who was living with you at the time any help with personal care because of their long-term physical or mental condition, illness, or disability?" Respondents answering, "yes," were asked, "Who did you give the most personal care of this kind?"

To assess out-of-household caregiving at NSFH2, respondents were asked, "Sometimes because of a physical or mental condition, illness, or disability, people require the assistance of friends or relatives. During the last 12 months have you, yourself, given anyone not living with you at the time any help or assistance because of their health problem or disability?" Respondents answering "yes" were further queried, "Who did you provide with the most help?"

Based on answers to all these questions, a dichotomous variable for *primary kin care T1–T2* was created where a respondent was coded 1 if (1) they had answered at NSFH1 that they lived with a person with a disability and/or provided out-of-household care and/or (2) they answered at NSFH2 that they provided in-household or out-of-household care to a disabled biological/step/adopted/or foster child or child-in-law, spouse, or biological or adoptive parents. In other words, respondents reporting any caregiving provided at either NSFH1 or NSFH2 for these categories of primary family relationships during the last 12 months were coded 1 as providing primary kin care T1–T2. All others were coded 0 – no primary kin care T1–T2.

Secondary kin care T1–T2 was constructed in a similar way, only the categories of persons included for this variable were stepparents, parents-in-law, grandparents, sibling, step-sibling, half-sibling, sibling-in-law, grandchild, and other relatives. Thus, if a respondent to NSFH1 indicated they lived with or provided out-of-household care for a relative in these categories, and/or if a respondent to NSFH2 indicated they provided in-household or out-of household care to a relative in these categories they were coded 1 for secondary kin care T1–T2; otherwise, they were coded 0 – no secondary kin care T1–T2.

Nonkin care T1–T2 was constructed as a dichotomous variable where respondents were coded 1 if they had indicated they lived with and/or provided out-of-household care at NSFH1 and/or provided in-household or out-of-household caregiving at NSFH2 to a disabled roommate, friend, or other nonrelative. All other respondents were coded 0 – no nonkin care T1–T2.

Finally, a composite *total kin/nonkin care T1–T2* variable was created. This dichotomous variable was coded 1 for any respondent who had indicated they had provided either primary kin care, secondary kin care, or nonkin care at either NSFH1 or NSFH2. Table 5.3 shows the results of analyses showing overall weighted percentages of persons providing caregiving to family members and friends at either NSFH1 or NSFH2.

Caregiving for primary kin. The bottom row of Table 5.3 shows the rates of providing caregiving overall at one or both of the survey time points separated by about five years. The results in the primary kin care columns indicate that about one in five (18.9%) US adults age 19 and over reported providing some level of caregiving for a disabled primary kin member within the last 12 months of being interviewed at NSFH1 or

Table 5.3 Unweighted N and Weighted Percentage of Persons Providing Caregiving to Family and Friends Measured at Two Times Over Five Years by Gender, Age, Race/Ethnicity, Education, and Household Income

	Unweighted N			Primary kin care (weighted %)			Secondary kin care (weighted %)			Nonkin care (weighted %)			Total kin or nonkin care (weighted %)		
	Total	Women	Men	Total	Women	Men	Total	Women	Men	Total	Women	Men	Total	Women	Men
Age															
19–24	1242	735	507	10.5[a]	13.3[a]	7.8[a]	18.0[a]	19.5[a]	16.4	5.4[a]	6.7[a]	4.1	30.8[a]	35.5[a]	26.2[a]
25–34	2882	1696	1186	18.0	21.7	14.2	15.5	17.3	13.6	7.0	8.0	5.9	36.3	42.2	30.2
35–44	2155	1301	854	23.1	26.6	19.6	14.7	16.2	13.3	7.8	8.4	7.1	40.5	45.5	35.8
45–54	1211	757	454	25.7	29.7	20.7	14.9	15.4	14.1	7.4	9.2	5.1	42.8	48.0	36.2
55–64	1005	625	380	19.5	23.7	14.3	13.0	12.8	13.2	9.8	12.7	6.2	37.8	43.5	30.9
65–74	778	523	255	18.1	21.0	14.3	11.1	11.0	11.3	9.7	13.0	5.3	33.7	38.8	27.2
75+	343	252	91	11.7	10.9	12.5	9.0	9.9	6.3	5.9	6.1	5.4	25.3	25.9	24.1
Race/ethnicity															
Non-Hispanic White	7192	4328	2864	19.3[b]	23.0	15.3	15.0[a]	16.4[a]	13.6	7.6	9.3	5.8	37.6[a]	43.2[a]	31.5[a]
African American	1655	1083	572	18.5	21.4	14.7	16.1	16.5	15.8	7.4	8.1	6.4	37.9	41.9	32.9
Latino	434	264	170	13.7	17.9	9.7	10.2	10.3	10.1	4.8	6.0	3.6	24.7	29.5	20.6
Other race/ethnicity	327	210	117	18.0	17.5	18.7	10.8	6.8	16.3	8.4	11.2	4.8	33.6	31.6	35.8

Education														
Less than 12 years	1834	1173	661	17.2	19.0	14.9	9.2[a]	9.9[a]	8.3[a]	6.9[a]	8.6[a]	4.7[b]	29.5[a]	33.4[a]	24.5[a]
12 years	3493	2260	1233	19.4	23.1	14.7	16.1	15.8	16.5	6.8	8.1	5.3	38.0	41.9	33.0
13–15 years	2225	1372	853	19.1	23.1	14.7	17.2	19.7	14.5	6.9	8.8	4.8	38.2	45.2	30.6
16 years and more	2037	1069	968	19.1	22.9	16.0	14.5	16.5	12.8	9.5	11.8	7.5	39.2	46.3	33.4
Household income														
Lowest quarter	2599	1891	708	19.7	21.9	15.7	11.8[a]	12.4[a]	10.8[b]	9.5[a]	10.9[b]	6.8	36.9	40.4[b]	30.2
2nd quarter	2276	1374	902	19.9	24.1	15.5	14.7	17.3	12.0	8.6	10.0	7.0	38.4	44.9	31.4
3rd quarter	2194	1272	922	20.0	23.3	16.5	15.5	15.9	15.1	6.3	7.3	5.3	37.1	41.2	32.7
Highest quarter	1280	680	600	17.4	22.3	13.3	16.9	20.6	13.6	6.6	8.8	4.7	36.8	46.1	28.9
Total	9620	5893	3727	18.9	22.3[c]	15.1	14.8	15.7[c]	13.7	7.5	9.1[c]	5.7	36.9	41.9[c]	31.3

Note. Percentages across care recipient types for total kin and nonkin care can total less than total of subcomponents because 409 respondents reported providing care to more than one person in and/or out of their household at T1 or T2. US National Survey of Families and Households, primary respondents (T1:1987–1988, T2:1992–1993).

[a] Chi-square test revealed significant group differences (within column) in proportions at p < .01 (two-tailed).

[b] Chi-square test revealed significant group differences (within column) in proportions at p < .05 (two-tailed).

[c] Chi-square test revealed significant gender differences (across bottom row) in proportions at p < .01 (two-tailed).

NSFH2. The rates were significantly higher for women than for men (22.3% vs. 15.1%).

Primary kin care rates differed across age groups, with highest rates overall during the midlife decades from ages 35–54, when about one in four US women and one in five US men reported providing primary kin care. Total rates also differed across race/ethnicity, with fewer Latinos reporting primary kin care. It is unclear why Latinos reported lower primary kin caregiving rates in this study, given that they reported more normative obligation to primary kin and more hours of instrumental help to primary kin in MIDUS. One possibility is that owing to more recent immigration to the United States many Latinos may be living separate from older and/or more disabled family members who have remained in their "home" countries and are therefore not living in close enough proximity to be provided with hands-on caregiving help. Rates did not differ by education or household income.

Caregiving for secondary kin. Rates of secondary kin care were somewhat lower than for primary kin care but were still sizable. Overall, about 14.8% of US adults reported providing care to a secondary kin member either at T1 or T2 of the NSFH; rates were higher for women than men (15.7 vs. 13.7%). Total group difference tests suggested more secondary kin care at younger ages, among non-Hispanic whites and African Americans, among persons with at least a high-school education, and among persons not in the lowest income quarter.

Caregiving for nonkin. Care for persons outside of family is likely to be more voluntary, and therefore is of particular interest in terms of considering acts of compassionate love. Overall, 7.5% of adults – almost one in ten women (9.1%) and slightly more than one in twenty men (5.7%) – reported providing care for a disabled friend, neighbor, or other non-family member at one or both times of assessment. Total rates were highest among women, adults ages 55–74, and respondents with the highest education, yet also among respondents with the lowest income.

These results demonstrate considerable rates of compassionate acts by friends and neighbors to provide help to others in times of need owing to disablement (see also Himes & Reidy, 2000; Liebler & Sandefur, 2002). In considering these numbers it is also important to remember this analysis estimates caregiving only at two time points about five years apart; lifetime incidence rates of care for nonkin others would be expected to be much higher.

Total caregiving for kin or nonkin. Overall, the last columns of Table 5.3 for combined kin or nonkin care demonstrate that more than one-third of respondents (36.9%) reported providing some caregiving for a disabled family member or friend either at NSFH1 or NSFH2. More than two in five women (41.9%) reported such caregiving. Almost one in three men reported kin or nonkin caregiving (31.3%) at one or both time points. Again, it is important to note that lifetime incidence of caregiving would be expected to be much higher.

The relatively high rates of caregiving for kin as well as nonkin reported here are also relatively convergent with results from a US national sample study conducted in 2003 by the American Association for Retired Persons and the National Alliance for Caregiving, which estimated there were 44.4 million US caregivers aged 18 and older (21% of the population at these ages) providing unpaid care to one or more adults who needed help due to some level of functional limitation (Caregiving in the US, 2004). Women reported caregiving more often than men, yet four of ten caregivers were men. While 83% of the instances of caregiving reported were for family members, a sizable percentage of care recipients named were nonkin (17%). Overall, these prevalence rates from two national studies suggest the importance of family as well as friend and neighbor caregiving as increasingly important manifestations of compassionate acts in adulthood.

Conclusions and Suggestions for Future Research

This chapter aimed to provide linkages between theory guiding the empirical study of compassionate love and theory and research in the fields of adult development and life-course studies. It also sought to contribute to a population perspective on how cultural and sociodemographic contextual characteristics contribute to differences in selected compassionate norms and compassionate acts in the contemporary US adult population.

We have suggested that there is compatibility between the biopsychosocial model of compassionate love guiding this volume and contemporary biopsychosocial theoretical frameworks in human development, including bioecological systems theory and the life-course perspective. Human development theories that emphasize psychological readiness (e.g., Eriksonian theory) and material readiness (e.g., Maslovian theory) can provide additional insights in understanding the antecedents of internalized compassionate norms and compassionate action. Structural social exchange theory can also inform the science of compassionate love, through its consideration of how societal and subcultural social norms can influence patterns of expectable giving and receiving in a society.

Biopsychosocial theoretical frameworks emphasize developmental contextualism – that is, individual development occurs within specific sociocultural milieux. The model guiding the science of compassionate love likewise posits the importance of physical, social, and cultural contextual factors in shaping compassionate motives and behaviors. We found a number of sociocultural (as indexed by gender, age, race/ethnicity, educational status, and income status) differences in compassionate normative obligation and action. Future research in the science of compassionate love might benefit from continuing to consider such sociodemographic differences and to further "unpack" the processes whereby such differences occur. For example, there was relatively consistent evidence across the compassionate norms and acts considered here that women report higher levels than men. This is a finding that deserves more research exploration. Is this finding a result of gender differences in biological proclivity toward compassionate norms and acts and/or differences in normative socialization regarding obligations regarding giving to kin and nonkin? Are gender differences due to differences in expectations in social roles (e.g., in enacting the role of adult child as a daughter vs. a son), and/or differences in other societal opportunity structures that enhance compassionate norms and allow for compassionate acts (e.g., more emphasis on giving to others in the jobs that women are more likely to occupy than men)?

Age differences in compassionate norms suggested greater altruistic normative obligation at midlife and older ages vs. younger ages, yet normative obligation as well as emotional and instrumental support to secondary kin and friends was highest at youngest ages. Overall contribution to others was rated highest among midlife adults (ages 35–64), when we might expect societal expectations and opportunities for social contributions to others to be greatest. Future work might further explore how much age differences in norms and acts reflect developmental differences as might be suggested by Eriksonian theory, structural differences in role expectations as might be suggested by sociological norm theory, cohort differences, or some combination of developmental, structural, and cohort differences.

African Americans are noteworthy in their high levels of reported altruistic normative obligation, even in the face of considerable discrimination and disadvantage in US society (Kessler, Mickelson, & Williams, 1999). African Americans also were found to report the highest levels of normative obligation to friends and overall personal contribution to the wellbeing of others. Other research that has suggested that African American culture emphasizes inclusiveness, cooperation, interdependence, and collective responsibility (Baldwin & Hopkins, 1990).

Latinos, another relatively disadvantaged group in US society, were found to report the highest normative obligation to primary kin and the highest mean number of hours per month of instrumental support to primary kin. Does this reflect a greater ideological "familism" in Latino culture (Vega, 1990), which is influencing compassionate norms and compassionate acts toward primary kin?

To better understand the antecedents of compassionate normative obligation it would be worthwhile for future research to investigate the question: How much is internalized compassionate normative obligation a result of ideological factors, such as a culture-based value orientation (e.g., communitarianism or familism), in contrast to structural factors, such as access to greater resources (e.g., income, education)?

Education and household income are structural factors that might be expected to constrain compassionate normative obligation and action at the lower end of the socioeconomic status spectrum and to enhance opportunities for compassionate normative obligation and action at the higher end of the socioeconomic status spectrum, yet the patterns reported here did not consistently reflect this expectation. For example, higher education was associated with higher rates of volunteering, but also with lower rates and fewer mean hours per month of instrumental support to primary kin. Higher income was associated with higher normative obligation to primary kin, but lower levels of obligation to secondary kin and friends. More research is needed to understand why adults with higher education (in contrast to lower education) reported lower normative obligation to primary kin, less emotional support to kin and nonkin, and less instrumental support to primary kin. Additionally, it would be worthwhile to explore why persons with higher income (in contrast to lower income) reported lower normative obligation to friends and rates of nonkin caregiving.

Large population surveys can continue to be useful for the scientific study of compassionate love. For example, use of longitudinal survey data that allow for analyses of change in compassionate normative obligation and compassionate actions over time in relation to other time-invariant as well as time-varying biological, psychological, and social factors would be useful in further clarifying causal processes related to compassionate love. Multivariate analyses were beyond the scope of this descriptive chapter, but future, more targeted population research, which develops models that better account for the confounding of sociodemographic factors (e.g., race/ethnicity and income) will yield more precise conclusions.

In sum, this theoretical overview and population perspective suggests that US adults are reporting generally high levels of compassionate normative obligation and action; therefore, such motivational norms and actions are relatively "typical" for adults. These results fit with developmental theories such as those of Erikson and Maslow, as well as sociological theories that emphasize the widespread socialization of norms in all societies to increase an internalized sense of obligation, and therefore motivation, to provide support to others. Our results suggest that levels of compassionate norms and compassionate acts often differ by sociocultural location; therefore, it is important to continue to take into account such sociocultural differences in future research, as well as develop further research to help better account for these differences. Developmental and life-course scholars are well situated to contribute to the science of compassionate love through further analysis of existing data with relevant constructs, and through the inclusion of new measures like the Compassionate Love Scale (Sprecher & Fehr, 2005) in future surveys. Likewise, additional scholarship concerning the biopsychosocial antecedents, correlates, and consequences of compassionate love will make an important contribution to the fields of adult development and life-course studies by providing a more complete understanding of the biopsychosocial conditions that foster the development of more compassionate individuals and more compassionate societies.

Acknowledgments

Support for this research was provided by the National Institute on Aging (AG12731, AG 206983, AG20166), and the National Institute on Mental Health (MH61083).

References

Allison, L. D., Okun, M. A., & Dutridge, K. S. (2002). Assessing volunteer motives: A comparison of open-ended probe and Likert rating scales. *Journal of Community and Applied Social Psychology, 12,* 243–255.

Almeida, D. M., & McDonald, D. A. (2005). The national story: How Americans spend their time on work, family, and community. In J. Heymann & C. Beem (Eds.), *Unfinished work: Balancing equality and democracy in an era of working families* (pp. 180–203). New York: New Press.

Aspinwall, L. G., & Staudinger, U. M. (Eds.). (2003). *A psychology of human strengths: Fundamental questions and future directions for a positive psychology.* Washington, DC: American Psychological Association.

Baldwin, J. A., & Hopkins, R. (1990). African-American and European-American cultural differences as assessed by the Worldviews Paradigm: An empirical analysis. *Western Journal of Black Studies, 14,* 38–52.

Batson, C. D. (2002). Addressing the altruism question experimentally. In S. G. Post, L. G. Underwood, J. P. Schloss, & W. B. Hurlbut (Eds.), *Altruism and altruistic love: Science, philosophy, and religion in dialogue* (pp. 89–105). Oxford, England: Oxford University Press.

Biegel, D., Sales, E., & Schulz, R. (1991). *Family caregiving in chronic illness: Heart disease, cancer, stroke, Alzheimer's disease, and chronic mental illness.* Newbury Park, CA: Sage.

Blake, J., & Davis, K. (1964). Norms, values and sanctions. In R. E. L. Faris (Ed.), *Handbook of modern sociology* (pp. 456–484). Chicago: Rand McNally.

Brim, O. G., Ryff, C. D., & Kessler, R. C. (2004). The MIDUS National Survey: An overview. In O. G. Brim, C. D. Ryff, & R. C. Kessler (Eds.), *How healthy are we? A national study of well-being at midlife* (pp. 1–34). Chicago: University of Chicago Press.

Bronfenbrenner, U. (1989). Ecology systems theory. In R.Vasta (Ed.), *Annals of Child Development: Vol. 6* (pp. 187–249). Greenwich, CT: JAI Press.

Bronfenbrenner, U., & Morris, P. A. (1998). The ecology of developmental processes. In R. M. Lerner (Ed.), *Handbook of child psychology: Theoretical models of human development* (5th ed., Vol. 1, pp. 993–1028). New York: John Wiley.

Caregiving in the US Study. (2004). Bethesda, MD and Washington, DC: National Alliance for Caregiving and AARP.

Cohen, S., & Wills, T. A. (1985). Stress, social support, and the buffering hypothesis. *Psychological Bulletin, 98*, 310–357.

Davey, A., & Eggebeen, D. J. (1998). Patterns of intergenerational exchange and mental health. *Journal of Gerontology: Psychological Sciences, 53*, P86–P95.

de St. Aubin, E., McAdams, D. P., & Kim, T., (Eds.). (2004). *The generative society: Caring for future generations*. Washington, DC: American Psychological Association.

Eggebeen, D., & Hogan, D. P. (1990). Giving between generations in American families. *Human Nature, 1*, 211–232.

Elder, G. H., Jr., Johnson M. K., & Crosnoe, R. (2003). The emergence and development of life course theory. In J. T. Mortimer and M. J. Shanahan (Eds.), *Handbook of the life course* (pp. 3–22). New York: Plenum.

Erikson, E. H. (1950). *Childhood and society*. New York: Norton.

Erikson, E. H. (1969). *Gandhi's truth: On the origins of militant nonviolence*. New York: Norton.

Featherman, D. L. (1983). The life-span perspective in social science research. In P. B. Baltes & O. G. Brim, Jr. (Eds.), *Life-span development and behavior: Vol. 5* (pp. 1–57). New York: Academic Press.

Fischer, C. S. (1982). *To dwell among friends*. Chicago: University of Chicago Press.

Fleeson, W. (2001). Judgments of one's own overall contribution to the welfare of others. In A. S. Rossi (Ed.), *Caring and doing for others: Social responsibility in the domains of family, work, and community* (pp. 75–96). Chicago: University of Chicago Press.

Gerstel, N., & Sarkisian, N. (2006). Marriage: The good, the bad, and the greedy. *Contexts, 5*, 16–21.

Greenfield, E. A., & Marks, N. F. (2004). Formal volunteering as a protective factor for older adults' psychological well-being. *Journal of Gerontology: Social Sciences, 59B*, S258–S264.

Himes, C. L., & Reidy, E. B. (2000). The role of friends in caregiving. *Research on Aging, 22*, 315–336.

Hirst, M. (2005). Carer distress: A prospective, population-based study, *Social Science and Medicine, 61*, 2005, 697–708.

Homans, G. C. (1961). *Social behavior: Its elementary forms*. New York: Harcourt, Brace and Jovanovich.

Kessler, R. C., Mickelson, K. D., & Williams, D. R. (1999). The prevalence, distribution, and mental health correlates of perceived discrimination in the United States. *Journal of Health and Social Behavior, 40,* 208–230.

Keyes, C. L. M., & Haidt, J. (Eds.). (2003). *Flourishing: Positive psychology and the life well lived.* Washington, DC: American Psychological Association.

Keyes, C. L. M., & Ryff, C. D. (1997). Generativity in adult lives: Social structural contours and quality of life consequences. In D. P. McAdams & E. de St. Aubin (Eds.), *Generativity and adult development: Psychosocial perspectives on caring for and contributing to the next generation* (pp. 227–264). Washington, DC: American Psychological Association.

Krause, N., Herzog, A. R., & Baker, E. (1992). Providing support to others and well-being in later life. *Journal of Gerontology: Psychological Sciences, 47,* P300–P311.

Lévi-Strauss, C. (1969). *The elementary structures of kinship.* Boston: Beacon Press.

Liebler, C. A., & Sandefur, G. D. (2002). Gender differences in the exchange of social support with friends, neighbors, and co-workers at midlife. *Social Science Research, 31,* 364–391.

Marks, N. F. (1995). Midlife marital status differences in social support relationships with adult children and psychological well-being. *Journal of Family Issues, 16,* 5–28.

Marks, N. F. (1996). Caregiving across the lifespan: National prevalence and predictors. *Family Relations, 45,* 27–36.

Marks, N. F., Bumpass, L. L., & Jun, H. (2004). Family roles and well-being during the middle life course. In O. G. Brim, C. D. Ryff, & R. C. Kessler (Eds.), *How healthy are we? A national study of well-being at midlife* (pp. 514–549). Chicago: University of Chicago Press.

Maslow, A. H. (1954). *Motivation and personality.* New York: Harper & Row.

Maslow, A. H. (1968). *Toward a psychology of being* (2nd Ed.). New York: Van Nostrand.

Maslow, A. H. (1971). *The farther reaches of human nature.* New York: Viking.

Mauss, M. (1954). *The gift.* New York: Free Press.

McAdams, D. P. (2001). Generativity in midlife. In M. Lachman (Ed.), *Handbook of midlife development* (pp. 395–443). New York: John Wiley & Sons.

McAdams, D. P. (2006). *The redemptive self.* Oxford: Oxford University Press.

McAdams, D. P., & de St. Aubin, E. (1992). A theory of generativity and its assessment through self-report, behavioral acts, and narrative themes in autobiography. *Journal of Personality and Social Psychology, 62,* 1003–1015.

McAdams, D. P., Hart, H. M., & Maruna, S. (1998). The anatomy of generativity. In McAdams, D. P., & de St. Aubin, E. (Eds.), *Generativity and adult development: Psychosocial perspectives on caring for and contributing to the next generation* (pp. 7–43). Washington, DC: American Psychological Association.

McPherson, M., Smith-Lovin, L., & Brashears, M. E. (2006). Social isolation in America: Changes in core discussion networks over two decades. *American Sociological Review, 71,* 353–375.

McPherson, M., Smith-Lovin, L., & Cook, J. M. (2001). Birds of a feather: Homophily in social networks. *Annual Review of Sociology, 27,* 415–444.

Mikulincer, M., & Shaver, P. R. (2005). Attachment security, compassion, and altruism. *Current Directions in Psychological Science, 14*, 34–38.

Moen, P., Dempster-McClain, D., & Williams, R. M., Jr. (1992). Successful aging: A life course perspective on women's multiple roles and health. *American Journal of Sociology, 97*, 1612–1638.

Moore, G. (1990). Structural determinants of men's and women's personal networks. *American Sociological Review, 55*, 726–735.

Morrow-Howell, N., Hinterlong, J., Rozario, P. A., & Tang, F. (2003). Effects of volunteering on the well-being of older adults. *Journal of Gerontology: Social Sciences, 58B*, S137–S145.

Musick, M. A., Herzog, A. R., & House, J. S. (1999). Volunteering and mortality among older adults: Findings from a national sample. *Journal of Gerontology: Social Sciences, 54B*, S173–S180.

Mutran, E., & Reitzes, D. C. (1984). Intergenerational support activities and well-being among the elderly: A convergence of exchange and symbolic interaction perspectives. *American Sociological Review, 49*, 117–130.

Oman, D., Thoresen, C. E., & McMahon, K. (1999). Volunteerism and mortality among the community-dwelling elderly. *Journal of Health Psychology, 4*, 301–316.

Peterson, C., & Seligman, M. E. P. (2004). *Character strengths and virtues: A handbook and classification.* Washington, DC: American Psychological Association.

Post, S. G., Underwood, L. G., Schloss, J. P., & Hurlbut, W. B. (Eds.). (2002). *Altruism and altruistic love: Science, philosophy, and religion in dialogue.* Oxford, England: Oxford University Press.

Preston, S. D., & de Waal, F. B. M. (2002). The communication of emotions and the possibility of empathy in animals. In S. G. Post, L. G. Underwood, J. P. Schloss, & W. B. Hurlbut (Eds.), *Altruism and altruistic love: Science, philosophy, and religion in dialogue* (pp. 284–308). Oxford, England: Oxford University Press.

Rossi, A. S. (2001). Domains and dimensions of social responsibility: A sociodemographic profile. In A. S. Rossi (Ed.), *Caring and doing for others: Social responsibility in the domains of family, work, and community* (pp. 97–134). Chicago: University of Chicago Press.

Rossi, A. S., & Rossi, P. H. (1990). *Of human bonding: Parent–child relations across the life course.* New York: Aldine de Gruyter.

Sabatelli, R. M., & Shehan, C. L. (1993). Exchange and resource theories. In P. G. Boss, W. J. Doherty, R. LaRossa, W. R. Schumm, & S. K. Steinmetz (Eds.), *Sourcebook of family theories and methods* (pp. 385–411). New York: Plenum Press.

Seligman, M. E. P., & Csikszentmihalyi, M. (Eds.). (2000). Positive psychology. [Special Issue] *American Psychologist, 55 (1).*

Seligman, M. E. P., Steen, T. A., Park, N., & Peterson, C. (2005). Positive psychology progress: Empirical validation of interventions. *American Psychologist, 60*, 410–421.

Settersten, R. A., Jr. (2003). Propositions and controversies in life-course scholarship. In R. A. Settersten (Ed.), *Invitation to the life course: Toward new understandings of later life* (pp. 15–45). Amityville, NY: Baywood Publishing Company.

Snyder, C. R., & Lopez, S. J. (Eds.). (2002). *Handbook of positive psychology.* Oxford, England: Oxford University Press.

Spitze, G., & Logan, J. (1992). Helping as a component of parent–adult child relations. *Research on Aging, 14,* 291–312.

Sprecher, S., & Fehr, B. (2005). Compassionate love for close others and humanity. *Journal of Social and Personal Relationships, 22,* 629–651.

Stoller, E. P. (1985). Exchange patterns in the informal support networks of the elderly: The impact of reciprocity on morale. *Journal of Marriage and the Family, 47,* 335–342.

Sweet, J. A., & Bumpass, L. L. (1996). *The National Survey of Families and Households Waves 1 and 2: Data description and documentation.* Center for Demography and Ecology, University of Wisconsin-Madison (http://www.ssc.wisc.edu/nsfh/home.htm).

Sweet, J. A., Bumpass, L. L., & Call, V. (1988). *The design and content of the National Survey of Families and Households.* NSFH Working Paper #1. Madison, WI: Center for Demography and Ecology, University of Wisconsin.

Taylor, S. E., Klein, L. C., Lewis, B. P., Gruenewald, T. L., Gurung, R. A. R., & Updegraff, J. A. (2000). Behavioral responses to stress in females: Tend-and-befriend, not fight-or-flight. *Psychological Review, 107,* 411–429.

Thibaut, J. W., & Kelley, H. H. (1959). *The social psychology of groups.* New York: Wiley.

Turner, M. J., Killian, T. S., & Cain, R. (2004). Life course transitions and depressive symptoms among women in midlife. *International Journal of Aging and Human Development, 58,* 241–265.

Underwood, L. G. (2002). The human experience of compassionate love. In S. G. Post, L. G. Underwood, J. P. Schloss, & W. B. Hurlbut (Eds.), *Altruism and altruistic love: Science, philosophy, and religion in dialogue* (pp. 72–105). Oxford, England: Oxford University Press.

Vega, W. A. (1990). Hispanic families in the 1980s: A decade of research. *Journal of Marriage and the Family, 52,* 1015–1024.

Wilson, J. (2000). Volunteering. *Annual Review of Sociology, 26,* 215–240.

Wilson, J., & Musick, M. A. (1997). Work and volunteering: The long arm of the job. *Social Forces, 76,* 251–272.

Wolff, J. L., & Kasper, J. D. (2006). Caregivers of frail elders: Updating a national profile. *Gerontologist, 46,* 344–356.

Part III

Compassionate Love in Close Relationships

6

Empathy and Compassionate Love in Early Childhood: Development and Family Influence

Brenda L. Volling, Amy M. Kolak, and Denise E. Kennedy

Imagine if you will the following scenarios. In the first instance, the family consists of a mother, father, and two little girls. The older sister, Catherine,[1] is around 6 years old and the younger, Anne, is approaching 2½ years. Catherine seems jealous of her younger sister and avoids her as much as possible as they walk around examining the laboratory playroom. When asked to play together with a Fisher-Price play set, the two girls squabble continuously throughout the 15-minute session. Catherine pushes Anne away from the toy several times until Anne eventually gets up and begins to whine and complain to her mother, who is sitting nearby completing a questionnaire, that her sister won't let her play with the toys. The mother requests that Catherine share, and Anne once again joins her sister on the floor to play. Eventually, the two begin to pull the toy as if in a tug-of-war, fighting over who should have it, until the younger girl finally throws herself onto the floor and starts to have a tantrum, kicking her feet and crying. Her older sister, now the triumphant victor, continues to play with the toy nearby and gleefully watches her younger sister cry. The mother must now intervene not only to calm the younger child, but also to prevent the two girls from further conflict and aggression.

The second family also consists of a mother and father, but with two little boys. The older brother, Nathan, is around 5 and his younger brother, Jared, is also 2½ years of age. From the moment the two children walk into the laboratory, Nathan looks out for his younger brother, making sure he has toys to play with and showing him how things work. Jared listens attentively and follows his older brother around the room. During the cooperative play session with the Fisher-Price play set, the two sit side by side, taking turns running the small cars up and around, moving little people, and pretending to be firemen. They laugh repeatedly and clearly enjoy each other's company. As Nathan is being escorted to the door

---

[1]   Names have been changed in order to protect the confidentiality of the participants.

so he can complete a social-cognitive perspective-taking task in a nearby room, Jared begins to cry, calling out for his older brother and telling the experimenter he wants his older brother to stay. Nathan, hearing his younger brother crying, turns to him, tells him it will be OK and that he will be right back. While he is gone, Jared sits on the floor and plays, but watches the door intently for his older brother's return, even though his parents sit nearby completing questionnaires. When Nathan does return, Jared greets him with a big smile and runs to him at the door.

The exchanges described above were actually witnessed in our research laboratory as part of a study designed to address the family factors that contribute to the development of compassionate behavior, empathy, and early moral development. In both cases, the experimenter asked the mothers at the end of the visit whether the interactions that occurred in the laboratory were typical of the children's interactions in the home. Both mothers claimed they were, with one mother emphasizing how exhausting it was to constantly supervise the two children and the other, now pregnant with her third child, explaining how easy it was to parent them because they got along so well. The vastly different interactions between the children in these two families underscore the individual differences that exist within families and the manner in which young children share and cooperate, show concern for another's distress, help one another, and care for each other. Not only are the interactions between siblings in these families so completely different, but as the mothers' comments attest, so, too, is the experience of parenting. One family is constantly negotiating sibling rivalry and conflict and the other family enjoys the harmony and peace of two young children mutually engaged in cooperative play.

One of the central aims of this chapter is to examine the earliest beginnings of compassionate love in the family. From a developmental standpoint, compassionate behavior in adulthood must, in part, stem from the experiences that the individual had as a child. We are particularly interested in whether young children are capable of demonstrating compassionate behavior toward others, at what age this concern for another becomes apparent, and what early socialization experiences facilitate such behavior. This chapter focuses specifically on the development of compassionate behavior and empathic concern in very young children from infancy into preschool. Along the way, we will note some of the difficulties in attempting to do research with such young children and the unique methodologies that are often used to capture the emergence of compassion and empathic concern in the early years.

We provide a brief overview of the development of children's compassionate behavior within a broader framework of moral development, before presenting a model of young children's compassionate behavior based on Underwood's (2002) model designed to understand compassionate love in adulthood. We then turn to a review of the development of empathy and related prosocial behaviors in early childhood, spanning from infancy into the preschool years. This section is then followed with a presentation of our research, designed to investigate the development of compassionate love in the toddler and preschool years and the family factors that either encourage or undermine a young child's expression of compassion and empathic concern for others. The chapter ends by noting current gaps in our knowledge of early compassionate behavior and some suggestions for future research directions.

Early Moral Development and the Emergence of Conscience

Compassion and concern for another have long been the focus of research on moral development. Young children's empathy and concern in response to another's distress, their feelings of guilt after wrongdoing, and their attempts to make amends, are indicators of emerging moral awareness and internalized conscience. Expressing compassion for another must involve not only the ability to feel another's emotions (empathy), but also the ability to understand that there are moral rules (standards of conduct) that govern one's behavior. As Turiel (1998) notes, when someone comes to the aid of another in distress, it may be because they feel the other's distress (i.e., empathy), but also because they know it is wrong to do nothing and allow another to suffer (i.e, moral understanding). Although parents provide the external support early on that teaches a child right from wrong and, hopefully, the proper response to harmful behavior, the child must eventually develop the ability to internally regulate his or her conduct in line with society's values, norms, and rules in the absence of parental surveillance (i.e., an internalized conscience). The period between 2 to 3 years of age is a critical developmental stage for the emergence of conscience, including empathy, thus making the second year of life a significant developmental period in which to study early compassionate behavior and moral emotions (Emde, Biringen, Clyman, & Oppenheim, 1991; Kagan & Lamb, 1987; Kochanska, 1993; Kopp, 1982).

Compassionate Love in Early Childhood

Underwood (2002) defines altruistic or compassionate love in adulthood as a self-giving, caring love that values the other person highly and is intended to give full life to the other. According to her model, the key components of compassionate love include a cognitive understanding of the self, an awareness of being part of something beyond oneself, and an evaluation of another's situation and the ability to act accordingly. In her model, each person is situated in a larger sociocultural context. As such, external sources such as the family, the peer group, and even the media can influence the expression of compassionate behavior toward others. According to Underwood, emotional expressions and acts of compassion are motivated not only by these external social forces, but also by internal processes within the individual that balance the desires of the self with a sense of concern for others. When the internal motivation is positive and focused on others, not only will the individual show a capacity for compassionate love, but the essence of showing compassion toward others can have beneficial effects on one's own development. Conversely, when motives of the self outweigh those of the other, individuals may act inappropriately or harshly. Such behavior may have negative consequences for the individual as well as for others, because his or her inept behavior alters the social landscape and affects the formation of close social relationships. Behavior that may appear helpful or altruistic on the surface cannot be deemed an expression of compassionate love if the underlying motivation is for selfish, rather than selfless, reasons.

Because an advanced understanding of the self and others appears central to the concept of compassionate love, some may mistakenly believe that young children are unable to express concern for another's well-being or demonstrate compassionate behaviors. On the contrary, as we will show, small children are quite capable of expressing behaviors and emotions that reflect the earliest beginnings of compassionate love. As Zahn-Waxler and her colleagues (Zahn-Waxler, Radke-Yarrow, Wagner, & Chapman, 1992) note, 2-year-old children have "the cognitive capacity to interpret the physical and psychological states of others, the emotional capacity to affectively experience the other's state, and the behavioral repertoire that permits the possibility of trying to alleviate discomfort in others" (p. 127).

A Model of Compassionate Love in Early Childhood

We have taken the basic model of compassionate love formulated by Underwood (2002) and replaced the mature adult forms with children's prosocial behaviors, emotions, and cognitive understanding (see Figure 6.1). The left-hand side represents the young child nested in the social and physical environment. The family environment consisting of parent–child, sibling, and in some cases, marital relationships, is the

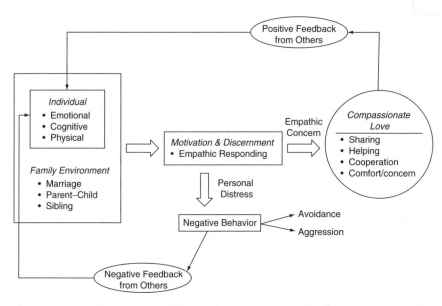

Figure 6.1 A Model of Compassionate Love in Early Childhood

most proximal environment for the young child and exerts a significant influence on the child's social and emotional development. On the far right are the prosocial behaviors (i.e., helping, sharing, comforting) that reflect compassionate love expressed by the young child. The middle box represents the motivations or internal processes involved that are responsible for the expressed behaviors, including the moral emotions of guilt and empathy, as well as cognitive advances in self–other understanding and affective perspective-taking. The link from empathy to prosocial behaviors is not necessarily a direct one. Batson (Batson, Fultz, & Schoenrade, 1987) suggested that there are two different forms of empathic responding for adults, and Eisenberg and her colleagues later applied these concepts to children (see Eisenberg, Fabes, & Spinrad, 2006, for a review). The first, *sympathy,* is an other-oriented emotional reaction to another's emotional state that consists of feelings of sorrow or empathic concern. Given the other-orientation, sympathy or empathic concern as noted in Figure 6.1 is expected to motivate altruistic behavior (e.g., comforting or helping another). The second, *personal distress,* is a self-focused aversive emotional reaction (e.g., anxiety) and reflects an egoistic motivation. Children experiencing sympathy often will try to alleviate the distress of another, whereas children experiencing personal distress often will try to avoid the distressing situation or respond aggressively toward the other

(Eisenberg et al., 1989; Eisenberg, Fabes, Miller, & Shell, 1990). Children experiencing personal distress may help or comfort another, but if so, it is based on an egoistic motivation with the goal of alleviating their own distress rather than the distress of the other. Whether empathic concern or personal distress is the underlying motivation will determine whether the child acts altruistically or otherwise, and these differences in the child's actions also will be met with different responses from others (see Figure 6.1). As the earlier descriptions of sibling interaction in our laboratory suggested, the responses from others in the child's immediate environment will be very different, depending on whether children act prosocially or antisocially.

A Developmental Framework for the Emergence of Empathy and a Concern for Others

Hoffman (1982, 2000) proposed a theoretical framework highlighting the development of children's empathy by delineating four stages. In the first stage, *global empathy*, young infants are unable to differentiate between the self and others' emotional states and may often experience personal distress in response to another's distress. Newborn infants will cry in response to another infant's cry, and this emotional contagion is viewed as an early precursor to global empathy. In later infancy, infants actually may seek out others in an effort to calm their own distress when exposed to another's distress, but they also may ignore the distress of another (Hay, Nash, & Pederson, 1981; Volling, 2001).

Starting in the second year, *egocentric empathy* emerges. At this stage, toddlers are able to distinguish between their own and others' emotional states and often have a simple understanding of others' emotions. Toddlers can now experience empathic concern for another person and can offer assistance to another in distress rather than seeking comfort from an adult to diminish their own distress. Still, toddlers' understanding of others' internal emotional states is relatively limited. Even though they may offer assistance or aid in response to a distressed other, their behaviors reflect an egoistic orientation. In this case, they may offer the other person items that they themselves would find comforting and not necessarily what would provide comfort to the other in need. For instance, a toddler might offer a distressed sibling his or her own blanket or security object rather than discern what the older sibling might want or need (see Dunn, 1988).

The third stage of *empathy for another's feelings* is apparent as early as the second and third years of life and reflects children's abilities to take the perspective of others and an appreciation that others may experience different emotions and desires than they do. Here, children are capable of engaging in prosocial behaviors that reflect their understanding of another's emotional needs rather than the egocentric focus of the previous stage. Further, children become increasingly capable of empathizing with a wider range of emotions and can now engage in more elaborate prosocial responses to victims of distress or others in need of assistance.

In the fourth stage, *empathy for another's life condition*, children's growing cognitive understanding allows them somewhere around the period of late childhood to experience empathic concern outside the immediate situation. Children are able to feel empathy for individuals not immediately present and to understand the social circumstances surrounding another's misfortune. In this case, they may have empathic feelings for the suffering and adversity of entire social groups based on their more sophisticated understanding of self, other, and the wider society (e.g., homeless, abused children, impoverished individuals).

In the next section, we provide a brief review of the literature in the infant, toddler, and preschool years underscoring young children's empathic concern for others and their sense of responsibility for others in distress. Along the way, we will compare these findings with Hoffman's model, noting whether there is support for these different developmental periods. Because of the young age of these children, much of the research uses creative paradigms conducted either in the research laboratory or in the home environment. Direct observations allow the researcher to actually witness the child's empathic responses to others, in contrast to research in which empathy or compassion are assessed with self-reports, where social desirability may be a threat. Throughout this section, we will highlight many of these observationally based methods and the findings resulting from them.

Empathy Research with Infants and Toddlers

Research examining distress reactions during infancy suggests that infants respond differentially to the sound of cries from another infant (Sagi & Hoffman, 1976; Simner, 1971). For example, infants tend to be more distressed by a real baby cry than a synthetic cry. Infants in the real baby cry condition cry more frequently and for longer than those infants assigned to other conditions (Sagi & Hoffman, 1976). Hoffman (1982) suggested that from birth, humans are biologically predisposed to respond to others' distress. The research in this area suggests that these innate, involuntary reactions, more specifically, infants' crying in response to real baby cries, during the first few days of life may in fact be the earliest indicator of empathy toward others' distress. Though these first signs may be remarkably unsophisticated initially, distress reactions eventually give rise to more sophisticated and complex empathic reactions toward the end of the first year (Zahn-Waxler & Radke-Yarrow, 1982).

Research by Zahn-Waxler and colleagues (Zahn-Waxler & Radke-Yarrow, 1982; Zahn-Waxler, Radke-Yarrow, & King, 1979; Zahn-Waxler et al., 1992), in which mothers were trained to be observers of their own toddler children's reactions to naturalistic distress occurring in the home, revealed a wide range of behaviors, including self-focused distress reactions and prosocial interventions that were interpreted as empathic concern for others. Prosocial interventions took a number of forms, with toddlers providing verbal comfort (e.g., reassuring a person that he or she will be OK), physical comfort (e.g., patting, hugging, or kissing), and/or help (e.g. getting Band-Aid) in an effort to alleviate another's distress. Moreover, they documented developmental changes in children's emotional responding from 10 months to 2½ years, with children becoming less self-focused in their responses (Zahn-Waxler & Radke-Yarrow, 1982). In fact, at around 18 months of age, there was a considerable shift in toddlers' empathic responding, with distress reactions increasingly accompanied by, or altogether replaced with, children's efforts to interact positively with those in distress (Zahn-Waxler & Radke-Yarrow, 1982).

Toddlers' empathic reactions also have been observed during distress simulations (Zahn-Waxler & Radke-Yarrow, 1982; Zahn-Waxler et al., 1979). In this case, either the mother or an unfamiliar adult simulated distress and the toddlers' reactions to the distress were noted. Although toddlers' reactions differed somewhat across naturalistic and simulated distress situations (i.e., toddlers exhibited greater personal distress to naturally occurring distress in the home than during simulations), toddlers' reactions across the two contexts were highly correlated. For example, toddlers who were unresponsive to naturalistic distress also were unresponsive to simulated distress, and toddlers' personal distress reactions in the home and in simulations were correlated (Zahn-Waxler & Radke-Yarrow, 1982). Moreover, there was strong correspondence in toddlers' prosocial interventions (e.g., verbal and/or physical behavior intended to alleviate another's distress) to naturalistically occurring distress and simulated distress (Zahn-Waxler & Radke-Yarrow, 1982; Zahn-Waxler et al., 1979). The emergence of empathy during the second year of life appeared to be associated with toddler's increasing self-awareness and their rudimentary ability to differentiate themselves from others. Toddlers as young as 23 months were more likely to respond to their mother's distress when they had higher scores on self–other understanding (Zahn-Waxler et al., 1992).

Researchers consistently have found that toddlers tend to express more empathic behavior toward their mothers than toward unfamiliar adults during these distress simulations, regardless of the toddler's age

(Spinrad et al., 2006; Young, Fox, & Zahn-Waxler, 1999; Zahn-Waxler & Radke-Yarrow, 1982), although some research found this only to be the case as children approached 2 years of age (van der Mark, van IJzendoorn, & Bakermans-Kranenburg, 2002). For 16-month-old children, van der Mark et al. (2002) found no difference in the amount of empathy expressed toward mothers and unfamiliar adults. These studies underscore the importance of the interpersonal context in which children witness distress, with toddlers far more likely to respond to their mothers than to an unfamiliar adult. It is perhaps not surprising that children would be more distressed by and empathic toward a parent with whom they have formed a close relationship, yet it is noteworthy that even though toddlers express more empathy toward their mothers than an unfamiliar adult, they do not dismiss the unfamiliar adult's distress. Spinrad and Stifter (2006), for instance, found that 18-month-old toddlers actually showed more concerned attention toward the unfamiliar adult and exhibited more personal distress during these simulations than during the mother simulations, even though they provided more help to their mothers. Taken together, the research on the emergence of empathy during toddlerhood indicates that, consistent with Hoffman's perspective, even young children are observant of another's distress and act accordingly, either by inquiring about the harmful incident or by offering comfort to the distressed other.

In addition to this research with mothers and unfamiliar adults, naturalistic home observations conducted by Dunn and Munn (1986) provide descriptive data on naturally occurring sibling distress. In this case, they distinguished between distress that was either caused or not caused by the sibling. As might be expected, the younger siblings experienced considerably more distress when they were 18 and 24 months of age than their older siblings, who were 2 years older, on average. Although rates of ignoring and comforting behavior were fairly similar regardless of whether the sibling was the cause or not, watching another's distress occurred more frequently when the child had not caused the distress. But, children were more likely to exacerbate the distress of their sibling and laugh if they had actually caused the distress.

Researchers have yet to extensively examine toddlers' reactions to distress simulated by their fathers and within the broader family context. However, some work has indicated that young children respond with a variety of positive and negative emotions, including distress, to background anger between unfamiliar adults (Cummings, 1987; Cummings, Iannotti, & Zahn-Waxler, 1985; Cummings, Zahn-Waxler, & Radke-Yarrow, 1981), anger displayed in the home (Cummings, Zahn-Waxler, & Radke-Yarrow, 1984), and marital discussions (Easterbrooks, Cummings, & Emde, 1994).

Empathy Research with Preschoolers

According to Hoffman's (2000) theory, by the time children reach the preschool period they develop more advanced cognitive abilities, are capable of empathizing with a broader range of emotions, and are using more sophisticated means in responding to another's distress. Between the ages of 2 and 3, children become aware that other individuals' feelings differ from their own (Denham, 1998; Dunn, 1988; Harris, 1989; Saarni, 1999; Wellman & Liu, 2004). Moreover, toddlers of around 2 years of age can talk about the internal emotional and cognitive experiences of self and others (Bretherton, Fritz, Zahn-Waxler, & Ridgeway, 1986; Kendrick & Dunn, 1982). As children become more mature and sophisticated in their language ability and their ability to understand more complex emotions (e.g. disappointment, betrayal, guilt), they become better equipped to respond empathically. For example, when exposed to an empathy-eliciting film, 4- to 6-year-old children expressed facial/gestural cues and reported emotions that were consistent with empathic reactions to another's distress (Eisenberg, McCreath, & Ahn, 1988). Miller, Eisenberg, Fabes, and Shell (1996) also found that preschool children's self-reports and facial measures during exposure to others' distress (e.g., a film portraying a boy/girl falling and getting injured) were related to increased levels of moral reasoning and empathy. Perspective-taking and the ability to understand others' thoughts and emotions emerge in the preschool period (Denham, 1986). Research with preschool children has demonstrated that by the ages of 3 and 4, children are developmentally able to display an advanced capacity for empathy that is not demonstrated in earlier developmental periods (e.g., Eisenberg et al., 1988).

With advances in empathic responding now possible, studies of preschool children's vicarious emotional responsiveness (i.e., feeling another's emotions vicariously) have used a variety of methodologies (e.g., self-report, parent report, observations, physiological indices). Personal distress and sympathy reactions, both vicarious emotional responses to potential distress, have been assessed by showing preschool children a videotape of other children or adults in distressing circumstances (e.g., hurt in an accident: Barnett, 1984; Eisenberg et al., 1988; Miller et al., 1996). Children's facial reactions of sadness and concern, their physiological responses (e.g., heart rate acceleration or deceleration), and their self-reported emotions (i.e., pointing to emotion faces) to the video clips have been used to differentiate sympathy from personal distress responses.

In one study designed to examine 4- to 7-year-olds' empathic responding to different emotions, Eisenberg et al. (1988) showed preschoolers and second-graders three short films designed to elicit: anxiety (e.g., a boy and girl were frightened by a thunderstorm), sadness (e.g., a girl was sad over the death of a pet bird), and cognitively induced empathy (e.g., a handicapped girl discussed her handicap in a neutral tone of voice and attempted to walk). The cognitive sympathy film required the viewer to interpret situational cues rather than to attend only to the facial expressions or tone of voice of the protagonist in the film. Children's facial expressions (e.g., fear, sadness, gaze aversion) were coded while viewing each film clip. In addition, children's nonverbal self-reports of the intensity of emotion they experienced were obtained by having children point to a set of pictures displaying facial expressions (e.g., sadness, happiness, sorrow). Seven-year-old children were better able to differentiate their reports of emotions and empathic responsiveness to the cognitive sympathy film, whereas the 4-year-old preschool children were not. Physiological measures also were employed in this study to differentiate sympathy from personal distress reactions. Heart rate (HR: beats per minute) accelerated when 4- to 7-year-old children expressed personal distress and decelerated when a child expressed sadness (i.e., sympathy) while watching the emotion-inducing video clips. Different patterns of HR response were reported for each of the three emotion-eliciting films (sadness, anxiety, and concern), suggesting that different emotions were related to distinct patterns of autonomic response. Heart rate consistently accelerated when children in the study watched the anxiety-evoking film and decelerated linearly during the sadness and cognitive sympathy-inducing films. Heart rate also was associated with children's facial responses in that boys' facial sadness during the sad film was associated with heart rate deceleration. More generally, Eisenberg and her colleagues have shown that preschoolers' personal distress and sympathy reactions can be distinguished by using different methods (facial, heart rate, self-report) that converge in systematic and predictable ways.

In another study, Miller et al. (1996) studied the relations of moral reasoning and vicarious emotion to prosocial behavior in 4- to 5-year-old children by obtaining verbal and nonverbal self-reports of emotions (e.g., neutral, sad, happy, or sorry) and facial responses (e.g., fearful, sad, or happy affect) to two short films of children getting hurt on a playground. Children were told that although the children in the film were now in hospital and doing fine, they needed something to do. They were then given the option to sort and package crayons for the hospitalized children so these children could color while in the hospital, or they could choose to play with toys in the room instead. Helping behaviors were scored based on the number of crayons sorted and boxed in a 3-minute period. Children's prosocial moral reasoning also was assessed and the children's facial and behavioral responses to simulations of mother and experimenter distress (e.g., mother pretends to bang her knee while getting up from a chair, experimenter pretends to prick finger with a pin) were coded. Overall, preschool children's self-reports and facial/gestural indices of other-oriented vicarious responsiveness were positively related to more advanced moral reasoning and greater engagement in peer-directed prosocial responding. They did not find a positive relation between needs-oriented reasoning and empathic responding which has been found in studies with older children and adolescents (Eisenberg, Miller, Shell, McNally, & Shea, 1991; Eisenberg, Shell, Pasternack, & Lennon, 1987). Thus, preschoolers with limited moral reasoning abilities do not respond empathically as one would expect for older children.

In a study designed to address empathy in preschoolers, Barnett (1984) had 3- to 5-year-olds play one of two games (e.g., Puzzle Board or Buckets) and children were told they had (a) won, (b) lost, or (c) nothing (the no-outcome control group). Children were then shown a 4-minute videotape of another child failing at the same game the child played. Children's emotional responses were coded after they played the game and again after they watched the child in the film play the game. Preschoolers reported more empathy for a saddened peer when the pre-schooler was in a similar condition (both children lost) than in a different condition (one child won the game, but the other lost), suggesting that preschool children may have limited perspective-taking and, thus, ability to empathically respond in situations in which people experience different emotional outcomes.

Naturalistic and semi-naturalistic observational techniques also have been employed to study prosocial interactions and vicarious emotional responsiveness in preschoolers. Eisenberg et al. (1988) placed two 3- to 5-year-old children in a room with one desirable toy that they were sup-posed to share and then left the preschoolers alone to look for more toys. Eisenberg et al. (1988) hypothesized that sad/concerned reactions in response to sharing one desirable toy, as opposed to anxious reactions, would be positively related to spontaneous prosocial responsiveness (e.g., sharing the toy). There was a significant positive relation between sympathy and the frequency of spontaneous prosocial actions. Also, girls' (not boys') sympathetic reactions were positively correlated with requested sharing behaviors. Overall, the relations between empathy and prosocial behavior appeared to be contingent on the child's motives, with empathic responses associated with prosocial behavior when they were a result of other-oriented concern (i.e., sympathy) as opposed to egoistic or compliance-related concerns.

In general, the research with children in the preschool to early elementary school years indicates that children of this age are quite sophisticated in using situational information to evaluate the emotional experience of others. Further, researchers are able to reliably distinguish between children's personal distress and sympathy reactions in a number of laboratory paradigms and naturalistic settings using multiple research methods. Sympathy appears to be related to children's prosocial responses and as children mature, to more other-oriented moral reasoning. Personal distress reactions, on the other hand, do not predict young children's prosocial orientation toward others. Children experiencing personal distress often avoid the distressed other.

Family Socialization and the Development of Empathic Concern

Even though young children are capable of expressing concern and providing help to others, there are large individual differences between children (Dunn, 1987; Eisenberg, Fabes, Schaller, & Miller, 1989; Zahn-Waxler & Robinson, 1995), as demonstrated by the scenarios with which this chapter opened. Some children engage in prosocial interaction and require little coaxing to apologize or confess when they have transgressed, whereas other children are easily engaged in conflict, use angry aggression toward others indiscriminately, and express little concern or sympathy for others. Socialization experiences in the family are significant predictors of the marked individual differences seen between children. In the early years of childhood, several areas of family socialization have been considered, including the security/insecurity of early attachment relationships, disciplinary strategies, and parents' socialization of negative emotional experiences. Although each of these areas has received some research attention, we focus here on emotion-socialization experiences within the family and their role in the development of empathic responding and concern for others in the early years of childhood.

Emotion Socialization in the Family

Empathy and vicarious emotional responding are shaped by specific emotion-socialization practices within the family context. Parents purposefully direct children's behaviors and respond to children's emotions in line with cultural display rules or family display rules that govern the appropriate expression of emotions in specific social situations. For instance, some parents may punish the expression of such negative emotions as anger or sadness, whereas others may actively encourage the open expression of such emotions so the child can learn how to cope with a range of emotional experiences. Such differences in parental practices no doubt play a role in whether children will express empathy and respond to another's distress, whether they will actively avoid a distressed other, or worse, further victimize and perpetuate another's distress. As the descriptive scenarios at the beginning of this chapter attest, young children are very aware of the distress of others. Whereas Nathan responded to his younger brother's tears with comfort and compassion, Catherine sat nearby and not only ignored her younger sister's upset, but delighted in it. How is it that children learn to respond so differently to the distress of others?

Research with infants has shown that parents begin to socialize emotional responses at a very young age (Malatesta, Culver, Tesman, & Shepard, 1989; Tronick, 2003). If young infants are to develop and move from Hoffman's early phase of global distress to a point where they are able to modulate their own distress and begin to respond to the distress of others, it is imperative that parents provide the early external supports to do so. According to Kopp (1989), parental responses to infant distress provide the external support for emotion regulation and allow infants to connect the caregiver with the relief of their own distress. In this regard, infants as young as 1 month of age quiet and soothe themselves at the sight and sound of an approaching caregiver (Lamb & Malkin, 1986) and by 4 to 5 months of age, infants actually will protest and cry louder if their mothers do not pick them up. The assumption here is that infants come to expect that mothers will pick them up, and when they do not, they cry louder to gain their mothers' attention. The caregivers' sensitivity and responsiveness to infant distress and emotional signals help infants learn to modulate their own arousal (Cassidy, 1994) and eventually, through repeated associations of caregiver responsiveness and distress relief, the infant becomes other-oriented and comes to trust the availability of others to assuage his or her own arousal. When parents are not responsive to the infant's distress and the young child is left to self-soothe in the midst of an emotionally arousing situation, he or she learns to rely on self-oriented regulation and use strategies to self-soothe (i.e., finger- or thumb-sucking). These self-focused strategies can indeed serve the infant well in some situations, but given the young age and dependency of the infant on adult intervention, the number of situations under which self-soothing will allow the infant to cope independently with negative arousal is surely limited.

Given the extant research on maternal sensitivity and the emergence of young children's self-regulation (Feldman, Greenbaum, & Yirmiya, 1999; Kochanska & Murray, 2000; Raver, 1996; Volling, McElwain, Notaro, & Herrera, 2002), it is surprising to find so little research linking the emergence of self- and other-oriented emotion regulation in infancy to the self- and other-oriented vicarious emotional responding (i.e., sympathy, personal distress) in older children. Nonetheless, there are several studies looking at emotion-socialization practices and preschool and early elementary school-age children's vicarious emotional responding.

In this line of work, Eisenberg, Fabes, and colleagues (Eisenberg, Fabes, & Murphy, 1996; Eisenberg et al., 1999; Fabes, Leonard, Kupanoff, & Martin, 2001; Fabes, Poulin, Eisenberg, & Madden-Derdich, 2002) have focused on supportive (i.e., emotion-focused, comforting, and problem-focused reactions) and nonsupportive (e.g., punitive, dismissing, or minimizing reactions) emotion-socialization strategies and their relations to children's sympathy and personal distress. Eisenberg and her colleagues suggest that when parents punish the expression of negative emotions, children will heighten their level of emotional arousal in future emotion-evoking situations in which distress is encountered. The increased arousal might overwhelm children, leading to personal distress, which could undermine children's social functioning and lead to dysregulated behavior. Similarly, when parents punish or discourage the expression of negative emotions, children will learn to view their own and others' emotions as threatening or frightening and will choose to avoid situations in which negative affect is experienced.

The influence of parents' punitive reactions on children's empathic concern and comforting behavior may differ as a function of the age of the child and which negative emotion is at the center of the parent–child interaction – sadness or anger, for instance. If parents punish children for feelings of sadness, children may not wish to express such emotions for fear of further punishment. They may become dysregulated and unsure of how to cope with their own distress. On the other hand, parents who punish or discourage children's expressions of anger, particularly anger directed toward another, may use the moment to teach children about the harm their actions have for others, leading children to reflect on the consequences of their actions for the well-being of another (Eisenberg, Fabes, Schaller, Carlo, & Miller, 1991). These two socializing experiences would have very different outcomes with respect to the development of young children's empathic concern and early moral awareness. The findings with regard to punitive parental reactions are not simple or direct because the effect of parental restrictiveness on harmful emotions such as anger appears to differ, depending on the age and gender of children. For instance, maternal restrictiveness of kindergarten girls is related to physiological indicators of personal distress in a sympathy induction, but this is not the case for older children or for boys, in general (Fabes et al., 1994).

Other nonsupportive parental responses to children's negative emotions include the parents' attempts to minimize the seriousness of children's distress, as well as parental distress reactions in which the parents themselves become uncomfortable or overaroused with the children's negative emotions. Parents who become distressed in response to their children's distress are expected to avoid their children during distressing situations when the children may need them most, or engage in other nonsupportive and nonresponsive parenting behaviors. Although much of the research examining parental minimizing and distress reactions has been conducted with older children in elementary school, the findings reveal that nonsupportive parental reactions are associated with negative outcomes in children (e.g., low peer acceptance, social competence, and coping skills; see Eisenberg et al., 1996).

In contrast to nonsupportive emotion-socialization practices, parents also may support and encourage the expression of children's negative emotions and provide comfort when children are sad or distressed. When parents respond sensitively to their children's emotional arousal, offer them support and encourage them to seek solutions to the problems they face, children can learn to regulate distressing emotions and eventually cope with stressful situations in the future. In addition, such sensitive and responsive reactions to children's emotional upset can enhance the attachment relationship between parents and their children, leading to feelings of security and a sense of trust that others will respond to their needs in moments of despair. Encouragement of the expression of negative emotions legitimizes children's emotional experiences, and allows them to express their distress openly and shamelessly and to learn that an individual in distress needs to be nurtured and offered assistance.

Research in the early years on supportive emotional reactions by parents has indicated that 4- to 5-year old-children's perceptions of their parents' comforting behaviors to their negative emotions, assessed through the use of vignettes and dolls for children to act out parental responses, are positively related to teachers' reports of empathy and cooperativeness with peers (Denham, 1997). Further, parental positive responsiveness to emotional expression is positively correlated with preschoolers' understanding of others' emotions (Denham, Zoller, & Couchoud, 1994), which others have found predict young children's responses to a distressed sibling (Garner, Jones, & Palmer, 1994; Stewart & Marvin, 1984).

Supportive and nonsupportive parental reactions to the child's negative emotions may change over time in line with parents' different expectations about the age-appropriateness of emotional expression. Whereas parents of preschool boys may be inclined to comfort and emotionally respond to the boy's distress, parents may come to expect more mature forms of self-regulation as children get older and be far less likely to use emotion-focused or comforting behaviors with older children, especially boys. However, Eisenberg, Fabes, and Murphy (1996) found that even for boys in Grades 3 to 6, maternal emotion-focused reactions to negative emotions (e.g., comforting) were positively related to the boys' comforting behavior in response to an infant's distress. Further, maternal encouragement of emotion expression and problem-focused reactions to negative emotions also were positively associated with boys' comforting behavior, whereas low to moderate levels of paternal encouragement of emotional expression were related to girls' comforting behavior toward an infant.

In general, the literature provides evidence that supportive emotion-socialization practices are positively related, and nonsupportive emotion-socialization practices are negatively related, to a host of prosocial outcomes for children from preschool through elementary school. Research in this area, however, would benefit from examining younger cohorts of children in the toddler and preschool years to determine if emotion-socialization practices (a) change over time and (b) differ across mothers and fathers. Eisenberg et al. (1996) did find that mothers of children in Grades 3 to 6 reported greater encouragement of emotional expression, as well as emotion-focused and problem-focused reactions to children's negative emotions than did fathers, who reported more punitive and minimization reactions. We turn next to the role of fathers in the development of children's empathic concern.

Fathers and Children's Empathic Concern

Even though studies have considered the role that emotion-socialization practices have on young children's development of empathy and empathic concern (Eisenberg, Cumberland, & Spinrad, 1998), these investigations have focused almost exclusively on mothers. Nonetheless, research investigations that have included fathers find that fathers also contribute to children's empathic responding and prosocial behavior. For example, fathers' participation in childcare (Bernadett-Shapiro, Ehrensaft, & Shapiro, 1996; Koestner, Franz, & Weinberger, 1990), their responsiveness to children's distress (Davidov & Grusec, 2006; Roberts & Strayer, 1987), their expression of positive emotions (Boyum & Parke, 1995; Cassidy, Parke, Butkovsky, & Braungart, 1992; Garner, Robertson, & Smith, 1997), and their responses to children's negative emotions (Eisenberg et al., 1996) have been linked to 4- to 13-year-old children's expressions of positive and negative emotions, as well as to empathic concern into adulthood (see Koestner et al., 1990).

Most studies including fathers and their role in the development of empathic responding have not focused on young children in infancy, toddlerhood, or the preschool years, but rather, on older children in early elementary school or middle school. Next, we briefly summarize some of these studies in an effort to discern how fathers may contribute to the emergence of empathy in early childhood and what areas future research may need to explore in this regard.

Studies of children's empathic behavior that have considered fathers' contributions have found both direct (Eisenberg et al., 1991) and indirect links (Strayer & Roberts, 1989, 2004) between paternal emotional expressions and their children's empathic behavior. For example, Eisenberg et al. (1991) found that when fathers reported more sympathy, their elementary school-aged sons displayed less distress and scored higher on both dispositional sympathy and empathy. Strayer and Roberts (1989) did not find associations between fathers' and children's empathy for 6-year-old children, but they did find that fathers' empathy was positively related to children's prosocial behavior in the home (e.g., child is helpful and cooperative, child tends to give, lend, and share). One comprehensive multi-method study examined both mothers' and fathers' empathy and their emotional expression with respect to children's empathic behavior in a sample of children ranging from 5 to 13 years of age (Strayer & Roberts, 2004). Strong links were found between parents' empathy and emotional expressiveness and children's empathy; however, these associations appeared to be mediated by parenting behaviors such as the parents' use of control, warmth, and discipline and their encouragement of emotions (Strayer & Roberts, 2004). Taken together, these findings suggest that fathers' empathy and emotional expressiveness are important correlates of children's empathic responding during middle childhood.

Because fathers' contributions to children's empathic development during infancy and toddlerhood largely have been unexplored, we know little about the father's role in young children's development of empathy. Yet given that this period in the emotional lives of children is filled with dramatic changes, as children move from self-focused behaviors to prosocial interventions when witnessing another's distress (Zahn-Waxler & Radke-Yarrow, 1982; Zahn-Waxler et al., 1979), fathers are likely to be important in influencing whether children's empathic responding increases in complexity. In order to gain a more nuanced understanding of fathers' contributions to children's early empathy development, future research investigations in this area should consider fathers' expression of emotion and their socialization practices when empathy-related abilities begin to emerge during the first few years of life.

Siblings as Socializing Agents

The sibling relationship is enduring, lasting from birth to old age, yet there is a dearth of research that looks at the socialization of children's empathy in the sibling context. McHale and Crouter (1996) found that middle-school children spend most of their time with siblings (33%) as opposed to time spent alone (12%), with peers (13%), or parents (23% mothers, 19% fathers). This also appears to be true of relationships between young siblings. For example, in a study during early infancy of the second-born child, at 1 year of age, children spent almost as much time interacting with a sibling as they did with their mother, and considerably more time than with their father (Lawson & Ingleby, 1974). Finally, in a study of 4- to 6-year-old siblings, Bank and Kahn (1975) found that siblings spent twice as much time with one another than with their parents.

Sibling relationships are an excellent context for learning how to constructively solve disagreements, to modulate emotions in the presence of conflict, and to develop prosocial behaviors. Sibling relationships are first managed and modulated by caregivers when children are too young to do so themselves. As children grow, they become more involved in managing their sibling relationships (Bedford & Volling, 2004). Dunn and Kendrick (1981, 1982) studied the period after the arrival of a second child and examined the older sibling's behavior toward the infant sibling at several points after the birth. Forty percent of the mothers reported that older siblings wanted to comfort the younger siblings when they were distressed and that by 8 months after the birth, the older siblings exhibited empathic concern for their younger siblings. By the final visit at 14 months, 65% of mothers reported that older siblings expressed empathic concern toward a younger sister or brother. Mothers also reported that the younger, 14-month-old siblings displayed concern about, or understanding of, the older child's emotional state, which might be viewed as an early form of empathy and perspective-taking ability.

Because older siblings are more advanced cognitively than their younger sibling counterparts, they also display more prosocial behaviors (e.g., helping, sharing, and comforting) toward a younger sister or brother than vice versa (Dunn & Munn, 1986). As the examples of sibling interaction presented at the beginning of this chapter indicate, siblings can be involved in mutually positive exchanges that promote the development of a cooperative and close sibling relationship, which in turn, can promote prosocial behavior and empathic concern for one another. On the other hand, siblings' mutual hostility and aggression toward one another can contribute to a competitive and agonistic relationship that, over time, undermines individual competencies, including a lack of concern for the welfare of others. Through their interactions with one another, each sibling socializes the other. In their longitudinal study of siblings and the development of prosocial behavior, Dunn and Munn (1986) found that at 18 months, younger siblings have the ability to share, help, or comfort an older sibling 3 to 6 years of age, as well as identify distress and frustration in their older sisters or brothers and to actively attempt to assuage their problems. Further, young children with an older sibling who cooperatively plays with them develop into more cooperative individuals than children without cooperative older siblings (Dunn & Munn, 1986). It appears, then, that those older siblings who are more cognitively capable of displaying prosocial behaviors can have a positive socializing influence on their younger siblings.

Several studies have examined sibling caregiving by preschool children and the factors that predict whether older siblings provide care to a younger one. A laboratory separation paradigm has been used in most of these studies in which parents are asked to separate and leave the older preschooler alone with their younger toddler or infant sibling. Often, younger siblings will become distressed upon parental separation and the older siblings' caregiving responses to the distress are observed (Garner, Jones, & Miner, 1994; Stewart, 1983; Stewart & Marvin, 1984; Teti & Ablard, 1989; Volling, 2001; Volling, Herrera, & Poris, 2004). These studies have shown that by the end of the preschool period, children can become an effective surrogate attachment figure for their infant sibling and provide comfort in response to the infant's distress (Stewart, 1983; Stewart & Marvin, 1984). For instance, Stewart (1983) found that 52% of 4-year-old siblings responded to the distress of their infant sibling and offered some form of caregiving when their mother left the room. Several investigators also have found that emotional role-taking and cognitive perspective-taking positively predict the older sibling's caregiving behavior (Garner et al., 1994; Stewart & Marvin, 1984).

In comparison to research on parenting, there is far less research examining the effect of sibling relationships on the development of young children's prosocial behavior, in general, and empathic concern, specifically. Yet, the research to date suggests that siblings by virtue of the time they spend with one another and the types of interactions in which they engage, may play a significant, but largely ignored, role in the development of empathy in young children.

The Present Study

The primary goal of the current research was to consider children's emerging empathic responding and prosocial behavior within the context of the family environment. Our review of the literature illustrates that few studies have considered either fathers' or siblings' influence on young children's empathic development. The research reported here was designed as a first step in remedying this oversight. To this end, mothers, fathers, and siblings were included in our investigation of young children's early development of compassionate behavior.

Study Design and Methods

The sections that follow present the methods used with our children and their parents to assess empathy and early prosocial responding in line with the model presented earlier. The different laboratory paradigms that were developed to assess compassionate love in the form of concern, cooperation, sharing, and helping between young children will be described. Unique observational methods were required to capture the empathic concern and prosocial orientations of children between the ages of 2 and 6 years.

The participants for this study were 57 families consisting of a biological mother and father and at least two young children. The younger child in all cases was 2 years old, on average, given the significance of this age period for the emergence of a "moral sense" (Kagan & Lamb, 1987). Families were recruited through various means: a university subject pool for developmental psychology, birth records from the university hospital, advertisements in local newspapers and community organizations, flyers and pamphlets placed in health clinics, pediatricians' offices, and local churches. Study criteria included: (1) married spouses with (2) a 2-year-old child, with (3) at least one older sibling between the ages of 4 and 6. All participating families were invited to the research laboratory for two observational visits.

The first visit involved only the spouses and the second, occurring approximately a month later, involved all family members (mother, father, and siblings). We focus here only on the assessments conducted at the second visit. During that visit, after a brief 15-minute warm-up period of family interaction, all family members viewed a series of short video clips to assess parents' and children's sympathy and personal distress reactions. Mothers and fathers were then videotaped interacting with children in several triadic (each parent with both children) freeplay sessions and siblings were observed in very brief paradigms to assess cooperation, sharing, and helping. Each family was paid $50 for their participation and children received small gifts at the end of the second visit.

Compassionate Behavior in Early Childhood

Based on our model in Figure 6.1, socialization experiences in the family predict empathic responding which can take the form of either empathic concern for others (i.e., sympathy) or personal distress. Children expressing empathic concern are more likely to engage in compassionate behaviors observed in our laboratory paradigms. Children experiencing personal distress are more likely to avoid distressed others or actually be aggressive toward them. For present purposes, we focus predominantly on the links between parental reports of the children's empathic concern, the children's compassionate behavior, and family socialization.

We examined four domains of compassionate behavior: comfort (i.e., alleviating another's emotional distress), helping (i.e., alleviating another's non-emotional needs by offering aid or assistance), sharing (i.e., giving or allowing another child temporary use of a toy), and cooperation (i.e., the ability to engage in joint and cooperative play)

Comfort. A research assistant (RA) entered the laboratory and helped the experimenter move a small table in front of a sofa to a side area, telling parents and children that they needed to make room so the children could play with the toys they were about to bring out. As they moved the table, the RA pretended to drop the table leg on her foot. Both parents were told that we wanted to see the children's spontaneous reactions to the distress and were asked to therefore refrain from prompting their children to assist. A standard script was recited in which the experimenter inquired about the RA's injury. Both children's reactions to the distress simulation were coded on a six-point rating scale that was based on earlier work of Hastings, Zahn-Waxler, Robinson, Usher, and Bridges (2000) and assessed overall global concern with another's distress: (1) *No concern is evident* to (6) *Combined expressions of strong concern* (i.e., showing more than one behavioral or emotional expression).

Helping. Helping an adult in need of assistance was assessed with a task adapted from Yarrow and Waxler (1976). The experimenter entered with a clipboard, some papers, and a box of paper clips and sat down to talk to the children about the next "game" they were about to play. While looking through her instructions, the experimenter "accidentally" dropped the box of paper clips on the floor and it spilled. The experimenter exclaimed "Oh no! I can't believe I did that! Let me see if I can find my instructions here first" and continued to look through her papers. After 10 seconds, if the children had not helped, the experimenter provided the first prompt: "I just can't seem to get this all together here today" and began to pick up some clips. After another 10 seconds, if the children still hadn't helped, the experimenter turned to them and provided the second prompt: "Do you think you might be able to help me?" Children's helping was scored 3 if they helped spontaneously within the first 10 seconds after the clips spilled, 2 if they helped after the first prompt, 1 if they helped after the second prompt, and 0 if they never helped to pick up the paper clips.

Sharing. Sibling sharing was assessed using a fishing game adapted from Yarrow and Waxler (1976). An inflatable children's swimming pool was placed in the middle of the room and 10 plastic fish were placed inside (each fish had a magnet attached to its nose). The experimenter explained that the children were to take turns "fishing" and would win small prizes based on how many fish each of them caught: if they caught 1 fish they won 1 prize, 5 fish would get them 5 prizes, and 10 fish would get them 10 prizes. Only one fishing pole was supplied and the experimenter handed it to the older sibling first to start and then took a nearby seat where she was engaged in work. If squabbling or conflict arose, the experimenter gently reminded the children "Remember, you need to take turns," and then returned to her work. The sharing game was coded along several dimensions, including (1) *conflict* (the extent of disagreements, conflict, and hostility between siblings while they were to take turns) and (2) *cooperation* (the extent to which each sibling eagerly cooperated with the other in taking turns), which was coded separately for each of the two siblings.

Cooperative sibling play. After the distress simulation, the experimenter returned to the room with a Fisher-Price Mainstreet play set and proceeded to help the children assemble the toy, showing them how each piece worked. Parents were seated at a nearby table and completed questionnaires. They were asked to refrain from initiating interaction with their children, but were free to respond to them as they would at home if the children initiated interaction with them. The siblings were allowed to play with the toy for 15 minutes. Five-point global ratings from "not at all" to "extremely" were used to capture (a) *cooperative play involvement* (i.e., the extent to which both siblings were involved in joint play or joint pretend play), and (b) *conflict* (i.e., the extent and severity of conflict between siblings).

Children's Empathic Concern

Both mothers and fathers completed Kochanska's *My Child* questionnaire, a measure of conscience development, for both the older and younger siblings (Kochanska De Vet, Goldman, Murray, & Putnam, 1994). Although there are eight subscales (e.g., guilt, concern over good feelings with parent, apology), we focus here on the 13-item subscale of *empathic, prosocial response to another's distress* (e.g., "child will try to comfort or reassure another in distress", $\alpha = .78$ to .83 for the current sample). Because mothers' and fathers' reports for both the older sibling ($r = .63$, $p < .001$) and younger sibling ($r = .43$, $p < .001$) were significantly correlated, we averaged mothers' and fathers' reports to create a single score of empathic concern for the older and younger siblings. The younger siblings' age (in months) was significantly correlated with the parent composite of empathic concern for the younger sibling, $r = .51$, $p < .001$, but the older siblings' age was not correlated with parents' reports of the older siblings' empathic concern, $r = -.01$. Further, composites of empathic concern for older and younger siblings were correlated, $r = .44$, $p < .001$, indicating that younger siblings showed more empathic concern when parents also reported the older siblings were high in empathic concern.

Gender and age differences in empathic concern. A 2(sibling) by 4(gender dyad: older/younger sibling gender) ANCOVA controlling for the younger siblings' age and using parents' reports of empathic concern as the dependent variable revealed a significant main effect for sibling, $F(1,53) = 33.00$, $p < .001$, and a significant sibling by gender dyad interaction, $F(3,53) = 3.81$, $p < .05$. As expected, older siblings had higher empathic concern scores than did younger siblings, $M = 4.69$ and 4.30. Younger siblings in brother/brother (younger/older) and brother/sister dyads had lower empathic concern scores ($M = 4.23$ and 4.08, respectively) than younger siblings in sister/sister dyads ($M = 4.60$). There were no significant differences in the older siblings' empathic concern across the four gender dyads. Further, there were differences between older and younger siblings' empathic concern scores within gender dyads, except for the sister/sister dyad. In other words, older siblings in the brother/brother, brother/sister, and sister/brother dyads had higher empathic concern scores ($M = 4.53, 4.82$, and 4.66, respectively) than their younger siblings ($M = 4.22, 4.08$, and 4.29, respectively). Because younger sisters with older sisters showed more empathic concern than younger siblings in the other gender groups, they were more similar to their older sisters, suggesting that involvement with a highly empathic older sister may promote empathic concern, especially for younger sisters.

Because the sibling effect could be due to differences in age or the birth order of the siblings, we reran the analyses three times, once controlling for the age of the siblings (older and younger), the second time controlling for the birth order of the siblings, and the third time controlling for the age space between siblings. If the sibling effect was due to age, then the effect should be nonsignificant once age is controlled. A similar logic applies to birth order and the age space between siblings. The sibling effect remained significant regardless of whether we controlled for age or birth order, but became nonsignificant when controlling for age space, suggesting that it was the relative difference between siblings and not their absolute age or the birth order that was responsible for the sibling differences in empathic concern.

Relations between Empathic Concern and Laboratory Observations of Compassionate Behavior

Correlational analyses (and partial correlations controlling for the age of the younger sibling) examined the relations between parents' reports of the children's empathic concern and our observations of children's compassionate behaviors in the laboratory, in line with our model in Figure 6.1. Significant associations were found for the older siblings' empathic concern and the older siblings' helping score during the paper-clip task, $r = .47$, $p < 001$. The younger siblings' helping score also was correlated with parents' reports of the older siblings' empathic concern, $r = .39$, $p < .01$. Children's empathic concern was not correlated significantly with any of the other observational measures of compassionate behavior.

Family Environment and Early Socialization

Several questionnaires were used to assess family context variables in line with our model in Figure 6.1, including parental emotion-socialization practices, marital love, parents' empathic responding, and sibling relationship quality.

Emotion socialization. Mothers and fathers reported on emotion-socialization practices used with both the older and younger siblings in the family using the Coping with Children's Negative Emotions questionnaire (CCNES: Fabes et al., 2002). The measure contains the following six subscales (represented here by a single item example): *distress reactions* (e.g., "If my child becomes angry because he/she is sick or hurt and can't go to his/her friend's birthday party, I would get angry at my child"); *punitive reactions* (e.g., "If my child is panicky and can't go to sleep after watching a scary TV show, I would tell him/her to go to bed or he/she won't be allowed to watch any more TV"); *expressive encouragement* (e.g., "If my child falls off his/her bike and breaks it, and then gets upset and cries, I would tell my child it is OK to cry"); *emotion-focused reactions* (e.g., "If my child loses some prized possession and reacts with tears, I would distract my child by talking about happy things"); *problem-focused reactions* (e.g., "If my child is playing with other children and one of them calls him/her names, and my child then begins to tremble and become tearful, I would help my child think of constructive things to do"); and *minimize reactions* (e.g., "If my child is going over to spend the afternoon at a friend's house and becomes nervous and upset because I can't stay there with him/her, I would tell my child to quit overreacting and being a baby"). Alpha reliability for the scales ranged from .57 to .93, with a mean of .78.

We first examined parent and sibling differences in our emotion-socialization scores to determine if mothers and fathers differed in how they responded to young children's negative emotions. Based on earlier work with older children (Eisenberg et al., 1996) and research on gender differences in adults' emotional expression (Brody & Hall, 1993),

Table 6.1 Means (Standard Deviations) of Emotion Socialization as a Function of Parent and Sibling (n = 53)

Emotion socialization	Mother	Father	F (1, 52)	η_p^2	Older	Younger	F (1, 52)	η_p^2
1. Minimize reactions	2.26 (.10)	2.72 (.14)	9.94**	.16	2.50 (.12)	2.50 (.10)	ns	.00
2. Punitive reactions	2.08 (.08)	2.25 (.10)	ns	.00	2.19 (.09)	2.14 (.07)	ns	.05
3. Distress reactions	2.87 (.08)	2.89 (.10)	ns	.00	2.94 (.08)	2.81 (.08)	5.71*	.10
4. Emotion-focused	5.75 (.08)	5.39 (.10)	7.45**	.13	5.52 (.07)	5.62 (.08)	ns	.02
5. Problem-focused	5.56 (.08)	5.19 (.10)	10.09**	.16	5.44 (.07)	5.30 (.08)	4.28*	.08
6. Encourage expression	4.92 (.13)	4.20 (.16)	16.54***	.24	4.67 (.12)	4.45 (.14)	4.69*	.08

*$p < .05$, **$p < .01$, ***$p < .001$.
η_p^2 = effect size (partial eta squared).

we hypothesized that fathers would be more punitive and more likely to minimize negative emotions, whereas mothers would be more likely to encourage the expression of negative emotions, use more emotion-focused strategies to comfort their children, and perhaps be more likely to use problem-focused strategies to change the emotional experience. We conducted 2(parent) by 2(sibling) repeated measures ANOVAs with parent and sibling as repeated factors and the emotion-socialization scores as dependent variables. Table 6.1 presents the findings from these analyses. Significant parent effects were found for: minimize reactions, emotion-focused, problem-focused, and encourage expression. Mothers were less likely to minimize negative emotions than were fathers and more likely to encourage the expression of negative emotions, as well as use more emotion-focused and problem-focused strategies to help children cope with their emotions than were fathers.

Significant sibling effects were found for: distress reactions, problem-focused, and encourage expression. Here, parents reported being more distressed by the older siblings' negative emotions than the younger siblings', but also used more problem-focused strategies and openly encouraged the expression of emotions for older, as compared to younger, siblings (see Table 6.1). Again, the sibling effects could be attributed to either age differences between siblings or to birth order. We reran all analyses controlling for age of siblings and birth order to determine if the significant sibling and parent effects would no longer be significant. In both analyses, controlling for either age or birth order, all sibling effects became nonsignificant, as did all but one parent effect; the exception was minimize reactions which remained significant. These analyses reveal that the sibling differences in this case were due to both age differences and birth-order differences. Differences in how parents treat older and younger siblings in the family also appear to be due primarily to developmental differences between siblings.

Emotion socialization and children's empathic concern. We conducted correlations between emotion-socialization practices and siblings' scores on empathic concern. Only the mothers' reports of their distress reactions were significantly and negatively correlated with the older siblings' empathic concern, $r = -.32$, $p < .05$. There were two marginally significant correlations between the older siblings' empathic concern and the mothers' punitive reactions, $r = -.23$, $p = .10$, and her encouragement of expressiveness, $r = .26$, $p = .06$. For the younger sibling, partial correlations (controlling for the younger sibling's age) revealed that only the fathers' encouragement of expression of negative emotions was significantly and positively related to children's empathic concern, $r = .32$, $p < .05$; mothers' encouragement of expression showed a marginally positive association, $r = .24$, $p = .08$.

Marital love in the family. Mothers and fathers also completed the marital love scale from Braiker and Kelley's (1979) Intimate Relations Questionnaire, which assesses feelings of love toward one's spouse. Individuals rated the degree to which statements (e.g., "How close do you feel to your partner?") were characteristic of their relationship with their spouse (1 = "very little or not at all" to 9 = "extremely or very much"). Alpha coefficients were .83 and .82 for wives and husbands, respectively.

For older siblings, mothers' and fathers' reports of marital love were positively and significantly correlated with the older siblings' empathic concern, $r = .28$, $p < .05$ and $r = .34$, $p < .01$, respectively. There were no associations between marital love and the younger siblings' empathic concern.

Parental empathy and young children's empathic concern. Parents also completed the Interpersonal Reactivity Index (Davis, 1996), which consists of two subscales, each comprising seven items: *empathic concern* – the tendency for one to experience feelings of empathy and compassion for less fortunate others (e.g., "I am often quite touched by things that I see happen") and *personal distress* – one's experience of distress and discomfort at seeing others in distress (e.g., "I sometimes feel helpless when I am in the middle of a very emotional situation"). The subscales are internally consistent with alphas of .67 and .84 for mothers' and fathers' empathic concern and .77 and .75 for mothers' and fathers' personal distress. In the current study, only the fathers' empathy score was positively correlated with the older siblings' empathic concern, $r = .37$, $p < .01$.

Sibling relationships and children's empathic concern. Parents also completed the Sibling Inventory of Behavior (see Volling & Blandon, 2005) for the older siblings. The positive involvement scale which included items such as "has fun at home with sibling," "teaches sibling new things," and "shows sympathy when things are hard for sibling" was used. Internal consistency was excellent; $\alpha = .91$ and .90 for mothers and fathers. In order to create a more robust composite of the older siblings' positive involvement with their younger siblings, and because mothers' and fathers' scores were significantly correlated, $r = .45$, $p < .01$, a composite was created by averaging mothers' and fathers' scores. We ran partial correlations (controlling for the age of both siblings) addressing the relations between parents' reports of the older siblings' positive involvement with the younger sibling and both the older and younger siblings' empathic concern. This analysis allowed us to consider whether or not the older siblings' behaviors toward a younger sibling play a role in the development of empathic concern. Parents' reports of the older siblings' positive involvement with the younger sibling was positively related to both the older siblings' ($r = .43$, $p < .01$) and the younger siblings' empathic concern ($r = .57$, $p < .001$).

Table 6.2 Family and Parent Factors Predicting Older and Younger Siblings' Empathic Concern

Older sibling		Younger sibling	
Predictors	β	*Predictors*	β
Age of older sibling	.10	Age of younger sibling	.48***
Father's empathy	.28*	Father's encourage expressive	.27*
Mother's distress reactions	–.26*	Positive sibling involvement	.28*
Wife's marital love	.18		
Husband's marital love	.04		
Positive sibling involvement	.23†		
Adj. R2	.25	Adj. R2	.39
F (6, 49)	4.03**	F (3, 50)	12.37***

†p = .08, *p < .05, **p < .01, ***p < .001.

Multiple prediction of children's empathic concern from family factors. In the final analysis, we examined the multiple predictors of the children's empathic concern by using all family-level variables from the univariate analyses that showed significant relations with the outcome variables. For older siblings, multiple regression analyses were performed that included the age of the older sibling, the fathers' empathy, mothers' distress reactions, mothers' and fathers' reports of marital love, and positive sibling involvement. For younger siblings, this included the age of the younger sibling, fathers' encouragement of emotional expressiveness, and positive sibling involvement. The results are shown in Table 6.2. Whereas the overall model explained a significant 25% of the variance in the older siblings' empathic concern, only the father's empathy and the mother's distress reactions to negative emotions were unique predictors. For younger siblings, a significant 39% of the variance was explained, and all variables in the model were significant predictors of the younger siblings' empathic concern (see Table 6.2).

Conclusions and Future Research Directions

The analyses presented here examining the development of empathic concern among very young children revealed that not only are children of this age capable of expressing concern for another, but also that this concern is related to aspects of the family environment. First, as expected, we found that there were developmental differences in empathic concern for older and younger siblings in the family such that older siblings had higher scores on empathic concern than did their younger siblings.

Although the main effect of sibling in our ANOVA models could be due to either birth order or age, our follow-up analyses indicated that the sibling difference was due to the relative age difference between siblings and not whether one is first- or second- born. These results are clearly in line with earlier developmental research finding an increase in young children's empathic concern and interest in others' distress across the toddler and preschool years.

These developmental differences in empathic concern for older and younger siblings coincided with the sibling differences we also found with respect to parents' emotion-socialization practices. As one might expect, mothers and fathers were more distressed in response to the negative emotions of the older sibling than those of the younger sibling. These findings are consistent with the idea that parents expect children to be better at regulating emotions as they get older and that when an older sibling is perhaps not doing so, parents tend to become distressed. Parents also reported more problem-solving reactions to the older siblings' negative emotions than to the younger siblings, and also encouraged the expression of emotion for older siblings – more so than for younger siblings. Again, the difference in age between siblings appeared to be responsible for these sibling effects, but, so too, was birth order. Parents focused more on helping older siblings to find ways of remedying the problem situation giving rise to the negative emotions than they did with younger siblings, and actually reported that they encouraged the emotional expression of negative emotions more for older, than younger, siblings.

Although the original model of compassionate love formulated by Underwood does not emphasize developmental change, our results indicate that siblings of different ages express more or less empathic concern in line with developmental models underscoring children's increasing ability to express empathic concern as they mature. Further, parents may actually change their behavior in response to children as they get older. Thus, continuing longitudinal research is needed to examine whether there are stable individual differences in children's empathic concern over time and whether parents socialize negative emotions differently at older and younger ages. Such developmental differences may have important implications for the influence of family factors on the development of children's empathic concern.

We were surprised to find so few relations between the parents' reports of empathic concern, which we included as a motivational element in Underwood's model, and the children's compassionate behaviors as observed in the various laboratory paradigms designed to capture helping, sharing, cooperation, and comforting. Only the older and younger siblings' helping scores during the paper-clip task were correlated with the older siblings' empathic concern. It is not entirely clear why there were so few significant relations. The development of prosocial behaviors as diverse as helping a stranger pick up paper clips, responding to a stranger's distress during a simulation, playing cooperatively, and sharing with one's sibling may have different underlying motivations that are not simply a reflection of the individual child's empathic responding. Our model in Figure 6.1 focused only on empathic responding as an indicator of motivation and discernment, yet clearly there are other internal processes that are responsible for whether or not children act prosocially, take responsibility for their actions, and respond to distressed others. Such internal processes in young children could include self–other understanding, feelings of guilt after wrongdoing, and emotional perspective-taking, all of which have been linked to young children's social behaviors with others and moral awareness (Barrett, Zahn-Waxler, & Cole, 1993; Denham, 1986; Pipp-Siegel & Foltz, 1997). Quite possibly, the prosocial behaviors observed in our laboratory are related to these other internal predilections. Also, we relied on parents' reports of empathic concern and have not yet looked at children's facial expressions of sympathy and personal distress during video clips of distress situations. These direct observations of the children's facial distress and sympathy may better predict their compassionate behavior during the laboratory paradigms than parents' reports. In any event, both siblings in the current research were inclined to help a stranger spontaneously if parents reported higher empathic concern on part of the older sibling. In this case, having an older sibling with higher empathic concern appeared to benefit the younger sibling as well. Perhaps exposure to an empathic older sibling even when as young as 2 years of age provides a model of compassionate behavior for younger siblings. It is also quite possible, in line with the research of Dunn and Munn (1986), that empathic older siblings may direct their compassionate behaviors toward their younger siblings as early as the first year and as the toddlers mature, they begin to reciprocate.

In our model adapted from Underwood to understand the development of compassionate behavior among young children, the individual child is nested within a social and cultural context. For young children, the most immediate social context is that of the family. In contrast to earlier research that has focused predominantly on mothers and their influence on children's empathic concern and vicarious emotional responding, we were also interested in the quality of other family relationships including the father–child, marital, and sibling relationship. We believe that children come to learn about kindness, sharing, cooperation, and compassion through the daily interactions they have with all family members. Mothers may discipline an older sibling for hitting and hurting a younger sibling, pointing out the harmful consequences of his or her behavior, and perhaps demand firmly, yet warmly, that the older sibling make amends and apologize for the harm he or she has just caused. It is also through sibling interactions that older siblings learn to be kind to someone younger than themselves, share their personal belongings, and practice skills of negotiation, and younger siblings, as the recipients of acts of both kindness and hostility, learn to trust and forgive. It was not surprising to find that the positive involvement of an older sibling with a younger sibling, based on parents' reports, was related to the empathic concern of both siblings. The positive exchanges between older and younger siblings may facilitate the development of young children's empathic concern, but at the same time, the empathy, concern, and helping of the siblings toward one another no doubt enhances the development of a cooperative and caring sibling relationship. Individual development is intricately linked to the quality of relationships children have with significant others, and these relationships, in turn, are influenced by the individuals involved.

Fathers, on average, appeared to minimize children's negative emotional reactions more than mothers for both the older and younger siblings. It is possible that fathers feel more uncomfortable with their children's negative emotions or simply have greater expectations, than do mothers, that children should learn to control and regulate their negative emotions at earlier ages. Although fathers' minimization or control of children's emotional reactions might reflect age-inappropriate expectations for children, fathers' firm control might also help children learn to regulate their negative emotions in a socially acceptable manner. Regardless of the fathers' emphasis on minimizing and restricting the expression of negative emotions, the current research also found that fathers' encouragement of negative emotional expression was positively associated with the younger siblings' empathic concern, but not the older siblings'. Also, older siblings showed more empathic concern if fathers reported that they were high in empathic concern. Without longitudinal research, we are not in a position to know if these findings are due to developmental differences in response to older and younger siblings, due simply to the lack of statistical power in our small sample, or due to chance. Whatever the reason, these findings underscore the need for future research examining the role that fathers play in the socialization of empathic concern in very young children.

Finally, the marital relationship, and specifically the love reported by husbands and wives for each other, was positively related to the older siblings', but not the younger siblings', empathic concern. These findings are remarkably similar to an earlier study that found a negative association between spousal reports of marital love and the older siblings' jealousy of a younger sibling during a triadic interaction in the laboratory (Volling, McElwain, & Miller, 2002). We are aware of no other study that has examined the link between marital relationship quality and the development of young children's empathic concern for others. We do know that young children are acutely aware of the emotional exchanges between their parents (Cummings et al., 1981, 1984) and experience emotional distress after witnessing conflict between adults (Cummings et al., 1985). Whereas marital conflict may give rise to emotional distress, marital love may give rise to a child's sense of emotional security within the family (Davies, Cummings, & Winter, 2004). Although there is considerable research examining links between interparental conflict and children's dysregulated affect and adjustment problems, this is the first study to show that love between spouses may provide a family context that facilitates the development of children's empathic concern, at least in the case of older siblings. Needless to say, more research is needed to address the influence of positive marital relationship functioning on young children's empathic concern.

In conclusion, the findings reported here support Underwood's model in which aspects of an individual's social and cultural context influence his or her motivation to respond empathically, and in turn, to engage in compassionate behaviors. We found, in some cases, that the emotion-socialization practices of mothers and fathers, the parents' empathy, their reports of marital love, and positive sibling relationship involvement were related to young children's empathic concern. Further, empathic concern on the part of the older sibling was related to observations of helping behavior for both older and younger siblings. Based on these findings, we might conclude that Catherine's hostility and apparent lack of empathy toward her younger sister, as described at the beginning of this chapter, were fueled by a family system in which marital love was low, there was little positive engagement between siblings, and the mother experienced distress in response to Catherine's anger and attempted to punish her daughter's negative emotions. In contrast, Nathan's concern for his younger brother's welfare and his attempts to comfort him when distressed may have developed in the context of family interactions characterized by high levels of marital love, a highly empathic father, a mother who openly encouraged him to express his negative emotions, and a sibling relationship high in teaching, empathy, and companionship.

Of course, the cross-sectional nature of the current study does not allow us to draw firm conclusions about the direction of effects. It is just as likely that a mother becomes distressed when she witnesses her older child's ferocious anger and aggression toward her younger child, as it is that her distress reactions give rise to the older siblings' antisocial behavior. Similarly, marital conflict may result when parents have to constantly supervise and intervene in sibling abuse just as much as interparental hostility contributes to children's distress and aggressive actions. No doubt these relations are bidirectional and change over time, creating transactional processes involving family members and dynamic family interaction (Sameroff & MacKenzie, 2003). Longitudinal research is required to further our understanding of the ways in which the early family environment influences the development of young children's empathic concern and compassionate behavior toward others.

Acknowledgment

The research presented in this chapter was funded by the John E. Fetzer Institute.

References

Bank, S., & Kahn, M. D. (1975). Sisterhood–brotherhood is powerful: Sibling subsystems and family therapy. *Family Process, 14*(3), 311–337.

Barnett, M. A. (1984). Similarity of experience and empathy in preschoolers. *Journal of Genetic Psychology, 145*, 241–250.

Barrett, K. C., Zahn-Waxler, C., & Cole, P. M. (1993). Avoiders vs. amenders: Implications for the investigation of guilt and shame during toddlerhood? *Cognition & Emotion, 7*(6), 481–505.

Batson, C. D., Fultz, J., & Schoenrade, P. A. (1987). Distress and empathy: Two qualitatively distinct vicarious emotions with different motivational consequences. *Journal of Personality, 55*(1), 19–39.

Bedford, V. H., & Volling, B. (2004). A dynamic ecological systems perspective on emotion regulation development within the sibling relationship context. In F. R. Lang & K. L. Fingerman (Eds.), *Growing together: Personal relationships across the life span* (pp. 76–102). New York: Cambridge University Press.

Bernadett-Shapiro, S., Ehrensaft, D., & Shapiro, J. L. (1996). Father participation in childcare and the development of empathy in sons: An empirical study. *Family Therapy, 23*(2), 77–93.

Boyum, L. A., & Parke, R. D. (1995). The role of family emotional expressiveness in the development of children's social competence. *Journal of Marriage & the Family, 57*(3), 593–608.

Braiker, H., & Kelley, H. (1979). Conflict in the development of close relationships. In R. Burgess & T. Huston (Eds.), *Social exchange in developing relationships* (pp. 135–167). New York: Academic Press.

Bretherton, I., Fritz, J., Zahn-Waxler, C., & Ridgeway, D. (1986). Learning to talk about emotions: A functionalist perspective. *Child Development, 57*(3), 529–548.

Brody, L. R., & Hall, J. A. (1993). Gender and emotion. In M. Lewis & J. M. Haviland (Eds.), *Handbook of emotions* (pp. 447–460). New York: Guilford Press.

Cassidy, J. (1994). Emotion regulation: Influences of attachment relationships. In N. A. Fox (Ed.), *The development of emotion regulation*. Monographs of the Society for Research in Child Development, *59*(2–3), 228–283.

Cassidy, J., Parke, R. D., Butkovsky, L., & Braungart, J. M. (1992). Family-peer connections: The roles of emotional expressiveness within the family and children's understanding of emotions. *Child Development, 63*(3), 603–618.

Cummings, E. M. (1987). Coping with background anger in early childhood. *Child Development, 58*(4), 976–984.

Cummings, E. M., Iannotti, R. J., & Zahn-Waxler, C. (1985). Influence of conflict between adults on the emotions and aggression of young children. *Developmental Psychology, 21*(3), 495–507.

Cummings, E. M., Zahn-Waxler, C., & Radke-Yarrow, M. (1981). Young children's responses to expressions of anger and affection by others in the family. *Child Development, 52*(4), 1274–1282.

Cummings, E. M., Zahn-Waxler, C., & Radke-Yarrow, M. (1984). Developmental changes in children's reactions to anger in the home. *Journal of Child Psychology and Psychiatry, 25*(1), 63–74.

Davidov, M., & Grusec, J. E. (2006). Untangling the links of parental responsiveness to distress and warmth to child outcomes. *Child Development, 77*(1), 44–58.

Davies, P. T., Cummings, E. M., & Winter, M. A. (2004). Pathways between profiles of family functioning, child security in the interparental subsystem, and child psychological problems. *Development and Psychopathology, 16*(3), 525–550.

Davis, M. H. (1996). *Empathy: A sociopsychological approach*. Boulder, CO: Westview Press.

Denham, S. A. (1986). Social cognition, prosocial behavior, and emotion in preschoolers: Contextual validation. *Child Development, 57*(1), 194–201.

Denham, S. A. (1997). 'When I have a bad dream mommy holds me': Preschoolers' conceptions of emotions, parental socialisation, and emotional competence. *International Journal of Behavioral Development, 20*(2), 301–319.

Denham, S. A. (1998). *Emotional development in young children*. New York: Guilford Press.

Denham, S. A., Zoller, D., & Couchoud, E. A. (1994). Socialization of preschoolers' emotion understanding. *Developmental Psychology, 30*(6), 928–936.

Dunn, J. (1987). The beginnings of moral understanding: Development in the second year. In J. Kagan & S. Lamb (Eds.), *The emergence of morality in young children*. (pp. 91–112). Chicago: University of Chicago Press.

Dunn, J. (1988). *The beginnings of social understanding*. Cambridge, MA: Harvard University Press.

Dunn, J., & Kendrick, C. (1982). Siblings and their mothers: Developing relationships within the family. In M. L. B. Sutton-Smith (Ed.), *Sibling relationships: Their nature and significance across the lifespan* (pp. 39–60). Mahwah, NJ: Lawrence Erlbaum.

Dunn, J., & Kendrick, C. (1981). Interaction between young siblings: Association with the interaction between mother and firstborn child. *Developmental Psychology, 17*(3), 336–343.

Dunn, J., & Munn, P. (1986). Siblings and the development of prosocial behaviour. *International Journal of Behavioral Development, 9*(3), 265–284.

Easterbrooks, M. A., Cummings, E. M., & Emde, R. N. (1994). Young children's responses to constructive marital disputes. *Journal of Family Psychology, 8*(2), 160–169.

Eisenberg, N., Cumberland, A., & Spinrad, T. L. (1998). Parental socialization of emotion. *Psychological Inquiry, 9*(4), 241–273.

Eisenberg, N., Fabes, R., Miller, P. A., Fultz, J., Shell, R., Mathy, R. M., et al. (1989). Relation of sympathy and personal distress to prosocial behavior: A multi-method study. *Journal of Personality and Social Psychology, 57*(1), 55–66.

Eisenberg, N., Fabes, R., Miller, P. A., & Shell, R. (1990). Preschoolers' vicarious emotional responding and their situational and dispositional prosocial behavior. *Merrill-Palmer Quarterly, 36*(4), 507–529.

Eisenberg, N., Fabes, R. A., Bustamante, D., Mathy, R. M., Miller, P. A., & Lindholm, E. (1988). Differentiation of vicariously induced emotional reactions in children. *Developmental Psychology, 24*(2), 237–246.

Eisenberg, N., Fabes, R. A., & Murphy, B. C. (1996). Parents' reactions to children's negative emotions: Relations to children's social competence and comforting behavior. *Child Development, 67*(5), 2227–2247.

Eisenberg, N., Fabes, R. A., Schaller, M., Carlo, G., & Miller, P. A. (1991). The relations of parental characteristics and practices to children's vicarious emotional responding. *Child Development, 62*, 1393–1408.

Eisenberg, N., Fabes, R. A., Schaller, M., & Miller, P. A. (1989). Sympathy and personal distress: Development, gender differences, and interrelations of indexes. *New Directions in Child Development, 44*, 107–126.

Eisenberg, N., Fabes, R. A., Shepard, S. A., Guthrie, I. K., Murphy, B. C., & Reiser, M. (1999). Parental reactions to children's negative emotions: Longitudinal relations to quality of children's social functioning. *Child Development, 70*(2), 513–534.

Eisenberg, N., Fabes, R. A., & Spinrad, T. L. (2006). Prosocial development. In N. Eisenberg, W. Damon & R. M. Lerner (Eds.), *Handbook of child psychology: Vol. 3, Social, emotional, and personality development (6th ed.).* (pp. 646–718). New York: John Wiley.

Eisenberg, N., McCreath, H., & Ahn, R. (1988). Vicarious emotional responsiveness and prosocial behavior: Their interrelations in young children. *Personality and Social Psychology Bulletin, 14*, 298–311.

Eisenberg, N., Miller, P. A., Shell, R., McNally, S., & Shea, C. (1991). Prosocial development in adolescence: A longitudinal study. *Devlopmental Psychology, 27*, 849–857.

Eisenberg, N., Shell, R., Pasternack, J., & Lennon, R. (1987). Prosocial development in middle childhood: A longitudinal study. *Developmental Psychology, 23*(5), 712–718.

Emde, R. N., Biringen, Z., Clyman, R. B., & Oppenheim, D. (1991). The moral self of infancy: Affective core and procedural knowledge. *Developmental Review, 11*(3), 251–270.

Fabes, R. A., Eisenberg, N., Karbon, M., Bernzweig, J., Speer, A., & Carlo, G. (1994). Socialization of children's vicarious emotional responding and prosocial behavior: Relations with mothers' perceptions of children's emotional reactivity. *Developmental Psychology, 30*(1), 44–55.

Fabes, R. A., Leonard, S. A., Kupanoff, K., & Martin, C. L. (2001). Parental coping with children's negative emotions: Relations with children's emotional and social responding. *Child Development, 72*(3), 907–920.

Fabes, R. A., Poulin, R. E., Eisenberg, N., & Madden-Derdich, D. A. (2002). The Coping with Children's Negative Emotions Scale (CCNES): Psychometric properties and relations with children's emotional competence. *Marriage & Family Review, 34*(3), 285–310.

Feldman, R., Greenbaum, C. W., & Yirmiya, N. (1999). Mother-infant affect synchrony as an antecedent of the emergence of self-control. *Developmental Psychology, 35*(1), 223–231.

Garner, P. W., Jones, D. C., & Miner, J. L. (1994). Social competence among low-income preschoolers: Emotion socialization practices and social cognitive correlates. *Child Development, 65*, 622–637.

Garner, P. W., Jones, D. C., & Palmer, D. J. (1994). Social cognitive correlates of preschool children's sibling caregiving behavior. *Developmental Psychology, 30*, 905–911.

Garner, P. W., Robertson, S., & Smith, G. (1997). Preschool children's emotional expressions with peers: The roles of gender and emotion socialization. *Sex Roles, 36*(11), 675–691.

Harris, P. L. (1989). Children's understanding of emotion: An introduction. In *Children's understanding of emotion* (pp. 3–24). New York: Cambridge University Press.

Hastings, P. D., Zahn-Waxler, C., Robinson, J., Usher, B., & Bridges, D. (2000). The development of concern for others in children with behavior problems. *Developmental Psychology, 36*(5), 531–546.

Hay, D. F., Nash, A., & Pederson, J. (1981). Responses of 6-month-olds to the distress of their peers. *Child Development, 52*, 1071–1075.

Hoffman, M. L. (1982). Affect and moral development. *New Directions for Child Development, 16*, 83–103.

Hoffman, M. L. (2000). *Empathy and moral development: Implications for caring and justice.* New York: Cambridge University Press.

Kagan, J., & Lamb, S. (1987). *The emergence of morality in young children.* Chicago: University of Chicago Press.

Kendrick, C., & Dunn, J. (1982). Protest or pleasure? The response of first-born children to interactions between their mothers and infant siblings. *Journal of Child Psychology and Psychiatry, 23*(2), 117–129.

Kochanska, G. (1993). Toward a synthesis of parental socialization and child temperament in early development of conscience. *Child Development, 64*, 325–347.

Kochanska, G. & Murray, K. T. (2000). Mother-child mutually responsive orientation and conscience development: From toddler to early school age. *Child Development, 71*(2), 417–431.

Kochanska, G., DeVet, K., Goldman, M., Murray, K. T., & Putnam, S. P. (1994). Maternal reports of conscience development and temperament in young children. *Child Development, 65*, 852–868.

Koestner, R., Franz, C., & Weinberger, J. (1990). The family origins of empathic concern: A 26-year longitudinal study. *Journal of Personality and Social Psychology, 58*(4), 709–717.

Kopp, C. B. (1982). Antecedents of self-regulation: A developmental perspective. *Developmental Psychology, 18*(2), 199–214.

Kopp, C. B. (1989). Regulation of distress and negative emotions: A developmental view. *Developmental Psychology, 25*, 249–265.

Lamb, M. E., & Malkin, C. M. (1986). The development of social expectations in distress-relief sequences: A longitudinal study. *International Journal of Behavioral Development, 9*(2), 235–249.

Lawson, A., & Ingleby, J. D. (1974). Daily routines of pre-school children: Effects of age, birth order, sex and social class, and developmental correlates. *Psychological Medicine, 4*(4), 399–415.

Malatesta, C. Z., Culver, C., Tesman, J. R., & Shepard, B. (1989). The development of emotion expression during the first two years of life. *Monographs of the Society for Research in Child Development, 54*(1), 1–104.

McHale, S. M., & Crouter, A. C. (1996). The family context of children's sibling relationships. In G. Brody (Ed.), *Sibling Relationships: Their causes and consequences* (pp. 173–196). Norwood, NJ: Ablex.

Miller, P. A., Eisenberg, N., Fabes, R. A., & Shell, R. (1996). Relations of moral reasoning and vicarious emotion to young children's prosocial behavior toward peers and adults. *Developmental Psychology, 32*(2), 210–219.

Pipp-Siegel, S., & Foltz, C. (1997). Toddlers' acquisition of self/other knowledge: Ecological and interpersonal aspects of self and other. *Child Development, 68*(1), 69–79.

Raver, C. C. (1996). Relations between social contingency in mother-child interaction and 2-year-olds' social competence. *Developmental Psychology, 32*(5), 850–859.

Roberts, W. L., & Strayer, J. (1987). Parents' responses to the emotional distress of their children: Relations with children's competence. *Developmental Psychology, 23*(3), 415–422.

Saarni, C. (1999). *The development of emotional competence*. New York: Guilford Press.

Sagi, A., & Hoffman, M. L. (1976). Empathic distress in the newborn. *Developmental Psychology, 12*(2), 175–176.

Sameroff, A. J., & MacKenzie, M. J. (2003). Research strategies for capturing transactional models of development: The limits of the possible. *Development and Psychopathology, 15*(3), 613–640.

Simner, M. L. (1971). Newborn's response to the cry of another infant. *Developmental Psychology, 5*(1), 136–150.

Spinrad, T. L., Eisenberg, N., Cumberland, A., Fabes, R. A., Valiente, C., Shepard, S. A., et al. (2006). Relation of emotion-related regulation to children's social competence: A longitudinal study. *Emotion, 6*(3), 498–510.

Spinrad, T. L., & Stifter, C. A. (2006). Toddlers' empathy-related responding to distress: Predictions from negative emotionality and maternal behavior in infancy. *Infancy, 10*(2), 97–121.

Stewart, R. B. (1983). Sibling attachment relationships: Child-infant interaction in the strange situation. *Developmental Psychology, 19*(2), 192–199.

Stewart, R. B., & Marvin, R. S. (1984). Sibling relations: The role of conceptual perspective-taking in the ontogeny of sibling caregiving. *Child Development, 55*(4), 1322–1332.

Strayer, J., & Roberts, W. (1989). Children's empathy and role taking: Child and parental factors, and relations to prosocial behavior. *Journal of Applied Developmental Psychology, 10*(2), 227–239.

Strayer, J., & Roberts, W. (2004). Children's anger, emotional expressiveness, and empathy: Relations with parents' empathy, emotional expressiveness, and parenting practices. *Social Development, 13*, 229–254.

Teti, D. M., & Ablard, K. E. (1989). Security of attachment and infant–sibling relationships: A laboratory study. *Child Development, 60*(6), 1519–1528.

Tronick, E. Z. (2003). Emotions and emotional communication in infants. In J. Raphael-Leff (Ed.), *Parent–infant psychodynamics: Wild things, mirrors and ghosts* (pp. 35–53). London: Whurr.

Turiel, E. (1998). The development of morality. In W. Damon (Ed.), *Handbook of child psychology: Vol. 3, Social, personality, and emotional development* (pp. 863–932). New York: John Wiley.

Underwood, L. G. (2002). The human experience of compassionate love: Conceptual mapping and data from selected studies. In S. G. Post, L. G. Underwood, J. P. Schloss & W. B. Hurlbut (Eds.), *Altruism & altruistic love: Science, philosophy, & religion in dialogue.* (pp. 72–88). New York: Oxford University Press.

van der Mark, I. L., van IJzendoorn, M. H., & Bakermans-Kranenburg, M. J. (2002). Development of empathy in girls during the second year of life: Associations with parenting, attachment, and temperament. *Social Development, 11*(4), 451–468.

Volling, B. L. (2001). Early attachment relationships as predictors of preschool children's emotion regulation with a distressed sibling. *Early Education and Development, 12*(2), 185–207.

Volling, B. L., & Blandon, A. Y. (2005). Positive indicators of sibling relationship quality: The Sibling Inventory of Behavior. In K. A. Moore & L. H. Lippman (Eds.), *What do children need to flourish? Conceptualizing and measuring indicators of positive development* (pp. 203–219). Heidelberg: Springer Science + Business Media.

Volling, B. L., Herrera, C., & Poris, M. P. (2004). Situational affect and temperament: Implications for sibling caregiving. *Infant and Child Development, 13*(2), 173–183.

Volling, B. L., McElwain, N. L., & Miller, A. L. (2002). Emotion regulation in context: The jealousy complex between young siblings and its relations with child and family characteristics. *Child Development, 73*(2), 581–600.

Volling, B. L., McElwain, N. L., Notaro, P. C., & Herrera, C. (2002). Parents' emotional availability and infant emotional competence: Predictors of parent-infant attachment and emerging self-regulation. *Journal of Family Psychology, 16*(4), 447–465.

Wellman, H. M., & Liu, D. (2004). Scaling of theory-of-mind tasks. *Child Development, 75*(2), 523–541.

Yarrow, M., & Waxler, C. (1976). Dimensions and correlates of prosocial behavior in young children. *Child Development, 47,* 118–125.

Young, S. K., Fox, N. A., & Zahn-Waxler, C. (1999). The relations between temperament and empathy in 2-year-olds. *Developmental Psychology, 35*(5), 1189–1197.

Zahn-Waxler, C., & Radke-Yarrow, M. (1982). The development of altruism: Alternative research strategies. In N. Eisenberg (Ed.), *The development of prosocial behavior* (pp. 109–139). San Diego, CA: Academic Press.

Zahn-Waxler, C., Radke-Yarrow, M., & King, R. A. (1979). Child rearing and children's prosocial initiations toward victims of distress. *Child Development, 50,* 319–330.

Zahn-Waxler, C., Radke-Yarrow, M., Wagner, E., & Chapman, M. (1992). Development of concern for others. *Developmental Psychology, 28*(1), 126–136.

Zahn-Waxler, C., & Robinson, J. (1995). Empathy and guilt: Early origins of feelings of responsibility. In J. P. Tangney & K. W. Fischer (Eds.), *Self-conscious emotions: The psychology of shame, guilt, embarrassment, and pride* (pp. 143–173). New York: Guilford Press.

7

Compassionate Love in Early Marriage

Lisa A. Neff and Benjamin R. Karney

*I, (name), take you, (name), to be my (husband/wife). I promise to
be true to you in good times and in bad, in sickness and in health.
I will love you and honor you all the days of my life. (—excerpt from
traditional wedding vows)*

In their wedding vows, couples publicly announce before their friends,
family members, and authority figures that they will spend a lifetime
loving their partner for better or for worse. Research on newlyweds confirms that most couples do enter marriage with the intent to fulfill this
promise. Studies of newlywed couples reveal that these spouses profess a
deep love for their partner, describe their partner in extremely positive
and glowing terms, report being highly committed to the relationship,
and have an almost unbridled optimism about the future of the marriage
(e.g., Neff & Karney, 2005). For most newlyweds, it is inconceivable that
their marriage will not last. Yet, a poignant fact about marriages is, that
despite this seemingly strong foundation of love and the uniformly positive outlook of newlyweds, many marriages eventually end (Bumpass,
1990; Cherlin, 1992). Why is this the case?

Answering this question involves recognizing that there are many ways
to love a partner. Early in a relationship, each of these types of love may
manifest itself in similar ways. For instance, all newlyweds appear motivated to engage in positive behaviors toward their partners. However, as
the relationship continues, the precise nature of spouses' initial feelings of
love is likely to influence the way the marriage develops or deteriorates
over time (e.g., Noller, 1996; Sternberg & Barnes, 1988). As noted in
Figure 1.1 in Chapter 1 of this book (see also Underwood, 2002), the
motivation underlying spouses' love for their partner may vary between
couples. While some spouses' love may be guided by more selfish desires
(e.g., "I will behave positively in order to gain some favor"), for others,
positive behaviors may stem from a true concern for the well-being of

the other. The former is often described as a more romantic, immature type of love (Noller, 1996). As seen in the figure, because a self-focus lies at the core of this love, ultimately it may be associated with miscarried or inappropriate relationship behaviors. The latter, on the other hand, represents compassionate love: a love based on selflessness in which the partner is fundamentally valued and promoted regardless of costs to the self. Theories of compassionate love suggest this form of love is based on a more mature awareness and understanding of the other. It is thought to encompass a caring, altruistic attitude in which the other is valued to such a degree as to put the needs of the other before one's own (Underwood, 2002). As a result, expressions of this love are more likely to truly benefit the partner.

Yet, a closer look at common definitions of compassionate love reveals what seems to be, at first glance, a paradox. Compassionate lovers not only unconditionally value the other, but also may gain a sense of happiness and fulfillment from doing so. For instance, prior work on compassionate love suggests that one feature of loving compassionately is deriving a sense of meaning from engaging in activities that benefit the other (Sprecher & Fehr, 2005). In this way, compassionate love incorporates an element of selfishness in even the most selfless love for another person. Compassionate love is rooted in selflessness, yet also rewarding at a higher level.

Consequently, the question guiding the current chapter is: How can we distinguish the pleasures of selfless love from the pleasures of a selfish one? We approach this topic from the perspective of researchers who have devoted our careers to studying the early years of marriage. We consider marriage to be an especially relevant domain within which to study compassionate love. Prior work on compassionate love indicates that this love should inspire behaviors such as compromise, tolerance, empathy, and support (Underwood, 2002). Consequently, compassionate love should be a critical element of a healthy marriage. We should expect married couples who love compassionately to last longer, be happier, and support each other more effectively than couples who do not love each other compassionately. Conversely, it is hard to imagine a successful marriage in which spouses were not able, at least occasionally, to put each other's needs before their own. Thus, conventional wisdom argues that compassionate love should be at the heart of marital success.

Newlyweds in particular are an appropriate sample to distinguish between compassionate love and other kinds of love. In order to understand fully how marriages develop and change over time, it is necessary to understand how and where they begin. As mentioned, all newlyweds report a deep and abiding love for the partner, yet not all of these couples may love each other in the same way. Examining newlyweds closely may suggest ways of teasing apart the compassionate lovers from the other lovers as well as provide insight into the types of love that lead to better marital outcomes over time.

The goal of the current chapter, then, is to present a model for distinguishing the initial love professed by all newlyweds from the compassionate love that should lead to healthier, more stable marriages. To accomplish this goal, the remainder of the chapter is organized into three sections. The first section more precisely defines compassionate love in marriage as a love for the partner that is based on an accurate understanding of a partner's specific strengths and weaknesses. The second section will describe some data indicating that newlyweds who love their partners compassionately think and behave in more positive ways within the marriage as well as experience better marital outcomes over time. Finally, the last section will describe the next steps for examining compassionate love in marriage as well as draw out some of the broader implications of this model for fostering compassionate love more generally, between strangers, groups, or nations.

A Model of Compassionate Love

The first step for identifying compassionate love in early marriage involves defining what exactly it means to love a partner compassionately. Our model of compassionate love is based on two premises. Drawing from other perspectives on love (Noller, 1996; Rubin, 1970), the first premise is that love can be thought of as an attitude toward a particular individual, and thus shares the structure that other sorts of attitudes have been shown to have (Fabrigar, Smith, & Brannon, 1999). In other words, assuming that love is an attitude suggests that spouses' feelings of love are founded on a variety of perceptions and judgments of the partner that range from perceptions of the partner's specific traits and abilities (e.g., "My partner is a fabulous cook") to global evaluations of the partner as a whole (e.g., "My partner is the greatest"; Hampson, John & Goldberg, 1986; Neff & Karney, 2002a, 2002b). Consequently, these perceptions and judgments of a relationship can be arranged in a hierarchical structure from very general and global to very specific. For instance, as seen in Figure 7.1, the global perception that my partner is fabulous may subsume the more specific perceptions that my partner is thoughtful, trustworthy, and successful. In this way, global perceptions might include evaluations of the partner's general worth, whereas specific perceptions refer to the particular traits and behaviors that comprise the foundation on which global evaluations are based (Pelham & Swann, 1989; Rosenberg, 1979).

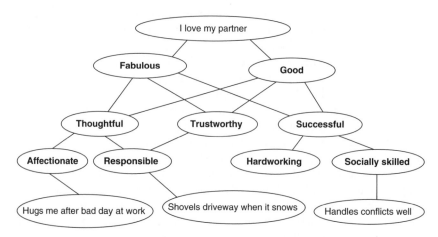

Figure 7.1   Hierarchical Representation of Spouses' Perceptions

The second premise of the model is that spouses' motivation to view the partner positively may vary at different levels of this hierarchy. This premise is based on research suggesting that people generally care more about, and derive more pleasure from, their global perceptions compared to their specific perceptions (John, Hampson, & Goldberg, 1991; Neff & Karney, 2002a). As perceptions become more global, they tend to subsume a greater number of specific perceptions and behaviors. As a result, global perceptions should carry more emotional weight and be considered more important for marital happiness. Confirming this idea, prior research suggests that spouses tend to rate global perceptions, such as "my partner is kind," or "my partner is caring," as more important to their overall relationship satisfaction than specific perceptions, such as "my partner is intelligent," or "my partner is socially skilled" (Neff & Karney, 2002a). In other words, it seems more important for spouses to believe that their partners are good, worthy people than to believe that their partners are talented in any specific way.

An implication of this greater importance given to global perceptions is that spouses should be more invested in seeing the best in their partners at the global level. That is, in order to maintain their feelings of marital satisfaction, spouses should be highly motivated to perceive their partners as wonderful, kind, loving individuals. In this way, spouses' self-interests may influence their global perceptions of the partner. However, the motivation to view the partner in a positive light may not operate quite as strongly when spouses are evaluating their partners' more specific qualities, because acknowledging faults and imperfections at the specific level should have relatively few negative consequences for marital satisfaction. For instance, spouses may be willing to recognize their partners as disorganized or as lacking in social skills, as these negative specifics should do little to hurt spouses' satisfaction with the marriage as long as spouses possess a number of positive global perceptions of the partner. In this case, spouses can note that their partner is disorganized, but also is a very caring person overall (Murray & Holmes, 1993). Thus, self-interest need not play as large a role in shaping spouses' specific perceptions.

Supporting this idea, our research indicates that, on average, spouses tend to view their partners' specific qualities in a less positively biased manner than they view their partners' global qualities. In one study, 82 newlywed couples were asked to rate both themselves and their partners on a variety of attributes that varied in their specificity (Neff & Karney, 2002a). We then compared spouses' views of their partner to the partner's self-views on the attributes. Results indicated that as the attributes became more global (e.g., good, understanding), spouses were more likely to enhance their partner's self-views, seeing the partner even more positively than the partner viewed him/herself. Thus, spouses viewed their partners in a highly positive light when evaluating their partner on global qualities. On the other hand, as the attributes became more specific (e.g., organized, socially skilled), spouses tended to agree with their partner's self-views, even if agreeing with the partner involved seeing the partner in a somewhat negative light. In this way, spouses were less likely to put a positive spin on their partners' specific qualities compared to their partners' global qualities.

Recognizing this hierarchical structure in relationship perceptions has two important implications for understanding the types of love found in early marriage. First, this perspective suggests that spouses who may all look identical in their global perceptions of their partners (e.g., they all view their partners in a highly positive light) may still look quite different from one another when examining their specific partner perceptions. In other words, while all newlywed spouses are likely to view their partners as wonderful people overall, they also may hold a variety of both positive and negative perceptions of their partner's specific qualities and abilities (McNulty & Karney, 2001). Second, these perceptions at the specific level may be more or less accurate reflections of the partner's self-image. In other words, even though on average, spouses may be less positively biased in their specific perceptions compared to their global perceptions, for some spouses these specific perceptions of the partner may be unrealistically positive or negative compared to their partners' self-views, whereas other spouses may see their partners as their partners see themselves (e.g., Swann, De La Ronde, & Hixon, 1994).

This reasoning suggests that among happily married, newlywed couples, some spouses may base their overall positive view of the partner on an accurate understanding of their partners' specific qualities, whereas other spouses may have little insight into their partners' qualities. We suggest that it is the former individuals, those who affirm and adore the partner globally, yet also recognize the partner's specific positive *and* negative qualities, who are providing their partners with compassionate love. In other words, the compassionate lover does not gloss over the partner's specific negative qualities, but rather holds the partner in high esteem while at the same time acknowledging specific faults and weaknesses.

What makes this love compassionate? Consider that if individuals truly believed that every specific aspect of their partners was fabulous, then loving them would not be very difficult. Indeed, some spouses may not be able to love their partners unless they view each of their partners' specific traits very positively, suggesting their love may be grounded in more selfish concerns (see Figure 1.1 in Chapter 1). In this case, the spouse may be unwilling to accept a partner's faults, and once the partner's less-than-perfect traits come into awareness, the spouse's love for the partner may dissipate. However, understanding and accepting a partner's specific strengths and weaknesses may represent a selfless act, in that spouses endure the costs of their partner's faults, weaknesses, and limitations but love them anyway. These spouses set aside any desires to view the partner in a particular manner and acknowledge the strengths and imperfections of their partners. In other words, consistent with other definitions of compassionate love (e.g., Underwood, 2002), these spouses are unconditionally valuing their partner at a fundamental level. Thus, compassionate love is more than simply caring for the partner; it is a love founded on an accurate understanding of the partner. Compassionate love is personally fulfilling, in that spouses can reap the rewards of their love, but it is also selfless, in that spouses accept their partners, the good and the bad, for who they are.

The Implications of Compassionate Love for Marital Processes and Development

The goal of our research, then, has been to examine spouses who compassionately love their partners and to investigate the implications of compassionate love for marital well-being over the early years of marriage (for a more detailed description of this research see Neff & Karney, 2005). To accomplish this goal, we collected data from a total of 251 newlywed couples at several points during the first 4 years of their marriages. All couples were in the first 6 months of their marriage when the study began and it was the first marriage for both members of the dyad. Examining compassionate love within a sample of newlywed couples provided several advantages. First, selecting newlyweds ensured that all couples were at a similar marital duration and that the motivation to evaluate a partner positively should be strong and fairly uniform across spouses. In this way, the use of newlyweds allowed us to study the advantages of compassionate love within a sample of couples who all proclaim to love their partners deeply. Second, newlywed couples are an appropriate sample in which to examine issues of relationship change and dissolution. Compared to more established marriages, newlyweds experience more dramatic changes in relationship quality and are at elevated risk of marital disruption (Cherlin, 1992).

Examining Compassionate Love

To examine compassionate love, it was necessary to assess spouses' global and specific perceptions of their partner and the relationship. At the beginning of the study, when these couples were first married, we measured their global perceptions by asking them to rate their marital satisfaction using a 15-item version of the Semantic Differential (Osgood, Suci, & Tannenbaum, 1957). Thus, spouses were asked to indicate their current feelings about the marriage on seven-point scales placed between two opposing adjectives (e.g., "satisfied–dissatisfied," "unpleasant–pleasant," "rewarding–disappointing"). Spouses also were asked to report on the extent to which they considered their partners to be good, worthy people overall using a version of the Rosenberg Self-Esteem Questionnaire (Rosenberg, 1965). This measure was reworded such that spouses completed it with regard to the esteem in which they held their partners (e.g., "I feel my partner has a number of good qualities"). To assess spouses' specific perceptions, spouses were asked to rate both themselves and their partners on numerous specific traits and abilities, taken from the Specific Attributes Questionnaire (Swann et al., 1994) and the Big Five Personality Inventory (Goldberg, 1999), such as intellect, extroversion, conscientiousness, and social skills. It should be noted that although the specific qualities on these measures are generally considered to be positive, spouses varied in the degree to which they claimed these qualities for themselves. In other words, spouses were acknowledging particular weaknesses in themselves (e.g., low degrees of social skills). As such, if partners agree with their spouse's self-reports across all dimensions (e.g., those in which they rate themselves high and those on which they rate themselves low), this would seem to indicate that partners are acknowledging their spouse's strengths *and* limitations. Based on our model of compassionate love, it was expected that while all newlyweds would report highly positive global evaluations of their partners, these happy spouses would nevertheless vary significantly in their understanding of each other's specific strengths and weaknesses, indicating variability in compassionate love even among recently married couples.

To assess the assumption that newlywed couples are uniformly happy with their partner and the relationship, we first examined the distribution of scores on the measures of global perceptions. As is often seen in samples of newlyweds, virtually all couples reported being extremely satisfied in their marriage. In fact, even though scores on the satisfaction measure could range from 15 to 105 (with higher scores indicating greater satisfaction), close to 50% of the sample had a perfect score on the measure of marital satisfaction (for husbands, $M = 96.1$, $SD = 9.5$; for wives, $M = 97.8$, $SD = 9.9$). Similarly, virtually all spouses viewed their partners as extremely good and worthy people. Close to 60% of the sample gave their partner the highest rating possible on the measure of the partner's global worth (possible range was 4 to 40). The average score was 38.2 ($SD = 2.5$) for husbands and 38.6 ($SD = 2.2$) for wives. Thus, results revealed very little variability in spouses' global perceptions.

Given that spouses reported strongly positive global impressions of their marriages and their partners, we next examined whether, within this sample of uniformly happy couples, spouses varied in the accuracy with which they viewed their partners' specific traits and abilities. To do this, the within-couple association between a spouse's perceptions of the partner's specific attributes and the partner's self-perceptions on these attributes was examined. In other words, we examined the relative degree to which spouses' perceptions agreed with their partners' perceptions across the attributes. It was predicted that while on average spouses would tend to agree with their partners' self-perceptions, there would nonetheless be significant variability in the extent of this agreement across spouses.

Results revealed that, on average, both husbands and wives were demonstrating a relatively accurate view of their partners' self-perceived traits and abilities. However, there was notable variability across spouses in the extent of this accuracy, such that some spouses were demonstrating a more accurate understanding of their partners' specific qualities than were others. Thus, only a subset of these loving, newly married couples seemed to be engaging in compassionate love, in which a globally positive view of the partner is linked to an accurate understanding of the partner's specific strengths and weaknesses.

Having found variability in the degree in which these happy spouses were engaging in compassionate love, we next examined the implications of compassionate love for marital well-being. If compassionate love does in fact provide a deeper, more solid foundation for marriage, then spouses who view their partners in this manner should enjoy better marital outcomes than spouses whose love is not based on an understanding of the partner's specific qualities. In particular, we addressed three specific questions: First, is compassionate love associated with the manner in which spouses support one another in the marriage? Second, is compassionate love associated with spouses' feelings of efficacy when faced with marital difficulties? Finally, is compassionate love associated with the stability of marriage over time?

Compassionate Love and the Provision of Social Support

One of the primary needs served by intimate relationships is providing a source of social support (Coyne & DeLongis, 1986). Relationship partners are expected to help each other attain their goals and surmount the challenges encountered in daily life. Accordingly, support from a partner has been associated not only with personal well-being, but also with relationship satisfaction (Cutrona, 1996). Spouses receiving greater levels of support from their partner report greater marital happiness (Pasch & Bradbury, 1998), and spouses often cite a lack of support as prominent factor underlying relationship dissatisfaction (Baxter, 1986). Furthermore, support received from an intimate partner is unique, such that support from other sources generally cannot compensate for lack of support from a partner (Ruehlman & Wolchik, 1988). Yet, despite the fact that supportive, compassionate interactions appear critical to marital success, little is known about the conditions that promote such positive interactions within marriage.

A common assumption within the counseling literature is that a key component of effective support provision is providing the other with "unconditional positive regard" (Kelly, 2000). Consistent with the idea that successful support occurs when individuals maintain a high positive regard for one other, research on established marriages has found positive associations between supportive behavior and relationship satisfaction (Cutrona, 1996). However, studies of newlywed couples reveal that, despite their generally high regard for each other, newlyweds nevertheless vary considerably in their ability to provide positive support to their partners (Pasch & Bradbury, 1998). Thus, while providing a partner with positive regard may help create a safe, loving environment for spouses to express their needs, this finding indicates that positive regard alone may not be sufficient for spouses to effectively support their partners in reaching their goals.

Rather, spouses may be effective in helping and supporting their partners only when they also demonstrate an accurate understanding of their partner's specific qualities and attributes. Spouses who understand their partner's qualities should be better able to predict how their partner will respond to them, which should serve to facilitate successful interactions (Swann, Stein-Seroussi, & Giesler, 1992). On the other hand, a discrepancy between spouses' views and partners' self-views may indicate that interactions will be characterized by misunderstanding, as partners' behaviors may frequently counter spouses' expectations (Swann et al., 1992). Thus, accurate insight into when the partner needs support, as well as what kind of support would be most effective, may result from positive regard that is coupled with specific understanding. In this way, compassionate love may foster more behaviors that effectively promote and support the partner than a love lacking in specific understanding.

To examine this idea, when couples were first married, they were asked to attend a laboratory session in which we had them engage in two 10-minute videotaped discussions. For each discussion, one spouse was asked to choose a personal problem or difficulty they were facing and discuss that problem with their partner. The partner was instructed to respond in any way he or she felt appropriate. Thus, each spouse had the opportunity to play the role of the support provider. A panel of independent observers then rated the supportiveness of the partner's behaviors during the discussions using the Social Support Interaction Coding System (Bradbury & Pasch, 1992). Specifically, observers were trained to identify three general types of supportive behaviors: behaviors where the partner reassured, consoled, or otherwise encouraged the spouse, letting the spouse know that he or she is loved (i.e., positive emotional behaviors); behaviors that offered the spouse specific suggestions on how to reach desired goals (i.e., positive instrumental behaviors); and behaviors that provided insight into the cause of the problem (i.e., other positive behaviors that were neither emotional nor instrumental in nature).

Results revealed that husbands' compassionate love was not associated with their support behaviors. However, wives who based their love for their partner on a more accurate understanding of the partner's specific qualities were rated as providing better support during the interactions than wives lacking in compassionate love. Importantly, this result held even when controlling for how positively wives viewed their husbands' specific qualities. In other words, wives were more supportive when they viewed their husbands' qualities in an accurate manner, not necessarily in a positive manner. Given that all wives reported being very happy with their partner and the marriage, these results provide further evidence that caring for a partner may not be sufficient for providing positive support. Rather, having a compassionate love for the partner may allow spouses to give both the loving encouragement and the specific information necessary to effectively support a partner.

Compassionate Love and Feelings of Marital Efficacy

In addition to predicting spouses' actual behaviors, we also expected that compassionate love would be associated with spouses' feelings of marital efficacy when faced with conflicts or difficulties in the relationship. In other words, compassionate love may be associated with spouses' beliefs that they are able to execute the behaviors necessary for resolving relationship conflicts. Individuals' feelings of efficacy and control often influence coping responses to stressful situations (e.g., Fincham, Harold, & Gano-Phillips, 2000). For instance, while spouses high in efficacy beliefs, feeling confident in their abilities, may respond to marital conflicts by taking active, constructive steps toward resolving the issue, spouses with low efficacy beliefs are likely to "give up" and engage in more passive or even destructive responses to conflict (e.g., withdrawing from the problem), thereby leaving the couple vulnerable to further relationship problems. Thus, maintaining a sense of marital efficacy can be essential for protecting marital happiness over the long term (Swann, 1984; Swann et al., 1994).

Theories of identity negotiation in relationships argue that when spouses accurately understand their partners' qualities, they will be better able to predict how their partner will respond to them in various situations (Swann et al., 1992). As a result, when spouses recognize each other's particular strengths and weaknesses, marital interactions should proceed smoothly, and cooperative efforts to overcome conflicts and difficulties are likely to be successful (Schlenker, 1984; Swann, 1984). These experiences of successfully surmounting challenges should, in turn, serve to bolster spouses' feelings of efficacy. Consequently, we expected that spouses exhibiting compassionate love would experience the greatest increases in their feelings of marital efficacy as the marriage progressed over time.

To examine this idea, we measured spouses' feelings of efficacy both at the beginning of the study when couples were first married, and again 6 months after their initial assessment using the Relationship Efficacy Measure (Fincham et al., 2000). Example items from this measure include, "When I put my mind to it, I can resolve just about any disagreement that comes up between my partner and I" and "I have little control over the conflicts that occur between my partner and I" (reverse-scored). Controlling for initial feelings of efficacy, wives who loved compassionately reported greater feelings of marital efficacy 6 months later than wives whose love was not based on specific accuracy. As with the previous results, this finding held when controlling for how positively wives viewed their husbands' specific qualities. The association between compassionate love and feelings of efficacy was not significant for husbands. Thus, at least for wives, loving a partner compassionately seemed to increase marital efficacy beliefs over the course of the marriage.

Compassionate Love and Marital Stability

As mentioned previously, despite the fact that newly married spouses uniformly profess a strong love for their partners, a large percentage of marriages end in divorce (Bumpass, 1990). Though a large literature has argued that the nature of spouses' love for one other may help account for this change in marital quality, such that a love that is initially "deeper" should be more stable over time, exactly what constitutes a deeper love has been the source of some debate (Noller, 1996). The current model of compassionate love argues that love should be stronger and more resilient over time when positive global evaluations of the partner are coupled with an accurate understanding of the partner's specific traits and abilities.

Namely, perceiving a partner with global adoration should serve to maintain positive partner evaluations and protect the relationship from doubt (e.g., Murray, Holmes, & Griffin, 1996a, 1996b). In other words, spouses who view their partners with global adoration should feel confident in their belief that their partner is the "right one." However, holding a partner in high positive regard may be necessary, but not sufficient to ensure better marital outcomes. For instance, spouses who adore their partners, but lack an understanding of their partners' specific traits and abilities, may find themselves prone to disappointment in the marriage. These spouses are unlikely to have their expectations for their partners met, as maintaining a false view of partners' qualities places partners in the uncomfortable position of having to live up to an identity they may be unwilling or unable to confirm (Schlenker, 1984). On the other hand, spouses who love compassionately enter the marriage recognizing their partners' limitations and accepting them anyway. As a result, when partners' negative qualities inevitably surface as the relationship progresses, these spouses should be more likely to respond adaptively in the face of this negativity.

To address the idea that couples who love compassionately should have more stable marriages, we examined whether compassionate love was associated with the likelihood of divorce over the first 4 years of marriage (approximately 20% of couples divorced during this time). Results indicated that husbands' compassionate love was not associated with marital outcomes. However, when wives loved their husbands compassionately, the couple was less likely to divorce. As with the previous analyses, this finding held even when controlling for the general positivity of wives' specific views of their husbands. In other words, it was only when wives understood their partner's traits, not when they viewed those specific traits positively, that the marriage fared better over time. Overall, it seems that love at the global level may be even more powerful when coupled with an understanding of a partner's specific qualities.

Gender Differences in Compassionate Love?

The results described thus far indicate that although a subset of both husbands and wives engaged in compassionate love, only for wives was this type of love able to predict positive outcomes. In other words, husbands' compassionate love was not associated with their supportive behaviors, their feelings of marital efficacy, or the couple's likelihood of divorce. Does this suggest that it is not important for husbands to love compassionately? There is some evidence in the broader literature on marriage that women's relational processes may be particularly important for marital quality and stability. Prior research indicates that women are more likely to think about relationship issues, and are more likely to actively work on improving aspects of the marriage (Acitelli & Young, 1996; Christensen & Heavey, 1990). If women take on more responsibility for relationship maintenance activities, then it would be more important for them to base their love for the partner on an accurate understanding of the partner's qualities in order to facilitate marital processes.

However, it may be premature simply to conclude that husbands' compassionate love is less meaningful for marital success. For instance, by necessity, the current research measured a limited number of qualities when examining specific understanding and its implications. It is possible that husbands and wives may differ in the types of qualities they need to understand in order to enhance marital success. Future research may want to examine which specific qualities men and women report as particularly important for a relationship partner, and determine if an accurate perception of those qualities deemed important predicts positive outcomes for both husbands and wives.

Similarly, perhaps husbands' compassionate love influences the marriage in ways not measured in the current research. In the current studies, we measured only a limited number of the many possible processes that have been shown to affect marital outcomes (e.g., social support, feelings of marital efficacy). It is possible that husbands' compassionate love may influence different marital processes than does wives' compassionate love. For example, prior research indicates that spouses who enter a marriage with overly positive, unrealistic expectations of the partner (e.g., "My partner will never disappoint me" or "My partner and I will always communicate well") tend to experience the most dramatic declines in their satisfaction over the early years of marriage (e.g., McNulty & Karney, 2004).

If spouses hold more accurate specific perceptions of their partner (e.g., recognizing the partner's strengths and weaknesses), this may lead them to align their marital expectations closer to reality, thus preventing spouses from becoming disappointed and dissatisfied in the marriage. In other words, husbands' compassionate love may affect marital outcomes by influencing the nature of the expectations they bring to the marriage. Thus, additional research is necessary to clarify the role of husbands' compassionate love in marital development.

Integrating Compassionate Love with Alternative Theories of Marital Success

> *If you want a person's faults, go to those who love him. They will not tell you, but they know. And herein lies the magnanimous courage of love, that it endures this knowledge without change. (—Robert Louis Stevenson)*

Arguably, a compassionate, selfless love should be at the core of a healthy marriage. The trick is reconciling how love can be selfless, yet also rewarding and personally fulfilling. Similar to Robert Louis Stevenson's musing on love, we argue that what makes love compassionate is the fact that love endures despite the recognition of the other's specific weaknesses. Consistent with other theories of compassionate love (Underwood, 2002), our research confirms that a love founded on an accurate understanding of the partner's strengths and weaknesses, in other words a love in which the partner is valued at a fundamental level, may have several important benefits for marriage. First, compassionate love has benefits for the beloved. While it may be good to be the object of love, it is better to be the object of a love that is coupled with understanding. Compared to husbands who were only globally adored, when husbands were both loved and understood, they received better support from their wives. Second, compassionate love has benefits for the lover. Wives who loved compassionately experienced increases in their feelings of marital efficacy as the relationship progressed. As a result, these spouses may be better equipped to respond to marital difficulties in an adaptive manner. Finally, compassionate love benefited the couple as a unit, as marriages characterized by compassionate love were less likely to dissolve over time. Thus, as indicated in Figure 1.1 in Chapter 1, a love motivated by compassion and selflessness seems to lead to the expression of more positive relationship behaviors.

This view of compassionate love ties together research and theory on the types of marital evaluations associated with more lasting, satisfying relationships. In the close relationships literature, there has been a long-standing debate regarding the types of relationship perceptions associated with better relationship quality. Some theorists have argued that a critical part of maintaining a relationship involves viewing the partner through rose-colored spectacles. That is, positive feelings toward the partner should remain high if spouses are positively biased in the way they view the partner (Murray et al., 1996a, 1996b). On the other hand, other theorists argue that the essential ingredient for long-term happiness is to hold a more tempered, accurate view of the partner's qualities (Swann et al., 1994). The current model of compassionate love reconciles these positions by formally delineating how the best relationships may be characterized by both positive biases and accuracy.

Complementing research on positive biases in relationships, our perspective on compassionate love argues that a degree of positive bias in perceptions at the global level is a necessary element of successful marriages. However, our results indicated that globally adoring the partner was not sufficient to produce better marital well-being. Likewise, viewing the partner's specific qualities in a positive light did not ensure happier, more stable marriages. Thus, positive biases alone seemed to result in marriages that may be fragile. Rather, it was only when that global adoration of the partner was founded on an accurate understanding of who the partner really is that the marriage fared better over time. Consequently, our model of compassionate love also argues for the critical role of specific accuracy within relationships. Contrary to the old adage, true love is not blind. It seems that spouses in healthy marriages love their partners in spite of (or perhaps because of) their less than perfect specific traits.

Fostering Compassionate Love in Marriage and Beyond

The Origins of Compassionate Love in Marriage

If compassionate love, or a love that is based on specific understanding, produces marriages that are happier and less fragile than love without this understanding, an important direction for future research is to examine the antecedents of specific understanding and how it may be fostered within relationships. One could speculate that certain aspects related to the history of the relationship (e.g., length of courtship) may allow individuals to witness a wider variety of behaviors from the partner, and thus enhance the accuracy of their perceptions of their partners' qualities. Yet, in our studies, the length of time couples knew one another prior to marriage, whether couples were friends prior to dating, whether the couple cohabited prior to marriage, and whether the couple received premarital counseling all failed to predict which spouses loved their partners compassionately (Neff & Karney, 2005). Thus, having more opportunities to learn about and interact with the partner did not seem to ensure spouses would have more accurate perceptions of the partner's specific qualities.

Rather, future research may want to examine a number of individual difference factors that may be associated with spouses' ability to love compassionately. For instance, individuals' attachment style may play a significant role in shaping their perceptions of their partners. Anxious/ambivalent individuals, who tend to be less happy and trusting in their relationships, may be particularly threatened by the presence of negative relationship aspects, even at the level of their specific perceptions (e.g., Mikulincer & Shaver, 2005). Consequently, these individuals may be motivated to "misperceive" their partners, and thus be less likely than securely attached individuals to accurately view their partners' positive and negative qualities. Supporting this idea, Feeney and Noller (1991) have found that when asking intimates to describe their romantic partners, anxious/ambivalent individuals are more likely to idealize their partners than are securely attached individuals. This reasoning is consistent with other research (Gillath, Shaver, & Mikulincer, 2005) arguing that secure individuals are better equipped than non-secure individuals to provide compassionate love to others.

Spouses' cognitive complexity also may affect spouses' specific perceptions of their partners. The ability to acknowledge specific negative aspects of the partner and then reconcile those negative perceptions into an overall positive view of the partner and the relationship is likely to require a certain degree of cognitive skill. In other words, prior research has shown that the effects of a specific perception on the global relationship evaluation depend on how that perception is linked to the overall evaluation (Showers & Kevlyn, 1999). When a specific perception is negative, linking that perception to the global evaluation will likely result in a deterioration of relationship satisfaction. On the other hand, maintaining a cognitive structure that serves to minimize the impact of the negative perception on the global evaluation would allow satisfaction to remain high despite the presence of negative relationship aspects. For instance, spouses may acknowledge the presence of a negative perception (e.g., "My partner is disorganized"), yet view that perception as unimportant, thereby weakening the link between that negative perception and their feelings of marital happiness (Neff & Karney, 2003). Alternatively, spouses may dilute the meaning of their partner's faults by linking them to their partner's many strengths (Murray & Holmes, 1999). Spouses lower in cognitive complexity may be unable to engage in this process of minimizing negative perceptions. Consequently, these spouses may find themselves unable to maintain global feelings of love while also understanding and accepting the partner's specific strengths and weaknesses.

Looking beyond Marriage: Compassionate Love in Other Domains

Although the current research examined compassionate love in early marriage, this model of compassionate love may have implications for other types of relationships as well. For instance, some theories of effective parenting suggest that parents should strive to protect their children's self-esteem through unconditional positive regard. The "self-esteem movement" of recent decades recommends that parents and teachers cultivate a sense of uniqueness and worth in children by refraining from criticizing children, and instead praising them for even trivial accomplishments. The idea is that if children feel good about themselves as a result of this feedback, a number of desirable outcomes will ensue (e.g., they will achieve more in school, avoid drugs and smoking, etc.). Unfortunately, a growing body of work has called this assumption into question, demonstrating that self-esteem formed in this manner not only has few actual benefits, but also may lead to undesirable outcomes (e.g., narcissism; for a review see Baumeister, Campbell, Krueger, & Vohs, 2003).

The current research complements alternative perspectives to the self-esteem movement, which argue that the benefits of having high self-esteem may only appear when those feelings of worth are explicitly linked to an accurate understanding of one's specific strengths and weaknesses (Baumeister et al., 2003). From this perspective, it may be more productive for parents to promote accurate self-knowledge in children, provided that this knowledge is offered in a context of global acceptance. In fact, Schlenker (1984) has argued that for feedback to be perceived as supportive and trustworthy, it must be perceived as both sincere and believable. While giving the child unconditional positive regard may provide the sincerity, by itself this regard may not create a context in which feedback is believable. That is, if the positive feedback parents provide is removed from an honest recognition of children's limitations, children may fail to understand the logic behind the feedback, thereby undermining its effectiveness (cf. Swann & Predmore, 1985). Thus, raising happy, healthy, and successful children may require compassionate love.

Finally, the current research dovetails well with contact theories of prejudice and intergroup relations. These theories argue that simply providing groups with the opportunity to interact with one another is not enough to reduce prejudicial feelings and create positive attitudes toward outgroup members. Rather, certain conditions must be met in order for contact to generate positive intergroup relations (for a review see Dovidio, Gaertner, & Kawakami, 2003). One critical feature necessary for contact to be effective is that the contact must provide individuals with opportunities to learn new information about outgroup members. Acquiring greater knowledge of others has been shown to increase understanding and sensitivity toward the outgroup, as well as reduce discomfort and uncertainty when interacting with outgroup members (Dovidio et al., 2003). Thus, consistent with the current model of compassionate love, this research suggests that acceptance and tolerance of others must be based on accurate knowledge of others' specific qualities. Before compassionate love can take hold, there must be understanding.

Conclusions

We began the chapter by highlighting the tremendous difficulty many newlywed couples have when trying to adhere to their vow to love and honor their partner for all the days of their lives. Despite even the best of intentions, many couples fail to keep this promise. Understanding why this is the case seems to require a deeper examination of the kind of love spouses have for their partners. The current research argues that in order to alleviate or prevent marital distress, the advice to love the partner, to view the partner with unconditional positive regard, is too simple. Love that is not founded on understanding is not enough and not likely to improve marital processes. Rather, an accurate understanding of the partner may be a prerequisite for truly compassionate love, which leads to enhanced marital success.

References

Acitelli, L. K., & Young, A. M. (1996). Gender and thought in relationships. In G. J. O. Fletcher & J. Fitness (Eds.), *Knowledge structures in close relationships: A social psychological perspective* (pp. 147–168). Mahwah, NJ: Lawrence Erlbaum.

Baumeister, R. F., Campbell, J. D., Krueger, J. I., & Vohs, K. D. (2003). Does high self-esteem cause better performance, interpersonal success, happiness or healthier lifestyles? *Psychological Science in the Public Interest, 4*, 1–44.

Baxter, L. A. (1986). Gender differences in the heterosexual relationship rules embedded in break-up accounts. *Journal of Social and Personal Relationships, 3*, 289–306.

Bradbury, T. N., & Pasch, L. A. (1992). *The Social Support Interaction Coding System*. Unpublished coding manual. University of California, Los Angeles.

Bumpass, L. L. (1990). What's happening to the family? Interactions between demographic and institutional change. *Demography, 27*, 483–498.

Cherlin, A. J. (1992). *Marriage, divorce, remarriage* (2nd ed.). Cambridge, MA: Harvard University Press.

Christensen, A., & Heavey, C. L. (1990). Gender and social structure in the demand/withdraw pattern of marital interaction. *Journal of Personality and Social Psychology, 59*, 73–81.

Coyne, J. C., & DeLongis, A. (1986). Going beyond social support: The role of social relationships in adaptation. *Journal of Personality and Social Psychology, 54*, 454–460.

Cutrona, C. E. (1996). *Social support in couples.* Thousand Oaks, CA: Sage.

Dovidio, J. F., Gaertner, S. L., & Kawakami, K. (2003). Intergroup contact: The past, present, and the future. *Group Processes and Intergroup Relations, 6*, 5–20.

Fabrigar, L. R., Smith, S. M., & Brannon, L. A. (1999). Applications of social cognition: Attitudes as cognitive structures. In F. T. Durso (Ed.), *Handbook of applied cognition* (pp. 173–206). New York: John Wiley.

Feeney, J. A., & Noller, P. (1991). Attachment style and verbal descriptions of romantic partners. *Journal of Social and Personal Relationships, 8*, 187–215.

Fincham, F. D., Harold, G. T., & Gano-Phillips, S. (2000). The longitudinal association between attributions and marital satisfaction: Direction of effects and role of efficacy expectations. *Journal of Family Psychology, 14*, 267–285.

Gillath, O., Shaver, P. R., & Mikulincer, M. (2005). An attachment-theoretical approach to compassion and altruism. In Gilbert. P. (Ed.), *Compassion: Conceptualisations, research and use in psychotherapy,* (pp. 121–147). New York: Routledge.

Goldberg, L. R. (1999). A broad-bandwidth, public domain, personality inventory measuring the lower-level facets of several five-factor models. In I. Mervielde, I. Deary, F. De Fruyt, & F. Ostendorf (Eds.), *Personality psychology in Europe: Vol. 7* (pp. 7–28). Tilburg, The Netherlands: Tilburg University Press.

Hampson, S. E., John, O. P., & Goldberg, L. R. (1986). Category breadth and hierarchical structure in personality: Studies of asymmetries in judgments of trait implications. *Journal of Personality and Social Psychology, 51*, 37–54.

John, O. P., Hampson, S. E., & Goldberg, L. R. (1991). The basic level in personality-trait hierarchies: Studies of trait use and accessibility in different contexts. *Journal of Personality and Social Psychology, 60*, 348–361.

Kelly, A. E. (2000). Helping construct desirable identities: A self-presentational view of psychotherapy. *Psychological Bulletin, 126*, 475–494.

McNulty, J. K., & Karney, B. R. (2001). Attributions in marriage: Integrating specific and global evaluations of close relationships. *Personality and Social Psychology Bulletin, 27*, 943–955.

McNulty, J. K., & Karney, B. R. (2004). Positive expectations in the early years of marriage: Should couples expect the best or brace for the worst? *Journal of Personality and Social Psychology, 86*, 729–743.

Mikulincer, M., & Shaver, P. R. (2005). Attachment theory and emotions in close relationships: Exploring the attachment-related dynamics of emotional reactions to relational events. *Personal Relationships, 12*, 149–168.

Murray, S. L., & Holmes, J. G. (1993). Seeing virtues in faults: Negativity and the transformation of interpersonal narratives in close relationships. *Journal of Personality and Social Psychology, 65,* 707–722.

Murray, S. L., & Holmes, J. G. (1999). The (mental) ties that bind: Cognitive structures that predict relationship resilience. *Journal of Personality and Social Psychology, 77,* 1228–1244.

Murray, S. L., Holmes, J. G., & Griffin, D. W. (1996a). The benefits of positive illusions: Idealization and the construction of satisfaction in close relationships. *Journal of Personality and Social Psychology, 70,* 79–98.

Murray, S. L., Holmes, J. G., & Griffin, D. W. (1996b). The self-fulfilling nature of positive illusions in romantic relationships: Love is not blind but prescient. *Journal of Personality and Social Psychology, 71,* 1155–1180.

Neff, L. A., & Karney, B. R. (2002a). Judgments of a relationship partner: Specific accuracy but global enhancement. *Journal of Personality, 70,* 1079–1112.

Neff, L. A., & Karney, B. R. (2002b). Self-evaluation motives in close relationships: A model of global enhancement and specific verification. In P. Noller & J. A. Feeney (Eds.), *Understanding marriage: Developments in the study of couple interaction* (pp. 32–58). London, England: Cambridge University Press.

Neff, L. A., & Karney, B. R. (2003). The dynamic structure of relationship perceptions: Differential importance as a strategy of relationship maintenance. *Personality and Social Psychology Bulletin, 29,* 1433–1446.

Neff, L. A., & Karney, B. R. (2005). To know you is to love you: The implications of global adoration and specific accuracy for marital relationships. *Journal of Personality and Social Psychology, 90,* 480–497.

Noller, P. (1996). What is this thing called love? Defining the love that supports family and marriage. *Personal Relationships, 3,* 97–115.

Osgood, C. E., Suci, G. J., & Tannenbaum, P. H. (1957). *The measurement of meaning.* Urbana: University of Illinois Press.

Pasch, L. A., & Bradbury, T. N. (1998). Social support, conflict and the development of marital dysfunction. *Journal of Consulting and Clinical Psychology, 66,* 219–230.

Pelham, B. W., & Swann, W. B. (1989). From self-conceptions to self-worth: On the sources and structure of global self-esteem. *Journal of Personality and Social Psychology, 57,* 672–680.

Rosenberg, M. (1979). *Conceiving the self.* New York: Basic Books.

Rosenberg, S. (1965). *Society and the adolescent self-image.* Princeton, NJ: Princeton University Press.

Rubin, Z. (1970). Measurement of romantic love. *Journal of Personality and Social Psychology, 16,* 265–273.

Ruehlman, L. S., & Wolchik, S. A. (1988). Personal goals and interpersonal support and hindrance as factors in psychological distress and well-being. *Journal of Personality and Social Psychology, 55,* 293–301.

Schlenker, B. R. (1984). Identities, identifications, and relationships. In V. Derlega (Ed.), *Communication, intimacy, and close relationships* (pp. 71–104). New York: Academic Press.

Showers, C., & Kevlyn, S. (1999). Organization of knowledge about a relationship partner: Implications for liking and loving. *Journal of Personality and Social Psychology, 76,* 958–971.

Sprecher, S., & Fehr, B. (2005). Compassionate love for close others and humanity. *Journal of Social and Personal Relationships, 22,* 629–651.

Sternberg, R. J., & Barnes, M. L. (Eds.). (1988). *The psychology of love.* New Haven, CT: Yale University Press.

Swann, W. B., Jr. (1984). Quest for accuracy in person perception: A matter of pragmatics. *Psychological Review, 91,* 457–477.

Swann, W. B., Jr., De La Ronde, C., & Hixon, J. G. (1994). Authenticity and positivity strivings in marriage and courtship. *Journal of Personality and Social Psychology, 66,* 857–869.

Swann, W. B., Jr., & Predmore, S. C. (1985). Intimates as agents of social support: Sources of consolation or despair? *Journal of Personality and Social Psychology, 49,* 1609–1617.

Swann, W. B., Jr., Stein-Seroussi, A., & Giesler, R. B. (1992). Why people self-verify. *Journal of Personality and Social Psychology, 62,* 392–401.

Underwood, L. G. (2002). The human experience of compassionate love: Conceptual mapping and data from selected studies. In S. G. Post, L. G. Underwood, J. P. Schloss, & W. B. Hurlbut (Eds.), *Altruism and altruistic love: Science, philosophy, and religion in dialogue,* (pp. 72–88). New York: Oxford University Press.

Part IV

Compassionate Love for Non-Close Others

8

A Behavioral Systems Perspective on Compassionate Love

Mario Mikulincer, Phillip R. Shaver, and Omri Gillath

Is it possible for a person to be compassionate and kind without also being selfish at some level? After all, Dawkins's (1976/1989) metaphor, "the selfish gene," has been associated in many intellectual circles with the assumption that selfish genes lead to selfish people. Can a person really love others in an unguarded way if she does not also love herself? What is the best way to foster compassion and loving-kindness, especially toward people from outside one's network of close relationships?

As noted throughout this volume, there are many approaches to these questions – and several relevant levels of analysis, from genes to culture. In our work (e.g., Mikulincer & Shaver, 2003, 2004, 2007a; Shaver & Mikulincer, 2002, 2005) we use Bowlby and Ainsworth's attachment theory as a framework for studying love and compassion, because it has already proven of inestimable value in the study of various forms of love (for an overview, see Cassidy & Shaver, 1999). Using this framework, we focus on the "substrate" component of Underwood's (Chapter 1, this volume) model of compassionate love and deal with the effects of being loved, protected, and comforted by others, beginning with parents during infancy, and on the capacity to love others and react sensitively and compassionately to their needs.

For more than 30 years, since the publication of Bowlby's (1969/1982) foundational book, attachment theory has guided research on the development of love and empathy in parent–child relationships. Since 1987, when Hazan and Shaver first applied the theory to the study of romantic and marital love (see Feeney, 1999; Shaver & Clark, 1994, for reviews), researchers have continued to make remarkable discoveries about the system of mental processes that governs attachment behavior (which Bowlby (1969/1982) called the attachment behavioral system) and the complementary system that governs caregiving in close relationships (the caregiving behavioral system).

In recent studies, for example, we (Mikulincer, Gillath, & Shaver, 2002) found that when a young adult is presented subliminally with threatening words such as "failure" or "separation," his or her mind turns automatically to mental representations of caregivers, or "attachment figures." This is the mental equivalent of an infant's behavior in Ainsworth's famous "strange situation" laboratory procedure (Ainsworth, Blehar, Waters, & Wall, 1978): When an infant is frightened, he or she drops previously engaging toys and moves quickly toward a parent to be picked up, protected, and soothed. Interestingly, in the case of adults as well as infants, individuals whose caregivers have been relatively inaccessible, insensitive, or unreliable have a difficult time using attachment figures confidently and effectively. They therefore tend to be chronically insecure. This insecurity, we argue, makes it more difficult for them to be compassionate and altruistic. Moreover, insecurely attached people tend to be deficient in what Underwood (Chapter 1, this volume) views as the motivational signature of compassionate love; their motives for helping others are not really centered on others' welfare.

We begin this chapter with a summary of Bowlby's conceptualization of the attachment and caregiving behavioral systems. Specifically, we describe the normative features and individual-difference parameters of the attachment and caregiving behavioral systems, as well as the nature of their interaction. We then summarize research on the ways in which individual differences in the attachment system affect caregiving behavior in various kinds of relationships. Finally, we describe new studies of attachment-related differences in altruistic helping, community volunteering, prosocial motives and behaviors, and emotional, cognitive, and behavioral reactions to other people's distress – all viewed as aspects or forms of compassionate caregiving.

The Attachment and Caregiving Behavioral Systems

Although Bowlby (1969/1982, 1973, 1980) focused mainly on the formation of attachment bonds in childhood, he also attempted to understand how evolutionary mechanisms shape other kinds of human behavior (e.g., exploration, parental caregiving, and affiliative and sexual behaviors). For this purpose, he borrowed from ethology the concept of *behavioral system*, a species-universal neural program that organizes an individual's behavior in ways that increase the likelihood of survival and reproductive success in the face of environmental dangers and demands. Responses to these demands – such as dealing with threats to life and well-being by relying on "stronger, wiser" attachment figures, exploring and learning how to cope with the environment, caring for dependent offspring – led to the evolution of distinct but interrelated behavioral systems (e.g., attachment, exploration, caregiving, and sexual systems), each with its own functions and characteristic behaviors.

A behavioral system is an inborn, goal-oriented neural program that governs the selection, activation, and termination of behavioral sequences that produce a functional change in the person–environment relationship, a change that has generally yielded adaptive advantages for survival and reproduction. Each behavioral system involves a set of contextual activating triggers (e.g., attaining a sense of safety and security, relieving others' distress, and promoting their welfare) and a set of interchangeable, functionally equivalent behaviors that constitute the *primary strategy* of the system for attaining its particular goal (e.g., attaining safety and security through proximity-seeking, protecting or comforting another person). These behaviors are automatically "activated" by certain stimuli or kinds of situations that make a particular goal salient (e.g., loud noises that signal danger, an encounter with a distressed or needy person), and "deactivated" or "terminated" by other stimuli or outcomes that signal attainment of the desired goal. Each behavioral system also includes cognitive operations that facilitate the system's functioning and specific excitatory and inhibitory links with other behavioral systems.

Bowlby (1973) also discussed individual differences in the functioning of behavioral systems, especially the attachment system. Although behavioral systems are innate circuits or mental modules, they are manifested in actual behavior, guide people's transactions with the social world, and can be affected or shaped by close others' responses. Over time, social encounters mold the parameters of a person's behavioral systems in ways that produce individual differences in strategies and behaviors. Bowlby (1973) assumed that social interactions gradually correct a behavioral system's primary strategies and produce more effective action sequences. According to him, the residues of such experiences are stored as mental representations of person–environment transactions, which he called *working models of self and others*. With repeated use, these models can become automatic and serve as an important source of within-person continuity in behavioral system functioning.

The Attachment Behavioral System

The presumed biological function of the attachment system is to protect a person (especially during infancy and childhood) from danger by assuring that he or she maintains proximity to caring and supportive others (*attachment figures*). The attachment system is activated by perceived (real or imagined) threats and dangers, which cause a threatened person to seek actual or symbolic proximity to protective others (Bowlby,

1969/1982). In infants, attachment-system activation includes nonverbal expressions of neediness and desire for proximity, such as crying and pleading, as well as active behaviors aimed at reestablishing and maintaining actual proximity, such as moving toward the caregiver or clinging to him or her (Ainsworth et al., 1978). In adulthood, however, attachment-system activation does not necessarily entail actual proximity-seeking behavior. Instead, protection and relief can be obtained by the activation of soothing, comforting, mental representations of relationship partners who have regularly provided care and protection (Mikulincer & Shaver, 2003, 2004).

The attainment of proximity and protection promotes an inner sense of attachment security (based on expectations that key people will be available and supportive in times of need) and results in the consolidation of optimistic beliefs about distress management; faith in others' goodwill; a sense of being loved, esteemed, understood, and accepted by relationship partners; and a sense of self-efficacy with respect to gaining proximity to a loving partner when support is needed. Bowlby (1988) considered the optimal functioning of this behavioral system to be crucial for mental health, the development of a positive self-image, and the maintenance of positive attitudes toward others. A large number of studies provide strong empirical support for the existence of these benefits of an optimal functioning attachment system (for reviews, see Feeney, 1999; Mikulincer & Shaver, 2003, 2007a; Shaver & Mikulincer, 2002).

When a person's attachment figures are not reliably available and supportive, a sense of attachment security is not attained and the distress that initially activated the system is compounded by doubts and fears about the feasibility of attaining a sense of security. Moreover, negative interactions with attachment figures indicate that the primary attachment strategy, proximity and support seeking, has to be replaced with an alternative ("secondary") strategy. Attachment theorists (e.g., Cassidy & Kobak, 1988; Mikulincer & Shaver, 2003; Shaver & Mikulincer, 2002) emphasize two such secondary strategies: hyperactivation and deactivation of the system. Hyperactivation of the attachment system is manifested in energetic, insistent attempts to get a relationship partner, viewed as insufficiently available or responsive, to pay more attention and provide better care and support. Hyperactivating strategies include clinging to and attempting to control a relationship partner, cognitive and behavioral efforts to establish greater physical and emotional closeness, and overdependence on relationship partners as a source of protection (Shaver & Mikulincer, 2002). Hyperactivation keeps the attachment system chronically activated, constantly on the alert for threats, separations, and betrayals, thereby exacerbating relational distress and conflicts (Mikulincer & Shaver, 2003).

Deactivation of the attachment system includes inhibition of proximity-seeking and the adoption of a personal style that Bowlby (1980) called "compulsive self-reliance." Deactivating strategies require a person to deny attachment needs; avoid closeness, intimacy, commitment, and dependence; and increase cognitive, emotional, and physical distance from others (Shaver & Mikulincer, 2002). They also involve active inattention to threatening events and personal vulnerabilities as well as inhibition and suppression of thoughts and memories that evoke distress and feelings of vulnerability, because such thoughts might cause unwanted reactivation of the attachment system (Fraley, Davis, & Shaver, 1998).

When studying individual differences in the functioning of the attachment behavioral system during adolescence and adulthood, attachment researchers have measured *attachment style* – the chronic pattern of relational expectations, emotions, and behaviors that results from a particular history of attachment experiences (Fraley & Shaver, 2000). Beginning with Ainsworth et al.'s (1978) studies of infant–caregiver attachment, continuing through Hazan and Shaver's (1987) conceptualization of romantic love as an attachment process, and followed up in many studies by social and personality psychologists (e.g., Bartholomew & Horowitz, 1991; Brennan, Clark, & Shaver, 1998; Fraley & Waller, 1998; see Mikulincer & Shaver, 2007a, for a comprehensive review), researchers have found that individual differences in attachment style can be measured along two orthogonal dimensions, attachment-related *avoidance* and *anxiety*. The first dimension, attachment *avoidance*, reflects the extent to which a person distrusts relationship partners' goodwill, deactivates the attachment system, and strives to maintain behavioral independence and emotional distance from partners. The second dimension, attachment *anxiety*, reflects the degree to which a person worries that a partner will not be available in times of need and engages in hyperactivating strategies. People who score low on both dimensions are said to be secure or securely attached.

The two dimensions can be measured with reliable and valid self-report scales, such as the Experience in Close Relationships scale (ECR; Brennan et al., 1998), the Adult Attachment Questionnaire (AAQ; Simpson, Rholes, & Phillips, 1996), or the Adult Attachment Scale (AAS; Collins, 1996). These dimensions have been consistently found to be associated in theoretically predictable ways with affect regulation, self-esteem, psychological well-being, and interpersonal functioning (for reviews, see Mikulincer & Shaver, 2003, 2007a; Shaver & Clark, 1994; Shaver & Hazan, 1993). Several studies have shown consistently that a person's positions on the attachment dimensions also influence his or her motives (causing him or her to be more or less self-focused vs. altruistic) during social interactions, valuing or devaluing of others' needs and desires, and the actions taken in response to others' needs and feelings (for an extensive review, see Mikulincer & Shaver, 2007a). As in Underwood's (Chapter 1, this volume) model of compassionate love, the attachment behavioral system (the substrate) is shaped by familial forces and personal history, and it can, in turn, shape a person's social motives, attitudes, decisions, and actions.

Attachment styles begin to be formed in interactions with primary caregivers during early childhood (Cassidy & Shaver, 1999), but Bowlby (1988) claimed that impactful interactions with others throughout life can alter a person's working models and move him or her from one region of the two-dimensional (anxiety by avoidance) space to another. Moreover, although attachment style is often conceptualized and measured as a single global orientation toward close relationships, a person's attachment orientation is actually rooted in a complex cognitive and affective network that includes many different episodic, context-related, and relationship-specific, as well as fairly general, attachment representations (Mikulincer & Shaver, 2003). In fact, research shows that attachment style can change, subtly or dramatically, depending on context and recent experiences (e.g., Baldwin, Keelan, Fehr, Enns, & Koh Rangarajoo, 1996; Mikulincer & Shaver, 2001).

Beyond focusing on the tendency to seek protection and support from close others in times of need, attachment theory also deals with the complementary tendency to provide protection and support to needy others. One of the major contributions of attachment theory and research is the identification and delineation of the normative features and individual-differences parameters of the caregiving behavioral system, which seem to underlie and organize a person's motives, feelings, attitudes, and actions when he or she witnesses another person suffering. This is another component of Underwood's (Chapter 1, this volume) conception of the substrate of compassionate love, which guides a person's choice to protect, support, and comfort others in times of need, or instead to ignore them without helping.

The Caregiving Behavioral System

According to Bowlby (1969/1982), human beings are born with a nascent capacity to provide protection and support to others who are either chronically dependent or temporarily in need. Bowlby (1969/1982) claimed that these caregiving behaviors, as they emerge in development, are organized around an innate *caregiving behavioral system* that emerged over the long course of evolution because it increased the inclusive fitness of human beings by increasing the likelihood that children, siblings, mates, and tribe members with whom one shared genes (or offspring) would survive (Hamilton, 1964). Although the caregiving ֙ presumably evolved primarily to increase the viability of an individuaı offspring and close relatives (George & Solomon, 1999), its products can be made more widely available to all suffering human beings, and even to members of other species. That is, through moral education and socialization, people can be induced to provide protection and support even to strangers – a goal of all major religions. In this way, caregiving motives can be extended to apply to anyone in need. If a person's caregiving system develops under favorable social conditions, compassion, loving kindness, and generosity become the norm.

The goal of the caregiving system is to reduce other people's suffering, protect them from harm, and foster their growth and development (e.g., Collins, Guichard, Ford, & Feeney, 2006; George & Solomon, 1999; Gillath, Shaver, & Mikulincer, 2005; Kunce & Shaver, 1994.) That is, the caregiving system is designed to accomplish the two major functions of a security-providing attachment figure: to meet another person's needs for protection and support in times of danger or distress (Bowlby, 1969/1982, called this "providing a safe haven") and to support others' exploration, autonomy, and growth when exploration is safe and viewed by the explorer as desirable. (Bowlby called this "providing a secure base for exploration.") According to Collins et al. (2006), caregiving motives and behaviors are likely to be activated (a) when another person has to cope with danger, stress, or discomfort and is either seeking help or would clearly benefit from it; and (b) when another person has an opportunity for exploration, learning, or mastery and either needs help in taking advantage of the opportunity or seems eager to talk about and be validated for his or her efforts and accomplishments. In either case, a person's caregiving system is activated, and he or she calls upon a repertoire of behaviors aimed at relieving a needy person's distress, supporting his or her coping efforts, or providing a secure base for exploration, growth, and development.

A key part of the caregiving system's primary strategy is the adoption of what Batson (1991) called an empathic stance toward another person's needs, such as taking the other's perspective in order to help him or her reduce suffering and distress or pursue growth and development. According to Collins et al. (2006), an empathic stance includes sensitivity and responsiveness, the two aspects of parental caregiving emphasized by Bowlby, Ainsworth, and subsequent attachment researchers. Sensitivity includes attunement to, and accurate interpretation of, another person's signals of distress, worry, or need, and responding in synchrony with the person's proximity- and support-seeking behavior. Responsiveness includes generous intentions; validating the troubled person's needs and feelings; respecting his or her beliefs, attitudes, and values; and helping him or her feel loved, understood, and cared for (Reis & Shaver, 1988). Lack of sensitivity and responsiveness can cause a careseeker to feel misunderstood, disrespected, or burdensome, which exacerbates distress rather than providing a secure base.

According to Batson (1991), another person's visible suffering can evoke two different kinds of emotional reactions in a potential caregiver: compassion (or compassionate love) and personal distress. Although both compassion and personal distress are signs that one person's distress has triggered emotional reactions in another, the two states are quite different in attentional focus and motivational implications. The main focus of compassion is the other person's needs or suffering, and the natural implication is that the distress should be alleviated for the sufferer's benefit. In contrast, the main focus of personal distress is the self's own discomfort, which might be alleviated either by helping or by ignoring or fleeing the situation. Moreover, whereas compassion sustains caregiving without any direct payoff to the caregiver (*unconditional caregiving*), personal distress is likely to be translated into helping only if helping is the best way to reduce the caregiver's own discomfort (Batson, 1991). Under conditions of "easy escape," when potential caregivers can reduce their distress by means other than helping, personal distress does not motivate empathic care (Batson, 1991).

Although Bowlby (1969/1982) assumed that everyone is born with the potential to become an effective care provider, optimal functioning of the caregiving system depends on several different intra- and inter-personal factors. Caregiving can be impaired by feelings, beliefs, and concerns that dampen or conflict with sensitivity and responsiveness. It also can be impaired by a care seeker's failure to express needs appropriately, by his or her rebuff of a caregiver's helping efforts, or by external obstacles to support provision. Effective care also can be disrupted by problems in emotion regulation that cause a caregiver to feel overwhelmed by the other person's pain and suffering, to slip into the role of the needy person oneself rather than serving as a care provider, or to distance oneself physically, emotionally, or cognitively from the person in need in order to soothe one's own personal distress. Collins et al. (2006) discussed four factors that hamper optimal caregiving: (1) social skill deficits; (2) depletion of psychological resources; (3) lack of motivation to help; and (4) acting on egoistic motives while supposedly "helping." Social skill deficits interfere with accurate decoding of a needy person's signals and communications. Without sufficient psychological resources, it is difficult to attend empathically to a needy person's distress while developing effective plans to intervene. Whereas an absence of motivation to help disrupts caregiving from the start, acting on egoistic motives can disrupt empathy and sensitivity toward a suffering other, which is likely to interfere with effective helping.

The Interplay of the Attachment and Caregiving Systems

Bowlby (1969/1982) noticed that because of a person's urgent need to protect himself or herself from imminent threats, activation of the attachment system can inhibit activation of other behavioral systems and thus interfere with nonattachment activities, such as exploration. In early childhood, this interference results in nonoptimal learning and skills development. The same kind of interference can disrupt the caregiving system, because potential caregivers may feel so threatened that obtaining care for themselves seems more urgent than providing care to others. At such times, people are likely to be so focused on their own vulnerability that they lack the mental resources necessary to attend sensitively and compassionately to others' needs. Only when a degree of safety is attained, and a sense of security is restored, can most people perceive others to be not only sources of security and support, but also worthy human beings who need and deserve comfort and support themselves.

Reasoning along these lines, attachment theorists (e.g., Gillath et al., 2005; Kunce & Shaver, 1994; Mikulincer & Shaver, 2003; Shaver & Hazan, 1988) have hypothesized that a sense of attachment security allows a person to shift attention to caregiving and provides a psychological foundation for accurate empathy and effective helping. In addition, secure adults generally have witnessed and benefited from the good care provided by their attachment figures, and this gives them positive models for their own behavior (Collins & Feeney, 2000). By processes of identification and internalization, a person who perceived an attachment figure as sensitive and caring can view himself or herself as a sensitive and caring person, as well, and then maintain sensitive, empathic, and altruistic attitudes toward others.

We expect, therefore, that secure adults' social interaction goals and positive models of self and others will foster effective caregiving. Secure adults' comfort with intimacy and interdependence (Hazan & Shaver, 1987) allows them to approach others in need, because in order to be comforting and helpful, a care provider typically has to acknowledge and accept other people's needs for closeness, sympathy, and support (Lehman, Ellard, & Wortman, 1986). Secure adults' positive expectations concerning other people's goodwill and cooperativeness make it easier for them to construe a distressed person as deserving sympathy and compassion. Moreover, positive models of self may help secure people feel confident about their ability to handle another person's distress and maintain emotional balance while addressing the person's needs, a task that might otherwise generate an overwhelming degree of personal distress (e.g., Batson, 1987).

Insecure adults, in contrast, are likely to have difficulty providing effective care (Collins et al., 2006; George & Solomon, 1999; Shaver & Hazan, 1988). Although anxiously attached people may have some of the skills and qualities needed for effective caring (e.g., comfort with intimacy and closeness), their characteristic focus on their own vulnerabilities and unsatisfied attachment needs may draw important mental resources away from attending to the needs of others. Moreover, their strong desire for closeness and approval may cause them to become overly involved and enmeshed, intensifying their experience of personal distress and blurring the distinction between the other person's welfare and their own. Attachment anxiety also can taint caregiving motives with egoistic desires for intense closeness, acceptance, inclusion, and other people's gratitude. According to Collins et al. (2006), these self-centered motives encourage compulsive caregiving, based on lack of sensitivity to the needy other's signals. Anxious people may try to get too close or too involved when a partner doesn't want much help or any help of the kind insistently offered, and this can generate resentment, anger, and conflict.

An avoidant person's lack of comfort with closeness and negative models of others may also interfere with sensitive and responsive care. Their dislike of, and discomfort with, expressions of need and vulnerability may cause them to back away rather than get involved with someone whose needs are all too evident. For them, a distressed person sometimes provides a mirror that reminds them of their own vulnerabilities, causing them to detach and escape rather than offer help. In some cases, negative models of others and associated hostile attitudes toward them may even transform sympathy or pity into contemptuous gloating, causing them actually to enjoy others' unfortunate fate.

The Attachment-Caregiving Link in the Context of Close Relationships

These theoretical ideas have received strong support in studies assessing caregiving responses to close relationship partners' needs (i.e., the needs of one's children, parents, dating partners, or spouse). In studies of parent–child relationships, secure parents are consistently found to be more attentive, sensitive, and responsive to their infant's needs and less distressed when interacting with their infant, as compared with insecure parents (e.g., Bosquet & Egeland, 2001; Crowell & Feldman, 1988; Grossmann, Fremmer-Bombik, Rudolph, & Grossmann, 1988; Haft & Slade, 1989; Pederson, Gleason, Moran, & Bento, 1998). For example, Haft and Slade (1989) videotaped interactions between mothers and their infant children and found that secure mothers were attuned to both positive and negative emotions expressed by their babies. They were also consistent in reacting to their baby's needs. In contrast, anxious mothers reacted inconsistently to both positive and negative emotions, and avoidant mothers did not seem to attend or react coherently to negative emotions at all. In another study, Crowell and Feldman (1988) found that secure mothers were rated by independent judges as warmer, more supportive, and more helpful toward their preschool children in a problem-solving situation than were insecure mothers. Crowell and Feldman (1998) also found that whereas avoidant mothers were cool and controlling when interacting with their child, anxious mothers gave confusing instructions and were intrusive when trying to help their children.

In a later study, Crowell and Feldman (1991) videotaped mothers' behavior when their child was exposed to an attachment-related threat – separation from mother in a laboratory setting – and found that secure mothers were more affectionate toward their children and prepared them better for a separation than did insecure mothers. Avoidant mothers showed little distress and affection toward their child; anxious mothers were agitated, found it difficult to leave the room, and were highly distressed during a subsequent reunion, making it more difficult for their children to recover from the separation. In another study, Goodman, Quas, Batterman-Faunce, Riddlesberger, and Kuhn (1997) asked parents to describe their interactions with their child after the child underwent a threatening and painful medical procedure. They found that secure parents were more likely than insecure parents to discuss the procedure with their child and physically comfort the child afterward. Edelstein et al. (2004) videotaped children's and parents' behavior when the children received an inoculation at an immunization clinic and found that more avoidant parents were less responsive to their distressed children. Thus, as expected based on attachment theory, insecure parents appear to be less effective caregivers.

The attachment-caregiving link has been studied at the other end of the age continuum as well, when adult children may be called upon to care for their aging parents. For example, Cicirelli (1993) and Townsend and Franks (1995) found that adult children who were more securely attached to their aging parents reported providing more care to their parents while experiencing less caregiver burden. In other studies, adult children who scored higher on attachment anxiety or avoidance reported experiencing more caregiver burden and providing less emotional support to their aging parents (e.g., Carpenter, 2001; Crispi, Schiaffino, & Berman, 1997). There is also evidence that relatively avoidant adult children whose parents suffer from progressive dementia are more likely than less avoidant ones to institutionalize their parents rather than provide care at home (Markiewicz, Reis, & Gold, 1997). Sörensen, Webster, and

Roggman (2002) asked middle-aged adults about their preparation for caring for their aging parents in the future and found that attachment anxiety and avoidance were associated with being less prepared.

Attachment-related differences in caregiving have also been assessed in the context of dating and marital relationships. Using the Caregiving Questionnaire (Kunce & Shaver, 1994), several researchers have assessed caregiving attitudes toward a dating partner or spouse. This questionnaire measures responsive, controlling, and compulsive patterns of caregiving in couple relationships. Responsive caregiving is defined by *proximity maintenance* to a partner in times of need (e.g., "When my partner is troubled or upset, I move closer to provide support or comfort") and *sensitivity* to a partner's signals and needs (e.g., "I am very attentive to my partner's nonverbal signals for help and support"). *Controlling* caregiving includes maintenance of a domineering, non-mutual stance when offering "help" and failure to respect a partner's ability to solve the problem at hand (e.g., "When I help my partner with something, I tend to do things my way"). *Compulsive* caregiving is indicated by over-involvement with the partner's distress and a tendency to merge with the needy partner (e.g., "I frequently get too 'wrapped up' in my partner's problems and needs").

Findings consistently indicate that secure individuals are more likely to provide support to their partner and be sensitive to the partner's needs, and less likely to be controlling or over-involved in caregiving (e.g., Feeney, 1996; Feeney & Collins, 2001; Feeney & Hohaus, 2001; Kunce & Shaver, 1994). Moreover, whereas avoidant individuals score lower on responsive caregiving and higher in controlling caregiving, anxious individuals score higher on compulsive caregiving, reflecting their over-involvement with a partner's problems. Importantly, Feeney (2005) found that attachment insecurities also interfered with providing a secure base for a dating partner's exploration: More avoidant people reported being less available when their partner pursued important personal goals, and more anxious people reported compulsive caregiving that disrupted a partner's activities.

Beyond identifying insecure adults' caregiving patterns within romantic and marital relationships, Feeney and colleagues (Feeney, 2005; Feeney & Collins, 2003) assessed motives for providing care to a romantic partner and found that secure adults tended to endorse more altruistic reasons for helping (e.g., helping out of concern for the partner needs). In contrast, avoidant adults reported more egoistic reasons for helping (e.g., to avoid a partner's negative reactions, to get something explicit in return). Moreover, they disliked coping with a partner's distress, lacked a sense of responsibility for their partner, and perceived the partner as too dependent. Attachment-anxious adults endorsed altruistic reasons for helping (helping because of concern for the partner), but they also reported helping in order to gain a partner's approval and increase the partner's relationship commitment. In addition, anxious people attributed their reluctance to provide a secure base for their partner's exploration to worries that the partner's independent pursuits might damage the relationship. In terms of Underwood's (Chapter 1, this volume) model, insecurely attached persons seem to be lacking in the altruistic motives characteristic of compassionate love.

Insecure people's patterns of caregiving have also been observed in laboratory studies (e.g., Collins & Feeney, 2000; Feeney & Collins, 2001; Rholes, Simpson, & Orina, 1999; Simpson, Rholes, & Nelligan, 1992; Simpson, Rholes, Orina, & Grich, 2002). For example, Simpson et al. (1992) unobtrusively videotaped dating couples while the female partner waited to undergo a stressful procedure, finding that secure men recognized their partner's worries and provided more emotional support and more supportive verbal comments if their partner showed higher levels of distress. In contrast, men who scored high on avoidance actually provided less support as their partner's distress increased. To give another example, Collins and Feeney (2000) videotaped dating couples while one member of the couple disclosed a personal problem to the partner. Among participants who were assigned the role of caregiver (listening to a partner's disclosures), the attachment-anxious ones were less likely to provide instrumental support and were less responsive and more negative toward the distressed partner than participants who scored low on attachment anxiety.

Overall, these studies show that attachment insecurities interfere with caregiving in both parent–child relationships and adult couple relationships. In both kinds of relationship, avoidant people's deactivating defenses interfere with sensitive and responsive caregiving. Attachment-anxious people also have difficulties providing sensitive care to a partner. Their self-focus and insensitivity, combined with a wish that their partner would occupy the role of "stronger and wiser" caregiver, bury anxious people's good intentions in a welter of ineffective behaviors.

The Attachment-Caregiving Link in the Wider Social World

The establishment of empirical links between adult attachment styles and caregiving patterns in both parent–child and couple relationships led researchers to explore the possibility that attachment insecurity interferes with compassion toward suffering strangers, members of minority groups, and community members with special needs. It led us in particular to explore the possibility that attachment security, whether assessed as an individual-difference characteristic or enhanced experimentally, would be associated with compassion and empathy beyond the realm of well-established close relationships.

Several correlational studies have shown that avoidance is associated with less empathic concern for others' needs, a weaker inclination to adopt the perspective of a distressed person, less ability to share another person's feelings, less sense of communion with others, and less willingness to take responsibility for others' welfare (e.g., Corcoran & Mallinckrodt, 2000; Feeney & Collins, 2001; Joireman, Needham, & Cummings, 2002; Shaver et al., 1996; Zuroff, Moskowitz, & Cote, 1999). More avoidant people are less likely to be cooperative and to write comforting messages to a distressed person, and are perceived by peers as less supportive in a variety of hypothetical scenarios where someone was in need (e.g., Priel, Mitrany, & Shahar, 1998; Van Lange, de Bruin, Otten, & Joireman, 1997; Weger & Polcar, 2002). People who score high on attachment anxiety, on the other hand, report high levels of personal distress while witnessing another person's distress (Britton & Fuendeling, 2005; Joireman et al., 2002), and they score high on a measure of "unmitigated communion" – a compulsive need to help others even when they are not asking for assistance (Fritz & Helgeson, 1998; Shaver et al., 1996). In an observational study, Westmaas and Silver (2001) videotaped people while they interacted with a confederate who had (according to the experimenter) recently been diagnosed with cancer. Whereas more avoidant participants were less verbally and nonverbally supportive during the interaction, more anxious participants reported greater discomfort while interacting with the confederate and were more likely to report self-critical thoughts after the interaction.

In an attempt to examine the link between attachment and altruistic helping behavior more directly, we (Gillath, Shaver, Mikulincer, Nitzberg et al., 2005) assessed young adults' attachment orientations, their involvement in voluntary altruistic activities in their communities (in Israel, the Netherlands, or the United States), and their motives for volunteering. Participants completed the ECR (a measure of attachment anxiety and avoidance) and a scale assessing volunteer activities (e.g., teaching reading, counseling troubled people, providing care to the sick). They also completed the Volunteer Functions Inventory (VFI; Clary et al., 1998), a measure of the extent to which participants volunteered for either selfish, egoistic reasons (self-protection, career promotion, ego-enhancement, achieving a sense of togetherness that benefits the self) or more exploration-oriented and altruistic reasons (other-focused values, achieving a more mature understanding of the world and the self). In addition, participants completed scales tapping self-esteem and interpersonal trust, so that we could evaluate competing explanations for the results.

The findings were similar across the three countries. Avoidant attachment was consistently associated with engaging in fewer volunteer activities, devoting less time to such activities, and being less motivated by desires to express altruistic values and to understand, learn, and explore oneself and the world. Attachment anxiety generally was not related to engaging in volunteer activities or to devoting more or less time to such activities, but it was associated with more egoistic reasons for volunteering. That is, highly anxious individuals were not less likely to engage in volunteer activities than their less anxious counterparts, but their reasons for volunteering were often tinged with wishes to fit in, be thanked and appreciated, or be distracted from, or relieved of, their own problems. We also found that the associations between attachment and volunteering could not be explained by other factors, such as self-esteem or interpersonal trust.

Subsequently, we turned to experimental tests of causal predictions concerning the links between attachment security, compassion, and caregiving. In these experiments, we used well-validated priming techniques such as exposing participants to security-related words (love, hug, close) or names of their security-enhancing attachment figures (e.g., their mother or spouse), leading them through a guided imagery scenario in which they felt safe and secure, or asking them to visualize the face of a security-enhancing attachment figure in order to contextually activate mental representations of attachment security. Then, we assessed the effects of these priming procedures on feelings and attitudes toward needy people (Mikulincer et al., 2001, 2003; Mikulincer, Shaver, Gillath, & Nitzberg, 2005). We tried both subliminal priming (e.g., presentation of an attachment figure's name for only 20 milliseconds, which was not long enough to allow participants to recognize the name) and supraliminal priming (e.g., asking participants to visualize the face of an attachment figure or to think about a particular interaction with him or her) to be sure that the effects occurred whether or not the person knew how he or she was being influenced. Although this might have resulted in perceived "demand characteristics" in the case of supraliminal priming, the results were quite similar, regardless of the priming method used.

In the first of these studies, we (Mikulincer et al., 2001, Study 1) performed an experiment assessing compassionate responses to others' suffering. Dispositional attachment anxiety and avoidance were assessed with the ECR scale. (We use the term "dispositional" to refer to participants' general, stable, attachment orientations in close relationships, as measured by the ECR, which we distinguish from attachment-related mental representations and reactions triggered by specific situational forces, including the ones we create deliberately in our experiments.) Mental representations of attachment security were activated by having participants read a story about a loving attachment figure who provides sensitive, responsive social support. This experimental condition was compared with ones that induced either neutral or positive affect (reading a set of instructions for installing a high-fidelity stereo system; a series of brief jokes about comical social interactions and their consequences). Following the priming procedure, all participants rated their mood, read a brief story (similar to the one used by Batson et al., 1989) about a student whose parents had been killed in an automobile accident, and rated how much they experienced compassion (e.g., compassion, sympathy, tenderness) and personal distress (e.g., tension, worry, distress) when thinking about the student. The results confirmed that the security induction yielded higher levels of compassion than the neutral and positive affect conditions.

In addition, dispositional attachment anxiety and avoidance were inversely related to compassion, and anxiety was positively related to personal distress in response to another's suffering. That is, attachment anxiety, as expected based on theory, seems to amplify a form of distress that, while possibly aroused via empathy, fails to motivate a person to take care of a needy other. These findings were conceptually replicated in four additional studies (Mikulincer et al., 2001, Studies 2–5), using different methods of priming mental representations of attachment security (e.g., asking people to recall personal memories of supportive care, subliminally exposing them to positive attachment-related words) and measuring different dependent variables (e.g., coded descriptions of feelings elicited by others' suffering, accessibility of memories in which participants felt compassion or distress).

We also showed that the effects of security priming and the correlates of attachment-style dimensions could not be explained in terms of conscious mood (Mikulincer et al., 2001). Although the priming of positive affect reduced personal distress, this priming procedure did not significantly affect compassion. In addition, mood reports did not mediate the effects of security priming and dispositional attachment scores on compassion and personal distress. The effects of attachment security were not the same as the effects of the positive affect induction and were not explicable in terms of mood.

In another set of three experiments, we (Mikulincer et al., 2003) documented links between attachment security and two self-transcendent values, benevolence (concern for close others) and universalism (concern for all humanity). The values were measured either with standardized scales (Schwartz, 1992) or by asking participants to list their most important values. Dispositional attachment anxiety and avoidance were assessed with the ECR scale and mental representations of attachment security were experimentally activated by asking participants to recall personal memories of supportive care or by exposing them unobtrusively to a picture of a supportive interaction. Higher scores on the ECR avoidance scale were associated with lower scores on the two self-transcendent values, showing again that avoidant attachment is not conducive to concern for others' feelings. More important from a practical standpoint, priming mental representations of attachment security led to higher scores on the two prosocial values (compared with priming neutral or positive affect).

In a recent series of experimental studies, we (Mikulincer et al., 2005) examined the decision to help or not to help a person in distress. In the first two experiments, American and Israeli participants watched a confederate while she performed a series of increasingly aversive tasks. As the study progressed, the videotaped confederate became increasingly distressed by the aversive tasks, finally becoming quite upset about the prospect of having to pet a large, live tarantula in an open-topped glass tank. After a short break in the procedure, supposedly to allow the confederate to calm down, and after being told that she refused to continue performing the aversive tasks but would be willing to exchange roles, the actual participant was given an opportunity to take the distressed person's place.

Shortly before the scenario just described, participants were primed with either mental representations of attachment security (the names of a participant's security-enhancing attachment figures) or attachment-unrelated representations (the names of close people who did not function as an attachment figure or the names of mere acquaintances). To obtain the names of each participant's security-enhancing attachment figures, all of them completed a six-item WHOTO scale developed by Fraley and Davis (1997). Participants provided the first names of people to whom they sought proximity (e.g., "Who is the person you most like to spend time with?") and people who provided a safe haven and/or secure base for them (e.g., "Who is the person you want to talk to when you are worried about something?," "Who is the person you know will always be there for you?"). The three kinds of primes were administered either subliminally (via very rapid presentations of a person's name while participants performed a computerized cognitive task) or supraliminally (by explicitly asking participants to recall an interaction with a particular person). At the point of making a decision about replacing the distressed confederate, people completed brief measures of compassion and personal distress (based on Batson et al.'s 1989 research).

In both studies, security priming (either subliminally or supraliminally) caused participants to report higher levels of compassion toward the woman in distress and greater willingness to help her than attachment-unrelated priming (close person, acquaintance). More important, participants in the security priming conditions were more than twice as likely (~70% vs. ~30%) than those in the control conditions to actually replace the suffering woman and take on her remaining aversive tasks. Since these findings were obtained even when the primes were administered subliminally, we can be sure that the heightening of compassion and altruism produced by mental representations of attachment security did not require conscious mediation or deliberation. Rather, the attachment-caregiving link seemed to occur at a preconscious, automatic level. In addition, in line with previous findings, dispositional avoidance was negatively associated with compassionate and helpful responses, whereas attachment anxiety was associated with higher ratings of personal distress, but not greater compassion, while watching another person suffering. These effects were all obtained in both the American and Israeli samples.

Despite the theoretical cogency of the findings, they might also be explained in terms of modeling, because the priming procedure might directly arouse thoughts of helping without any mediation by attachment representations. That is, subliminal exposure to the name of a security provider might prime mental representations of a caring, supportive role model, who has repeatedly exhibited effective helping behavior, which in turn might facilitate one's own compassion and altruism. Although such modeling might facilitate caregiving, and might be part of what happens even in early childhood (e.g., when a child imitates a loving parent), the range and form of the security-priming effects we have obtained across various studies (for a review, see Mikulincer & Shaver, 2007b) cause us to believe that the main and most direct effect of security priming is to activate feelings of being protected and comforted. We do not think security priming activates caregiving representations and impulses directly. Rather, we believe they potentiate these representations and impulses only if they occur in conjunction with seeing a person in need. In other words, in the presence of a person in need, security priming promotes the smooth activation and functioning of the caregiving system by virtue of weakening or eliminating attachment-related worries and defensive (avoidant) tendencies. Several of our studies have demonstrated this anxiety and defense reducing effect of security priming (Mikulincer & Shaver, 2007b).

Because there were no statistical interactions between security priming and dispositional attachment orientations, we know that increasing a person's sense of security increases his or her tendency to provide effective care, regardless of attachment style. This implies that temporary activation of the sense of attachment security allows even chronically insecure people to react to others' needs in ways similar to those of people with a more secure attachment style. Contextual augmentation of security may remind people of similar experiences stored in memory, inhibit incongruent memories of attachment insecurity, and bring to mind cognitive and action schemas that are congruent with security. In this way, a particular mental representation of attachment security may spread throughout a person's memory network, causing the person temporarily to become more compassionate or helpful. It is important to note, however, that the findings suggest that temporary effects of security enhancement coexist with the effects of dispositional attachment orientations. That is, reactions to others' needs are concurrently affected by experimentally-enhanced attachment security and chronically accessible schemas related to attachment anxiety and avoidance.

In two additional studies, we (Mikulincer et al., 2005, Studies 3–4) asked whether contextual activation of mental representations of attachment security could override egoistic motives for helping, such as mood enhancement (Schaller & Cialdini, 1988) and empathic joy (Smith, Keating, & Stotland, 1989). Participants were randomly assigned to one of two priming conditions (security priming, neutral priming), read a true newspaper article about a woman in dire personal and financial distress, and rated their emotional reactions to the article (compassion, personal distress). In one study, half of the participants anticipated mood-enhancement by means other than helping (e.g., expecting, immediately after this part of the experiment, to watch a comedy film). In the other study, half of the participants were told that the needy woman was chronically depressed and her mood might be beyond their ability to improve (*no empathic joy* condition). Schaller and Cialdini (1988) and Smith, Keating, and Stotland (1989) found that these two conditions, expecting to improve mood by other means or anticipating no sharing of joy with the needy person, reduced egoistic motivations for helping because a person gains no special mood-related benefit from helping the needy person. However, in our studies, these conditions failed to inhibit security-induced altruistic motives for helping, which arose even when the manipulated egoistic motives were absent (Batson, 1991).

We found that expecting to improve one's mood by means other than helping or expecting not to be able to share a needy person's joy following the provision of help reduced compassion and willingness to help in the neutral priming condition, but not in the security priming condition. Instead, security priming led to greater compassion and willingness to help even when there was no egoistic reason (no empathic joy, no mood relief) for helping.

Of special interest, both studies also indicated that expecting to improve one's mood by watching a comedy film or anticipating no sharing of joy with the needy person reduced compassion and willingness to help *only among relatively avoidant people*. Only they provided evidence for the assumption that helping is an outgrowth of selfishness when it occurs at all. Egoistic concerns held less sway over people who were either dispositionally less avoidant or under the influence of a security prime. It seems, therefore, that attachment security counteracts some of the egoistic motives underlying avoidant people's failure to help.

The combined evidence from our experimental studies and the correlational studies reviewed earlier in this chapter indicates that attachment security, whether established in a person's long history of close relationships or induced experimentally by priming procedures, makes compassion and altruistic caregiving more likely. Although there are other reasons for one person to help another, the prosocial effects of attachment security do not depend on alternative egoistic motives, such as a person's desire to improve his or her own mood or the desire to share a suffering person's relief. We think it is likely that the sense of attachment security reduces one's need for defensive self-protection and allows a person to activate his or her caregiving behavioral system, direct attention to others' distress, and engage in altruistic behavior with the primary goal of benefiting other people, rather than oneself. For secure people, helping others does not seem to be selfishly motivated and is not aimed at self-protection or self-enhancement, presumably because they already feel sufficiently safe and secure. The sense of security frees attention and mental energy to be used by the caregiving system, allowing a person to adopt a truly empathic attitude toward others' distress.

This conclusion fits with our two-level model of psychological defenses (Mikulincer & Shaver, 2005). In this model, attachment-figure availability and the resulting sense of attachment security provide a stable and secure foundation for psychological resilience and mental health. Being able to count on available, caring, and supportive attachment figures during times of need provides an important sense of personal safety and protection, and a solid and authentic sense of self-worth. Security-related mental representations and social skills act as resilience resources that maintain emotional balance and effective psychological functioning without the need for defenses. Attachment security, which sustains self-esteem and reduces selfish defenses, facilitates the functioning of other behavioral systems, including the caregiving system, which maintains compassionate, generous, loving attitudes toward others even when providing care produces no direct personal benefit other than achieving the natural goals of the caregiving system.

A second level of defenses is required when a person fails to form secure attachments and is unable to maintain a solid and stable psychological foundation. For an insecurely attached person, many everyday experiences challenge the sense of safety and threaten the person's already tenuous hold on life, self, and identity. At this secondary, defensive level, a "prevention motivational orientation" (Higgins, 1998) and the use of ego-protective defenses can sometimes compensate for a shortage of loving and accepting attachment figures, create a façade of self-esteem, and contribute some degree of emotional equanimity and personal adjustment. But the natural functioning of the caregiving system can be damaged by such a defensive stance, subordinating its operation to self-protective goals and strategies. In such cases, the caregiving system is activated mainly when helping others promises to improve one's own mood or enhance one's own self-esteem.

We believe, in unison with Bowlby (1969/1982) and Batson (1991), that the caregiving system is guided by the altruistic, benevolent goal of promoting other people's welfare, and that egoistic motives for helping arise from the absence of attachment security. Our findings and reasoning suggest that the caregiving behavioral system that evolved to assure adequate care for vulnerable, dependent children can be extended, through kind social treatment and effective moral modeling, to include care and concern for other people, even if we generally tend to care more for people with whom we are closely related, either psychologically or genetically. The attachment behavioral system affects the caregiving system, making it likely that heightening security will yield benefits in the realm of compassionate, altruistic behavior.

The research reviewed here indicates that caregiving can be generalized or extended to strangers and that attachment security facilitates a generalized compassionate attitude toward all humanity. Although the prototypical biological function of the caregiving system is to facilitate the survival of offspring, which should cause it to be most strongly applied to people with whom one has a close relationship, recurrent functioning of the caregiving system in favorable, security-providing environments may transform empathy, compassion, and altruism into chronically accessible dispositions, traits, or skills that can be contextually activated by the presence of a distressed person, even a stranger in need. That is, what begins as caring for specific individuals (especially offspring) can become transformed and generalized into a prosocial disposition or trait that is applied very broadly. The availability of sensitive, loving, and caring attachment figures contributes greatly to this extension and expansion of compassion, caring, and altruism. Future studies should examine in greater depth the process by which compassionate love is generalized from close relationship partners to strangers and the extent to which security-enhancement through media or school systems can increase a compassionate attitude towards others' needs.

In following Bowlby and Ainsworth's lead, we have portrayed attachment security as a likely prerequisite for the optimal functioning of other behavioral systems. One reason for doing so is that attachment behavior and attachment styles appear early in infant development, whereas caregiving (e.g., as first indicated, for example, by empathy in 3-year-olds; Kestenbaum, Farber, & Sroufe, 1989) appears next. Another reason for giving prominence to the attachment system is that its biological function – assuring protection (i.e., survival) – is obviously necessary if one is to provide support and comfort to needy others. Once a child has a functioning attachment system and has begun to adapt to the local caregiving environment (i.e., once a stable attachment style has developed), the child's caregiving system comes online to deal with sibling and peer relationships and to allow the child to be influenced by enculturation and moral socialization.

Given that children with different attachment styles act in, and experience, social relationships differently, the operating parameters of the caregiving system may be shaped in directions compatible with the parameters of the attachment system. Also potentially important, as discussed earlier, are direct imitation and modeling of primary caregivers, which might create similarities between a child's attachment system (shaped by the parents) and his or her caregiving system (modeled on those of the parents). Future developmental research should examine the trajectories of attachment and caregiving from childhood to adulthood and determine how parenting behavior, a parent's personality, and other familial, social, and cultural factors shape these trajectories. For example, researchers could examine the extent to which parents' attachment orientations, caregiving practices, interpersonal skills, values, and norms contribute to the development of their offspring's compassionate love during childhood and adolescence. Moreover, research could determine whether and how early influences on compassion shape adults' later involvement in altruistic and philanthropic activities.

There are at least two ways to think about the connections between the attachment and caregiving systems. One possibility is that the two systems are affected by individual differences in temperament or personality. Several studies have been conducted to see whether global attachment styles, or attachment-style dimensions, are redundant with one or more of the "big five" personality traits: openness to experience, conscientiousness, extroversion, agreeableness, and neuroticism. The evidence so far suggests that they are related, but not redundant (e.g., Carver, 1997; Noftle & Shaver, 2006; Shaver & Brennan, 1992). Attachment measures have frequently outperformed global personality measures in predicting caregiving behaviors (e.g., Mikulincer et al., 2001, 2005; Simpson et al., 1996). In addition, we have controlled for neuroticism, self-esteem, and interpersonal trust in several of our studies and still obtained predicted effects of attachment anxiety and avoidance (Gillath, Shaver, Mikulincer, Nitzberg et al., 2005; Mikulincer et al., 2005).

Nevertheless, attachment and caregiving may be influenced by genes. To date, there have been only a few behavior genetic studies of attachment in infancy and adulthood, and their findings are inconsistent. Some suggest a role for genetic, temperamental factors in shaping individual differences in attachment and some do not (e.g., Bakermans-Kranenburg, van IJzendoorn, Bokhorst, & Schuengel, 2004; Brussoni, Jang, Livesley, & MacBeth, 2000; Crawford et al., in press; O'Connor & Croft, 2001). It is likely that similarities, degrees of overlap, and differences in what is tapped by measures of adult attachment and caregiving can eventually be better understood by discovering the extent to which they have similar or different genetic and social-environmental roots. Much more research is needed to determine how, and to what extent, security-enhancing experiences interact with genes and patterns of gene expression to influence caregiving motives and behavior.

A second alternative is that caregiving behavior feeds back on attachment security. This alternative fits with Underwood's (Chapter 1, this volume) model, according to which being compassionate, loving, and caring toward others can alter the substrate of compassionate love, which we believe includes the attachment system. Even if the operating parameters of the caregiving system are shaped by variations in attachment security, they may also be influenced by specific life circumstances that facilitate or block effective caregiving (e.g., attending religious services or a school that fosters empathy, compassion, and benevolence). Moreover, adult attachment styles are not mere reflections of early parent–infant interactions, but can be affected by later social experiences (e.g., Davila & Cobb, 2004; Fraley, 2002). Hence, expressions of the caregiving system (e.g., volunteering to help others and becoming more self-confident as a result) and experiences in close relationships (e.g., caring effectively for a romantic partner and thereby enhancing relationship satisfaction and stability) can feed back on a person's attachment security.

At present we know relatively little about the extent to which the caregiving system affects the attachment system. However, we have preliminary evidence from a cross-sectional, correlational study in which attachment-anxious people who volunteered in the community reported less loneliness and lower levels of interpersonal problems than attachment-anxious people who did not engage in such activities (Gillath, Shaver, Mikulincer, Nitzberg et al., 2005). We need more sophisticated longitudinal and experimental designs that allow us to delineate the boundaries and mediators of these effects. For example, further research is needed to identify the self-esteem benefits that people receive from engaging in philanthropic activities, and to see whether these benefits influence attachment security. Research is also needed that evaluates the effects of engaging in altruistic activities on a person's sense of being valued, admired, approved, and accepted by others. Among these effects might be the strengthening of person's sense of attachment security.

Concluding Comments: A Broader Perspective

The process we have described in this chapter, whereby attachment security supports compassionate, altruistic love is referred to, either explicitly or implicitly, in many religious sayings and practices. In Buddhism, for example, a common form of compassion meditation involves remembering what it feels like to receive unconditional love from an attachment figure and then turn that love, in one's mind (and eventually in one's behavior), toward other targets. Chödrön (2003) describes the procedure as follows:

> To begin, we start just where we are. We connect with the place where we currently feel loving-kindness, compassion, joy, or equanimity, however limited they may be ... Then we gradually extend [this] to a widening circle of relationships ... "May I be free from suffering and the root of suffering. May you be free from suffering and the root of suffering. May all beings be free of suffering and the root of suffering." (pp. 66–67)

This is remarkably similar to the security inductions we used in our research to foster compassion and altruism, even though we had not heard about the Buddhist technique. We began with reminders of others who had provided study participants with love and kindness, and we then checked to see whether greater compassion arose as a result – and it did. Our manipulations were based on attachment theory rather than Buddhism, but the two approaches are similar in this and other respects.

Buddhism also recognizes the importance of love to the development of a healthy mind. According to Chödrön (2003):

> The essential practice is to cultivate maitri, or loving-kindness ... [An] image for maitri is that of a mother bird who protects and cares for her young until they are strong enough to fly away. People sometimes ask, "Who am I in this image – the mother or the chick?" The answer is *both* ... Without loving-kindness for ourselves, it is difficult, if not impossible, to genuinely feel it for others. (pp. 9–10)

This is similar to our ideas about the importance of attachment figures' love and secure self-representations to the ability to be compassionate toward oneself and other people. However, attachment theory and research point to the social origins of this ability and show that it is much more difficult for some people than for others to apply "maitri" to themselves or anyone else.

Our approach is also relevant to Judeo-Christian religions. The golden rule of these religions, for example, which enjoins people to treat others as they would like to be treated themselves, is obviously easier to follow if one knows what it is like to be treated well, can accurately empathize with other people's need for kind treatment, and can provide for others without feeling cheated, robbed, or entitled to praise. Moreover, religious "models" (Oman & Thoresen, 2003) are generally portrayed in Judeo-Christian scriptures and stories as security-enhancing attachment figures who love their followers and enjoin them to treat others lovingly as well. Jesus, for example, is described by John (13:35) as saying, "By this all will know that you are my disciples, if you have love for one another." Luke (6:30–36) describes Jesus as giving the following instructions: "Give to everyone who asks of you ... Love your enemies, do good, and lend, hoping for nothing in return." Thinking about a caring and loving God or such a God incarnate, praying to a security-enhancing God, and acknowledging God's protective and comforting power may be effective ways to promote compassionate love and altruistic behavior because they enhance a believer's sense of security. Future research should test this intriguing possibility.

Seeing the similarity between attachment theory and religious traditions suggests that attachment theory (like other humanistic theories in psychology) grows out of a core set of ideas that appear repeatedly in human history and in psychology. The potential advantages of attachment theory, when seen in the context of previous psychological, religious, and philosophical approaches, are its roots in evolutionary biology and its growing body of empirical research evidence. Our hope, for both our work and the present volume more generally, is that it will prove possible to integrate the valid insights of previous and current thinkers while providing useful details concerning psychological and neural mechanisms. This should lead to valuable policies and practices for parents, educators, therapists, and political and religious leaders, all of whom play a role in moving humanity closer to universal compassionate love and world peace.

References

Ainsworth, M. D. S., Blehar, M. C., Waters, E., & Wall, S. (1978). *Patterns of attachment: Assessed in the strange situation and at home.* Hillsdale, NJ: Lawrence Erlbaum.

Bakermans-Kranenburg, M. J., van IJzendoorn, M. H., Bokhorst, C. L., & Schuengel, C. (2004). The importance of shared environment in infant–father attachment: A behavioral genetic study of the attachment Q-sort. *Journal of Family Psychology, 18*, 545–549.

Baldwin, M. W., Keelan, J. P. R., Fehr, B., Enns, V., & Koh Rangarajoo, E. (1996). Social-cognitive conceptualization of attachment working models: Availability and accessibility effects. *Journal of Personality and Social Psychology, 71*, 94–109.

Bartholomew, K., & Horowitz, L. M. (1991). Attachment styles among young adults: A test of a four-category model. *Journal of Personality and Social Psychology, 61*, 226–244.

Batson, C. D. (1987). Prosocial motivation: Is it ever truly altruistic? In L. Berkowitz (Ed.), *Advances in experimental social psychology: Vol. 20* (pp. 65–122). New York: Academic Press.

Batson, C. D. (1991). *The altruism question: Toward a social-psychological answer.* Hillsdale, NJ: Lawrence Erlbaum.

Batson, C. D., Batson, J. G., Griffitt, C. A., Barrientos, S., Brandt, J. R., Sprengelmeyer, P., & Bayly, M. J. (1989). Negative-state relief and the empathy-altruism hypothesis. *Journal of Personality and Social Psychology, 56*, 922–933.

Bosquet, M. & Egeland, B. (2001). Associations among maternal depressive symptomatology, state of mind, and parent and child behaviors: Implications for attachment-based interventions. *Attachment and Human Development, 3*, 173–199.

Bowlby, J. (1973). *Attachment and loss: Vol. 2. Separation: Anxiety and anger.* New York: Basic Books.

Bowlby, J. (1980). *Attachment and loss: Vol. 3. Sadness and depression.* New York: Basic Books.

Bowlby, J. (1969/1982). *Attachment and loss: Vol. 1. Attachment* (2nd ed.). New York: Basic Books.

Bowlby, J. (1988). *A secure base: Clinical applications of attachment theory.* London: Routledge.

Brennan, K. A., Clark, C. L., & Shaver, P. R. (1998). Self-report measurement of adult attachment: An integrative overview. In J. A. Simpson & W. S. Rholes (Eds.), *Attachment theory and close relationships* (pp. 46–76). New York: Guilford Press.

Britton, P. C., & Fuendeling, J. M. (2005). The relations among varieties of adult attachment and the components of empathy. *Journal of Social Psychology, 145*, 519–530.

Brussoni, M. J., Jang, K. L., Livesley, W., & MacBeth, T. M. (2000). Genetic and environmental influences on adult attachment styles. *Personal Relationships, 7*, 283–289.

Carpenter, B. D. (2001). Attachment bonds between adult daughters and their older mothers: Associations with contemporary caregiving. *Journals of Gerontology: Series B: Psychological Sciences and Social Sciences, 56B*, 257–266.

Carver, C. S. (1997). Adult attachment and personality: Converging evidence and a new measure. *Personality and Social Psychology Bulletin, 23*, 865–883.

Cassidy, J., & Kobak, R. R. (1988). Avoidance and its relationship with other defensive processes. In J. Belsky & T. Nezworski (Eds.), *Clinical implications of attachment* (pp. 300–323). Hillsdale, NJ: Lawrence Erlbaum.

Cassidy, J., & Shaver, P. R. (Eds.). (1999). *Handbook of attachment: Theory, research, and clinical applications.* New York: Guilford Press.

Chödrön, P. (2003). *Comfortable with uncertainty.* Boston, MA: Shambhala.

Cicirelli, V. G. (1993). Attachment and obligation as daughters' motives for caregiving behavior and subsequent effect on subjective burden. *Psychology and Aging, 8,* 144–155.

Clary, E. G., Snyder, M., Ridge, R. D., Copeland, J., Stukas, A. A., Haugen, J., & Miene, P. (1998). Understanding and assessing the motivations of volunteers: A functional approach. *Journal of Personality and Social Psychology, 74,* 1516–1530.

Collins, N. L. (1996). Working models of attachment: Implications for explanation, emotion, and behavior. *Journal of Personality and Social Psychology, 71,* 810–832.

Collins, N. L., & Feeney, B. C. (2000). A safe haven: An attachment theory perspective on support seeking and caregiving in intimate relationships. *Journal of Personality and Social Psychology, 78,* 1053–1073.

Collins, N. L., Guichard, A. C., Ford, M. B., & Feeney, B. C. (2006). Responding to need in intimate relationships: Normative processes and individual differences. In M. Mikulincer & G. S. Goodman (Eds.), *Dynamics of romantic love: Attachment, caregiving, and sex* (pp. 149–189). New York: Guilford Press.

Corcoran, K. O., & Mallinckrodt, B. (2000). Adult attachment, self-efficacy, perspective taking, and conflict resolution. *Journal of Counseling and Development, 78,* 473–483.

Crawford, T. N., Livesley, W. J., Jang, K. L., Shaver, P. R., Cohen, P., & Ganiban, J. (in press). Insecure attachment and personality disorder: A twin study of adults. *Journal of Personality Disorders.*

Crispi, E. L., Schiaffino, K., & Berman, W. H. (1997). The contribution of attachment to burden in adult children of institutionalized parents with dementia. *Gerontologist, 37,* 52–60.

Crowell, J. A., & Feldman, S. S. (1988). Mothers' internal models of relationships and children's behavioral and developmental status: A study of mother–child interaction. *Child Development, 59,* 1273–1285.

Crowell, J. A., & Feldman, S. S. (1991). Mothers' working models of attachment relationships and mother and child behavior during separation and reunion. *Developmental Psychology, 27,* 597–605.

Davila, J., & Cobb, R. J. (2004). Predictors of changes in attachment security during adulthood. In W. S. Rholes & J. A. Simpson (Eds.), *Adult attachment: Theory, research, and clinical implications* (pp. 133–156). New York: Guilford Press.

Dawkins, R. (1976/1989). *The selfish gene.* New York: Oxford University Press.

Edelstein, R. S., Alexander, K. W., Shaver, P. R., Schaaf, J. M., Quas, J. A., Lovas, G. S., & Goodman, G. S. (2004). Adult attachment style and parental responsiveness during a stressful event. *Attachment and Human Development, 6,* 31–52.

Feeney, B. C. (2005). *Individual differences in secure base support provision: The role of attachment style, relationship characteristics, and underlying motivations.* Unpublished manuscript, Carnegie Mellon University, Pittsburgh, PA.

Feeney, B. C., & Collins, N. L. (2001). Predictors of caregiving in adult intimate relationships: An attachment theoretical perspective. *Journal of Personality and Social Psychology, 80,* 972–994.

Feeney, B. C., & Collins, N. L. (2003). Motivations for caregiving in adult intimate relationships: Influences on caregiving behavior and relationship functioning. *Personality and Social Psychology Bulletin, 29,* 950–968.

Feeney, J. A. (1996). Attachment, caregiving, and marital satisfaction. *Personal Relationships, 3,* 401–416.

Feeney, J. A. (1999). Adult romantic attachment and couple relationships. In J. Cassidy & P. R. Shaver (Eds.), *Handbook of attachment: Theory, research, and clinical applications* (pp. 355–377). New York: Guilford Press.

Feeney, J. A., & Hohaus, L. (2001). Attachment and spousal caregiving. *Personal Relationships, 8,* 21–39.

Fraley, R. C. (2002). Attachment stability from infancy to adulthood: Meta-analysis and dynamic modeling of developmental mechanisms. *Personality and Social Psychology Review, 6,* 123–151.

Fraley, R. C., & Davis, K. E. (1997). Attachment formation and transfer in young adults' close friendships and romantic relationships. *Personal Relationships, 4,* 131–144.

Fraley, R. C., Davis, K. E., & Shaver, P. R. (1998). Dismissing-avoidance and the defensive organization of emotion, cognition, and behavior. In J. A. Simpson & W. S. Rholes (Eds.), *Attachment theory and close relationships* (pp. 249–279). New York: Guilford Press.

Fraley, R. C., & Shaver, P. R. (2000). Adult romantic attachment: Theoretical developments, emerging controversies, and unanswered questions. *Review of General Psychology, 4,* 132–154.

Fraley, R. C., & Waller, N. G. (1998). Adult attachment patterns: A test of the typological model. In J. A. Simpson & W. S. Rholes (Eds.), *Attachment theory and close relationships* (pp. 77–114). New York: Guilford Press.

Fritz, H., & Helgeson, V. S. (1998). Distinctions of unmitigated communion from communion: Self-neglect and over-involvement with others. *Journal of Personality and Social Psychology, 75,* 121–140.

George, C., & Solomon, J. (1999). Attachment and caregiving: The caregiving behavioral system. In J. Cassidy & P. R. Shaver (Eds.), *Handbook of attachment: Theory, research, and clinical applications* (pp. 649–670). New York: Guilford Press.

Gillath, O., Shaver, P. R., & Mikulincer, M. (2005). An attachment-theoretical approach to compassion and altruism. In P. Gilbert (Ed.), *Compassion: Conceptualizations, research, and use in psychotherapy* (pp. 121–147). London: Brunner-Routledge.

Gillath, O., Shaver, P. R., Mikulincer, M., Nitzberg, R. A., Erez, A., & van IJzendoorn, M. H. (2005). Attachment, caregiving, and volunteering: Placing volunteerism in an attachment-theoretical framework. *Personal Relationships, 12,* 425–446.

Goodman, G. S., Quas, J. A., Batterman-Faunce, J. M., Riddlesberger, M. M., & Kuhn, J. (1997). Children's reactions to and memory for a stressful event: Influences of age, anatomical dolls, knowledge, and parental attachment. *Applied Developmental Science, 1,* 54–75.

Grossmann, K., Fremmer-Bombik, E., Rudolph, J., & Grossmann, K. E. (1988). Maternal attachment representations as related to patterns of infant–mother attachment and maternal care during the first year. In R. A. Hinde & J. Stevenson-Hinde (Eds.), *Relationships within families* (pp. 241–260). Oxford, England: Oxford Science Publications.

Haft, W., & Slade, A. (1989). Affect attunement and maternal attachment: A pilot study. *Infant Mental Health Journal, 10,* 157–172.

Hamilton, W. D. (1964). The genetical evolution of social behavior. I and II. *Journal of Theoretical Biology, 7,* 1–52.

Hazan, C., & Shaver, P. R. (1987). Romantic love conceptualized as an attachment process. *Journal of Personality and Social Psychology, 52,* 511–524.

Higgins, E. T. (1998). Promotion and prevention: Regulatory focus as a motivational principle. In M. P. Zanna (Ed.), *Advances in experimental social psychology: Vol. 30* (pp. 1–46). New York: Academic Press.

Joireman, J. A., Needham, T. L., & Cummings, A. L. (2002). Relationships between dimensions of attachment and empathy. *North American Journal of Psychology, 4,* 63–80.

Kestenbaum, R., Farber, E. A., & Sroufe, L. A. (1989). Individual differences in empathy among preschoolers: Relation to attachment history. In N. Eisenberg (Ed.), *Empathy and related emotional competence (New Directions for Child Development, No. 44,* pp. 51–64). San Francisco, CA: Jossey-Bass.

Kunce, L. J., & Shaver, P. R. (1994). An attachment-theoretical approach to caregiving in romantic relationships. In K. Bartholomew & D. Perlman (Eds.), *Advances in personal relationships: Vol. 5* (pp. 205–237). London, England: Jessica Kingsley.

Lehman, D. R., Ellard, J. H., & Wortman, C. B. (1986). Social support for the bereaved: Recipients' and providers' perspectives of what is helpful. *Journal of Consulting and Clinical Psychology, 54,* 438–446.

Markiewicz, D., Reis, M., & Gold, D. P. (1997). An exploration of attachment styles and personality traits in caregiving for dementia patients. *International Journal of Aging and Human Development, 45,* 111–132.

Mikulincer, M., Gillath, O., Halevy, V., Avihou, N., Avidan, S., & Eshkoli, N. (2001). Attachment theory and reactions to others' needs: Evidence that activation of the sense of attachment security promotes empathic responses. *Journal of Personality and Social Psychology, 81,* 1205–1224.

Mikulincer, M., Gillath, O., Sapir-Lavid, Y., Yaakobi, E., Arias, K., Tal-Aloni, L., & Bor, G. (2003). Attachment theory and concern for others' welfare: Evidence that activation of the sense of secure base promotes endorsement of self-transcendence values. *Basic and Applied Social Psychology, 25,* 299–312.

Mikulincer, M., Gillath, O., & Shaver, P. R. (2002). Activation of the attachment system in adulthood: Threat-related primes increase the accessibility of mental representations of attachment figures. *Journal of Personality and Social Psychology, 83,* 881–895.

Mikulincer, M., & Shaver, P. R. (2001). Attachment theory and intergroup bias: Evidence that priming the secure base schema attenuates negative reactions to out-groups. *Journal of Personality and Social Psychology, 81,* 97–115.

Mikulincer, M., & Shaver, P. R. (2003). The attachment behavioral system in adulthood: Activation, psychodynamics, and interpersonal processes. In M. P. Zanna (Ed.), *Advances in experimental social psychology: Vol. 25* (pp. 53–152). San Diego, CA: Academic Press.

Mikulincer, M., & Shaver, P. R. (2004). Security-based self-representations in adulthood: Contents and processes. In W. S. Rholes & J. A. Simpson (Eds.), *Adult attachment: Theory, research, and clinical implications* (pp. 159–195). New York: Guilford Press.

Mikulincer, M., & Shaver, P. R. (2005). Mental representations of attachment security: Theoretical foundation for a positive social psychology. In M. W. Baldwin (Ed.), *Interpersonal cognition* (pp. 233–266). New York: Guilford Press.

Mikulincer, M., & Shaver, P. R. (2007a). *Attachment in adulthood: Structure, dynamics, and change.* New York: Guilford Press.

Mikulincer, M., & Shaver, P. R. (2007b). Boosting attachment security to promote mental health, prosocial values, and intergroup tolerance. *Psychological Inquiry, 18,* 139–156.

Mikulincer, M., Shaver, P. R., Gillath, O., & Nitzberg, R. A. (2005). Attachment, caregiving, and altruism: Boosting attachment security increases compassion and helping. *Journal of Personality and Social Psychology, 89,* 817–839.

Noftle, E. E., & Shaver, P. R. (2006). Attachment dimensions and the big five personality traits: Associations and comparative ability to predict relationship quality. *Journal of Research in Personality, 40,* 179–208.

O'Connor, T. G., & Croft, C. M. (2001). A twin study of attachment in preschool children. *Child Development, 72,* 1501–1511.

Oman, D., & Thoresen, C. E. (2003). Spiritual modeling: A key to spiritual and religious growth? *International Journal for the Psychology of Religion, 13,* 149–165.

Pederson, D. R., Gleason, K. E., Moran, G., & Bento, S. (1998). Maternal attachment representations, maternal sensitivity, and the infant–mother attachment relationship. *Developmental Psychology, 34,* 925–933.

Priel, B., Mitrany, D., & Shahar, G. (1998). Closeness, support and reciprocity: A study of attachment styles in adolescence. *Personality and Individual Differences, 25,* 1183–1197.

Reis, H. T., & Shaver, P. R. (1988). Intimacy as an interpersonal process. In S. Duck (Ed.), *Handbook of research in personal relationships* (pp. 367–389). London: John Wiley.

Rholes, W. S., Simpson, J. A., & Orina, M. M. (1999). Attachment and anger in an anxiety-provoking situation. *Journal of Personality and Social Psychology, 76,* 940–957.

Schaller, M., & Cialdini, R. B. (1988). The economics of empathic helping: Support for a mood management motive. *Journal of Experimental Social Psychology, 24,* 163–181.

Schwartz, S. H. (1992). Universals in the content and structure of values: Theoretical advances and empirical tests in 20 countries. In M. P. Zanna (Ed.), *Advances in experimental social psychology: Vol. 25* (pp. 1–65). Orlando, Fl: Academic Press.

Shaver, P. R., & Brennan, K. A. (1992). Attachment styles and the "big five" personality traits: Their connections with each other and with romantic relationship outcomes. *Personality and Social Psychology Bulletin, 18,* 536–545.

Shaver, P. R., & Clark, C. L. (1994). The psychodynamics of adult romantic attachment. In J. M. Masling & R. F. Bornstein (Eds.), *Empirical perspectives on object relations theory (Empirical studies of psychoanalytic theories: Vol. 25,* pp. 105–156). Washington, DC: American Psychological Association.

Shaver, P. R. & Hazan, C. (1988). A biased overview of the study of love. *Journal of Social and Personal Relationships, 5,* 473–501.

Shaver, P. R., & Hazan, C. (1993). Adult romantic attachment: Theory and evidence. In D. Perlman & W. Jones (Eds.), *Advances in personal relationships: Vol. 4* (pp. 29–70). London, England: Jessica Kingsley.

Shaver, P. R., & Mikulincer, M. (2002). Attachment-related psychodynamics. *Attachment and Human Development* [Special Issue: The psychodynamics of adult attachments – Bridging the gap between disparate research traditions], *4,* 133–161.

Shaver, P. R. & Mikulincer, M. (2005). Attachment theory and research: Resurrection of the psychodynamic approach to personality. *Journal of Research in Personality, 39,* 22–45.

Shaver, P. R., Papalia, D., Clark, C. L., Koski, L. R., Tidwell, M., & Nalbone, D. (1996). Androgyny and attachment security: Two related models of optimal personality. *Personality and Social Psychology Bulletin, 22,* 582–597.

Simpson, J. A., Rholes, W. S., & Nelligan, J. S. (1992). Support seeking and support giving within couples in an anxiety-provoking situation: The role of attachment styles. *Journal of Personality and Social Psychology, 62,* 434–446.

Simpson, J. A., Rholes, W. S., Orina, M. M., & Grich, J. (2002). Working models of attachment, support giving, and support seeking in a stressful situation. *Personality and Social Psychology Bulletin, 28,* 598–608.

Simpson, J. A., Rholes, W. S., & Phillips, D. (1996). Conflict in close relationships: An attachment perspective. *Journal of Personality and Social Psychology, 71,* 899–914.

Smith, K. D., Keating, J. P., & Stotland, E. (1989). Altruism revisited: The effect of denying feedback on a victim's status to an empathic witness. *Journal of Personality and Social Psychology, 57,* 641–650.

Sörensen, S., Webster, J. D., & Roggman L. A. (2002) Adult attachment and preparing to provide care for older relatives. *Attachment and Human Development, 4,* 84–106.

Townsend, A. L. & Franks, M. M. (1995). Binding ties: Closeness and conflict in adult children's caregiving relationships. *Psychology and Aging, 10,* 343–351.

Van Lange, P. A. M., de Bruin, E. M. N., Otten, W., & Joireman, J. A. (1997). Development of prosocial, individualistic, and competitive orientations: Theory and preliminary evidence. *Journal of Personality and Social Psychology, 73,* 733–746.

Weger, H., Jr., & Polcar, L. E. (2002). Attachment style and person-centered comforting. *Western Journal of Communication, 66,* 84–103.

Westmaas, J. L., & Silver, R. C. (2001). The role of attachment in responses to victims of life crises. *Journal of Personality and Social Psychology, 80,* 425–438.

Zuroff, D. C., Moskowitz, D. S., & Cote, S. (1999). Dependency, self-criticism, interpersonal behavior and affect: Evolutionary perspectives. *British Journal of Clinical Psychology, 38,* 231–250.

9

Compassionate Acts: Motivations for and Correlates of Volunteerism among Older Adults

Allen M. Omoto, Anna M. Malsch,
and Jorge A. Barraza

In many different ways and contexts, people take individual actions that have a large and collective impact on society. Not all of these efforts are necessarily motivated by an explicit desire to benefit society, certainly, but their combined effects have profound and far-reaching consequences. For example, people may recycle and conserve energy, as well as use mass transit, in order to preserve and conserve natural resources, save money, or simply to avoid the stress of driving at rush hour. They may engage in lobbying and advocacy efforts to rouse other people to work for the passage of legislation of concern to them. They may join and actively work for social movements that are dedicated to causes they believe in, such as improving the living conditions for disadvantaged individuals, protecting and expanding human rights, and working for peace at home and abroad.

In this chapter, we focus on volunteerism as an exemplar of social action; importantly, we also consider volunteerism as one possible behavioral manifestation of compassionate love. Volunteerism includes activities such as providing companionship to the elderly, tutoring the illiterate, counseling the troubled, or assisting sick individuals to care for themselves. In the United States, it is estimated that over 61 million people, or close to 30% of the US population, volunteered through or for an organization at least once during 2005–2006 (Bureau of Labor Statistics, 2007). And approximately 25% of older adults aged 65 or over are active volunteers (Bureau of Labor Statistics, 2007). Whereas the United States has long been marked by relatively high rates of volunteerism, voluntary action can be found in countries throughout the world (e.g., Allik & Realo, 2004; Curtis, Grabb, & Baer, 1992; Van Vugt, Snyder, Tyler, & Biel, 2000).

Volunteerism is only one of the many and varied ways in which people attempt to help other people. However, there are important ways in which volunteerism stands apart from other forms of prosocial action. For example, volunteerism can be distinguished from charitable giving and philanthropy in that the work of volunteers goes beyond simply donating money or goods (although, on average, people who volunteer also donate substantially more money to charity than non-volunteers; Independent Sector, 2001). Philanthropic efforts are crucial to the success of many organizations and service programs, but our focus is on volunteer behavior itself. In addition, we distinguish between "forced" and freely chosen volunteer efforts. Many schools, businesses, and other institutions provide volunteer opportunities that are mandatory for students or employees or perceived as all-but required (e.g., service learning programs, some corporate–community partnerships). And, although the recipients and societal benefits of these programs may be similar to freely chosen volunteer efforts (e.g., Clary, Snyder, & Stukas, 1998; Stukas, Snyder, & Clary, 1999), our interests are in the instances and organizations in which individuals provide assistance to other people and causes without receiving compensation or having been obviously coerced.

In short, volunteerism is a unique form of prosocial action in which people actively and freely seek out opportunities to provide non-monetary assistance to others perceived to be in need and in which helpers do not expect to be compensated for their work. These efforts can be costly in terms of time and resources, can extend over long periods of time, and generally occur in an organizational context. Furthermore, and unlike much other prosocial action and social support, there are generally no prior interpersonal bonds or obligations to help between volunteers and recipients of services (Omoto & Snyder, 1995; see also Penner, Dovidio, Piliavin, & Schroeder, 2005; Wilson, 2000).

Theory and Research on Volunteerism

The Volunteer Process Model (see Omoto & Snyder, 1995; Snyder & Omoto, 2007) is a conceptual model that includes the defining features of volunteerism and focuses on volunteerism as a process that unfolds over time. This model specifies psychological and behavioral features associated with each of three sequential and interactive stages (i.e., antecedents, experiences, and consequences) and speaks to activity at multiple levels of analysis (i.e., the individual, the interpersonal, the organizational, and the social system). A simplified schematic of this model with illustrative examples for each "cell" of the model is shown in Figure 9.1. This model has guided our research on volunteering, but has also been used in other empirical work on volunteering (e.g., Davis et al.,

Levels of analysis	Stages of the volunteer process		
	Antecedents	Experiences	Consequences
Individual	Personality, motivation, life circumstances	Satisfaction, stigma, organizational integration	Knowledge and attitude change, health
Interpersonal/ social group	Group memberships, norms	Helping relationship, collective esteem	Composition of social network, relationship development
Organization	Recruitment strategies, training	Organizational culture, volunteer placement	Volunteer retention, work evaluation
Societal/ cultural context	Ideology, service programs, institutions	Service provision, program development	Social capital, economic savings

Figure 9.1   Schematic of the Volunteer Process Model

1999; Penner & Finkelstein, 1998) and as a framework for understanding prosocial behavior more generally (e.g., Penner, 2002; Penner et al., 2005).

At the first, *antecedents*, stage, the model identifies personality, motivational, and circumstantial characteristics of individuals that predict who becomes involved as volunteers. In research focused on this stage, researchers have sought to identify specific personality characteristics and motivational tendencies, as well as characteristics of people's life circumstances, that are related to volunteerism and that predict who becomes more effective and satisfied in their work (see Omoto & Snyder, 1990, 1993, 1995; Omoto, Snyder, & Martino, 2000; Snyder & Omoto, 1992a, 1992b; Snyder, Omoto, & Smith, in press).

At the *experiences* stage, the model explores psychological and behavioral aspects of the interpersonal relationships that develop between volunteers and recipients of their services, and pays particular attention to the behavioral patterns and relationship dynamics that facilitate the continued service of volunteers and positive benefits to the recipients of their services (Crain, Snyder, & Omoto, 2000; Lindsay, Snyder, & Omoto, 2003; Omoto, Gunn, & Crain, 1998). In addition, research at this stage examines correlates of satisfaction for volunteers and recipients of service, as well as factors that may make for more pleasant and rewarding experiences (such as organizational integration) and those that detract from enjoyment (such as stigmatization by others); Kiviniemi, Snyder, & Omoto, 2002; Snyder, Omoto, & Crain, 1999.

Finally, at the *consequences* stage, the model focuses on the impact of volunteer service at different levels and especially on changes in attitudes, knowledge, and behavior. As such, research has examined the impact of volunteer service on the attitudes and behaviors of volunteers, the recipients of their services, and the members of their social networks, including such "bottom-line" behaviors as continuing involvement and willingness to recruit others to the volunteer service organization (Barraza, 2007; O'Brien, Crain, Omoto, & Snyder, 2000; Omoto & Snyder, 1995; Omoto, Snyder, Chang, & Lee, 2001; Snyder et al., 1999).

In addition to these sequential stages, the Volunteer Process Model characterizes volunteerism as a phenomenon that is situated at, and builds bridges between, many levels of analysis. At the level of the *individual*, the model calls attention to the activities and psychological processes of individual volunteers and recipients of volunteer services. Thus, volunteers make decisions to get involved, seek out service opportunities, engage in volunteer work for some period of time, and eventually cease their efforts. At the *interpersonal* level, the model expands this focus, incorporating the dynamics of the helping relationships between volunteers and recipients of service. At an *organizational or agency* level, the model focuses on the goals associated with recruiting, managing, and retaining an unpaid workforce, including the related concerns about work performance, compensation, and evaluation. These concerns come about because volunteer efforts typically take place through or in cooperation with community-based organizations or other agencies (and can therefore be distinguished from informal helping). Thus, the Volunteer Process Model includes aspects of organizational structure, roles, and operations. Finally, at a *societal* level, the model considers the linkages between individuals and broader social structures and institutions. In addition, it takes account of collective and cultural dynamics that impact and are influenced by events and activities at "lower" levels of analysis. To date, and as the examples noted above attest, most of the empirical work derived from the Volunteer Process Model has focused on variables and constructs at the individual level of analysis. However, the model is clearly much broader and integrative; it should prove useful for future research rooted in different disciplinary perspectives.

Conceptualizing Volunteerism as an Expression of Compassionate Love

In this chapter, we seek to connect research on volunteerism and the Volunteer Process Model to recent theorizing on compassionate love. Specifically, we view acts of volunteerism, and especially an individual's provision of care and support to others, as *potential* expressions of compassionate love. In our view, and for the purposes of this chapter, compassionate love enacted involves actions primarily motivated by concern about another person or group and that are intended to benefit the other. Thus, compassionate love may be expressed in many ways, and is not restricted only to instances of volunteerism. Similarly, not all volunteerism is necessarily enacted compassionate love, especially because volunteerism is known to be motivated by many different reasons or needs (e.g., Clary et al., 1998; Omoto & Snyder, 1995). In considering the links between volunteerism and compassionate love, therefore, we start by identifying beneficent acts and then examine the motivations as well as consequences of these actions. In other words, we ask, "what motivates volunteerism?" and "what are the effects of having engaged in volunteerism not only for those who receive help, but also for the individuals who provide it?" In empirical work, to be discussed later, we begin with the simple behavioral observation of people helping others, again for extended periods of time and without compensation or obligation, and consider this activity to be one possible behavioral manifestation of compassionate love. Our interest then turns to possible differences in motivation for what appear to be similar actions, and whether and how the different motivations may relate to different effects of volunteerism.

In keeping with the Volunteer Process Model, our emphasis on volunteerism includes the motivational antecedents and consequences of volunteer actions. However, we note that compassionate love has been the starting point for others (e.g., Sprecher & Fehr, 2005; Underwood, 2002, Chapter 1, this volume), and that their definitions and descriptions of compassionate love may encompass some acts of volunteerism. For example, Sprecher and Fehr (2005) define compassionate love as an *attitude* that focuses on "caring, concern, tenderness, and an orientation toward supporting, helping, and understanding" (p. 630) without necessarily focusing on any of the specific actions that may derive from this attitude. Underwood (2002, Chapter 1, this volume), meanwhile, offers a fuller model of compassionate love that outlines situational and contextual factors that set the stage for a range of behaviors that can be considered expressions of compassionate love, as well as some of the consequences that follow from them (primarily the benefit to the recipient, and the side effect of spiritual growth, moral development, and gaining of insight for the enactor). In this model, certain motivations as well as discernment are critical in defining whether or not different behaviors can be considered expressions of compassionate love. Finally, this model also incorporates feedback to the broader social and cultural context in which expressions of compassionate love occur; these expressions are predicted to increase the capacity for future acts of caring and compassionate love.

A closer examination of this model suggests aspects that can be related to our conceptualization of volunteerism. For example, Underwood

(2002, Chapter 1, this volume) proposes that one definitional aspect of compassionate love is free choice in that individuals exercise choice in offering their love to others. As noted above, one defining feature of volunteerism according to the Volunteer Process Model is that it occurs without obligation or expectation, and therefore invites exploration of the particular motivations that lead people to engage in it (see Omoto & Snyder, 1995; Snyder & Omoto, 2007). In short, choice seems to play a central role both in defining what compassionate love is and in distinguishing volunteerism from other forms of helping behavior.

Moreover, cognitive and emotional understanding of situations and individuals is central to Underwood's definition of compassionate love. True compassionate love does not occur without some degree of understanding. Similarly, in volunteer work, as in much social support, volunteers must calibrate their help to the needs of the recipient. Not all support has positive effects (e.g., Rook, 1984), and depending on the context, timing, and extent of help offered, can convey unflattering messages of dependence and incompetence to the help recipient or reinforce power differentials between the helper and help recipient (e.g., Nadler, 2002; Nadler & Fisher, 1986; Nadler & Halabi, 2006). Not surprisingly, then, volunteer efforts are likely to be most well received and beneficial to the extent that there is good understanding between the volunteer and recipient of services. Thus, both compassionate love and volunteer efforts are built upon and made more effective through understanding between helper and recipient.

Continuing with Underwood's (2002) model, being aware of and open to influences outside of and larger than oneself is another important component of compassionate love, and in many instances, this encompassing framework includes divine inspiration or religious and spiritual beliefs. Not incidentally, a good deal of volunteer work occurs in the context of religious institutions and organizations (e.g., Wilson, 2000). While not essential to understanding volunteerism, for many people volunteerism seems to be prompted by or tied to religious and faith-based concerns and institutions. Furthermore, value-based reasons, some of which are religious values, have been shown to be common in motivating volunteerism and other social action (e.g., Clary et al., 1998; Malsch, 2005; Omoto & Snyder, 1995). Thus, religious and spiritual beliefs often, but not always, play a role in both compassionate love and volunteerism.

To this point, then, we have noted some of the ways that volunteerism may "fit" within the framework of compassionate love offered by Underwood (2002, Chapter 1, this volume), as well as some important differences in emphasis between her model and the foci and research of the Volunteer Process Model. In the remainder of this chapter, we present the results of a study of older adults, many of whom were actively and currently engaged as volunteers. These results help illustrate potential connections between the models and perspectives. Specifically, we begin our empirical analyses at the point at which positive behavior occurs, using volunteerism as the positive behavior of interest. We investigate the extent to which volunteerism is understood by laypersons as involving compassion or as being an expression of compassionate love. Next, we explore some of the motivational underpinnings for volunteerism, but with special focus on motivations that are relatively selfish or altruistic in nature. That is, we distinguish between self-focused and other-focused motivations and the extent to which they are linked to volunteerism. We also attempt to connect these motivations to different personal dispositions and propensities; that is, we attempt to empirically assess the extent to which different "substrates" are related to different motivations. Finally, we examine a select set of correlates of volunteer behavior, namely subjective health assessments. In doing so, we attempt to establish some of the potential positive consequences of expressing compassionate love, and also to test if these effects are greater when compassionate acts are motivated by one type of motivation or another. To be clear, Underwood's model makes no claim about potential health consequences of compassionate love expressed; instead, we draw from the growing body of research on the health correlates of helping behavior (e.g., Post, 2007) in examining subjective health in relation to volunteer activity.

A Research Study on Compassionate Acts among Older Adults

The data included in this chapter come from a program of psychological research exploring volunteerism among older adults, and specifically how volunteerism may be linked to religious and spiritual beliefs, feelings of empathy and compassion, and indicators of health. The data, taken from questionnaire responses, allow us to describe the characteristics and motivations of older volunteers, the extent of their volunteer activity, including volunteer activity in religious contexts (whether or not religiously motivated), and selected health correlates of these compassionate acts.

A total of 228 people completed the questionnaire. They were residents of four retirement communities ($n = 141$, 62%) and attendees at two different community senior centers (living independently) ($n = 87$, 38%) in greater Los Angeles County, California. All four communities were roughly the same size, and provided a continuum of care ranging from independent living in on-campus apartments or houses to long-term custodial care in a designated health center. The two senior centers from which participants were recruited are located in the same towns as the retirement communities, and all recruitment sites are within 15 minutes of each other.

Participants ranged from 54 to 94 years of age ($M = 78.60$, $SD = 7.15$). The sample consisted of 72.7% women and 27.3% men, and was predominately white (84.4%). Participants were well-educated; 84.3% of them had attained some post-high school education. Most of the participants were either married (41.5%) or widowed (40.1%), with 11.6% divorced or separated, and 6.9% single or never married. The majority of the sample was retired (90%), and most participants (81%) reported an annual household income of at least $25,000. Participants were also predominately Christian, with 73% claiming a Protestant religious affiliation and 10% saying they were Catholic.

At the beginning of the questionnaire, participants were provided with the following definition of volunteering: "By volunteering, we mean any type of *unpaid work* that you do or have done *that helps others*. Some examples of this type of activity include preparing and delivering meals to homebound individuals, coaching a youth sports team, staffing a crisis hotline, providing care and support to people in need, and so on." They were then asked, "Do you currently volunteer?" and were provided with a *yes/no* response option. If they checked the *yes* box, they were instructed to answer a more detailed set of questions, indicating the quantity and range of their current volunteer work. Specifically, using a five-point scale (1 = not at all; 5 = extremely), participants rated how active they were currently in the following types of organizations: "church," "other faith-based," "school- or youth-related," "health-related," "seniors," "political, service, or philanthropic," "civic or neighborhood," "professional/ employment," and "social." Responses to these items were summed to form a *volunteer activity* composite ($\alpha = .56$).

We also created indices of religious-based volunteer work and non-religious volunteer activity. Specifically, for *religious-based volunteer activity*, we averaged the activity ratings for "church" and "other faith-based" volunteering ($r = .28$). For *non-religious volunteer activity*, we averaged the ratings for the remaining eight organization types ($\alpha = .46$). Because people can be very involved in volunteer work in one domain or even with one organization without necessarily being highly involved in other domains or with other organizations, high internal consistency reliabilities were not necessarily expected across the different indices of volunteer activity. Thus, the relatively low reliabilities obtained for the composite volunteerism measures were not surprising; however, they may have weakened our ability to detect relationships among some of the variables.

Perceptions of Volunteerism as Compassionate Love

We first explored the possibility that individuals who were current volunteers and those who were not currently volunteering might view volunteering differently. In particular, we compared the extent of their agreement with statements suggesting that they believe that volunteerism is strongly linked to compassionate love. These analyses might be considered a test of one of our key assumptions – that volunteerism can be and is often thought of as an expression of compassionate love. We expected that to the extent that individuals "walk the talk" of their beliefs, that endorsement of the link between compassion and volunteerism would be higher among active volunteers than non-volunteers. The questionnaire contained four items that tapped this link: "To me, volunteering is an expression of love," "For me, compassion and volunteering are closely linked to each other," "Love motivates me to act on behalf of my community," and "Volunteering allows people to express a sense of compassion." These items were strongly related to each other ($\alpha = .88$) and were averaged to form an index of *perceptions of volunteerism as compassionate love.*

Although all participants tended to view volunteerism as indicative of compassionate love ($M = 3.72$ on the 5-point scale), this tendency was significantly greater among participants who were currently volunteering ($n = 137$, $M = 3.79$) than individuals who were not currently volunteering ($n = 40$, $M = 3.38$); $t = 2.37$, $p < .05$. Of course, we cannot know the causal direction in this cross-sectional comparison (i.e., whether perceiving volunteerism as an expression of compassionate love leads people to volunteer or if engaging in volunteer work enhances these perceptions). However, the reliable difference suggests that individuals who engage in compassionate acts of volunteerism see a strong connection between what they do and compassionate love.

We also examined if ratings of perceptions of volunteerism as compassionate love were differentially related to volunteering in religious or faith-based organizations and volunteering in other, secular organizations among active volunteers only. Approximately 55% of volunteers claimed to do at least some volunteer work in religious organizations, whereas the remaining volunteers claimed to work only in non-religious contexts. There was no difference in the perceptions of volunteerism as compassionate love between people who volunteered in religious versus non-religious contexts; $t < 1.0$, *ns*.

Next, we correlated the ratings of perceptions of volunteerism as compassionate love with ratings of volunteer activity in both religious and non-religious contexts. We found a positive but relatively small correlation for religious volunteer activity ($r = .12$, $p < .10$) and a significant and positive relationship for non-religious volunteer activity ($r = .17$, $p < .05$). These correlations were of similar magnitude and did not differ significantly from each other. Thus, it seems that to the extent that people perceive volunteering to be an expression of compassionate love, they are also likely to report greater volunteer activity in both religious and non-religious organizations. Perceiving volunteering as closely linked to compassionate love was not necessarily more characteristic of religiously-based volunteerism.

The first simple point these results highlight, therefore, is that active volunteers (as well as non-volunteers to a lesser extent) perceive volunteerism to be associated with feelings of compassion and compassionate love. It is possible, in fact, that feelings of compassionate love may be a prime motivation for volunteering among older adults, although this speculation goes beyond the current data. We do know that to the extent that individuals consider volunteerism to be an expression of compassion and love, they report devoting more time and energy to helping others as volunteers.

The second, and intriguing, finding is that perceptions of volunteerism as an expression of compassionate love were related to volunteer activity in both religious and non-religious domains. That is, we found no evidence that perceptions of volunteerism as an expression of compassionate love were more strongly linked to work in religious than non-religious contexts. Our participants understood volunteerism as closely linked to compassion and compassionate love, and the strength of these perceptions did not vary with the context of their volunteerism. We recognize that the context of volunteerism (religious or non-religious organizations) is not the same as the inspiration or motivation for volunteerism. It is entirely possible, for example, that people divinely inspired to volunteer may choose to help others in non-religious settings. The point we are emphasizing is that the volunteers in our sample saw their work as expressions of compassion, and this was true regardless of the context in which they were volunteering.

Motivations for Volunteerism

Because motivations are crucial to definitions of compassionate love and potentially in predicting the consequences of compassionate love expressed, we next looked at the underlying motivations that our participants reported for their compassionate acts. In Underwood's (2002) model, discernment and other-focused motivation are important for producing positive effects, such as the development of the person who expresses compassionate love. (e.g., moral and spiritual growth) In fact, the balance or relative importance of motives focused on the self (such as desire for social praise or personal reward) and those focused on caring for, valuing, and doing good for another is suggested to be critical in determining the nature of the effects on the caregiver or helper. Said another way, the core motives that push an individual to engage in helpful actions are thought to play a large role in determining the effects of those actions on the individual.

This line of logic is consistent with theory and research on volunteerism that has sought to distinguish different types of motivations for volunteer work, the relevance of different motivations for different periods of life or circumstance (e.g., Boling, 2005; Omoto et al., 2000), and to isolate the effects of different motivations for the amount of time served, satisfaction with volunteer work, persistence in volunteer efforts, and even effectiveness as a volunteer (e.g., Barraza, 2007; Lindsay et al., 2003; Omoto & Snyder, 1995; Omoto et al., 2000; Penner & Finkelstein, 1998). As suggested by research from the Volunteer Process Model, the very same motivations can, in fact, produce different patterns of effects, depending on the individual and context.

For example, engaging in volunteer work for self-focused reasons may be natural and important, and lead to substantial personal growth at one developmental period (e.g., in early or mid adulthood, when education and career goals are important), whereas other-focused motivations may be more likely to lead to beneficial effects at other developmental periods (e.g., in older adulthood, when generativity and legacy are important; see Boling, 2005; Omoto et al., 2000). Or, the influences and benefits of other-focused motivations may be stronger for individuals with certain dispositional tendencies (such as empathic, kind-hearted, and communal) than for individuals with other personality traits or characteristics (less empathic, more selfish, more agentic; e.g., Davis, Hall, & Meyer, 2003; Davis et al., 1999). Self-focused and other-focused motivations also may be more important in sustaining volunteers in some contexts than in others (Omoto & Snyder, 1995; Penner & Finkelstein, 1998), or even at different stages of the volunteer process (see Snyder et al., in press). The conceptual point is that different motivations may lead to expressions of compassionate love, and different effects for both helper and recipient may result, with the specific motivations that are important varying by person, context, culture, and so on (see also van de Vliert, Huang, & Levine, 2004).

In addressing these issues empirically, we decided to consider possible motivations for volunteerism that were more general and did not necessarily revolve around only compassion per se. We examined measures of self-reported motivations for volunteering that have been shown to reliably assess volunteer motivations across multiple dimensions (i.e., items from Clary et al., 1998; Omoto & Snyder, 1995). Specifically, participants used a five-point scale in rating the importance of a list of different reasons for their volunteer work.

One type of motivation relates to personal *values*, and includes humanitarian concern and other personal guiding values that promote and encourage volunteerism. This motivation is exemplified by relatively high ratings for reasons such as "Because of my personal values, convictions, and beliefs," and "Because of my humanitarian obligation to help others." Another important type of motivation focuses on *community concern*, or the desire to support and assist a specific community of people, whether or not the volunteer considers himself or herself to be a member of that community. Sample items for this motivation include, "Because of my concern and worry about a particular community," and "To help members of a particular community."

Other reasons for volunteering are relatively more self-focused. These motivations focus on *career* considerations, such as volunteering in order to bolster career skills and experiences or to broaden employment-relevant networks (e.g., "Because I can make new contacts that might help my business or career"), or volunteering in order to gain greater *understanding* or knowledge about a problem, cause, or set of people (e.g., "To learn more about how to prevent certain problems"). Other motivations for volunteerism include *personal development* concerns (e.g., "To challenge myself and test my skills"), ego or *esteem enhancement* (e.g., To feel better about myself") or to bring stability to one's life, and *social* concerns such as expanding one's social network and meeting similar others (e.g., "To meet new people and make new friends.").

Rather than examining this large and differentiated set of motivations, however, and in keeping with the simple distinction between giving to others versus motives for the self, we created two aggregate measures of motivation. One type of motivation, *other-focused motivation*, was tapped by averaging participant responses to the items in the values and community concern motivation scales. An index of *self-focused motivation* was calculated by averaging responses to the remaining motivation scales. Both of these aggregate measures proved to be highly reliable (α_{other} = .75, α_{self} = .81). They were also significantly related to each other (r = .56, $p < .001$), a finding that is not surprising because they are both measures of motivation for volunteerism. However, the fact that the correlation is only moderate in size suggests that acts of volunteerism can be motivated by different considerations and, perhaps, that at least some volunteers have multiple motives for the help they provide (see Kiviniemi et al., 2002). In summary, the motivations for volunteer service included concerns about benefiting others and concerns for benefiting the self.

Next, we correlated the self-focused and other-focused motivation scores and the measure of perceptions of volunteerism as compassionate love, as well as examining the connections between the different types of motivation and indices of volunteer activity. Following up on earlier analyses, we also explored possible differences in the connections between motivations for volunteerism in religious and secular contexts. These analyses were intended to provide initial evidence for the potential connections between motivations for volunteerism and religious outlets (if not inspiration) for this work.

We found that, across all volunteers, other-focused motivation was closely related to conceptualizing volunteerism as acts of compassionate love, $r = .74$, $p < .001$. That is, to the extent that participants claimed that values and community concern were important motivations for them to volunteer, they also saw volunteerism as connected to feelings of love and compassion for others. This finding is perhaps not surprising, but the magnitude of this correlation is quite large and could be interpreted as suggesting that holding a view of volunteerism as compassionate love functions very much like a motivation to volunteer. In fact, the correlation between these two measures is of sufficient magnitude that they might be able to be incorporated into a single scale or assessment of other-focused compassionate love as an impetus for volunteering.

In comparison, the correlation between the self-focused motivation aggregate and the perception measure was $r = .47$, $p < .001$. Although this relationship is substantial, it is significantly weaker than the connection between the measures of other-focused motivation and perception of volunteerism as compassionate love, $z = 5.06$, $p < .001$. It is not simply the case, therefore, that all motivations for volunteerism are interchangeable. From the results reported here, there were important distinctions between other- and self-focused motivations in their relationships with volunteerism conceptualized as compassionate love.

But, do the different motivations relate differentially to volunteer activity? To address this question, we computed correlations between the motivation measures and participants' ratings of their degree of volunteer activity. We found that both greater other-focused motivation ($r = .28$, $p < .001$) and self-focused motivation ($r = .29$, $p < .001$) were related to more volunteer activity. And, breaking down volunteer activity into separate indices of religious/faith-based activity and all other (secular) activity revealed a similar pattern of relationships. All four of these correlations (each motivation measure with each volunteer index) were small to moderate in size and of similar magnitude (all rs between .20–.26, ps < .01). In summary, both other- and self-focused motivation were positively related to volunteer activity, and there were no significant differences between the two types of motivation in their associations with activity in religious and non-religious contexts.

This pattern of results suggests that there are multiple routes rather than one single path to volunteerism; several different motivations can lead people to engage in volunteer work. This point has been made by others (e.g., Clary et al., 1998; Omoto & Crain, 1995; Omoto & Snyder, 1995; Omoto et al., 2000; Schondel, Shields, & Orel, 1992; Simon, Stürmer, & Steffens, 2000; van de Vliert et al., 2004), but it bears repeating here. Although volunteer work and organizations that utilize volunteers in delivering services may promote the "selfless" nature of these actions, volunteer efforts appear to be motivated just as strongly by motivations that benefit the self. From the perspective of help recipients, in fact, it may matter less *why* they receive help than that they receive it at all (but see Nadler & Fisher, 1986; Nadler & Halabi, 2006). For the help giver, however, the positive actions that are undertaken may have different implications, depending on why the actions were engaged in the first place. We empirically address this issue later in the chapter.

Potential Substrates of Motivation and Volunteerism

To this point, we have investigated people's perceptions of volunteerism as compassionate love, as well as broad motivations for volunteerism and the correlations between motivations and volunteer activity. In the remainder of this chapter, we continue to draw parallels and potential connections between Underwood's (2002) model of compassionate love and the Volunteer Process Model first by considering "substrates" or "individual antecedents" for compassionate acts of volunteerism and then later by assessing some of the potential effects of these acts on the individuals who perform them. In our consideration of substrates, we focus on potentially relevant individual differences and how other- and self-focused motivations as we have defined them may naturally flow from different dispositional characteristics and past experiences.

One individual difference measure that was included in the questionnaire completed by participants was a multiple-item measure of empathic concern. Specifically, the questionnaire contained five items from the Interpersonal Reactivity Index (Davis, 1983, 1996) that measured dispositional tendencies to experience empathic concern for others. Empathy, and empathic concern in particular, has been positively related to helping behavior, and volunteering, in prior research (see Davis et al., 1999, 2003). Participants rated their agreement with items such as, "I often have tender, concerned feelings for people less fortunate than me;" and "Sometimes I *don't* feel very sorry for other people when they are having problems") on a five-point scale. We averaged the scores to form an *empathic concern* composite. The internal consistency of this index was lower than might be expected ($\alpha = .63$), but because reliability analyses indicated that the alpha could not be improved by deleting any items, we retained all five items in the final measure.

In addition to this individual difference measure, we investigated another potential substrate, namely, psychological sense of community (see McMillan, 1996; McMillan & Chavis, 1986; Omoto & Malsch, 2005; Omoto & Snyder, 2002). This multidimensional construct was tapped by 23 items and assessed the extent to which participants felt connected to, proud of, and invested in their retirement communities or senior center (e.g., "I feel a sense of attachment and belonging to my senior center/retirement community," "I am proud to be part of my senior center/retirement community"). Participants rated their agreement with these items (again, using a five-point scale), and after scoring responses in a consistent direction, we averaged the items to create an overall index of *psychological sense of community* (PSOC, $\alpha = .91$). This measure does not so much assess an individual difference in motivation and volunteerism, but rather reflects the nature of participants' environments or experiences that are likely to encourage them to feel concern and take action for others. Taken together, then, two different possible "substrates" for motivation and action were considered: one is presumably stable and idiographic (empathic concern) and one is relatively more changeable and situational in nature (PSOC).

The results of our analyses revealed that both substrates were correlated with motivations for volunteerism. Specifically, both empathic concern ($r=.35$, $p<.001$) and PSOC ($r=.25$, $p<.01$) were significantly related to other-focused motivation. However, only empathic concern ($r=.23$, $p = .01$) was related to self-focused motivation (PSOC, $r=-.06$, *ns*). In addition, the links between both substrates and other-focused motivation were stronger than between the substrates and self-focused motivation ($zs>1.52$, $ps<.07$). This pattern of results held for volunteers working in religious or faith-based organizations as well as for those working only in secular contexts.

Taken together, these results support speculation that different motivations for volunteerism flow from or are rooted in different dispositional tendencies and life experiences. The specific pattern of results for empathy is also consistent with findings from research in which a substantial correlation was reported between compassionate love (conceptualized and measured as an attitude) and individual difference assessments of empathy (Sprecher & Fehr, 2005). Finally, our results are generally consistent with the approach and framework of Underwood (2002) by identifying two specific constructs that may function as potential substrates from which different motivations and compassionate love emerge. Individuals who easily and often feel empathy for others seem more likely to develop motivations for volunteerism that focus on serving others, meeting their needs, and expressing concern. Similarly, individuals who feel connected to their communities, find value in them, and see these communities as sources of companionship may be motivated to volunteer for other-focused reasons.

Our findings are based on correlational data. Thus, the causal connections that we are intimating remain in need of rigorous empirical testing. In addition, our results appear to have less to say about the reliable determinants of self-focused motivation and volunteerism than about other-focused motivation. These caveats notwithstanding, our evidence and speculation on the potential personal and situational determinants of motivations for volunteerism suggest that interventions intended to encourage such compassionate acts would do well to carefully attend to whom they target, their past experiences and current environments, and a range of possible motivations.

Volunteerism and Health

Having considered answers to the first question we posed earlier in this chapter, "what motivates volunteerism?," we now consider our second question: "what are some of the effects of volunteerism on those who engage in it?" In answering this question, we continue to focus on the individual level of analysis from the Volunteer Process Model, but now move to consider potential consequences of volunteerism. Underwood's model suggests not only that certain individual and social substrates might set the stage for different motivations for and expressions of compassionate love, but that individuals are likely to be impacted by their expressions of compassionate love. Specifically, compassionate love that flows from positive motivation and discernment (i.e., a motivation similar to other-focused motivation in our analyses) is likely to lead to moral and spiritual growth, along with attendant benefits of wisdom and insight. On the other hand, actions engaged in for negative reasons (i.e., similar to our self-focused motivation) are thought to have benign or potentially deleterious effects on individuals who engage in them.

Past research originating from the Volunteer Process Model has not necessarily shown direct negative effects of volunteerism motivated by self-focused concerns. Rather, this research suggests the greatest benefits and volunteer persistence occur when there is a close correspondence or match between an individual's motivations and the outcomes derived from volunteer work (see Clary et al., 1998; Snyder & Omoto, 2007; Snyder et al., in press) or when volunteers are motivated by relatively few and non-completing motivations than by many different motivations (Kiviniemi et al., 2002). Nonetheless, the possibility remains that the same compassionate acts, when enacted for different reasons, have differential effects on individuals. In our research, we examined the relationships between motivations and volunteerism and several measures of respondents' current and projected health that were included in the questionnaire. These measures permit us to conduct initial tests of hypotheses about differential effects of volunteering motivated by self- and other-focused concerns, and to address an individual-level consequence of volunteerism from the Volunteer Process Model that also has been the focus of increased attention in research on prosocial behavior.

In fact, there is a growing body of psychological and sociological research suggesting that volunteerism is related to an array of positive health outcomes for those who volunteer (House, 2001; House, Robbins, & Metzner, 1982; Piliavin, 2005). Research has found, for example, that older adults who volunteer compared to those who do not believe they are in better physical health (Young & Glasgow, 1998). Volunteerism also has been related to greater longevity (Moen, Dempster-McClain, & Williams, 1992; Musick, Herzog, & House, 1999), including lower mortality rates for volunteers relative to non-volunteers (Oman, Thoresen, & McMahon, 1999; see also Brown, Nesse, Vonokur, & Smith, 2003, for similar findings on the provision of informal help).

Volunteering also is related to better mental health. In fact, the results of several studies reveal that older volunteers are more satisfied with their lives than older adults who do not donate their time to helping others (e.g., Hunter & Linn, 1980–1; Thoits & Hewitt, 2001; van Willigen, 2000; see also Wheeler, Gorey, and Greenblatt, 1998, for a meta-analysis). In addition, compared to older adults who are non-volunteers, older adult volunteers have a greater will to live, lower levels of anxiety and depression (Hunter & Linn, 1980–1; Musick & Wilson, 2003), and higher morale, self-esteem, positive affect, and general well-being (Midlarsky & Kahana, 1991). Many older adults also formally or informally volunteer their time through religious groups or organizations (Krause, Ingersoll-Dayton, Liang, & Sugisawa, 1999; Musick et al., 1999). There is some evidence suggesting that the beneficial effects of volunteering on health may be stronger or enhanced for older adults who are also more religious (Musick & Wilson, 2003; Oman et al., 1999; Omoto, Schlehofer, Adelman, & Blagg, 2007). In short, research suggests considerable health benefits of helping others, although the causal direction of these effects (are healthier individuals more likely to volunteer, or does volunteering improve health?) and the specific mechanisms by which they occur are not yet clearly established (for a review of recent research on this topic, see Post, 2007).

Among the questionnaire items completed by participants in our research were three items in which they rated their current health as well as their current health "compared to 3 months ago" and "compared to most other people your age." These items were combined into a single composite measure of subjective health ($\alpha = .72$) that we used in attempting to track some of the individual-level benefits that might accrue to people as a result of engaging in compassionate acts of volunteerism.

Consistent with the research literature, the current volunteers in our sample ($M = 3.26$ on a four-point scale) reported better subjective health than non-volunteers ($M = 3.11$), although the difference was only marginally significant; $t = 1.66$, $p < .10$. However, total volunteer activity was unrelated to ratings of health; $r = .012$, ns. Likewise, our continuous measures of religious volunteer activity and non-religious volunteer activity were not reliably related to subjective health; $rs = .034$ and $-.084$, ns, respectively. Thus, in predicting subjective health, what seemed to matter most was whether or not participants volunteered at all, and not the extent of the volunteer activity they reported (see also Piliavin, 2005). As with all of the data reported in this chapter, our ability to ascertain the potential causal connections between these measures is limited. It could be that individuals who are or feel healthier are more likely to volunteer, or alternatively, volunteering and helping others may serve to increase the health and functioning of individuals over time. It is this latter possibility that intrigues us most, especially because of its implications for interventions targeted at enhancing the life expectancy and outcomes of individuals as they age.

In our questionnaire, we did ask participants how actively they were involved with each of the ten different types of organizations/causes they had previously used to rate their current volunteer activity, but this time with reference to "over the course of your life." By combining responses to these items as before, we created indices of lifetime activity in religious and non-religious volunteer organizations and causes. Next, we computed correlations between the lifetime volunteerism measures and the subjective health index. Overall, and across all participants, lifetime volunteer activity ($\alpha = .79$) was unrelated to ratings of subjective health; $r = .07$, ns. However, lifetime activity in religious/faith-based organizations was related to better current health ($r = .15$, $p < .05$), whereas lifetime volunteerism in non-religious organizations was not reliably related to health ($r = .07$, ns).

Although these findings emerge from self-report data, the significant relationship between lifetime activity in religious organizations and current health provides suggestive evidence that volunteering leads to better health, especially when volunteering is performed in religious and faith-based contexts. As suggested by the findings of other research, then, the impact of volunteering on those who volunteer may not be equal; religious-based volunteering may be especially beneficial (e.g., Musick & Wilson, 2003; Oman et al., 1999; Omoto & Schlehofer, 2007; Omoto et al., 2007). Specifically, the positive effects of compassionate love expressed would include perceptions of better, if not actual, health, and these effects seem to be clearest when compassionate acts are performed in religious or faith-based contexts, to say nothing of the benefits that might be derived from divinely inspired prosocial action.

Summary and Conclusions

Taken together, our conceptual and empirical analyses suggest potentially important implications for expressing compassionate love through volunteerism. We found, for example, that different motivations for volunteerism (i.e., other-focused and self-focused) were differentially related to personal and situational "substrates." Specifically, dispositional tendencies to feel empathy were more strongly related to other-focused than self-focused motivation for volunteerism. Psychological sense of community, meanwhile, was reliably related to other-focused motivation but not to self-focused motivation. There are clearly other substrates or individual-level antecedents that could be investigated and hypothesized, but our research provides empirical validation for these substrates and points to their potential roles in producing compassionate acts.

We also obtained evidence that people construe volunteerism as emblematic of compassionate love and that this tendency is strongly related to having other-focused motivation for volunteer work. We suspect that these beliefs may predate acts of volunteerism, but given the cross-sectional nature of our data, we cannot rule out the possibility that current volunteerism leads people to see stronger connections between helping others and compassionate love. Furthermore, it may be that coming to view volunteerism as tied to compassion and expressions of love is one mechanism by which people persist in volunteer efforts even in the face of trying circumstances and costs sometimes encountered during the course of their work. As another possibility, there may be no or only relatively small differences between people who volunteer and those who do not, at least at the outset of service. Differences in perceptions and motivations may emerge as a consequence of volunteerism, and these differences, in turn, may take on practical significance of their own.

Adopting a functional perspective (Snyder, 1993; Snyder & Cantor, 1998), we also suggest that researchers might start with observable behaviors, but should also consider the reasons or motivations that produce compassionate acts. Some volunteerism is motivated primarily to help another (e.g., other-focused motivation), but some volunteerism seems to be primarily motivated by self-focused desires or goals such as to increase understanding or esteem, or to develop and expand the self. Thus, it appears that one meaningful difference in motivations for volunteerism includes the distinction between acts that are other-focused versus self-focused.

Where there was less distinction among the motivations for volunteerism was in the extent to which they predicted volunteer activity. The different motivation measures predicted both religiously and non-religiously-based volunteer activity equally well. Thus, in our data it made little difference what specific reasons people espoused for volunteering to help others; regardless of whether people reported self-focused or other-focused motivations, the extensiveness of their volunteer activity and subsequent effects of this work were similar. Regarding this last point, however, it should be noted that we examined volunteer activity in religious and non-religious contexts and not necessarily the religiousness or religious motivations of volunteers. One goal for future research, therefore, is to disentangle religious and non-religious motives, contexts, and behaviors, as well as their potential implications for volunteerism and other helping behavior. Furthermore, this type of research could help build additional bridges between theory and research on volunteerism and Underwood's model of compassionate love.

One consequence of volunteerism that we explored was subjective health. And, in fact, current volunteerism was related to better reported health, but in a relatively simple way. Specifically, people who currently volunteered reported better health than non-volunteers; the degree or amount of volunteer activity was not reliably related to better or worse subjective health. Finally, we found some evidence that lifetime, rather than current, volunteering in religious or faith-based contexts predicted better health. This result suggests that there might be a cumulative or lagged effect of volunteerism that is only discernible in aggregated (i.e., lifetime) measures.

It is important to note that our measure of health was a subjective assessment rendered by participants and was not validated through physician reports, observer ratings, or other objective measures. Likewise, the ratings of volunteer motivations, empathy, and psychological sense of community were self-report measures. As such, it is possible that these data were influenced by a number of different factors, including memory fallibility and recall problems, self-presentational concerns, and response biases. However, we have little reason to believe that these sources of bias might have produced the pattern of results we obtained, especially given that the patterns we observed were consistent with findings reported elsewhere in the literature.

Linking back to Underwood's (2002) model of compassionate love, we started with a conceptual analysis that identified parallels between this model and the Volunteer Process Model (Omoto & Snyder, 1995, 2002; Snyder & Omoto, 2007). The connections we explicated depended on conceptualizing volunteerism as one form or manifestation of compassionate love. We identified several ways in which volunteerism shares key features with Underwood's working definition of compassionate love. The data we described empirically tested some of the links among constructs that could be derived from these models and that addressed two key questions about the motivations for and effects of expressions of compassionate love. The results of our analyses yielded little evidence that our measures of other- and self-focused motivations differentially predicted different types of volunteerism. In addition, subjective health was better among volunteers than non-volunteers, and it seemed to matter little how much people volunteered or in what contexts (i.e., religious or secular).

In short, compassionate acts were not restricted to one motivation type. Moreover, in considering consequences of volunteerism, why people volunteered did not seem to make nearly as much difference as that they chose to help at all. There are many and good reasons why people do not, and perhaps should not, help others. However, there is little doubt that when such actions occur, they can affect not only those who engage in them but the recipients of the actions and society at large.

This point brings us full circle. We began this chapter by noting that volunteerism is important for social action, cultural change, and quality of life. Whereas the possible transformative effects of volunteerism for individuals in terms of personal growth, spiritual development, and insight are important for a variety of reasons, our focus on grassroots efforts of community mobilization and volunteerism highlights the fact that these concerns may be shared and pondered by only a select few in the world. That is, people focused on meeting their basic human and survival needs may not be in position to extensively help others or to worry about their spiritual development and emerging insight. We are by no means denigrating these consequences, but rather, simply pointing out that compassionate love enacted as volunteerism, derived from whatever motivation, has a myriad of benefits.

Moreover, and as suggested by the subjective health data in our research, volunteers benefit from their helpful actions. We do not believe that these consequences should be minimized, nor should they be overlooked in favor of consequences exclusively at more ethereal, spiritual, and philosophical levels. Rather, we advocate for further theorizing and research that recognizes and explores the practical, spiritual, psychological, and health correlates of compassionate acts, both for recipients and providers. A strong tradition already exists in many cultures and countries, whereby people are encouraged to give back to society and to engage in prosocial actions. We believe that greater understanding of the causes, correlates, and consequences of these actions, at multiple levels of analysis, is needed in order to ensure their continued occurrence, as well as to put into place programs and interventions that maximize their positive effects.

Acknowledgments

The research described in this chapter was supported by the Fetzer Institute and the Institute for Research on Unlimited Love; preparation of this chapter was also supported by a grant from the National Institute of Mental Health. The authors thank the following individuals for their assistance with this project: Christina D. Aldrich, Anita Boling, Michèle M. Schlehofer, Viviane Seyranian, Tanya Valery, and the participants who took part.

References

Allik, J., & Realo, A. (2004). Individualism-collectivism and social capital. *Journal of Cross-Cultural Psychology, 35,* 29–49.

Barraza, J. A. (2007). *Volunteer persistence: The role of individual and group processes.* Unpublished MA thesis, Claremont Graduate University, Claremont, CA.

Boling, A. (2005). *Motivations for volunteerism over the lifespan.* Unpublished doctoral dissertation, Claremont Graduate University, Claremont, CA.

Brown, S., Nesse, R. M., Vonokur, A. D., & Smith, D. M. (2003). Providing social support may be more beneficial than receiving it: Results from a prospective study of mortality. *Psychological Science, 14,* 320–327.

Bureau of Labor Statistics (2007, January 10). *Volunteering in the United States, 2006.* Washington, DC: United States Department of Labor.

Clary, E. G., Snyder, M., Ridge, R. D., Copeland, J. T., Stukas, A. A., Haugen, J. A., & Miene, P. K. (1998). Understanding and assessing the motivations of volunteers: A functional approach. *Journal of Personality and Social Psychology, 74,* 1516–1530.

Clary, E. G., Snyder, M., & Stukas, A. A. (1998). Service-learning and psychology: Lessons from the psychology of volunteers' motivations. In R. G. Bringle & D. K. Duffy (Eds.), *With service in mind: Concepts and models for service-learning in psychology* (pp. 35–50). Washington, DC: American Association of Higher Education.

Crain, A. L., Snyder, M., & Omoto, A. M. (2000, May). *Volunteers make a difference: Relationship quality, active coping, and functioning among PWAs with volunteer buddies.* Paper presented at the annual meeting of the Midwestern Psychological Association, Chicago, IL.

Curtis, J. E., Grabb, E., & Baer, D. (1992). Voluntary association membership in fifteen countries: A comparative analysis. *American Sociological Review, 57,* 139–152.

Davis, M. H. (1983). The effects of dispositional empathy on emotional reactions and helping: A multidimensional approach. *Journal of Personality, 51,* 167–184.

Davis, M. H. (1996). *Empathy: A social psychological approach.* Boulder, CO: Westview.

Davis, M. H., Hall, J. A., & Meyer, M. (2003). The first year: Influences on the satisfaction, involvement, and persistence of new community volunteers. *Personality and Social Psychology Bulletin, 29,* 248–260.

Davis, M. H., Mitchell, K. V., Hall, J. A., Lothert, J., Snapp, T., & Meyer, M. (1999). Empathy, expectations, and situational preferences: Personality influences on the decision to participate in volunteer helping behaviors. *Journal of Personality, 67,* 469–503.

House, J. (2001). Social isolation kills, but how and why? *Psychosomatic Medicine, 63,* 273–274.

House, J. S., Robbins, C., & Metzner, H. L. (1982). The association of social relationships and activities with morality: Prospective evidence from the Tecumseh Community Health Study. *American Journal of Epidemiology, 116,* 123–140.

Hunter, K. I., & Linn, M. W. (1980–1). Psychosocial differences between elderly volunteers and non-volunteers. *International Journal of Aging and Human Development, 12,* 205–213.

Independent Sector (2001). *Giving and volunteering in the United States: Key findings.* Washington, DC: Author.

Kiviniemi, M. T., Snyder, M., & Omoto, A. M. (2002). Too many of a good thing? The effects of multiple motivations on task fulfillment, satisfaction, and cost. *Personality and Social Psychology Bulletin, 28,* 732–743.

Krause, N., Ingersoll-Dayton, B., Liang, J., & Sugisawa, H. (1999). Religion, social support, and health among the Japanese elderly. *Journal of Health and Social Behavior, 40,* 402–421.

Lindsay, J. J., Snyder, M., & Omoto, A. M. (2003, May–June). *Volunteers' impact on psychological and physical functioning of persons living with HIV.* Paper presented at the annual meeting of the American Psychological Society, Atlanta, GA.

Malsch, A. M. (2005). *Prosocial behavior beyond borders: Understanding a psychological sense of global community.* Unpublished doctoral dissertation, Claremont Graduate University, Claremont, CA.

McMillan, D. W. (1996). Sense of community. *Journal of Community Psychology, 24,* 315–325.

McMillan, D. W., & Chavis, D. M. (1986). Sense of community: A definition of theory. *Journal of Community Psychology, 14,* 6–23.

Midlarsky, E., & Kahana, E. (1991). *Altruism in later life*. Thousand Oaks, CA: Sage.

Moen, P., Dempster-McClain, D., & Williams, R. M., Jr. (1992). Successful aging: A life-course perspective on women's multiple roles and health. *American Journal of Sociology, 97*, 1612–1638.

Musick, M. A., Herzog, A. R., & House, J. S. (1999). Volunteering and mortality among older adults: Findings from a national sample. *Journals of Gerontology: Psychological Sciences and Social Sciences, 54B*, S173–S180.

Musick, M. A., & Wilson, J. (2003). Volunteering and depression: The role of psychological and social resources in different age groups. *Social Science and Medicine, 56*, 259–269.

Nadler, A. (2002). Inter-group helping relations as power relations: Maintaining or challenging social dominance between groups through helping. *Journal of Social Issues, 58*, 487–502.

Nadler, A., & Fisher, J. D. (1986). The role of threat to self-esteem and perceived control in recipient reactions to aid: Theory development and empirical validation. In L. Berkowitz (Ed.), *Advances in experimental social psychology: Vol. 19* (pp. 81–123). New York: Academic Press.

Nadler, A., & Halabi, S. (2006). Intergroup helping as status relations: Effects of status stability, identification, and type of help on receptivity to high-status group's help. *Journal of Personality and Social Psychology, 91*, 97–110.

O'Brien, L. T., Crain, A. L., Omoto, A. M., & Snyder, M. (2000, May). *Matching motivations to outcomes: Implications for persistence in service*. Paper presented at the annual meetings of the Midwestern Psychological Association, Chicago, IL.

Oman, D., Thoresen, E., & McMahon, K. (1999). Volunteerism and mortality among the community-dwelling elderly. *Journal of Health Psychology, 4*, 301–316.

Omoto, A. M., & Crain, A. L. (1995). AIDS volunteerism: Lesbian and gay community-based responses to HIV. In G. M. Herek & B. Greene (Eds.), *Contemporary perspectives on lesbian and gay issues (Vol. 2): AIDS, identity, and community* (pp. 187–209). Thousand Oaks, CA: Sage.

Omoto, A. M., Gunn, D. G., & Crain, A. L. (1998). Helping in hard times: Relationship closeness and the AIDS volunteer experience. In V. J. Derlega & A. P. Barbee (Eds.), *HIV infection and social interaction* (pp. 106–128). Thousand Oaks, CA: Sage.

Omoto, A. M., & Malsch, A. M. (2005). Psychological sense of community: Conceptual issues and connections to volunteerism-related activism. In A. M. Omoto (Ed.), *Processes of community change and social action* (pp. 83–102). Mahwah, NJ: Lawrence Erlbaum.

Omoto, A. M., & Schlehofer, M. M. (2007). Volunteerism, religiousness, spirituality, and the health outcomes of older adults. In S. G. Post (Ed.), *Altruism and health: Perspectives from empirical research* (pp. 394–409). New York: Oxford University Press.

Omoto, A. M., Schlehofer, M. M., Adelman, J. R., & Blagg, R. D. (2007). *Older adults' mental health: Direct and interactive influences of volunteerism, religious identity, and spiritual identity*. Manuscript submitted for publication.

Omoto, A. M., & Snyder, M. (1990). Basic research in action: Volunteerism and society's response to AIDS. *Personality and Social Psychology Bulletin, 16,* 152–165.

Omoto, A. M., & Snyder, M. (1993). AIDS volunteers and their motivations: Theoretical issues and practical concerns. *Nonprofit Management and Leadership, 4,* 157–176.

Omoto, A. M., & Snyder, M. (1995). Sustained helping without obligation: Motivation, longevity of service, and perceived attitude change among AIDS volunteers. *Journal of Personality and Social Psychology, 68,* 671–686.

Omoto, A. M., & Snyder, M. (2002). Considerations of community: The context and process of volunteerism. *American Behavioral Scientist, 45*(5), 846–867.

Omoto, A. M., Snyder, M., Chang, W., & Lee, D. H. (2001, August). *Knowledge and attitude change among volunteers and their associates.* Paper presented at the annual meetings of the American Psychological Association, San Francisco, CA.

Omoto, A. M., Snyder, M., & Martino, S. C. (2000). Volunteerism and the life course: Investigating age-related agendas for action. *Basic and Applied Social Psychology, 22,* 181–198.

Penner, L. A. (2002). Dispositional and organizational influences on sustained volunteerism: An interactionist perspective. *Journal of Social Issues, 58,* 447–467.

Penner, L. A., Dovidio, J. F., Piliavin, J. A., & Schroeder, D. A. (2005). Prosocial behavior: Multilevel perspectives. *Annual Review of Psychology, 56,* 365–392.

Penner, L. A., & Finkelstein, M. A. (1998). Dispositional and structural determinants of volunteerism. *Journal of Personality and Social Psychology, 74,* 525–537.

Piliavin, J. A. (2005). Feeling good by doing good: Health consequences of social service. In A. M. Omoto (Ed.), *Processes of community change and social action* (pp. 29–50). Mahwah, NJ: Lawrence Erlbaum.

Post, S. G. (2007) (Ed.). *Altruism and health: Perspectives from empirical research.* New York: Oxford University Press.

Rook, K. S. (1984). The negative side of social interaction: Impact on psychological well-being. *Journal of Personality and Social Psychology, 46,* 1097–1108.

Schondel, C., Shields, G., & Orel, N. (1992). Development of an instrument to measure volunteers' motivation in working with people with AIDS. *Social Work in Health Care, 17,* 53–71.

Simon, B., Stürmer, S., & Steffens, K. (2000). Helping individuals or group members? The role of individual and collective identification in AIDS volunteerism. *Personality and Social Psychology Bulletin, 26,* 497–506.

Snyder, M. (1993). Basic research and practical problems: The promise of a "functional" personality and social psychology. *Personality and Social Psychology Bulletin, 19,* 251–264.

Snyder, M., & Cantor, N. (1998). Understanding personality and social behavior: A functionalist strategy. In D. T. Gilbert, S. T. Fiske, & G. Lindzey (Eds.), *The handbook of social psychology: Vol. 1.* (4th ed., pp. 635–679). Boston: McGraw-Hill.

Snyder, M., & Omoto, A. M. (1992a). Volunteerism and society's response to the HIV epidemic. *Current Directions in Psychological Science*, *1*, 113–116.

Snyder, M., & Omoto, A. M. (1992b). Who helps and why? The psychology of AIDS volunteerism. In S. Spacapan & S. Oskamp (Eds.), *Helping and being helped: Naturalistic studies* (pp. 213–239). Newbury Park CA: Sage.

Snyder, M., & Omoto, A. M. (2007). Social action. In A. W. Kruglanski & E. T. Higgins (Eds.), *Social psychology: A handbook of basic principles* (2nd ed., pp. 940–961). New York: Guilford Press.

Snyder, M., Omoto, A. M., & Crain, A. L. (1999). Punished for their good deeds: Stigmatization of AIDS volunteers. *American Behavioral Scientist, 42,* 1175–1192.

Snyder, M., Omoto, A. M., & Smith, D. M. (in press). The role of persuasion strategies in motivating individual and collective action. In E. Borgida, J. L. Sullivan, & C. Federico (Eds.), *The political psychology of democratic citizenship*. New York: Oxford University Press.

Sprecher, S., & Fehr, B. (2005). Compassionate love for close others and humanity. *Journal of Social and Personal Relationships, 22,* 629–651.

Stukas, A. A., Snyder, M., & Clary, E. G. (1999). Service learning: Who benefits and why. *Social Policy Report, 13,* 1–19.

Thoits, P. A., & Hewitt, L. N. (2001). Volunteer work and well-being. *Journal of Health and Social Behavior, 42,* 115–131.

Underwood, L. G. (2002). The human experience of compassionate love: Conceptual mapping and data from selected studies. In S. G. Post, L. G. Underwood, J. P. Schloss, & W. B. Hurlbut (Eds.), *Altruism and altruistic love: Science, philosophy, and religion in dialogue* (pp. 72–88). New York: Oxford University Press.

Van de Vliert, E., Huang, X., & Levine, R. V. (2004). National wealth and thermal climate as predictors of motives for volunteer work. *Journal of Cross-Cultural Psychology, 35,* 62–73.

Van Vugt, M., Snyder, M., Tyler, T., & Biel, A. (Eds.) (2000). *Cooperation in modern society: Promoting the welfare of communities, states, and organizations.* London, England: Routledge.

Van Willigen, M. (2000). Differential benefits of volunteering across the life course. *Journal of Gerontology: Social Sciences, 55B,* S1–S11.

Wheeler, J. A., Gorey, K. M., & Greenblatt, B. (1998). The beneficial effects of volunteering for older volunteers and the people they serve: A meta-analysis. *International Journal of Aging and Human Development, 47,* 69–79.

Wilson, J. (2000). Volunteering. *Annual Review of Sociology, 26,* 215–240.

Young, F. W., & Glasgow, N. (1998). Voluntary social participation and health. *Research on Aging, 20,* 339–362.

10

Compassionate Love for Individuals in Other Social Groups

Salena Brody, Stephen C. Wright, Arthur Aron, and Tracy McLaughlin-Volpe

When hip-hop artist Kanye West veered off script during a 2005 Hurricane Katrina celebrity telethon proclaiming "George Bush doesn't care about black people," he created more than a memorable television moment. The United States, still reeling after the natural disaster, reacted divisively. West's comments angered many Americans who felt the accusation slandered the Bush administration and humanitarian efforts to provide aid. On the other hand, many other Americans identified with his outrage toward the current administration and what they considered an appalling attempt at relief efforts. Subsequent news stories focused on the depth of poverty in many parts of Louisiana and the disproportionate number of black Americans with substandard living conditions. Talking heads on cable news networks openly discussed race and class relations and the United States experienced polarization reminiscent of the O. J. Simpson case. The country seemed divided into hostile camps, each sure of its truth and openly attacking the other.

Couple West's comments with international headlines about the ongoing crises involving Israel and the Palestinians, warring factions in Iraq, the diffusion of nuclear weapons technology, sex trafficking in Cambodia, or ethnic cleansing in Sudan, and the situation begins to seem hopeless for humanity. With every turn of the newspaper page, we see examples of groups hating, avoiding, abusing, disliking, and even killing one another in the name of nation, ethnicity, or ideology. As concerned citizens, we wonder how to reverse the tide of hostility and broker a lasting peace. Since the mid-twentieth century, social science research in intergroup relations has tackled just this issue. Researchers, observant of the real-life conflicts in the world, have sought to identify the conditions under which hostility between groups might be reduced. The research has resulted in programs and interventions aimed at generating tolerance between hostile groups.

Recently, however, some social scientists have adopted a more "positive" approach to researching the relations between social groups. Inspired by the development of "Positive Psychology," a few researchers, while acknowledging the myriad conflicts in the world, also recognize numerous examples of truly positive intergroup relations. With these examples providing hope, these researchers seek to complement traditional intergroup relations research with a more positive approach: Perhaps it is possible to move beyond tolerance as the end goal. Perhaps it is possible to create a world in which truly positive attitudes toward other groups, such as respect, admiration – and even compassionate love – might become the norm.

Such an optimistic possibility means starting to see the world through a different lens. It does not mean disparaging the sharp critics of the relief efforts (e.g., Mayor Ray Nagin of New Orleans) or ignoring the almost omnipresent realities of prejudice, discrimination, conflict, and hatred between all too many groups. But it does mean, for example, taking the opportunity to examine some of the extraordinary acts of compassion and love offered by people of diverse backgrounds. Following the New Orleans disaster, people throughout the world reached deep into their pocketbooks to provide help. In fact, the private donations after Hurricane Katrina created history by surpassing all previous records of charitable giving, according to philanthropy researchers (Christian Century, 2006).

As a more personal example, some individuals responded to the disaster by including others into their most sacred quarters, the home. Forrest King, an Attleboro, Massachusetts resident, ignored the advice of the American Red Cross and government disaster agency personnel and offered a family of evacuees shelter in his home (Ripley, 2005). King, a lifelong conservative, decided to share his home with an unlikely family, the Meehan-Hoos. Yolanda and Jan Meehan-Hoo are a same-sex couple with three children. When interviewed about his experience, Mr. King discussed how sharing his home with the couple and their children provided learning opportunities for everyone involved. Regarding his new extended "family," he joked, "The other day I heard them arguing with each other in the stairway. It proves to me that same-sex couples are just as miserable as the rest of us" (p. 31).

The Kings and Meehan-Hoos are but one example of compassionate love directed toward members of another group. We see it in how they treat each other like family, take care of each other's children and poke friendly jibes – a heartening show of compassion. We see other examples that illustrate our human motivation to express compassionate love as well. Jill Fitch, a volunteer in San Antonio, Texas, took care of infant evacuees in a temporary shelter. She described her work as tending to the evacuees as she would for her own brother or sister (della Cava, 2005). Or, consider Erin Burns's decision to spend spring break rebuilding homes in post-Katrina New Orleans. She described her own motivation to spend her vacation from Santa Clara University as being fueled by "love and compassion" (Burns, 2006).

These examples give us an opportunity to explore the conditions under which individuals might show compassionate love for another, even when the other is clearly a member of a group other than their own. In this chapter we will focus mainly on relations among members of different ethnic groups. However, we want to emphasize that the same issues apply to relations between genders, age groups, nationalities, religions, social classes, political parties, sexual orientations, the disabled and enabled, different political parties, and so forth. But ethnicity has been the context for most social-science intergroup research and thinking. It is also, of course, an excellent example of a very serious source of intergroup prejudice and tension – and thus a prime arena in which to examine the possibilities for compassionate love between members of different groups.

According to Underwood (see Chapter 1, this volume), compassionate love involves both feeling and cognition. In our examples about helping after Hurricane Katrina, the "feeling" element of compassionate love involves positive affect and closeness with the other. With the Kings and Meehan-Hoos, this might even be described as a feeling of friendship. The "cognitive" element of compassionate love in these examples, we would argue, can be expressed as treating the other as connected to the self. Ms. Fitch, for example, perceived those she was helping as connected to herself as a sibling would be. Compassionate love suggests an authentic connection to the other, where the other becomes to some extent "part of the self."

Underwood (2005) highlights several key ideas central to the study of compassionate love, including "understanding of self, knowing ourselves and our agendas, valuing the other at a fundamental level, [and] openness and receptivity" (pp. 293–294). In this chapter we hope to build on these ideas and contribute to the study of compassionate love by reviewing theory and research on how closeness to a person in another group can promote compassionate love for members of that person's group more generally. People quite commonly express love to those to whom are they are closest, such as family members and friends. However, in this chapter our focus is on how this same process can be extended to compassionate love for members of other groups, even groups against whom we may be initially prejudiced. Most important, moving away from traditional intergroup relations research that proposes tolerance as our "best shot" toward peace and harmony, our model focuses on the potential for truly positive orientations toward the other groups, with compassionate love as our new benchmark for success.

In the following sections, we will make a case for the positive transformative power of close cross-group friendships to create compassionate love for members of other groups. We will begin by introducing the self-expansion model, the theoretical underpinning of our arguments, which has been applied, until recently, primarily in the context of close relationships. We will then consider in some detail its implications for improving relations between members of different groups. Next, we will review research supporting four key predictions from this application of the self-expansion model to intergroup relations, and to the creation of compassionate love (or at least more positive attitudes) for other groups in particular. Finally, we will consider practical implications of this work for creating compassionate love among different groups outside the laboratory, concluding with directions for future research.

The Self-Expansion Model

A friend is, as it were, a second self. (—Cicero)

Aron and Aron's self-expansion model (1986; see also Aron et al., 2005) provides a framework for examining the motivation behind and psychological consequences of forming close interpersonal relationships. There are two main parts of the model. The first proposes that individuals are motivated to self-expand, in the sense of increasing their ability to achieve whatever they desire by seeking out resources that help them meet future challenges. This motivation is further promoted because the process of self-expansion is affectively positive (when rapid, very highly positive).

The second part of the model is that when individuals form a close relationship with another person, they "expand" themselves by including aspects of the other within the self (Aron, Mashek, & Aron, 2004). This "inclusion of other in the self" can be represented as the degree of perceived or felt overlap between self and other. According to the model, the closer individuals become to each other, the more overlap there is between the mental representation of self and other. To some extent, the two become one.

In one test of the overlap hypothesis, Aron, Aron, Tudor, and Nelson (1991, Study 3) first had participants indicate whether each of a large set of personality traits was representative of themselves, and then whether each of the traits was representative of a close other (e.g., a spouse). Participants then made "me/not me" judgments about these sets of traits as quickly as possible while a computer recorded their reaction time. If self and close other were cognitively overlapped, quicker response times were predicted for when there was consistency between self and other for the trait being judged, as compared to when self and the other were seen to be inconsistent on that trait. The reasoning was that if the other was overlapped with self, then if the other was different from self on a trait, this would generate some confusion – as if part of me is one way and part of me is another way. This confusion was expected to slow response times for these traits. The results clearly supported the overlap hypothesis. In further research (Aron & Fraley, 1999; Smith, Coats, & Walling, 1999), it was found that the strength of this effect was strongly correlated with reported closeness to the other. These kinds of effects have been found in a variety of other cognitive, memory, perspective, and other research paradigms (see Aron et al., 2005, for a review). It has even been seen in the brain. For example, Aron and colleagues found that the closer one was to a friend, the more similar was the pattern of brain response between hearing the friend's name and one's own name (Aron, Whitfield-Gabrieli, & Lichty, in press).

The overlap between self and close others has several consequences. As the lines between self and other are blurred, another person becomes part of one's self-identity, and the other is treated more like the self. The "golden rule" is the spontaneous response to the needs of the other. A number of studies have illustrated the effect of treating the other like the self. For example, it is well documented that people tend to see others' actions as due to fixed predispositions, but their own actions as due to the situation (e.g., Ross & Nisbett, 1991). However, Aron et al. (1991, Study 2) showed that close others are treated like the self; their actions are more likely to be seen as due to the situation than to fixed personality, and the closer they are, the stronger the effect (Aron & Fraley, 1999). Also, including the other in the self can benefit self-concept when good things happen to the other (so long as self is not competing with the other), as individuals find themselves spontaneously basking in the reflected glory of the other (Cialdini et al., 1999; Tesser, 1999). When a close friend experiences a promotion, compliment, or other good fortune and shares it, individuals have the benefit of experiencing joy and elation as the event is now self-relevant. Such closeness can bring pain as well. When someone psychologically hurts a friend, the self can feel the pain as it, too, is self-relevant. Individuals can become happy, proud, hurt, or offended all due to experiences of their close others.

In addition to sharing the affective experiences of close others, individuals who are cognitively overlapped with another tend to share material resources. For example, in one set of experiments (Aron et al., 1991), participants allocated monetary rewards equally to themselves and a close friend; when the other was a stranger, participants allocated more to themselves. Crucially, this occurred even when participants understood that friend or stranger would not know the money came from them.

We should emphasize that inclusion of other in the self does not mean that when another person is quite thoroughly included in the self, one cannot distinguish self from other. Both your arms and legs are part of yourself, but you can certainly tell one limb from the other. Indeed, people will even sacrifice one part of themselves for the good of the whole, as when it is necessary to amputate a limb to save the rest of the body. That is, the more inclusion, the more care we take for the whole, with the whole including both self and other.

Can Love Be Selfish?

As Underwood (2005) notes, unselfishness is a central feature of compassionate love. So is this compassionate love or just sophisticated selfishness? We would answer that when self includes other, these are the same thing! That is, to the extent another person is truly part of the self, individuals spontaneously weigh the other person's benefits as much as their own. Individuals could even weigh the other person's needs more heavily than their own, if those needs are greater or if the other is the more important part of the whole. Hence, people sacrifice themselves for members of their family or larger group when it is threatened. Actions to benefit the other are "selfish" in the sense that they benefit this enlarged self. But they are *not* selfish in the sense that they are not being done for the unique benefit of the individual self of the actor, but rather they are being done for the benefit of this larger self that includes the other. Indeed, if one carried this logic to its extreme, this larger self would include all of humanity and even nature. This corresponds to what many mystical traditions in both the East and West describe as "enlightenment" or "individuation." Indeed, some of these approaches use a capitalized "Self" for this kind of "selfishness" (e.g., the Hindu spiritual texts called 'Upanishads').

The process of self-expansion through including others in the self, such as self-expansion of all kinds (e.g., learning), is said to proceed in alternating phases of expansion and integration (Aron, Norman, & Aron, 1998). Expansion involves the taking in of new experiences, perspective, and identities provided by the partner during relationship formation. For example, in a new friendship, partners might try new foods, visit new places, and meet new people. If one partner is a lifelong vegetarian, during expansion, the more carnivorous friend might begin frequenting vegetarian restaurants and learning why the new relationship partner became a vegetarian. Even if the meat-eater continues to enjoy filet mignon over "Tofurkey," he may find himself talking knowledgeably about the energy used to produce meat, humane slaughterhouses, and the health benefits of a meat-free diet. Because of the relationship with the new friend, vegetarianism has become part of the self.

We perceive new relationships, particularly when they develop over a short time, to be exciting, in part, because they create rapid self-expansion, and rapid self-expansion generates high levels of positive affect (Aron et al., 1998). Even rapid expansion with a long-standing relationship partner can generate high levels of positive affect that then become associated with the partner, rejuvenating initial strong feelings for the other (Aron, Norman, Aron, McKenna, & Heyman, 2000). Of course, too-rapid expansion can be stressful. When individuals lack the cognitive resources to integrate these new aspects into the self, a mismatch between the rate of expansion and the rate of integration can occur, and may lead to feelings of stress and burnout (Aron et al., 1998). In the case of a new friendship, this can translate into the feeling of "too much, too soon." Expansion-related burnout also may be experienced as a function of too many new expansion experiences happening at once (e.g., starting a new job, a new relationship, and living in a new city) leading to "overload" when attempting to integrate these many new aspects of the self.

It is important to choose new relationships carefully – although a new relationship brings potential benefits, it also presents an opportunity for self-loss; self-identity can become swamped by the other or by the other's problems and difficulties that are now included in the self (Mashek & Sherman, 2004). Returning to our earlier example, the individual "trying on" vegetarianism does so at the cost of a personal identity of being someone who jokes with his hunting buddies about vegetarians being granola, hippie, crunchy, tree-hugger types. Thus, in addition to the situational and interpersonal factors influencing friendship formation, the decision to become close with another involves a cost-benefit analysis where the benefits to self outweigh the potential losses.

However, in general, access to the other's resources and identities increases self-efficacy, and the self-expansion process provides opportunities to view the world from a new perspective – from the perspective of the close other. Indeed, forming a new relationship quite literally expands the self: In one longitudinal study (Aron, Paris, & Aron, 1995, Study 1), people's self-descriptions became significantly more complex from before to after forming a significant new relationship; another longitudinal study (Aron et al., 1991, Study 2) showed a significant increase in feelings of competence and the ability to accomplish whatever one desires.

People relish this new exposure to the other's world and, in this way, self-expansion can be described as the engine that drives the desire to form relationships with others. In particular, recent work has examined how self-expansion might be the engine that drives people to form relationships with members of other groups and how these relationships might positively impact relations between different groups, leading in the direction of compassionate love. The next section explores how self-expansion and including the other in the self has been connected to work in intergroup relations aimed at changing attitudes toward other groups.

Close Relationships and Contact

What happens when one has a friend who is a member of another group? Our work has focused on how friendships can be a particularly potent form of intergroup contact, being especially effective in reducing prejudice, and particularly important for going beyond reducing prejudice to enhancing positive attitudes.

The classic intergroup contact hypothesis, formulated by Gordon Allport (1954), focuses on the factors influencing whether an interaction between members of different groups will lead to improved attitudes. Specifically, Allport's hypothesis was that prejudice may be reduced through contact between members of two groups, provided that contact involves: (a) cooperative interdependence toward a common goal; (b) equal status within the contact situation; and (c) support for the contact from authorities, law, or custom. However, in his review of the substantial research literature arising from the original contact hypothesis, Pettigrew (1998) noted that most contact studies report positive contact effects, and many of these studies report positive outcomes even in the absence of some or all of Allport's key conditions (see also Pettigrew & Tropp, 2000). Pettigrew argued that "writers have overburdened the hypothesis with too many facilitating, but not essential, conditions" (p. 80). In other words, while it is clear that all contact does not necessarily lead to positive attitude change, the absence of certain specific conditions for optimal contact does not necessarily ensure negative outcomes.

In our work (e.g., Wright, Brody, & Aron, 2005), we have proposed that the facilitating conditions that Pettigrew (1998) and many others have discussed might be better understood as conditions that are likely to lead to the development of feelings of friendship between the contact partners. The parameters for optimal contact appear to set the stage for friendship development, from initial attraction (pre-friendship) to liking (early friendship) to intimacy (established friendship). That is, feelings of friendship for a member of another group may be the critical outcome of contact that will lead to positive affect and positive attitudes directed toward the friend's group. Juxtaposing the research literature on close relationships with the intergroup contact literature suggests some interesting linkages. For example, expecting future interactions is a key factor in friendship formation (Berg & Clark, 1986); the intergroup contact literature indicates that this is also an important factor in creating optimal contact situations (Brewer & Miller, 1996; Pettigrew, 1998). Additionally, the self-disclosure that is central to becoming close friends (e.g., Altman & Taylor, 1973; Collins & Miller, 1994) mirrors discussions of learning about the other in the intergroup contact literature (Cook & Selltiz, 1955, Pettigrew, 1997).

Our work has focused on bringing these literatures together in a comprehensive framework wherein intergroup contact meets self-expansion (Wright et al., 2005; see also Aron et al., 2005; Wright, Aron, & Tropp, 2002). Extending the inclusion-of-other-in-self model to the context of intergroup contact offers a new perspective on how and why the positive feelings generated toward the single individual – the contact partner – can then be generalized to the partner's group as a whole. Our suggestion is that individuals who make friends with a member of another group increasingly include aspects of that person in the self (Wright et al., 2002). One aspect of the friend is his or her social identity as a member of the other group. Thus, as the friendship grows and circumstances inevitably make this aspect of the friend's identity salient, this identity aspect of the other, like everything else about the friend, also becomes part of the self. With increasing closeness, there is an increasing psychological connection with the friend's group. Because of this psychological connection, the friend's group is accorded some of the benefits usually reserved for the self, such as the benefit of the doubt in making attributions for causes of actions, sharing of resources, and positive regard. A person may never gain actual membership in the friend's group; in the case of racial groups, it may not even be possible. However, the friendship may allow individuals to gain, vicariously or even actually, some of the resources, perspectives, and other benefits associated with being a member of the other group. (Even if I am not a vegetarian, I still may gain some of the resources, perspectives, and identities of a vegetarian; and in this case, of vegetarians as a group.) The main point here is not about changing group memberships; rather the focus is on the psychological process that leads individuals to treat the other group as though it were more like the self.

By including the member of the other group in the self, the individual makes a psychological connection with that group that can lead to improved intergroup relations. This process involves interactions that emphasize personal identities as well as group, or social, identities. Researchers and intergroup contact theorists have debated the specifics of the role that personal and social identities play during intergroup contact (e.g., Brewer & Miller, 1984; Hewstone & Brown, 1986; Pettigrew, 1997). Specifically, the issues have revolved around whether raising awareness of group memberships during cross-group contact will lead to positive or negative outcomes. To illustrate this distinction, it is helpful to consider a hypothetical example involving ethnic groups. Let's assume that Lila, a Mexican-American college student, is getting to know Kathryn, an Anglo-American. Lila's identity as a Chicana is important to her, but should she discuss the struggles of Chicanos with Kathryn? Doing so might cause conflict in the relationship as the history between the groups is not entirely positive. However, since this is an important part of Lila's identity, self-disclosure may bring the relationship to a deeper level of intimacy, making the pair better friends.

Lila and Kathryn's situation relates directly to the psychology of social categorization and the distinction between interpersonal and intergroup interactions. The salience of personal or group identities during a contact situation determines whether the situation will be construed by the partners in interpersonal or intergroup terms (Tajfel, 1981; Turner, Hogg, Oakes, Reicher, & Wetherell, 1987). Interpersonal interactions occur when group memberships are downplayed and individuals interact in terms of their personal characteristics. In the context of Lila and Kathryn, sharing hobbies, interests, likes, and dislikes would generally fall under the umbrella of interpersonal interactions. In contrast, intergroup interactions occur when individuals clearly recognize and interact in terms of their relevant group memberships. For Lila and Kathryn, discussing race relations or attending a Chicano cultural event would raise the salience of their divergent ethnic (social) identities, leading them to interact in terms of these group memberships.

Contact theorists have debated whether it is interpersonal or intergroup contact that is more likely lead to the generalization of positive contact outcomes to new people and new situations. Brewer and Miller (1984) argue that interpersonal contact should contribute to positive interactions with new members of the other group and that consistent personalization of the member of that group will lead the person to be less likely to categorize other members of that group. According to this approach, the personalization process leads to treating everyone more as individuals. Thus, personalized contact will reduce prejudice by reducing the use of group memberships more generally. Hewstone and Brown (1986) argue, however, that interpersonal interactions often fail to lead to generalized attitude change toward the group as a whole precisely because group memberships are ignored. They argue that in order to generalize positive contact effects from the specific contact partner to the group as a whole, it is fundamental that group memberships be a central part of the interactions. According to this perspective, in order for individuals to develop positive attitudes toward the entire group, individuals in the contact interaction must recognize the others' group memberships and thus recognize that their positive attitudes toward the single individual are relevant to their attitudes about the group as a whole.

Returning to Lila and Kathryn's new friendship, is there an ideal way to develop a close relationship while also acknowledging important social identities? To answer this question, Owen, Wright, and Brody (2001) experimentally manipulated the timing of group membership salience during a cross-group friendship encounter. Participants in the study were paired with a stranger of a different ethnicity, and participated in 4 hour-long sessions over the course of 8 weeks. The sessions were designed to mimic the processes usually involved in real friendship formation (see Fehr, 1996). The experiment had two conditions. For the pairs randomly assigned to the "Group Salience Early" condition, the issue of race relations was one of the structured discussion topics during the very first session, just as the friendship was starting to get established. However, for those in the "Group Salience Late" condition, this topic was not introduced until the third session, after a friendship was well on its way. By the end of the fourth session, all participants reported that their partner was a "friend," and that they had fairly strong feelings of closeness and comfort with their partners, but they arrived by different routes. Participants in the Group Salience Early condition reported lower levels of friendship, closeness, and comfort following the first two sessions, but then began to "catch up" to those in the Group Salience Late condition in the third and fourth session.

These findings give us a glimpse into the importance of personal and social identities in the development of cross-group friendships. It appears that cross-group friendships can become close even if group identities are made salient from the onset, but that this early salience of group membership may slow the pace of friendship formation. On the other hand, if group memberships are brought to the forefront after personalized interactions have produced fairly strong feelings of interpersonal closeness, the sharing of social identity information does not disrupt or undermine the friendship.

However, one caveat needs to be raised. The current study involved considerable encouragement for participants to return to subsequent sessions. They had committed themselves to a four-session process and were expected to return even if the initial interactions were not particularly comfortable and rewarding. In more typical contexts in which decisions to engage in future interactions are much more voluntary, the lack of comfort and closeness found in the Group Salience Early condition might have ended the development of a friendship before it could begin. Thus, this study suggests that both personal and social identities can be shared during cross-group friendships; but it also points out that the timing of group membership salience may make a difference, especially if the decision to engage in continued interaction is voluntary.

Returning to the general theme of how intergroup contact can affect intergroup relations, theorists (e.g., Pettigrew, 1998) have argued that optimal contact involves a number of processes: learning about the other group, changing behavior, generating affective ties, and a reappraisal of one's own group and its values and perspectives. Our research suggests that close cross-group friendships may be a form of intergroup contact that can powerfully produce each of these four outcomes. First, close relationships involve self-disclosure, and we would propose that learning about the other group is actually a byproduct of these normal self-disclosure processes that occur during friendship development. This was seen in the earlier example of the King and Meehan-Hoo families where Mr. King's acquisition of new knowledge about lesbian couples resulted from the normal exchange of information that occurs when people develop interpersonal relationships. As we include the other group in the self, we also change our behaviors. This can come in the form of "trying on" new identities (e.g., vegetarian) or treating the other group with a newfound respect. This results from treating the other group more like the self, as was the case of Ms. Fitch treating evacuees like her own siblings. Generating affective ties also occurs during cross-group friendships as individuals first become emotionally connected to their friend and then to the friend's group as a whole. Using the example of Ms. Burns building homes in New Orleans during Spring Break, we would argue that the love and compassion she describes apply both to her one-on-one relationships with families and to evacuees as a group. Finally, including another group in the self reduces the distinctiveness of one's own group from the other group, thus leading to reappraisal of one's own group. This is illustrated when people with cross-group friendships are now bothered by the apparent ignorance or narrowmindedness of other members of their own group and begin to question the norms of their own group for relating to the other group (as when I now wince when my hunting buddies disparage those hippie, tree-hugger "types").

Thus, at the heart of the thesis advanced in this chapter is the idea that cross-group friendships serve as a vehicle for inclusion of the other group in the self, and that this in turn is a crucial ingredient for developing compassionate love for the other group. That is, a friend's social identity (group membership) can be included in an individual's self-concept much as other aspects of the friend's identity are. The inclusion of this group identity in the self is then the mechanism by which friendship across social groups leads to more positive attitudes and more positive behaviors toward that group and its members.

In addition, the broader self-expansion model, on which the concept of including others in the self is based, proposes that the desire to include aspects of the other (including the other's group identity) results from a self-expansion motive. This motive is inspired by a desire to increase feelings of efficacy by increasing one's resources, perspectives, and identities. It is also proposed that the motivation to include others in the self is supported by the positive emotional experience that is associated with the rapid expansion of the self that comes when the other is included in the self. So, beyond providing an explanation for why cross-group friendships can lead to more positive intergroup attitudes, we propose that the self-expansion motive may also represent one basic human motivational process that would lead us to approach with interest members of other groups.

The social science literature is filled with explanations for why we should be suspicious of and avoid, or even hate and harm, members of other groups (e.g., Brewer & Brown, 1998). There are evolutionary explanations based on group competition, discussions of basic human cognitive and motivational processes that lead to biases toward one's own group, theories of personality and political ideology that explain competition and efforts to subjugate others. All of these paint a picture of the near-inevitability of group conflict and animus. In contrast, we find virtually no discussions of why people might tolerate other groups, let alone why they might seek out opportunities to have positive interactions with them. If one looked only at this literature, one might come to the conclusion that nothing other than abstract, even esoteric, beliefs about justice and equality stem the tide of intergroup conflict.

Why then, despite the obvious terrible examples of group conflict, do most groups seem to coexist quite peacefully? Conflict is conspicuous by the problems it creates, but, fortunately, it is more the exception than the rule. Yet, for the most part, the intergroup relations literature remains silent in explaining the positive side of intergroup relations. Perhaps the self-expansion motive provides one example of a psychological process that might work in opposition to those that lead to negative intergroup relations. That is, self-expansion may represent a basic human process that would, at times, lead to an appetitive interest in other groups. The logic follows directly from the basic premise of the model – people seek to expand the self by building relationships with others who can increase their current complement of resources, perspectives, and identities. Someone who shares most of what we currently are will offer little opportunity for self-expansion, while forming a relationship with someone who has a different set of perspectives and identities provides a much greater potential for expansion of the self (Aron, Steele, Kashdan, & Perez, 2006). Thus, if we are not too afraid of being rejected or that a relationship simply could not work out, we should be drawn to others quite different from ourselves, making members of other groups particularly appealing. This application of the self-expansion model to the context of intergroup relations may help to explain both mundane experiences such as venturing out to eat "exotic" foods, as well as more dramatic examples of behaviors oriented toward other groups, such as travel, humanitarian aid, foreign adoptions, and interracial marriage. In all these cases, the inclination *toward*, rather than *away from*, those who are different follows directly from self-expansion motives.

In summary, our model brings together work in the close relationships and intergroup contact arenas and proposes an extension of the self-expansion model. We argue that because of the new perspectives, identities, and resources possessed by members of other groups, we are motivated by self-expansion to develop relationships with them. By doing so, we include aspects of the members of these other groups in the self – including the others' social identities – as we become closer. And that inclusion of others' social identities in the self leads us to think, feel, and act toward the friends' groups more as we think, feel, and act toward ourselves. The following section systematically addresses various parts of our model and presents supporting research in relation to four critical predictions of our model.

Supporting Research

The claims made by our application of the self-expansion model and the associated concept of including others in the self to the context of intergroup friendships and intergroup relations lead to several hypotheses. Four of the critical predictions are: (1) cross-group friendships lead to more positive intergroup attitudes; (2) cross-group friendships provide a special opportunity for self-expansion; (3) cross-group friendships lead to the inclusion of the other in the self, and this inclusion leads to an increase in generalized positive affect; and (4) self-expansion needs actually motivate individuals to seek out members of other groups.

Prediction 1: Cross-Group Friendships Lead to more Positive Intergroup Attitudes

In a landmark study of contact and cross-group friendship (Pettigrew, 1997), a sample of six minorities in Western Europe completed survey measures of friendship, contact, and attitudes toward other ethnic minorities. The study found that having a friend in another group was associated with lower blatant and subtle prejudice, more support for policies aimed at helping that group, and a "spillover" positive effect to additional groups besides one's own. Pettigrew found stronger effects as the closeness between members of the different groups increased. That is, there were larger effects when the member of the other group was a friend rather than merely a neighbor or co-worker.

Likewise, we have conducted two questionnaire studies that examined the relationship between cross-group friendships and positive attitudes (McLaughlin-Volpe, Aron, Wright & Reis, 2000). In the first, students at a diverse university who had friends in various ethnic groups reported on how many friends they had and the level of closeness with their closest friend in each of three specific ethnic groups other than their own. They then answered questions about their attitudes toward those groups. Closeness to the friends was measured by the Inclusion of Other in Self (IOS) Scale (Aron, Aron, & Smollan, 1992); from a set of seven pairs of increasingly overlapping circles, respondents select the pair that best describes their relationship with the other person. Results indicated that participants who had more friends in a particular group had more positive attitudes toward that group; the closer participants were to their closest friend in a group, the more positive they felt to that group. Analysis of the correlational patterns involving a series of related variables suggested that effects were stronger from closeness to positive attitudes than from positive attitudes to closeness. The same pattern of results was found in the second questionnaire study. This study focused on intergroup contact in the context of rival universities, a context that is interesting because it reverses the usual biases in US student samples. (That is, in this context, participants are more willing to admit to negative attitudes toward the other group and reluctant to admit to positive attitudes.)

An additional result found in both studies was that closeness was a moderator of the contact–attitude relationship. When closeness to their closest friend in a group was high, the more interactions participants had with members of that group, the more positive the attitudes they had toward the group. When closeness was low, however, there was a slight but significant *negative* relationship between contact and attitudes – the more interactions with members of the other group, the *less* positive attitudes!

Recent experimental work (Wright & Van Der Zande, 1999) supports these correlational findings and presents some evidence for the causal path from friendship to attitudes. In a unique experimental paradigm, Wright and Van Der Zande (1999) manipulated whether participants formed a friendship with a member of their own ethnic group or with a member of a different ethnic group. Specifically, white participants were assigned either a white partner (same-group condition) or an Asian or a Latina partner (cross-group condition) for a study that required each pair (initially strangers) to make four consecutive visits to the lab. (All participants in this study were women.) In the experiment, high levels of closeness and friendship were created in both the same-group and cross-group friendship conditions. (These were the same procedures used in the Owen et al., 2001 study described earlier, but using the late salience condition for all participants.) Later, white participants in the cross-group friendship condition showed significantly more positive attitudes toward the ethnic group of their partner – and to a slightly lesser extent, even to minorities in general – than white participants paired with another white participant. This finding, in conjunction with correlational research illustrating the relation between cross-group friendships and attitudes toward the other groups as reviewed above, supports the hypothesis that in addition to the usual positive benefits accorded to close relationships, the inclusion of members of other groups in the self leads to improved intergroup attitudes.

Prediction 2: Cross-Group Friendships Provide a Special Opportunity for Self-Expansion

In a longitudinal study conducted at the University of Queensland, Australia (McLaughlin-Volpe & Wright, 2002), students filled out questionnaires on four occasions over the first six weeks of the semester. In addition to a number of other questions about new experiences that they had during the period since the last test, they provided the initials of any new friends that they had made. They also completed several measures of *self-change;* these included a standard measure of self-efficacy and a free response listing in response to "who are you today?," which was coded for a number of different aspects of the self. At the end of the project, they also provided demographic information, including ethnicity, nationality, religion, and residence (urban/rural) about each of the new friends that they had reported on in each of the four sessions. Participants then rated the degree to which these friends were different from them on a variety of dimensions. By having these measures at the end of the study, participants were never made aware that the study was in any way related to differences between themselves and their friends when they were nominating new friends or when they were completing the measures of self-change.

The results showed a clear connection between making friends with someone who was very different from oneself and changes in the self (self-expansion). On those occasions when a participant indicated that he or she had made a new friend who they later indicated was different from themselves in meaningful ways, he or she also reported increased feelings of social self-efficacy and a greater number of new self-domains in the free response listing. In addition, the degree to which the newly made friend was seen to be different from self was positively associated with continuing changes in the self-concept over subsequent testing occasions. So, while making new friends of any kind was associated with self-expansion and increased self-efficacy, making cross-group friends heightened these effects. Thus, there is some initial evidence that cross-group relationships may provide a particularly good opportunity for self-expansion.

Prediction 3: Cross-Group Friendships Lead to the Inclusion
of the Other in the Self, and this Inclusion Leads to an Increase
in Generalized Positive Affect

This hypothesis was tested in a study involving undergraduate students at Boston College who were participating in a service-learning program (Brody, 2003). Service-learning programs generally require students to participate in regular service in the local community and, through active reflection, to tie their concrete experiences in the community to broader theoretical concepts they are learning about in their coursework. In this program, students committed to a year-long weekly service at a Boston social service agency. They also participated in mandatory reflection meetings with others who were also serving at the same agency in which they discussed their experiences in the context of social justice and public policy. The participating agencies were chosen because they served disadvantaged groups and because they provided students with an opportunity to interact with individuals whom they might otherwise not meet.

Questionnaires were distributed before and after the service learning experience. The pre-experience questionnaire included a measure of the participants' feelings of social closeness with the group with which they were most likely to interact in their service-learning program. Social closeness assessed how comfortable participants felt with increasing levels of intimacy with that group (measured using Crandall's (1991) scale of social distance). In the questionnaire that followed the service learning experience, participants indicated how much direct contact they had with members of the relevant group. They also completed the IOS Scale (the overlapping circles measure) for how much participants included in themselves each of the individuals with whom they had interacted, plus the same measure of feelings of social closeness with that group that was on the pre-experience questionnaire. Finally, they completed a measure of their generalized positive affect that assessed levels of pleasure, enthusiasm, and excitement associated with the service experience.

Again, the data supported the claims made by our application of self-expansion theory to cross-group friendships. First, more direct contact with members of another group was associated with a general increase in feelings of social closeness with that group. In addition, more direct contact was associated with greater inclusion of the member of the other group in the self. Further, the amount of direct contact with members of the other group also predicted greater generalized positive affect about the experience, suggesting the kind of emotional experience associated with compassionate love. Finally, from a theoretical perspective, an especially important result was that the positive relation between amount of contact and generalized positive affect was fully mediated by the increase in the inclusion of the other group member in the self. Put another way, the pattern of results was consistent with the scenario in which more contact led to greater inclusion of the other in the self, and it was this greater inclusion of the other in the self that led to the increase in generalized positive feelings. So, the self-expansion associated with cross-group friendship does indeed appear to be associated not only with positive changes in attitudes toward the other group, but also with generalized positive emotions similar to those found in other research on interpersonal closeness.

Prediction 4: Self-Expansion Needs Actually Motivate Individuals to Seek out Members of Other Groups

The model predicts that fluctuations in the need for self-expansion lead to changes in the degree to which one prefers interactions that could lead to the formation of cross-group friendships. To investigate this hypothesis we designed a laboratory experiment involving white undergraduate students (Wright, McLaughlin-Volpe, & Brody, 2004). First, participants completed a short self-description and then a bogus personality test, the ostensible results of which were used to alter the level of their self-expansion needs. In the high self-expansion need condition, participants were told that the personality test demonstrated that their life was rather predictable and stagnant – that they were in a bit of a "rut," and that they demonstrated concern that they were not getting the resources needed to meet potential upcoming challenges. In the low self-expansion need condition, they were told that the personality test indicated that they had recently experienced considerable psychological change, that they were somewhat overwhelmed with the number of new things they were trying to manage in their life, and that they probably needed time to sort out these changes. Importantly, although participants were randomly assigned one of these two conditions, they were equally and fairly strongly convinced that the description accurately represented their current feelings. After reading the feedback, they were told that they would now interact with one of six other same-gender participants who were currently working in other cubicles in the lab, and that they would first rate their interest in meeting each of these participants. They then received seven handwritten self-descriptions, each with a name at the top (the names and descriptions were counterbalanced so that all the names appeared equally with all of the self-descriptions). One of the descriptions was their own and the other six included two white/Caucasian, two Chinese, and two Latino names.

Our manipulation of perceived self-expansion need clearly influenced participants' interest in interactions with others and, more specifically, with members of other ethnic groups. Compared to participants who received the feedback designed to decrease their self-expansion motivation, those who received the high self-expansion motivation feedback generally showed greater interest in interacting with all of the other people. However, and most importantly, this greater degree of interest was most pronounced for members of other ethnic groups. Put another way, white undergraduates who were experiencing high self-expansion needs showed greater interest in interacting with Latino and Chinese students than did those who were experiencing low self-expansion needs.

This research supports the claim that people are, at times, motivated to develop cross-group friendships and these relationships with members of other groups generally lead not only to prejudice reduction, but also to opportunities for self-expansion and positive affect. Given that the research suggests that there is an appetitive interest in other groups, it seems timely to consider reevaluating our current thinking about the range of emotions that might be experienced during intergroup interactions.

Some Final Thoughts

We suggest promoting cross-group friendships as a mechanism for moving beyond tolerance and toward compassionate love. We see cross-group friendship as the fertile ground where cross-group compassionate love can blossom. Friends perceive each other as equals, but when times are tough, lean on each other for support. Because the dynamics in real relationships (e.g., equal status within the friendship) do not necessarily mirror actual intergroup dynamics, friendships provide an opportunity to interact with the other group in new ways. For the member of a disadvantaged group, participation in a cross-group friendship makes it possible to have a give-and-take relationship, rather than simply being the target of sympathy or pity. For the member of a more advantaged group, a cross-group friendship can provide the opportunity to be the recipient of the other's help and assistance. As Underwood (Chapter 1, this volume) notes, one way to show compassion is to allow the other to help you. Compassionate love can include emotions such as sympathy and empathy, but in a true friendship, there are reciprocal opportunities to be both the recipient and the purveyor of these emotions.

Astrophysicist Stephen Hawking recently posed this question to the internet cosmos: "In a world that is in chaos politically, socially, and environmentally, how can the human race sustain another 100 years?" While some responded by suggesting the elimination of nuclear weapons or suggestions to inhabit space, others focused on improving relations between groups as the ultimate solution (Jesdanun, 2006). We share this view and are hopeful about creating real social change through the cultivation of close cross-group friendships. At the macro-level, we need to structure contact situations in ways that facilitate friendship formation.

To facilitate opportunities for cross-group friendships, we propose specific changes in arenas where intergroup contact is likely. In particular, people are likely to interact with other groups at school, at work, and in the community. In schools, our approach requires a recognition of social categorization processes. Multicultural education that involves learning about history and celebrating of cultural traditions and customs is only part of the solution. While much of the educational literature focuses on the role of the teacher in multicultural education (Banks, 2006), our approach focuses on how relationships among peers can be more effective in creating positive intergroup relations.

Interventions in schools might incorporate aspects of the procedure used in our laboratory work to achieve closeness (Aron, Melinat, Aron, Vallone, & Bator, 1997; Owen et al., 2001; Wright & van Der Zande, 1999). This procedure consists of structured activities, each designed to replicate the natural processes involved in friendship formation and development such as self-disclosure, cooperation, and teamwork. Essentially, this "fast-friends procedure" is a fast track to developing closeness between strangers. The first activity asks participants to reciprocally disclose increasingly intimate thoughts, feelings, and past experiences, to compliment and support each other, and to find and describe similarities between themselves. Other activities designed to develop closeness focus on cooperation in meeting a joint goal, discussing issues of importance, activities that require that one partner rely on and trust the other, and simply have fun. The procedure in these studies easily could be adapted for use in classrooms where cross-group pairings could be arranged.

Adaptations of these laboratory procedures could be utilized in the workplace with functional work groups. Work teams are real groups who share collective responsibility for an outcome and members have differentiated roles (Wageman, 1997). Outside of quality concerns, two measures of work-team success are whether team members would like to work together again and whether individual members experienced personal growth (Yeatts, Hyten, & Barnes, 1996). In this sense, building friendships within diverse work teams as part of a teambuilding exercise can potentially improve work-team effectiveness, morale, and productivity. Employers may not have improved social relations outside of the office as their main priority, but these other benefits of creating cross-group friendships in diverse work groups may be enough to inspire organizational practices that could become part of this broader social change agenda.

Community relations also could be structured in ways that facilitate close cross-group friendships. Ideally, members of different groups could work together on community projects under equal status conditions (e.g., building a house for Habitat for Humanity). In many cases, however, service work emphasizes social identities to such a degree that forming close personal relationships across groups is difficult. For example, a college student may opt to engage in service-learning at a soup kitchen as part of her academic coursework. At the soup kitchen, she may find that standing behind a table serving soup is the extent of her social interactions with patrons of the kitchen. It is very likely that in these circumstances, the self-expansion motive that may well have inspired her interest in the service learning program in the first place (Brody & Wright, 2004) will not be satisfied by these limited interactions and the resulting lack of opportunity to get to know the guests. Consistent with this analysis, research indicates that following a service-learning experience, students indicate that developing interpersonal relationships was the highest ranked "peak experience" (Brody & Brody, 2004). Unless community relations are structured in a way that promotes interpersonal relationships, service-learners are unlikely to have experiences that fulfill their self-expansion motive and that lead to optimal contact outcomes.

For community service work to be an optimally transformative experience, individuals should be given opportunities to interact with others in ways that could lead to feelings of interpersonal closeness. The uneven distribution of power and resources in many other service-provider settings (e.g., soup kitchens), coupled with highly salient group boundaries, makes it particularly important that the organization structure the situation such that disadvantaged group members (e.g., guests at the kitchen) have opportunities to represent themselves as individuals, and that will encourage one-to-one interactions across group lines.

Haley House, an agency providing services to the disadvantaged and homeless living in Boston, Massachusetts, nicely illustrates how cross-group friendships can be formed in the context of volunteer–guest interactions. Haley House is committed to empowering individuals who are marginalized, unemployed, and underemployed, and having difficulty making ends meet. The agency runs a soup kitchen and has opened a bakery as an economic development initiative. In each of the programs, workers are a mix of local college students, community members, and regular guests at Haley House. Volunteers at Haley House work together to prepare meals and often develop friendships with members of their shift. When they work, there also are many opportunities to "hang out" with guests in a real-life version of our laboratory procedure. College student David Moorhead published a reflection piece that describes his budding friendship with Prince, one of the regular guests at Haley House. He wrote:

> Haley House ... became a part of me ... There was that cold January morning when I took a break from washing the dishes. Sitting down next to two men playing checkers, I met Prince. As he quickly devoured his opponent,

his bragging that he was the best in Boston made me want to play. Finally getting the opportunity after Prince produced another victim, I sat down for the first of many games ... After several blowouts, I barely beat Prince, by some amazing luck. Throughout the months that followed, I never did beat Prince again. Yet each time I played him, I was reminded that even though our worlds appeared very different, we were still human beings who could enjoy each other's company ... one morning ... I read a newspaper article about all the different candidates running for the presidential nomination ... Standing in Haley House, it was hard to agree with cuts in support of welfare or tax breaks for the rich. Haley House [affected my] thinking about what to stand for and whom to vote for ... It was these experiences and many more that made Haley House a part of me. Not only did I think about Haley House when I was there, I thought about the guests' situation a lot. [For example, w]hen someone told me that it was supposed to snow, I thought of the three guys who told me they sleep by the dumpster at the Burger King on Huntington Avenue ... When people on the news and in the newspapers talk about cutting SSI, I think about the men who hobble into Haley House each day. When people speak about injustice in this world, I think about the men at Haley House and their struggles. When it is late at night and I'm trying to get comfortable under my comforter on my bed, I think of the men of Haley House curled up under a street light on some corner ... Haley House has been a part of me. (http://www.haleyhouse.org/volunteer.htm)

Mr. Moorhead's narrative describes many of the aspects of successful intergroup contact that we have proposed – a context that creates opportunities for friendship by encouraging interactions in which individuals have chances to interact in terms of their unique, personal characteristics – while recognizing their group differences and similarities. The result is relationships that build over time and lead to the inclusion of other – and the other group – in the self, as well as generalized positive attitudes from those relationship partners to the groups to which they belong. Moorhead's words describing Haley House as "a part of me" mirror precisely the feeling of psychological connection that the inclusion of other in the self-model describes. For Mr. Moorhead, the self-expansion experienced with the people he met at Haley House led him to reconsider his current worldviews, to question the values and beliefs of his previous group identification, and perhaps even to alter his behavior in terms of casting his ballot. The close relationships he developed at Haley House made not only the experience of his specific friend, Prince, relevant to him, but also the experience of thousands of others who share Prince's economic status.

As researchers, we can do much more, of course, to sort out mechanisms and the conditions under which cross-group friendships are most effective. We have only just begun to scratch the surface of the field of intergroup relations in moving from reducing prejudice to promoting compassionate love. But the state of intergroup relations is among the world's foremost sources of misery, and the possibility of compassionate love is among the most hopeful visions of our future. Thus, we cannot wait for all the results to be in: As researchers we may also want to study these methods in the real world, testing applications where it can make a real difference without further delay. In fact, recently we have begun two projects in which we are attempting to apply the "fast-friends procedure" in the real world. One is a study applying these methods with the entire entering freshman class at a major university to attempt to create a more compassionate intergroup atmosphere throughout the campus; the other is a pilot program bringing together police and community members to build mutual trust and admiration.

Thus, returning to Hawking's question about the future of the human race, we respond hopefully. The real-life examples of compassionate love presented in this chapter, coupled with the research evidence on cross-group friendships, lead us to see this approach as a valuable contribution to solving some of the most important social problems that face us. Some may see outer space as the answer to Hawking's question, but we focus on a different kind of space – the psychological space between human beings. People's self-expansion motives may provide the basic fuel that will motivate us to cross the spaces that divide us, but it will be those who structure social situations to cultivate and support meaningful cross-group relationships who may be most influential, not only in bringing individuals closer, but in building the bridges that bring groups together as well. By creating small changes in everyday life situations, there is the potential to create large changes in our social world, and to move the rhetoric and the reality of intergroup relations from talk of tolerance to feelings of genuine respect, admiration – and perhaps – even compassionate love.

References

Allport, G. W. (1954). *The nature of prejudice*. Menlo Park, CA: Addison-Wesley.

Altman, I., & Taylor, D. (1973). *Social penetration: The development of interpersonal relationships*. Oxford, England: Holt, Rinehart & Winston.

Aron, A., & Aron, E. N. (1986). *Love as the expansion of self: Understanding attraction and satisfaction*. New York: Hemisphere.

Aron, A., Aron, E. N., & Smollan, D. (1992). Inclusion of other in the self scale and the structure of interpersonal closeness. *Journal of Personality and Social Psychology, 63*, 596–612.

Aron, A., Aron, E. N., Tudor, M., & Nelson, G. (1991). Close relationships as including other in the self. *Journal of Personality and Social Psychology, 60*, 241–253.

Aron, A., & Fraley, B. (1999). Relationship closeness as including other in the self: Cognitive underpinnings and measures. *Social Cognition, 17*, 140–160.

Aron, A., Mashek, D., & Aron, E. (2004). Closeness as including other in the self. In D. Mashek & A. Aron (Eds.), *Handbook of closeness and intimacy* (pp. 27–41). Mahwah, NJ: Lawrence Erlbaum.

Aron, A., McLaughlin-Volpe, T., Mashek, D., Lewandowski, G., Wright, S. C., & Aron, E. (2005). Including others in the self. In W. Stoebe & M. Hewstone (Eds.), *European Review of Social Psychology, Vol. 14* (pp. 101–132). Hove, England: Psychology Press.

Aron, A., Melinat, E., Aron, E. N., Vallone, R., & Bator, R. (1997). The experimental generation of interpersonal closeness: A procedure and some preliminary findings. *Personality and Social Psychology Bulletin, 23*, 363–377.

Aron, A., Norman, C. C., & Aron, E. N. (1998). The self-expansion model and motivation. *Representative Research in Social Psychology, 22*, 1–13.

Aron, A., Norman, C. C., Aron, E. N., McKenna, C., & Heyman, R. E. (2000). Couples' shared participation in novel and arousing activities and experienced relationship quality. *Journal of Personality and Social Psychology, 72*, 273–284.

Aron, A., Paris, M., & Aron, E. N. (1995). Falling in love: Prospective studies of self-concept change. *Journal of Personality and Social Psychology, 69*, 1102–1112.

Aron, A., Steele, J. L., Kashdan, T., & Perez, M. (2006). When similars do not attract: Tests of a prediction from the self-expansion model. *Personal Relationships, 13*, 387–396.

Aron, A., Whitfield-Gabrieli, S. L., and Lichty, W. (in press). *Whole brain correlations: Examining similarity across conditions of overall patterns of neural activation in fMRI real data analysis.* American Educational Research Association SIG/Educational Statisticians book.

Banks, J. A. (2006). *Cultural diversity and education: Foundations, curriculum and teaching.* Boston, MA: Pearson/Allyn & Bacon.

Berg, J. H., & Clark, M. S. (1986). Differences in social exchange between intimate and other relationships: Gradually evolving or quickly apparent? In V. J. Derlega & B. A. Winstead (Eds.), *Friendship and social interaction* (pp. 101–128). New York: Springer.

Brewer, M. B., & Brown, R. J. (1998). Intergroup relations. In D. T. Gilbert & S. T. Fiske (Eds.), *The handbook of social psychology, Vol. 2* (4th ed.) (pp. 554–594). Boston, MA: McGraw-Hill.

Brewer, M. B., & Miller, N. (1984). Beyond the contact hypothesis: Theoretical perspectives on desegregation. In N. Miller & M. B. Brewer (Eds.), *Groups in contact: The psychology of desegregation* (pp. 281–302). Los Angeles, CA: Academic Press.

Brewer, M. B., & Miller, N. (1996). *Intergroup relations.* Buckingham, England: Open University Press.

Brody, S. M. (2003). *Serving a higher purpose: How service-learning leads to improved intergroup relations.* Unpublished doctoral dissertation, University of California, Santa Cruz.

Brody, S. M., & Brody, B. T. (2004, September 26–28). *Peak experiences: Bridging the gap between service-learning and student-centered learning.* Paper presented at the Conference for Civic Education Research, Reno, NV.

Brody, S. M., & Wright, S. C. (2004). Expanding the self through service-learning. *Michigan Journal of Community Service Learning, 11,* 14–24.

Burns, E. (2006, April 3). Spread love, compassion for Katrina victims. *USA Today,* p. 14A.

Christian Century. (2006, January 10). Post-hurricane donors show record generosity. *Christian Century, 123(1),* 13.

Cialdini, R., Borden, R., Thorne, A., Walker, M., Freeman, S., & Sloan, L. (1999). Basking in reflected glory: Three (football) field studies. In R. F. Baumeister (Ed.), *The self in social psychology* (pp. 436–445). New York: Psychology Press.

Collins, N., & Miller, L. (1994). Self-disclosure and liking: A meta-analytic review. *Psychological Bulletin, 116,* 457–475.

Cook, S. W., & Selltiz, C. (1955). Some factors which influence the attitudinal outcomes of personal contacts. *International Sociological Bulletin, 7,* 51–58.

Crandall, C. S. (1991). Multiple stigma and AIDS: Medical stigma and attitudes towards homosexuals and IV-drug used in AIDS-related stigmatization. *Journal of Community and Applied Social Psychology, 32,* 39–70.

della Cava, M. R. (2005, September 7). In Katrina's wake, generosity. *USA Today,* p. 1D.

Fehr, B. (1996). *Friendship processes.* London: Sage.

Hewstone, M., & Brown, R. (1986). Contact is not enough: An intergroup perspective on the "Contact Hypothesis." In M. Hewstone & R. Brown (Eds.), *Contact and conflict in intergroup encounters* (pp. 1–44). New York: Basil Blackwell.

Jesdanun, A. (2006). Hawking seeks answers on humanity. *Associated Press.*

Mashek, D., & Sherman, M. (2004). Desiring less closeness with intimate others. In D. J. Mashek & A. P. Aron (Eds.), *Handbook of closeness and intimacy* (pp. 343–356). Mahwah, NJ: Lawrence Erlbaum.

McLaughlin-Volpe, T., Aron, A., Wright, S. C., & Reis, H. T. (2000). *Intergroup social interactions and intergroup prejudice: Quantity versus quality.* Manuscript under review.

McLaughlin-Volpe, T., & Wright, S. C. (2002). *The hidden rewards of cross-group friendship: Self-expansion across group membership.* Paper presented at the European Association of Experimental Social Psychology, San Sebastián, Spain.

Moorhead, D. (2006). Get involved. Retrieved July 14, 2006, from http://www.haleyhouse.org/volunteer.htm

Owen, K. I., Wright, S. C., & Brody, S. M. (2001). *Bicultural friends: When group membership salience matters.* Poster presentation at the meeting of the Western Psychological Association. Maui, HI.

Pettigrew, T. (1997). Generalized intergroup contact effects on prejudice. *Personality and Social Psychology Bulletin, 23,* 173–185.

Pettigrew, T. (1998). Intergroup contact theory. *Annual Review of Psychology, 49,* 65–85.

Pettigrew, T. F., & Tropp, L. R. (2000). Does intergroup contact reduce prejudice?: Recent meta-analytic findings. In Stuart Oskamp et al. (Eds.), *Reducing prejudice and discrimination* (pp. 93–114). Mahwah, NJ: Lawrence Erlbaum.

Ripley, A. (2005, September 26). Guess who's coming. ... *Time, 166(13),* 30–31.

Ross, L., & Nisbett, R. E. (1991). *The person and the situation: Perspectives of social psychology.* New York: McGraw-Hill.

Smith, E. R., Coats, S., & Walling, D. (1999). Overlapping mental representations of self, in-group, and partner: Further response time evidence and a connectionist model. *Personality and Social Psychology Bulletin, 25,* 873–882.

Tajfel, H. (1981). *Human groups and social categories.* Cambridge, England: Cambridge University Press.

Tesser, A. (1999). Toward a self-evaluation maintenance model of social behavior. In R. F. Baumeister (Ed.), *The self in social psychology* (pp. 446–460). New York: Psychology Press.

Turner, J. C., Hogg, M. A., Oakes, P. J., Reicher, S. D., & Wetherell, M. S. (1987). *Rediscovering the social group.* Oxford, England: Basil Blackwell.

Underwood, L. (2005). Interviews with Trappist monks as a contribution to research methodology in the investigation of compassionate love. *Journal for the Theory of Social Behaviour, 35,* 285–302.

Wageman, R. (1997). Critical factors for creating superb self-managing teams. *Organizational Dynamics, 26(1),* 49–61.

Wright, S. C., Aron, A., & Tropp, L. R. (2002). Including others (and their groups) in the self: Self-expansion theory and intergroup relations. In J. P. Forgas & K. Williams (Eds.), *The social self: Cognitive, interpersonal and intergroup perspectives* (pp. 343–363). Philadelphia, PA: Psychology Press.

Wright, S. C., Brody, S. A., & Aron, A. (2005). Intergroup contact: Still our best hope for reducing prejudice. In C. S. Crandall & M. Schaller (Eds.), *The social psychology of prejudice: Historical perspectives* (pp.115–142). Seattle, WA: Lewinian Press.

Wright, S. C., McLaughlin-Volpe, T., & Brody, S. M. (2004, January). *Seeking and finding an expanded "me" outside my ingroup: Outgroup friends and self change.* Paper presented at the annual convention of Society for Personality and Social Psychology, Austin, TX.

Wright, S. C., & van Der Zande, C. C. (1999, October). *Bicultural friends: When cross-group friendships cause improved intergroup attitudes.* Paper presented at the annual convention of the Society for Experimental Social Psychology, St. Louis, MO.

Yeatts, D. E., Hyten, C., & Barnes, D. (1996). What are the key factors for self-managed team success? *Journal for Quality & Participation, 19,* 68–76.

Part V

Compassionate Love in Health Care and Other Caregiving Contexts

11

Compassionate Family Caregiving in the Light and Shadow of Death

Linda J. Roberts, Meg Wise, and Lori L. DuBenske

The dark background which death supplies, brings out the tender colors of life in all their purity. (—Santayana (quoted in Yalom, 1980, p. 163))

Receiving a terminal diagnosis triggers an acute awareness of human fragility and personal vulnerability. As the physician Ira Byock (2002, p. 280) put it, "From the moment an individual is diagnosed with an incurable illness, death becomes the alarm that will not stop ringing." The alarm signifies the entrance to what McQuellon and Cowan (2000) call "mortal time" – the psychological state humans enter when they directly or vicariously are confronted with the prospect of death. The alarm of mortal time rings not only for the patient with a terminal diagnosis, but for the patient's family and other loved ones as well. Like the dying person, close others are forcefully reminded of their own mortality and vulnerability. Moreover, they are called on to give support, care, and empathy to the dying person, all while preparing for a significant loss in their own life. While the alarm of death is ringing, both dying persons and their families experience profound needs for physical, emotional, relational, spiritual, and existential care. It is a context for compassion.

In this chapter, we focus on compassionate love as it is expressed in this end-of-life caregiving context. Following Underwood (2005; Chapter 1, this volume) and others (e.g., Sprecher & Fehr, 2005), we understand compassionate love to encompass feelings and actions that provide support and care to another in a way that respects and values the other-as-other. Compassion is predicated on awareness and appreciation of the other's experience, particularly the other's suffering and fundamental needs (see also Batson, 1991). Compassion and altruism are motivated by the desire to promote the good of the other, and as such, require setting aside one's personal agenda for the sake of the good of the other. Compassionate love is distinguished from compassion and altruism in its explicit involvement of what Underwood (2002) calls "a response of the heart." Compassionate love is not a dispassionate, detached, or dutiful act, but rather, as the word "love" suggests, a tender, moving, and positive emotional experience. To acknowledge the end-of-life caregiving context that is our focus, we will use the term *compassionate caregiving* interchangeably with compassionate love. The term *caregiving* is chosen purposefully to suggest a connection to two different relevant research literatures that use the term: the family and informal caregiving literature, and the adult attachment theory literature.

It is estimated that there are currently more than 50 million "informal caregivers" providing care for the disabled, elderly or ill in the United States (US Department of Health and Human Services, 1998). An important and burgeoning literature has developed documenting the experiences of informal caregivers and importantly, the substantial sacrifices and costs associated with the caregiver role (Gallagher-Thompson et al., 1998; Hunt, 2003; Pinquart & Sorensen, 2003). A smaller literature directly addresses end-of-life caregiving, where caregivers are predominantly family members (Emanuel et al., 1999; Hebert & Schulz, 2006). These family caregivers often experience significant decrements in their quality of life and emotional functioning (e.g., Hull, 1990; Weitzner, McMillan, & Jacobsen, 1999), sometimes reporting more distress than the terminally ill patient (Axelsson & Sjödén, 1998; Eldredge, 2004). In the family caregiving literature, the interpersonal caregiving context is usually conceptualized narrowly – caregiving is depicted as a unidirectional process going from a self-sacrificing "caregiver" to a passive care recipient (Midlarsky & Kahana, 1994). However, it is clear that even very frail patients are often able to make instrumental contributions to the household and provide critical emotional support to others (Midlarsky & Kahana, 1994). For our purposes, we conceptualize end-of-life caregiving as a "two-way street" marked by the potential for caregivers and patients to both give and receive care. Caregivers, too, need care and love; and patients, even dying patients, can and do give care and love.

This broader notion of caregiving as a bidirectional interpersonal process is consistent with the use of the term caregiving in the adult attachment literature (Bowlby, 1969/1982, 1988; Collins & Feeney, 2000; Kunce & Shaver, 1994). Attachment theory, Bowlby's influential theory of human nature and development, suggests that the ability to engage in both care-seeking and caregiving is essential to a mature, healthy, intimate relationship. According to attachment theory, the need for care and the ability to give care are both grounded in "behavioral systems" that evolved to enhance the probability of survival, reproduction, and successful parenting. The "caregiving behavioral system" is an innate system that prompts us to respond to the needs of others

(Bowlby, 1969/1982). The caregiving system, however, is not always activated, and even when it is, the care provided is not always effective, appropriate, or moved by compassion (Collins & Feeney, 2000; Feeney & Collins, 2003; Mikulincer, Shaver, & Gillath, Chapter 8, this volume). Following our definition of compassionate love and caregiving, whether attending to another's needs is compassionate caregiving depends on what "moves" it, what the underlying motivation and emotional experience is (Underwood, Chapter 1, this volume). Caregiving can be motivated by self-serving, defensive goals, or by genuine, other-oriented goals. Crocker and her colleagues (Crocker, 2008; Crocker, Nuer, Olivier, & Cohen, 2006) contrast these two different types of motives, proposing that they are supported by two underlying motivational frameworks, the "egosystem" and "ecosystem," corresponding, respectively, with two biologically based motivational systems of self-preservation and species preservation. Crocker (2008) has produced evidence to suggest that it is ecosystem motivation that enhances well-being and fosters feelings of closeness and social support. Similarly, research from an attachment-theory perspective has found that caregiving that is motivated by feelings of love and concern and is sensitive and responsive to the needs of the other increases relationship quality (e.g., Feeney & Collins, 2003). Thus the expression of compassionate love in the end-of-life caregiving context is expected to be associated with enhanced relational quality and intimacy.

Although compassionate love may be manifest in a range of contexts (Sprecher & Fehr, 2005), our focus here is on the expression of compassionate love within a close, familial relationship, specifically between a "patient" with terminal illness and a family "caregiver."[1] In terms of Underwood's (Chapter 1, this volume) model of compassionate love, the diagnosis of terminal illness represents a situational context that opens individuals to a choice about compassionate responding. Within this situational context, both *intrapersonal processes* (within the person) as well as *interpersonal processes* (between persons) are important determinants of the expression of compassionate love. The interpersonal context is implicit in Underwood's model, as the act of compassionate love is by definition an interpersonal act. In addition to examining intrapersonal processes, we focus explicitly on compassionate love as an interpersonal process, acknowledging the reality of the relational context of caregiving behavior and the importance of situating each person's behavior in the context of the other's. It is

---

[1] For ease of discussion we will continue to refer to the person with terminal illness as the *patient* and the close family member(s) of the patient as the *caregiver*(s), although we do not mean to suggest by this terminology that care and love are the exclusive domain of the "caregivers."

assumed that the behavioral acts and feelings of each partner both provoke and respond to the other's behaviors and feelings, potentially propelling or dampening compassionate responding.

Our goals in this chapter are threefold: (1) to review philosophical, religious, and theoretical perspectives on a confrontation with death, highlighting implications for an understanding of the manifestation of compassionate love; (2) to examine manifestations of compassionate love in the lived experiences of caregivers and terminally ill patients; and (3) to begin to identify intrapersonal and interpersonal processes that enable and support fully expressed compassionate love and caregiving in light of death.

In Mortal Time: Confronting Death and Dying

The Denial of Death: Modernity's Paradox

Until the modern era, the season of human life was short and unpredictable; death was accepted as an inevitable and ever-present aspect of life, beyond human control (Ariès, 1974; Friel, 1982; Zimmermann & Rodin, 2004). Shrouded in mystery, death was imbued with transcendent qualities – the deceased were often seen as living on in our hearts and/or in an afterlife. With the Enlightenment, science and rational positivism replaced the mystery surrounding disease and death with a hope of prediction and control. Science and medicine have had astonishing success in curing disease and extending the human life span, but with these advances has come the hubris that we can banish death – and greater fear and anxiety related to death and dying (Becker, 1973; Kuebler-Ross, 1970). Paradoxically, the fruits of scientific rationalism have mercifully cured disease and delayed death but may have threatened the relational, compassionate, and spiritual aspects of the end-of-life experience (Block, 2001; Byock, 1997).

Modern medicine has indeed afforded us some bargaining power, but not the power to cheat death. Denial, even when bolstered by science, does not alter the fundamental inevitability of death. Yet the most rational among us are all too eager to trade the scientific fact of death for the "magical thinking" (Didion, 2005) that science can render our bodies, if not our souls, immortal (Becker, 1973). Indeed, it has been widely argued that the denial of death is a natural feature of the human condition (e.g., Becker, 1973; Freud, 1930; Glaser & Strauss, 1965; Greenberg, Pyszczynski, & Solomon, 1986). A terminal cancer patient who participated in our research put it this way: "You're immortal until you find out how mortal you are." In his influential book, *The Denial of Death*, Ernst Becker creates a "network of arguments based on the universality of the fear of death, or 'terror,' … in order to convey how all-consuming it is when we look it full in the face" (p. 15). Becker argues that human behavior needs to be understood in the context of this fundamental terror and the concomitant human propensity to vigorously avoid looking at death "full in the face." Death and its associated terror represent a powerful motivating force – in Becker's simple and oft-quoted words: "Of all things that move man, one of the principal ones is his terror of death" (p. 11). Acts of extreme cruelty, greed, and selfishness, as well as acts of all-giving compassion and love may be moved, or motivated, by the terror-infused awareness of death.

Following Becker's lead, "Terror Management Theory" (TMT; Greenberg et al., 1986; Solomon, Greenberg, & Pyszczynski, 1991) argues that people manage the paralyzing terror engendered by the awareness of death by using two symbolic defense mechanisms, worldview validation and self-esteem enhancement. By validating their own culturally constructed worldviews and by adopting culturally accepted behaviors to increase their self-esteem, people are protected from the anxiety and terror associated with death. In a series of experimental studies in which mortality is made salient by exposing research participants to death-related content (gory videos, a funeral parlor, subliminal presentation of death-related words), TMT researchers have found empirical support for these hypothesized defensive strategies (for a review, see Pyszczynski, Greenberg, Solomon, Arndt, & Schimel, 2004). For example, when mortality is made salient, people have been found to exhibit more greed and to resort to "ingroup" behaviors, stereotyping others, and punishing those who do not share their worldviews. Thus, death awareness has the potential to activate "egosystem" motivations and evoke self-serving, defensive reactions.

In a commentary on TMT theory, Crocker and Nuer (2004) argue that a fear-motivated embrace of culturally sanctified values and meaning structures is not the only response to death salience:

> We suggest that although this is a common strategy for dealing with the problem of death, there is a different paradigm, one in which death is not a source of anxiety and paralysis but a source of energy, resolve, and enthusiasm. … With a clear sense of purpose and strong goals, the possibility that one might have only 1 year or 1 day or 20 min to live can be a reminder to focus on the most essential goal at every moment. In this paradigm, awareness of one's mortality is not a source of fear but a source of inspiration. Thoughts of death are not something to avoid but a precious reminder of the limited time each person has to accomplish his or her goals, as well as a reminder not to waste the time one has. (pp. 469–470)

Looking death "full in the face" can provoke selfish, protective, defensive actions, but it also can initiate positive transformation buoyed by proactive other-oriented rather than defensive self-preserving motivations. Indeed, like Crocker and Nuer, religious, philosophical, and popular writings have long extolled a "bright side" to death's shadow.

Positive Transformation in the Light of Death

From Buddha, to Kiekegaard, to Stephen Levine, it has been argued that it is facing rather than denying the existential condition of suffering and death that brings a rich and fulfilling life (e.g., Byock, 2002; Frankl, 1964; Heidegger, 1927/1996; Levine, 1997; Martin, Campbell, & Henry, 2004; Staton, Shuy, & Byock, 2001; Yalom, 1980). For example, bestselling author Stephen Levine (1997) popularized the idea that increasing mortality salience is transformative in books such as *A Year to Live: How to Live this Year as if It Were Your Last*. As Levine points out, his ideas are not new, Socrates, for example, is reported to have recommended that his followers "practice dying" as the highest form of wisdom. Buddhism posits impermanence as a central tenet of existence; death and suffering need to be fully acknowledged to enter the path of enlightenment. Indeed, the Buddha proclaims "of all mindfulness meditations, that on death is supreme." The Stoics embrace a similar aphorism: "Contemplate death if you would learn how to live" (cited in Yalom, 1980, p. 169).

The idea of integrating death into life has perhaps found its most complete expression in existentialism. Existential philosophy begins unabashedly with suffering and death as essential conditions of human life. From an existential perspective (e.g., Frankl, 1964; Kierkegaard, 1983; Nietzsche, 1955), we best understand what it means to live when we contemplate what it means to die, to not exist. Kierkegaard asserts that accepting the ultimate fragility of our own being is the antidote to despair. The integration of death into life underscores the preciousness of time and paradoxically increases vitality. As the existential psychotherapist Irvin Yalom put it: "by keeping death in mind one passes into a state of gratitude for the countless givens of existence" (1980, p. 163). Not only are suffering and death not denied, but existentialism brings acute focus to experiences such as alienation, anxiety, inauthenticity, dread, sickness-unto-death, sense of nothingness, and terror – all without regressing to pre-Enlightenment notions of predetermination and prescriptive paths to transcendence. Accepting these basic negative conditions of existence as the springboard for authentic living, existentialists hold that it is by making personal meaning of death-and-life that people can achieve joy and transcendence. Individuals must find their own paths to such meaning and are endowed with the capacity to change and grow to meet the existential challenges of suffering and death.

Consistent with this philosophical backdrop, posttraumatic growth research (PTG; Tedeschi, Park, & Calhoun, 1998) supports the notion that facing trauma, suffering, or mortality has the potential to spawn personal growth and transformation (for recent reviews, see Calhoun & Tedeschi, 2006; Linley & Joseph, 2004). Posttraumatic growth is the subjective sense of positive psychological change as a result of trauma or suffering, thus it encompasses but is not limited to experiences of "mortal time" or a confrontation with death. Rather than manipulating cues to evoke mortality salience as in the TMT tradition, this research tradition studies individuals facing or surviving adverse life conditions. Further, in contrast to the predictions of terror management theory of a heightened reliance on externally sanctioned worldviews, when death is made salient, posttraumatic growth studies point to a shift from extrinsic to intrinsic values. PTG researchers (Tedeschi et al., 1998) have documented a range of positive transformations in the interpersonal domain in light of death, including increased compassion, connection, and giving to others.

Recentering on Love, Compassion, and Caregiving in the Light of Death

The theme of awakening compassion in the light of death is embodied in the well-known transformation of Dickens's Ebenezer Scrooge after he confronts the reality of suffering and death at the Ghosts' mystical prompting – he changes from a self-centered and miserly, well, "scrooge" to a loving, giving, and compassionate benefactor. Similarly, the movie *Shadowlands* poignantly depicts the well-known author C. S. Lewis's transformation in light of his new wife's terminal cancer diagnosis – he becomes able to move outside of his own world to hers; in light of the shadow of death, he learns to love. And at the base of this love is compassion, as his character in the film explains:

> I'm not sure that God particularly wants us to be happy. I think He wants us to be able to love … and be loved, wants us to grow up. We think our childish toys bring us all the happiness there is and our nursery is the whole wide world. But something must drive us out of the nursery … to the world of others … and that something is suffering. See, if you love someone, you don't want them to suffer. You can't bear it. You want to take their suffering onto yourself.

Compassionate love in the face of death and suffering is an ideal across a range of cultural, religious, and philosophical systems. Both Eastern and Western religions elevate love and compassion, or fundamentally, a shift from "egosystem" values to "ecosystem" values, to the pinnacle of spiritual ideals. In Judeo-Christian traditions, humans are exhorted to love the other as oneself and to perform acts of loving kindness without expectation of return. Buddhism teaches that "God" is within all beings and that suffering is central to the human condition because of our attachment to that which is impermanent (e.g., people, fortune, life). Suffering is relieved through the paradoxical acceptance of detachment and loving kindness. Existential philosophers suggest that coming to terms with suffering and death (nonexistence) leads to a more purposeful life, and that caring relationships are central to an ethically and affectively meaningful life. For example, Frankl (1964) asserted that one "wills meaning" by choosing how one thinks, and by loving others: "The more one forgets oneself – by giving to another person – the more human he is" (p. 115). Living in the constant shadow of death in a Nazi prison camp, Frankl personally experienced a transformation, and love was at its core. His epiphany came in an icy pre-dawn march to the camp worksite:

> My mind clung to my wife's image, imagining it with an uncanny acuteness. I found her answering me; saw her smile, her frank and encouraging look. Real or not her look was then more luminous than the sun which was beginning to rise. … I saw the truth – that love is the ultimate and highest goal to which man can aspire. Then I grasped the meaning of the greatest secret that human poetry and human thought and belief have to impart *"The salvation of man is through love and in love."* (pp. 48–49)

Love, compassion, giving to others, and the fundamental importance of relationships are also core themes in contemporary literature on positive responses to death awareness (e.g., Block, 2001; Carstensen, Isaacowitz, & Charles, 1999; Mikulincer, Florian, & Hirschberger, 2003; Tedeschi et al., 1998). For example, recent experimental studies from the TMT perspective have demonstrated that death salience can bring close relationships to the foreground (Mikulincer et al., 2003). Expanding TMT to incorporate insights from Attachment Theory, Mikulincer and his colleagues (et al., 2000; Mikulincer Florian, & Hirschberger, 2004) found that heightened death salience increases a desire for close relationships and, additionally, that close relationships effectively buffer death anxiety.

Although the background material we have reviewed suggests the possibility of positive transformation and a recentering on relationships and love in the end-of-life caregiving context, it is important to acknowledge that many people decidedly do not have transformative or loving experiences in the context of terminal illness or other confrontations with death. Death and relationships with others may be two fundamental existential conditions of our lives, but their existence certainly does not guarantee their transformative power. Humans may have an innate "caregiving system"

(Bowlby, 1969/1982) and even a biologically wired "compassionate instinct" (Keltner, 2004), but responding with compassionate love rather than indifference, defensiveness, or self-interest is far from ubiquitous, whether in intimate or global interactions. When does a confrontation with suffering and mortality evoke compassionate love between a family caregiver and a terminally ill patient? What intrapersonal and interpersonal processes might enable and support responsive compassionate caregiving? In the remainder of the chapter we turn to the context of terminal illness and the lived experiences of caregivers and patients to begin to address these questions.

Lived Experiences in the Light of Death

To explore the manifestations of compassionate love in the relationship between a family caregiver and terminally ill patient, we undertake an analysis of data from three related studies we have conducted on patient and caregiver experiences with life-limiting illness (primarily advanced, or terminal, cancer). The three studies we draw on are each briefly described below.

The *Assets Study* (AS; Roberts & Wise, 2006; Wise & Marchand, in preparation; Wise, Roberts, & Marchand, in preparation) uses grounded theory and in-depth interviewing with advanced cancer patients and/or their partners to further our understanding of coping processes in the context of the threat of death and loss. Patients and caregivers were recruited from a comprehensive cancer center according to a Human Subjects Committee-approved protocol. They were invited to join the study by their oncologist or support group leader. Interview questions focused on the informants' sources of strength and support as they faced terminal cancer. Informants were ten patients with advanced lung or colorectal cancer and seven spousal caregivers.

Additional in-depth interviews were conducted in conjunction with the *Couples Facing Advanced Cancer Together (C-FACT) Study* (Roberts, 2007; Roberts & Wise, 2006). The C-FACT study is designed to further our understanding of relationship functioning, dyadic coping processes, and the adaptational correlates and sequelae of communication processes for couples facing a death as a result of cancer. In addition to in-depth interviews, couples were videotaped while having a naturalistic conversation with each other about their concerns related to the illness. Recruitment was conducted through physician referral at a comprehensive cancer center or through support groups. Preliminary data from the interviews with six couples (twelve individual interviews) are the focus here.

A third study, the *Cancer Caregiver Study* (CCS; Bernard-DuBenske et al., under review; Roberts, Faust, & DuBenske, in preparation), includes both current (n = 38) and bereaved (n = 133) family caregivers of advanced cancer patients who completed surveys assessing relationship characteristics, caregiving behaviors, and information and support needs. In addition, prompted by three open-ended questions, informants provided narrative descriptions of the effects of the illness on their close relationship. The prompts asked them to write about the effects, both positive and negative, the illness had on their relationship and then to reflect on "what brought about" the positive and negative changes. Half of the patients were male and half were female, but consistent with the greater likelihood that women are in a caregiving role (Miller & Cafasso, 1992), a majority of the respondents were female. Forty-four percent of the sample were partners or spouses, another 38% a son or daughter of the patient, and the remaining were other family caregivers, for example, parents, grandchildren, or siblings (the original sample contained 11 non-familial caregivers who are not considered here).

Combining data from the three studies yielded qualitative data (either interview transcripts or written narratives) reflecting the lived experiences of patients (16) and caregivers (184) struggling with the reality of mortal time. The sample was predominantly white, reflecting the demographics of the recruitment area, but somewhat heterogeneous with respect to level of education (the majority had at least some college education) and age. Data were analyzed using analytic induction methods (Strauss & Corbin, 1998). The data were thematically coded using NVivo 7 software (QSR International, 2007) as a tool to manage and organize them as well as to develop and assign codes. Coding qualitative data is an intensive process involving multiple readings of the data and numerous modifications of the catalog of codes. Constant comparison and collaboration were used to check and recheck coding decisions and to refine patterns and themes in the data. In addition to relying on analyses from the separate studies here, we highlight themes related to compassionate love that we identified across the three data sets. When using direct quotes from our research participants, we indicate the study source by using the acronyms introduced above (i.e., AS, C-FACT, CCS) and further denote caregiver (C) or patient (P) for the AS and C-FACT informants.

Experiences of Compassionate Love

Based on our analyses of the qualitative data provided by terminally ill patients and their family caregivers, we report on three types of experiences of compassionate love: *compassionate love as caring for the other*, *compassionate love as healing and forgiving*, and *compassionate love as letting go of the other*. Although other manifestations of compassionate love are possible and were reported, we focus on these three because they emerged from the data as the most common types, and importantly, they emerged in all three data sets and in patient as well as caregiver descriptions.

Compassionate Love as Caring for the Other

For centuries, family members were the primary care providers to people with terminal illness. However, as the field of medicine grew and end-of-life care became more institutionalized, the majority of people with terminal illness spent their final days in hospitals or nursing homes. Owing to recent technological advances and rising health-care costs, the pendulum has swung again and end-of-life care has returned to the family (Arno, Levine, & Memmott, 1999). The landscape of home-based care, however, has changed and caregiving for a dying family member is not the same experience it was a century ago when caring for the dying was a normative and expected part of family life (Lynn, 2004). Modern-day terminal illness can involve an extended period of caregiving, over months or years rather than days or weeks, and family members are generally unprepared for the tasks, or for death itself (Becker, 1973). Further, families today are smaller and the responsibility for care is often placed on a single family member rather than a large support network. Family caregivers struggle to balance caregiving with other responsibilities both inside and outside the home (i.e., work, community activities), leading to experiences of financial, physical, and emotional strain (Covinsky et al., 1994; Hebert & Schulz, 2006). Caregivers often give tirelessly of themselves, often in the face of their own emotional and physical difficulties.

The family caregiving role, however, is not simply synonymous with compassionate caregiving. Motivations for caregiving are diverse, ranging from compassion and love, to indebtedness, obligation, pressure from others, and a desire to get something in return (Linsk & Poindexter, 2000; Noonan, Tennstedt, & Rebelsky, 1996). Some caregivers are driven by "egosystem" or self-serving motivations, giving care begrudgingly, being insensitive to the other's real needs, or holding resentments toward the other (Feeney & Collins, 2003; Linsk & Poindexter, 2000). Although caregiving springing from self-serving motives may nonetheless be helpful to the patient, it would not embody compassionate love. Other-oriented motivational factors, appreciation of the real needs of the other, and warm caring emotion characterize family caregiving grounded in compassionate love.

Similarly, caregiving that patients provide to their caregivers may or may not be compassionate caregiving. The dying can express compassionate love to others in many ways. In interviews with terminally ill patients, Proot et al. (2004) identified the most common caregiving activity for end-of-life patients as "directing." For example, the patient may settle financial matters, talk with their spouse about finding a new partner after their death, or in other ways make arrangements for the comfort of their family in the future. They may try to hand down their knowledge and skills related to household or financial management, or complete will and funeral arrangements (Martens & Davies, 1990). Patients also try to give emotional support to others to decrease their feeling of being a burden. However, being nice or supportive to the caregiver simply to assure continued care and attention is not expressing compassionate love, nor is care driven by discomfort with dependency or feeling that one is a burden. On the other hand, deep recognition and appreciation of the other and expressions that are genuinely responsive to the caregiver's emotional needs would represent acts of compassionate caregiving on the part of the dying patient.

Compassionate caregiving was not evident in all of the caregiver–patient dyads in our data sets. In the CCS study, the only one of our studies large enough to provide meaningful quantification, about one in nine family caregivers had a decidedly negative experience in their caregiving role. Consistent with the large literature on the burdens of caregiving, some of these caregivers expressed feelings of helplessness, frustration and resentment related to their role. As one caregiver put it: "Some nights I just want to scream at the top of my lungs." Another caregiver, now bereaved, reported that she was plagued by pangs of guilt for wishing that her husband would die because she felt she could not "handle him anymore." Many caregivers reported feeling resentment related to their role as caregiver. In one such response, the caregiver reflected: "I think I became somewhat resentful at this new life where I feel like I have to take care of everything; from supporting us financially, to household chores, to managing his care." Or as one woman noted, she felt sad and angry that she had become her husband's "caretaker rather than his wife." The act of caregiving took a significant toll on the personal lives of this group of caregivers; they described themselves as being depressed, exhausted, lonely, and even suicidal. For these caregivers, caring for a dying family member was not described as grounded in feelings of compassionate love.

However, a majority of the patients and caregivers across all three studies spontaneously described experiences that we have identified as reflecting at least glimmers of compassionate love as they faced death together. A smaller proportion of the study respondents experienced mutual and fully expressed compassionate love. In contrast to the dark experience some caregivers reported, the sentiment that the end-of-life caregiving experience was profound, a gift, or a "blessing" was common among both spousal and non-spousal family caregivers:

> *I can honestly say that taking care of Mom at home was one of the best, most purposeful times in my life. (CCS, 1119)*

> *Having my mother-in-law in our home was a blessing. ... Spending time together, learning to give and meet her needs was great. She learned to receive. The experience was rich for me, her, my husband, and my children. (CCS, 1090)*

> *Although the process of end-of-life care is difficult – emotional – it is one of the things in life I'm most proud of. (CCS, 1113)*

> *A person that ... has seen their wife or husband through and taken care of them right up until the day they die – it turns out that that's the most satisfying thing they've ever done in their life, when they think about it. And that's true, it is. (AS, P9)*

Although some of the individuals who found benefit in their experience may nonetheless have experienced severe strain while caring for a dying loved one, many caregivers in our studies explicitly denied feeling burdened. One woman put it this way: "I felt stressed by the fact that I could not stop what was happening to him. I would do it all again, but I know he felt he was a burden and nothing could be further from the truth." A husband acknowledged the physical stress of caregiving, but at the same time, articulated his strong desire to perform:

> *Attending to her needs was exhausting – cleaning bowel movements, inserting suppositories, medications, etc,. required many hours of lost sleep. I performed happily. (CCS, 1053)*

Although the general family caregiving literature has documented overwhelming psychological stresses for long-term caregivers, studies that focus explicitly on end-of-life caregivers (e.g., Eldredge, 2004; Linsk & Poindexter, 2000; Nelms, 2000, 2002; Wolff, Dy, Frick, & Kasper, 2007) have found evidence of benefits, similar to our findings here. For example, in Nelms's interview-based study of mothers who cared for their adult sons dying from AIDS, the mothers described caregiving as "not pretty work," but none of them reported experiencing the caregiving as a burden. One mother explained that she had never felt more love in her life than during that time and she "woke each day she cared for her son and asked 'What can I do today to make his life better?'" According to the authors, the depth of the mothers' commitment to their sons, their desire to provide care, the love and care they felt in return from their sons, and their awareness that caregiving was limited and would end with the death of their sons overshadowed any burden they experienced. Similarly, in a second study of AIDS caregivers, Linsk and Poindexter (2000) found that while caregivers acknowledged difficulties and considerable personal cost and effort, they also felt their caregiving led to positive results. The ability to find day-to-day personal meaning through caregiving can buffer caregivers against depression and role strain (Farran, Miller, Kaufman & Davis, 1997).

In the course of our interviews, both patients and caregivers repeatedly expressed the desire to give of themselves to others. Some focused on the welfare of their children, others on volunteer work or plans to leave gifts to charities, but the most prevalent theme was an expression of the desire to be a "giver" in the dyadic relationship of patient and family member. The majority of our caregiver informants were spouses, often lifelong partners in living. These spousal caregivers' words capture the feeling of compassionate love:

> *Her illness made me realize just how much I loved her; and needed her. I wanted to be with her as much as possible; to attend to her every need ... I kissed her and hugged her and told her I was proud to be able to be of help to make her as comfortable as possible. (CCS, 1053)*

> *I catered to him as much as possible. Not because I had to but because I loved him so much and wanted to make him comfortable and happy. (CCS, 1092)*

> *It has made me cling tighter than ever to each day he's alive, grateful that each morning he is alive. I get excited to see him each evening I return from work and thrilled when he actually accomplished something at home, however small the task. (It) has drawn me back to him the same way as when we first dated – couldn't wait to see him in person. (CCS, 0105)*

For these couples, the love described was not the love buoyed by passion, but by compassion – by the kindling of a strong motivation to respond to the needs of close others in the face of ultimate vulnerability.

Consistent with the few existing studies addressing the helpfulness and caregiving of the ill and frail (Midlarsky & Kahana, 1994; Proot et al., 2004), we found ample evidence of patient caregiving in our data. Most of the terminally ill patients we interviewed were no longer working, but their spouses often maintained work outside of the home and, as a result, some patients took on major responsibilities at home, despite their illness. For example, four months before his death, Karl described the ways he was supporting his working wife:

> *our roles are reversed from what we've been used to for the last, for the prior 35 years. We're learning role reversal and I am trying to do as much as I can,*

around the house, ... because now she has to go out full-time and work and so now I'm at home. I try to take as much of the load off of her, to help her. (*C-FACT, P-106*)

In addition to his instrumental work in the home, Karl also described his attempts to hide his own pain from his wife, out of a desire to be compassionate toward her:

The other thing I try and not to do is, unless I really need to, I try not to show her if I'm having a bad time physically. Like, for instance, right now one of the side effects of my last chemo is neuropathy. So I'm having to deal with neuropathy also, but she doesn't know exactly – she doesn't know 100%. (*C-FACT, P-106*)

In their work on end-of-life caregiving, Martens and Davies (1990) found that patients who were aware of caregiver needs worked to maintain a positive presentation of themselves in order to not burden those around them. As a C-FACT patient put it: "There was a lot of smiling when you are too tired to smile." This "protective buffering" (Coyne & Smith, 1991) was described by both caregivers and patients frequently in our data sets and represents an important manifestation of compassionate caregiving.

Another way that patients evidenced compassionate caregiving was in their direct expressions of care and concern for their family members. Although they were clearly dealing with their own mortality and pain, they often asserted that seeing – or anticipating – the pain of their family was more difficult for them than dealing with their own suffering:

One of the biggest concerns I've had since I was told I had cancer was ... how am I going to take care of my wife? ... So I think the family is the hardest thing, probably, to deal with, you know, how it affects them, how it affects other people. That's probably harder than how it affects myself. (*AS, P-09*)

Compassionate love can also be expressed by making the space for others to give (Underwood, 2002). By compassionately letting others in to help them, patients presented their family with the gift of being of help. A female patient experienced her husband's presence and support during her treatments as a "blessing," but went on to share that it was also "a blessing for the marriage because not all of my needs involve things he can actually do, so for him to feel as though what I needed was what he could give" helped them both. She was giving the gift of appreciatively receiving his support, allowing him to experience the rewards of giving and of feeling needed.

In our studies, compassionate love was expressed in acts of affection, touch, and soothing as well as acts of instrumental care, and often simply in the act of being physically and emotionally present, "being there" for the other:

> *I was there to help him out in all aspects – physical, mental, emotional. I learned when to listen, to talk and most of all to be silent; sometimes to just be there without talking or touching (CCS, 1036)*

> *The hugs and all have always been there, but since this has happened they're a little bit longer, a little bit more meaningful now than they were a year ago ... We've been spending a lot of time being closer in our quiet way ... He likes having me close by, so we crawl into bed early. He'll just nuzzle up next to me, ... and go to sleep while I watch TV. (AS, C-5)*

Corrina, a patient in the C-FACT study, passionately and appreciatively described her husband's loving attention to her personal hygiene as "the kiss":

> *He had to wash my hair most of the time ... He brushed my teeth for me. You know, that level of caregiving. There's fluid love there being exchanged by the brushing of your teeth. Like kissing your head and saying you're beautiful when your eyes have disappeared and your face is mauled and chemo-blistered, and somebody is still doing that. How do people live without that?.... What he was was fluid love. And getting what you need, I think it made the difference between my living or dying. It was life milk that you get ... he gave me everything I needed ... all through the "kiss." (C-FACT, P-104)*

Compassionate Love as a Process of Healing and Forgiving

For many caregiver–patient dyads, love and compassion seemed to naturally intensify as they faced death together. However, the dyadic family relationships of our informants were not immune from relationship tensions and transgressions – extramarital affairs, alcoholism, gambling, coercion and control, interpersonal conflict, and other hurts and transgressions were all reported to us in the course of these studies. Closure and reconciliation in intimate relationships is seen as an important task for the dying person and their family (Byock, 2004; Keeley, 2007; Steinhauser et al., 2000). Some of our informants found that the end-of-life context presented an interpersonal challenge, and some of them embraced this as an important opportunity to resolve relationship problems and heal previous hurts and wounds.

Forgiving someone can be seen as an act of compassionate love. A leading forgiveness researcher, Robert Enright, describes forgiveness as a volitional act that substitutes compassion for resentment (Enright, 1996; Enright, Freedman, & Rique, 1998). Enright emphasizes that forgiveness is a personal choice, not a relational phenomenon. It is an unconditional gift to the transgressor and does not rely on a dialogue or specific acts by the transgressor. In contrast, reconciliation is considered a process of negotiation or dialog with the other. Our informants engaged in both forgiving and reconciliation processes, although we concentrate here on the intrapersonal process of forgiving as an act of compassionate love. We identified two distinctly different processes in our data, both of which involved an experience of compassion for the other: forgiving as an effortful process of personal, purposive work, and forgiving as a relatively effortless process in which grievances simply fell away.

Forgiving as effortful. For some, forgiving and working through negative feelings about the dying person required concentrated effort. Forgiveness is a process that involves empathy and cognitive reframing and it was often incomplete. For instance, one adult child of an alcoholic reported that she was trying to understand, avoid judgment, and get professional help for her father:

> *When my father gets depressed and starts drinking, I used to get mad at him. But now I am learning to not pass judgment against him for it; to try and understand it and get him professional help if he will accept it. (CCS, 0119)*

Her focus on "learning" and "trying" suggests an active, deliberate process that, at the time of her report, was not yet fully resolved forgiveness or fully expressed compassionate love. Another adult child caregiver described specific behaviors she used to work through her negative feelings and to forgive. She also identified a purpose for this personal work – to prepare herself to give care to her dying parent:

> *I did a lot of journaling and reflecting on what I needed to forgive him for, it helped me be less angry with him and be ready to care for him. I talked with my friends and sisters about these things,[that] helped me work through my negative feelings about him. (CCS, 1109)*

However, it is unclear from her account whether her efforts at forgiving resulted in fully realized compassionate love for her father.

One caregiver in the C-FACT study did find that effortful forgiving resulted in compassionate love for her husband. With considerable encouragement from her end-of-life clinical team, she decided to dismantle the "protective wall she had built brick by brick" over 40 years of a marriage challenged by her husband's alcoholism and their financial insecurity. Once she decided to forgive, "the wall of immense anger came tumbling down, leaving a surge of unconditional love." She felt amazed and grateful for the healing she experienced in their relationship before his death, a healing enabled by a process of forgiving and opening to compassionate love.

Grievances fell away. Several people reported that with the impending death, rough edges and resentments in the relationship simply disappeared, thus allowing family members to become closer and renew their connection to one another. The "falling away" was often experienced as effortless and rather inexplicable:

> *It seemed that we forgot the "rough" times we went through. (CCS, 1106)*
>
> *We became very close. Any previous tension dissipated between us (CCS, 1119)*
>
> *There's not bitterness. I mean the bitterness seems to have gone away. (AS C-7)*

For many informants, what once seemed unacceptable came to be seen as "petty" in the light of mortal time. In the stark light of death, previous tensions and conflicts were mutually forgiven:

> *(We) stopped being petty and getting upset about little things, stopped fighting/ bickering. (CCS, 1088)*
>
> *Prior to her diagnosis the relationship with my mother was complicated ... We had many disagreements, political and religious. After the diagnosis and until her death many of these disagreements seemed to fall away as unimportant. We became very close again. (CCS, 1010)*
>
> *I think the cancer diagnosis made us leave most petty arguments behind. (CCS, 1030)*

Even large transgressions were simply left behind in the face of terminal illness: "his illness initiated an end to his affair and another beginning to our relationship." When relationships had been strained in the past, forgiving or working through negative feelings toward each other seemed to be a prerequisite for sustaining the comfortable expression of compassionate love in the end-of-life context. A C-FACT caregiver whose husband had a series of extramarital affairs prior to his diagnosis gave credit to the illness experience for precipitating the fundamental change she and her husband made, moving from "a marriage of convenience to a marriage of care."

Compassionate Love as Letting Go

For caregivers of someone with a life-limiting illness, the ultimate act of compassionate love may be letting go, allowing and accepting death. When you love someone, letting go involves self-sacrifice. Caregivers may dread the grief, loneliness, pain, or emptiness that death will bring. When families have focused so much time, energy, and hope on treatment and a cure, letting go of a hope for a cure – for a way to "cheat death" – can represent a dramatic and difficult shift. Dying patients, too, can resist letting go, especially when they sense it will cause pain to those around them (Callanan & Kelley, 1992; Keeley, 2007). It takes both courage and compassion to support someone in their dying.

It was clear that many caregivers across the data sets felt challenged to put aside their own fears to allow more comfort and peace for the dying person. Although interviews in two of our studies generally occurred prior to the patient's death, in the Cancer Caregiver Study we have data from a number of caregivers who had already lost their family member. Failing to let go and to accept death was a common regret this group experienced. One caregiver shared the tension she realized her denial created for her husband, who was acutely aware of his own impending death:

> *3½ days before he died, I suggested he buy a new winter jacket and he got very angry with me and yelled at me. We knew his lung cancer was terminal. I guess I was in denial, I think until that day. (CCS, 1125)*

Reticence to accept an approaching death is common. As one caregiver put it simply: "I just didn't believe she would die, until she did" (CCS, 1102). In a study of hospice cancer patients and their close family members followed over time, by the last month of life, less than 50% of the patients and caregivers showed indications of being aware of the impending death (Hinton, 1999).

Some caregivers, however, did report experiences of compassionately "letting go" of their dying family member. One of our bereaved caregivers describes his compassionate letting go with pride:

> *After awhile all I could do was hug her and sit with her. It was a hard but wonderful time of my life. I know I helped her accept death and leave the life she loved. (CCS, 1110)*

While it takes great strength to let go of a deeply loved family member, giving permission to die can be a final act of love (Berns & Colvin, 1998). Research suggests that patients and families are increasingly realizing the importance of "life completion" and the need to offer the reassurance or support the patient may need to let go, letting the patient know that it is OK to die – that it is all right to leave them behind (Berns & Colvin, 1998; Heyland et al., 2006; Richards & Folkman, 1997; Wheeler, 1996). Such positive interactions with a partner shortly before death have been found to be associated with less anger during bereavement (Carr, 2003).

Processes that Enable and Support Compassionate Love

What was clear across the three data sets was that the end-of-life context precipitated significant personal transformations and, at the same time, transformed the pre-illness relationship between caregiver and patient. Based on our analyses of the data, we identified four interrelated processes that directly supported compassionate responding in this dyadic end-of-life context. Two of the processes were intrapersonal, involving personal changes in either the patient, the caregiver, or both: (1) *a goal shift to prioritize relationship*; and (2) *a prosocial shift from ego to eco motives*; and two were interpersonal processes: (3) *a shift to deeper intimate connection*; and (4) *a positive cyclical growth process of spiraling compassionate love*. We discuss each of these processes in turn.

Prioritizing Relationship

The reprioritization of life goals was an overarching theme identified in each of the three data sets. For the informants who were able to experience compassionate caregiving and love, a prioritization of relationship with others seemed to be at the core. Consistent with the theoretical and research literatures we reviewed earlier, mortality salience accentuates the importance of close relationships for both caregivers and patients. One caregiver captured the shift simply: "Positive changes resulted from realizing that nothing is as important as love and friendship" (CCS, 0109). A male patient articulated the conclusion he came to, that "it's people" that matter:

> *You really find out what's important. ... Before, people are so busy and caught up in their lives, and you're trying to work as much as you can, make as much money as you can, save money for retirement, all this sort of thing, and it turns out ... the most important things are just the simple things – your family, the wife and kids, grandchildren, things like that. It's people. It's family and friends, is what's important. That's what means everything.* (AS, P-9)

The shift to the perspective of "mortal time" can create a clear view of what is trivial and what is important, and caregivers and patients alike focused on love and relationship as paramount.

At the same time that people and close relationships took center stage, relationship issues and differences that may have at one time seemed important become inconsequential or trivial in the light of death. Informants repeatedly characterized the positive transformation they experienced in their relationship as due to the fact that "we no longer sweat the small stuff":

> *We've come a long ways ... [we] don't sweat the small things anymore. Your priorities totally change. It made us realize how meaningless some of our prior stresses were.* (C-FACT, C-106)

This reprioritization seemed to contribute to the effortless form of forgiveness where "grievances simply fell away." Supporting this process was a basic reorientation to the relationship and an appreciation of the other. As one caregiver put it: "His illness made me totally care and love him and not think about the bad parts of the relationship" (CCS, 0125). Disagreements, long-term conflicts, and even affairs simply were put aside or forgiven "in the greater scheme of things."

> *[I'm] less apt to question her on, why did you do this? ... It's like, hey, she probably had a bad day or something happened and you know what, in the grand scheme of things, it's not worth bitching about. It's just not. I mean, this is tough, I won't deny that, but, I guess the good outweighs the bad now ... I think we really know what's important.* (C-FACT, C-105)

Our data suggest not only that close relationships become a priority, but that patients and caregivers begin to more fully recognize and appreciate the reality of the "other" as they confront mortality and the fragility of human existence. Patients and caregivers alike remarked on how they previously had taken each other for granted:

> *We stopped taking each other for granted. (CCS, 1088)*

> *I think we really realize how important each other is, I mean I realize how important she is. ... I can't take her for granted anymore because she might not be here tomorrow.* (C-FACT, C-105)

> *I learned all over again why I loved him, how much I admired him. I remember one particular conversation we had when I voiced that I felt I had taken him for granted – his reply was that he'd taken me for granted too.* (CCS, 1075)

> *And there's always that phrase "live each day as if it were your last" and since it might be in his case, I look at him and treat him as if it were his last. Every day of our marriage should have been with that philosophy.* (CCS, 0105)

The last comment captures a common refrain in the data, particularly among the bereaved caregivers, the wish that the lessons learned in light of death had been achieved much earlier.

A Prosocial Shift

Consistent with the literature on posttraumatic growth, our informants reported significant personal transformations as they faced mortality and loss. Both patients and caregivers reported these transformations, sometimes their own, other times their loved one's, sometimes profound and life-changing, other times minor, and, at times, more wishful than actual. Some caregivers found family members to be remarkably different people after facing terminal illness: "it's softened and humbled my brother"; "my husband's attitude changed so much"; "my mother, who was always difficult, became much nicer"; "while he was dying he became much kinder and more gentle." Jean, a caregiver in the Assets study, described a remarkably changed husband:

> Before he was diagnosed with cancer I always felt that he was a very bitter, unhappy person ... he would snap my head off for absolutely nothing. I couldn't win an argument if my life depended on it. If I said the sky is a beautiful blue today, he would say no, it's green ... Since he's had cancer I haven't heard this bitterness in his voice. For the first time in 30 years of marriage I have heard "I'm sorry, you didn't deserve what I just said." ... He's starting to think about how he's treating me and I like it. (AS, C-7)

Some caregivers reported dramatic changes in themselves as a result of their experiences:

> I'm a better person – more compassionate, loyal to family, and realize I have more outer and inner strength than I knew I had. (CCS, 1113)

Brett, a 28-year-old caregiver in the C-FACT study, spoke at length about the personal transformation he experienced as a result of his wife's illness. Although he was careful to say he would not "wish the experience" of dealing with a life-threatening illness on anyone, he also was sure he would never want to go back to the person he was before her illness: "It's just, face it, I'm a better husband, a better friend, a better dad, and I think I'm a better person." He feels he now has a greater sense of compassion and altruism and less focus on himself, it's "just the way I go through life now ... whatever I can do to help somebody, to make their life easier." As he shared his newfound commitment to compassionate caring, he was quietly crying, underscoring the strong emotional undercurrent for his transformation. To him, his personal change was "the miracle part of going through this." He explained that his wife's illness forced him to slow down and "reevaluate what is important ... No one could have told me two years ago, 'you know what, you don't need to play as much golf. You don't need to go out with the guys tonight.' No one could have told me that, and I couldn't have read it in a book." Struggling to put words to the profound transformation he felt he underwent, he described a sudden flip: "I don't know what that moment is that causes someone to flip, but it's like you flip over, it's like you're looking this way, you're looking this way, you're looking this way, and all of a sudden, something happens. It's this: I got to look the other way ... And I wouldn't trade it, I wouldn't go back." Consistent with Brett's description, our analyses suggest that central to the individual and relational transformations our informants experienced was a simple shift from a preoccupation with self to a focus on others, a switch from a chronic dominance of "egosystem" motives to a comfort with "ecosystem" motives.

A Shift to Deeper Intimate Connection

Our informants described many relationship changes as they faced an advancing illness and death, but the theme articulated most frequently and strongly was "the illness brought us closer." Both patient and caregiver reported experiencing stronger, more intimate and "deeper" bonds with their loved ones. For many, the closeness was experienced as "out of the ordinary," a closeness that Prager and Roberts (2004) have called "deep intimate connection." Analysis of the quantitative survey data collected in the Cancer Caregiver Study supported this theme of deeper intimate connection that we found in the qualitative data. Three-quarters of family caregivers responded affirmatively to items related to perceptions of increased closeness or intimacy with their loved one as a result of the terminal illness (Roberts et al., in preparation). This finding held for both current and bereaved caregivers and for both spouses as well as other family caregivers. Further, less than 10% of caregivers reported becoming less close or experiencing a deterioration in the relationship as they faced their loved one's death.

The following quotes represent typical written or interview responses of spousal caregivers describing their experiences of increased intimacy:

> *I have never felt closer emotionally or spiritually to anyone. We have a deep loving bond that I have never experienced before.* (CCS, 0120)

> *This whole situation has brought our relationship to a different level. We are closer than we have ever been in our lives. We do everything together and speak openly about everything. For the first time, we actually listen to each other and pay attention to what each of us want. [I'm] constantly telling her I love her, touching her, being there for her.* (CCS, 0142)

> *This illness has brought us closer together – our marriage is in much better shape now than it was 6 months ago.* (AS, C-7)

Although heightened intimacy seemed to be particularly strong in couple relationships, in their written descriptions of their experiences, non-spousal family caregivers also detailed experiences of new levels of closeness. At times, the closeness was facilitated by a new physical proximity. For example, a few parents mentioned that an adult child with a terminal diagnosis returned home to be taken care of after living at considerable distance prior to the illness. In other cases, caregivers already felt physically and emotionally close to their relatives, but found new depths of intimacy in their relationships when they became caregivers:

> *The illness deepened my attachment and understanding of my aunt incredibly. ... We developed a trust and love for one another that would not have happened otherwise.* (CCS, 1104)

> *My mother and I were always close but when I told her she had 5 brain tumors and 2 weeks to live a bond was formed. She asked me not to leave her because I was her rock ... we got closer and told each other things we never did before.* (CCS, 1110)

> *We were always very close, but Grandpa's illness made us closer ... There was a brief period of tension when his cancer began to advance and he needed more personal care due to both of our discomfort with the physical aspects of [caregiving]. But after a few words about it, we were both at ease and had an easy, quiet bond.* (CCS, 1046)

A Positive Cyclical Growth Process: Spiraling Compassionate Love

The caregiver and patient are situated in a mutually constructed interpersonal context. Changes in one person's attitudes, feelings, or behaviors had rippling effects on the other person. For example, personal transformations like the one Brett described had positive repercussions for his wife. Some of our informants described their own opening to feelings of compassion as a reaction to the other person's prosocial transformation. We earlier described Jean's perception of the radical change in her sick husband's treatment of her, but she goes on to describe the change it brought to her: "I'm just so happy to see who he is now that I don't think about who he used to be. I don't throw anything in his face." Her husband's deeper compassion for her led to changes in his behavior, which in turn led her to more compassionate responses to him. Similarly, another caregiver described how her husband's apologies allowed her to stop "holding grudges:"

> *[My husband] learned to say "I'm sorry." ... [we] stopped holding grudges, wasting time staying mad/upset at each other ... realized how lucky we were to have each other.* (CCS, 1088)

The process might be set in motion one step further back – caregivers sometimes attributed personal transformations in patients directly to the patient's receipt of care and love from compassionate caregivers. For example, a daughter attributed changes in her dying mother to the family's caregiving: "My mother, who was always difficult, became much nicer as she appreciated all the help we offered." (CCS, 1124). In a pattern of positive cyclical growth, her mother's newfound positivity may in fact spur more compassionate caregiving from the daughter.

The outpouring of love and care terminally ill patients experienced often opened them to gratitude, and the expression of this gratitude returned love to their caregiver, as these patients suggest:

> I tell her that I love her many many times a day. I tell her how pretty she is, because she works hard at that. Whatever she does, like, just changing this patch, I say thank you. And she knows that I'm grateful, and I appreciate it. But I say it. Every time. Not just once in a while, every time. (AS, P-11)

> We've had our ups and downs and in and outs. But when this life-threatening occurrence came our way, and my wife responded the way she did, to things that I would never expected her to help me with, she rose above and beyond the call of duty. I just hope my wife never gets ill, but if she does, I just hope I'm around to help her as much, or more – it's gonna be very difficult to do more – than what she has done for me in these last three years. I give her all the credit in the world for enduring all that stuff. She is just a wonderful person. (AS, P-11)

In turn, caregivers who were aware of the patient's care and concern for them deepened their own experience of love:

> She was such a loving and caring person that her thoughts and concerns were typically for her family rather than herself. (CCS, 1093)

> Our love and concern for each other became deeper ... my husband became deeply concerned about my welfare and how I could have a good life after he was gone. (CCS, 1057)

In our data, compassionate love seemed to be most easily supported and maintained when it was experienced as a process of mutual give and take. Many couples described their experience in terms of "we" and "our," explicitly acknowledging this mutuality: "Our love and concern for each other became deeper" (CSS, 1057), or "(it) made us both determined and strong, one for the other" (CCS, 1134). Acts of compassionate caregiving opened the door for reciprocating acts of compassionate care. Caregivers opened patients to new levels of gratitude, love, and compassion, and similarly, the patient's ability to act out of compassion opened the caregiver to continuing self-sacrifice, patience, and tending. Compassion from one person led to further compassion from the other, and so on, resulting in an escalating cycle of positive emotion, to mutual, fully expressed compassionate love.

In systems language, the dynamic interpersonal process we have been describing would be conceptualized as a "self-reinforcing feedback loop" where feedback increases the probability that the next event in the loop will occur. Corrina, the patient we introduced earlier who described her husband's loving attention to care of her personal hygiene as the "kiss," aptly captured this dynamic and reciprocal flow of compassionate love with her notion of *fluid love*: "There's fluid love there being exchanged by the brushing of your teeth." Using this personal metaphor, Corrina highlighted the importance of the feedback loop as she elaborated her simple notion of fluid love: "[it's] a current that runs between two people. And if one goes down, the other one can shoot a little more energy, but you have to send something back." Compassionate love is enabled, sustained, and grows through reciprocation. Again, the words of one of our informants convey the underlying love that was felt, caregiver to patient, patient to caregiver and back again:

> [*My husband*] *continued to care for me as best he could. He lovingly tried to reassure me especially when I couldn't sleep; he encouraged me to maintain social contacts, and accepted everything with so much patience, grace, and dignity. He's forever in my heart.* (CCS, 1075)

Although she was "the caregiver," and he the patient, she reflects on the care she received, the compassionate love they felt one for the other was intimately intertwined in a spiral.

Summary and Future Directions

While awareness of an approaching death and the associated changes in physical, cognitive, and emotional functioning can lead to spiraling suffering and negative interpersonal behavior, we found that the stark light of death also can be a powerful catalyst to mutually reciprocated, fully expressed compassionate love. In the face of the significant distress and suffering associated with an advancing illness, the patients and caregivers in our studies engaged in acts of compassionate caregiving, from disguising their pain, to feeding, brushing teeth and washing hair, to holding, kissing, touching, and just being there for one another. Moreover, despite the existence of pre-illness tensions, wounds, and transgressions, many – but certainly not all – of the dyads found the way to compassionate acts of healing and forgiveness in the light of death. We also found evidence for "letting go" of a life as a loving, compassionate act. Reinforcing the importance of the act, many bereaved caregivers reported regret when they had not found the way to accept an impending death and "say goodbye."

In terms of Underwood's model, it is important to remember that the situational context for the experiences of compassionate love described here is a very specific one: the confrontation with an impending death. The subjective experience of mortal time should be seen as a primary – although not sufficient – determinant of the opening to compassionate love in our respondents. The philosophical, theoretical, and empirical literature we have reviewed in this chapter in combination with our own findings suggest that awareness of human mortality may be a critical situational factor prompting compassionate responding. Coming face to face with mortality represents, we believe, a fertile context for explorations of compassionate love. More research is needed not only on experiences with life-threatening circumstances, but also on religious, spiritual, or other attitudinal positions that simultaneously embrace *both living and dying* (i.e., human mortality).

Our understandings of the roots of compassionate responding are still rudimentary and more "discovery-phase" science is needed to fully describe the phenomenon before model-building and theoretical work can become more sophisticated. Although we have identified some manifestations of compassionate love here (as have many others in this volume), more documentation of the ways in which compassionate love is expressed and experienced is needed. What cues would an observer use to understand that an act of compassion, grounded in the experience of love, was occurring? How is compassionate love experienced by the giver and, importantly, the receiver? What moves someone to compassionate responding? In addition to in-depth interviews and narrative analyses such as those conducted here, observational procedures can be used to capture "in-the-moment" experiences of compassionate love. For example, in the C-FACT study (Roberts, 2007), couples are videotaped discussing their "vulnerabilities" with each other, alone, for 10 minutes. The discussions involve an interpersonal process of open, emotional disclosure of a personal need or experience of suffering and the partner's behavioral response to the disclosure (see Roberts & Greenberg, 2002 for a full description of the paradigm). This observational paradigm captures *in vivo* expressions of compassionate love and thus provides the opportunity for descriptive analyses of the characteristics, antecedents, and consequences of compassionate responding. In addition to advancing our definitional and descriptive understanding of compassionate love, it is important to understand the long-term implications of compassionate love for the giver, the receiver, and the relationship. In the future, it will be important to undertake longitudinal research to more fully understand both the determinants and the consequences of the choice of compassion. What attitudes, personality variables, past experiences, and personal goals support compassionate responses? What relational or interpersonal experiences nurture and sustain compassionate responding in relationships?

Consistent with Underwood's model, our work has suggested that both intrapersonal and interpersonal processes are important determinants of expressions of compassionate love. We have identified two specific intrapersonal processes that fall under Underwood's notion of "Motivation and Discernment" in her model: an intense valuing of relationship and a shift to a prosocial "ecosystem" orientation. We believe that Crocker's theoretical work on ego- and eco-motivational systems represents a promising theory for understanding both selfish and compassionate responding and for framing future research efforts. In particular, the theory lends itself to experimental and hypothesis-testing investigations that may have wide applicability. Our analyses also identified two interpersonal processes: increased intimacy, and reciprocal caregiving. As the feedback loops in Underwood's model suggest, the expression of compassionate love itself may in turn support the further expression and escalation of compassionate love. The interpersonal nature of this escalation is not explicit in the Underwood model; the development of an "interpersonal process model" (see, e.g., Reis & Shaver, 1988) of compassionate love may help spur future research that furthers our understanding of the dynamic interplay of giver and receiver.

Conclusion

Over the past few decades several lines of clinical practice, scholarship, and research have challenged the "magical thinking" associated with a medicalization of death and dying that have made hospitals, in Ira Byock's (2002) words, secular "temples of death denial." The palliative care movement has advocated for death with dignity to balance science with soul and the search for cure with the gift of compassion. The confrontation with mortality through terminal illness can lead to greater terror and anxiety but also to greater purpose in life, to growth and transcendence – and, importantly, to loving compassion. Research on the responses of terminally ill patients and their family caregivers presented here provides evidence to support this movement toward a renewed interest in the psychological, spiritual, and existential issues that accompany death and dying, a movement toward the good and compassionate death. Together, the light and shadow of death provide a "bittersweet" hue – the approaching death illuminates a reality that holds loss and suffering on the one hand and the clarity of human love and relationship on the other.

Acknowledgments

The authors wish to express gratitude for support from the Fetzer Institute (2009.6), the National Cancer Institute (P50 CA095817–01A1), and the National Institute of Nursing Research (R01 NR008260–01).

References

Ariès, P. (1974). *Western attitudes toward death: From the middle ages to the present*. Baltimore, MD: Johns Hopkins University Press.

Arno, P. S., Levine C., & Memmott, M. M. (1999). The economic value of informal caregiving. *Health Affair, 18*, 182–188.

Axelsson, B., & Sjödén, P. O. (1998). Quality of life of cancer patients and their spouses in palliative home care. *Palliative Medicine, 12*, 29–39.

Batson, C. D. (1991). *The altruism question: Toward a social-psychological answer*. Mahwah, NJ: Lawrence Erlbaum.

Becker, E. (1973). *The denial of death*. New York: The Free Press.

Bernard-DuBenske, L. L., Wen, K. Y., Gustafson, D. H., Guarnaccia, C. A., Cleary, J. F., Dinauer, S. K., & McTavish, F. M. (under review). Caregivers' differing needs across key experiences of the advanced cancer disease trajectory.

Berns, R., & Colvin, E. (1998). The final story: Events at the bedside of the dying patients as told by survivors. *American Nephrology Nurses Association Journal, 25*(6), 583–587.

Block, S. D. (2001). Psychological considerations, growth, and transcendence at the end of life: The art of the possible. *JAMA: Journal of the American Medical Association, 285*, 2898–2905.

Bowlby, J. (1969/1982). *Attachment and loss*. New York: Basic Books.

Bowlby, J. (1988). *A secure base: Parent–child attachment and healthy human development*. New York: Basic Books.

Byock, I. (1997). *Dying well: Peace and possibilities at the end of life*. New York: Berkley Publishing Group.

Byock, I. (2002). The meaning and value of death. *Journal of Palliative Medicine, 5*, 279–288.

Byock, I. (2004). *The four things that matter most: Essential wisdom for transforming your relationships and your life*. New York: The Free Press.

Calhoun, L. G., & Tedeschi, R. G. (2006). *Handbook of posttraumatic growth: Research & practice*. Mahwah, NJ: Lawrence Erlbaum.

Callanan, M., & Kelley, P. (1992). *Final gifts*. New York: Bantam Books.

Carr, D. (2003). A 'good death' for whom? Quality of spouse's death and psychological distress among older widowed persons. *Journal of Health and Social Behavior, 44*, 215–232.

Carstensen, L. L., Isaacowitz, D. M., & Charles, S. T. (1999). Taking time seri-ously: A theory of socioemotional selectivity. *American Psychologist, 54,* 165–181.

Collins, N. L., & Feeney, B. C. (2000). A safe haven: An attachment theory per-spective on support seeking and caregiving in intimate relationships. *Journal of Personality and Social Psychology, 78,* 1053–1073.

Covinsky, K. E., Goldman, L., Cook, E. F., Oye, R., Desbiens, N., Reding, D., Fulkerson, W., Connors, A., Lynn J., Philips, R. S. (1994). The impact of seri-ous illness on patients' families. *JAMA: The Journal of the American Medical Association, 272,* 1839–1844.

Coyne, J. C., & Smith, D. A. (1991) Couples coping with a myocardial infarc-tion: Contextual perspective on wives' distress. *Journal of Personality and Social Psychology, 61,* 404–412.

Crocker, J. (2008). From egosystem to ecosystem: Implications for relationships, learning and well-being. In H. Wayment and J. Brauer (Eds.), *Transcending self-interest: psychological explorations of the quiet ego* (pp. 63–72). Washington, DC: American Psychological Association.

Crocker, J., & Nuer, N. (2004). Do people need self-esteem? Comment on Pyszczynski et al. (2004). *Psychological Bulletin, 130,* 469–472.

Crocker, J., Nuer, N., Olivier, M. A., & Cohen, S. (2006). *Egosystem and ecosys-tem: Two motivational orientations for the self* (working paper). University of Michigan.

Didion, J. (2005). *The year of magical thinking.* New York: Knopf.

Eldredge, D. (2004). Helping at the bedside: Spouses' preferences for helping critically ill patients. *Research in Nursing and Health, 27*(5), 307–321.

Emanuel, E. J., Fairclough, D. L., Slutsman, J., Alpert, H., Baldwin, D., & Emanuel, L. L. (1999). Assistance from family members, friends, paid care givers, and volunteers in the care of terminally ill patients. *The New England Journal of Medicine, 341,* 956–963.

Enright, R. D. (1996). Counseling within the forgiveness triad: On forgiving, receiving, forgiveness, and self-forgiveness. *Counseling and Values, 40,* 107–126.

Enright, R. D., Freedman, S., & Rique, J. (1998). The psychology of interper-sonal forgiveness. In Enright, R. D. & North, J. (Eds.), *Exploring forgiveness* (pp. 46–62). Madison: University of Wisconsin Press.

Farran, C., Miller, B., Kaufman, J., & Davis, L. (1997). Race, finding meaning and care distress. *Journal of Aging and Health, 9(3),* 316–333.

Feeney, B. C., & Collins, N. L. (2003). Motivations for caregiving in adult inti-mate relationships: Influences on caregiving behavior and relationship func-tioning. *Personality and Social Psychology Bulletin, 29,* 950–968.

Frankl, V. E. (1964). *Man's search for meaning.* London, England: Hodder & Stoughton.

Freud, S. (1930). *Civilization and its discontents* (J. Riviere, Trans.). New York: Hogarth Press.

Friel, P. B. (1982). Death and dying. *Annals of Internal Medicine 97*(5), 767–771.

Gallagher-Thompson, D., Coon, D. W., Rivera, P., Powers, D., Zeiss, A. M., Hersen, M. et al. (1998). Family caregiving: Stress, coping, and intervention.

In A. M. Hersen, & V. B. Van Hasselt (Eds.), *Handbook of clinical geropsychology* (pp. 469–493). New York: Plenum Press.

Glaser, B. G., & Strauss, A. L. (1965). *Awareness of dying.* Piscataway, NJ: Aldine Transaction.

Greenberg, J., Pyszczynski, T., & Solomon, S. (1986). The causes and consequences of a need for self-esteem: A terror management theory. In R. F. Baumeister (Ed.), *Public self and private self* (pp. 189–212). New York: Springer-Verlag.

Hebert, R. S., & Schulz, R. (2006). Caregiving at the end of life. *Journal of Palliative Medicine, 9,* 1174–1187.

Heidegger, M. (1927/1996) *Being and time: A translation of* Sein und Zeit (J. Stambaugh, Trans.). Albany, NY: SUNY Press.

Heyland, D. K., Dodek, P., Rocker, G., Groll, D., Gafni, A., Pichora, D. et al. (2006). What matters most in end-of-life care: Perceptions of seriously ill patients and their family members. *Canadian Medical Association Journal, 174,* O1–O9.

Hinton, J. (1999). The progress of awareness and acceptance of dying assessed in cancer patients and their caring relatives. *Palliative Medicine, 13,* 19–35.

Hull, M. M. (1990). Sources of stress for hospice caregiving families. *Hospice Journal, 6,* 29–54.

Hunt, C. K. (2003). Concepts in caregiver research. *Journal of Nursing Scholarship, 35,* 27–32.

Keeley, M. P. (2007). "Turning toward death together": The functions of messages during final conversations in close relationships. *Journal of Social and Personal Relationships,* 24, 225–253.

Keltner, D. (2004). The compassionate instinct. *Greater Good, 1,* 6–9.

Kierkegaard, S. (1983). *Fear and trembling* (H.V. Hong & E. H. Hong, Trans. & Eds.). Princeton, NJ: Princeton University Press.

Kuebler-Ross, E. (1970). *On death and dying.* New York: Collier Books/ Macmillan.

Kunce, L. J., & Shaver, P. R. (1994). An attachment-theoretical approach to caregiving in romantic relationships. In K. Bartholemew & D. Perlman (Eds.), *Advances in personal relationships, Vol. 5: Attachment processes in adulthood* (pp. 205–237). London, England: Jessica Kingsley.

Levine, S. (1997). *A year to live: How to live this year as if it were your last.* Boston: Beacon Press.

Linley, P. A., & Joseph, S. (2004). Positive change following trauma and adversity: A review. *Journal of Traumatic Stress, 17,* 11–21.

Linsk, N. L., & Poindexter, C. C. (2000). Older caregivers for family members with HIV or AIDS: Reasons for caring. *Journal of Applied Gerontology, 19,* 181–202.

Lynn, J. (2004). *Sick to death and not going to take it anymore: Reforming health care for the last years of life.* Berkeley, CA: University of California Press.

Martens, N., & Davies, B. (1990). The work of patients and spouses in managing advanced cancer at home. *Hospice Journal, 6,* 55–73.

Martin, L. L., Campbell, W. K., & Henry, C. D. (2004). The roar of awakening: Mortality acknowledgment as a call to authentic living. In *Handbook of Experimental Existential Psychology* (pp. 431–448). New York: Guilford Press.

McQuellon, R. P., & Cowan, M. A. (2000). Turning toward death together: Conversation in mortal time. *American Journal of Hospice & Palliative Care, 17*, 312–318.

Midlarsky, E., & Kahana, E. (1994). *Altruism in later life*. Thousand Oaks, CA: Sage.

Mikulincer, M., & Florian, V. (2000). Exploring individual differences in reactions to mortality salience: Does attachment style regulate terror management mechanisms? *Journal of Personality and Social Psychology, 79*, 260–273.

Mikulincer, M., Florian, V., & Hirschberger, G. (2003). The existential function of close relationships: Introducing death into the science of love. *Personality and Social Psychology Review, 7*, 20–40.

Mikulincer, M., Florian, V., & Hirschberger, G. (2004). The terror of death and the quest for love: An existential perspective on close relationships. In J. Greenberg, S. L. Koole, & T. Pyszczynski (Eds.), *Handbook of Experimental Existential Psychology* (pp. 287–304). New York: Guilford Press.

Miller, B., & Cafasso, L. (1992). Gender differences in caregiving: Fact or artifact? *The Gerontologist, 32*, 498–507.

Nelms, T. P. (2000). The practices of mothering in caregiving an adult son with AIDS. *Advances in Nursing Science, 22*, 46–57.

Nelms, T. P. (2002). A most wonderful, tragic experience: The phenomenon of mothering in caregiving an adult son with AIDS. *Journal of Family Nursing, 8*, 282–300.

Nietzsche, F. (1955). *Beyond good and evil* (M. Cowan, Trans.). Chicago: Henry Regnery.

Noonan, A., Tennstedt, S., & Rebelsky, F. (1996). Making the best of it: Themes and meaning among informal caregivers to the elderly. *Journal of Aging Studies, 10*(4), 313–327.

Pinquart, M., & Sorensen, S. (2003). Differences between caregivers and non-caregivers in psychological health and physical health: A meta-analysis. *Psychology and Aging, 18*, 250–267.

Prager, K. J., & Roberts, L. J. (2004). Deep intimate connection: Self and intimacy in couple relationships. In D. J. Mashek & A. P. Aron (Eds.), *Handbook of closeness and intimacy* (pp. 43–60). Mahwah, NJ: Lawrence Erlbaum.

Proot, I. M., Abu-Saad, H. H., ter Meulen, R. H. J., Goldsteen, M., Spreeuwenberg, C., & Widdershoven, G. A. M. (2004). The needs of terminally ill patients at home: Directing one's life, health and things related to beloved others. *Palliative Medicine, 18*, 53–61.

Pyszczynski, T., Greenberg, J., Solomon, S., Arndt, J., & Schimel, J. (2004). Why do people need self-esteem? A theoretical and empirical review. *Psychological Bulletin, 130*, 435–468.

Reis, H. T., & Shaver, P. R. (1988). Intimacy as an interpersonal process. In S. Duck, D. F. Hay, S. E. Hobfoll, W. Ickes, & B. M. Montgomery (Eds.), *Handbook of personal relationships: Theory, research, and interventions* (pp. 367–389). Oxford, England: John Wiley.

Richards, T. A., & Folkman, S. (1997). Spiritual aspects of loss at the time of a partner's death from AIDS. *Death Studies, 21*, 527–552.

Roberts, L. J. (2007). *Love and death: Couples coping at end of life.* Paper presented at Close Relationships and Health: Developing an Integrative Approach to Research and Theory, Vancouver, British Columbia, Canada.

Roberts, L. J., Faust, T. & DuBenske, L. L. (in preparation). Individual and dyadic coping strategies related to relationship changes: Perceptions of partners of advanced cancer patients.

Roberts, L. J., & Greenberg, D. R. (2002). Observational "windows" to intimacy processes in marriage. In P. Noller & J. A. Feeney, *Understanding marriage: Developments in the study of couple interaction* (pp. 118–149). Cambridge, England: Cambridge University Press.

Roberts, L. J., & Wise, M. E. (2006, July). *Living and loving in the shadow of death: Couple relationships at end of life.* Paper presented at the International Association for Relationship Research Conference, Crete, Greece.

Solomon, S., Greenberg, J., & Pyszczynski, T. (1991). A terror management theory of social behavior: The psychological functions of self-esteem and cultural worldviews. In M. P. Zanna (Ed.), *Advances in Experimental Social Psychology: Vol. 24* (pp. 93–159). New York: Academic Press.

Sprecher, S., & Fehr, B. (2005). Compassionate love for close others and humanity. *Journal of Social and Personal Relationships, 22,* 629–651.

Staton, J., Shuy, R., & Byock, I. (2001). *A few months to live: Different paths to life's end.* Washington, DC: Georgetown University Press.

Steinhauser, K. E., Christakis, N. A., Clipp, E. C., McNeilly, M., McIntyre, L., & Tulsky, J. A. (2000). Factors considered important at the end of life by patients, family, physicians, and other care providers. *JAMA: Journal of the American Medical Association, 284,* 2476–2482.

Strauss, A., & Corbin, J. (1998). *Basics of qualitative research: Techniques and procedures for developing grounded theory* (2nd ed.). Thousand Oaks, CA: Sage.

Tedeschi, R. G., Park, C. L., & Calhoun, L. G. (1998). *Posttraumatic growth: Positive changes in the aftermath of crisis.* Mahwah, NJ: Lawrence Erlbaum.

Underwood, L. G. (2002). The human experience of compassionate love: Conceptual mapping and data from selected studies. In S. G. Post, L. G. Underwood, J. P. Schloss, & W. B. Hurlbut, *Altruism & altruistic love: Science, philosophy, & religion in dialogue* (pp. 72–88). Oxford, England: Oxford University Press.

Underwood, L. G. (2005). Interviews with Trappist monks as a contribution to research methodology in the investigation of compassionate love. *Journal for the Theory of Social Behaviour, 35,* 285–302.

US Department of Health and Human Services (1998, June). *Informal caregiving: Compassion in action.* Washington, DC: US Department of Health and Human Services.

Weitzner, M. A., McMillan, S. C., & Jacobsen, P. B. (1999). Family caregiver quality of life: Differences between curative and palliative cancer treatment settings. *Journal of Pain and Symptom Management, 17,* 418–428.

Wheeler, S. R. (1996). Helping families cope with death and dying. *Nursing, 26,* 25.

Wise, M. E., & Marchand, L (in preparation) *Living fully in the shadow of mortal time*.

Wise, M. E., Roberts, L. J. & Marchand, L (in preparation). *Living and loving in the shadow of death: Couple relationships near end of life*.

Wolff, J. L., Dy, S. M., Frick, K. D., & Kasper, J. D. (2007). End-of-life care: Findings from a national survey of informal caregivers. *Archives of Internal Medicine, 167*, 40–46.

Yalom, I. (1980). *Existential psychotherapy*. New York: Basic Books.

Zimmermann, C., & Rodin, G. (2004). The denial of death thesis: Sociological critique and implications for palliative care. *Palliative Medicine, 18*, 121–128.

12

Compassionate Clinicians: Exemplary Care in Hospital Settings

David R. Graber and Maralynne D. Mitcham

As is commonly known, individuals are often fearful, anxious, and unhappy during times of sickness and disability, in addition to feeling physical symptoms and pain. By the time they are placed in a hospital, due to the extreme or escalating nature of the condition, their psychological, emotional, and physical well-being may be at their lowest point. This is the time when a word of encouragement, a smiling face, or an act of kindness are most needed and appreciated, and may have the most impact. Such behaviors and interpersonal support by hospital staff might even be considered to be synonymous with basic patient care. However, in the experience of the authors, many individuals who have been patients feel that empathic, supportive behavior is uncommon in hospital environments.

Although most hospitals pay lip service to caring and compassion, inevitably mentioning these in their mission statements, a number of forces or historical trends have made it difficult for health care clinicians who work in hospitals to be compassionate in their interactions with patients. Most hospital clinicians have myriad job responsibilities and work under pressing time demands, and many work long shifts on units that are chronically understaffed. Nevertheless, in the face of these obstacles, some individuals stand out and are noted by their co-workers and by patients as being consistently caring and compassionate. Certainly, their expression of compassion and positive actions that reflect compassion are not carried out at their convenience or when they have nothing else to do. Their exemplary patient care in such adverse circumstances makes the support they give to patients all the more remarkable. It is obvious that clinicians who are able to be consistently compassionate and caring to their patients in the fast-paced hospital environment must also possess considerable tact, self-control, and other inner resources.

What characterizes compassionate care, and how do a few clinicians, among the countless practicing physicians, nurses, and therapists, overcome the substantial obstacles to being caring in the current health-care environment? Current definitions of compassion generally do not depart significantly from the original Latin meaning – to sympathize and suffer with. Consequently, the word compassion necessarily implies more than just feeling sympathy; it also includes the active participation or experience of one individual in another individual's feelings or suffering. The inner feeling of compassion should not be over-intellectualized; it is a spontaneous feeling of love and unity that arises within the being of the individual who feels compassion. The ability to provide compassionate care clearly has its source in individual motivation and wisdom. Underwood states that motivation and discernment lead to "compassionate love fully expressed," which in turn leads to the appropriate words and actions of "positive behavior" (Underwood, 2002, p. 76). It is likely that the expression of compassionate love and subsequent positive behaviors form key elements in the affective foundation of good hospital care.

This chapter provides a brief summary of the current literature on empathic and compassionate love as expressed in hospitals by clinicians such as physicians, nurses, and therapists. American moral and spiritual values that have been linked to compassionate care are described. The chapter also addresses the ways in which professional cultures and organizational characteristics may foster or suppress the expression of empathic and compassionate behaviors within the clinical context, and how these attributes have evolved over time.

Because compassionate care is not practiced by all who work in hospitals, advancing our knowledge of the practice of compassion in hospitals may be best furthered by focusing on those clinicians who are noted for being caring and compassionate. This approach was used by the authors in an exemplar study of 24 hospital clinicians. The clinicians we talked to were asked to describe the nature of the compassionate care they provide and to give specific examples of the ways in which they demonstrate compassionate love. Thus, a key focus of our study was on the interpersonal style and affect adopted by these clinicians. Interview data from this study formed the basis for the emergence of a preliminary model of affective clinician–patient interactions involving four levels of clinician–patient interactions.

In many hospitals, the interpersonal culture is changing and becoming more supportive of clinicians who engage in more demonstrable acts of compassion with their patients. This chapter provides recommendations for designing education programs that enhance provision of compassionate care and for developing reward structures that acknowledge the affective components inherent in providing exemplary health care.

Antecedents of the Caring Environment in Hospitals

The public appears to have always valued selfless service and compassionate health care. Uplifting stories or anecdotes of individuals who have served the poor, sick, or disabled are often presented by the media. In the nineteenth century, the work of Florence Nightingale, and in the twentieth century, the work of Albert Schweitzer and Mother Teresa's Sisters of Charity received worldwide recognition. Many people are exposed from an early age to New Testament stories, which describe Christ healing lepers, the crippled, and the blind man, and the story of the Good Samaritan. The Old Testament, sacred in Judaism, Islam, and Christianity, has numerous passages extolling care and compassion toward the sick, widows and orphans, foreigners, and the poor. Several founders of other major religions, such as Mohammed and the Buddha, showed compassion for the sick and exhorted their followers to serve those who are ill. Among modern cultures, appreciation of caring and compassion for the sick appears to be a universal value.

It has not been easy for hospital patients to reconcile these values with their experiences in hospitals. A shift away from a humanistic, compassionate milieu for hospital care developed in the twentieth century and was related to a number of factors, including:

- The development of professional cultures that extolled rationality, science, and technical achievements and emphasized these in education and professional socialization.
- A bureaucratization of hospital care related to increasing size, for-profit ownership, and financial imperatives.
- A "reductionistic" approach in science and clinical care in which the focus is on the smallest elements of an organism and not the individual (Graber & Johnson, 2001).

Clinical Professional Cultures and Compassionate Care

In the twentieth century, clinical cultures and educational programs embraced technical knowledge and scientific achievements and implicitly or explicitly minimized the importance or value of compassion. From the later 1800s, medical writers and educators have advocated that clinicians demonstrate an affective equanimity or neutrality and maintain professional distance between themselves and patients (Cathell, 1890; Parsons, 1951). William Osler, often considered the most influential medical educator of the twentieth century, extolled physician imperturbability, impassiveness, and firmness in difficult situations (Osler, 1932).

The most common term for this posture, "detached concern," is seen repeatedly and advocated in medical literature throughout the twentieth century. A variety of reasons have been cited for maintaining interpersonal distance, such as physicians' desire for respect and patient compliance, a perceived lack of time for social relations, or the belief that interpersonal involvement will undermine clinical objectivity and prevent effective functioning (Borgenicht, 1984; Yeo & Longhurst, 1996). Thus, entire generations of physicians have been educated and socialized to keep some distance from and avoid being too friendly with their patients. With the entrenchment of physician cultures in hospitals characterized by detached concern, it is likely that those physicians who acted in a contrary fashion and demonstrated caring and compassion were considered aberrant.

Results from an Israeli study illustrate that empathy is not considered an important quality for advancement among hospital clinicians. Carmel and Glick (1996) used a sociometric questionnaire to explore physicians' compassionate-empathic behavior and to determine how organizational factors might affect such behavior. They found that those physicians viewed as "compassionate-empathic" typically have fewer years in medical practice "and score higher on pro-social, non-stereotypic attitudes toward patients and on empathy measures ... but they report more emotional exhaustion (burnout) than other physicians" (p. 1253). A more telling finding was that empathy was ranked as least important for getting promoted within the hospital, thereby highlighting the culture clash between what is desired by patients and what is rewarded by health-care organizations.

The highest percentage of clinicians in hospitals has always been nursing personnel. The training and professional culture of nurses has traditionally been more associated with caring and compassion as compared to physicians. However, by the late twentieth century, nursing education and practice also shifted. For example, in an influential book about the future of nursing curricula, Bevis and Watson (1989) described the twentieth-century model of nursing as "a neutral technical process, associated with biomedical science empiricism ... imparting a form of technocratic rationality, void of human meaning and values; void of moral commitment ... and moral ideals, or the covenantal relationship associated with human caring (healing and wholeness)" (p. 38). Bevis and Watson further noted that caring in nursing had become considered secondary or inferior to the technical and scientific aspects of care and they called for a return to "caring curricula" in nursing programs.

In recent years, the need for a professional demeanor of detachment and disengagement by clinicians has been increasingly questioned. One possible outcome of disengagement and emotional distancing by clinicians may be the failure to recognize the human individual with multiple and intertwined conditions. Thus, when treatment focuses on a dysfunction and not the person who has the dysfunction, it is often the reflection of a disengaged therapeutic relationship – one that ultimately may be harmful to the patient (Van Amberg, 1997).

By the 1980s and 1990s, commissions and conferences on the education of the health professions started to recognize the need to embrace a broader, more holistic paradigm for care. At that time, a number of influential groups began to call for greater emphasis in education on social and behavioral issues (Robert Wood Johnson Foundation, 1992; Shugars, O'Neil, & Bader, 1991). In 1992, the Pew Health Professions Commission–Fetzer Institute Task Force recommended the adoption of "relationship-centered care," which involves communicating openly with patients, and practicing with a healing and caring ethic (Tresolini, 1994). Although a greater humanism in health care (through what has been termed a biopsychosocial model) is not equivalent to including compassion in health care, it may be considered a stepping stone to support caring in the health-care environment. By 1998, the Pew Health Profession Commission stated that clinicians should listen openly and empathetically (O'Neil, 1998). The Pew Report recognized that health professionals must have the desire and ability to convey compassion for people's experience of health and illness. A major report on increasing the quality of patient care was released by the Institute of Medicine (IOM) in 2001 and contained six major aims for quality improvement. A key focus of the report was the need to develop patient-centered care that reflects the qualities of compassion, empathy, and responsiveness to the needs, values, and expressed preferences of the individual patient (IOM, 2001).

Although commissions and conferences emphasized the need for greater caring and compassion, by the new millennium, many hospitals and other health-care organizations had not adopted many of the recommendations. Due to the continuing deficiency of most hospitals in striving to provide compassionate care, greater understanding of the barriers to and enablers of compassionate care in health-care organizations is clearly needed. One avenue to understanding compassionate care lies in studying exemplary individual clinicians, who exist in virtually every hospital. However, empirical information about compassionate care has been largely unexplored. How is it provided? What are examples of compassionate care? What is the nature of the compassionate, caring relationship between clinicians and their patients? Such simple and fundamental questions have been largely overlooked in the literature. Therefore, the authors felt that it was an important endeavor to find out more about compassionate care as expressed by the clinicians and to understand more about their interactions with patients. Another goal was to examine whether there is an underlying typology or schema of compassionate interactions between clinicians and patients.

Study of Compassionate Hospital Clinicians

In 2002, we undertook a qualitative study of compassionate care among hospital clinicians at two hospitals in a metropolitan area of the southeast United States. Through individual interviews with exemplary hospital clinicians, we sought to understand how they enacted compassion on a daily basis in two separate settings, a nonprofit, religious-affiliated hospital and a public, teaching hospital.

Major Aims of the Compassionate Clinicians Study

The principal aims of the study were to understand the nature of the clinicians' interactions with patients and the meaning and value they found in their personal and professional lives. More specifically we sought to:

(1)   Identify the meaning or purpose in life as expressed by compassionate clinicians and how they achieved this in their daily interactions with patients. This aim explored the extent to which their spiritual beliefs gave meaning to life; how their understanding of God influenced their goals in life; how their religion or spirituality helped them in difficult circumstances and gave them purpose in life; and to what extent they felt that their lives conformed to God's wishes or plan.

(2)   Better understand what *caring* clinicians "gain" (or lose) from providing compassionate care.

(3)   Understand whether compassionate clinicians experience close relationships with their patients or if they seek to maintain some emotional distance. To better understand how clinicians who are emotionally close to their patients are able to cope with the death of or adverse outcomes for these patients.

(4)   Understand how clinicians express compassion and altruistic love while carrying out their job responsibilities and in their interactions with patients.

(5)   Understand the organizational enablers or obstructions to clinicians providing compassionate care.

Planning and Methodologies for the Compassionate Clinicians Study

In our efforts to understand the daily work experience of compassionate clinicians, we used a qualitative, phenomenological approach to elicit what is known as the "emic" or the insider perspective of the clinicians' lived experience (Pollio, Henley, & Thompson, 1999). In this case, we regarded the clinicians as the best sources for describing their world of experience (Carpenter & Hammell, 2000; Van Manen, 1990). We conducted the study at two hospitals in the southeastern United States: one was a large academic medical center with over 500 beds; the other was a 140-bed, religious-affiliated, community hospital. Review and approval from the Medical University of South Carolina Institutional Review Board was obtained prior to conducting the study.

The study was designed as an exemplar study (not a random selection of hospital clinicians). We wished to study those who excelled in caring and compassion in their work with patients; therefore a purposive, nonrandom, selection methodology was used. To identify the sample of compassionate clinicians in each hospital, e-mails and/or letters were sent to the unit directors and managers in all clinical departments. The directors and managers were asked to submit the names of "exemplary individuals – nurses, doctors, and other clinicians – who are really caring and compassionate in their interactions with patients." Clinicians were defined as health-care practitioners who provided treatment or support to patients. The managers provided a large number of names; these were reviewed by three different high-level clinical managers at each hospital. At this stage, the managers narrowed down the list based upon additional inclusion criteria such as a clinician being recommended more than once, a clinician being frequently commended in letters from families, and previous positive reports about the clinician provided by co-workers. For the final sample, 12 clinicians were selected for interviews at each hospital ($n = 24$). Each clinician received a letter inviting him or her to participate in the study. All clinicians who were contacted agreed to participate in the study. Table 12.1 shows the mix of clinical professions represented in our study. The largest group of clinicians interviewed was hospital nurses (10) and the second largest group was physicians (6).

Prior to developing content for the interviews, we engaged in a process of bracketing interviews with a team of three academics from the disciplines of anthropology, ethics, and divinity who were familiar with the process of interview design. Bracketing is a technique or process in which researchers are questioned before and during the study to obtain feedback about their attitudes, feelings, and preconceptions regarding the subject of their study (Pollio et al., 1999). Optimally, once this information is elicited or unveiled, the researchers are better prepared to undertake their research activities with minimal bias and conceptual projections.

We developed a semi-structured interview guide with 10 questions which entailed asking the selected hospital clinicians to describe the nature of their work, their formal and informal religious or spiritual practices, how their religious or spiritual beliefs might influence their interactions

Table 12.1   Compassionate Clinicians Interviewed in Two Hospital Settings

Profession	Academic medical center	Religious-affiliated hospital
Nurses	4	6
Physicians	4	2
Physical therapists	1	3
Occupational therapist	1	0
Nurses' aide	0	1
Dentist	1	0
Child life specialist	1	0
Total	12	12

Note. Adapted from "Compassionate clinicians: Taking patient care beyond the ordinary," by D. R. Graber & M. D. Mitcham, 2004, *Holistic Nursing Practice, 18*(2), p. 88. Copyright 2004 by Lippincott Williams & Wilkins.

with patients, difficulties or possible sacrifices involved in caring for patients, and organizational obstructions or facilitators to compassionate care. In this chapter, we primarily focus on the questions that were directly related to the provision of compassionate care. For full discussion and analysis of these questions, see Graber and Mitcham (2004).

- I can imagine in your position you have the opportunity to be caring and compassionate to your patients. Would you describe some of the things you do to be caring to your patients? Can you think of a specific example or two?
- Do you feel you have to sacrifice your own interests and comforts at times to serve your patients?
- Is it hard for you at times to balance this with completing your other job responsibilities?
- Could you describe one or two relationships you've had with patients that were fulfilling or meaningful to you?
- Do you feel you get close to and are able to have close personal relationships with patients, or do you try to keep some emotional distance and detachment?

During the spring and early summer of 2002, we conducted and audiotaped individual interviews in quiet rooms in each hospital at times convenient for the clinicians; typically the interviews were completed within 45 minutes. During the fall of 2002, two research assistants transcribed the interviews verbatim and entered the narrative into a qualitative software package: Ethnograph v.5.0 (1998). Transcripts were coded by the authors and the two assistants, who subsequently analyzed them for content and emergence of major themes. After all interviews were completed, we held member-checking sessions at each hospital with a small group of participants to share overall results, review preliminary analyses, and receive feedback.

Key Findings of the Compassionate Clinicians Study

Feeling compassion. The foundation of the compassionate love of the clinicians toward patients is their ability to feel what the patient is feeling, to "put themselves in the patient's shoes." As one nurse assistant often reminded herself, "one day it's going to be me." Such thoughts and feelings reflect the discernment and motivation that support compassionate love (Underwood; see Chapter 1, this volume). Clinicians often described feeling compassion for patients. One nurse described how she started crying and admonished a physician for being slow in issuing an order for pain medications for a cancer patient. Another nurse shared a story:

> I was down in the CCU – just walking through there doing some education stuff the other day, and a lady was sitting in a chair outside a room, and she had a smile on her face, and I just kind of put my hand on her shoulder and said, "Are you all right?" And she just started to cry. She told me, "My husband won't make it this time." And I wound up sitting on the floor holding this lady's hand for about an hour. Well the man made it; the patient made it. And every time I would walk through that unit that lady would say, "There's my friend when I needed her." Now that is really ... my positive stroke.

The clinicians described many similar situations where they felt and acted from the heart and reached out to patients. They were not too preoccupied with their responsibilities and duties to notice and respond to patients' needs and feelings.

Clinicians enacting caring and compassion to patients. There is a multitude of ways that the clinicians express caring and compassion to patients, many of which involve attentiveness and good communication. Several nurses mentioned that they try to introduce themselves to patients, let them know that they will take care of them that day, and often ask if there is anything they can do to help them. There might be a smile or pat on the back, an expression of interest, and a friendly tone of voice. One nurse said, "For new admissions, you can just make up some soup and crackers. You'll go that extra mile, to get a tray – a regular lunch or supper tray." The clinicians also try to foster personal relationships with new patients.

One told us, "If you meet them and are outgoing and say, 'How many kids do you have? Oh, look at these pictures up here ...' and you human-ize them, you get a much better response when you deal with the medical issues." A physical therapist stated that if you don't develop a relationship with patients early on, they won't trust you or relax so you can treat them. Another approach mentioned by several clinicians is to ask for permission to sit on the patient's bed to foster relaxed interaction and rapport. Almost all the clinicians we interviewed said that they enjoyed getting to know patients and that friendly patient relationships were the usual ones. They often mentioned that knowing their patients personally also helped in treatment.

Meaningful patient relationships. The clinicians we interviewed were from a number of health professions and the extent and nature of their contact with patients varied considerably. An emergency-room nurse might typically interact with a patient over a few hours. Many of the clinicians had long-term relationships with patients and family members that might extend over several years. One physician described his satisfaction at seeing some children with arthritis grow up to be healthy and even athletic. "I have a patient who is on a full golf scholarship at her university, and who was rookie of the year last year on the ladies' golf team. So, things like that stand out, but it's just as fulfilling to me to see the child participate in Little League or youth basketball." A therapist described treating a young boy with a head injury and continuing outpatient therapy with him into adolescence. She stated, "I was telling his mom the other day ... it's like he's my little brother, in a way."

Long-term relationships with patients often involved reciprocal com-munication involving telephone calls, letters, cards, and sharing of photo-graphs. On the other hand, some of the clinicians interviewed did not typically experience long-term relationships with their patients, unless a patient happened to return or be readmitted. However, these clinicians invariably described conversations with patients that were not limited to superficial topics or discussions about care and treatment, but involved a sharing of personal information.

The temporal dimension of compassion. The long-term relationships described above are one of many clinician–patient relationships in a tem-poral continuum that ranges from momentary encounters to enduring interactions based on the nature of the care (Mitcham, Graber, & Blue, 2002). For short-term encounters (staccato) clinicians mentioned the importance of personal recognition, eye contact, a smile, positive affect, and friendly words. The longer-term interactions (legato) included these elements, but also involved greater personal knowledge and familiarity between the patient and the clinician.

Tasks and interactions between compassionate clinicians and patients vary throughout the different periods or stages of engagement. The initial meeting or meetings with patients may involve establishing rapport, providing information, and reassuring patients through body language, speech, and actions that the clinician is there to help and can be trusted. During the patient's stay, education and advocacy may be offered, as well as a response to requests and building a richer relationship with the patient. For many clinicians, once the patient is discharged the interaction ends, but for some clinicians (as described above) the care relationship may continue to involve patient advocacy, education, and personal friendship. These actions or tasks do not so much represent the actual feeling of compassion, but the positive behaviors described by Underwood that are the expression of compassionate love (see Chapter 1, this volume).

Virtually all of the clinicians acknowledged the busyness and time demands of their jobs, but such constraints did not keep them from acting compassionately. As described above, even in a short-term encounter, warmth and friendliness can be displayed. Several clinicians mentioned the importance of communication, for example, letting a patient know you need to leave to attend to your work, but that you will not forget him or her and will return when you can.

Emotional closeness vs. professional detachment. Virtually none of the clinicians adopted a demeanor of professional detachment. Several communicated that such an approach was foreign to their personalities or to their self-image as health-care professionals. However, several clinicians noted that interpersonal distance may be necessary, depending on the situation and the patient. The following verbatim narratives from two nurses and a physical therapist give a sense of their views on close relationships with patients.

1.   Again, when I was young, we were taught you were supposed to maintain your objectivity. As I have gotten older and grown up, you can't. The only way you can share your humanity with people is to show your vulnerability. When someone hurts ... when someone cries, I cry right along with them. It takes too much energy to hide myself from people. And having said that, of course there are people – patients and families and other nurses ... you don't get close to everybody. But it's not because I hide myself. Life's too short to do that.

2.   There's a team effort [working with patients who are children and their parents], and we share a lot. And they're interested to know what's going on in my life, too. So they'll ask me questions. "How's your house coming?" So it's a friendship, and it's hard sometimes, because you want to have that line too. I know people say, "Oh, you're getting too involved."

But, I think that if it was my child, I would want to know that the people that were working with them really cared about them: that it wasn't just a job.

3.   I don't [keep a distance between myself and patients] because I find it fulfilling to talk to patients and to learn from patients. I can't say that I put up emotional walls and try not to get close, because I think it is rewarding. That is part of the field. If I wanted to sit behind a computer all day I would have gone into a different field. I like interacting with people.

A number of clinicians distinguished between involvement that was normal, healthy, functional, and considered desirable; and emotional or dysfunctional involvement. An emergency room nurse noted, "I think on a professional level, you have to keep that distance to not become so involved that you can't take care of that patient the way that they need you to. They don't need a crying, hysterical person. They need a caring person in a quiet sort of way. So it's a fine line where it becomes emotional involvement." A few clinicians felt that there are some situations where closeness is inadvisable, such as with unstable or manipulative patients, but in general were open to emotional closeness between themselves and their patients. However, social distancing was not necessarily advocated by all the clinicians. One physician said about patients who are demanding and unrealistic in their expectations, "The path of least resistance would be to distance yourself from difficult patients. It's a challenge and sometimes trying, but you can foster a relationship, and often the difficult patient ceases to be as difficult and confrontational as he first appeared to be."

These interviews revealed that the clinicians are warm and familiar with their patients. They generally seem to enjoy getting to know them and do not seek to maintain emotional distance or detachment, although (when needed in a specific situation) they may adopt this posture.

Spirituality and compassionate care. Study results indicated that 23 of the 24 clinicians had strong beliefs or experiences related to a higher power. During the interviews, participants often described their daily spiritual experiences. These included feeling God's presence and guidance and an inner intuition, and finding comfort in one's religion or relationship with God. The clinicians also completed a spirituality scale (Underwood, 1999, 2006). The Daily Spiritual Experiences Scale contains 15 statements concerning one's spirituality, religion, or relationship to God, such as: I feel God's presence; I find strength in my religion or spirituality; I ask for God's help in the midst of daily activities. The response options are (1) Many times a day; (2) Every day; (3) Most days; (4) Some days; (5) Once in a while; (6) Never or almost never. The most frequent response option chosen by the clinicians for each of the 15 statements of the Daily Spiritual Experiences Scale was option 1 (many times a day). Option 1 was the most frequently selected option for nine statements, and option 2 (every day) was selected most frequently for five statements. Note that option 1 indicates having a feeling or experience (involving spirituality or one's relationship with God) *many times a day*. Option 2 indicates this experience *every day*. These responses indicate high levels of daily spiritual experiences among the clinicians. Thus, at least in our sample of 24, a strong spiritual orientation and daily spiritual experiences are characteristic of compassionate clinicians.

A Preliminary Model of Affective Clinician/Patient Interactions

An analysis of the exemplar clinician transcripts provided evidence that there are four levels at which clinician–patient interactions take place (Graber & Mitcham, 2004). In Table 12.2 we present a model that does not categorize individuals per se but rather illustrates a continuum along which clinicians may interact with patients. There are four levels along this continuum, ranging from the everyday or mundane (Level I) to the transcendental (Level IV). For each level we identify a series of attributes that characterize the parameters of the clinician–patient interactions.

- Primary form of expression between the clinician and the patient, which reflects the degree of intimacy or closeness between them.
- Inner motivational source for the clinician's interpersonal and affective behaviors.
- Degree of personal focus or concern as compared to a focus or concern for the patient.

Because hospitals are busy places and clinicians working in them have considerable demands on their time, some patient encounters will necessarily be brief and will primarily focus on the performance of a clinical or work-related task. Other interactions may occur when a clinician has more time to communicate in depth and relax with the patient. Therefore, clinicians may operate on more than one level, even within a single day, but will generally have a specific level where they most often relate to patients. It is also possible for clinicians in a single patient encounter to manifest elements of more than one of the four levels. These levels are discussed below:

Level I: Everyday/practical. Work-related and practical interactions typify the first level of clinician–patient interaction. In general, our exemplary clinicians communicated that if their professional practice was largely limited to such interactions, it would be barren and unfulfilling. Interactions at this level are not typically unfriendly interactions; however,

Table 12.2   A Model of Affective Clinician–Patient Interactions

Levels of clinician–patient interaction	Primary forms of expression	Primary motivational sources	Foci of concern
IV. Transcendent	Love and compassion	Feeling and intuition	Primary concern for patient; minimal concern for self
III. Personal/ feeling	Intimacy and friendly patient relations	Secular or religious values; sense of duty (higher); altruism; personal social needs;	Concern for patient and self
II. Personal/ social	Friendly patient relations; some emotional involvement	Personal social needs; altruism	Concern for self and patient
I. Everyday/ practical	Fulfilling job responsibilities; superficial patient relations; detached concern	Material reward; sense of duty (lower)	Concern for self

Note. Adapted from "Compassionate clinicians: Taking patient care beyond the ordinary," by D. R. Graber & M. D. Mitcham, 2004, *Holistic Nursing Practice, 18*(2), p. 91. Copyright 2004 by Lippincott Williams & Wilkins.

conversations between the clinician and the patient generally focus on care or treatment issues. Clinician–patient conversations not related to care or treatment will usually be superficial, such as discussions about the weather. Owing to their focus on the task and not the patient, clinicians who are based primarily in the everyday/practical level are relatively less concerned about the well-being and happiness of the patient compared to clinicians who more commonly operate from the other levels. These clinicians are often motivated to quickly accomplish their work responsibilities and may consider the patient to be more of a "work unit" than an individual. Another motivation may be to protect themselves from imagined jarring influences arising from greater patient intimacy. Some clinicians may lack the inner resources to engage and be empathic to patients owing to "isolation, sadness at prolonged human tragedies, long hours of service, chronic lack of sleep, and depression at futile … therapeutic maneuvers" (Spiro, 1993, p. 10). For protection, the clinician may, over time, create a persona that reflects detachment and communicates a measured show of concern.

Clinicians operating at the everyday/practical level often consider patient relations to be part of a paid job. Doing this, they carry out patient interactions based on a sense of duty, i.e., the perceived need to work and interact with patients as part of the job and salary. These clinicians tend to be focused on personal concerns and responsibilities and have suppressed the warmth and spontaneity necessary for meaningful human interchange. At the worst, such clinicians are armored and distant from their patients.

Level II: Personal/social. At the personal/social level, the most typical patient interactions involve clinicians having friendly relations with patients and other clinicians primarily to meet personal social needs. Social interactions based on human needs have been expounded in earlier psychological and motivational theories – for example, the *belongingness* need described by Abraham Maslow in the 1940s (Maslow, 1943) and the *affiliation* need conceptualized by David McClelland in the 1960s (McClelland, 1961).

The personal/social level may involve clinicians fulfilling their social needs, but this level also involves giving and receiving warmth and affection from patients. Concomitant with warm, interpersonal exchanges and the development of personal relationships is also the emergence of altruistic concern by clinicians for their patients. Sometimes, relationships become difficult when dealing with troubled, unstable, or angry patients. When this occurs, clinicians often will resort to the everyday/practical position – one that adopts a posture of detached concern or minimal patient interaction.

Level III: Personal/feeling. In comparison to Level II, clinicians at Level III are motivated to a greater degree by empathic or altruistic concern for their patients, and less by the personal self-concern or focus that is predominant at the two lower levels. It is likely that clinicians at this level possess high degrees of altruism, although this was not explicitly measured in this study. A number of definitions of altruism exist and most of them incorporate some dimension of selflessness and sacrifice. Kagan (2002) considers altruism to be "the helping agent's awareness of the need of another and the intention to be of assistance" (p. 43). Such an interpersonal perspective involves a focus on the other (or patient) and less concern for oneself.

From the interviews that formed the basis for this study, it was readily apparent that the closeness that occurs between patients and clinicians that reflects the clinician's altruism and concern for the patient is of a different quality from interactions based on emotional involvement with the patient. A number of the clinicians we interviewed considered it best to avoid emotional involvement with *some* patients, which could detract from providing good care and carrying out their job responsibilities. These patients might be the unusual or exceptional ones, who are unstable or unreasonable. In general, clinicians who operate at the higher levels (and these comprised our study sample) typically have warm relationships with patients; however, they are also quite capable of interpersonal distancing when they feel it is best for patients and their care.

The interviews indicated that at the personal/feeling level, positive interactions with patients are supported by the clinicians' belief system and values. Our subjects often cited a value that guided them in their work, such as the golden rule. One clinician stated, "Maybe our only purpose is to make life livable for those around us. That's how our life becomes livable." Another mentioned that she tried to be caring to patients, because "One day it will probably be me lying in that hospital bed." So, for the clinicians we studied, their values appeared to be the foundation for consistent behaviors to help and comfort patients. These were not superficially held values, but ones that were held for many years and embraced on a deep level. The values also appeared to be linked to a sense of duty among the clinicians we interviewed who, perhaps more than other health-care professionals, felt compelled to translate their beliefs into practice in their interactions with patients. However, the clinicians enacting these values and expressing compassion in their daily work life did not do so merely from a rigid sense of duty. The exemplary individuals we interviewed have a strong sense of duty and values about what is important in serving patients, but their caring is also enlivened by the heart – the spontaneous expression of love, feeling, and altruism.

Level IV: Transcendent. Although compassion may be considered an emotion or feeling, numerous philosophers and religious figures have considered compassion to be identical to love or an expression of love. Dante noted the transcendent nature of compassion and asserted that it is not a human passion, but arises from an individual's soul (Hilliard, 1889). Similarly, Williamson (2002) stated that compassion is not just an emotion, but has its own innate force.

Compassion is closely related to intuition; Rogers (1951) noted that empathic listening in counseling often leads to a hunch or insight that sheds greater light on the client's experience or condition. Such an insight may, in turn, provide the basis or impetus for greater feelings and expressions of compassion. In our analysis of the transcripts, we noted numerous instances in which clinicians experienced a deep sense of compassion for their patients. They also experienced an exchange of sharing and support that appeared qualitatively distinct from ordinary emotional or social interactions.

At the transcendent level, clinicians feel great closeness and even unity with the patient. Clinicians who have the capacity for transcendent experiences in their work do not operate on this level at all times. This is neither practical nor appropriate, as clinicians must be focused on their work and carry out a number of responsibilities in the face of severe time demands. However, most of the clinicians did relate stories of interactions with patients that involved great sharing, compassion, and unity. Often, the stories that were narrated involved experiences that were challenging for patients and their family members. A maternity nurse described her experiences with a young female patient whose first two childbirths were unsuccessful. This nurse even attended the funeral of one of the patient's infants. A year later, there was a third pregnancy. The nurse allowed the woman to attend free childbirth classes (as she did not have insurance cover or funds to pay for the classes). This time the pregnancy was successful and the nurse was present during the delivery. She said that the successful delivery "was a celebration of our spirits – of our very beings. That's probably one of the most fulfilling births that I've had. There was a long time that we just cried ... it was kind of bittersweet, but also a celebration at the same time."

The results of our study of compassionate care in hospitals support Underwood's contention that individual motivation is a foundation for compassion (see Chapter 1, this volume). Our four levels of clinician–patient interactions are based on different levels or types of motivation in interpersonal interactions. Compassion occurs primarily and most often when clinicians' focus is not on themselves, but on the well-being and interests of their patients. Therefore, at Levels III and IV the clinician's main focus and concern are for the patient; in fact, at Level IV, the greater experience of empathy involves almost no preoccupation or focus on the individual self or ego (of the clinician). At Level II, the focus of concern is for the "self and the patient," indicating a comparatively greater self-orientation or personal focus compared with Levels III and IV. Thus, improving or increasing compassionate care in hospitals appears closely related to one path of human development: growing beyond a narrow preoccupation with oneself to what has been termed "other-centered love," which is directed toward the needs and issues of others. Underwood (2002) notes that those who have an other-centered focus also tend to be more satisfied and have better quality of life. She describes the observations of a working group of individuals from various cultures and religions who met in the late 1990s to develop an instrument to measure spiritual contributions to quality of life. In her words:

> One of the important preliminary findings of this project is that qualities that are not obviously oriented toward self-interest can be important in improving satisfaction with life for people in their everyday lives throughout the world. Quality of life is not only determined by physical health,

> mental health, and economic status but also by some other-oriented features. Giving of self for the other has been rated as important to the quality of one's life, in a variety of settings and cultural contexts, to people throughout the world. (Underwood, 2002, p. 79)

To what extent can a focus on others' needs and compassion for them be developed? If compassion is a relatively fixed, personal attribute then it may be difficult to evoke in adults, especially those working in demanding environments, such as hospitals. However, to embrace this position is tantamount to believing that humans are not capable of becoming better, more loving individuals, a position which the authors of this chapter are unwilling to take and do not subscribe to. The next section describes programs that may be useful in developing compassion in hospital environments.

Increasing or Augmenting Compassionate Care in Hospitals

The current conundrum in the health profession is developing strategies in educational and training programs that integrate disparate and sometimes conflicting sets of "virtues" in a way that honors their complexity and their continuity within health-care delivery environments. This is particularly salient in hospital care, where both the providers and the patients have not yet realized the proper balance between the art and the science, the cure and the care. As described in this chapter, some practitioners act empathetically or more distantly, with detached concern and an air of technical rationality. Health-care educational programs and their curricula have been heavily influenced by reductionism and logical positivism, but many programs are now trying to redress prior imbalances by searching for more demonstrative measures of caring and compassion. These challenges loom large against a backdrop of increased demands for evidence-based practice, cost-containment, and technological sophistication. Nevertheless, much can be done on the organizational, professional, and personal levels to uplift the culture and enhance caring and compassion among those working in hospitals.

On the organizational level, executives and leaders of large hospitals or hospital systems could strive to develop a culture of caring and compassion. In the experience of one of the authors of this chapter, one proprietary hospital chain in the 1980s explicitly discouraged and sought to not hire managers who expressed values relating to compassion and who valued service to the community and to the underserved. Obviously, such organizations do not provide fertile ground for developing compassionate care. However, many hospital executives have realized that staff and physicians who manifest human warmth and compassion are usually those who also are highly effective in satisfying patients and marketing the hospital to the community. The concept of developing a strong culture of compassionate care is compatible with an enormous body of literature that focuses on organizational leaders developing, sharing, and institutionalizing key values and their vision with members of the organization (Blanchard & O'Connor, 1997; Burns, 1978; Conger, 1998; Covey, 1991). If organizations such as Nordstrom or L. L. Bean can develop and sustain cultures that support very high levels of customer service, can hospitals not emulate them in developing cultures that support compassionate care?

The current motivational and reward systems in hospitals can be vastly improved. Hospitals may extol compassion and caring in their mission statements and in other official pronouncements, but do little to reward workers who embody compassion in their daily working lives. Such organizational inconsistency was noted by Kerr (1995) in a reprint of his classic article, "On the Folly of Rewarding A, While Hoping for B." This article summarizes the results of a survey of executives and describes common conflicts between expressed organizational values and the reward system (e.g., "We hope for innovative thinking and risk-taking, but we reward proven methods and not making mistakes"; "We hope for employee involvement and empowerment, but we reward tight control over operations and resources"). Kerr's folly also applies to those hospitals that hope for caring and compassion by their clinicians and staff, but tend to reward technical skills or the amount of services produced. Some organizations are already measuring such qualities as perspective-taking and empathic concern and using these for individual development or employee evaluations (Organizational Diagnostics Online, 2006, Personality section). Therefore, caring and compassion can be measured or objectified in reward systems, perhaps imperfectly, but well enough to reward individuals who consistently manifest these in their interactions with others.

In addition to developing motivators for compassionate care, hospitals also can develop programs to foster compassionate care. Oman and Thoresen (2003) developed a program of spiritual modeling, wherein health-care clinicians read about the lives of exemplars such as Christ, Buddha, Mohammed, Gandhi, Lillian Wald, and Mother Teresa. Programs such as this may foster compassion and a greater sense of caregiving self-efficacy (Oman, Hedberg, Downs, & Parsons, 2003). Some medical schools have instituted courses with literary readings designed to evoke humanism or compassion in students (Shapiro, Morrison, & Boker, 2004).

Although such courses may help to increase empathy, as these courses are generally electives, they can only have limited influence.

Professional socialization and education were described earlier in this chapter as being related to the propensity of members of a heath-care profession to be compassionate. Due to previous socialization and education, new clinicians enter a hospital with an established self-image about the type of affect and demeanor they will manifest in their interactions with patients. Obviously, the influences in shaping this self-image are numerous: societal norms and values about clinicians; influences during formal education, residencies, and clinical rotations; conscious and unconscious imitation of clinical role models; a perceived need to conform to an organizational culture; and peer pressure from other clinicians. In the earlier-cited Carmel and Glick study (1996), the medical professional culture in Israeli hospitals did not value or consider compassion to be an important or valuable quality among member physicians. A key assumption in a conceptual model of altruism in health care developed by McGaghie, Mytko, Brown, & Cameron (2002) is that "Reinforcement increases the probability of future altruistic acts and strengthens one's compassionate core" (p. 375). A medical or health-care culture that does not value compassion also will not reinforce compassionate or altruistic care. Therefore, both hospital organizational cultures and professional cultures must begin to value compassionate care and build rewards for those clinicians who are not only proficient but also caring and compassionate.

In the view of the authors, Western culture is largely supportive of and values compassionate care from clinicians. The task, then, for hospitals and health-care educational programs is to develop caring cultures that conform to these values. Clearly, the development of a caring culture must begin in professional educational programs. Strategies for instilling these values of caring and compassion are discussed next.

Instilling Compassionate Care in Health-Care Education

Although the public has historically valued compassionate care, many disciplines in the twentieth century, particularly medicine, deemphasized warmth, caring, and compassion in their educational programs. In more recent years, many medical schools and other health-profession programs have modified their admission criteria to encourage greater admissions of students with varied backgrounds and experiences (e.g., liberal arts or humanities degrees, experience working with the poor). In prior decades, male students far outnumbered female students in medical schools. The percentage of female students in medical schools climbed to about 46 percent in 2001–2002 from only 27 percent in 1980–1981 (HRSA, 2004).

Greater diversity in the pool of students entering health-care professions will ultimately be reflected in hospitals and other health-care settings, and may serve to loosen established professional cultures and gradually alter the stereotypical images of clinicians. Such diversity also may contribute to a more receptive environment for the practice of compassionate care.

Demographic changes related to the admission of students in the health professions may be influential in changing the culture of health care. What is probably more important is what is subsequently communicated in the course of health-care education. Educational programs that seek to foster compassionate care and strive to graduate caring clinicians can offer required courses on this topic in the curriculum. Another educational approach is to integrate the construct of compassionate care across the curriculum, thereby building a corpus of expertise. Unfortunately, unless the ideals of compassionate care are explicitly embedded in course objectives, the integration of course content often will become attenuated over time.

Shapiro (2002) looked at ways in which physicians teach empathy to medical students and residents in primary-care settings and concluded that teaching empathy must go far beyond skill development and requires a strong affective component if it is to reflect the complexity of what actually transpires in the clinical setting. Consequently, recent examples in medical education have stressed simulation experiences such as hospitalization (Wilkes, Milgrom, & Hoffman, 2002), in which students gain direct experience of what it is like to be in the patient's shoes, and drama (Deloney & Graham, 2003), designed to provoke strong emotional responses that may be instrumental in bringing about attitudinal change, or nonclinical experiences, such as visiting or serving as big brothers/big sisters for children with disabilities (Tess, Baier, Eckenfels, & Yogev, 1997). These types of experiences are likely to be remembered by students, compared to nonexperiential forms of learning associated with the early didactic portion of a medical curriculum.

Stepping outside of medicine and looking at health professions such as nursing, occupational therapy, and physical therapy, it is more common to find educational curricula that are designed around holistic concepts associated with patient or client-centered care (e.g., Jamieson et al., 2006). Factors influencing curriculum design decisions as a whole include a commitment to honoring the processes by which one becomes a caring practitioner, as much as the knowledge and skills one needs for entry-level competence in one's chosen field. Learning about empathy is usually much more explicit, and explicit attempts are made to integrate affective and cognitive learning (Goulet & Owen-Smith, 2005; Misch & Peloquin, 2005). Recent examples of instructional strategies devoted to teaching and developing empathy include art (Peloquin, 1996), simulation (Wikstrom,

2003), gaming (Reagan, 2000), role-playing (Norman, 2001), reflective journaling (Jung & Tryssenaar, 1998), service learning (Bailey & Angell, 2005; Bentley & Ellison, 2005; Hoppes, Bender, & DeGrace, 2005), and specific skills training in communication (Oz, 2001).

Specific skills training, such as communicating, listening, and showing respect to patients may provide an important foundation for compassionate care. While these skills are not the same thing as compassion, they do represent some of the "positive behaviors" related to compassion (see Underwood, Chapter 1, this volume). For example, Benbassat and Baumal (2004) assert that important steps in developing empathy are first to deflect the desire to focus immediately on the "chief complaint" and second to detect the patient's concerns through a carefully structured "patient-centered" interview. Once students understand these concerns, they can empathize with the patient. Teaching the detection of the patient's concerns is accomplished through practice of patient-centered interviews in which students also record the patient's concerns. Cohen-Cole and Bird (1991) identified five different empathic responses, each of which may be appropriate in different circumstances. These empathic responses denote reflection, legitimation, support, partnership, or respect. For example, a statement reflecting legitimation might be, "I can understand why you're feeling very stressed at work." A statement involving reflection and support could be, "It sounds like your prostate cancer has made life feel very uncertain for you. I'd like to help if I can." Suchman, Roter, Green, & Lipkin (1993) note that patients do not always directly express an emotion. However, they do make disclosures, referred to as "trial balloons," which are potential empathic opportunities for an alert, compassionate clinician. These aspects of communication can and should be incorporated in training students and health professionals. With this knowledge, clinicians can begin their own "experiments" in patient encounters and determine what works best and is most practical in caring for patients.

A 1999 Bayer Institute–Fetzer Institute conference identified five key communication tasks in the physician–patient encounter, including *building the doctor–patient relationship* and *understanding the patient's perspective* (Makoul, 2001). Other organizations, such as Kaiser Permanente, administer questionnaires to patients that assess each physician's communication skills, including his or her understanding of patients and their problems (Janisse & Vuckovic, 2002). Better understanding of the patient requires effort on the part of the clinician; however, this understanding leads to greater compassion and more intelligent and effective treatment.

If hospitals and health-profession schools adopt programs to teach skills such as communication and empathic listening, will students and clinicians become more compassionate? This may be a question of the chicken and the egg. However, it does seem reasonable that compassion may be enhanced by developing specific patient-centered skills. Learning and applying these skills should lead to greater understanding of the patient, which in turn will elicit compassion in many, if not all, clinicians. Compassion or empathy also may be considered an aspect of emotional intelligence, which is related to and supportive of many interpersonal skills, such as tact, sensitivity, and listening (Goleman, 1995). In the view of the authors, clinicians with empathy are more likely to develop and use practical, interpersonal skills to better understand and help their patients.

The strategies described above are often employed preparatory to students' participation in full-time clinical placement. Clinical education programs generally involve clerkships or residencies wherein students are able to work alongside practicing clinicians. These clinicians and sites can be selected by the educational programs on a number of criteria, including the presence of caring clinicians or the stipulation that the site should have a caring environment. Thus, without lecturing students on the importance of compassion, students may naturally begin to embrace compassionate care by having their role models carefully chosen by faculty in their educational program. In the view of the authors, the compassionate clinicians who were the subject of our study would be impressive and influential preceptors for students in health professions. Students and professionals could benefit from videos of, or presentations by, such compassionate clinicians. Similar to expert panels on various topics, a presentation at a conference or educational setting might include exemplary clinicians who could answer questions or brainstorm, and discuss how to manage challenging jobs or difficult patient situations while still exhibiting compassion and caring.

Areas for Future Research

We believe our qualitative study (Graber & Mitcham, 2004) makes a modest contribution to our knowledge of compassionate care in hospitals. A limitation of the study is that our sample was limited to exemplary hospital clinicians working in two southern US hospitals. Certainly, much health care is provided elsewhere and similar or related studies in such settings as nursing homes, primary-care clinics, and health departments would be useful and could serve to support or add clarity to the findings of our study.

In identifying the nature of personal relationships between compassionate clinicians and patients, and the variety and nature of specific acts of compassion, our study provided basic and practical information for those who would like to design programs for compassionate care. Similar studies could be carried out in the future in other geographic areas, and focusing on compassionate clinicians from a variety of racial, ethnic, and religious backgrounds.

In this chapter we have described various approaches to increase compassionate care in education and in hospitals. A number of interventions or programs have been studied by researchers, but the evaluation of results often has been limited to one or two post-intervention measurements. We really do not know how lasting are the effects of different programs to enhance compassion or exactly what interventions might be the most effective. Nor are we aware of programs that seek to improve compassionate care over the long-term involving multiple methods and strategies. These should not only be fruitful areas for research but also will help managers learn what might work or not work in their hospitals.

An important research and organizational consideration is how compassion is improved in organizations, such as hospitals, with various health-care professionals. As mentioned previously, professional cultures may tend to value compassionate care, or may consider it inconsequential and unimportant. Influencing physicians, who typically are not even employees of the hospitals in which they work, remains a challenge. Programs and research studies that focus on improving the compassionate behavior of physicians who are practicing in hospitals may be highly useful for hospitals and other health-care organizations. More research also is needed that evaluates curricula and experiential learning programs to foster compassionate care among students in health professions. Broad, interprofessional, educational programs that seek to inculcate compassionate care in a number of health-professional disciplines may have more impact on health-care cultures than programs targeted to a single discipline. It is essential to begin integrating compassion into health-care curricula. Students who graduate from health-care programs that value compassionate care have enormous potential to transform the caring environment in the hospitals of the future.

References

Bailey, R. L., & Angell. M. E. (2005). Service-learning in speech-language pathology: Stakeholders' perceptions of a school-based feeding improvement project. *Contemporary Issues in Communication Science and Disorders, 32*, 126–133.

Benbassat, J., & Baumal, R. (2004). What is empathy, and how can it be promoted during clinical clerkships? *Academic Medicine, 79*(9), 832–839.

Bentley, R., & Ellison, K. J. (2005). Impact of a service-learning project on nursing students. *Nursing Education Perspective, 26*(5), 287–290.

Bevis, E., & Watson, J. (1989). *Toward a caring curriculum: A new pedagogy for nursing.* New York: National League for Nursing.

Blanchard, K., & O'Connor, M. (1997). *Managing by values.* San Francisco: Berrett-Koehler.

Borgenicht, L. (1984). Richard Selzer and the problem of detached concern. *Annals of Internal Medicine, 100,* 923–934.

Burns, J. M. (1978). *Leadership.* New York: Harper and Row.

Carmel, S., & Glick, S. M. (1996). Compassionate-empathic physicians: Personality traits and social-organizational factors that enhance or inhibit this behavior pattern. *Social Science and Medicine, 43*(8), 1253–1261.

Carpenter, C., & Hammell, K. (2000). Evaluating qualitative research. In K. Hammell, C. Carpenter & I. Dyck (Eds.), *Using qualitative research* (pp. 107–119). New York: Churchill Livingstone.

Cathell, D. (1890). *The physician himself.* Philadelphia, PA: F. A. Davis.

Cohen-Cole, S. A., & Bird, J. (1991). Building rapport and responding to patient emotions. In Cohen-Cole, S. A. (Ed.), *The medical interview: The three function approach* (pp. 21–27). St. Louis, MO: Mosby Year Book.

Conger, J. (1998). *Winning 'em over.* New York: Simon and Schuster.

Covey, S. (1991). *Principle-centered leadership.* New York: Free Press.

Deloney, L. A., & Graham, C. J. (2003). Wit: Using drama to teach first-year medical students about empathy and compassion. *Teaching and Learning Medicine, 15*(4), 247–251.

The Ethnograph v5.0. (1998). [Computer software]. Salt Lake City, UT: Qualis Research Associates.

Goleman, D. (1995). *Emotional intelligence: Why it can matter more than IQ.* New York: Bantam Books.

Goulet, C., & Owen-Smith, P. (2005). Cognitive-affective learning in physical therapy education: From implicit to explicit. *Journal of Physical Therapy Education, 19*(3), 67–72.

Graber, D., & Mitcham, M. (2004). Compassionate clinicians: Taking patient care beyond the ordinary. *Holistic Nursing Practice, 18*(2), 87–94.

Graber, D. R., & Johnson, J. A. (2001). Spirituality and healthcare organizations. *Journal of Healthcare Management, 46,* 39–52.

Health Resources and Services Administration (HRSA). Women's Health USA. (2004). Retrieved from http://www.mchb.hrsa.gov/whusa04/pages/ch1.htm#schools

Hilliard, K. (1889). *The banquet of Dante Alighieri.* London: Kegan.

Hoppes, S., Bender, D., & DeGrace, B. W. (2005). Service learning is the perfect fit for occupational and physical therapy education. *Journal of Allied Health, 43*(1), 47–50.

IOM. (2001). *Crossing the quality chasm: A new health care system for the 21st century.* Washington, DC: National Academy Press. Retrieved August 18, 2006, from http://darwin.nap.edu/books/0309072808/html.

Jamieson, M., Krupa, T., O'Riordan, A., O'Connor, D., Paterson, M., Ball, C., & Wilcox, S. (2006). Developing empathy as a foundation for client-centered practice: Evaluation of a university curriculum initiative. *Canadian Journal of Occupational Therapy, 73*(2), 76–85.

Janisse, T., & Vuckovic, N. (2002). Can some clinicians read their patients' minds? Or do they just really like people? A communication and relationship study. *The Permanente Journal, 6*(3), 35–40.

Jung, B., & Tryssenaar, J. (1998). Supervising students: Exploring the experience through reflective journals. *Occupational Therapy International, 5*(1), 35–48.

Kagan, J. (2002). Morality, altruism, and love. In S. Post, L. G. Underwood, J. P. Schloss, & W. B. Hurlbut (Eds.), *Altruism and altruistic love* (pp. 40–50). New York: Oxford University Press.

Kerr, S. (1995). On the folly of rewarding A, while hoping for B. *Academy of Management Executive, 9*(1), 7–14.

Makoul, G. (2001). Essential elements of communication in medical encounters: the Kalamazoo consensus statement. *Academic Medicine 76*(3), 390–3.

Maslow, A. (1943). A theory of human motivation. *Psychological Review, 50,* 370–396.

McClelland, D. (1961). *The achieving society.* Princeton, NJ: Van Nostrand.

McGaghie, W., Mytko, J., Brown, W. N., & Cameron, J. (2002). Altruism and compassion in the health professions: A search for clarity and precision. *Medical Teacher, 24*(4), 374–378.

Misch, D. A., & Peloquin, S. M. (2005). Developing empathy through confluent education. *Journal of Physical Therapy Education, 19*(3), 41–51.

Mitcham, M., Graber, D., & Blue, A. (2002, May 23–24). Doing compassionate care: Making sense of the spiritual component. First Canadian Occupational Science Symposium, Halifax, Nova Scotia.

Norman, R. (2001). Experiential learning in drug and alcohol education. *Journal of Nursing Education, 40*(8), 371–374.

Oman, D., Hedberg, J., Downs, D., & Parsons, D. (2003). A transcultural spiritually based program to enhance caregiving self-efficacy: A pilot study. *Complementary Health Practice Review, 8*(3), 201–224.

Oman, D., & Thoresen, C. E. (2003). Spiritual modeling: A key to spiritual and religious growth? *International Journal for the Psychology of Religion,13* (3), 149–165.

O'Neil, E. H., & the Pew Health Professions Commission. (1998, December). *Recreating health professional practice for a new century.* San Francisco, CA: Pew Health Professions Commission.

Organizational Diagnostics Online. *Personal diagnostics.* Retrieved September 5, 2006 from http://www.od-online.com/prsndiag.asp

Osler, W. (1932). *Aequanimitas with other addresses to medical students, nurses, and practitioners of medicine* (3rd ed.). Philadelphia, PA: Blakiston.

Oz, F. (2001). Impact of training on empathic communication skills and tendency of nurses. *Clinical Excellence for Nurse Practitioners, 5*(1), 44–51.

Parsons, T. (1951). *The social system.* Glencoe, IL: Free Press.

Peloquin, S. M. (1996). Art an occupation with promise for developing empathy. *American Journal of Occupational Therapy, 50*(8), 655–661.

Pollio, H., Henley, T. B., & Thompson, C. (1999). *The phenomenology of everyday life.* Cambridge: Cambridge University Press.

Reagan, R. (2000). *The effects of gaming on the empathic communication of associate degree nursing students.* Unpublished doctoral dissertation, Widener University School of Nursing.

Robert Wood Johnson Foundation Commission on Medical Education, Robert Wood Johnson Foundation. (1992). *The science of medical practice*. Princeton, NJ: Author.

Rogers, C. A. (1951). *Client-centered therapy: Its current practice, implications, and theory*. Boston: Houghton Mifflin.

Shapiro, J. (2002). How do physicians teach empathy in the primary care setting? *Academic Medicine, 77*(4), 323–328.

Shapiro, J., Morrison, E., & Boker, J. (2004). Teaching empathy to first-year medical students: Evaluation of an elective literature and medicine course. *Education for Health, 17*(1), 73–84.

Shugars, D. A., O'Neil, E. H., & Bader, J. D. (1991). (Eds.). *Healthy America: Practitioners for 2005*. Durham, NC: Pew Health Professions Commission.

Spiro, H. (1993). What is empathy and can it be taught? In H. M. Spiro, M. G. McCrea Curnen, E. Peschel, & D. St. James (Eds.), *Empathy and the practice of medicine* (pp. 7–14). New Haven, CT: Yale University Press.

Suchman, A., Roter, D., Green, M., & Lipkin, M. (1993). Physician satisfaction with primary care office visits. Collaborative Study Group of the American Academy of the Physician and the Patient. *Medical Care, 31*, 1083–92.

Tess, J., Baier, C., Eckenfels, E. J., & Yogev, R. (1997). Medical students act as big brothers/big sisters to support human immunodeficiency virus-infected children's psychosocial needs. *Archives of Pediatrics and Adolescent Medicine, 151*, 189–192.

Tresolini, C. P. (1994). *The Pew–Fetzer Task Force. Health professions education and relationship-centered care*. San Francisco, CA: Pew Health Professions Commission.

Underwood, L. G. (1999). Daily spiritual experiences. In R. Ables, C. Ellison, L. George, E. Idler, N. Krause, J. Levin, M. Ory, K. Pargament, L. Powell, L. Underwood, & D. Williams (Eds.), *Multidimensional measurement of religiousness/spirituality for use in health research: A report of the Fetzer Insitute/National Insitute on Aging Working Group*. Kalamazoo, MI: John E. Fetzer Institute.

Underwood, L. G. (2002). The human experience of compassionate love: Conceptual mapping and data from selected studies. In S. G. Post, L. G. Underwood, J. P. Schloss, & W. B. Hurlbut (Eds.), *Altruism and altruistic love: Science, philosophy, and religion in dialogue* (pp. p72–88). New York: Oxford University Press.

Underwood, L. G. (2006). Ordinary spiritual experience: Qualitative research, interpretive guidelines and population distribution for the Daily Spiritual Experience Scale. *Archive for the Psychology of Religion/Archiv für Religionpsychologie, 28*(1), 181–218.

Van Amberg, R. (1997). A Copernican revolution in clinical ethics: Engagement versus disengagement. *American Journal of Occupational Therapy, 51*, 186–190.

Van Manen, M. (1990). *Researching lived experience: Human science for an action sensitive pedagogy*. Albany, NY: State University of New York Press.

Wikstrom, B. (2003). A picture of a work of art as an empathy teaching strategy in nurse education complementary to theoretical knowledge. *Journal of Professional Nursing, 19*(1), 49–54.

Wilkes, M., Milgrom, E., & Hoffman, J. R. (2002). Towards more empathic care medical students: A medical student hospitalization experience. *Medical Education, 36*(6), 528–533.

Williamson, M. (2002). *Everyday grace.* New York: Riverhead Press.

Yeo, M., & Longhurst, M. (1996). Intimacy in the patient–physician relationship. *Canadian Family Physician, 42*, 1505–1508.

13

Caregiving in Sociocultural Context

Norman D. Giesbrecht

The language of love has many dialects. One person may draw close and affirm their care with gentle words, another may move away so as to provide freedom to grow, and yet another may sit in silence simply sharing his or her presence. These behavioral expressions of compassionate love are influenced not only by psychosocial characteristics of the individual, but also by macro-system factors such as sociocultural worldview (Bronfenbrenner, 1979). The present study explores the role of psychological and sociocultural factors in facilitating compassionate love for persons with developmental disabilities. Compassionate care is understood in terms of Bowlby's (1969/1982) caregiving system, an innate behavioral system in which a "stronger, wiser" caregiver responds to the physical, psychological, and social needs of another, provides protection, comfort, and support, and serves as a "secure base" for the other to explore the world. A theoretical path model of caregiving is proposed, incorporating constructs from attachment-caregiving theory (Bowlby, 1969/1982) and cross-cultural research (e.g., Carlson & Harwood, 2003; Rothbaum, Weisz, Pott, Miyake, & Morelli, 2000), and evaluated using empirical data from 594 support staff for persons with cognitive, physical, and/or psychiatric impairments. This theoretical model focuses on the substrate of cognitive, affective, and sociocultural factors proposed by Underwood (Chapter 1, this volume) in the behavioral expression of compassionate love for adults with cognitive impairments.

Attachment and Caregiving

According to Bowlby (1969/1982), human beings are equipped with innate attachment and caregiving behavioral control systems, because emotional attachment to caregivers (e.g., parents) and providing care to dependent individuals (e.g., children, elderly family members) enhances the chances survival, reproduction, and successful parenting. The function of the attachment system is to respond to requests for help and provide protection and support to others who are dependent or unable to fend for themselves. The caregiver and dependent other establish a "goal-directed partnership" (Bowlby, 1969/1982) in which the caregiver provides a "safe haven" of protection to help alleviate the other's distress and a secure base to support the other's exploration, growth, and development.

Research indicates that Bowlby's (1969/1982) theory of attachment and caregiving has important implications for a dependent adult's health and psychobiological functioning (Diamond & Hicks, 2004) and the caregiving relationship between health professionals and patients (Ciechanowski, Katon, Russo, & Walker, 2001; Fricchione, 2002). The ability to provide effective care to another is a consequence of having witnessed and benefited from good care provided by one's own attachment figures, which increases one's sense of security and provides models of good caregiving (Collins & Feeney, 2000, Kunce & Shaver, 1994). A plethora of studies have shown that an individual's attachment style, assessed along two dimensions of attachment-related avoidance and attachment-related anxiety (Brennan, Clark, & Shaver, 1998), is related to psychological phenomena that promote effective caregiving. Attachment security (i.e., low scores on avoidance and anxiety) is related to positive conceptions of self and others, cognitive openness and information-processing flexibility, relationship commitment, willingness to provide caregiving to a relationship partner, compassionate responses to others' suffering, and willingness to interact with threatening outgroup members (see Mikulincer & Shaver, 2004 for a review).

Current theory suggests that attachment security does not activate the caregiving system directly, but rather provides a solid and stable psychological foundation that enables an individual to respond empathically without being overwhelmed by another's suffering or threatened by the interdependence entailed by caregiving (Mikulincer, Shaver, Gillath, & Nitzberg, 2005). In contrast, attachment avoidance is negatively associated with empathic reactions to others' suffering, including willingness to help a distressed person (e.g., Feeney & Collins, 2001; Joireman, Needham, & Cummings, 2002; Lopez, 2001; Wayment, 2006). Research indicates that avoidant people report less inclination to take the perspective of a distressed person (Corcoran & Mallinckrodt, 2000; Joireman et al., 2002), less ability to share another person's feelings (Trusty, Ng, & Watts, 2005), less sense of communion with others, less willingness to take responsibility for others' welfare (Collins & Read, 1990; Shaver, Collins, & Clark, 1996; Zuroff, Moskowitz, & Cote, 1999), and endorse fewer other-focused, altruistic motives for volunteering (Gillath et al., 2005). Avoidant people are less likely to be cooperative and other-oriented (Van Lange, Otten, DeBruin, & Joireman, 1997), write comforting messages to a distressed person (Weger & Polcar, 2002), offer effective help in relation to hypothetical scenarios (Drach-Zahavy, 2004), or engage in volunteer, philanthropic activities (Gillath et al., 2005).

Attachment anxiety is associated with personal distress in response to another's suffering, but not actual helping. It appears to promote arousal and self-preoccupation with the needy role but mitigates against the objective perspective-taking necessary for effective caregiving responses. As a consequence, anxiously-attached individuals tend to engage in caregiving that lacks sensitivity to the expressed need of another and tends to result in intrusiveness and higher levels of personal distress (Feeney & Collins, 2004). People who score relatively high on measures of attachment anxiety report higher levels of personal distress while witnessing others' distress (Britton & Fuendeling, 2005; Joireman et al., 2002), offer less effective help to physically ill people in hypothetical scenarios (Drach-Zahavy, 2004), rate intrusive and neglectful caregiving responses to elderly people's needs as less abusive and more typical than these responses are viewed by less anxious people (Malley-Morrison, You, & Mills, 2000), and score higher on a measure of unmitigated communion (Fritz & Helgeson, 1998; Shaver et al., 1996). Internal attachment representations thus appear to play an important role in the accurate discernment of another's need, and the effective response (or lack of response) to this perceived need.

Attachment also has been linked to a caregiver's ability to cope with the psychological, social, and physical demands that arise from caregiving responsibilities. Appropriate self-care appears to an important element in mitigating the negative effects of caregiving stress on general well-being (Acton, 2002). Attachment anxiety is associated with higher levels of compulsive caregiving and lower levels of self-care (Feeney, 1996; Kunce & Shaver, 1994). In the context of spousal caregiving, secure attachment and comfort with closeness is related to support-seeking, whereas attachment anxiety is related to self-centered caregiving that seeks to meet one's own relational needs rather than those of a partner (Feeney & Hohaus, 2001). Attachment is related not only to an individual's ability to care for others, but also to the self-care skills of defusing the personal distress response that activated the caregiving system, distinguishing between the needs of the self and another, and effectively soliciting social support to meet one's own needs for help, comfort, or reassurance.

Caregiving in Sociocultural Context

The role of sociocultural context in the development of attachment and caregiving representations is an important but underresearched consideration (Rothbaum et al., 2000). Although Bowlby (1969/1982) theorized that the caregiving system is an innate biologically evolved regulatory system, these "globally adaptive behavioral propensities ... become realized in a specific way dependent on the cultural niche" (van IJzendoorn & Sagi, 1999, p. 714). Social norms influence caregiving behavior both explicitly and implicitly. Normative expectations about the caregiving role are usually explicitly stated in the policies and procedures of health-care organizations, government legislation, and training curricula. Social representations of the idealized caregiver are internalized at the individual level and shape the affective-laden beliefs and cognitive appraisals that activate a person's caregiving responses (Carlson & Harwood, 2003).

Cross-cultural research (e.g., Carlson & Harwood, 2003; Rothbaum et al., 2000) has documented significant differences in caregiving representations and behaviors across two primary dimensions, that of independent and interdependent self-construal. Western nations, such as North America and Europe, are characterized by an emphasis on individual rights and responsibilities, whereas many other cultures and nations are guided by a focus on the relationships and social roles that connect individuals together as a group. As a consequence, caregiving in an interdependent sociocultural context is focused on the goals of promoting emotional closeness and social harmony, and care recipients are encouraged to develop multiple social relationships and accommodate themselves to the larger social group. (Matsumoto & Juang, 2004). Caregiver responses are proactive rather than reactive, guided by anticipatory cognitive appraisals and attentiveness to situational cues, and are characterized by positive other-oriented affect (e.g., sympathy, empathy, respect) that promote relatedness and minimize disagreement. In contrast, caregivers in an independent sociocultural context focus on the goal of facilitating individuation and autonomous exploration. Caregiver responses are restrained by respect for the recipient's independent efforts to satisfy his or her own needs and activated in response to explicit requests or overt indications of need. Care recipients are encouraged to develop self-assertion and self-advocacy skills, including the overt emotional expression of pride, frustration, and disagreement, which enable them to successfully interact in a competitive independent society.

Caregiving Norms in Health-care Organizations

Organizations that fulfill a socially mandated caregiving role, such as group homes for individuals with disabilities, also are characterized by sociocultural values and norms that may reflect an interdependent or independent ethic of care. Adults with cognitive and/or physical impairments who live in a group-home environment have accumulated considerable life experience, developed their own individual personality, and engage in relatively long-term relationships with the support staff. These factors provide caregivers with a unique opportunity to develop mutual friendships and reciprocal relationships, and embrace the person beyond the disability. Alternately, caregivers may view relational engagement as intrusive and instead seek to foster self-sufficiency and independent decision-making. Although not mutually exclusive, organizational caregiving norms of relational engagement versus independent living have important consequences for the cognitive representations, affective expression, social interaction, and instrumental behaviors that characterize the caregiving relationship.

To investigate the influence of an organization's sociocultural caregiving norms on caregiving behavior, I conducted a study of 594 support staff for persons with disabilities. These participants were recruited from organizations reflecting either an independent sociocultural ethic of care (two large multi-site Community Living organizations on the west coast of Canada) or an interdependent sociocultural ethic of care (40 l'Arche sites across the United States and Canada). The two large multi-site Association for Community Living organizations that participated in this study were characterized by an independent caregiving ethic. The stated mission of these organizations was to assist individuals with disabilities to "participate and contribute fully and to be recognized and accepted as valued members in the community" (Mission and Vision Statement). Caregiving interactions were guided by a Declaration of Rights, which included the rights of persons with disabilities to "Be treated as an equal; Make your own choices; Take responsibility for the choices you make ... Receive help only when you ask for it; Choose who helps you; Complain without getting into trouble; Be heard, listened to; Have a formal process for appealing decisions."

In contrast, the interdependent l'Arche communities that participated in this study were characterized by vision statements and explicit organizational principles that reflected an interdependent caregiving ethic. L'Arche is a worldwide network of communities in which support staff and individuals with disabilities share a common life together. The stated mission of l'Arche is to create communities which "welcome people with a mental handicap ... [as] a sign that a society, to be truly human, must be founded on welcome and respect for the weak and downtrodden" (Charter). In l'Arche homes, caregiving interactions are guided by an ethic of interpersonal relationship and mutuality that holds:

> Whatever their gifts or their limitations, people are all bound together in a common humanity ... [and] the deepest need of a human being is to love and be loved. ... To develop their abilities and talents to the full, realizing all their potential as individuals, they need ... to live in an atmosphere of

trust, security, and mutual affection. They need to be valued, accepted and supported in real and warm relationships. (l'Arche Charter: Fundamental Principles)

Altruistic Caregiving

The caregiving system is inherently altruistic (van den Mark, van IJzendoorn, & Bakermans-Kranenburg, 2002) and is considered to be the locus and foundation of empathy and compassion in situations in which one person reacts to another's pain, need, or distress (Mikulincer et al., 2005). Theory and research on altruism provide valuable insights into the nature of compassionate caregiving. For example, Batson's (1991) theoretical distinction between personal distress and empathy provides a useful conceptual framework for understanding the self-preoccupied responses of anxiously-attached caregivers versus the empathic assistance provided by securely-attached caregivers. In an integrative review of the literature, Krebs and Van Hesteren (1994) highlight the developmental nature of altruism and the role of social cognition in effective helping. Caregiving behavior is contingent upon social cognition about another's need, since good caregivers must sensitively and flexibly respond to attachment needs; be aware of the other's point of view, feelings, and intentions, and adjust their own behavior in response to the contingencies of the situation (Bowlby, 1988). The altruism literature consistently confirms the importance of empathic sensitivity and perspective-taking ability in helping behaviors. These characteristics parallel the qualities of emotional sensitivity and affective responsiveness, and cognitive appraisal of another's need, that the attachment literature indicates are essential to effective caregiving (e.g., Bowlby, 1988).

The underlying motivations that people have for helping others also play an important role in determining the quality of care that is provided. Conceptually, the provision of support may reflect either egoistic or altruistic motives which may be rooted in an other-oriented empathic reaction or a self-oriented aversive response that seeks to alleviate personal distress (Mikulincer et al., 2001). Research indicates that responsive caregivers report altruistic motives (Feeney & Collins, 2004) and endorse benevolent and transcendent ideals (Mikulincer et al., 2001, 2003). Altruistic motivations also are linked to increased relationship satisfaction between individuals over time, and decreased compulsive and/or controlling caregiving (Feeney & Collins, 2003). Research suggests that relational spirituality, reflected in a commitment to love, interpersonal relatedness, and sources of meaning beyond the self, also can serve to motivate and sustain effective caregiving (Faver, 2004).

Self-Transformative Outcomes of Caregiving

Research has shown that helping others can accrue benefits to the self, including greater life satisfaction, larger social networks, better mental health, and further expansion of altruistic behavior (e.g., Morrow-Howell, Hinterlog, Rozario, & Tang, 2003). Many philosophical and theological traditions are founded on the premise that it is "more blessed to give than to receive," and there is an extensive body of spiritual literature that describes how the apparent loss of self in "self-giving love" paradoxically becomes the source of a deeper life. Underwood (Chapter 1, this volume) observes that the expression of compassionate love can result in dynamic feedback that impacts one's sense of identity and enhances the capacity to love. In attachment-theoretical terms, just as a secure attachment style promotes effective caregiving, positive caregiving behaviors may provide positive feedback to the caregiver's attachment system that facilitates the reparation of unresolved attachment traumas (Mikulincer & Shaver, 2004). Attachment experiences provide the basis for internal working models that guide the expression of caregiving behaviors for others, and these mental representations are instrumental in developing the capacity to comfort and care for the self (Mikulincer & Shaver, 2004). It would seem reasonable to expect that the empathic and perspective-taking abilities developed in the caregiving role also would be internalized in an increased capacity to care for the self, and to repatriate aspects of the caregiver's own internal attachment representations. Gillath et al. (2005) report results that suggest that frequent engagement in volunteer activities moderates the association between insecure attachment and loneliness and interpersonal problems among individuals high in attachment anxiety (but not among those high in attachment avoidance). Gillath et al. (2005) also report that altruistic motives (e.g., compassion, humanitarian concern) and understanding motives (e.g., new learning experiences, exercising skills and abilities) were positively related to social well-being and negatively related to attachment avoidance among samples in three different countries.

Phelps, Belsky, and Crnic (1998) observed that the essential element in attachment reparation appears to be a supportive relationship that provides the individual with the safety to access and acknowledge painful emotions and beliefs. This "corrective emotional experience" can promote cognitive restructuring, flexible problem-solving, and adaptive behavioral changes. Noam (1993) proposed several "windows of change" that facilitate self-transformation, including childlike playfulness, emotional authenticity, emotional and relational perspectives on "truth," and free-flowing interplay between the public and private self; these are often characteristic features of persons with a cognitive impairment. Although the caregiver functions as a "stronger and wiser other" for the individual with a cognitive disability, human nature is characterized by "normative vulnerabilities" and continued struggles between strength and weakness across the life span, regardless of the level of cognitive, social, or ego development (Noam, 1996). The childlike playfulness, emotional authenticity, and freedom from a "public persona" modeled by persons with cognitive impairment can facilitate a "corrective emotional experience" that enables a caregiver to reconnect with these vital aspects of the self and explore alternate ways of being in the world. The acceptance of weakness in the care recipient can enhance the caregiver's acceptance of his or her own vulnerability, and thus serve as a catalyst for greater self-integration. The belief that caregiving relationships between able-bodied assistants and core members with disabilities can facilitate self-transformation is a fundamental principle of the l'Arche caregiving ethic, which states:

> People with mental handicaps often possess qualities of welcome, wonderment, spontaneity, and directness ... able to touch hearts and call others to unity through their simplicity and vulnerability. ... [modeling] the essential values of the heart without which knowledge, power, and action lose their meaning and purpose. ... [so we can] rediscover what is essential: Committed relationships, openness and the acceptance of weakness, a life of friendship and solidarity. (l'Arche Charter: Fundamental Principles)

Purpose of the Study

The purpose of this study was to explore specific characteristics within the substrate of psychological and sociocultural factors (Underwood, Chapter 1, this volume) that facilitate compassionate caregiving for adults with developmental disabilities. The specific aims of the research were to: (a) investigate the influence of sociocultural context on psychosocial predictors of compassionate care; (b) formulate and test a theoretical model of caregiving that integrates the literature on sociocultural context, attachment-caregiving, and altruism; and (c) to examine participant narratives of self-transformative outcomes arising from caregiving interactions.

Sociocultural Context, Psychosocial Characteristics, and Attachment-Caregiving

Cross-cultural research (e.g., Matsumoto & Juang, 2004; Rothbaum et al., 2000) led me to expect that an interdependent versus independent sociocultural context would be reflected in significant differences in participants' self-reported psychosocial characteristics and attachment representations of the caregiver–client relationship. To confirm that participants in the two samples maintained a self-representation consistent with an interdependent (or communal) or independent sociocultural ethic, I hypothesized:

> H1: *l'Arche participants would evidence significantly higher endorsement of an interdependent self-construal and Community Living participants would evidence a significantly higher endorsement of an independent self-construal.*

Consistent with cross-cultural theory that an interdependent ethic is guided by values emphasizing interpersonal closeness and positive other-oriented affect, I also hypothesized that:

> H2: *l'Arche caregivers would evidence significantly higher endorsement of the psychosocial characteristics of altruistic love and empathy than Community Living caregivers.*

> H3: *l'Arche caregivers would evidence significantly lower endorsement of attachment avoidance in the caregiver–client relationship than Community Living caregivers.*

Theoretical Model of Caregiving

A theoretical model (see Figure 13.1) was formulated that integrated current theory and research on sociocultural context, attachment-caregiving, and altruism. Cross-cultural theory and research led me to expect that an interdependent self-construal would positively predict altruistic love. Informed by Vanier's (1997) spiritual and philosophical perspective on caring for people with disabilities, I expected that relational spirituality also would positively predict altruistic love. Altruistic love was hypothesized to be a positive predictor, both directly and indirectly through the facilitation of empathy and perspective-taking, of caregiving. Drawing from the attachment-caregiving litera-ture (e.g., Bowlby, 1988), attachment avoidance and anxiety were expected to be negative predictors, both directly and indirectly through the facilitation of empathy and perspective-taking, of caregiving. Attachment anxiety also was expected to be a negative predictor of self-care in the enactment of caregiving behaviors. Based on the altruism literature (e.g., Batson, 1991), empathy and perspective-taking were identified as affective and cognitive predictors, respectively, of effective caregiving behaviors.

The experience of self-transformation shown in Figure 13.1 was mod-eled as a feedback process whereby (a) altruistic love facilitates positive caregiver–client attachment; (b) positive caregiver–client attachment prompts experiences of relational spirituality; and (c) relational spirituality positively contributes to altruistic love. The rationale for this feedback model was informed by the l'Arche caregiving principle that persons with mental handicaps often possess unique qualities of spontaneity, directness, and acceptance that can facilitate self-transformation in the assistant (i.e., caregiver). These self-transformative experiences result when the assistant is willing to enter into a mutual, egalitarian, attachment relationship with the core member (i.e., person with a disability), and their primary outcome is a deeper sense of compassion for himself or herself and others. This synergistic relationship and mutual experience of transformation is conceptualized in terms of relational spirituality, wherein each partner offers forgiveness and an expression of Divine love to the other. Since attachment anxiety has been implicated in attentive, but at times intrusive, caregiving (Feeney & Collins, 2004), caregivers high in anxiety may be perceived by clients as either responsive or intrusive; caregivers low in anxiety also may be high in avoidance. As a result, I surmised that low attachment avoidance scores would provide a conceptually clearer and more reliable indicator of positive attachment than the measure of attachment anxiety.

Based on attachment-caregiving theory and altruism theory, I hypothesized that:

> H4: The theoretical model would be empirically supported in both the l'Arche sample and the Community Living sample.

Informed by the value placed on other-oriented affect in an interdependent worldview, and the integration of spiritual values in the l'Arche caregiving ethic, I expected that an interdependent caregiving ethic would be evidenced in the following differences in the strength of path relationships across the two groups:

> H5: Altruistic love would exert a stronger influence on caregiving and empathy among l'Arche participants than among Community Living participants.

> H6: Relational spirituality would exert a stronger influence on altruistic love among l'Arche participants than among Community Living participants.

Recognizing the value placed on autonomy and self-validation in an independent worldview, I expected that the influence of an independent caregiving ethic would be evidenced in a difference in the strength of the following path relationship:

> H7: Self-care would exert a stronger influence on caregiving among Community Living participants than among l'Arche participants.

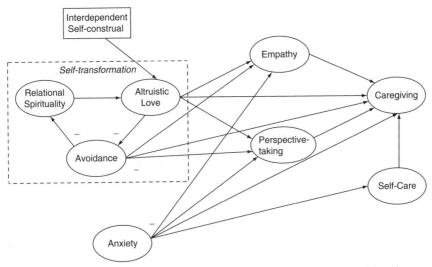

All paths connected with the Avoidance and Anxiety constructs hypothesize a negative relationship.

Figure 13.1   Theoretical Model of Caregiving

Self-Transformation Narratives

Participants responded to an open-ended question: "What changes have you experienced in your life as a result of being with people with disabilities?" In light of the parallels between Noam's (1993) theory of "windows of change" and the l'Arche philosophy of self-transformation through mutual relationships with persons with disabilities, I hypothesized the following:

> *H8: The self-transformation narratives of l'Arche participants would evidence significantly higher endorsement of experiences of self-acceptance and integration, relational mutuality, emotional authenticity, affirmation of life, and spirituality than the self-transformation narratives of Community Living participants.*

Method

In order to test these hypotheses, I recruited 594 participants from 14 American l'Arche communities, 26 Canadian l'Arche communities, and 2 large, multi-site Canadian Community Living organizations. A cover letter and survey were distributed to support staff in all 40 l'Arche communities across North America, and to multiple sites connected to 2 large

Community Living organizations in the Canadian Pacific Northwest. Participants completed standardized measures of caregiving and self-care (Kunce & Shaver, 1994), attachment anxiety and avoidance (Brennan et al., 1998), altruistic love (Underwood, O'Connell, & Saxena, 2001), empathic concern and perspective-taking (Davis, 1983), independent and interdependent self-construal (Singelis, 1994), and relational spirituality (McCullough, Pargament, & Thoresen, 2000; Underwood & Teresi, 2002). Participants also responded to open-ended questions regarding the rewards and challenges of caregiving, and experiences of transformation arising from caregiving interactions. Based on information available about staff levels, it is estimated that close to 100% of l'Arche staff across North America and 65–70% of Community Living staff participated in the study. Table 13.1 presents demographic information for the l'Arche and Community Living samples. Statistical comparisons indicated that Community Living participants evidenced a significantly higher mean age ($t = 3.1$; $p < .01$), more years of experience ($t = 6.7$; $p < .001$), and

Table 13.1   Demographic Information about Survey Participants

	Community Living (n = 207)	l'Arche (n = 364)
Age	39.6 (9.8)	36.5 (13.7)
Experience (years)	9.3 (6.5)	5.5 (6.4)
Preparation		
Professional training	131 (74%)	98 (27%)
Volunteer experience	74 (42%)	79 (22%)
Previous work experience	76 (43%)	101 (28%)
Gender		
Female	149 (72%)	235 (65%)
Male	58 (28%)	129 (35%)
Ethnicity		
Caucasian	156 (75%)	270 (74%)
Non-Caucasian	51 (25%)	94 (26%)
Marital status		
Married	120 (59%)	85 (23%)
Not married	84 (41%)	277 (77%)
Education		
High school	21 (10%)	81 (22%)
College/university	184 (90%)	281 (78%)
Religion		
Catholic	53 (27%)	226 (64%)
Protestant	61 (31%)	92 (26%)
Other/none	84 (42%)	36 (10%)

Note: Percentages are of those people who actually answered this question.

a significantly higher percentage of participants with professional training ($X^2 = 21.9$; $p<.001$). The l'Arche sample had a significantly higher percentage of participants who were not married ($X^2 = 11.0$; $p<.001$) and who had a Catholic religious affiliation ($X^2 = 15.0$; $p<.001$) than the Community Living sample.

Results

Sociocultural context, psychosocial characteristics and attachment-caregiving. Cross-cultural theory and research provided the basis for several hypotheses regarding differences in caregivers' psychosocial characteristics and attachment-caregiving as a function of sociocultural self-construal. The first hypothesis was that l'Arche caregivers and Community Living caregivers would evidence significantly greater endorsement of an interdependent or independent self-construal, respectively. This hypothesis was supported; independent samples t-tests indicated that l'Arche participants had a significantly higher mean score on the measure of interdependent self-construal and Community Living participants had a significantly higher mean score on the measure of independent self-construal (see Table 13.2). These results confirmed that caregivers in each sample maintained a self-construal consistent with their organization's sociocultural ethic, and support the conceptualization of these healthcare organizations as representing an interdependent or independent sociocultural caregiving ethic.

The second hypothesis was that the influence of an interdependent caregiving ethic would be evidenced in participants' psychosocial characteristics of altruistic love and empathy. This hypothesis also was supported; l'Arche participants had significantly higher mean scores on measures of altruistic love and empathy (see Table 13.2). Although no a priori hypothesis was formulated, Community Living participants had a significantly higher mean score on the measure of perspective-taking. These results are consistent with cross-cultural research concerning the primary values of each sociocultural ethic, and the embodiment of these values in social conceptions of the ideal caregiver. The emphasis on positive other-oriented affect and relational closeness in an interdependent caregiving ethic can facilitate the development and expression of altruistic concern for others and empathic sensitivity to their needs. In contrast, an independent caregiving ethic emphasizes the uniqueness of each individual. Perspective-taking would be an important skill in acknowledging this distinctiveness and providing opportunities for individual expression and negotiation of differences of opinion.

The third hypothesis was that the influence of an interdependent ethic would be evident in lower attachment avoidance. This hypothesis was confirmed; l'Arche caregivers had a significantly lower mean score on the measure of attachment avoidance. This result is consistent with the emphasis on relational closeness in an interdependent ethic. Although no a priori hypothesis had been formulated, l'Arche participants also had a significantly higher mean score on the measure of attachment anxiety. It is possible that the interdependent emphasis on relational closeness, particularly in situations in which a caregiver has limited training (as was the case with many l'Arche assistants) and/or care recipients have extremely limited communication skills (e.g., core members with autism spectrum disorder or co-morbid psychiatric diagnoses), may lead to heightened anxiety in assistants. Finally, l'Arche participants also had a significantly higher mean score on the Relational Spirituality measure than did Community Living participants. This result is consistent with the integration of spiritual values into the l'Arche caregiving ethic, which helps to strengthen and sustain their commitment to mutual relationships by placing these into a broader philosophical and moral context.

Community Living caregivers had a significantly higher mean score on caregiving than did l'Arche caregivers. Consistent with previous research (Feeney, 1996), the caregiving measure comprised three subscales that assessed *proximity versus distance, sensitivity versus insensitivity,* and *cooperation versus control.* Comparisons of these subscales indicated that

Table 13.2   Means, Standard Deviations, and Independent t-Test Values for Measures across Independent Community Living and Interdependent l'Arche Samples

	ACL (n = 207)	L'Arche (n = 364)	t-value
Sociocultural ethic			
Interdependent	16.8 (2.5)	17.6 (2.3)	4.1***
Independent	17.8 (2.2)	16.7 (2.9)	5.2***
Psychosocial characteristics			
Altruistic love	39.1 (4.3)	40.9 (4.0)	5.0***
Empathy	27.4 (3.1)	28.4 (3.4)	3.5***
Perspective-taking	28.1 (2.9)	27.0 (3.2)	4.2***
Relational spirituality[1]	34.5 (11.1)	39.3 (7.9)	5.1***
Caregiver attachment			
Avoidance	23.0 (4.3)	19.2 (4.5)	10.2***
Anxiety	17.9 (4.6)	20.4 (4.6)	6.5***
Caregiving	89.5 (8.1)	87.4 (9.5)	2.1**
Self-care	29.2 (4.0)	28.8 (4.3)	1.2

* = $p<.05$; ** = $p<.01$; ***= $p<.001$
[1] 36 Community Living participants did not complete the Relational Spirituality scale ($N=171$).

Community Living participants ($M = 31.5$; s.d. = 3.3) had a significantly higher mean score than l'Arche participants ($M = 29.5$; s.d. = 4.0) on the *cooperation versus control* subscale ($t = 6.3$; $p<.001$). The emphasis on facilitating autonomous decision-making in the Community Living sample may have prompted greater attentiveness to caregiver–client discussion and collaborative decision-making.

Theoretical model of caregiving. The LISREL 8.3 program was used to test the fourth hypothesis that the path model of caregiving (see Figure 13.1) would be empirically supported across both samples. After reviewing the modification indices, a path between interdependent self-construal and relational spirituality was added because it could be justified on both theoretical and statistical grounds (Jöreskog & Sorbom, 1993). The LISREL results for the initial theoretical model indicated an adequate fit for both the l'Arche sample (*GFI* = .93, *AGFI* = .86, *RMR* = .09) and the Community Living sample (*GFI* = .93; *AGFI* = .85, *RMR* = .09). The final path models for the Community Living and l'Arche samples are outlined in Figures 13.2 and 13.3, respectively. Path beta coefficients were tested for statistical significance by referencing a table for the t-values (computed as beta path coefficient divided by standard error of measurement) using the appropriate degrees of freedom for each sample.

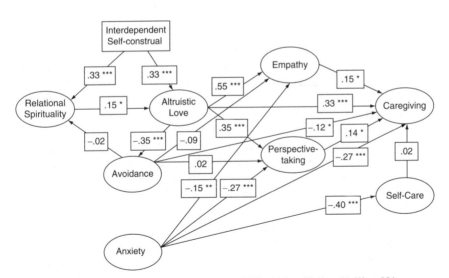

Normal Theory WLS $\chi^2_{16df} = 72.5$; *GFI* = .93; *AGFI* = .82; *RMR* = .09 $^*p<.05$; $^{**}p<.01$; $^{***}p<.001$.

Figure 13.2   LISREL path model for independent Community Living organizations (N = 207)

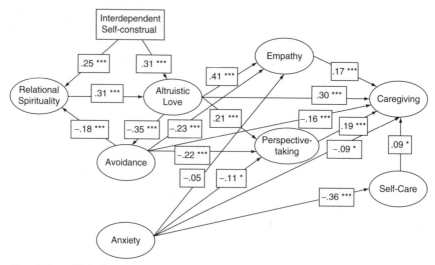

Normal Theory WLS χ^2_{16df} =129.0; *GFI*=.93; *AGFI*=.82; *RMR*=.09 *p<.05; **p<.01; ***p<.001.

Figure 13.3   LISREL path model for interdependent l'Arche organizations (N = 364)

Path models for both samples had a good fit, as indicated by Goodness of Fit (GFI) indices above .90 and Root Mean Square Residuals (RMR) below .10.

An examination of the beta coefficients across both path models indicated that altruistic love was a powerful predictor of caregiving, both directly and indirectly through its effects on empathy and perspective-taking. These results are consistent with a long-standing principle across many spiritual and philosophical traditions which holds that love is (or should be) at the heart of effective helping behavior, and that without love such actions may be as discordant as a "resounding gong or clanging cymbal" (KJ ver. Bible, 1 Cor. 13:1). The significant path relationships among altruistic love, caregiving, empathy, perspective-taking, and avoidance suggests that altruistic love exerts its effects in at least three ways, namely:

(a)   as a motivational impetus to engage in caregiving behaviors that entail sensitivity to another's needs and signals for help, physical and emotional availability (i.e. proximity), and cooperative caregiving interactions;

(b)   in facilitating the empathic concern and perspective-taking skills that foster effective caregiving responses that are sensitive to, and accurately reflect, the expressed needs of the care recipient; and

(c)   in facilitating attachment representations and behaviors that mini-
      mize detachment and avoidance in the caregiver–care recipient
      relationship.

An examination of the path relationships also indicates that an interdependent self-construal had a significant effect on altruistic love and relational
spirituality across both samples. This finding was somewhat surprising, as
I had expected these relationships to be significant only among l'Arche
participants. These results suggest that, even within the context of an
organizational caregiving ethic emphasizing professional distance, the
adoption of an other-oriented interdependent approach has positive
implications for one's motivation to care for others and one's spirituality.

The fifth and sixth hypotheses were that the influence of an interdependent sociocultural ethic would be evidenced in the stronger influence
of altruistic love on caregiving and empathy (H5), and the stronger influence of relational spirituality on altruistic love (H6), among l'Arche participants. These hypotheses were evaluated with t-tests on the beta
coefficients for these path relationships across samples. An examination of
the path coefficients in each model suggested that there also would be
value in statistically comparing the avoidance and anxiety path relationships across samples, although no a priori hypotheses had been formulated. Table 13.3 presents the t-values and significance associated with
differences in the path beta coefficients across the l'Arche and Community
Living samples.

With regard to the fifth hypothesis that altruistic love would exert a
stronger influence on caregiving and empathy among l'Arche participants, the strength of the relationship between altruistic love and caregiving was comparable among l'Arche participants ($\beta=.30$; $p<.001$) and
Community Living participants ($\beta=.33$; $p<.001$). The relationship
between altruistic love and empathy was stronger among Community
Living participants ($\beta=.55$; $p<.001$) than l'Arche participants ($\beta=.41$;
$p<.001$), and this difference approached statistical significance. Since
both path comparisons were not significant at $p<.05$, the fifth hypothesis
was rejected. However, the strength of these relationships across both
samples suggests that altruistic love exerts a powerful effect on caregiving, both directly and indirectly through the facilitation of empathy,
regardless of sociocultural context. An examination of the path models
indicated that altruistic love was arguably the most powerful predictor in
the model, exerting significant positive effects on caregiving, empathy, and
perspective-taking, and a significant negative effect on avoidance, across
both samples. Although the behavioral expression of altruistic love may
have cultural variants, its motivational power and positive direct and indirect effects on caregiving behavior may transcend cultural differences.

With regard to the sixth hypothesis, relational spirituality had a stronger influence on altruistic love among l'Arche participants (β=.31; p<.001) than among Community Living participants (β=.15; p<.05) but this effect was only marginally significant (p=.06). The seventh hypothesis that self-care would be a significantly more important influence on caregiving among Community Living participants was not supported. In fact, this path was not statistically significant in the Community Living sample. It may be that the significantly higher attachment avoidance in the caregiver–client relationships of Community Living participants served to reduce potential caregiver stress, and thus mitigate the relation between self-care and caregiving.

Although no a priori hypotheses had been formulated with regard to paths related to attachment avoidance and anxiety, an examination of the path coefficients suggested there might be value in conducting exploratory comparisons. T-tests revealed several interesting differences in the role of attachment avoidance and anxiety across samples (see Table 13.3). Attachment anxiety was a significantly more powerful predictor of both caregiving and perspective-taking in the independent Community Living

Table13. 3   Beta, Standard Error of Measurement, and t-Value for Path Comparisons

Path	Community Living	L'Arche	t-value
Altruistic love predicting			
Caregiving	.33 (.07)	.30 (.05)	0.4
Empathy	.55 (.06)	.41 (.05)	1.8+
Perspective-taking	.35 (.08)	.21 (.05)	1.5
Self-care predicting caregiving	.02 (.06)	.09 (.04)	0.9
Self-transformation			
Avoidance predicting relational spirituality	−.02 (.06)	−.18 (.05)	2.0*
Relational Spirituality predicting altruistic love	.15 (.07)	.31 (.05)	−1.9+
Attachment anxiety predicting			
Caregiving	−.27 (.06)	−.09 (.04)	−2.5*
Empathy	−.15 (.06)	−.05 (.04)	−1.4
Perspective-taking	−.27 (.06)	−.11 (.05)	−2.0*
Attachment avoidance predicting			
Caregiving	−.12 (.06)	−.16 (.04)	0.6
Empathy	−.09 (.06)	−.23 (.05)	1.8+
Perspective-taking	.02 (.07)	−.22 (.05)	2.8**

+ = p<.07; * = p<.05; ** = p<.01; *** = p<.001.

sample. In contrast, attachment avoidance was a significantly more powerful predictor of caregiving and perspective-taking in the interdependent l'Arche sample, and approached statistical significance as a more powerful predictor of empathy. These results are perhaps best interpreted in light of the sociocultural norms of each sample. Within an independent caregiving ethic, the norm of "professional distance" in the caregiving relationship is consistent with higher levels of attachment avoidance. However, the expectation that caregivers facilitate independent decision-making among individuals struggling with cognitive and communication impairments could heighten caregivers' anxiety and self-doubt about the accuracy of their signal-interpretation and perspective-taking with clients. In contrast, the social norm of relational intimacy in an interdependent caregiving ethic may allow for higher levels of anxiety and uncertainty. However, attachment avoidance or distancing oneself from a person with a disability may have an immediate and noticeable impact on caregiving interactions because it violates a fundamental principle.

Self-transformation narratives. A thematic analysis identified eight areas of growth and transformation in participants' narratives of change, namely: self-acceptance and integration, relational intimacy, spiritual growth, authenticity and affirmation of life, professional development, compassionate love, acceptance of others, and patience. Each participant's response was binary-coded to indicate the presence or absence of these themes. (All participants who provided data were included in this analysis.) A Discriminant Function Analysis (DFA) identified a statistically significant function (*Wilk's* $\Lambda_{8, 557}$=.72; $p<.001$), differentiating the transformative experiences endorsed by l'Arche versus Community Living participants (see Table 13.4). L'Arche participants were significantly more likely than community Living participants to report experience of self-acceptance and integration (X^2=15.7; $p<.001$), relational intimacy (X^2=18.5; $p<.001$), spiritual growth (X^2=11.3; $p<.001$), and authenticity and affirmation of life (X^2=9.7; $p<.01$). There were no significant differences between l'Arche and Community Living participants in the other themes of transformation; one-third or so of each group reported experiences of acceptance of others, professional development, and compassionate love.

The results supported the eighth hypothesis that l'Arche caregivers would evidence significantly higher endorsement of transformative experiences related to self-acceptance and integration, relational intimacy, emotional authenticity and affirmation of life, and spirituality. Participant accounts of self-acceptance and integration were consistent with Phelps et al.'s (1998) notion of a "corrective emotional experience" that facilitates restructuring of the internal attachment working model. An essential element appeared to be the opportunity to access past traumas and

Table 13.4   Self-Transformative Experiences Reported by Caregivers

Self-transformative experiences	DFA function loading	L'Arche (N = 363)	Community Living (N = 209)
Self-acceptance and integration	.63	62%	24%
Relational intimacy	.59	53%	17%
Spiritual growth	.49	24%	2%
Authenticity and affirmation of life	.46	58%	28%
Professional development	−.12	36%	41%
Compassionate love	.08	32%	27%
Acceptance of others	−.03	42%	42%
Patience	.01	21%	20%

internal contradictions, and integrate these into a coherent perspective of the self. A 31-year-old female assistant with five and a half years' experience described this process as follows:

> *I've discovered and faced my own dark side: my impatience sometimes, my high expectations of others and self … Some of my own personal problems emerged and I had to deal with them – being with people who are deeply wounded brings to surface my own wounds pain which was previously hidden so I can open myself for God's healing. Through pain I have discovered hidden treasures – in myself and in others … to see beauty, love in people around me – core members.*

Discussion

The findings of this study provide valuable insights into our understanding of the substrate of cognitive, affective, and sociocultural factors that facilitate compassionate care (Underwood, Chapter 1, this volume). The path model results confirmed that altruistic love, attachment avoidance and anxiety, empathy, and perspective-taking are all significant predictors of individual differences in the quality of caregiving provided to individuals with disabilities. There were significant differences in the mean scores on each of these psychosocial characteristics across groups, and significant differences in the effects of attachment avoidance and anxiety on caregiving as a function of sociocultural context. Among l'Arche participants, caregiver narratives and results for the self-transformation portion of the path model provided support for the thesis that compassionate care for others can facilitate self-transformation.

Consistent with findings reported by Mikulincer, Shaver, and Gillath (Chapter 8, this volume), attachment representations were an important element in the substrate of individual characteristics predicting compassionate care (Underwood, Chapter 1, this volume). This research extends this insight by highlighting the influence of sociocultural context on attachment-caregiving dynamics. From an attachment perspective, the sociocultural context findings provide valuable insights into our understanding of how "globally adaptive behavioral propensities ... become realized in a specific way dependent on the cultural niche" (van IJzendoorn & Sagi, 1999, p. 714). The results of this study suggest that an independent versus interdependent ethic has important consequences for the mental representation of the caregiving role, and lend support to the proposition that there are both universal and culture-specific aspects to attachment and caregiving processes (Rothbaum et al., 2000). Compassionate concern and sensitivity to an individual's unique signals, for example, are universal characteristics of the caregiving system. However, a caregiver's cognitive appraisal of, and affective sensitivity to, a signal, and subsequent behavioral response (or lack of response), are likely conditioned by sociocultural norms regarding desirable developmental outcomes and appropriate caregiving behaviors (Carlson & Harwood, 2003). The results of this study also reveal that attachment avoidance and anxiety exhibit different effects on caregiving as a function of sociocultural context.

Among Community Living participants, cognitive representations of the caregiving role were guided by an explicit Declaration of Rights that emphasized the rights of persons with disabilities to "Be treated as an equal; Make your own choices; Receive help only when you ask for it." This caregiving emphasis on autonomous client decision-making and "professional distance" is consistent with the significantly higher avoidance score evidenced among these participants' mental representation of the staff–client attachment-caregiving relationship. Perspective-taking and cooperative negotiation of client goals are essential caregiver skills in the goal-directed partnership designed to facilitate a client's independent exploration of the world, as evidenced in the significantly higher perspective-taking score. Professional training also is an essential prerequisite in understanding the perspective of the client, particularly when clients have cognitive and verbal impairments that hinder their ability to communicate their needs and desires, evidenced by the significantly higher proportion of Community Living caregivers who had professional training. Affective concerns were of secondary importance in the appraisal of clients' needs, as evidenced by the significantly lower mean scores on altruistic love and empathy.

Community Living participants exhibited significantly higher attachment avoidance, consistent with a socio-cultural emphasis on independence. Avoidance could be considered a normative response in the context of a caregiving ethic that emphasized professional distance, objective perspective-taking, and self-determination. However, attachment anxiety would be expected to negatively impact a caregiver's ability to accurately interpret client signals and underlying needs, and to provide decision-making support and social advocacy to facilitate the independent living of a person with a disability. This was empirically supported; attachment anxiety was a significantly more powerful negative predictor of caregiving quality and perspective-taking among Community Living caregivers than among l'Arche caregivers.

Among l'Arche participants, cognitive representations of the caregiving role were guided by an interdependent ethic of all people "bound together in a common humanity ... valued, accepted and supported in real and warm relationships." These affect-laden beliefs were important elements in the construction of the caregiver–core member relationship and in the appraisal of attachment-caregiving needs, evidenced in the significantly higher scores on empathy and altruistic love and the significantly lower attachment avoidance score. Within an interdependent caregiving ethic, the desirable end-state is a closely-knit community, and this goal is facilitated by positive other-oriented affect (e.g., sympathy, empathy, respect) that promotes relatedness, anticipatory appraisals of another's needs based on attentiveness to situational cues, and proactive caregiving responses. Altruistic love and empathic concern, rather than professional training and skills, are perceived to be an important motivation and psychological characteristic of an effective caregiver.

Relational mutuality and reciprocity are essential elements of an interdependent caregiver-dependent relationship, and a comparison of path model results across groups indicated that attachment avoidance was a powerful negative predictor of empathy and perspective-taking among l'Arche caregivers. The significantly lower attachment avoidance scores of l'Arche caregivers are consistent with an interdependent ethic in which caregivers seek to promote relational mutuality and community connection. An interdependent ethic also is characterized by the expectation that caregivers engage in anticipatory appraisals and proactive interventions. However, this may increase caregiver anxiety, particularly when working with individuals characterized by serious cognitive and verbal limitations, and may explain the significantly higher anxiety score among l'Arche participants.

Sociocultural norms provide caregiving ideals and normative behavioral expectations that shape the identification and discernment of a need, and define the repertoire of appropriate behavioral responses (including decisions regarding action or no action). As such, sociocultural context may exert an important influence on the motivation and discernment process, and subsequent behavioral response, in the model proposed by Underwood (Chapter 1, this volume). For example, an interdependent sociocultural context primes individuals to focus on the goals of emotional closeness and social harmony, and to utilize anticipatory cognitive appraisals and attentiveness to situational cues in the discernment of a need. The expression of compassionate care emphasizes positive other-oriented affect (e.g., sympathy, empathy, respect). An "appropriate action" is considered to be one that promotes interpersonal relatedness and minimizes disagreement. In contrast, an independent sociocultural context focuses attention on the goals of individuation and autonomous exploration, and caregivers' behavioral responses are activated by explicit requests or overt indications of need. It is likely that the care recipient's determination of whether a behavioral response was effective or ineffective in meeting a need also would be influenced by sociocultural expectations. Further research on the role of sociocultural values in the motivation and discernment process would be beneficial.

One of the most important findings of this study was that altruistic love was the most powerful predictor of caregiving, both directly and indirectly through facilitation of empathic concern and perspective-taking, regardless of sociocultural context. This result is consistent with the altruism literature, in which altruistic motivation is a consistent predictor of empathy and helping behavior (Batson, 1991). Giving of oneself for the good of another is a succinct definition of altruistic love, and the significant positive effect of altruistic love on caregiving suggests that it functions as a powerful motivational impetus for caring behaviors. The indirect effects of altruistic love on caregiving, mediated by empathy and perspective-taking, suggest that altruistic love also promotes the cognitive appraisals and affective responsiveness that enable caregiving behaviors to effectively meet the care recipient's needs.

Altruistic love evidenced a significant negative relationship with attachment avoidance. Griffin and Bartholomew (1994) identified the avoidant attachment style as characterized by a negative perception of the other and an overtly positive (but unconsciously negative) perception of the self. Although causal conclusions cannot be drawn from a cross-sectional design, it is possible that altruistic concern for others may counteract the negative representation of the other that characterizes an avoidant attachment style. Altruistic concern may introduce a positive representation of the other that subsequently enhances empathy, perspective-taking, and the quality of caregiving provided to others. Attachment theory proposes that attachment representations not only influence the quality of caregiving provided to others, but also are instrumental in developing the capacity to comfort and care for the self (Mikulincer & Shaver, 2004). As such, the positive representation of the other that arises from altruistic love, in combination with the enhanced empathic and perspective-taking abilities it facilitates, may promote greater compassion for the self and increased capacity to care for the self. The l'Arche results for the self-transformation feedback loop outlined in Figure 13.1 indicate that altruistic love is associated with decreased caregiver–client avoidance, which in turn facilitates experiences of relational spirituality. Further research should explore whether conscious participation in volunteer activities or compassionate care for others facilitates reparative attachment experiences as well as enhanced caregiving ability.

The thesis that compassionate caregiving for others can facilitate reparative experiences in the self also finds support in participant narratives of self-transformation. Caregivers across both samples reported that their caregiving interactions resulted in increased acceptance of others, compassionate love, and patience. More than half of l'Arche caregivers also reported transformative outcomes of self-acceptance and integration, authenticity and affirmation of life, relational intimacy, and spiritual growth. These accounts of self-acceptance and integration were consistent with Phelps et al.'s (1998) notion of a "corrective emotional experience" in which individuals access past traumas and internal contradictions, and integrate these into a positive and coherent perspective of the self. The self-transformative experiences arising from expression of compassionate love appear to be part of the feedback loop in Underwood's model (Chapter 1, this volume), reinforcing motivation and strengthening the substrate of cognitive and affective characteristics that facilitate compassionate care.

The l'Arche philosophical perspective appears to be an important element in facilitating caregiving interactions that promote self-transformation. L'Arche maintains a caregiving ethic that is centered around what Buber (1970) describes as an "I–Thou" relationship. In such a relationship, the other is embraced as a "Thou" in all his or her personhood, rather than being reduced to an "It" or object of our perception. When supporting people who have physical, cognitive, and/or psychiatric impairments, there is a danger that we may view them as an object of our sympathy rather than as a fellow human being from whom we have much to learn. Jean Vanier, the founder of l'Arche, effectively reframes the weakness of cognitive disability as a gift, noting that "Weakness is not something bad, to be shunned. It can become a path to communion – or rather a place of communion. People with handicaps teach us not to be afraid of our own vulnerability" (1997, p. 10). This philosophical perspective promotes enhanced altruistic concern, empathy, and relational mutuality in caregiving interactions, and also creates an atmosphere conducive to reparative attachment experiences.

The l'Arche narratives suggest that the unsophisticated defense mechanisms that characterize individuals with cognitive impairment appear to serve as a catalyst for increased awareness of unresolved attachment traumas in caregivers' own lives. The childlike playfulness, emotional authenticity, and freedom from a "public persona" modeled by core members also enable assistants to reconnect with vital aspects of the self and explore alternate ways of being in the world. In the context of a caregiving philosophy that holds that core members have learned and now model important life lessons about living in vulnerability and weakness, assistants have the opportunity to work through the pain of the past and undergo "corrective emotional experiences" (Phelps et al., 1998). This hypothesized transformation process is succinctly captured in the narrative account of a young female l'Arche assistant, who observed that: "Core members show me that I can't hide from what is broken inside of me and cause me to walk with that and slowly accept myself in all of my tainted beauty."

These preliminary results suggest that research needs to explore questions related to attachment reparation and experiences that motivate and sustain compassionate caregiving behaviors. With the exception of a few studies exploring an "earned secure" attachment style (e.g., Blair, Cox, Burchinal, & Payne, 1999; Phelps et al., 1998), there has been limited theoretical reflection and empirical investigation of factors that may mitigate the effects of negative attachment experiences or enhance the caregiving skills of individuals with insecure attachment schemas. Research also should explore practical implications of these results, such as whether the introduction of an interdependent caregiving philosophy, combined with role-modeling and social interaction training, can enhance empathic skills and altruistic motivation among caregivers and diminish avoidance in the caregiver–client relationship.

The results of this study, along with the contributions of Underwood and the other authors in this volume, provide a valuable contribution to our understanding of the psychological and sociocultural dynamics that facilitate compassionate love. In a global community increasingly caught up in regional conflicts, social and economic disparities, and hostile perceptions of the other, these insights offer hope and provide valuable signposts toward a positive alternative. The findings of this study also suggest that commitment to caring for others not only benefits others, but also has the potential to make our own lives more meaningful.

Acknowledgments

I would like to gratefully acknowledge the funding provided by the Fetzer Institute in support of the research outlined in this chapter. The helpful editorial feedback of Beverley Fehr, Susan Sprecher, and Lynn Underwood are much appreciated, as were the suggestions offered by Mario Mikulincer and three anonymous reviewers on an earlier version of this manuscript. I would also like to thank Bill Hunter, Kevin Reimer, Frank van Hesteren, and Lawrence Walker for their inspiration and support.

References

Acton, G. J. (2002). Health-promoting self-care in family caregivers. *Western Journal of Nursing Research, 24,* 73–86.

Batson, C. D. (1991). *The altruism question: Toward a social-psychological answer.* Hillsdale, NJ: Lawrence Erlbaum.

Blair, P., Cox, M. J., Burchinal, M. R., & Payne, C. C. (1999). Attachment and marital functioning: Comparison of spouses with continuous-secure, earned-secure, dismissing, and preoccupied attachment styles. *Journal of Family Psychology, 13*(4), 580–597.

Bowlby, J. (1969/1982). *Attachment and loss: Vol. 1, Attachment.* New York: Basic Books.

Bowlby, J. (1988). *A secure base: Parent–child attachment and healthy human development.* New York: Basic Books.

Brennan, K. A., Clark, C. L., & Shaver, P. R. (1998). Self-report measures of adult attachment: An integrative overview. In J. A. Simpson & W. S. Rholes (Eds.), *Attachment theory and close relationships* (pp. 46–76). New York: Guilford.

Britton, P. C., & Fuendeling, J. M. (2005). The relations among varieties of adult attachment and the components of empathy. *Journal of Social Psychology, 145,* 519–530.

Bronfenbrenner, U. (1979). *The ecology of human development.* Cambridge, MA: Harvard University Press.

Buber, M. (1970). *I and thou.* New York: Charles Scribner's Sons.

Carlson, V. J., & Harwood, R. L. (2003). Attachment, culture, and the caregiving system: The cultural patterning of everyday experiences among Anglo and Puerto Rican mother–infant pairs. *Infant Mental Health Journal, 24*(1), 53–73.

Ciechanowski, P. S., Katon, W. J., Russo, J. E., & Walker, E. A. (2001). The patient–provider relationship: Attachment theory and adherence to treatment in diabetes. *American Journal of Psychiatry, 158,* 29–35.

Collins, N. L., & Feeney, B. C. (2000). A safe haven: An attachment theory perspective on support-seeking and caregiving in adult romantic relationships. *Journal of Personality and Social Psychology, 78,* 1053–1073.

Collins, N. L., & Read, S. J. (1990). Adult attachment, working models, and relationship quality in dating couples. *Journal of Personality and Social Psychology, 58,* 644–663.

Corcoran, K. O., & Mallinckrodt, B. (2000). Adult attachment, self-efficacy, perspective taking, and conflict resolution. *Journal of Counseling & Development, 78,* 473–483.

Davis, M. H. (1983). Measuring individual differences in empathy: Evidence for a multidimensional approach. *Journal of Personality and Social Psychology, 44,* 113–126.

Diamond, L. M., & Hicks, A. M. (2004). Psychobiological perspectives on attachment: Implications for health over the lifespan. In W. S. Rholes & J. A. Simpson (Eds.), *Adult attachment: Theory, research, and clinical implications* (pp. 240–263). New York: Guilford.

Drach-Zahavy, A. (2004). Toward a multidimensional construct of social support: Implications of provider's self-reliance and request characteristics. *Journal of Applied Social Psychology, 34*, 1395–1420.

Faver, C. A. (2004). Relational spirituality and social caregiving. *Social Work, 49*(2), 241–249.

Feeney, B. C., & Collins, N. L. (2001). Predictors of caregiving in adult intimate relationships: An attachment-theoretical perspective. *Journal of Personality and Social Psychology, 80*, 972–994.

Feeney, B. C., & Collins, N. L. (2003). Motivations for caregiving in adult intimate relationships: Influences on caregiving behavior and relationship functioning. *Personality and Social Psychology Bulletin, 29*(8), 950–968.

Feeney, B. C., & Collins, N. L. (2004). Interpersonal safe haven and secure base caregiving processes in adulthood. In W. S. Rholes and J. A. Simpson (Eds.), *Adult attachment: Theory, research, and clinical implications* (pp. 300–338). New York: Guilford Press.

Feeney, J. A. (1996). Attachment, caregiving, and marital satisfaction. *Personal Relationships, 3*, 401–416.

Feeney, J. A., & Hohaus, L. (2001). Attachment and spousal caregiving. *Personal Relationships, 8*, 21–39.

Fricchione, G. L. (2002). Separation, attachment, and altruistic love: The evolutionary basis for medical caring. In S. G. Post, L. G. Underwood, J. P. Schloss, & W. B. Hurlbut (Eds.), *Altruism and altruistic love: Science, philosophy, and religion in dialogue* (pp. 346–361). New York: Oxford University Press.

Fritz, H. L., & Helgeson, V. S. (1998). Distinctions of unmitigated communion from communion: Self-neglect and overinvolvement with others. *Journal of Personality and Social Psychology, 75*, 121–140.

Gillath, O., Shaver, P. R., Mikulincer, M., Nitzberg, R. E., Erez, A., & van IJzendoorn, M. H. (2005). Attachment, caregiving, and volunteering: Placing volunteerism in an attachment-theoretical framework. *Personal Relationships, 12*, 425–446.

Griffin, D., & Bartholomew, K. (1994). Models of the self and other: Fundamental dimensions underlying measures of adult attachment. *Journal of Personality and Social Psychology, 67*, 430–445.

Joireman, J. A., Needham, T. L., & Cummings, A. (2002). Relationships between dimensions of attachment and empathy. *North American Journal of Psychology, 4*, 63–80.

Jöreskog, K. G., & Sorbom, D. (1993). LISREL 8: Structural equation modeling with the SIMPLIS command language. Chicago, IL, US: Lawrence Erlbaum.

Krebs, D. L., & Van Hesteren, F. (1994). The development of altruism: Toward an integrative model. *Developmental Review, 14*(2), 103–158.

Kunce, L. J., & Shaver, P. R. (1994). An attachment-theoretical approach to caregiving in romantic relationships. In K. Bartholomew & D. Perlman (Eds.),

Advances in interpersonal relationships: Vol. 5, Attachment processes in adulthood (pp. 206–237). London: Jessica Kingsley.

Lopez, F. G. (2001). Adult attachment orientations, self-other boundary regulation, and splitting tendencies in a college sample. *Journal of Counseling Psychology, 48*, 440–446.

Malley-Morrison, K., You, H. S., & Mills, R. B. (2000). Young adult attachment styles and perceptions of elder abuse: A cross-cultural study. *Journal of Cross-Cultural Gerontology, 15*, 163–184.

Matsumoto, D., & Juang, L. (2004). *Culture and psychology* (3rd ed.). Belmont, CA: Wadsworth/Thompson Learning.

McCullough, M. E., Pargament, K. I., & Thoresen, C. E. (Eds.). (2000). *Forgiveness: Theory, research, and practice.* New York: Guilford Press.

Mikulincer, M., Gillath, O., Halevy, V., Avihou, N., Avidan, S., & Eshkoli, N. (2001). Attachment theory and reactions to others' needs: Evidence that activation of the sense of attachment security promotes empathic responses. *Journal of Personality and Social Psychology, 81*(6), 1205–1224.

Mikulincer, M., Gillath, O., Sapir-Lavid, Y., Yaakobi, E., Arias, K., Tal-Aloni, L., & Bor, G. (2003). Attachment theory and concern for others' welfare: Evidence that activation of the sense of secure base promotes endorsement of self-transcendence values. *Basic and Applied Social Psychology, 25*(4), 299–312.

Mikulincer, M., & Shaver, P. R. (2004). Security-based self-representations in adulthood. In W. S. Rholes & J. A. Simpson (Eds.), *Adult attachment: Theory, research, and clinical implications* (pp. 159–195). New York: Guilford Press.

Mikulincer, M., Shaver, P. R., Gillath, O., & Nitzberg, R. A. (2005). Attachment, caregiving, and altruism: Boosting attachment security increases compassion and helping. *Journal of Personality and Social Psychology, 89*(5), 817–839.

Morrow-Howell, N., Hinterlog, J., Rozario, P. A., & Tang, F. (2003). Effects of volunteering on the well-being of older adults. *Journals of Gerontology: Psychological Sciences and Social Sciences, 58B*, 173–180.

Noam, G. G. (1993). "Normative vulnerabilities" of self and their transformation in moral actions. In G. G. Noam & T. E. Wren (Eds.), *The moral self* (pp. 209–238).Cambridge, MA: MIT Press.

Noam, G. G. (1996). Reconceptualizing maturity: The search for deeper meaning. In G. G. Noam & K. W. Fischer (Eds.), *Development and vulnerability in close relationships* (pp. 135–172). Mahwah, NJ: Lawrence Erlbaum.

Phelps, J. Lichtenstein, Belsky, J., & Crnic, K. (1998). Earned security, daily stress, and parenting: A comparison of five alternate models. *Development and Psychopathology, 10*, 21–38.

Rothbaum, F., Weisz, J., Pott, M., Miyake, K., & Morelli, G. (2000). Attachment and culture: Security in the United States and Japan. *American Psychologist, 55*(10), 1093–1104.

Shaver, P. R., Collins, N., & Clark, C. L. (1996). Attachment styles and internal working models of self and relationship partners. In G. J. O. Fletcher & J. Fitness (Eds.), *Knowledge structures in close relationships: A social psychological approach* (pp. 25–61). Hillsdale, NJ: Lawrence Erlbaum.

Shaver, P. R., Papalia, D., Clark, C. L., Koski, L. R., et al. (1996). Androgyny and attachment security: Two related models of optimal personality. *Personality and Social Psychology Bulletin, 22*, 582–597.

Singelis, T. M. (1994). The measurement of independent and interdependent self-construals. *Personality and Social Psychology Bulletin, 20*, 580–591.

Trusty, J., Ng, K. M., & Watts, R. E. (2005). Model of effects of adult attachment on emotional empathy of counseling students. *Journal of Counseling and Development, 83*, 66–77.

Underwood, L., O'Connell, K., & Saxena, S. (2001, November 7). *World Health Organization measure of subjective quality of life: Inclusion of values, meaning and spiritual aspects of life: Instrument development and testing*. Paper presented at the International Society of Quality of Life Research, Amsterdam, the Netherlands.

Underwood, L. G., & Teresi, J. A. (2002). The Daily Spiritual Experience Scale: Development, theoretical description, reliability, exploratory factor analysis, and preliminary construct validity using health-related data. *Annals of Behavioral Medicine, 24*(1), 22–33.

Van den Mark, I. L., van IJzendoorn, M. H., & Bakermans-Kranenburg, M. J. (2002). Development of empathy in girls during the second year of life: Associations with parenting, attachment, and temperament. *Social Development, 11*, 451–468.

van IJzendoorn, M. H., & Sagi, A. (1999). Cross-cultural patterns of attachment: Universal and contextual dimensions. In J. Cassidy & P. R. Shaver (Eds.), *Handbook of attachment: Theory, research, and clinical applications* (pp. 713–734). New York: Guilford Press.

Van Lange, P. A. M., Otten, W., De Bruin, E. M. N., & Joireman, J. A. (1997). Development of prosocial, individualistic, and competitive orientations: Theory and preliminary evidence. *Journal of Personality and Social Psychology, 73*, 733–746.

Vanier, J. (1997). L'Arche – a place of communion and pain. In F. Young (Ed.), *Encounter with mystery: Reflections on l'Arche and living with disability*. London: Darton, Longman and Todd.

Wayment, H. A. (2006). Attachment style, empathy, and helping following a collective loss: Evidence from the September 11 terrorist attacks. *Attachment & Human Development, 8*, 1–9.

Weger, H., Jr., & Polcar, L. E. (2002). Attachment style and person-centered comforting. *Western Journal of Communication, 66*, 84–103.

Zuroff, D. C., Moskowitz, D. S., & Cote, S. (1999) Dependency, self-criticism, interpersonal behaviour and affect: Evolutionary perspectives. *British Journal of Clinical Psychology, 38*, 231–250.

Part VI

Compassionate Love in an Intercultural Context

14

Testing Aspects of Compassionate Love in a Sample of Indonesian Adolescents

Julie Vaughan, Nancy Eisenberg, Doran C. French, Urip Purwono, Telie A. Suryanti, and Sri Pidada

Recently the construct of compassionate love has been discussed in depth in the social science literature (see Underwood, 2002; see Underwood, Chapter 1, this volume, for definition of compassionate love). The construct of compassionate love overlaps conceptually with the more frequently discussed and studied psychological constructs of empathy, sympathy, and prosocial behavior. Both the cognitive and emotional capabilities involved in sympathy are similar to those involved in compassionate love. Moreover, voluntary behaviors focused on the needs of others (e.g., prosocial and altruistic behaviors) are conceptualized to be related to (and possibly predictors of) compassionate love.

In this chapter, we first discuss the constructs of empathy, sympathy, perspective-taking, ethnocultural sensitivity, and prosocial behavior. Then we briefly review research on the relevance of caring behavior for ingroup and outgroup members and discuss how divisions among people might undermine empathy and prosocial behavior. Issues related to whether people do or do not help outgroup members and factors that foster across-group empathy are important for understanding the development and maintenance of compassionate love. Next, we present our heuristic model in which the constructs of sympathy, perspective-taking, and ethnocultural sensitivity are predictors of compassionate love and in which prosocial behavior and compassionate love have a reciprocal relationship. Then we discuss values related to caring in Indonesian culture – a culture in which we have been studying other-oriented emotion and behavior. Next, we present and discuss results on Indonesian adolescents' empathy-related responding (e.g., sympathy and perspective-taking), motivation and discernment (e.g., ethnocultural sensitivity), and positive behavior (e.g., prosocial behavior; cross-religion friends). Finally, we offer several suggestions for future research in this area.

Conceptual Definitions

Empathy has been defined in numerous ways over the decades, but in the last 20 to 30 years many social developmental psychologists have conceptualized it as having an emotional as well as a cognitive basis (e.g., Batson, 1991; Feshbach, 1978; Hoffman, 1977, 2001). We define empathy as an "affective response that stems from the apprehension or comprehension of another's emotional state or condition, and that is identical or very similar to what the other person is feeling or would be expected to feel" (Eisenberg & Fabes, 1998, p. 702). Unless empathy is weak or dissipates quickly, it is expected to evoke either sympathy or personal distress, or perhaps both sequentially.

Sympathy is an affective response that often stems from empathy, but can emerge directly from perspective-taking or other cognitive processes (e.g., retrieving information from memory about a needy group of people). Sympathy consists of feelings of sorrow or concern for distressed or needy others rather than merely experiencing the same emotion that others experience or the same emotion that others could be expected to experience in a given context. In contrast, personal distress is a self-focused, aversive emotional reaction to the vicarious experience of the emotions of others (e.g., discomfort or anxiety; see Batson, 1991; Eisenberg, Shea, Carlo, & Knight, 1991).

Several researchers have argued that individuals must recognize and understand others' feelings, needs, and desires if they are to care for others and to experience empathy and sympathy (Batson, 1991; Feshbach, 1978; Hoffman, 2000; Strayer, 1987). Individuals must also conceptualize others in a manner that is worthy of caring and helping behavior (e.g., Bandura, 1991; Weiner, 1980). According to this perspective, the rationale for why perspective-taking (seeing one's self in another person's shoes) can be conceptualized as an aspect of empathy-related responding is clear.

Ethnocultural sensitivity has been described as an acquired personality trait (Ridley & Lingle, 1996). Wang and colleagues (2003) defined ethnocultural empathy (a particular aspect of sensitivity) as "empathy directed toward people from racial and ethnic cultural groups who are different from one's own ethnocultural group" (p. 221). Ethnocultural sensitivity consists of a concern experienced or an awareness of when people from other religious or ethnic groups are insulted or mistreated (see Wang et al., 2003).

Relations of Sympathy and Perspective-Taking to Prosocial Behavior

Altruism is often defined as intentional, voluntary behavior that is motivated by sympathy or moral values, and not the desire for social or concrete rewards or the desire to reduce feelings of personal distress. Altruism is one type of prosocial behavior; it includes prosocial behaviors motivated by sympathy or moral values. Other prosocial behaviors can be motivated by nonmoral concerns (e.g., self-gain; fear of social disapproval). Thus, it is altruistically motivated prosocial behavior – which is believed to often stem from sympathy – and not all prosocial behavior that is related to compassionate love. Batson (1991) argued that empathy (what we define as sympathy), but not personal distress, is expected to motivate altruism when there are no concrete or social rewards for helping and when it is easy to escape contact with the needy or distressed other.

Although it is often difficult to empirically differentiate altruistic from nonaltruistic helping motivation and behavior, researchers have found positive relations between various measures of sympathy and prosocial behavior in numerous studies with children, adolescents, and adults (Bandura, Caprara, Barbaranelli, Gerbino, & Pastorelli, 2003; Batson, 1991; Carlo & Randall, 2002; Eisenberg, Fabes, & Spinrad, 2006; Krevans & Gibbs, 1996). When investigators have differentiated between sympathy and personal distress, they generally have found that sympathy, rather than personal distress, is associated with higher levels of helping and sharing with others (e.g., Batson, 1991; Davis, 1994; Eisenberg & Fabes, 1990). Thus, sympathy seems to play an important role in caring behavior.

Eisenberg and colleagues (e.g., Eisenberg, Zhou, & Koller, 2001) argued that perspective taking without moral motivation (i.e., not based on sympathy or moral values) does not lead to caring behavior. Perspective-taking could be used for manipulation, as in the case of a scam artist who uses social insight to manipulate a victim. Indeed, Machiavellian individuals probably are more likely to accomplish their selfish goals if they are skilled in perspective-taking. In one study of Brazilian adolescents, perspective-taking was related to high levels of sympathy and moral reasoning about prosocial moral dilemmas (Eisenberg, Zhou, & Koller, 2001), but predicted prosocial behavior only when it was linked to sympathy or mature moral reasoning.

Thus, sympathy and perspective-taking appear to be positively related to caring behavior in many instances. Moreover, as already noted, sympathy is associated with prosocial behavior, especially altruistic behavior (see Batson, 1991; Eisenberg et al., 2006). Consequently, it is important to study the development and correlates of prosocial behavior in our efforts to understand the roots of compassionate love in childhood and adolescence.

Empathy and Ingroup/Outgroup Status

Identifying factors that foster a positive versus negative orientation toward others, especially in regard to the role of prejudice and discrimination in sympathy and altruism, can enhance our understanding of when caring and compassionate love are extended to persons outside of one's ingroup. Individuals' perceptions of and relations with other people are likely to influence whether or not they extend caring.

A theoretical perspective relevant to this issue is Social Identity Theory (SIT), which claims that other people are seen as belonging either to the ingroup or the outgroup and this sense of belonging creates society identity (see Tajfel, 1982). Researchers have found evidence of ingroup favoritism but have not consistently found outgroup discrimination (see Aboud, 2003; Bennett et al., 2004; Brewer, 1999; Negy, Shreve, Jensen, & Uddin, 2003; Tropp & Pettigrew, 2005). For example, Tarrant and colleagues found that adolescents displayed a consistent ingroup positive bias (i.e., favorable opinion), but did not exhibit a strong outgroup negative bias (i.e., unfavorable opinion; Tarrant et al. 2001; see also Tarrant, 2002). In another study, Tarrant and colleagues found adolescents rated peers in their ingroup (i.e., friends) more favorably than peers in an outgroup (Tarrant, North, & Hargreaves, 2004). Other researchers have found that older elementary school-aged children and preschoolers preferred members of their own ethnic group than members of other ethnic groups (Enesco, Navarro, Paradela, & Guerrero, 2005; Rutland, Cameron, Bennett, & Ferrell, 2005).

Individual differences in children's empathy and sympathy may play a role in ingroup bias. For example, Nesdale and colleagues assessed the relation between elementary school-aged children's empathy and ethnic group attitudes (Nesdale, Griffith, Durkin, & Maass, 2005) and found that children's empathy was unrelated to their liking for persons in their ethnic ingroup but was positively related to their liking for persons of different ethnic groups. Thus, individuals' empathy appears to be related to positive views of outgroup members. In addition, empathic youth are more likely than their less empathic peers to say that they are comfortable being near children who are different from them and who might be viewed negatively (e.g., a child who is depressed, immature, aggressive, overweight, or doing poorly academically; Bryant, 1982; Strayer & Roberts, 1997).

An unwillingness to help outgroup members can be construed as a form of discrimination. Eisenberg (1983) found that children who provided higher moral-level justifications for helping or not helping (e.g., helping because of a universal principle, such as improving the condition of society) were less likely to differentiate between friends or family and other people in need than those who provided lower moral-level justifications. Killen and Turiel (1998) found that compared to adults, adolescents were more likely to help a person with whom they had a distant relationship (e.g., a former sibling-in-law). In other words, adolescents were less likely to distinguish between people from close relationships and people from not close relationships (all age groups reported similar levels of helping a friend or another person who they knew well) in comparison with adults.

It is important to understand factors related to the facilitation or inhibition of discrimination. For example, invoking sympathy and perspective-taking may be one way of bridging the gap between ingroup and outgroup attitudes. Batson, Polycarpou, et al. (1997), for example, found that inducing empathy (participants were asked to imagine how another person felt in a particular situation) increased adults' positive attitudes for outgroup members (for similar results, see Pedersen, Walker, & Wise, 2005; Stürmer, Snyder, & Omoto, 2005). Galinsky and Moskowitz (2000) found that adults who exhibited more perspective-taking had less stereotyped responses and more favorable evaluations of outgroup members than adults who exhibited less perspective-taking. Batson, Sager, et al. (1997), however, did not find that perspective-taking altered ingroup and outgroup attitudes; adults' sympathy and helping behavior were positively related regardless of their perspective-taking ability. Thus, there appears to be consistent support for the hypothesis that there is a negative relation between sympathy and outgroup bias, whereas evidence for the relation between perspective-taking and outgroup bias is mixed.

Empathy emerges early in life, and the capacity for sympathy is evident in the toddler and preschool years (Eisenberg et al., 2006). Similarly, the ability to identify others' emotions and to engage in simple perspective-taking emerges relatively early (see Eisenberg, Murphy, & Shepard, 1997) and has been linked to helping behavior (Eisenberg et al., 2006). Thus, it is likely that sympathy and perspective-taking contribute to children's caring for people outside their inner circle. However, it is quite possible that children and adolescents who value the well-being of people from other groups – be it due to exposure to people from other groups, values taught to children by adults, or other factors (see Oliner & Oliner, 1988) – increasingly develop the capacity for sympathy with the plight of outgroup members. We would expect children and youths who exhibit concern for people from other religious or cultural groups to be relatively high in sympathy and perspective taking.

Heuristic Model

In our proposed heuristic model (see Figure 14.1), the constructs in our investigation are incorporated into the conceptual model put forth by Underwood (see Chapter 1, this volume). In our model, the associated cognitive component of compassionate love reflected in empathy-related responding (e.g., perspective-taking) and sympathy are initially activated and, in turn, lead to motivation and discernment (e.g., ethnocultural

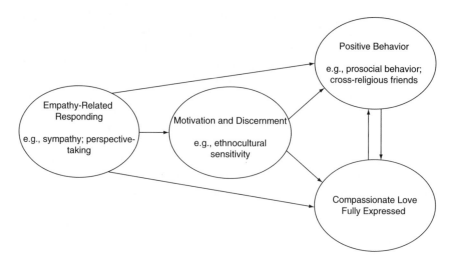

Figure 14.1   Conceptual Model of Aspects of Compassionate Love

sensitivity). Empathy-related responding, specifically sympathy, provides a motivational basis for the caring emotional responses and behaviors that are related to the core of compassionate love and are perhaps even predictive of compassionate love. Numerous researchers have found positive relations between sympathy and perspective-taking in childhood and adolescence (Batson, Early, & Salvarani, 1997; Davis & Franzoi, 1991; Eisenberg, Carlo, Murphy, & Van Court, 1995; Eisenberg, Zhou, & Koller, 2001; Estrada, 1995; Henry, Sager, & Plunkett, 1996; Karniol, Gabay, Ochion, & Harari, 1998; McWhirter, Besett-Alesch, Horibata, & Gat, 2002), and both have been conceptually and empirically linked to prosocial behavior (see Eisenberg et al., 2006). Thus, in our model we conceptualized empathy-related responding as including sympathy and perspective-taking.

Additionally, we propose that an individual's empathic tendencies and ethnocultural sensitivity lead to positive behaviors (e.g., prosocial behavior and cross-religion friendships) and the expression of compassionate love, and that the latter two capacities may stimulate one another. For example, prosocial behavior may stem from an initial, internal experience of compassionate love and/or the action of prosocial behavior (and the associated cognitions and experiences) may in turn foster future feelings of compassionate love. Ethnocultural sensitivity is considered an important characteristic of individuals' discernment and thought processes toward others of different ethnicities and religious backgrounds from their own. Lastly, ethnocultural sensitivity may mediate the relation between empathy-related responding and prosocial behavior. We conceptualize compassionate love as an outcome variable because compassionate love involves the integration of numerous complex processes (e.g., caring behavior based on other-oriented motivation; the capacities for sympathy and for other-oriented caring behavior). In this chapter, we discuss research in Indonesia, a country that provides a particularly interesting context for studying culture, empathy-related responding, and prosocial behavior.

Caring in Indonesian Culture

Levels of children's prosocial behavior appear to vary across cultures (see Eisenberg et al., 2006). In naturalistic observational studies, children who exhibited relatively high levels of helping and sharing tended to be from cultures in which people lived together with extended family, children at an early age received household chores and responsibilities involving the welfare of their family members, and parents emphasized connectedness with other members of their society (see Eisenberg et al., 2006). Therefore, it is important to investigate cultural variations in socio-emotional and socio-cognitive behaviors in order to better understand and identify potential universals in behavior.

Members of collectivist societies generally are viewed as concerned with the consequences of their behavior for other members of their group and as more willing than people in less collectivistic societies to engage in prosocial behavior for the good of the ingroup (i.e., people who belong to the same religious, ethnic, or social group are defined as members of an ingroup; people who belong to a different group are defined as members of an outgroup). Although the nature of collectivism varies somewhat across cultures (Triandis, 1995), maintaining personal relationships and interpersonal harmony with close others are key values in most collectivistic cultures (Markus & Kitayama, 1991; Oyserman, Coon, & Kemmelmeier, 2002; Triandis, 1995). There is evidence that Indonesia is a relatively collectivist culture (Marshall, 1997; Oyserman et al., 2002). Marshall (1997) found that Indonesian adults endorsed an interdependent view of the self (i.e., a view that incorporates a group perspective; an aspect of collectivism) more than an independent view of the self (there was also an interaction with socioeconomic class; lower SES Indonesian adults endorsed more interdependent beliefs than higher SES Indonesian adults).

Consistent with the general characteristics of collectivist cultures, the Javanese culture (the majority culture in Indonesia) emphasizes the display of overt interpersonal harmony and the avoidance of conflict (Koentjaraningrat, 1985; Williams, 1991). Additionally, traditional Indonesian society, including Javanese culture, has been described as emphasizing the ideals of cooperation, shared goals (Koentjaraningrat,

1985; Mulder, 1996; Peacock, 1973), and the virtues of helping, sharing, and empathizing with others (Williams, 1991). Thus, social scientists have described the Javanese culture as placing significance on sensitivity to others' needs and awareness of others' feelings (e.g., sympathy and prosocial behavior; see Eisenberg, Pidada, & Liew, 2001; Mulder, 1996), as well as self-control and the suppression of emotion (Geertz, 1976; Koentjaraningrat, 1985; Mulder, 1989, 1996; Van Beek, 1987; also see Magnis-Suseno, 1997). However, it is not clear if norms regarding the cultivation of feelings of caring and compassion translate into actions (i.e., if thoughts of helping turn in to actual helping).

Cultural psychologists have suggested that within collectivist groups, the differences between members of an ingroup become less distinct, but the distinction between ingroup and outgroup members becomes more pronounced (Iyengar, Lepper, & Ross, 1999). Consistent with this view, Iyengar et al. (1999) found that individuals from collectivist cultures made greater distinctions between ingroup and outgroup members on an attribution task (i.e., a task in which participants were asked to classify people's personality traits and behaviors) than did those from individualistic cultures. Although Indonesians (Javanese and those in other Indonesian ethnic groups) may be strongly encouraged to be caring and non-aggressive with members of their ingroup, these norms may not apply to interactions with outgroup members. Indeed, Indonesia is a country torn for decades by surges of ethnic and religious strife. Thus, it is important to examine sympathy and prosocial behavior in collectivist societies and whether compassion for people from other groups is related to individual differences in caring about the welfare of outgroup members.

In summary, Indonesia is an interesting culture in which to investigate the relations between various aspects of compassionate love. The significance of caring and social harmony within the Javanese culture would be expected to cultivate compassionate love (for ingroup members) in that society. More specifically, according to the conceptual model described by Underwood, we hypothesized that the aforementioned cultural values (i.e., situational factors) affect individuals' motivation and desire to be attuned to others' needs and to act in caring ways. This motivation, in turn, should be expected to predict the development of children's prosocial behavior and aspects of human functioning that are likely to play a role in compassionate love.

The Present Study

In this chapter, we present data from a study of adolescents from Java, Indonesia. These adolescents included youths from the majority culture (i.e., ethnic Javanese or Sundanese youths who are Muslim) and minority cultures (Christians and Muslim youths from ethnic minorities). There were two primary areas of interest with this study. First, because there are so few studies on the relations between sympathy and perspective taking and prosocial behavior in non-Western cultures, especially among adolescents, we examined these aspects across and within multiple reporters' (i.e., parents', teachers', and youths') assessments of youths' behavior. Findings of consistency across reporters and contexts would provide support for the existence of individual differences in an enduring prosocial personality – what has sometimes been labeled an altruistic personality. Lack of consistency between reports of youths' empathy-related responding and prosocial behavior could be explained by biases of different reporters or may indicate that adolescents' sympathy and prosocial behavior actually vary substantially across contexts such that few individuals are consistently more caring than others.

A second area of interest concerned the correlates of youths' caring tendencies. Based on what has been found in Western cultures, we expected adolescents who were sympathetic and skilled in perspective-taking to be more prosocial than their less responsive peers. This prediction is based on the assumption that sympathy provides the motivation for much other-oriented prosocial behavior. However, in a review of cultural differences, Lillard (1998) described variations in the degree to which cultures emphasize and process other people's thoughts and emotions. She reviewed work indicating that in some cultures, people are much less likely to try to understand others' psychological states and emotions. Extending Lillard's discussion to the constructs that we assessed, it is possible to imagine a culture in which prosocial behavior is valued due to cultural norms, but is not usually based on empathy-related responding (e.g., sympathy and perspective-taking).

We also examined the relation between youths' empathy-related responding (i.e., sympathy and perspective-taking skills) and self-reported ethnocultural sensitivity and between ethnocultural sensitivity and prosocial behavior. Consistent with our prior discussion, youths who were higher in empathy-related responding were expected to report higher concern about the treatment of people outside of their ethnic or religious group (i.e., higher ethnocultural sensitivity). Additionally, youths who reported higher ethnocultural sensitivity were expected to be higher in prosocial behavior. We studied this issue with a sample of adolescents because they generally find it easier to report on mental states and activities (e.g., perspective taking, attitudes) than do younger children.

Participants and Methods

The study had three phases: Time 1 (T1) – an initial screening in which we collected limited, preliminary data from a large sample of youths and selected a subsample for more intensive study; at Time 2 (T2), approximately three months later, data from parents and teachers were obtained; Time 3 (T3), approximately 4 to 5 months after T2, data from youths, parents, and teachers were obtained.

The sample was drawn from 7th-grade students in Bandung, Indonesia. Bandung, a city of approximately two million in Western Java, contains large populations of Chinese (an ethnic minority in Indonesia) as well as the Javanese and Sundanese majority. Whereas most of the population is Muslim, a substantial number of Christians live there as well. Javanese and Sundanese (ethnic majorities), Chinese (ethnic minority), other Muslim ethnic minorities, and Christian (a religious minority) populations often live in close proximity.

At T1, we surveyed (with student assent and parent consent) 1,254 7th-grade students ($M = 13$ years, 4 months; range: 11 years to 17 years, 6 months; girls = 636). They were recruited from a number of classrooms in 3 Christian schools and 4 public (primarily Muslim) schools, and included 959 Muslim youth (76.5% of the sample), 289 Christian youth, 1 Hindu, 3 Buddhists, and 2 youth of unidentified religious background. In terms of ethnicity, at T1 the sample included 776 Sundanese, 228 Javanese, 146 Batak, 33 Chinese, and 69 from another minority group (2 additional youth did not report ethnic status). Based on their ethnic and religious background, we formed two groups: 358 minority youth (religious or ethnic) and 896 majority youth (religious or ethnic). About 40% of the parents had graduated from junior high school, 14% had graduated from high school, and the remaining percentage had attended at least college or attained some form of higher education. Information on families' SES was not available at T1.

From the participants at T1, we targeted a sample of Christians from the Christian schools and Muslims from the primarily Muslim public schools. Specifically, 285 youth (girls = 152) were followed into T2. Of these, 88 were in the minority group (59 youth were of ethnic minority status: 38 Batak, 10 Chinese, and 11 from other minority groups; 29 youth were of religious minority status). Thirty-nine percent of the parents had graduated from junior high school, 15% had graduated from high school, and the remaining percentage had some college or higher education. Approximately 31% of the families were considered lower or low class, 33% of the families were middle class, and 37% of the families were upper middle to upper class (4 parents did not report their income and work status; therefore SES could not be calculated).[1] At T2, children and their parents ($n = 278$) were interviewed in the home and teachers ($n = 32$) were contacted at school.

---

[1]   A list of jobs in the local economy was created and then was reliably ranked on a scale of 1 (lower class) to 5 (upper class) by two independent raters who were native to the local economy, $r(123) = .73$. Then, parents' jobs and education level were ranked according to

At T3, 250 children from T2 participated.[2] Of the 250 adolescents, 137 were girls, 175 were majority (136 Sundanese and 39 Javanese), and 75 were minorities. The sample changed little from T2 in terms of education and SES. Youths' parents ($n = 246$) and teachers ($n = 32$; not the same teachers as at T2) also participated.

Measures

Adolescents' self-reported empathy-related responding and ethnocultural sensitivity were assessed at T1 and empathy-related responding and prosocial behavior were assessed at T3. Additionally, teachers and parents reported on youths' empathy-related responding and prosocial behavior at T2 and T3. These measures were translated into Indonesian by a native bilingual speaker and back-translated by a second native speaker.

In order to obtain a more trait-like composite of youths' behavior and attitudes, we averaged data from the same reporter (e.g., parents' reports of adolescents' prosocial behavior at T2 and T3 were averaged together). Rushton, Brainerd, and Pressley (1983) recommend aggregating across multiple measures to achieve a more accurate representation of a trait-like quality. Rushton et al. (1983) were cautious about aggregating a low number of measures; therefore, we acknowledge that the aggregate composites may only be moderately representative of adolescents' actual traits. However, we believe that these composites are better than the independent measures of adolescents' attitudes and behaviors. Additionally, because reports were obtained close in time to one another, the measures could be considered repeated measures as much as longitudinal measures.

Empathy-related responding. Adolescents' sympathy and perspective taking were assessed using self, teachers', and parents' reports. At T1 and T3, youths rated ($1 = does\ not\ describe\ me$ to $7 = describes\ me\ very\ well$) their sympathy (e.g., "I often have tender, concerned feelings for people

---

the scheme developed by the raters, $r(149) = .88$. SES information was collected for all children who participated in T2 and T3.

[2] To examine attrition from T2 to T3, a series of MANOVAs with demographic variables (adolescents' sex, majority/minority status, and parent education) and socio-emotional measures (i.e., prosocial behavior and empathy-related responding) as the dependent variables and the attrition status (did not participate at T2 or T3) variable were conducted (attrition from T1 to T2 was not examined because a smaller sample was intentionally selected). Neither the multivariate F nor univariate analyses were significant for the MANOVA with the demographic variables and for the MANOVA with parent-reported measures. The multivariate F for a MANOVA with T2 teacher-reported prosocial behavior and empathy-related responding as the dependent variables was not significant; however, the univariate was significant for prosocial behavior, $F(1,281) = 4.35$, $p = .04$ (Ms for non-participants and participants = 3.71 and 3.94).

less fortunate than me") and perspective-taking (e.g., "I sometimes try to understand my friends better by imagining how things look from their perspective") using the empathic concern/sympathy and perspective-taking subscales of Davis's (1994) Interpersonal Reactivity Index (Davis's empathic concern subscale taps what we have labeled as sympathy.) At T1, youths' self-reported sympathy and perspective-taking were moderately correlated (r=.49) and were not reliably assessed as individual subscales (αs = .52 and .57; two items were dropped because of low item-scale correlations, perhaps due to translation issues). Therefore, the remaining 12 items in the empathic concern/sympathy and perspective-taking subscales – henceforth labeled as empathy-related responding – were combined at both T1 and T3 (αs=.71 and .73). Both of these scales are considered by Davis (1994) to tap empathy-related responding, broadly defined. Adolescents' reports at T1 and T3 of their empathy-related responding were moderately correlated, $r(248) = .49, p < .001$, and were averaged together to form a more trait-like construct.

At T2 and T3, teachers and parents rated youths' empathy-related responding using the same items from the self-report measure with slightly modified wording (e.g., "This child often has tender, concerned feelings for people less fortunate than him/her" versus "My child often has tender, concerned feelings for people less fortunate than him/her"; 12 items; αs = .82 and .72 at T1 and .85 and .76 at T2). Parents' reports at T2 and T3 were moderately correlated, $r(238) = .40, p < .001$, and were averaged.

Ethnocultural sensitivity. At T1, adolescents were asked to rate themselves on statements assessing their sensitivity to issues related to others' ethnic status using a five-point scale (1 = *not like me at all* to 5 = *very much like me*; α = .55 for two items; "I get angry when I learn that someone is mistreated because of their religion or their ethnic group" and "I am offended when people make insulting jokes or say bad things about people who have a different religion or differ from me in their ethnicity") on an adapted scale from Wang et al. (2003).[3]

Prosocial behavior. Prosocial behavior was assessed using adolescents', teachers', and parents' reports. Self-reported prosocial behavior was assessed at T1 and T3, whereas parent-reported and teacher-reported prosocial behavior was measured at T2 and T3.

At T1 and T3, adolescents reported their prosocial behavior using a 10 item measure (e.g., "I never wait to help others when they ask for it";

[3] Reversed items (three items) were dropped because of low item-scale correlations. An alpha of .55 is reasonable for two items; the correlation between the two items was moderate, $r = .38$.

$\alpha = .78$ and .82, respectively) answered using a five-point scale ($1 = does\ not$ *describe me at all* to $5 = describes\ me\ greatly$); these items were selected from the emotional (helping in situations that are emotionally evocative), dire (helping in situations of emergency or crisis), anonymous (helping without other people's knowledge), altruistic (helping when no or little perceived potential for explicit reward), and compliant (helping when asked to help) subscales from Carlo, Hausmann, Christiansen, and Randall (2003).[4] Youths' reports at T1 and T3 were combined to simplify data presentation because they were moderately correlated, $r(248) = .29$, $p < .001$.

At T2 and T3, teachers and parents rated adolescents' prosocial behavior using four items (e.g., "This child is helpful to peers"; "This child says supportive things to peers"; "This child tries to cheer up peers when they are sad or upset about something; "This child is kind to peers"; $\alpha s = .82$ and .62 at T2 and .83 and .64, respectively, at T3) rated on a five-point scale ($1 = never\ true$ to $5 = never\ false$) taken from Crick (1996). This scale was designed to elicit adults' reports of youths' general prosocial tendencies, whereas the Carlo et al. (2003) measure was constructed to assess youths' self-reports of specific prosocial behaviors (that adults may or may not observe). Parents' reports of prosocial behavior at T2 and T3 were combined because they were moderately correlated and close in time, $r(240) = .32$, $p < .001$. Teachers' reports at T2 and T3 were kept separate because different teachers participated at T2 and T3.

Friendship types: Cross- and non-cross-religion friends. During the screening assessment (T1), students with parental permission and who assented to participate nominated up to four of their closest friends at school or outside of school (students provided the name and religion of each friend who was nominated). Nominations from outside of the class were allowed because often there were few other-religion youths in a classroom. The top two nominations were used to classify students into those who had a close friendship that crossed religious boundaries (i.e., had at least one close cross-group friend) and those who did not. We used only the top two nominations because we wanted to focus on relatively close friends and because not all children nominated four friends. At T1, 95 children included in the sample at T2 reported having a cross-religion friend (41 Christian and 54 Muslim youth) and 190 children reported not having a cross-religion friend (39 Christian and 151 Muslim youth).

---

[4] These subscales were selected because they seemed to best tap prosocial behaviors motivated by sympathy or moral values (dire, anonymous, and altruistic) versus social concern (i.e., compliance). However, the findings were very similar when we dropped the items on the compliant prosocial behavior subscale and used only items from the other subscales, so we retained all items.

Table 14.1 Correlations among Empathy-related Responding, Ethnocultural Sensitivity, and Prosocial Behavior

	Youth ERR	T2: Teacher ERR	T3:Teacher ERR	Parent ERR	Youth ethnic sens.	Youth prosocial	T2:Teacher prosocial	T3:Teacher prosocial	Parent prosocial
Youth ERR	—								
T2: Teacher ERR	.16* (246)	—							
T3: Teacher ERR	.10 (243)	.44*** (254)	—						
Parent ERR	.13* (238)	.11+ (236)	.09 (234)	—					
Youth ethnic sens.	.30*** (248)	.14* (281)	-.03 (256)	.19** (238)	—				
Youth prosocial	.53*** (248)	.11+ (246)	.03 (243)	.04 (238)	.16* (248)	—			
T2: Teacher prosocial	.19** (248)	.56*** (281)	.23*** (256)	.09 (238)	.03 (283)	12+ (248)	—		
T3: Teacher prosocial	.13* (246)	.29*** (257)	.61*** (256)	.09 (236)	.01 (259)	.08 (246)	.23*** (259)	—	
Parent prosocial	.16* (240)	.21*** (238)	.06 (236)	.53*** (238)	.14* (240)	.06 (240)	.15* (240)	.07 (238)	—

Note. Degrees of freedom in parentheses; T1 = Time 1; T2 = Time 2; T3 = Time 3; ERR = Empathy-related responding; Ethnic sens. = ethnocultural sensitivity.

*** $p < .001$; ** $p < .01$; * $p < .05$; + $p < .10$.

Testing Components of the Heuristic Model

The relations among adolescents' empathy-related responding, ethnocultural sensitivity, and prosocial behavior were assessed through a series of correlational analyses (see Table 14.1). Additionally, these correlations were examined separately for majority and minority adolescents and tested for significant differences using the Fisher r-to-z transformation formula (see Cohen, Cohen, West, & Aiken, 2003). Because none of the findings differed significantly for majority and minority youth, results are presented for the combined sample. In a second set of analyses, aspects of the heuristic model were examined using linear regression analyses to determine the unique prediction of multiple indicators. In a final set of analyses, the prediction of adolescents' friendship types was assessed using logistic regressions.

Relations among Reporters for Measures with Multiple Assessments

The first series of correlations assessed the relations among reporters for adolescents' empathy-related responding and prosocial behavior. We were interested in assessing the consistency across home and school contexts for each measure. In studies of these constructs in Western samples, significant correlations have been found across reporters (e.g., Goodman, 2001), but not always (e.g., Eberly & Montemayor, 1999). Given the strong emphasis on empathy-related responding and prosocial behavior in Indonesia, we expected the salience of empathy-related responding and prosocial behavior to increase parents' and teachers' awareness of these constructs; thus, we predicted moderate to high correlations among reporters.

There was some evidence that different reporters agreed on adolescents' empathy-related responding. Adolescents' reports of empathy-related responding were positively related to teachers' reports at T2 and parents' reports (T2 and T3 combined). Additionally, reports by different teachers at T2 and T3 were substantially positively related. However, correlations between teachers' and parents' reports were at best marginally significant.

Overall, there was little agreement among adolescents' self-reports, teachers' reports, and parents' reports of prosocial behavior. Adolescents' self-reported prosocial behavior was only marginally related to teachers' reports at T2. There were positive relations between T2 teachers and T3 teachers and parents. These relatively modest and inconsistent correlations could be due to biases in children's or parents' reports of prosocial behavior or to differences in children's behavior across contexts.

In summary, agreement between youths and adults on ratings of empathy-related responding and prosocial behavior was somewhat weak. The lack of relations for prosocial behavior could be attributed to differences in measurement (adolescent and adult ratings of prosocial behavior were completed using different measures). In addition, many adolescents' reports of their own prosocial tendencies may have been distorted by concerns about appearing in a socially desirable light. Such concerns may be especially common in a culture that values prosocial behavior. Further, the modest agreement between teachers' and parents' reports of adolescents' empathy-related responding and prosocial behavior could be a result of context. The classroom environment is likely different than the home environment in its structure, norms, and the people present (e.g., peers versus family members). Therefore, teachers' and parents' bases for judgments about children's behavior could be different, which would attenuate relations between their ratings. Indeed, adolescents' teachers in two different school years tended to agree on adolescents' prosocial behavior and empathy-related responding, perhaps because adolescents' behavior was relatively consistent in the school context.

Relations between Empathy-Related Responding and Prosocial Behavior

We examined the relations between adolescents' empathy-related responding and prosocial behavior. Within reporters (i.e., adolescents, parents, teachers at T2, and teachers at T3) there was a significant positive relation between empathy-related responding and prosocial behavior. Thus, adults reported that youths who exhibited empathy-related responding also were likely to assist others. Additionally, adolescents who scored high in empathy-related responding also rated themselves as high in prosocial behavior. Examining the relations across reporters, there was some support for a positive relation between empathy-related responding and prosocial behavior. Teachers' reports of empathy-related responding at T2 and at T3 were positively related to the others' reports of prosocial behavior. In addition, adolescents' self-reported, but not parent-reported, empathy-related responding were positively related to teachers' reports of prosocial behavior at both time points. Moreover, adolescents' self-reported and T2 teacher-reported empathy-related responding were positively related to parent-reported prosocial behavior. In summary, there was evidence for a positive relation between reports of empathy-related responding and adult-reported prosocial behavior. However, there was little support for the relation between adult-reported empathy-related responding and self-reported prosocial behavior.

Overall, we found support for a positive relation between empathy-related responding and prosocial behavior, even when the two constructs were rated by different reporters – a finding that is consistent with the association between empathy-related responding and prosocial behavior in Western societies (Batson et al., 1997; Davis & Franzoi, 1991; Estrada, 1995; Henry et al., 1996; Karniol et al. 1998; McWhirter et al., 2002). These aspects of socioemotional adjustment (i.e., empathy-related responding and prosocial behavior) may stem from the same biologically-based capacities (e.g., emotional reactivity). Based on recent neuropsychological research of mirror neurons (neurons that are activated when an individual observes an action made by another individual; see Cambray, 2006), Gallese and Lakoff (2005) proposed that imagining and doing use similar if not the same neurological processes. Further research in the field of mirror neurons should help map pathways between mental simulation and behavior, and perhaps the pathways among sympathy, perspective-taking, and prosocial behavior.

Relations between Ethnic Sensitivity and Empathy-Related Responding and Prosocial Behavior

The relations between adolescents' reports of ethnocultural sensitivity and adolescents', parents', and teachers' reports of empathy-related responding and prosocial behavior were examined with correlations. Adolescents' ethnocultural sensitivity was positively related to all but one of the reports of their empathy-related responding (was unrelated to T3 teachers' reports). With regard to prosocial behavior, adolescents' ethnocultural sensitivity was positively related to adolescents' self-reported and parent-reported prosocial behavior but was unrelated to teacher-reported prosocial behavior at both time points.

Overall, there was evidence that adolescents who were high in empathy-related responding also were high in ethnocultural sensitivity and prosocial behavior. Perhaps these relations tap an underlying personality type, such as an altruistic personality. Alternatively, these aspects of functioning (empathy-related responding, ethnocultural sensitivity, and prosocial behavior) could be related predictors of compassionate love. Research specifically examining compassionate love and these constructs across multiple measures could provide insight into these relations.

It appears that ethnocultural sensitivity is more consistently related to the cognitive and emotional aspects of caring behavior (i.e., perspective-taking and sympathy, respectively) than to the behavioral aspect of caring (i.e., prosocial behavior). Adolescents' awareness and thoughts about others in need appear to be different than their actual reported helping behavior (in other words, imagining/feeling and doing were distinct). However, as previously discussed, there is support for the hypothesized positive relation between prosocial behavior and empathy-related responding.

Perhaps empathy-related responding is a necessary skill that adolescents need in order to develop ethnocultural sensitivity, which would support the first path in our heuristic model. Moreover, many of adolescents' prosocial behaviors may have been a result of desires for social approval or concrete rewards rather than caring for others. This may be particularly the case at school; teacher's reports of prosocial behavior were unrelated to youths' ethnic sensitivity. However, more research needs to be done in order to replicate our findings with a more reliable measure of ethnic sensitivity.

Assessing Mediation in the Heuristic Model

The role of ethnocultural sensitivity as a potential mediator of the relation between empathy-related responding and prosocial behavior was examined in regression analyses. Two types of regression equations were needed to test for a mediated effect (see MacKinnon, 2000). First, a set of regression analyses was conducted with self- and parent-reported empathy-related responding as predictors of ethnocultural sensitivity. Thus, in regression analyses, we examined the prediction of ethnocultural sensitivity from empathy-related responding and the prediction of prosocial behavior from ethnocultural sensitivity, as well as empathy-related responding.

Empathy-related responding predicting ethnocultural sensitivity. In order to examine adolescents' empathy-related responding as a predictor of ethnocultural sensitivity, four separate regression equations with each indicator of empathy-related responding (youth self-reported, T2 teacher-reported, T3 teacher-reported, and parent-reported empathy-related responding) and with youths' self-reported ethnocultural sensitivity as the dependent variable were conducted. Two of the four regression equations were significant. Youths' self-reported and parent-reported empathy-related responding positively predicted ethnocultural sensitivity, $F(1, 248) = 23.96$, $p < .001$, $R^2 = .09$, $\beta = .30$ and $F(1, 238) = 8.99$, $p < .01$, $R^2 = .04$, $\beta = .19$. Time 2 and Time 3 teacher-reported empathy-related responding were not significant unique predictors of ethnocultural sensitivity. Based on the regression analyses, we found support for the path from empathy-related responding to ethnocultural sensitivity in our heuristic model for parents' and adolescents' self-reports, but not for teachers' reports.

Ethnocultural sensitivity predicting prosocial behavior. Next, we examined the prediction of youths' prosocial behavior from their ethnocultural sensitivity. Four separate regression equations were conducted with each report of prosocial behavior (self-reported, T2 teacher, T3 teacher, and parent-reported) as the dependent variable. All four regression equations had the same predictor, namely youths' self-reported ethnocultural sensitivity. Two of the four regression equations were significant. Adolescents' self-reported ethnocultural sensitivity positively predicted self-reported prosocial behavior and parent-reported prosocial behavior, $F(1, 248) = 6.69$, $p < .01$, $R^2 = .03$, $\beta = .16$ and $F(1, 240) = 4.78$, $p = .03$, $R^2 = .02$, $\beta = .14$. Ethnocultural sensitivity did not predict T2 or T3 teachers' reports of prosocial behavior. In summary, we found partial support for the path from ethnocultural sensitivity to prosocial behavior in the heuristic model.

Ethnocultural sensitivity as a mediator. Based on the results above, there was support for the path between empathy-related responding and ethnocultural sensitivity. These analyses were used as the first set of regression analyses to examine mediation. Next, a set of regression analyses was conducted: (a) self-reported empathy-related responding and self-reported ethnocultural sensitivity as predictors of youths' self-reported prosocial behavior; (b) self-reported empathy-related responding and self-reported ethnocultural sensitivity as predictors of youths' parent-reported prosocial behavior; (c) parent-reported empathy-related responding and self-reported ethnocultural sensitivity as predictors of youths' self-reported prosocial behavior; and (d) parent-reported empathy-related responding and self-reported ethnocultural sensitivity as predictors of youths' parent-reported prosocial behavior. The overall equations were significant: (a) $F(2, 247) = 47.76$, $p < .001$, $R^2 = .28$, (b) $F(2, 239) = 4.41$, $p < .01$, $R^2 = .04$, (c) $F(2, 237) = 3.53$, $p = .03$, $R^2 = .03$, (d) $F(2, 237) = 46.39$, $p < .001$, $R^2 = .28$. However, only one predictor in each of the four equations was significant: (a) self-reported empathy-related responding, $\beta = .53$, $p < .001$; (b) self-reported empathy-related responding, $\beta = .13$, $p < .05$; (c) self-reported ethnocultural sensitivity, $\beta = .17$, $p = .01$; and (d) parent-reported empathy-related responding, $\beta = .52$, $p < .001$.

Based on the regression analyses, there generally is a lack of support for the role of ethnocultural sensitivity as a mediator in the relation between empathy-related responding and prosocial behavior. In only one case – for parent-reported empathy-related responding and self-reported ethnocultural sensitivity as predictors of youths' self-reported prosocial behavior – was there support for mediation. Although self-reported empathy-related responding and ethnocultural sensitivity were correlated with youths' self-reported prosocial behavior, the relation of ethnocultural sensitivity to prosocial behavior overlapped in variance with the prediction of prosocial behavior from self-reported empathy-related responding. Thus, rather than finding evidence of mediation, in most analyses there was support for a direct path between empathy-related responding and prosocial behavior. However, because there was only one measure of ethnocultural sensitivity, more research is needed in order to replicate these findings.

Moreover, ethnocultural sensitivity might mediate the relation of empathy-related responding to prosocial behaviors directed toward outgroup members; in this study, a global measure of prosocial behavior was used.

Prediction of Cross-Religion Friendships: Aspect of Positive Behavior

We conducted a series of logistic regressions to examine the extent to which ethnocultural sensitivity, prosocial behavior, and empathy-related responding predicted whether or not adolescents had friendships with another of a different religion. We hypothesized that youth who were relatively high in these characteristics also would be those who developed cross-religion friendships (regardless of ethnic or religious group status). Seven logistic regressions were computed, one for each report of socio-emotional characteristics (three reports of prosocial behavior, three reports of sympathy/perspective-taking, and one report of ethnocultural sensitivity) and all possible interactions of the three characteristics. All of these analyses were not significant. In other words, ethnocultural sensitivity, prosocial behavior, and empathy-related responding did not predict adolescents having a cross-religion friend.

In brief, even though we predicted some differences in adolescents' behavior based on adolescents' friendship selection, we did not find support for this prediction. In general, youth tend to select friends who have similar interests and behaviors to themselves (for a review of the literature on intergroup friendships see Brody, Wright, Aron, & McLaughlin-Volpe, Chapter 10, this volume; see also Rubin, Bukowski, & Parker, 2006). Proximity in the neighborhood may also have been a factor for the selection of friends. Perhaps ethnocultural sensitivity, empathy-related responding, and prosocial behavior are more closely related to maintenance of cross-group friendships in middle adolescence, when friendships are based more on intimacy, understanding, disclosure, and trust (e.g., Youniss, 1980). More research needs to be done to further investigate this possibility.

Limitations and Future Directions

As previously mentioned, our investigation provides insight into the socio-emotional behavior of Indonesian adolescents. There are so few data on the relation between empathy-related responding and prosocial behavior in non-Western cultures, especially in samples of adolescents. However, our investigation did have a few limitations. One limitation is related to measurement. All measures were questionnaires and some of the relations could be a result of self-presentation or reporter bias. Additionally, more research is needed to better understand the role of youths' ethnocultural sensitivity. In order to test the hypothesis that ethnocultural sensitivity is indeed related to more cognitive aspects of caring behavior (i.e., perspective-taking) compared to actual caring behavior (i.e., prosocial behavior), it would be useful to obtain reports from peers or other reporters of adolescents' ethnocultural sensitivity and to develop a more comprehensive measure of ethnocultural sensitivity for adolescents.

Another limitation is the time frame of our study. Even though we had three assessments, they were relatively close together in time (approximately 3 to 5 months apart from each other). Perhaps a follow-up assessment a full year later would tell a more complete story about the relations across time and development of differences or similarities in the adolescents' attitudes and behaviors.

Given the sophisticated cognitive, emotion-regulatory, and motivational capacities that likely are needed for compassionate love, few children or young adolescents would be expected to exhibit compassionate love. Nonetheless, the roots of compassionate love may begin in childhood, with compassionate love growing out of the capacities for empathy, sympathy, perspective-taking, and altruism. A goal for future research is to assess these constructs longitudinally and with multiple measures of each construct in order to test if childhood empathy-related responding and altruism predict older adolescent and adult compassionate love. The assessment of these constructs with multiple measures will capture a more accurate representation of adolescents' altruistic traits compared to one or two assessments as presented in this chapter.

Based on our findings, it appears that the Javanese culture (collectivist) is more similar to, than different from, Western cultures (individualist) in regard to adolescents' thoughts and attitudes about empathy-related responding, ethnocultural sensitivity, and prosocial behavior. Perhaps these constructs represent a more universal standard rather than a specific type of cultural standard. In the future, more research in other cultures (individualistic and collectivistic) needs to be conducted to examine the potential universal qualities of these constructs and whether the model is more strongly supported if the index of prosocial behavior were prosocial behavior directed toward members of an outgroup.

Conclusions

This study was unique in its focus on the socioemotional correlates of adolescents in a non-Western society. Overall, the elements of functioning likely involved in compassionate love – that is, prosocial behavior, empathy-related responding, and ethnic sensitivity – generally were significantly positively interrelated (especially within reporter; recall that adolescents who reported themselves as high in empathy-related responding also rated themselves as high in prosocial behavior). Additionally, these relations were similar for majority and minority adolescents. The positive interrelations of these variables in this sample are consistent with findings in Western samples (e.g., Batson, 1991; Carlo & Randall, 2002; Krevans & Gibbs, 1996).

In the examination of our heuristic model, we found some support for the paths between empathy-related responding and ethnocultural sensitivity, ethnocultural sensitivity and prosocial behavior, and empathy-related responding and prosocial behavior. These findings are important initial findings in the examination of potential predictors of compassionate love.

Acknowledgments

This project was supported by The Institute for Research on Unlimited Love – Altruism, Compassion, Service (located at the School of Medicine, Case Western Reserve University) and the Fetzer Institute.

References

Aboud, F. E. (2003). The formation of in-group favoritism and out-group prejudice in young children: Are they distinct attitudes? *Developmental Psychology, 39,* 48–60.

Bandura, A. (1991). Social cognitive theory of moral thought and action. In W. M. Kurtines & J. L. Gewirtz (Eds.), *Handbook of moral behavior and development: Vol. 1* (pp. 45–103). Hillsdale, NJ: Lawrence Erlbaum.

Bandura, A., Caprara, G. V., Barbaranelli, C., Gerbino, M., & Pastorelli, C. (2003). Role of affective self-regulatory efficacy in diverse sphere of psychosocial functioning. *Child Development, 74,* 769–782.

Batson, C. D. (1991). *The altruism question: Toward a social-psychological answer.* Hillsdale, NJ: Lawrence Erlbaum.

Batson, C. D., Early, S., & Salvarani, G. (1997). Perspective taking: Imagining how another feels versus imagining how you would feel. *Personality and Social Psychology Bulletin, 23,* 751–758.

Batson, C. D., Polycarpou, M. P., Harmon-Jones, E., Imhoff, H. J., Mitchener, E. C., Bednar, L. L., Klein, T. R., & Highberger, L. (1997). Empathy and attitudes: Can feeling for a member of a stigmatized group improve feelings toward the group? *Journal of Personality and Social Psychology, 72,* 105–118.

Batson, C. D., Sager, K., Garst, E., Kang, M., Rubchinsky, K., & Dawson, K. (1997). Is empathy-induced helping due to self-other merging? *Journal of Personality and Social Psychology, 73,* 495–509.

Bennett, M., Barrett, M., Karakozov, R., Kipiani, G., Lyons, E., Pavlenko, V., & Riazanova, T. (2004). Young children's evaluations of the ingroup and of outgroups: A multi-national study. *Social Development, 13,* 124–141.

Brewer, M. B. (1999). The psychology of prejudice: Ingroup love or outgroup hate? *Journal of Social Issues, 55,* 429–444.

Bryant, B. K. (1982). An index of empathy for children and adolescents. *Child Development, 53,* 413–425.

Cambray, J. (2006). Towards the feeling of emergence. *Journal of Analytical Psychology, 51,* 1–20.

Carlo, G., Hausmann, A., Christiansen, S., & Randall, B. A. (2003). Sociocognitive and behavioral correlates of a measure of prosocial tendencies for adolescents. *Journal of Early Adolescence, 23,* 107–134.

Carlo, G., & Randall, B. A. (2002). The development of a measure of prosocial behaviors for late adolescents. *Journal of Youth and Adolescence, 31,* 31–44.

Cohen, J., Cohen, P., West, S. G., & Aiken, L. S. (2003). *Multiple regression: Correlation analysis for the behavioral sciences* (3rd ed.). Mahwah, NJ: Lawrence Erlbaum.

Crick, N. R. (1996). The role of overt aggression, relational aggression, and prosocial behavior in the prediction of children's future social adjustment. *Child Development, 67,* 2317–2327.

Davis, M. H. (1994). *Empathy: A social psychological approach.* Madison, WS: Brown & Benchmark.

Davis, M. H., & Franzoi, S. L. (1991). Stability and change in adolescent self-consciousness and empathy. *Journal of Research in Personality, 25,* 70–87.

Eberly, M. B., & Montemayor, R. (1999). Adolescent affection and helpfulness toward parents: A 2-year follow-up. *Journal of Early Adolescence, 19,* 226–248.

Eisenberg, N. (1983). Children's differentiations among potential recipients of aid. *Child Development, 54,* 594–602.

Eisenberg, N., Carlo, G., Murphy, B., & Van Court, P. (1995). Prosocial development in late adolescence: A longitudinal study. *Child Development, 66,* 1179–1197.

Eisenberg, N., & Fabes, R. A. (1990). Empathy: Conceptualization, measurement, and relation to prosocial behavior. *Motivation and Emotion, 14,* 131–149.

Eisenberg, N., & Fabes, R. A. (1998). Prosocial development. In W. Damon (Series Ed.) & N. Eisenberg (Vol. Ed.), *Handbook of child psychology: Vol. 3. Social, emotional, and personality development* (5th ed.) (pp. 701–778). New York: John Wiley.

Eisenberg, N., Fabes, R. A., & Spinrad, T. L. (2006). Prosocial development. In W. Damon (Series Ed.) & N. Eisenberg (Vol. Ed.), *Handbook of child psychology: Vol. 3. Social, emotional, and personality development* (6th ed.) (pp. 646–718). New York: John Wiley.

Eisenberg, N., Murphy, B., & Shepard, S. (1997). The development of empathic accuracy. In W. Ickes (Ed.), *Empathic accuracy* (pp. 73–116). New York: Guilford Press.

Eisenberg, N., Pidada, S., & Liew, J. (2001). The relations of regulation and negative emotionality to Indonesian children's social functioning. *Child Development, 72,* 1747–1763.

Eisenberg, N., Shea, C. L., Carlo, G., & Knight, G. P. (1991). Empathy-related responding and cognition: A "chicken and the egg" dilemma. In W. M. Kurtines & J. L. Gewirtz (Eds.), *Handbook of moral behavior and development: Vol. 1* (pp. 63–88). Hillsdale, NJ: Lawrence Erlbaum.

Eisenberg, N., Zhou, Q., & Koller, S. (2001). Brazilian adolescents' prosocial moral judgment and behavior: Relations to sympathy, perspective taking, gender-role orientation, and demographic characteristics. *Child Development, 72,* 518–534.

Enesco, I., Navarro, A., Paradela, I., & Guerrero, S. (2005). Stereotypes and beliefs about different ethnic groups in Spain. A study with Spanish and Latin American children living in Madrid. *Applied Developmental Psychology, 26,* 638–659.

Estrada, P. (1995). Adolescents' self-reports of prosocial responses to friends and acquaintances: The role of sympathy-related cognitive, affective, and motivational processes. *Journal of Research on Adolescence, 5,* 173–200.

Feshbach, S. (1978). The environment of personality. *American Psychology, 33,* 447–455.

Galinsky, A. D., & Moskowitz, G. B. (2000). Perspective-taking: Decreasing stereotype expression, stereotype accessibility, and in-group favoritism. *Journal of Personality and Social Psychology, 78,* 708–724.

Gallese, V., & Lakoff, G. (2005). The brain's concepts: The role of the sensory-motor system in conceptual knowledge. *Cognitive Neuropsychology, 22,* 455–479.

Geertz, C. (1976). *The religion of Java.* Chicago: University of Chicago Press.

Goodman, R. (2001). Psychometric properties of the Strengths and Difficulties Questionnaire. *Journal of the American Academy of Child and Adolescent Psychiatry, 40,* 1337–1345.

Henry, C. S., Sager, D. W., & Plunkett, S. W. (1996). Adolescents' perceptions of family system characteristics, parent-adolescent dyadic behaviors, adolescent qualities, and adolescent empathy. *Family Relations, 45,* 283–292.

Hoffman, M. L. (1977). Personality and social development. *Annual Review of Psychology, 28,* 5–321.

Hoffman, M. L. (2000). *Empathy and moral development: Implications for caring and justice.* New York: Cambridge University Press.

Hoffman, M. L. (2001). Toward a comprehensive empathy-based theory of prosocial moral development. In A. C. Bohart & D. J. Stipek (Eds.), *Constructive & destructive behavior: Implications for family, school, & society* (pp. 61–86). Washington, DC: American Psychological Association.

Iyengar, S. S., Lepper, M. R., & Ross, L. (1999). Independence from whom? Interdependence with whom? Cultural perspectives on ingroups versus outgroups. In D. A. Prentice & D. T. Miller (Eds.), *Cultural divides: Understanding and overcoming group conflict* (pp. 273–301). New York: Russell Sage Foundation.

Karniol, R., Gabay, R., Ochion, Y., & Harari, Y. (1998). Is gender or gender-role orientation a better predictor of empathy in adolescence? *Sex Roles, 39,* 45–59.

Killen, M., & Turiel, E. (1998). Adolescents' and young adults' evaluations of helping and sacrificing for others. *Journal of Research on Adolescence, 8,* 355–375.

Koentjaraningrat. (1985). *Javanese culture.* New York: Oxford University Press.

Krevans, J., & Gibbs, J. C. (1996). Parents' use of inductive discipline: Relations to children's empathy and prosocial behavior. *Child Development, 67*, 3263–3277.

Lillard, A. (1998). Ethnopsychologies: Cultural variations in theory of mind. *Psychological Bulletin, 123*, 3–32.

MacKinnon, D. P. (2000). *Technical assistance report: Mediation analysis.* Unpublished manual.

Magnis-Suseno, F. (1997). *Javanese ethnics and world-view: The Javanese idea of the good life.* Jakarta: Gramedia Pustaka Utama.

Markus, H. R., & Kitayama, S. (1991). Culture and the self: Implications for cognition, emotion, and motivation. *Psychological Review, 98*, 224–253.

Marshall, R. (1997). Variances in individualism across two cultures and three social classes. *Journal of Cross-Cultural Psychology, 28*, 490–495.

McWhirter, B. T., Besett-Alesch, T. M., Horibata, J., & Gat, I. (2002). Loneliness in high risk adolescents: The role of coping, self-esteem, and empathy. *Journal of Youth Studies, 5*, 69–84.

Mulder, N. (1989). *Individual and society in Java: A cultural analysis.* Yogyakarta, Indonesia: Gadjah Mada University Press.

Mulder, N. (1996). *Inside Indonesian Society: Cultural change in Indonesia.* Amsterdam, Netherlands: Pepin Press.

Negy, C., Shreve, T. L., Jensen, B. J., & Uddin, N. (2003). Ethnic identity, self-esteem, and ethnocentrism: A study of social identity versus multicultural theory of development. *Cultural Diversity and Ethnic Minority Psychology, 9*, 333–344.

Nesdale, D., Griffith, J., Durkin, K., & Maass, A. (2005). Empathy, group norms & children's ethnic attitudes. *Applied Developmental Psychology, 26*, 623–637.

Oliner, S. P., & Oliner, P. M. (1988). *The altruistic personality: Rescuers of Jews in Nazi Europe.* New York: Free Press.

Oyserman, D., Coon, H. M., & Kemmelmeier, M. (2002). Rethinking individualism and collectivism: Evaluation of theoretical assumptions and meta-analyses. *Psychological Bulletin, 128*, 3–72.

Peacock, J. L. (1973). *Indonesia: An anthropological perspective.* Pacific Palisades, CA: Goodyear.

Pedersen, A., Walker, I., & Wise, M. (2005). "Talk does not cook rice": Beyond anti-racism rhetoric to strategies for social action. *Australian Psychologist, 40*, 20–30.

Ridley, C. R., & Lingle, D. W. (1996). Cultural empathy in multicultural counseling: A multidimensional process model. In P. B. Pederson & J. G. Draguns (Eds.), *Counseling across cultures* (4th ed., pp. 21–46). Thousand Oaks, CA: Sage.

Rubin, K. H., Bukowski, W. M., & Parker, J. G. (2006). Peer interactions, relationships, and groups. In W. Damon & R. M. Lerner (Series Eds.) & N. Eisenberg (Vol. Ed.), *Handbook of child psychology: Vol. 3. Social, emotional, and personality development* (6th ed.), (pp. 719–788). New York: John Wiley.

Rushton, J. P., Brainerd, C. J., & Pressley, M. (1983). Behavioral development and construct validity: The principle of aggregation. *Psychological Bulletin, 94*, 18–38.

Rutland, A., Cameron, L., Bennett, L., & Ferrell, J. (2005). Interracial contact and racial constancy: A multi-site study of racial intergroup bias in 3–5-year-old Anglo-British children. *Applied Developmental Psychology, 26*, 699–713.

Strayer, J. (1987). Affective and cognitive perspectives on empathy. In N. Eisenberg & J. Strayer (Eds.), *Empathy and its development* (pp. 218–244). New York: Cambridge University Press.

Strayer, J., & Roberts, W. (1997). Children's personal distance and their empathy: Indices of interpersonal closeness. *International Journal of Behavioral Development, 20*, 385–403.

Stürmer, S., Snyder, M., & Omoto, A. M. (2005). Prosocial emotions and helping: The moderating role of group membership. *Journal of Personality and Social Psychology, 88*, 532–546.

Tajfel, H. (1982). Social psychology of intergroup relations. *Annual Review of Psychology, 33*, 1–39.

Tarrant, M. (2002). Adolescent peer groups and social identity. *Social Development, 11*, 110–123.

Tarrant, M., North, A. C., Edridge, M. D., Kirk, L. E., Smith, E. A., & Turner, R. E. (2001). Social identity in adolescence. *Journal of Adolescence, 24*, 597–609.

Tarrant, M., North, A. C., & Hargreaves, D. J. (2004). Adolescents' intergroup attributions: A comparison of two social identities. *Journal of Youth and Adolescence, 33*, 177–185.

Triandis, H. C. (1995). *Individualism and collectivism.* Boulder, CO: Westview Press.

Tropp, L. R., & Pettigrew, T. F. (2005). Relationships between intergroup contact and prejudice among minority and majority status groups. *Psychological Science, 16*, 951–957.

Underwood, L. G. (2002). The human experience of compassionate love: Conceptual mapping and data from selected studies. In S. G. Post, L. G. Underwood, J. P. Schloss, & W. B. Hurlbut (Eds.), *Altruism and altruistic love: Science, philosophy, and religion in dialogue* (pp. 72–88). New York: Oxford University Press.

Van Beek, A. M. (1987). Pastoral counseling challenge in the Javanese hospital: A cross-cultural comparison. *Pastoral Psychology, 36*, 112–122.

Wang, Y. W., Davidson, M. M., Yakushko, O. F., Savoy, H. B., Tan, J. A., & Bleier, J. K. (2003). The scale of ethnocultural empathy: Development, validation, and reliability. *Journal of Counseling Psychology, 50*, 221–234.

Weiner, B. (1980). A cognitive (attribution)-emotion-action model of motivated behavior: An analysis of judgments of help-giving. *Journal of Personality and Social Psychology, 39*, 186–200.

Williams, W. (1991). *Javanese lives: Men and women in modern Indonesian society.* New Brunswick, NJ: Rutgers University Press.

Youniss, J. (1980). *Parents and peers in social development: A Sullivan-Piaget perspective.* Chicago: University of Chicago Press.

Part VII

Commentary

15

Compassionate Love: Concluding Reflections

Daniel Perlman and Rozzana Sánchez Aragón

As both web sites and films testify, compassionate love (CL) is a notion that exists in popular culture. For example, when typed into the Google search system (circa June 2007) with a request that the words be adjacent to each other, this phrase returned 52,000 web sites and 1,000 images. (A web search for the terms without them necessarily being adjacent words yielded 1.4 million documents and over 100,000 images.) Among the first images to appear were pictures of bread (tied to Jesus's infinite love for *all* people and saying "I am the bread of life"), Mother Teresa, a wedding, a rose, a temple in South India, Sisters of Notre Dame, a misinterpreted diagram of Sternberg's triangular model of love, a nun attending an elderly patient, the cover of a book entitled *Compassionate Love*, a rose-quartz mala (a sacred bead necklace purported to help strengthen "the development of compassionate love, both for yourself and for others"), and a large boat with sails (linked to Tyson Williams's blog site with an entry on compassion and love as the Buddhist way of handling stress).

The Doctor, a 1991 release based on the memoir of a real-life surgeon, Ed Rosenbaum, provides a good illustration of the theme of compassionate love in a film. The movie begins showing Jack McKee (William Hurt) as a gifted but technocratic heart surgeon with little concern for the emotional welfare of his patients. Juxtaposed with McKee is Eli Blumfield, a compassionate eye, ear, and throat specialist, concerned about his patients as people but often ridiculed by his fellow physicians (including McKee). The film traces McKee's own health crisis (throat cancer): his recognition of the disease, his frustrations in dealing with the health-care system as a patient, his bonding with another patient, his turning to Blumfield for treatment, and finally a physically recovered McKee becoming a compassionate healer.

Popular culture underscores compassionate love as a noteworthy phenomenon, identifies examples of it, and offers some insights into its dynamics. Yet popular views generally lack the systematic, empirically based approach that social scientists provide. The present book illuminates compassionate love from a social science perspective.

In taking this approach, the book is a first of its kind, heading into relatively new territory. Underwood (Chapter 1, this volume) notes: "One of the first places that this term 'compassionate love' emerged in the context of scientific research was at a meeting of a World Health Organization (WHO) working group to develop an assessment tool for quality of life for use in many diverse cultures." The instrument developed by this group was published only recently – in 2006 (WHOQOL SRPB Group, 2006). Journal publications are also a recent phenomenon: a check of the PsycInfo database shows that compassionate love was not used in the title of a psychological article until 2001. Prior to the present volume, this concept had not made its way into specific research domains such as adult development (Marks & Song, Chapter 5, this volume).

Our goal in this chapter is to comment on this incipient area, especially the chapters in this volume. We will begin with brief comments on origins of the book, then synthesize and reflect on Underwood's model of compassionate love that served as a springboard for the volume, highlight key findings in the volume itself as they relate to Underwood's model, consider the paradox of compassionate love vs. the dark side of human nature, and end with conclusions which include our suggestions for future directions of compassionate love research.

Origins of the Volume

Three events, which are at least indirectly linked to the development of this volume, are noteworthy. First, both the Fetzer Institute and the John Templeton Foundation's Institute for Research on Unlimited Love supported research on compassionate, unselfish love. Second, these foundations supported research meetings that brought together compassionate love researchers (e.g., Sprecher, 2003). Third, Underwood articulated a conceptual formulation of compassionate love, previously (Underwood, 2002) and as the first chapter of the current volume. Underwood's model has both guided research on the topic and played a seminal role in framing the current volume.

Not all of the contributors to the present volume received foundation funding, nor did all contributors attend the working meetings on compassionate love. Nonetheless, the aforementioned events leading to this volume strike us as a highly advantageous set of circumstances. Underwood's conceptualization and the meetings provide a degree of coherence and interplay among the contributors that edited volumes often lack.

The Fetzer Institute states as its mission "to foster awareness of the power of love and forgiveness in the emerging global community." The John Templeton Foundation rests its mission on the "conviction that efforts to address the world's critical issues must go beyond political, social, and economic strategies to their psychological and spiritual roots." In its statement about itself, the Institute for Research on Unlimited Love expresses a somewhat similar position. After defining what it means by unlimited love, the Unlimited Love Institute asks how various scientific approaches can productively be brought together "with great religious thought and practice, and with the moral vision of a common humanity to which all great spiritual traditions give rise ... Without that vision, the future of humankind is increasingly imperiled" (see http://www.unlimited-loveinstitute.com/aboutus/index.html). Both Foundations conceptualize compassionate love as a positive force that is linked with spirituality.

In a period in which many research endeavors receive substantial financial support, the question arises: How does funding shape the focus, findings, or interpretation of research? Such questions are especially prominent in drug research, where drug companies have a substantial financial stake in the outcomes of drug trials (see Lexchin, 2005). Infamous examples of efforts to curtail close relationship research easily come to mind (e.g., Senator Proximere's attack on Berscheid and Hatfield's love research [Shaffer, 1977], as well as the role of conservative members of Congress in blocking sex research [Michael et al., 1998]).

With regard to investigations of compassionate love, it is good that funding agencies have played a benign role. The Fetzer Institute and Templeton Foundation funding focused attention on compassionate love and helped scholars carry out their work. This was a winning partnership for both parties. Naturally, subtle influences on the presentation of research findings are possible but, at least in our subjective judgment, do not appear to be problematic. Although the funding agencies have an interest in the role of spirituality in compassionate love, based on the role of religiosity and spirituality in promoting well-being (Paloutzian & Kirkpatrick, 1995) and prosocial behavior, we believe researchers would have undoubtedly considered these factors independent of the funding they received.

Underwood's Model of Compassionate Love

Defining Compassionate Love

Underwood provides both a definition of compassionate love and a conceptual framework for analyzing it. To recap briefly, she defines compassionate love in terms of the "giving of self for the good of the other."

The other can be close or more distant others, even strangers. Underwood articulated five basic elements of this kind of love: (a) free choice for the other; (b) some degree of accurate cognitive understanding of the other, oneself, and the situation; (c) valuing the other at a fundamental level; (d) openness and receptivity; and, finally, (e) a "response of the heart" – a heartfelt, affective component in compassionate attitudes or actions. While Underwood's working definition is from the perspective of the giver of compassionate love, she also considers the perspective of the recipient, writing:

> It's that kind of love that feels so good to be on the receiving end of. Good in a lasting way, one that sticks to the ribs and doesn't give indigestion. To be loved for who you truly are. To be loved by someone who knows your faults. To be loved through thick and thin. To be loved at cost to the other. To be loved in a way that brings you more fully alive.

Underwood's Model

Figure 1.1 in Chapter 1 of this volume presents Underwood's working model. The model is designed to "bring together disparate research and translate from one discipline to another." In its simplest form, it consists of what she calls the substrate, then motivation and discernment, compassionate love, and finally, outcomes. The outcomes are joined with the substrate via a feedback loop. The substrate consists of individual differences (biological, developmental, personality) and contextual factors (cultural, historical, familial, and social). The substrate also takes into consideration the situation and the relationship. Some might call the substrate antecedent or predisposing factors. Motive and discernment are part of the process. For compassionate love to occur, the actor's motives must be centered on the good of the other rather than on self-centered motives. Discernment involves an analytic aspect of compassion, identifying what is good for the other, examining short-term and long-term considerations, taking appropriate self-care, etc. Motives and discernment are internal processes within the actor that may not always be easily assessable. Given discernment and motives centered on the other's good, compassionate love results. Finally, stemming from compassionate love, there are positive behavioral and attitudinal outcomes.

Two points regarding the possible manifestations of compassionate love are worth noting. First, as Underwood makes explicit, what may appear as altruistic, prosocial behavior is not compassionate if the underlying motive is largely self-centered. Second, Underwood writes that "the way that compassionate love is expressed in marriage is going to be different than in interactions with strangers." Presumably Underwood is implying that it is not only the strength of compassionate love that may vary across different types of relationships but also the dynamics as well as outcomes (behavioral and attitudinal) may vary.

The model does not fully spell out all the specific variables involved or interactions among various parts. Thus, Underwood leaves much to be done in terms of specifying specific variables within classes of variables. Nonetheless, the model is a bold initiative in many ways. Derlega and Margulis (1982) described three, possibly overlapping, steps in concept development. The first identifies interest in the concept by presenting observations, cases, and preliminary studies that demonstrate the viability and importance of the phenomenon. The second step accepts the importance of the concept and tries to demonstrate similarities and differences between it and related concepts. The third step involves systematic analysis with formally defined constructs plus interrelated propositions about the relationships among constructs. At this point, a testable hypothesis can be derived. Derlega and Margulis (1982, p. 152) state that at this stage "the hows and whys ... are directly and fully addressed." In other words, the dynamics of the phenomenon including antecedents, processes, and consequences are explained. In formulating her model of compassionate love. Underwood assumes the importance of the construct, deals with how compassionate love is similar and different from related concepts, and begins moving toward step three. After over forty years of research, Derlega and Margulis assessed the area of loneliness in the early 1980s as still primarily in the second stage. By comparison, work on compassionate love is off to a quick start.

Reflections on Variables in the Model

In thinking about Underwood's model, three aspects of the nature of the variables struck us: the assumption of compassionate love involving both intimate and more distant relationships, the measurement and manifestations of compassionate love, and the placement of specific variables (cross-group relations and empathy) in the model. We will address each of these in turn.

Love for intimate vs. distant others. As close relationships researchers, we are accustomed to thinking of love in terms of dyadic or family relations. Consistent with this view, definitions of love often specify it is toward a particular person. In this volume, for example, Neff and Karney argue that "love can be thought of as an attitude toward a *particular individual*" (emphasis added). Similarly, Aron and Aron (1991) defined love as "the constellation of behaviors, cognitions, and emotions associated with a desire to enter or maintain a close relationship with a *specific* other person" (p. 26; emphasis added). Given such definitions emphasizing dyadic relationships, it is not surprising, as Fehr and Sprecher observe, that love for distant others (e.g., strangers or all of humanity) has "generally been overlooked by researchers."

One possibility would be to drop the word love from Underwood's central concept. Underwood argues, however, that compassion by itself is inadequate. She maintains that it leaves out "some of the emotional and transcendent components which the word *love* brings in" (Underwood, 2002, p. 78).

What does research in the current volume and elsewhere suggest regarding the extent to which compassionate feelings and behaviors toward intimate and more distant people are one and the same? In terms of laypeople's views, Fehr and Sprecher claim the prototype of compassionate love is better represented in intimate than distant relationships. Actual expressions of compassion are stronger toward close than distant others (Mikulincer, Shaver, Gillath, & Nitzberg, 2005). In their scale development research, Sprecher and Fehr (2005) administered their Compassionate Love items twice: once with reference to close others and again with reference to distant others. The two versions were moderately correlated ($r = .56$ and $.47$; Studies 1 and 2). Furthermore, variables correlated with one version of the scale were correlated with the other, although the close version of the scale correlated more strongly with social support while compassionate love for humanity correlated more strongly with volunteering. Complementing these findings, Mikulincer, Shaver, and Gillath conclude that secure attachment generally is linked to caregiving, whether that caregiving is to intimate or non-intimate others. Finally, Marks and Song report that feelings of normative obligation to kin and to friends (motivational factors) are fairly strongly related ($r = .57$) and, similarly, emotional support to kin and to nonkin is fairly strongly related ($r = .42$).

Overall, it appears there may be subtle differences between compassionate love for intimate others and compassionate love for distant others, but there does seem to be overlap between them. Love researchers have long discussed types and the intensity of love. The work report in the current volume testifies to the value of combining love toward intimate and distant others into an overarching concept.

Measurement and manifestations of compassionate love. There are many ways people can give of themselves for the good of another. In their research and discussions, the authors in this volume cover a number of indicators to reflect compassionate love as well as the attitudes and actions that stem from it. Underwood offers the Daily Spiritual Experience Scale to assess the attitude component of compassionate love. The Daily Experience Scale has utility as a very short measure for large surveys and other similar uses. Fehr and Sprecher's Compassionate Love Scale has already been mentioned. Longer scales such as Fehr and Sprecher's generally have greater reliability and can more fully capture the nuances of complex concepts.

Measures of interpersonal properties such as intimacy and compassionate love can vary along two dimensions: temporal duration (trait vs. state) and level (individual vs. dyadic). Underwood's measure asks for frequency of feeling selfless caring, implying this is a state, yet one that some people experience more often than others. Fehr and Sprecher's scale asks how characteristic each statement is of the person, implying a more trait-like property. Both measures focus on the individual level rather than assessing compassionate love as a relationship property.

In their definition, Sprecher and Fehr (2005, p. 630) write:

> *Compassionate love* is an attitude toward other(s), either close others or strangers or all of humanity; containing feelings, cognitions, and behaviors that are focused on caring, concern, tenderness, and an orientation toward supporting, helping, and understanding the other(s), particularly when the other(s) is (are) perceived to be suffering or in need.

Current measures do not focus on the cognitive aspects of compassionate love. Springing from this definition, it would be beneficial to more fully assess the beliefs (or philosophy of life) components of compassionate love.

In several chapters of the book what might be considered the attitudes and actions stemming from compassionate love are presented. These include: caregiving (Giesbrecht; Marks & Song; Mikulincer, Shaver, & Gillath; Roberts, Wise, & DuBenske); volunteerism (Marks & Song; Omoto, Malsch, & Barraza), social support, marital efficacy and marital stability (Neff & Karney); emotional and instrumental support (Marks & Song); children's conscience development (Volling, Kolak, & Kennedy); exemplary care (Graber & Mitcham); ethnocultural sensitivity when people from other groups are mistreated, prosocial behavior, and cross-religious friendships (Vaughan et al.); positive attitudes toward members of other groups than one's own, motivation to seek out members of other groups, self-expansion, generalized positive affect (Brody, Wright, Aron, & McLaughlin-Volpe); and empathy, altruistic values, altruistic love, and altruistic behavior (Tom Smith).

Given the plethora of outcomes of compassionate love, how associated are these manifestations with one another? Tom Smith examines this question using data from the General Social Surveys. With the exception of empathy and altruistic values, the various measures had at best a small association. One test doth not make a firm truth. In any event, the weak associations among the numerous manifestations of compassionate love are not incompatible with Underwood's position. As already underscored, she questions whether every potentially compassionate action is done for compassionate reasons. Some are not. Furthermore, to the extent that possible manifestations of compassionate love are like other forms of social behavior, they are undoubtedly determined by multiple influences, of which compassionate love is only one. Given such a causal constellation, low correlations among indicators are probable.

What are the implications of there being a loosely interrelated set of numerous outcomes of compassionate love? Our expectation is that compassionate love is likely to have moderate rather than strong associations with each of the attitudes and acts to which it can lead.

Placement of cross-group relations and empathy within the model. There are some discrepancies among authors in where they locate variables in Underwood's model. For example, Brody et al. speak of "the positive transformative power of close cross-group friendships to create compassionate love." Thus, they place cross-group friendships as an antecedent condition. Vaughan et al., on the other hand, talk of cross-religious relationships as one of the ways caring and compassionate love is extended to people outside one's own group. Given this framing, cross-religious friendships are an outcropping of compassionate love, not an antecedent.

Similarly, different authors place empathy at different points in the model. Underwood herself refers to empathy when discussing substrate variables. Graber and Mitcham view the empathetic act of putting one's self in another person's shoes as part of "the discernment and motivation that support compassionate love." Tom Smith lumps empathy with various forms of altruism, presumably implying that empathy is a manifestation or outcome of compassionate love.

A few points are worth mentioning regarding the discrepant placement of variables. First, placing empathy in the substrate vs. as discernment and motivation may reflect conceptualizing empathy as an enduring predisposition of the individual vs. a momentary aspect of people's interactions. Second, given feedback loops, it is possible that variables can at different times be both antecedents and consequences. Third, the majority of research on compassionate love is correlational in nature. In the intergroup relations tradition there are some laudatory experiments in which the creation of outgroup friendships promotes positive outcomes (Brody et al.). But such studies are rare. Investigators in this area do, of course, have statistical procedures for identifying plausible casual models. Giesbrecht's path analysis showing antecedents of caregiving illustrates this approach. Nonetheless, even with sophisticated statistical procedures it is difficult to definitively decipher antecedents, spurious relationships, concomitants, and consequences. Although this is of concern for those seeking scientific clarity, in everyday life, knowing that these things often go together may be sufficient for many practical purposes.

Evidence Related to Underwood's Model

Underwood offered her model as a starting point. Not all of the authors in the volume directly built on it. Yet, the model does offer one schema for briefly highlighting aspects of what the contributors can conclude about compassionate love. We will focus on Underwood's substrate factors plus motivation and discernment. We will not focus on either the positive behavioral and attitudinal outcomes of compassionate love or the feedback process. We have already discussed outcomes, and contributors largely ignore the feedback loop aspect of Underwood's model.

Substrate Factors

Individual variations. Starting at the far left of Underwood's model, the contributors to this volume investigated the role of individual variations in compassionate love and the positive behaviors associated with it. For example, Mikulincer et al. provide considerable evidence for the hypotheses that secure attachment is associated with effective caregiving and helping. These effects are found in both close relationships and in the wider social world involving strangers, members of minority groups, and people with special needs. Sprecher and Fehr as well as Giesbrecht provide complementary findings.

One of Mikulincer et al.'s key methodological techniques is priming: experimental manipulations to influence what participants are thinking about prior to being in situations where compassion or compassion-related behaviors could be expressed. Promoting thoughts associated with attachment security is one way of enhancing the likelihood of compassionate love. Such studies are a laudable demonstration of the cognitive factors in Underwood's model (cf. Giesbrecht's use of perspective-taking).

As indicated above, Underwood classifies dispositional empathy as a substrate variable. Again, this factor emerges throughout the volume as being important. Fehr and Sprecher found their compassionate love scale correlated moderately strongly with multiple indicators of empathy. Mikulincer et al. underscore its role in caregiving. Complementing this, Giesbrecht found empathy was an immediate predictor of caregiving among staff working with individuals who have developmental disabilities.

In Omoto et al.'s study, greater empathetic concern was associated with stronger motivation for volunteerism. In reviewing past research, Vaughan et al. conclude that empathy is related to more positive views of outgroup members. In their own research among Indonesian youth, they found a positive relationship between empathetic responding and prosocial behavior, as well as some support for an association between empathetic responding and ethnic sensitivity (e.g., being concerned when someone is mistreated because of the ethnicity). Finally, Tom Smith reports empathy being correlated with both altruistic values and altruistic behavior. In sum, empathy is clearly associated with, and likely fosters, compassionate love.

Drawing on large, national data sets, Tom Smith and Marks and Song cover the associations between several demographic variables and compassionate attitudes and acts. The results show a few general patterns but are not altogether consistent. Consider first the basic variable of age: Tom Smith cites past research suggesting that helping is most common in mid-life. In the General Social Survey data, this pattern was manifest for empathy and altruistic values. However, for other indices of compassionate love, curvilinear relationships were not found. Feelings of normative obligation to help to kin (Marks & Song) and altruistic behaviors (Tom Smith) were quite high among young adults and altruistic love was high among older adults (Tom Smith). Apropos of socioeconomic status, Tom Smith describes the associations between stratification variables (i.e., education and income) and compassion measures as "mixed and generally weak."

Part of the reason for variability in results undoubtedly stems from the fact of there being multiple measures of compassionate attitudes and acts. Some demographic predictors were measure-specific. In addition to the aforementioned findings on age, consider as a second example Tom Smith's findings on how various manifestations of compassion related to marital status. For empathy, there was little relationship with marital status. Altruistic love was higher among the married than among the divorced/separated or never married. Altruistic values were greater among the married than the never married. Turning to altruistic acts, the never married were more likely to engage in altruistic acts on the longer scale, but marital status did not differentiate on the shorter scale.

Illustrating a more consistent pattern of findings, contributors predominantly report evidence of women being higher than men in compassionate love and altruism. Women score higher on compassionate love (Fehr & Sprecher), compassionate motivation and acts including volunteerism (Marks & Song), measures of altruistic values, and the 15-item altruistic behavior scale (Tom Smith). Even to this pattern, exceptions did emerge: there was no gender difference on Tom Smith's 11 altruistic behavior scale and men scored higher on the altruistic love index. As Tom Smith notes, gender differences in altruistic behavior may depend on the nature of the help requested. Dating back to the 1980s, social psychologists have suggested that men may engage in more heroic and chivalrous helping behaviors, while women may offer more emotionally supportive help (Eagly & Crowley, 1986).

Contextual variations. Another aspect of Underwood's substrate is the context that shapes the individual. Here Underwood includes such elements as cultural, religious, and family environments. We will start with cultural. Vaughan et al. look at compassionate love within Indonesia and other authors look at racial–ethnic variation (e.g., there is some evidence that blacks are high in altruistic motivation and behavior – Marks & Song, Tom Smith). Vaughan et al. claim that the significance Javanese culture places on caring and social harmony should cultivate compassionate love in that society.

Complementing Vaughan et al.'s approach of examining compassionate love within a non-English-speaking society, Sánchez Aragón, coauthor of the present chapter, has been exploring love among Mexicans (see Sánchez Aragón, 2000, 2007). She has a 9-item index capturing aspects of compassionate love. Illustrative items include behaviors such as helping the other person, being nice to them, understanding them, taking care of them and attempting to satisfy the other person's needs. In both males and females, compassionate love was predicted by a collaborative, compromising conflict style; a positive, open communication style; several of Lee's love styles (pragma, storge, eros, and agape); and Mexicans' proclivity toward abnegation (denying oneself and instead putting the other first). In addition, in females, feeling closeness toward another person was associated with compassionate love. In males, being well educated, high in self-esteem and self-actualization; being low in defensiveness, and having both masculine and feminine traits (e.g., intelligent, competitive, loving, and warm) was associated with compassionate love.

Neither Vaughan et al. nor Sánchez Aragón, however, had another culture for comparisons purposes. The present volume provides only limited evidence on how compassionate love might vary cross-culturally. Illustrating the limited cross-cultural research reported in the volume, Mikulincer et al. found that avoidant attachment was consistently related to low levels of volunteerism in three different countries. In our view, more multinational, cultural research is warranted. Not only is cross-cultural research needed, but also, given the contemporary importance of migration in many societies, we advocate examination of how the acculturation of immigrants influences compassionate love. Procidano and Levine's (2007) investigation of social support among Hispanic Americans in New York takes a step in that direction.

With four contributors exploring the role of religiosity or spirituality, that context (or that context as it is internalized by individuals) receives considerable attention. Fehr and Sprecher report its positive association with their compassionate love scale. In Tom Smith's analysis of the General Social Survey data, religiosity was one of the few variables that predicted all five measures of empathy and altruism. Volling et al. demonstrated links between parents' beliefs in the sacredness of marriage and children's early expression of compassionate behavior. Among Graber and Mitcham's compassionate medical caregivers, virtually all had strong beliefs and experiences (e.g., feeling God's presence) related to spirituality. Overall, religiosity and spirituality appear firmly connected to compassionate love.

Aspects of the familial and social contexts in which compassionate love might develop are analyzed in Chapter 3 by Stacy Smith et al. and in Chapter 6 by Volling et al. Using definitions varying in stringency, Smith and her colleagues studied the prevalence of altruistic acts and compassionate love in American television shows. They also coded for selected aspects of these episodes, especially aspects related to the likelihood that viewers might imitate media portrayals. Overall this project provides evidence (see below) on the prevalence of altruism on television shows and indicates that such acts are often portrayed in contexts that are likely to foster viewers imitating the acts shown on television.

Volling et al. investigated how parents' moral socialization practices were associated with children's conscience development. They consider conscience development as a childhood precursor to compassionate love. Overall, a pattern of positive discipline was associated with early conscience development. Such positive discipline involved praising the child's good qualities, expressing pleasure and joy in the child's good behavior, and making parental approval conditional on the child's good behavior. Punitively oriented child-rearing practices generally were not linked to children's expression of moral emotions.

Relationships and situations. In Underwood's model, the expression of compassionate love can be influenced by relationships and the situation. We have already cited research showing that compassionate love is stronger toward intimate than distant others. As also discussed above, the associated manifestations of compassionate love may differ in different relationships. For example, Roberts et al. discuss the forms caregiving takes in relationships between family caregivers and terminally ill individuals. In this kind of relationship, they identify three relationship-linked types of compassionate love experiences: caregiving to the other, healing and forgiving, and letting go. Another illustration of the place of relationships in compassionate love is Graber and Mitcham's observation that compassionate caregivers tend to establish long-term, personal relations with their patients. In this instance, it is perhaps the compassionate love leading to the nature of the relationships.

In his classic *Art of Loving*, Erich Fromm (1956) provides one formulation that might guide future research on how relationships influence love. His argument is that mothers provide unconditional love but fathers are conditional in their love. Complementing the aforementioned gender differences in compassionate love, Fromm's view suggests the prediction that mothers are more prone to compassionate love than fathers.

Turning to situational factors, Underwood cites time urgency as an inhibiting influence on compassionate love. Similarly, Graber and Mitcham note: "Most hospital clinicians ... work under pressing time demands." They consider these time pressures obstacles to exemplary patient care but consider such care "all the more remarkable" when it is provided in these adverse situations.

From an attachment perspective, caregiving is a manifestation of compassionate love. Therefore situational aspects that activate the caregiving behavioral system could be conceptualized as situational forces promoting compassionate love. According to Mikulincer et al., our caregiving system is likely to be activated when we realize another person has to cope with stress, discomfort, or danger and when the potential recipient of our caregiving has an opportunity for exploration, learning, or mastery. In either of these circumstances, the caregiver can relieve the other person's distress, support the other person's coping efforts, or provide a secure base from which the other person can explore.

Another factor that might be classified as a situational influence is the size of the community in which people live. In the General Social Surveys rural residents were higher in altruistic values and altruistic love but not in altruistic behaviors (Tom Smith). The latter finding is somewhat surprising in that a meta-analysis of 65 tests of urban–rural differences show urban dwellers to be less helpful (Steblay, 1987). Given the larger number of people in cities, Smith speculates that urban dwellers may come into contact with situations where others need help more often than do rural dwellers. Following his reasoning, one possible reconciliation of Smith's results vs. those of the meta-analysis is that the General Social Surveys tap the total number of times people give help, but other studies have assessed the likelihood of rural vs. urban dwellers acting altruistically in single episodes where help is needed. In single episodes, rural dwellers may be more likely to offer help, even though they come upon such episodes less often than urban dwellers. It is also possible that the data collected via the General Social Surveys are an anomaly.

Discernment and Motivation

We have already discussed Graber and Mitcham's seeing health-care workers putting themselves in their patient's shoes as an example of discernment. Vaughan et al.'s concern with ethnocultural sensitivity is another indicator of discernment. It was related to children's prosocial behavior as reported by parents and offspring but not by teachers.

Several contributors to this volume consider various motivational aspects of compassionate love. Brody et al. view self-expansion as the basic motivation for people to seek out and develop positive attitudes toward members of the outgroup. Giesbrecht argues that altruistic motivation fosters caregiving both directly and indirectly by facilitating empathy and perspective-taking. His data support this view. Marks and Song identify three normative obligation constructs they see as related to motivation for compassionate love: altruistic normative obligation, normative obligation to family, and normative obligation to friends. Neff and Karney work motivation into their model by arguing that motivations to positively perceive global qualities of a partner are stronger than motivations to see specific qualities of a partner. They equate compassionate love with having realistic perceptions of a partner's specific qualities seeing both positive and *negative* qualities. Wives', but not husbands', compassionate love assessed in this manner was associated with greater social support and feelings of marital efficacy.

At the core of Underwood's model is the idea that compassionate love is motivated by a concern for the other rather than the self. Omoto et al., Roberts et al., and Stacy Smith et al. refer to this distinction. Smith et al. coded concern for the other as a motivation in their analysis of television episodes. Roberts et al. discuss "egosystem" and "ecosystem" motivational systems, presuming that an other-oriented, ecosystem motivation is essential for compassionate love. Among those who manifest compassionate love, Roberts et al. found evidence of a shift to a prosocial, "ecosystem" orientation as death approached. Omoto et al. correlate ego- vs. other-centered motivation with helping. They found that other-oriented motivation was strongly associated with laypeople thinking of volunteering as a form of compassionate love and more modestly associated with people engaging in volunteer activities. Egocentric motives also predicted volunteerism, although from Underwood's model, such volunteering would not qualify as compassionate love fully expressed.

There are undoubtedly findings in this volume that are outside of Underwood's framework, but overall she has provided a heuristic model for stimulating work on compassionate love and a useful framework for synthesizing what has been found. The evidence testifies to the utility of substrate, discernment, and motivational factors in compassionate love and to the outcomes that stem from it.

The Paradox of Compassionate Love vs. the Dark Side of Relationships

Acts of compassionate love suggest a positive, benign, charitable view of how people conduct their relationships. Not everyone shares that view. Mikulincer et al. mention the selfish gene perspective. Freudian psychologists assume aggression is inherent in human nature. Social exchange theorists depict humans as making decisions based on an economic calculus in which typically the goal is to get the best outcomes possible for oneself (Sprecher, 1998). Stanley Milgram is one of the most famous of all social psychologists. His studies dramatically showed humans' proclivity to destructive obedience (Milgram, 1963). Relationships scholars in recent years have produced a series of books and articles on the so-called dark side of relationships (see Perlman, 2000; Spitzberg & Cupach, 1998). Gable and Reis (2001, p. 175) go so far as to proclaim "existing research focuses predominantly on negative aspects of social interaction and close relationships."

Such discrepant views on the positive vs. negative nature of relationships generate several questions: Which of these images is more correct? Can data tell us anything? How can they be reconciled? Let us start with data.

The prevalence of compassionate and dark interpersonal acts. The contributors to this volume generally depict the positive acts and attitudes associated with compassionate love as widespread. Attachment theorists see caregiving as an evolutionary adaptive system that is inherent in humans. Several authors provide prevalence data. For example, Marks and Song report that 92% of participants in the National Survey of Midlife in the United States (MIDUS) claimed to be giving emotional support to kin. Roughly three out of five participants claimed to be giving instrumental support. The prevalence of volunteering varies by sample, but in the United States, estimates range from approximately 30% (see Omoto et al.) to 56% (see Marks & Song). Based on the General Social Surveys, Tom Smith concludes: "empathic feelings, altruistic-love sentiments, altruistic values and helping behaviors are all common." For many of the items in the GSS, three-quarters or more of participants expressed such views. Turning to media portrayals, 73% of all shows include one or more instances of helping or sharing (2.92 per hour), although when stringent coding criteria are used, only 5% of shows portray compassionate love (Stacy Smith et al.).

Juxtaposed to the evidence on the more positive and compassionate aspects of our relationships, it is easy to cite evidence of our dastardly attitudes and actions. Intimate relations texts are replete with discussions of such behaviors as unrequited love, lying, betrayal, jealousy, mistrust, conflict, peer rejection, divorce, and the like (Miller, Perlman, & Brehm, 2007). A few statistics will suffice to illustrate this point:

- In a study of older adults living in Greensboro, North Carolina, 79% experienced negative aspects of their friendships (Blieszner & Adams, 1998).
- Bella DePaulo and her colleagues at the University of Virginia had students keep daily diaries of their lying behaviors. They reported telling an average of two lies per day, lying to roughly a third of the people with whom they interacted (DePaulo, Kashy, Kirkendol, Wyer, & Epstein, 1996).
- In a study of adults, 45% admitting having betrayed someone and 52% indicated they had been the victims of betrayal by at least one of the members of their social network (see Jones & Burdette, 1994, p. 253).
- Results from the National Violence Against Women Survey in the United States show that over 50% of American women have been assaulted at some point in their lives (Tjaden & Thoennes, 1999).
- Meta-analytic studies find that 22% of women and 14% of men have been sexually assaulted (Spitzberg, 1999).
- Although altruistic acts are common on television, aggressive acts are even more common, occurring at a rate of 4.41 per hour on prime-time shows (Parents Television Council, 2007).
- A full 80% of participants in Milgram's (1963) study continued to follow the experiment's order to shock another person even though they knew that person had a heart problem and was screaming, "My heart's bothering me. Let me out of here." Five of every eight participants (62.5%) delivered shocks marked 450 volts.

Reconciling contrasting views. In looking at paradoxes such as the compassionate vs. the negative views of social relations, it is tempting to debate whether human nature is good or bad. Our sense is that question is too absolute. The above evidence suggests it is both. A next question might be: Which is more prevalent, our compassionate side or our egocentric orientations? Even answering that question seems beyond our reach at present. A third question becomes: When are we most likely to act in a self-centered, egocentric way, and when are we more likely to act in a compassionate, altruistic manner? We believe it is this question that Underwood's model and the contributors to this volume are best able to address. They do so by shedding light on the factors that promote compassionate love. In very broad terms, they indicate that some people tend to be more compassionate than others (e.g., secure individuals), that situational factors (e.g., time urgency) matter, and that compassion is more likely in some relationships than others.

Conclusions

Tackling the question of which factors foster (or block) compassionate love is one of the triumphs of the present volume. By and large, the evidence on facilitating factors that other authors obtained are consistent with what Underwood's model suggests should happen. Collectively, the chapters draw attention to the concept of compassionate love and some authors have provided rich descriptions of it as a lived experience (Roberts et al., Graber & Mitcham). Other authors have provided information about the prevalence and correlates of compassion-related norms, attitudes, and values (Mark & Song, Tom Smith). The development of measures for assessing compassionate love (Underwood, Fehr, & Sprecher) will make it easier for future scholars to incorporate this topic in their research.

By summarizing work on topics such as compassionate love, edited books can serve as a backdrop against which to consider where future work might go. A few directions come to our minds.

- First, attachment theory is a recurrent theoretical framework in this volume. We think it is a good one but wonder: What other theoretical perspectives (e.g., evolutionary, social learning) and/or conceptual analyses of related topics might be useful? Contributors to this volume already touch on some other theoretical perspectives. For example, Marks and Song partially embed their understanding of compassionate love in the Maslovian motivational tradition. From that vantage point, a researchable expectation is that compassionate love should emerge only after more basic needs have been met. In terms of related domains of research, there is a rich literature on altruism that might be more thoroughly mined for relevance to compassionate love. Research on forgiveness has also come into vogue in the past decade, both within North America and cross-culturally (see Hanke & Fischer, 2007; McCullough & Witvliet, 2002). Roberts et al. and Giesbrecht touch on forgiveness in this volume but its links to compassionate love might be worth developing more systematically.
- Second, we believe it would be interesting and potentially useful to examine compassionate love in contexts where it would be less expected

(e.g., among profit-oriented businesses). Attribution theorists (Kelley, 1972) discuss the augmentation principle where laypersons give stronger credence to causal influences on behavior in situations where there are other factors present inhibiting the behavior. Akin to this, if social scientists can find factors promoting compassionate love in contexts hostile to it, those factors may be especially important and strong. In such a context, it would also be informative to look for ways in which compassionate individuals deal with the pressures against compassion.

- Third, from Underwood's perspective, feedback loops and interactions among variables are important but have not been a primary focus of research reported in this volume (see Giesbrecht's Chapter 13 for one attempt to address this part of Underwood's model).
- Fourth, Underwood starts her discussion of compassionate love by declaring it is good for the recipient. Fehr and Sprecher report that receiving compassionate love is positive for the recipient's self-esteem and mood. Aside from this, however, very little research has been done from the recipient's perspective. What cues do people monitor in deciphering if they are the beneficiaries of compassionate love? Are the effects of compassionate love beneficial, as expected?

As we think about compassionate love, we realize it is a concept found for centuries in religious and philosophical writings. For social scientists, however, it is a relatively new topic. Clearly this volume represents an important step in establishing compassionate love on the social science map. The editors and authors have wisely, in our judgment, articulated how compassionate love as a concept is interrelated with other concepts but is unique and goes beyond them. We feel that establishing these points is crucial in showing that compassionate love is not just old wine in new bottles or reducible to its facets. The editors have brought together scholars from multiple disciplines to illustrate the relevance of their perspectives. They have looked at compassionate love in several places: volunteerism, health care, intergroup relations, and the like. But, as we have intimated above, this work is only beginning, and there are many profitable avenues to be investigated.

In our view, humanity faces many challenges, including, broadly defined, environmental sustainability and world peace. Although there are technological aspects to humankind's most pressing problems, we believe that successfully meeting these challenges rests heavily on interpersonal, intergroup, and international relations. We believe compassionate love can contribute to these relations and hope that the prosocial force of such love will be abundant in the twenty-first century and beyond.

References

Aron, A., & Aron, E. N. (1991). Love and sexuality. In K. McKinney & S. Sprecher (Eds.), *Sexuality in close relationships* (pp. 25–48). Hillsdale, NJ: Lawrence Erlbaum.

Blieszner, R., & Adams, R. G. (1998). Problems with friends in old age. *Journal of Aging Studies, 12,* 223–238.

DePaulo, B. M., Kashy, D. A., Kirkendol, S. E., Wyer, M. M., & Epstein, J. A. (1996). Lying in everyday life. *Journal of Personality and Social Psychology, 70,* 979–995.

Derlega, V. J., & Margulis, S. T. (1982). Why loneliness occurs: The interrelationship of social-psychological and privacy concepts. In L. A. Peplau & D. Perlman (Eds.), *Loneliness: A sourcebook of current theory, research, and therapy* (pp. 152–165). New York: Wiley-Interscience.

Eagly, A. H., & Crowley, M. (1986). Gender and helping behavior: A meta-analytic review of the social psychological literature. *Psychological Bulletin, 100,* 283–308.

Fromm, E. (1956). *The art of loving.* New York: Harper.

Gable, S. L., & Reis, H. T. (2001). Appetitive and aversive social interaction. In J. M. Harvey & A. E. Wenzel (Eds.), *Close romantic relationships: Maintenance and enhancement* (pp. 169–194). Mahwah, NJ: Lawrence Erlbaum.

Hanke, K., & Fischer, R. (2007, July). Interpersonal forgiveness across cultures: A meta analytical approach. In R. Fischer (Chair), *Advancements in the study of work behavior, forgiveness and cultural values: Meta-analysis as an important tool for cross-cultural research.* Symposium conducted at the meeting of the IV Latin American Regional Congress of Cross-Cultural Psychology, Mexico City.

Jones, W. H., & Burdette, M. P. (1994). Betrayal in relationships. In A. L. Weber & J. H. Harvey (Eds.), *Perspectives on close relationships* (pp. 243–262). Boston: Allyn and Bacon.

Kelley, H. H. (1972). *Causal schemata and the attribution process.* Morristown, NJ: General learning Press.

Lexchin, J. R. (2005). Implications of pharmaceutical industry funding on clinical research. *The Annals of Pharmacotherapy, 39,* 194–197.

McCullough, M. E., & Witvliet, C. V. (2002). The psychology of forgiveness. In C. R. Snyder & S. J. Lopez (Eds.), *Handbook of positive psychology* (pp. 446–458). New York: Oxford University Press.

Michael, R. T., Wadsworth, J., Feinleib, J., Johnson, A. M., Laumann, E. O., & Wellings, K. (1998). Private sexual behavior, public opinion, and public health policy related to sexually transmitted diseases: A U.S.–British comparison. *American Journal of Public Health, 88,* 749–754.

Mikulincer, M., Shaver, P. R., Gillath, O., & Nitzberg, R. A. (2005). Attachment, caregiving, and altruism: Boosting attachment security increases compassion and helping. *Journal of Personality and Social Psychology, 89,* 817–839.

Milgram, S. (1963). Behavioral study of obedience. *Journal of Abnormal and Social Psychology, 67,* 371–378.

Miller, R. S., Perlman, D., & Brehm, S. S. (2007). *Intimate relationships* (4th ed.). Boston, MA: McGraw-Hill.

Paloutzian, R., & Kirkpatrick, L. (Eds.). (1995). Religious influences on personal and societal well-being [Special Issue]. *Journal of Social Issues, 51*(2).

Parents Television Council (2007). *Dying to entertain: Violence on prime time television 1998 to 2006.* Los Angeles, CA: Author. Retrieved June 25, 2007, via http://www.parentstv.org/PTC/publications/reports/violencestudy/exsummary.asp

Perlman, D. (2000). El lado oscuro de las relaciones [The dark side of relationships]. *Revista de Psicología Social y Personalidad, 16,* 95–121.

Procidano, M. E., & Levine, J. (2007, July). *Effects of acculturation on social-support item functioning in Hispanic American vs. European American college students in New York.* Paper presented at the IV Latin American Regional Congress of Cross-Cultural Psychology. Mexico City.

Sánchez Aragón, R. (2000). *Empirical validation of bio-psycho-socio-cultural theory of couple relationships.* Unpublished doctoral dissertation, National Autonomous University of México, Mexico City, Mexico.

Sánchez Aragón, R. (2007). *Pasión Romántica: Más allá de la intuición, una ciencia del amor* [Romantic passion: Beyond the intuition, a science of the love]. México: Ed. Miguel Ángel Porrúa y Universidad Nacional Autónoma de México.

Shaffer, L. S. (1977). The Golden Fleece: Anti-intellectualism and social science. *American Psychologist, 32,* 814–823.

Spitzberg, B. H. (1999). An analysis of sexual aggression, victimization, and perpetration. *Violence and Victims, 14,* 241–260.

Spitzberg, B. H., & Cupach, W. R. (Eds.). (1998). *The dark side of close relationships.* Hillsdale, NJ: Lawrence Erlbaum Associates.

Sprecher, S. (1998). Social exchange theories and sexuality. *Journal of Sex Research, 35,* 32–43.

Sprecher, S. (2003). Update on the first IARR co-sponsored special topics conference. *Relationship Research News, 1*(2), 22–23.

Sprecher, S., & Fehr, B. (2005). Compassionate love for close others and humanity. *Journal of Social and Personal Relationships, 22,* 629–652.

Steblay, N. M. (1987). Helping behavior in rural and urban environments: A meta-analysis. *Psychological Bulletin, 102,* 346–356.

Tjaden, P., & Thoennes, N. (1999). *Extent, nature, and consequences of intimate partner violence: Findings from the National Violence Against Women Survey.* Washington, DC: National Institute of Justice/Centers for Disease Control and Prevention.

Underwood, L. G. (2002). The human experience of compassionate love: Conceptual mapping and data from selected studies. In S. G. Post, L. G. Underwood, J. P. Schloss, & W. B. Hurlbut (Eds.), *Altruism and altruistic love* (pp. 72–78). New York: Oxford University Press.

WHOQOL SRPB Group (2006). A cross-cultural study of spirituality, religion, and personal beliefs as components of quality of life. *Social Science and Medicine, 62,* 1486–1497.

Index